"Information through Innovation"

Mastering and Using WordPerfect 5.1

for WINDOWS

H. Albert Napier
Philip J. Judd

bf

boyd & fraser publishing company

Senior Acquisitions Editor: James H. Edwards
Production Editor: Barbara Worth
Director of Production: Becky Herrington
Manufacturing Coordinator: Karen Truman

A Division of South-Western Publishing Company
One Corporate Place • Ferncroft Village
Danvers, Massachusetts 01923

Manufactured in the United States of America

Library of Congress Cataloging-in-Publication Data

Napier, H. Albert, 1944-
Mastering and using WordPerfect 5.1 for Windows / H. Albert Napier, Philip J. Judd.
p. cm.
Includes index.
ISBN 0-87835-816-1
1. WordPerfect for Windows (Computer program) 2. Word processing--Computer programs. 3. Desktop publishing--Computer programs.
I. Judd, Philip J., 1953- . II. Title.
Z52.5.W65N363 1993 92-14441
652.5'536--dc20 CIP

1 2 3 4 5 6 7 8 9 10 H 4 3 2

Dedication

This book is dedicated to the staff at NJI.

CONTENTS

PREFACE

INTRODUCTION

Today there are literally millions of people using personal computers. One of the most popular applications of personal computers is document preparation. Today, most organizations use word processing software to prepare all kinds of documents, from simple one-page letters to multi-page newsletters and brochures. WordPerfect for Windows was chosen as the framework for this book because it is one of the best-selling word processing software packages currently available under the Windows environment for IBM PCs and compatible personal computers.

OBJECTIVES OF THIS BOOK

This book has been developed for an introductory course on word processing that utilizes IBM PCs or compatible hardware on which WordPerfect for Windows is used. The objectives of this book are:

- To acquaint the student with the process of using personal computers to prepare a variety of documents with word processing software.
- To provide a working knowledge of the basic and advanced capabilities of WordPerfect for Windows.
- To permit learning through examples using an exercise-oriented approach.
- To provide students with an excellent source of reference to advance their knowledge of WordPerfect for Windows.

AUTHORS' EXPERIENCE

The authors have worked with personal computers since PCs came to the market in the late 1970s. More than 30,000 people have attended personal computer training classes for which the authors have been responsible. This book is based on proven materials that have been used extensively in these training activities. In addition, the authors have more than 40 years of combined teaching and consulting experience.

DISTINGUISHING FEATURES

Access Methods for WordPerfect for Windows

This book features a unique parallel treatment of WordPerfect's three user interfaces. The use of pull-down menus, *with or without a mouse*, is available in WordPerfect for Windows. WordPerfect for Windows also allows the student to use the traditional keyboard function and combination keys to access its features. This book shows the student how to access WordPerfect for Windows features using either the pull-down menu or the keyboard methods.

New and Improved WordPerfect for Windows Features

A number of new features appear in WordPerfect for Windows. One of these features is the ability to quickly access commands using the Button Bar. A Ruler is provided to make formatting your document easier. The File Manager is available to handle file and disk management tasks. Each of these new features is covered in this book.

Many important features in WordPerfect 5.1 for DOS have been changed in WordPerfect for Windows. Some of the features that have been modified are font selection, merging documents, macros, graphics, and WordPerfect characters. Each of these features is comprehensively covered in this book.

Quick Start Approach

In Chapters 1 and 2, the student is introduced to word processing and the basics of WordPerfect for Windows. Chapter 3 provides a quick start to the "create-edit-print" cycle in WordPerfect. After completing Chapter 3, the student can 1) create a document, 2) edit the document, 3) save the document on a floppy or hard disk, 4) print the document, 5) close the document, 6) open and edit a document, and 7) exit WordPerfect.

Learning Through Examples

The book is designed for students to learn through examples rather than learning a series of features or commands. The materials are built around a series of example problems. The student learns commands for one example, then the commands are reinforced in others. New features are covered in subsequent examples.

Step-by-Step Instructions and Screen Illustrations

All examples in this text include step-by-step instructions. Screen illustrations are used extensively to assist the student while learning WordPerfect for Windows. The authors have found this approach very useful for the novice student as well as more advanced users, who may consider the book as a reference tool.

Extensive Exercises

At the end of each chapter, realistic exercises provide comprehensive coverage of the topics introduced in the chapter. Each chapter typically includes eight to ten exercises. There are more than 200 pages of exercises in the book.

Student Keyboard Templates and Command Summary Card

The book includes punch-out versions of the WordPerfect for Windows keyboard templates for student use. A Command Summary page is also provided.

Instructor Manual and Resources

An Instructor Manual, which includes additional exercises, is available to adopters of this text. A set of Instructor's Resource Disks with complete solutions to all examples and exercises, and a test item file are also available.

■ LEVEL OF INSTRUCTION

This book is designed to introduce the beginning, intermediate, and advanced capabilities of WordPerfect for Windows. First, the basic skills needed to create, change, save, and print a new or existing document are introduced. Subsequent chapters cover more advanced subjects, and build on previously presented concepts and developed skills. Each chapter contains eight to ten exercises that will help students improve their skills. A variety of practical examples provide an understanding of how WordPerfect can be used. The book assumes the student has little or no personal computer experience.

However, individuals with some previous experience can also advance their knowledge of WordPerfect for Windows. This book is characterized by its continuity, simplicity, and practicality. This book does not replace the WordPerfect for Windows Reference Manual that accompanies the software package. Used in conjunction with the reference manual, this book will provide the user with a complete understanding of the capabilities of WordPerfect for Windows.

■ ORGANIZATION/FLEXIBILITY

This book is designed to first take the student through the fundamentals of WordPerfect for Windows. After developing a solid foundation, the student learns more advanced features. The book is useful for college courses, professional schools, training classes, individual learning, and as a reference manual.

Chapter 1 introduces the student to word processing and personal computers. Typical types of documents created using word processing software packages are mentioned. The basic components of personal computers are described. The text guides users regarding software requirements and supplies the students may need.

Chapter 2 describes the WordPerfect for Windows software package and the process of accessing the WordPerfect for Windows software. The pull-down menu and keyboard methods of accessing WordPerfect for Windows features are discussed and illustrated.

The important "create-edit-print" cycle is covered in Chapter 3. After completing Chapter 3, the student can 1) create a document, 2) edit the document, 3) save the document on a floppy or hard disk, 4) print the document, 5) close the document, 6) open and edit a document, and 7) exit WordPerfect.

More extensive coverage of the process for creating a document appears in Chapter 4. Methods for inserting and replacing text are covered. The select feature and steps for deleting and undeleting text are shown. The help feature is also described.

Additional editing features are covered in Chapter 5. Important features such as reveal codes, searching and replacing text, converting the case of letters, and moving and copying text are demonstrated.

The WordPerfect Button Bar is covered in Chapter 6. Methods for using, creating, editing, formatting, and selecting a Button Bar are demonstrated.

Chapter 7 shows alternative methods for saving and opening a document. The File Manager feature is also discussed in Chapter 7. The use of the speller and thesaurus features is covered in Chapter 8.

When a document is created or edited, it may need to be formatted in a specific manner. Chapter 9 shows the basic formatting features such as fonts, margins, tabs, line spacing, justification, hyphenation, and indents. Chapter 10 discusses how to apply formats to a document using the WordPerfect Ruler. Additional formatting features such as headers and footers, page numbering, and page breaks are illustrated in Chapter 11.

WordPerfect includes many features for enhancing the text in a document. Chapter 12 contains instructions for using the center, bold, and underline features. Additional text enhancement features such as formatting with flush right, using superscripts and subscripts, changing font size and changing font appearance are shown in Chapter 13.

The printing capabilities are illustrated in Chapter 14. The steps for printing a document that appears on a screen, printing a document from a disk, and previewing a document are specified. Printer options are also discussed in this chapter.

WordPerfect allows the use of more than one document window on the screen at a time. The methods for arranging, moving, and sizing multiple windows are discussed in Chapter 15.

In many situations, it may be necessary to merge two documents. For example, a form letter may need to be sent to all customers of a company. The steps for merging a file containing the document with another file containing addresses are covered in Chapter 16. The processes for merging a document with input from the keyboard and creating a merged list are discussed in Chapter 17.

Rather than repeat the same actions for certain tasks each time they are performed, a macro can be created in WordPerfect. The steps necessary for creating and using a macro are demonstrated in Chapter 18. The process for creating an interactive macro is also discussed.

When documents are prepared, envelopes and labels may be needed. Methods for printing envelopes and labels are shown in Chapter 19. Use of the document merge technique learned in Chapter 16 is also used to merge address labels in Chapter 19.

Sometimes it may be necessary to place information in a specific order within a document. The process for sorting information is covered in Chapter 20. Part of this chapter presents information on sorting text used in a document merge. The process for selecting text that matches certain information is also demonstrated.

Documents may require the use of newspaper-style or parallel columns. The steps for using these types of columns are demonstrated in Chapter 21. Creating newspaper-style columns using the Ruler is also covered.

Some documents require a table of information, such as sales data. In Chapter 22, the steps to create and edit a table are shown. Creating a table using the Ruler is also covered.

WordPerfect includes some "desktop publishing" capabilities. The method for including a graphic in a document is illustrated in Chapter 23. Other features such as specifying the graphics caption, anchor type, vertical position, horizontal position, and size are also demonstrated.

Other graphic options are available in WordPerfect. Options related to border style, border space, caption location, and gray shading are shown in Chapter 24.

Graphics can be rotated, scaled, and moved within a document. These features are covered in Chapter 25.

Graphic lines can also be used in WordPerfect. Chapter 26 includes methods for creating and editing lines.

Advanced graphic features such as placing a graphic on another graphic and creating text boxes are demonstrated in Chapter 27. WordPerfect's typesetting capabilities and the WordPerfect characters feature are also discussed in this chapter.

A complex mathematical equation may need to be included in some technical documents. Chapter 28 describes the processes for creating an equation, printing an equation, using the equation palette, saving an equation, retrieving an equation, and editing an equation.

Many documents use the same style or format. The processes for creating, editing, saving, retrieving, and deleting a style are illustrated in Chapter 29.

Outlines are used in preparing many types of documents. Chapter 30 covers the steps for creating and editing an outline.

Endnotes and footnotes are used in reports to document the author's sources of information used. These features are illustrated in Chapter 31.

Long reports may require a table of contents, index, and list of figures. The methods for creating, defining, and generating such items are illustrated in Chapter 32.

This book includes three appendices. A selection of proofreader's marks is included in Appendix A. The process of linking data between WordPerfect and other Windows applications is shown in Appendix B. Appendix C discusses the methods for converting a document to and from WordPerfect for Windows.

ACKNOWLEDGEMENTS

We would like to thank and express our appreciation to the many fine individuals who have contributed to the completion of this book. We have been fortunate to have a group of reviewers whose constructive comments have been so helpful in completing this book. Special thanks go to:

Professor Robert R. Zilkowski
William Rainey Harper College

Professor Anna Marie Brummett
Oakton Community College

Professor Ronald Kapper
College of DuPage

Professor Melvin R. Martin
Eton Technical Institute

Professor Thomas Lightner
University of Colorado at Boulder

Judy Cameron
Spokane Community College

Professor Janice C. Sipior
Villanova University

Professor Sally J. Stackhouse
North Orange County Community College District

Professor Cheryl A. Bowers
Wayne State College

Professor Joseph H. Karr
Capital University

Paula Ecklund
Duke University

Gracie King
Arizona Western

We also appreciate the copy editing completed by Sheryl Rose.

As noted earlier, an extensive set of exercises is included in this book. The authors are particularly appreciative to Professor Robert R. Zilkowski of William Rainey Harper College for his assistance in preparing most of the exercises for the chapters.

No book is possible without the motivation and support of an editorial staff. Therefore, we wish to acknowledge with great appreciation the following people at boyd & fraser: Tom Walker, Publisher; James H. Edwards, Senior Acquisitions Editor; Barbara Worth, Production Editor; Peggy Flanagan, Production Manager; and Becky Herrington, Director of Production for their keen assistance in preparing this book.

We are very appreciative of the personnel at Napier & Judd, Inc., who helped prepare this book. We acknowledge, with great appreciation, the assistance provided by Kristi A. Willis, Nancy Onarheim, and Russell W. Hall in preparing and checking the many drafts of this book.

Houston, Texas
July 1992

H. Albert Napier
Philip J. Judd

CHAPTER ONE

INTRODUCTION TO WORD PROCESSING AND THE PERSONAL COMPUTER

OBJECTIVES

In this chapter, you will learn to:

- Define word processing
- Specify various applications of word processing
- Describe a personal computer and its hardware components
- Define software

CHAPTER OVERVIEW

This chapter introduces the concept of word processing. Applications for word processing are mentioned. The WordPerfect for Windows software package is discussed. The hardware of a personal computer system is described. Computer hardware and software requirements for processing WordPerfect for Windows are given. Supplies that you need are listed.

WHAT IS WORD PROCESSING?

Word processing is the preparation and production of documents using automated equipment. Today, most word processing activities are done with personal computers and a computer program that is called word processing software.

At first, special equipment that used a video display unit, a magnetic storage device, a keyboard and a printer were used for word processing. These devices, often called dedicated word processors, could be used only for word processing. During the 1980s, the use of personal computers grew. Personal computers allow people to complete word processing tasks as well as a host of other duties, including desktop publishing. Most word processing is now done with personal computers.

WHAT IS WORDPERFECT FOR WINDOWS?

WordPerfect for Windows is a word processing software package. You will learn version 5.1 of WordPerfect for Windows using this book. It allows you to create and change documents. You can save a document on a storage device so you can retrieve it at a later time. WordPerfect for Windows allows you to see your document on the screen as it will look when it is printed.

WordPerfect for Windows is used by organizations as well as by individuals for personal use. WordPerfect for Windows can be used to create and edit:

Letters	Mailing labels
Memos	Forms
Reports	Address lists
Book manuscripts	Brochures
Newsletters	

In many organizations today, you need to know a word processing program to get a job with the organization.

HARDWARE REQUIREMENTS

To use the version of WordPerfect for Windows covered in this book, you must have an IBM or compatible personal computer. Your personal computer needs an 80286, 80386, or greater processor, at least 2 MB of RAM, and 6 MB of hard disk space. Your personal computer also needs an EGA, VGA, 8514/A, or high resolution graphics adapter and monitor, and Windows 3.0 or higher.

A personal computer consists of several parts: a central processing unit, a monitor, keyboard, storage device(s), and a printer. Figure 1-1 contains an illustration of a personal computer. Each of the parts is described following the illustration.

Figure 1-1

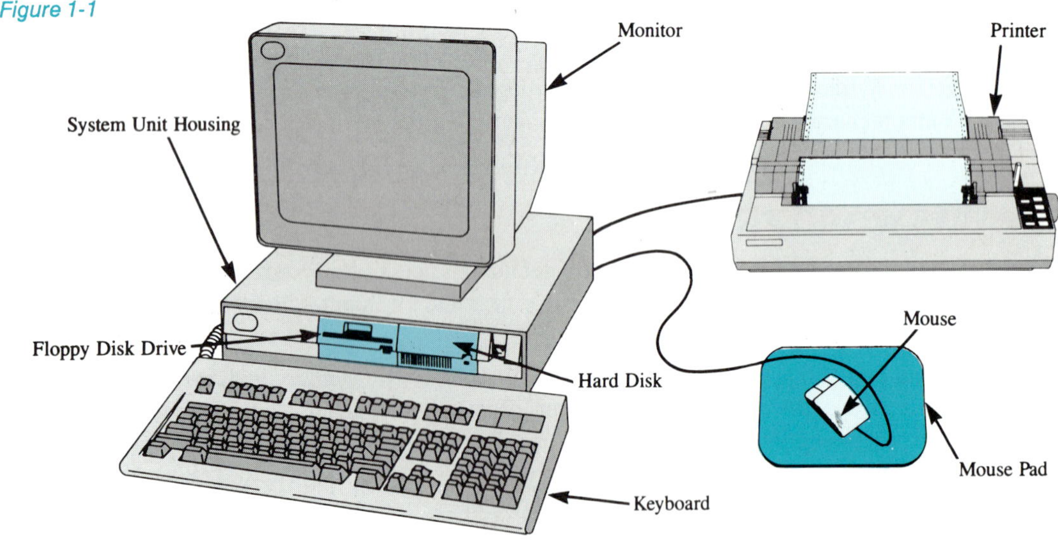

Central Processing Unit

The central processing unit (CPU) is like the brain of a personal computer. The CPU resides within the System Unit Housing. All of the word processing occurs within the CPU. Data is first entered into this unit by a person using a keyboard. The data is then processed by the software package. Finally, information is then output from the CPU to the monitor screen or to a printer. For example, you may enter the text for a letter from a keyboard. Then you can edit the document that appears on the monitor screen to make a few changes. Finally, you print the document.

Monitor

A monitor looks like a television screen. Commands and data that you enter, as well as responses from the CPU, appear on the monitor's screen.

There are two types of monitors: monochrome and color. A monochrome monitor usually displays a green or amber background with white or black characters. A color monitor permits the use of many colors on the monitor screen.

Most monitors are 13 inches across the diagonal. A standard monitor displays 24 lines of information, and each line can contain 80 characters.

Keyboard

A typical keyboard used on an IBM compatible personal computer appears in Figure 1-2. A keyboard is used to enter instructions, text, and data into a personal computer.

Figure 1-2

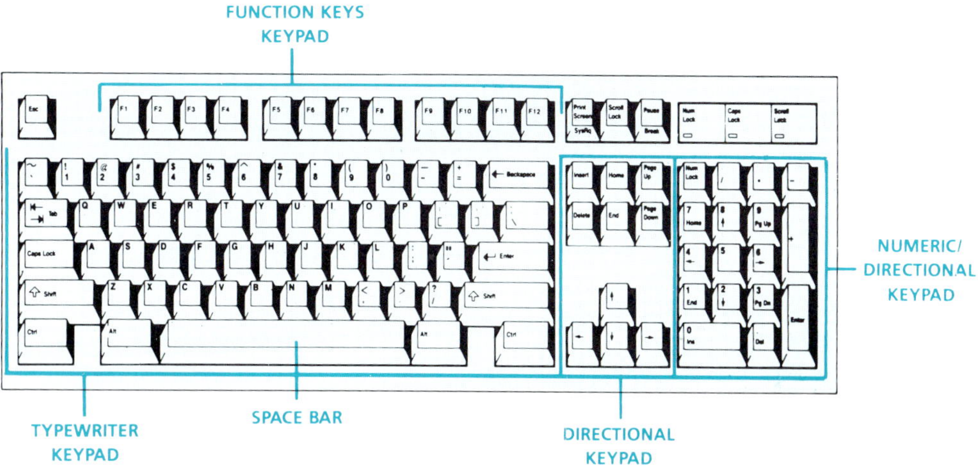

A keyboard usually has four keypads. The first keypad looks very much like a typewriter keyboard. It includes the alphabetic characters, numbers, and many special characters such as the $. The space bar appears at the bottom of the typewriter keypad.

The second keypad contains a set of 10 or sometimes 12 keys called function keys. Each of these keys starts with the letter F followed by a number. These keys are "programmed" by various software packages to give specific instructions to a computer. For example, the F5 key on the CUA Compatible template is used to print a document in WordPerfect for Windows. The function keys typically are above or to the left of the typewriter keypad.

The third keypad is called the numeric/directional keypad. The numeric keys are arranged like the keys on a calculator to facilitate entering numeric data. The Num Lock light above the keypad indicates whether the keypad is in numeric or directional mode. If the light is on, numbers will be entered if you press a key on the keypad. When the light is off, you can use the keys to move from one location on the monitor to another position. You can change the mode of the keypad from numeric to directional and vice versa by pressing the NumLock key.

The fourth keypad is positioned between the typewriter keypad and the numeric/directional keypad. These keys are used to move from one position on your monitor to another point. Some of the keys are used for inserting and deleting text. If your keyboard has this set of keys, it is suggested that you use these keys to move from place to place on your monitor. Assuming you have these directional keys available, it is recommended that you leave the numeric/directional keypad in numeric mode.

Mouse

A mouse is a piece of hardware that connects to your computer to perform various operations. You do not need a mouse to use WordPerfect for Windows, but the Windows environment was designed to be used with a mouse. You can use a mouse in WordPerfect for Windows to move the insertion point, to highlight text, and to select WordPerfect features and options. A typical mouse appears in Figure 1-3.

Figure 1-3

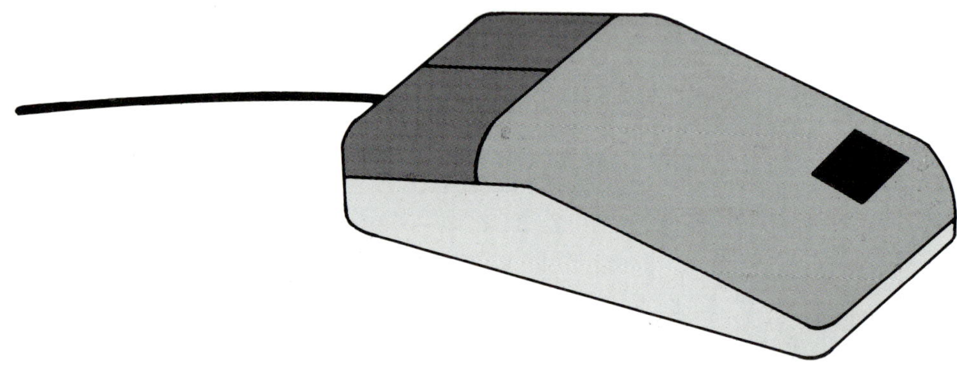

A mouse usually has two buttons. Most mouse procedures require the use of the left mouse button. Very few commands require the use of the right mouse button.

The mouse pointer indicates the position of the mouse in WordPerfect for Windows. The mouse pointer has many shapes. When the mouse pointer is in the document area, it appears as an I-beam. When the mouse pointer is in the menu bar, it appears as an arrow. Each shape indicates that the mouse performs a different function.

The mouse pointer that appears in the document area is shown in Figure 1-4.

Figure 1-4

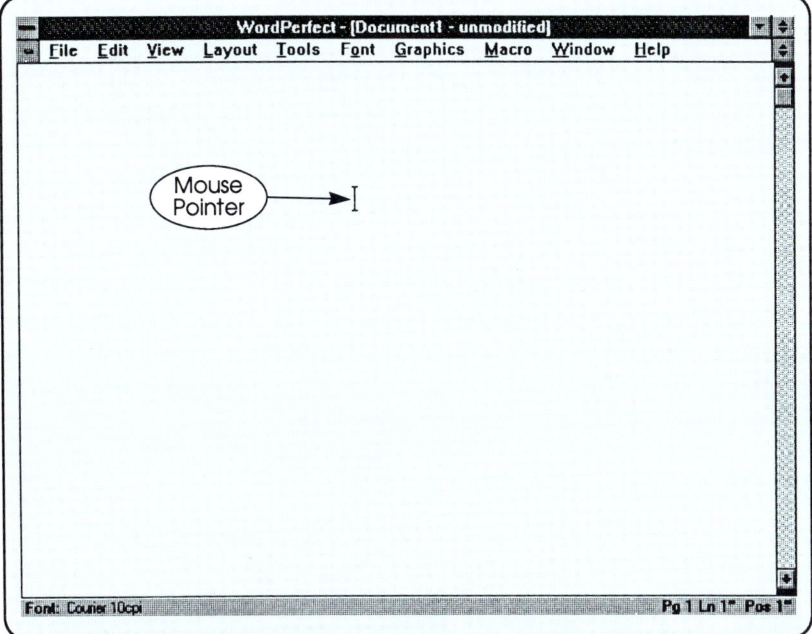

In This Book

For mouse instructions, the left mouse button will be referred to as the mouse button. If the right mouse button is to be used, it will be referred to as the alternate mouse button.

Storage Devices

When using a personal computer, you may need to save information for use at a later time. The two types of storage devices used most often with personal computers are the diskette and the hard disk. The WordPerfect for Windows software that you purchase is stored on diskettes.

Diskettes are the most common and transportable type of storage device. They sometimes are called floppy diskettes. They come in either 5.25 inch or 3.5 inch size. Depending on what type of diskette and personal computer is being used, the number of characters that can be stored on a diskette usually ranges from 360,000 to 1.4 million. For such storage devices, this means you can store approximately 180 to 700 double spaced typed pages.

A personal computer usually contains at least one floppy disk drive. If only one disk drive is available, it is referred to as Drive A. When a second floppy disk drive is present, it is called Drive B.

The most desirable and most expensive storage device on a personal computer is a hard disk. This type of disk drive is located within the cabinet housing the central processing unit of the personal computer and is often located next to the floppy disk drive(s).

Hard disks can store many times the amount of data that can be stored on a diskette. The hard disk on a personal computer can store 40, 60, 80 million, or more characters. The time it takes a personal computer to access data stored on a hard disk is much faster than for a diskette.

The word processing software that you use comes on diskettes. You must transfer the software from the diskettes to the hard disk on your personal computer. Through the use of a hard disk, you can make the process of creating, processing, and storing documents much more effective and efficient.

Printer

When you finish a document using a word processing software package, you will want to print it.

There are three common types of printers used with personal computers: dot matrix, letter quality and laser. A dot matrix printer builds each character by using a series of dots and prints the character through the use of an ink ribbon. Print speeds are in the range of 50 to 300 characters per second.

Letter quality printers make documents look as if they were typed on a high quality typewriter. Characters are printed with a daisywheel element (a round device with numbers, letters, and special characters on the end) and an ink ribbon. Speed for letter quality printers varies from 40 to 120 characters per second.

Laser printers provide the highest quality for printing documents. These printers use laser light to create the characters within the printer. The characters are then transferred to paper through the use of toner like the type used in copy machines. The speed of laser printers is much faster than that of other printers. It is measured in pages per minute rather than characters per second.

■ SOFTWARE REQUIREMENTS

This book focuses on WordPerfect for Windows. When you purchase the WordPerfect for Windows software, you are given a set of diskettes on which the software is stored. You will copy the software from the diskettes to the hard disk of a computer. Then you will access the software on the hard disk. For instructions for placing the WordPerfect for Windows software on a hard disk, see the reference manual that comes with the software.

■ SUPPLIES

When using a personal computer, you will need several items. You should have access to the WordPerfect for Windows reference manual that comes with the software.

You will also need to have some floppy diskettes to store documents. Make sure you have the proper type of diskette for the computer you are using. You can purchase them at office supply stores and campus bookstores. If you have never used diskettes, follow the instructions for handling that come with them. You may also want a disk storage box to protect your diskettes when you are not using them.

You will need to format the diskettes before you store documents on them. Refer to your DOS or Windows reference manual for the procedures used to format a diskette.

EXERCISE 1

INSTRUCTIONS: Define the following terms:

1. Central Processing Unit (CPU) ______________________________

   ____

2. Computer hardware ______________________________

   ____

3. Computer software ______________________________

   ____

4. Diskette ____________________

____

5. Dot matrix printer ____________________

____

6. Hard disk ____________________

____

7. Keyboard ____________________

____

8. Laser printer ____________________

____

9. Monitor ____________________

____

10. Mouse ____________________

____

EXERCISE 2

INSTRUCTIONS: Circle T if the statement is true and F if the statement is false.

T F 1. Books can be created with a word processing software package.

T F 2. There are two popular sizes of diskettes used with personal computers.

T F 3. You must use a laser printer with a personal computer.

T F 4. The CPU is used to input information into a computer.

T F 5. There are only two types of printers that can be used with a personal computer.

T F 6. The only difference between a diskette and a hard disk is the amount of data that can be stored on the device.

T F 7. Data can be stored on diskettes or a hard disk.

T F 8. Diskettes are not absolutely required to store data for use in the future.

T F 9. There are three keypads on a keyboard for most personal computers.

EXERCISE 3

Identify the kind of computer you will be using for this class (i.e., IBM PS/2 Model 30).

EXERCISE 4

What kind of monitor does your computer use (mono, color or amber)?

EXERCISE 5

How much memory does the computer (CPU) you will use contain?

EXERCISE 6

What size diskette will you use (3.5″ or 5.25″)?

CHAPTER TWO

GETTING STARTED WITH WORDPERFECT FOR WINDOWS

OBJECTIVES

In this chapter, you will learn to:

- Access the WordPerfect for Windows program
- Use the WordPerfect for Windows template
- Use the pull-down menus
- Change the default directory
- Exit the WordPerfect for Windows program

CHAPTER OVERVIEW

This chapter tells how to access WordPerfect for Windows. The items that appear on the WordPerfect for Windows screen are discussed. The WordPerfect for Windows template and the menu structure are explained and illustrated. The procedures for changing directories and for exiting WordPerfect for Windows are shown.

ACCESSING WORDPERFECT FOR WINDOWS

Before you attempt to access WordPerfect for Windows and place it into the memory of your personal computer, check all connections. The power cord should be plugged into an electrical outlet.

Turn on the computer

You access WordPerfect for Windows through the Windows program. You must first initiate the Windows program.

Assuming that Windows is installed in the directory WINDOWS on the C drive, use the following steps to load the software into your computer.

Type CD\WINDOWS (to change to directory WINDOWS)

Press ↵Enter

Type WIN

Press ↵Enter

The Windows software is loaded into the memory of your computer. Your screen should look similar to Figure 2-1.

Figure 2-1

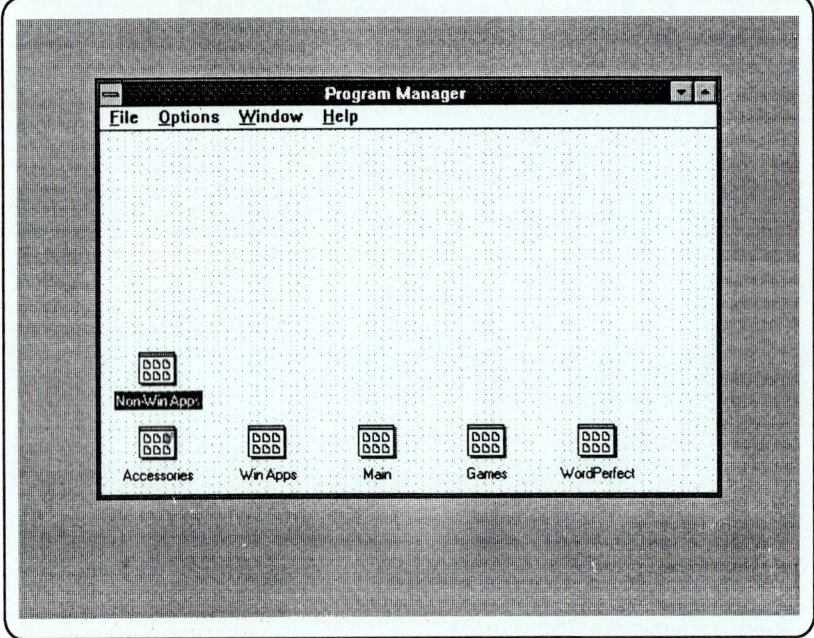

> **In This Chapter**
>
> The use of the menus with a mouse and with a keyboard are shown by using two columns. The directions in the left column are for the menus using a mouse. They appear in normal type. The instructions in the right column are for using the menus with a keyboard. They appear in *italic* type.

To access the WordPerfect for Windows software, you must open the WordPerfect group. To open the WordPerfect group:

Double-click the WordPerfect group icon

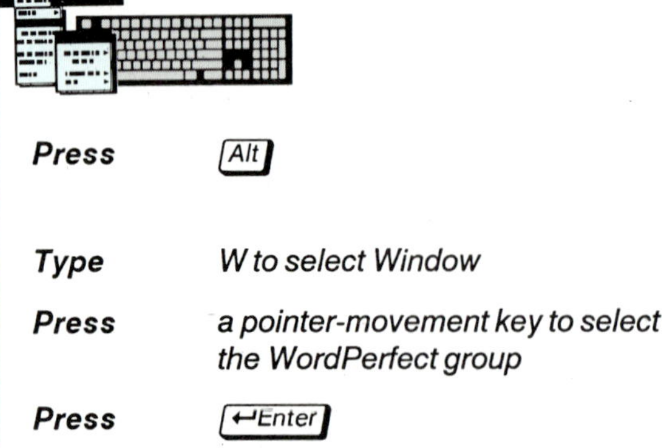

Press *Alt*

Type *W to select Window*

Press *a pointer-movement key to select the WordPerfect group*

Press *↵Enter*

To load WordPerfect for Windows into memory:

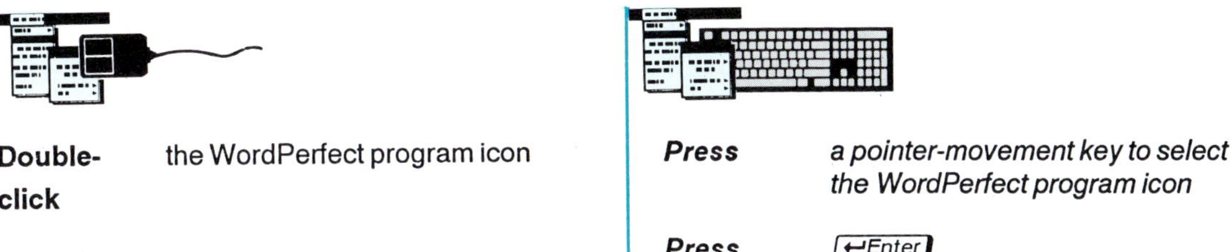

Double-click	the WordPerfect program icon	***Press***	*a pointer-movement key to select the WordPerfect program icon*
		Press	*↵Enter*

The WordPerfect for Windows copyright screen appears on your monitor. In a few seconds, your screen should look like Figure 2-2.

Figure 2-2

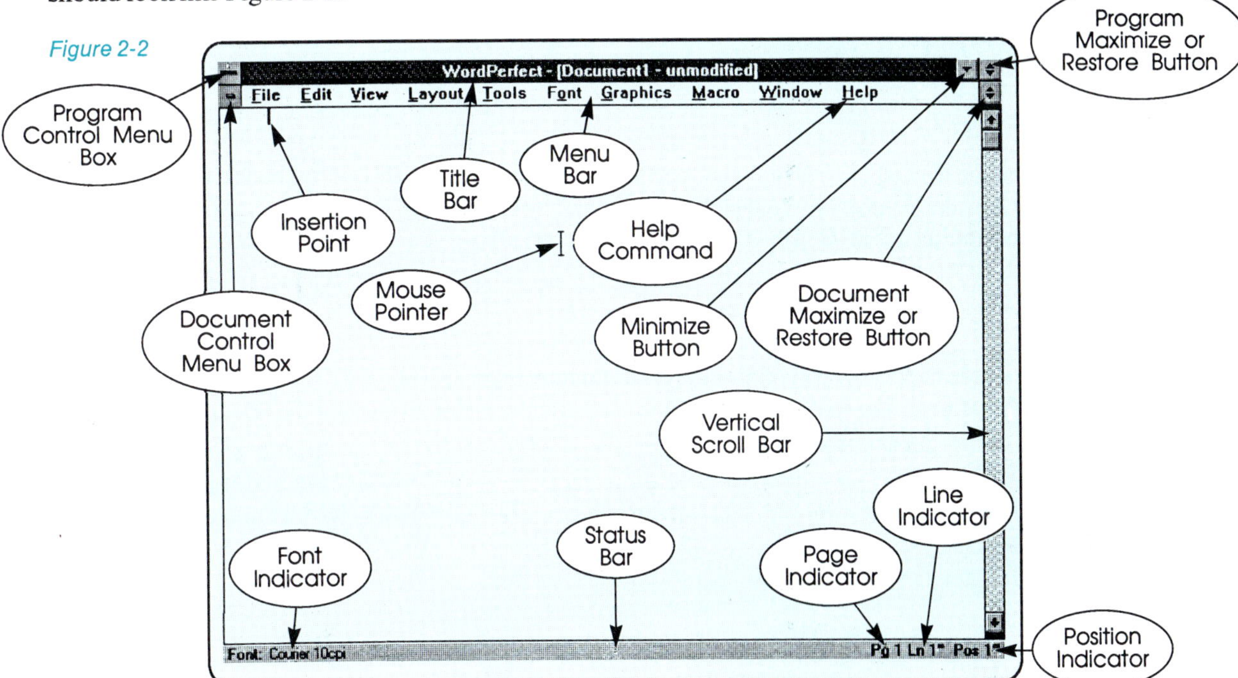

THE WORDPERFECT WINDOW

Figure 2-2 is an example of a WordPerfect for Windows screen. The WordPerfect for Windows program appears in a window. This window contains a blank document. The insertion point is the only item in the document area. There are no symbols. You can start typing as you would on a clean sheet of paper.

Control Menu Box

The control menu box is used to display the control menu. Every window has a control menu. The control menu typically contains options such as restore, maximize, minimize, move, size, close, and switch to. In some control menus, all of the options are not available to use. In this situation, the characters for the option are lighter than for options that can be used.

Title Bar

The WordPerfect for Windows title bar appears at the top of the window. It includes the control menu box, the software product name, the document name, the minimize button, and the maximize or restore button.

Minimize Button

The minimize button is used to reduce the WordPerfect window to an icon.

Maximize or Restore Button

The maximize or restore button is used to maximize the size of the window on your screen. If the window is already maximized the button is used to restore the window to its previous size.

Menu Bar

The menu bar is located below the title bar, and contains the initial WordPerfect for Windows commands available to you. Unlike the previous versions of WordPerfect, the menu always remains on the screen.

Help

The Help command is selected to use the WordPerfect for Windows Help feature.

Mouse Pointer

The mouse pointer is used to indicate what portion of your screen is affected by your next action. The mouse pointer has many shapes. When the mouse pointer is in the document area, it appears as an I-beam. When the mouse pointer is in the menu bar, it appears as an arrow. Each shape indicates that the mouse performs a different function.

Vertical Scroll Bar

The vertical scroll bar appears on the right side of the document area. This scroll bar includes scroll arrows as well as the scroll box. The vertical scroll bar is used to view different parts of the document.

Insertion Point

The blinking vertical bar at the top of the screen is the insertion point. It marks the location where you enter text on the screen.

Status Bar

The status bar appears at the bottom of the screen. It indicates the current page number (Pg), the vertical position of the insertion point (Ln), and the horizontal position of the insertion point (Pos). The current font being used also appears on the status bar.

■ DEFAULT SETTINGS

There are some initial settings called defaults that apply to the documents you prepare. You will learn ways to change the settings in later chapters.

In WordPerfect for Windows, margins are measured from the edges of a page. WordPerfect for Windows adjusts the text to fit within the current margins. The default setting is for a 1 inch margin for the top, bottom, left, and right side of a page.

Line Spacing determines the amount of space between lines. WordPerfect for Windows single spaces your document unless you change the line spacing.

Justification is used to align text. There are four types of justification. They are left, right, full, and center. Left justification is the default setting. When Left justification is used, WordPerfect for Windows aligns the text in your document on the left margin and has a "ragged right" margin.

Tabs are an exact measurement for indenting text in a document. A tab is displayed on the screen as a certain amount of space. WordPerfect for Windows defaults to setting tabs every 1/2 inch.

WordPerfect for Windows uses inches as the standard unit of measurement to position text on a page.

METHODS AVAILABLE FOR ACCESSING WORDPERFECT FOR WINDOWS FEATURES

WordPerfect for Windows provides three interface methods for accessing WordPerfect for Windows features. The methods are:

1. Menus using the mouse
2. Menus using the keyboard
3. Keyboard function keys

The menus can be used with a mouse. WordPerfect for Windows features are accessed by selecting words from the menu at the top of the screen. When a mouse is used with the menus, WordPerfect for Windows features are selected by pointing at the item with the mouse pointer and clicking the mouse button.

There are three basic mouse operations: clicking, double-clicking, and dragging. **Clicking** means to press the mouse button and then release it. **Double-clicking** means to press the mouse button twice quickly. **Dragging** means to press and hold down the mouse button while moving the mouse.

Menus can also be activated using the keyboard. You access the menu using the keyboard by pressing the Alt key.

When the keyboard function keys method is used, a template is placed on the keyboard. The template specifies which WordPerfect for Windows features are performed by each function key.

MENUS

WordPerfect for Windows has a menu interface, which allows you to select WordPerfect for Windows features using the menu bar. You can access the menus through the use of the mouse or from the keyboard.

The methods for accessing the menus with a mouse and with a keyboard are shown in this section.

Selecting Menus

The method you use to select a menu option from the menu bar depends on whether you are using the mouse or a keyboard.

For example, to select the Layout menu from the menu bar:

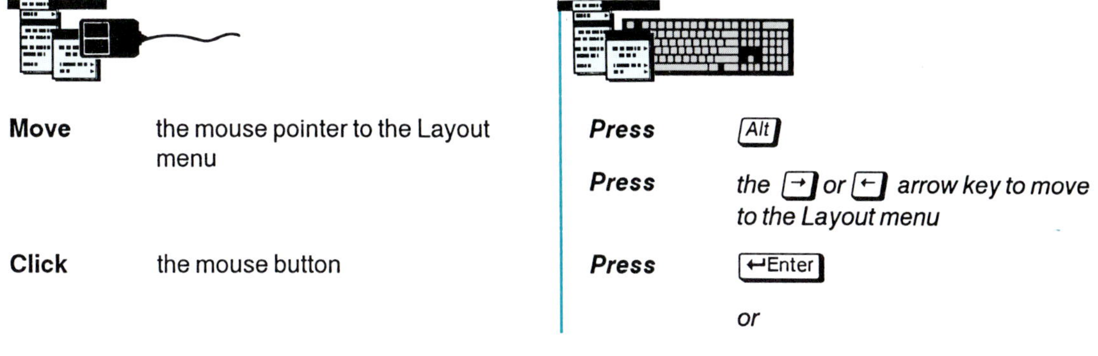

Move the mouse pointer to the Layout menu

Click the mouse button

Press *Alt*

Press *the → or ← arrow key to move to the Layout menu*

Press *↵Enter*

or

To select an option from the menu using the mouse, move the mouse pointer to the menu option and click the mouse button. Or, press and hold down the mouse button, drag the mouse pointer to an option, and then release the mouse button.

Press *Alt*

Type *L for Layout*

To select an option from the menu displayed using the keyboard, type the underscored letter associated with the menu option. Or, press the pointer-movement keys to highlight the option of your choice and press ↵Enter.

For example, to select the Columns option from the Layout menu:

Move	the mouse pointer to the Columns option
Click	the mouse button
	or
Press	and hold down the mouse button
Drag	the mouse pointer to the Columns option
Release	the mouse button

Press	*↓ to move to the Columns option*
Press	*↵Enter*
	or
Type	*C for Columns*

Your screen should look like Figure 2-3.

Figure 2-3

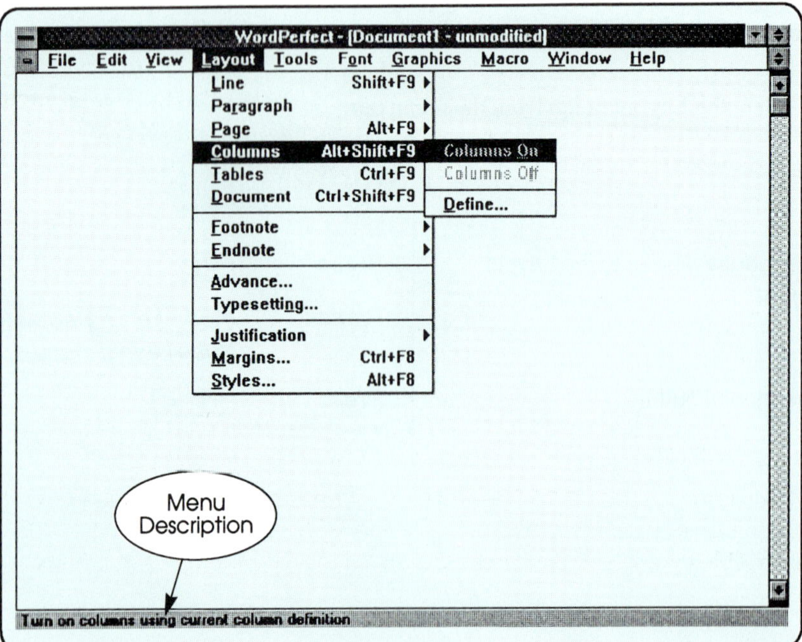

Notice that the left side of the status bar provides a brief explanation of the feature.

Exiting Menus

To escape the menus, click inside the document area or press Esc

To exit the Layout menu:

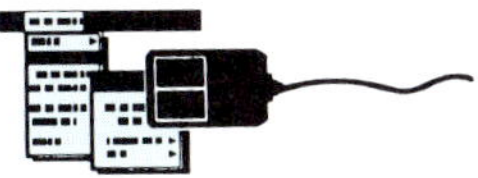

Move	the mouse pointer to the document area
Click	the mouse button

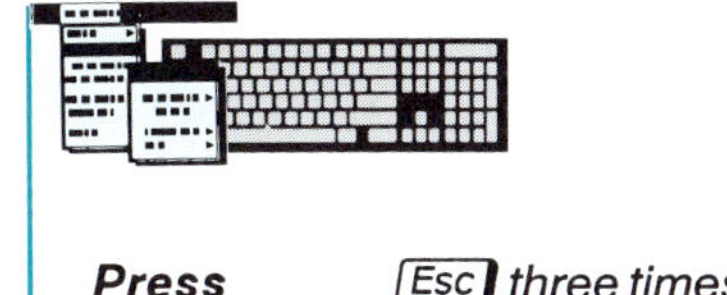

Press	*Esc three times*

■ TEMPLATE

A template is a diagram of the function keys. It includes a list of WordPerfect for Windows features that can be executed by using the function keys. The function keys, labeled F1 through F10 or F12, can be used by themselves or with the Control Ctrl, Alternate Alt, or Shift Shift keys. The WordPerfect for Windows template is color-coded. **Black** commands are issued by pressing only the function key. **Green** commands are issued by pressing the Shift key and then the corresponding function key. **Blue** commands are issued by pressing the Alt key and then the corresponding function key. **Blue commands with a green bullet** next to them are issued by pressing the Alt key, the Shift key, and then the corresponding function key. **Red** commands are issued by pressing the Ctrl key and then the corresponding function key. **Red commands with a green bullet** next to them are issued by pressing the Ctrl key, the Shift key, and the corresponding function key.

> **In This Book**
>
> The keyboard function key interface method is referred to as the keyboard method in the rest of the text.
>
> When you use the WordPerfect for Windows features with the keyboard method, you will often be asked to press one key, and while still holding the key down, to press another key. For example, you may be asked to hold down the Shift key, and then press the F7 key to get the Center feature. This type of instruction will appear in the text as:
>
> **Press**  Shift+F7

WordPerfect for Windows has two templates. The suggested template is the CUA (Common User Access) Compatible template. The CUA standard uses the same function keys to perform similar tasks in different applications. For example, the function key F4 performs the File, Open command in WordPerfect for Windows and other Windows applications that use the CUA standard. By default, WordPerfect for Windows is installed with the CUA Compatible template.

The second template is the WP 5.1 for DOS Compatible template. The function keys on this template are similar to the function keys used in WordPerfect 5.1 for DOS. More information is available about the WP 5.1 for DOS Compatible template in "Appendix G, Keyboards" of the Reference Manual.

> **In This Book**
>
> This book refers to the CUA Compatible template in all exercises and examples.
>
> Figure 2-4 is the WordPerfect for Windows CUA Compatible template.

Figure 2-4

Student Template for use with WordPerfect® for Windows™
CUA™ Version

Cancel	Esc	Top of Doc	Home
Undo	Z	Bottom of Doc	End
Cut	X	Column ←/→	←/→
Copy	C	Page Up	PgUp
Paste	V	Page Down	PgDn
Bold	B	Del EOL	Del
Italics	I	Hard Page	Enter
Underline	U	WP Characters	W
Normal	N	Print Doc	P

boyd & fraser publishing company

F1	*F2*	*F3*	*F4*		*F5*	*F6*	*F7*	*F8*		*F9*	*F10*	*F11*	*F12*
Preferences•		Draft Mode•	Clear•	*Ctrl + Sh*	Date Code•	Prev Doc•	Double Indent•		*Ctrl + Sh*	Document•	Macro Stop•	Vertical Line•	Sort•
Speller	Replace	Redisplay	Close	*Ctrl*	Date Text	Next Doc	Hanging Indent	Margins	*Ctrl*	Tables	Macro Record	Horizontal Line	Merge
		Ruler•		*Alt + Sh*	Paragraph Def•	Prev Window•	Decimal Tab•	Special Codes•	*Alt + Sh*	Columns•		Text Box Edit•	
Thesaurus	Search Prev	Reveal Codes	Exit	*Alt*	Paragraph Num	Next Window	Flush Right	Styles	*Alt*	Page	Macro Play	Text Box Create	Generate
Help: What Is?	Search Next	Save	New	*Shift*	Print Preview	Prev Pane	Center	Select Cell	*Shift*	Line		Figure Edit	Define
Help	Search	Save As	Open		Print	Next Pane	Indent	Select		Font	Menu Bar	Figure Retrieve	Mark Text

CHANGING THE DEFAULT DIRECTORY

A directory is a file that holds the names of a group of files. It helps you group your files to keep them organized. A directory name can have up to eight characters. The name should include only letters and numbers. Do not use special characters such as $, or - in a directory name. You may enter the alphabetic characters in a directory name using lowercase and uppercase letters. You can organize your directories and files with the File Manager feature.

All of the material you prepare with WordPerfect for Windows is saved on document files. Each time you start WordPerfect for Windows, a directory is selected by the computer for saving and retrieving document files. This directory is called the default directory.

You can find which directory is the default by using the File Preferences, Location of Files command sequence. The directory listed in the Documents text box is the current default directory. If no directory is listed in the Documents text box, then the WordPerfect for Windows directory is the default directory. Once you change the default directory, WordPerfect for Windows will refer to that directory until you change it again.

> **In This Book**
>
> The use of the menus with and without a mouse and the use of the keyboard function keys are shown using three columns. The directions in the left or first column are for using the menus with a mouse. They appear in normal type. The instructions for using the menus with a keyboard appear in the second column. They appear in *italics*. The directions in the third column are for the keyboard method. They appear in normal type.
>
> If a command cannot be performed using one of the three methods, the column for that method appears empty.

If you are not using a floppy disk to store your documents, please proceed to the section titled "Hard Disk."

Floppy Disk

To change the default directory to drive A, so you can save your document files on a diskette:

Insert a formatted diskette in drive A

To access the Preferences command:

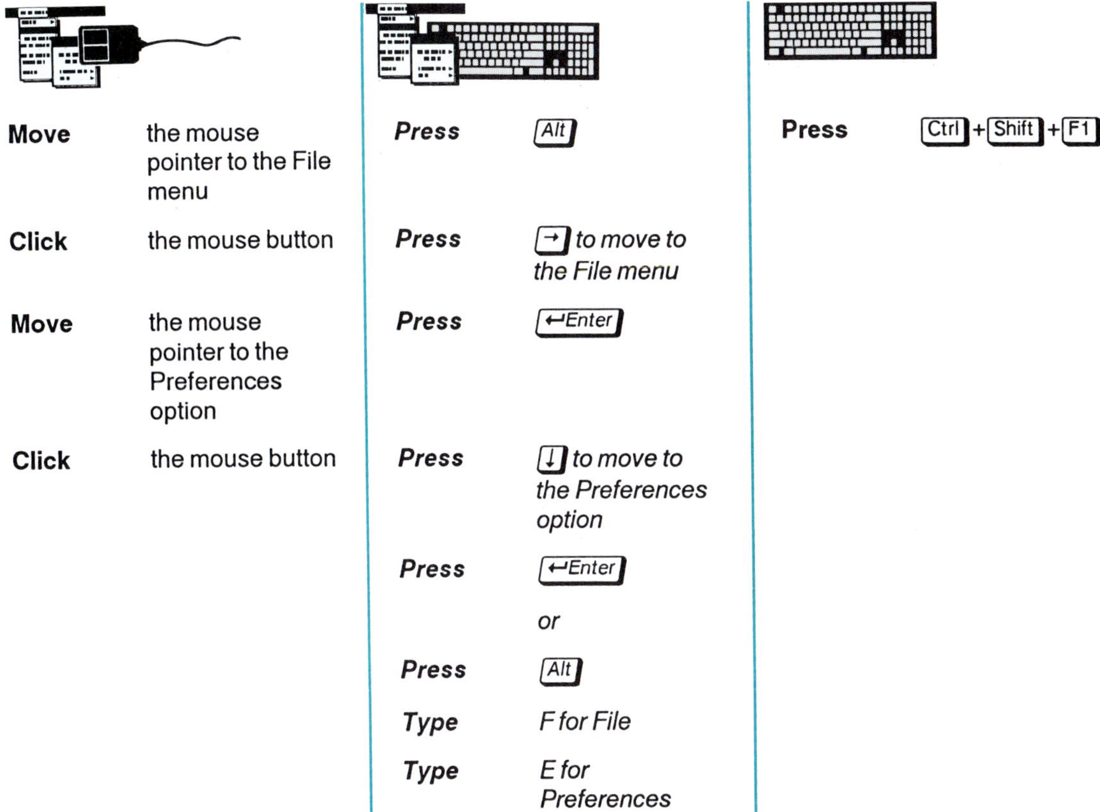

Mouse		Keyboard		Shortcut	
Move	the mouse pointer to the File menu	***Press***	*Alt*	**Press**	Ctrl + Shift + F1
Click	the mouse button	***Press***	*→ to move to the File menu*		
Move	the mouse pointer to the Preferences option	***Press***	*↵Enter*		
Click	the mouse button	***Press***	*↓ to move to the Preferences option*		
		Press	*↵Enter*		
			or		
		Press	*Alt*		
		Type	*F for File*		
		Type	*E for Preferences*		

Your screen should look like Figure 2-5.

Figure 2-5

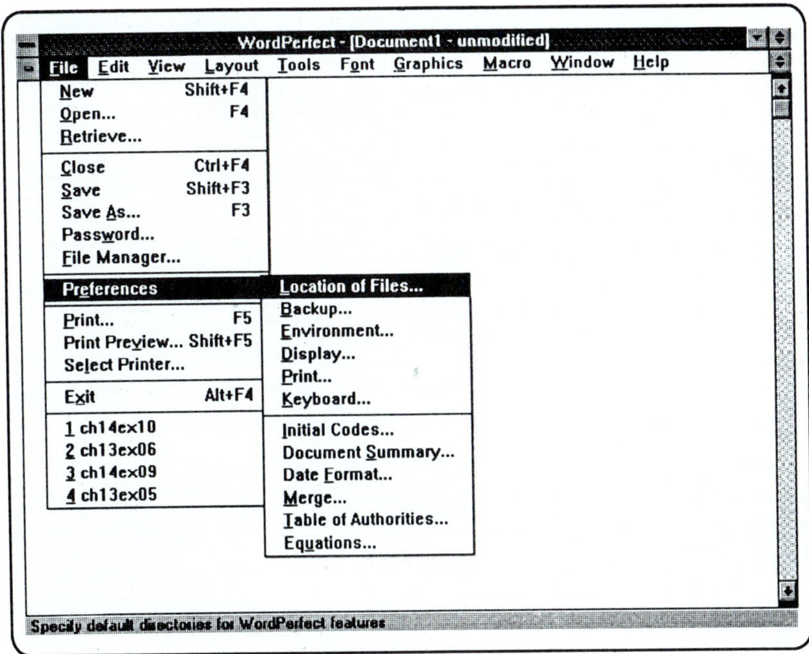

Many set up options are available under the File Preferences command. To change the location where files are being stored:

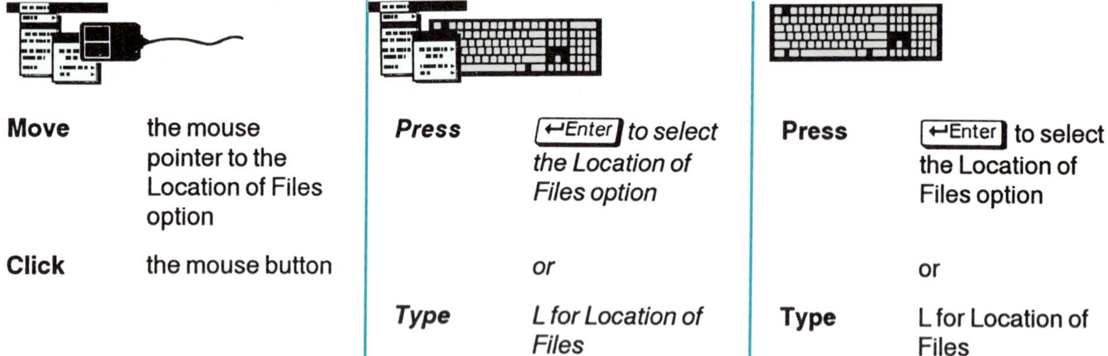

Move the mouse pointer to the Location of Files option
Click the mouse button
Press ↵Enter to select the Location of Files option
or
Type L for Location of Files
Press ↵Enter to select the Location of Files option
or
Type L for Location of Files

Your screen should look like Figure 2-6.

Figure 2-6

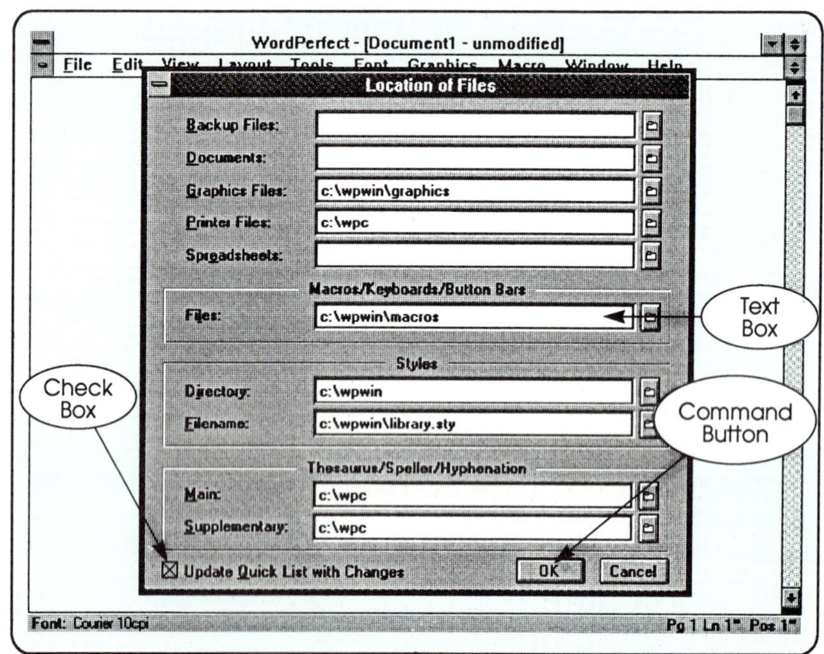

A dialog box appears on the screen. A dialog box provides options within a command. If a menu command provides a dialog box, it is followed by an ellipsis (...) in the menu. Dialog boxes often contain option buttons, check boxes, list boxes, text boxes, and command buttons.

Option buttons are round buttons. Whenever these round buttons appear in a dialog box, only one can be active. You can select the appropriate option button by clicking on the proper option button or by holding down the Alt key and pressing the underlined letter associated with that option.

Check boxes are small square boxes that you can check or place an X inside. If a check box contains an X, then that feature is on or active. If the check box is blank, then that feature is off or inactive. To activate a check box, click on the box until an X appears or hold down the Alt key and press the underlined letter associated with that check box until an X appears.

List boxes provide a list of names for you to choose from. Sometimes you cannot see the entire list. If you can not see the entire list, scroll bars appear next to the list for you to view the remaining options. To select an item from a list box using the mouse, click on the item in the list box. When using the keyboard, hold down the Alt key and press the underlined letter associated with the list box, then press the pointer-movement keys to select the proper item.

Text boxes allow you to type an option in them. For example, the Document text box allows you to type the directory of document files. To select the text box, double-click inside the text box area or hold down the Alt key and press the underlined letter associated with the text box.

Command buttons are rectangular buttons. Common command buttons are the OK and Cancel buttons. To select a button, click the button with the mouse or hold down the Alt key and press the underlined letter of the command button.

Another alternative for moving between the various items in a dialog box is to press the Tab key.

To select the Documents text box:

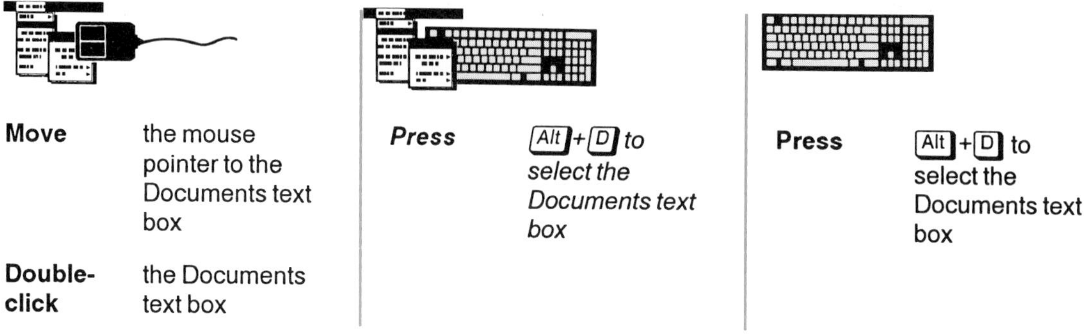

Move	the mouse pointer to the Documents text box	***Press***	*Alt+D to select the Documents text box*	**Press**	Alt+D to select the Documents text box
Double-click	the Documents text box				

To enter the drive and directory name:

Type	**a:\wpdocs**	***Type***	***a:/wpdocs***	**Type**	**a:\wpdocs**

To accept the name and close the dialog box:

Move	the mouse pointer to the OK command button	***Press***	*↵Enter to select the OK command button*	**Press**	↵Enter to select the OK command button
Click	the mouse button				

Your screen should now look like Figure 2-7.

Figure 2-7

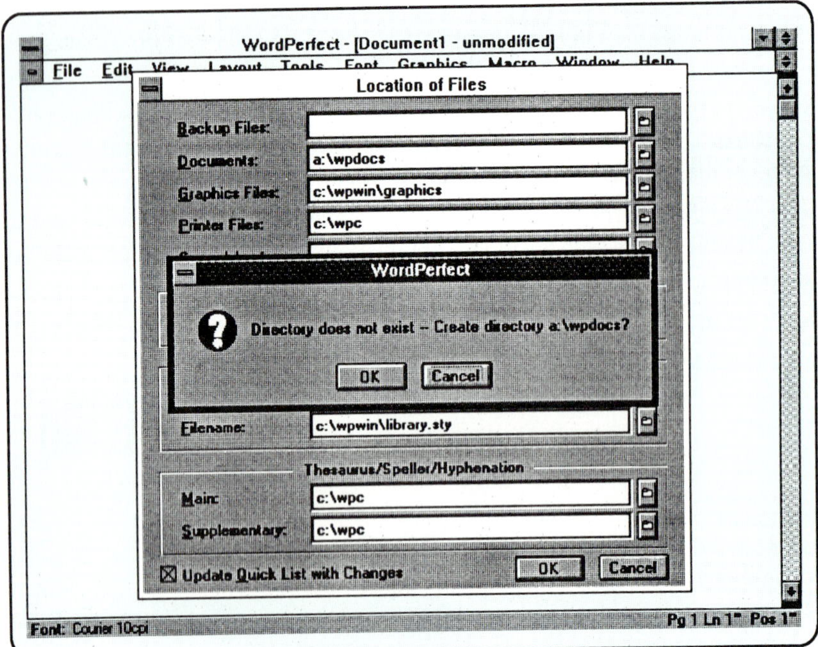

When you are prompted whether or not to create the directory "a:\wpdocs":

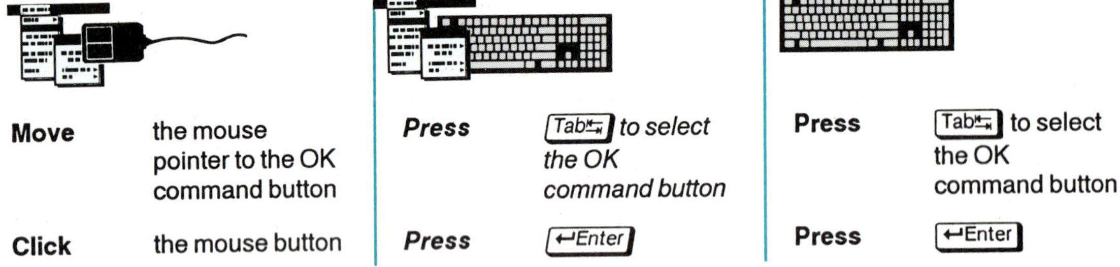

Move	the mouse pointer to the OK command button	***Press***	*Tab to select the OK command button*	**Press**	Tab to select the OK command button
Click	the mouse button	***Press***	*Enter*	**Press**	Enter

You have created a directory named "wpdocs" on the diskette in the A drive. You can store your document files using this directory. You are now ready to store documents on the diskette.

If you are not using a hard disk to store your documents, please proceed to the section titled "Exiting WordPerfect for Windows."

Hard Disk

On the hard disk, the WordPerfect for Windows software is usually stored in the directory named "wpwin." This directory name is also the initial default directory on which document files are saved. It is a good idea to store documents you create in a directory other than the default directory "wpwin." Once you change the default directory, WordPerfect for Windows refers to that directory until you change it again.

Suppose you want to save your documents in the directory "wpdocs" on your hard disk (that is, the C drive). To change the default directory to "wpdocs" on the C drive:

Move	the mouse pointer to the File menu	***Press***	*Alt*	**Press**	Ctrl+Shift+F1
Click	the mouse button	***Press***	*→ to move to the File menu*		

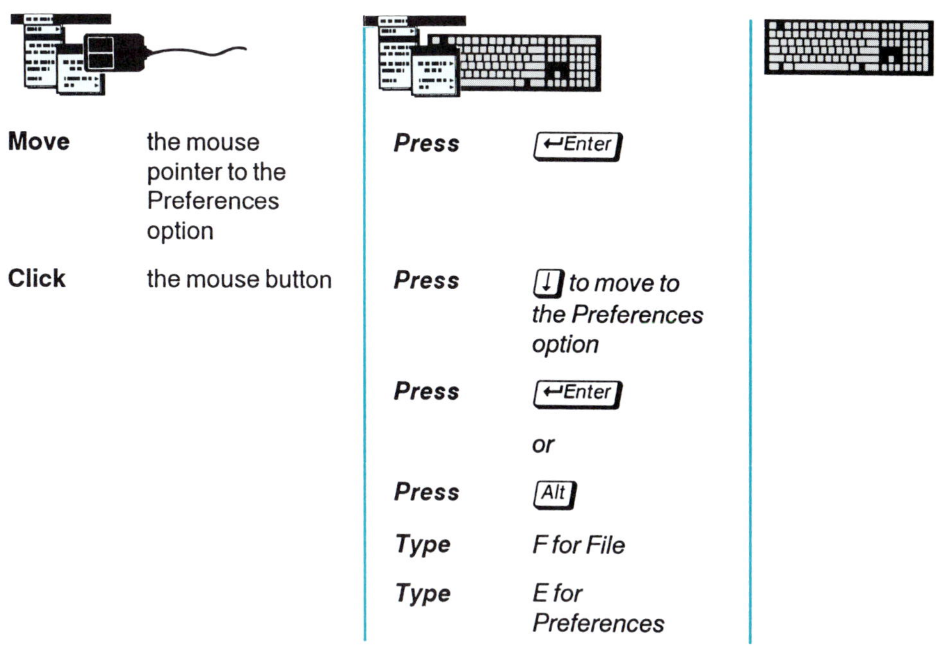

Move the mouse pointer to the Preferences option

Click the mouse button

Press *↵Enter*

Press *↓ to move to the Preferences option*

Press *↵Enter*

or

Press *Alt*

Type *F for File*

Type *E for Preferences*

Your screen should look like Figure 2-8.

Figure 2-8

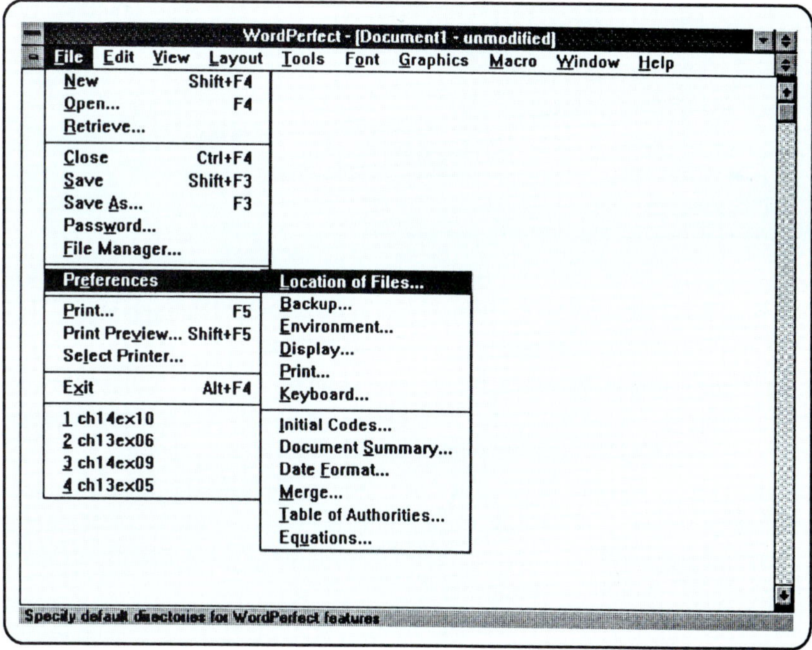

Many set up options are available under the File Preferences command. To change the location where files are being stored:

Move the mouse pointer to the Location of Files option

Press *↵Enter to select the Location of Files option*

Press ↵Enter to select the Location of Files option

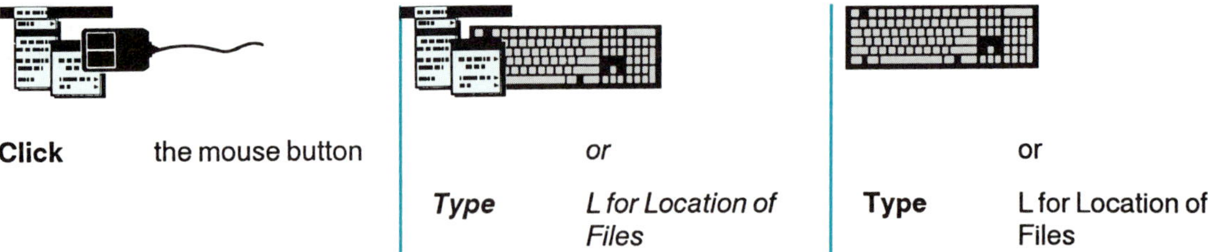

Click the mouse button

or

Type *L for Location of Files*

or

Type L for Location of Files

Your screen should look like Figure 2-9.

Figure 2-9

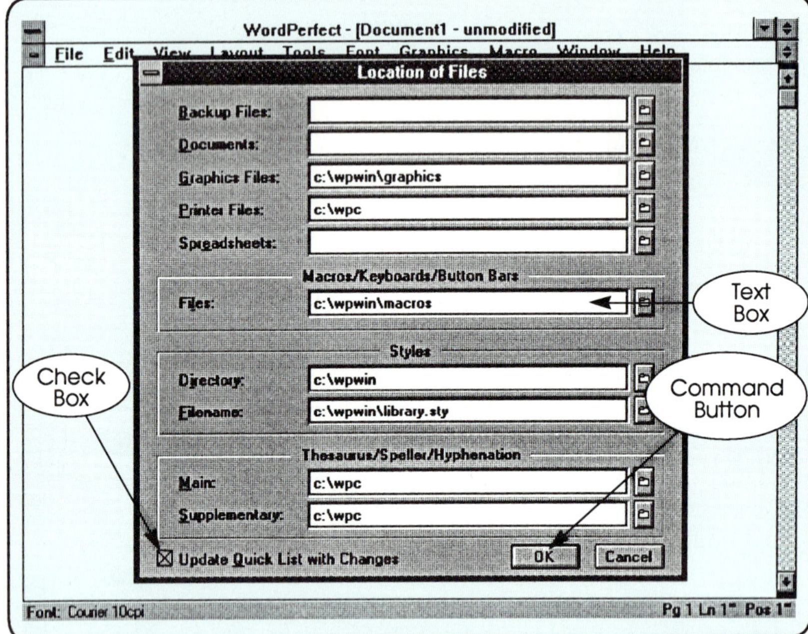

A dialog box appears on the screen. A dialog box provides options within a command. If a menu command provides a dialog box, it is followed by an ellipsis (...) in the menu. Dialog boxes often contain option buttons, check boxes, list boxes, text boxes, and command buttons.

Option buttons are round buttons. Whenever these round buttons appear in a dialog box, only one can be active. You can select the appropriate option button by clicking on the proper option button or by holding down the Alt key and pressing the underlined letter associated with that option.

Check boxes are small square boxes that you can check or place an X inside. If a check box contains an X, then that feature is on or active. If the check box is blank, then that feature is off or inactive. To activate a check box, click on the box until an X appears or hold down the Alt key and press the underlined letter associated with that check box until an X appears.

List boxes provide a list of names for you to choose from. Sometimes you cannot see the entire list. If you cannot see the entire list, scroll bars appear next to the list for you to view the remaining options. To select an item from a list box using the mouse, click on the item in the list box. When using the keyboard, hold down the Alt key and press the underlined letter associated with the list box, then press the pointer-movement keys to select the proper item.

Text boxes allow you to type an option in them. For example, the Document text box allows you to type the directory of document files. To select the text box, double-click inside the text box area or hold down the Alt key and press the underlined letter associated with the text box.

Command buttons are rectangular buttons. Common command buttons are the OK and Cancel buttons. To select a button, click the button with the mouse or hold down the Alt key and press the underlined letter of the command button.

Another alternative for moving between the various items in a dialog box is to press the Tab key.

To select the Documents text box:

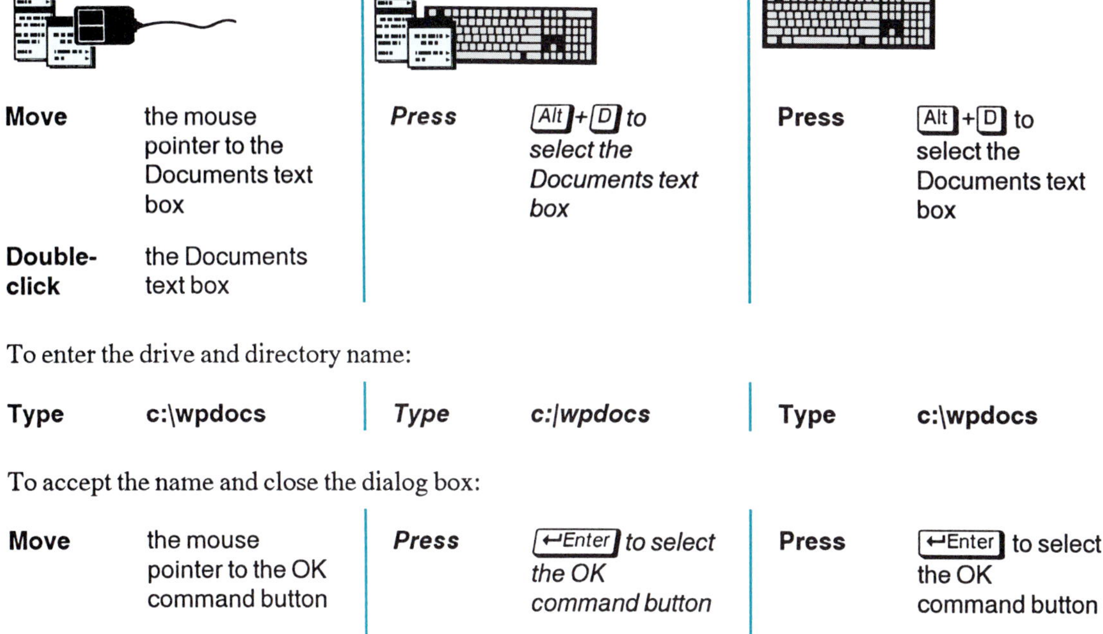

Move	the mouse pointer to the Documents text box	***Press***	*Alt+D to select the Documents text box*	**Press**	Alt+D to select the Documents text box
Double-click	the Documents text box				

To enter the drive and directory name:

Type	**c:\wpdocs**	***Type***	***c:/wpdocs***	**Type**	**c:\wpdocs**

To accept the name and close the dialog box:

Move	the mouse pointer to the OK command button	***Press***	*Enter to select the OK command button*	**Press**	Enter to select the OK command button
Click	the mouse button				

Your screen should now look like Figure 2-10.

Figure 2-10

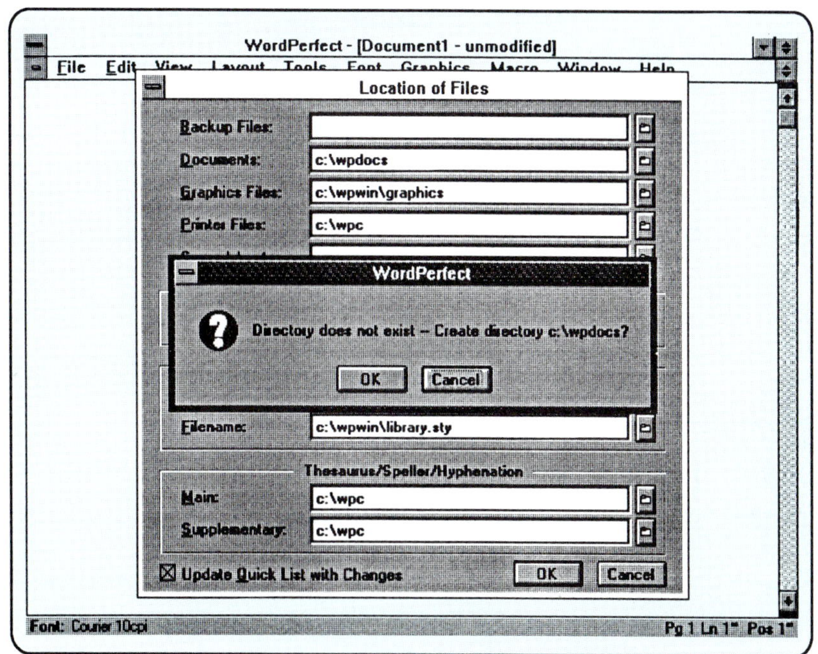

When you are prompted whether or not to create the directory "c:\wpdocs":

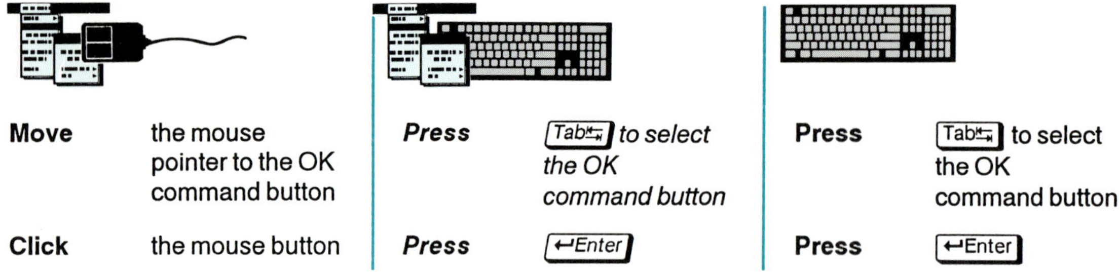

Move	the mouse pointer to the OK command button	***Press***	*Tab to select the OK command button*	**Press**	Tab to select the OK command button
Click	the mouse button	***Press***	*↵Enter*	**Press**	↵Enter

You have created a directory named "wpdocs" on the C drive. You can store your document files using this directory. You are now ready to store documents on the hard drive using this directory.

■ EXITING WORDPERFECT FOR WINDOWS

When you finish using WordPerfect for Windows, you need to exit from the software.

To exit WordPerfect for Windows:

Move	the mouse pointer to the File menu	***Press***	*Alt*	**Press**	Alt + F4
Click	the mouse button	***Press***	*→ to select the File menu*		
Move	the mouse pointer to the Exit option	***Press***	*↵Enter*		
Click	the mouse button	***Press***	*↓ to select the Exit option*		
		Press	*↵Enter*		
			or		
		Press	*Alt*		
		Type	*F for File*		
		Type	*X for Exit*		

EXERCISE 1

INSTRUCTIONS: Define the following terms:

1. Insertion point ______________________________

   ____

2. Function keys ______________________________

   ____

3. Pointer-movement keys ______________________________

____

4. Status bar ______________________________

____

5. Mouse pointer ______________________________

____

6. Template ______________________________

____

7. Default directory ______________________________

____

8. Menus ______________________________

____

EXERCISE 2

INSTRUCTIONS: Circle T if the statement is true and F if the statement is false.

T F 1. The blinking vertical bar on the screen is the insertion point.

T F 2. The status bar appears at the bottom of the screen. It shows the font you are using, the current page number, and the vertical position of the insertion point.

T F 3. A template is a diagram of the function keys and their operations.

T F 4. Black commands are issued by pressing the Shift key and then pressing the corresponding function key.

T F 5. Green commands are issued by pressing only the function key.

T F 6. Blue commands are issued by pressing the Ctrl key and then pressing the corresponding function key.

T F 7. Red commands are issued by pressing the Alt key and then pressing the corresponding function key.

T F 8. The menu can be accessed with a mouse or the keyboard.

T F 9. The names for a group of files can be stored in a special file called a directory.

T F 10. A dialog box appears when any menu command or function key is chosen.

EXERCISE 3

INSTRUCTIONS: Identify the circled items on the screen image below.

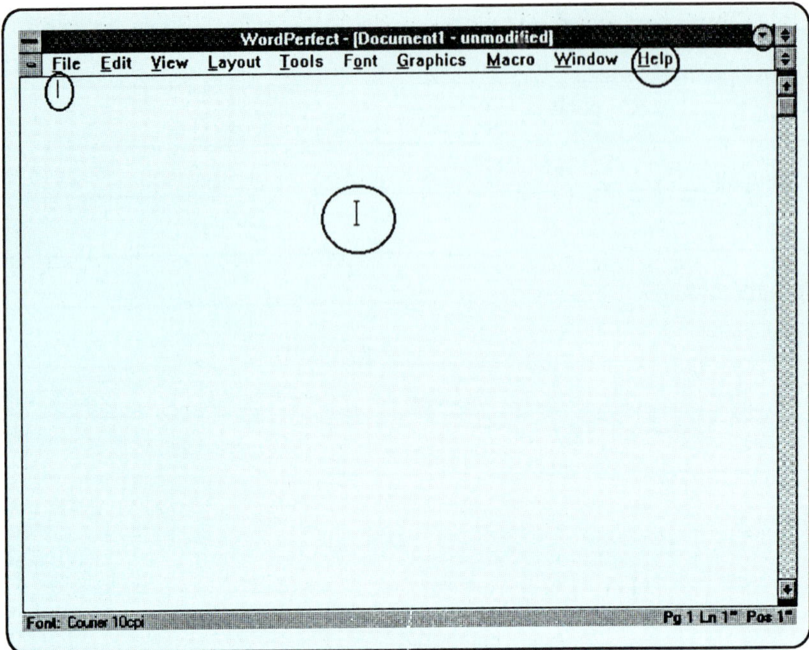

EXERCISE 4

INSTRUCTIONS: Access the WordPerfect for Windows software. Use the mouse to access the Tools menu choice from the menu bar. Your screen should look like the one below. Close the menu by clicking in the document area. Exit the WordPerfect for Windows software.

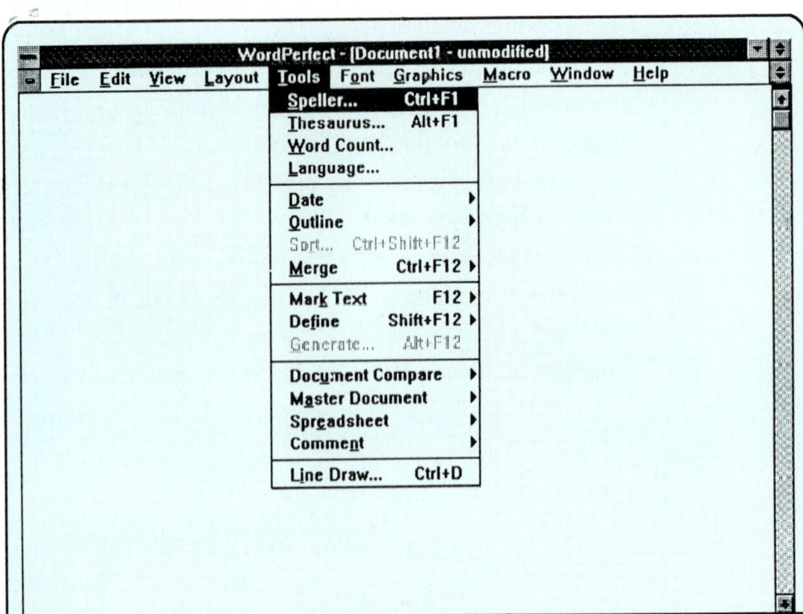

EXERCISE 5

INSTRUCTIONS: Access the WordPerfect for Windows software. Use the keyboard to access the Tools menu choice from the menu bar. Your screen should look like the screen in Exercise 4. Close the menu by using the Esc key. Exit the WordPerfect for Windows software.

EXERCISE 6

INSTRUCTIONS: Access the WordPerfect for Windows software. Use the mouse to access the Size options from the Font menu appearing on the menu bar. Your screen should look like the one below. Close the menu by clicking in the document area. Exit the WordPerfect for Windows software.

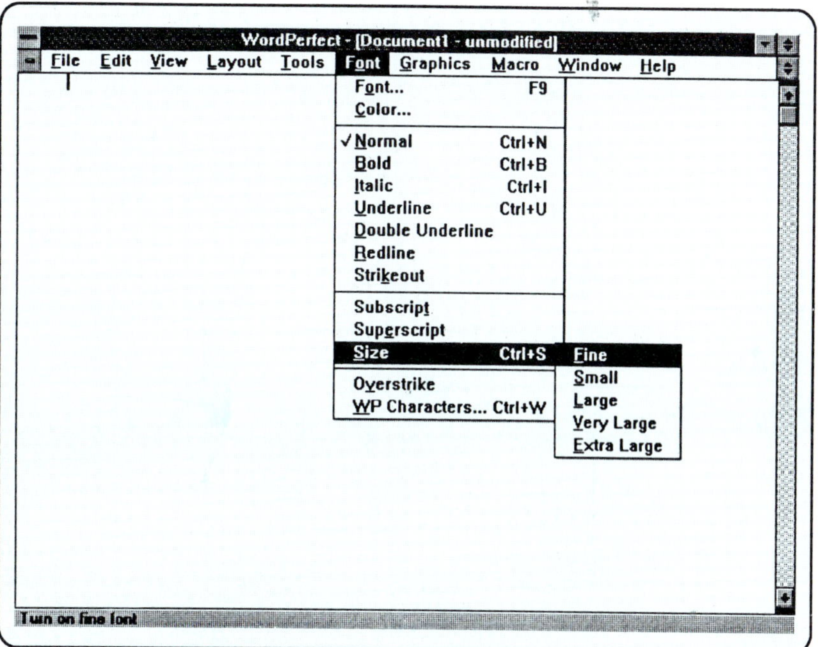

EXERCISE 7

INSTRUCTIONS: Access the WordPerfect for Windows software. Use the keyboard to access the Size options from the Font menu appearing on the menu bar. Your screen should look like the screen in Exercise 6. Close the menu by using the Esc key. Exit the WordPerfect for Windows software.

EXERCISE 8

INSTRUCTIONS: Access the WordPerfect for Windows software. Create a new default directory named "wpletter" using a floppy disk in drive A. Exit the WordPerfect for Windows software.

EXERCISE 9

INSTRUCTIONS: Access the WordPerfect for Windows software. Create a new default directory named "wpreport" using a hard disk drive. Exit the WordPerfect for Windows software.

EXERCISE 10

INSTRUCTIONS: Access the WordPerfect for Windows software. Create a new default directory named "wpmemos" using a floppy disk in drive A or on the hard disk drive. Exit the WordPerfect for Windows software.

EXERCISE 11

INSTRUCTIONS: Use the template and the menus to identify where you would find the following:

	Menu Used	Function Key Used
A. Preferences	______________	______________
B. Print	______________	______________
C. Reveal codes	______________	______________
D. Help	______________	______________
E. Exit	______________	______________

EXERCISE 12

INSTRUCTIONS: Use the template to identify which keys you would use to implement the following:

	Function Key
A. Date code	______________________
B. Font	______________________
C. Speller	______________________
D. Margins	______________________

CHAPTER THREE

QUICK START FOR WORDPERFECT FOR WINDOWS

OBJECTIVES

In this chapter, you will learn to:

- Create a document
- Edit a document
- Save a document
- Print a document
- Close the WordPerfect for Windows document
- Open a document
- Exit WordPerfect for Windows

CHAPTER OVERVIEW

When you create a document using WordPerfect for Windows, you go through the following steps:

1. Access the WordPerfect for Windows software
2. Create the document by keying in the material
3. Make modifications or changes to the document
4. Save the document in a file on a disk
5. Print the document

In other situations, you may open an existing document from a disk and make changes to it on your screen. After completing the changes, you save the document again. You may also print it.

When you are finished using one document, you need to close the document before you start working on another document. You must exit the WordPerfect for Windows software when you are completely finished.

In this chapter, you are given a quick overview of the processes of creating, editing, printing, and saving a document. You are also introduced to closing the WordPerfect for Windows document. You will open a document, make some changes, and save the document again. The procedure for exiting WordPerfect for Windows is presented.

■ CREATING A SIMPLE DOCUMENT

Access the WordPerfect for Windows software on your computer.

In this exercise you will type a short paragraph. As you type, the text will be displayed on the monitor screen and will reside in the memory of your computer. If you make a typing error, press [←Backspace] to delete the error and then enter the characters again. (You will learn other methods for correcting errors later.)

Word Wrap

You can type without worrying about how much text fits on a line. As you type, words automatically wrap to the next line. Do not press [↵Enter] at the end of each line. Press [↵Enter] only to create a blank line, to end a paragraph, or to end a short line.

Type the paragraph displayed in Figure 3-1. Remember, do not press [↵Enter] at the end of each line. You will make some needed changes in the next section.

Figure 3-1

```
With WordPerfect, you do not have too worry about pressing enter
the end of each line.  WordPerfect decides how much text can fit
on a line.  As you type, words automatically wrap to the next
line.
```

■ EDITING THE DOCUMENT

After you complete the process of creating a document, you may need to edit the document. In the paragraph you typed, the word "at" needs to be inserted at the beginning of the second line. Also, the second letter "o" in the word "too" on the first line needs to be deleted.

To insert the word "at" at the beginning of the second line:

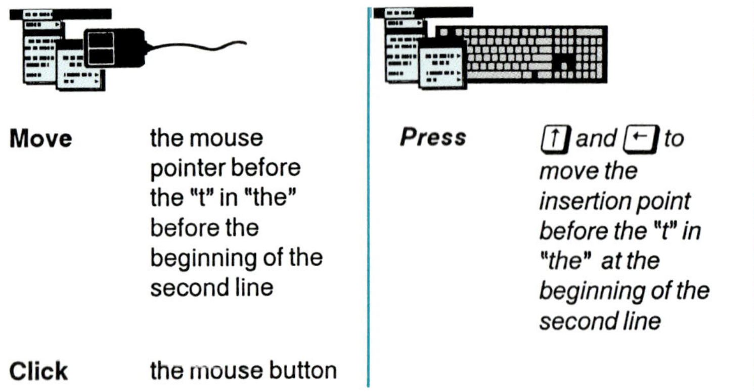

Move	the mouse pointer before the "t" in "the" before the beginning of the second line	***Press***	*[↑] and [←] to move the insertion point before the "t" in "the" at the beginning of the second line*
Click	the mouse button		

The top part of your screen should look like Figure 3-2.

Figure 3-2

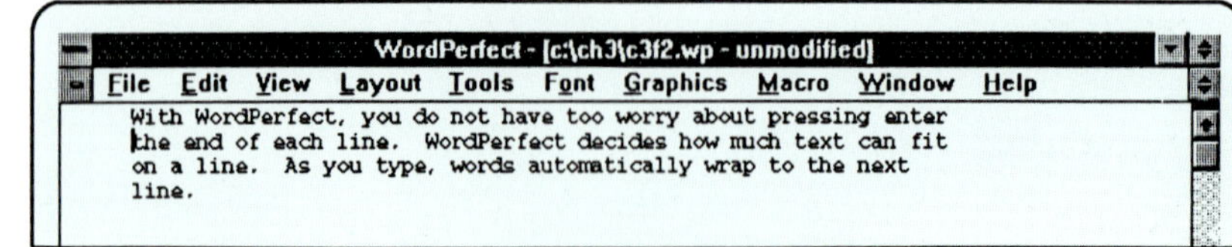

> **In This Book**
>
> The file name appearing on the WordPerfect for Windows title bar for most figures in the remaining portion of this book usually refers to the figure name. In most cases, your file name will be different.

Type	at	***Type***	*at*
Press	Spacebar	***Press***	*Spacebar*

The upper section of your screen should look like Figure 3-3.

Figure 3-3

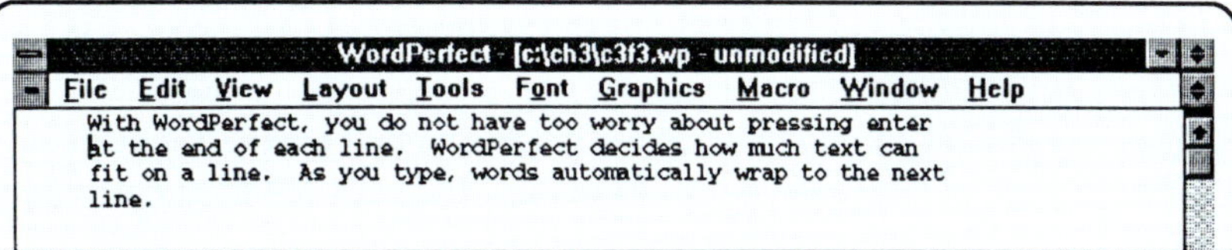

To delete the second "o" in the word "too" on the first line:

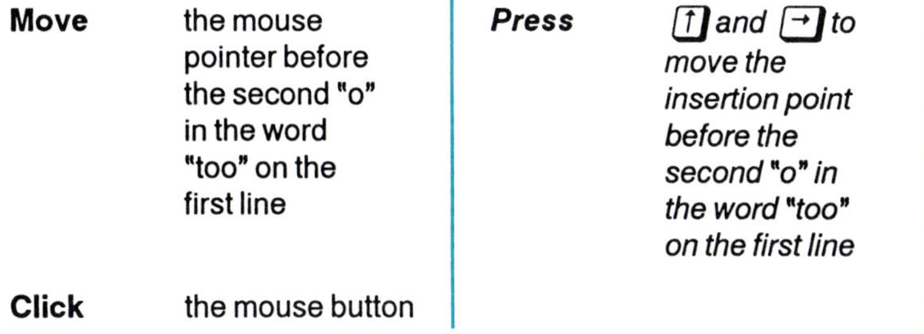

Move	the mouse pointer before the second "o" in the word "too" on the first line	***Press***	*↑ and → to move the insertion point before the second "o" in the word "too" on the first line*
Click	the mouse button		

The top portion of your screen should look like Figure 3-4.

Figure 3-4

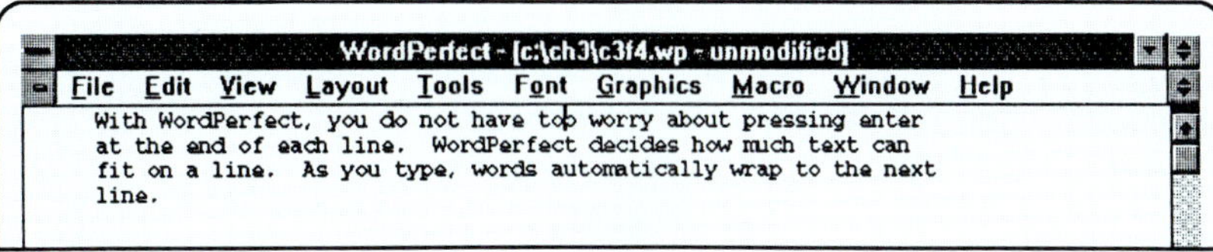

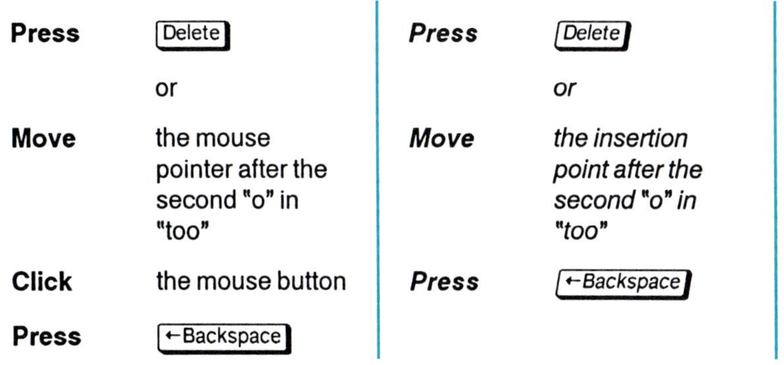

Press	Delete	***Press***	*Delete*
	or		*or*
Move	the mouse pointer after the second "o" in "too"	***Move***	*the insertion point after the second "o" in "too"*
Click	the mouse button	***Press***	*←Backspace*
Press	←Backspace		

The upper part of your screen should look like Figure 3-5.

Figure 3-5

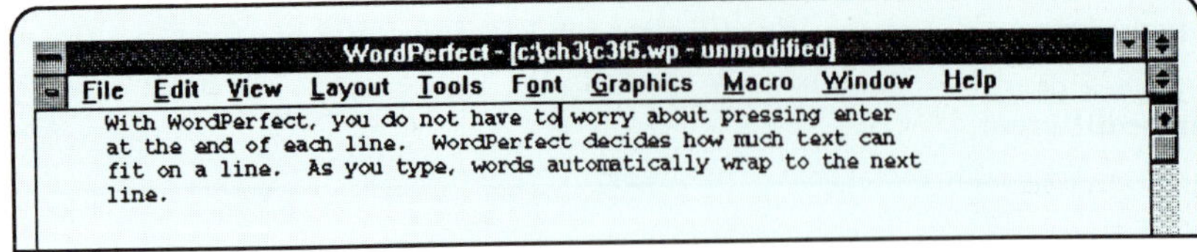

Additional editing features are presented in a later chapter.

■ SAVING THE DOCUMENT

While creating or editing a document, any changes you make are stored temporarily in your computer's memory. If the power to your computer fails, or if you turn off the computer, your work will be lost. You can prevent such a loss by using the Save As feature to place the document in a file on a disk. The disk can be a floppy disk or a hard disk. The Save As command is specified by selecting Save As from the File menu or by pressing the F3 key. The Save As feature allows you to save a document without losing your place on the screen, and then to continue creating or editing the document. As you work, it is a good idea to save the document every 10 to 15 minutes.

The first time you save a document, you must name it. A document name can have up to 8 characters followed by an optional period and up to 3 more characters. Use only letters and numbers in a file name. Do not include special characters such as $, or -.

If you are using a hard disk to store your documents, you can proceed to the Hard Disk section.

Floppy Disk

To change the default directory to the "wpdocs" directory you created on the A drive in Chapter 2:

Move	the mouse pointer to the File menu	***Press***	*Alt*	**Press**	Ctrl+Shift+F1
Click	the mouse button	***Press***	*→ to move to the File menu*		
Move	the mouse pointer to the Preferences option	***Press***	*↵Enter*		
Click	the mouse button	***Press***	*↓ to move to the Preferences option*		
		Press	*↵Enter*		
			or		
		Press	*Alt*		
		Type	*F for File*		
		Type	*E for Preferences*		

Your screen should look like Figure 3-6.

Figure 3-6

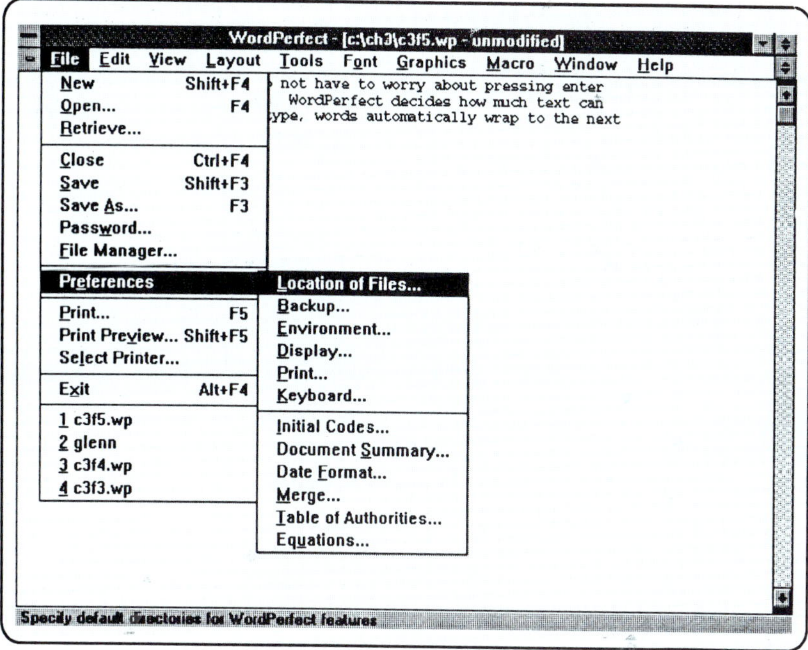

Move	the mouse pointer to the Location of Files option	***Press***	*↵Enter to select the Location of Files option*	**Press**	↵Enter to select the Location of Files option
Click	the mouse button		*or*		or
		Type	*L for Location of Files*	**Type**	L for Location of Files

Your screen should look like Figure 3-7.

Figure 3-7

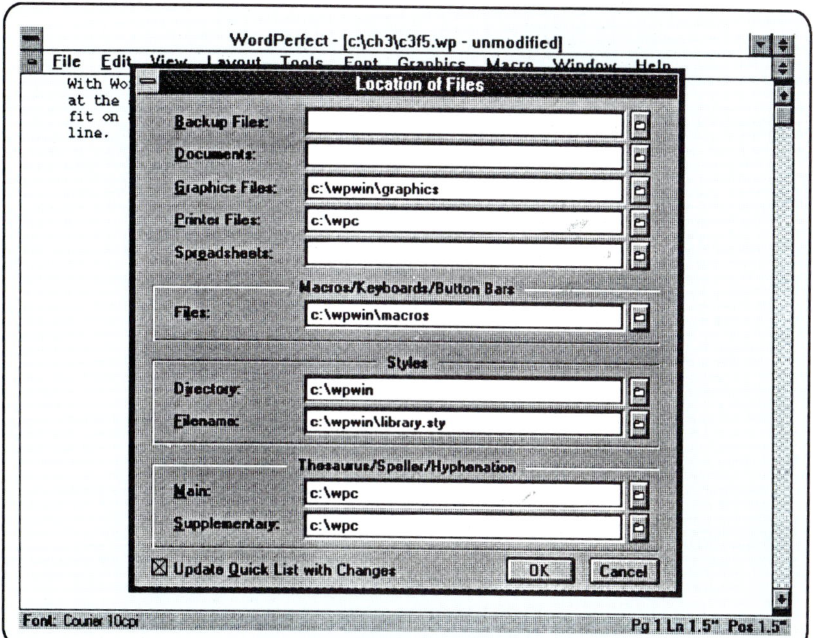

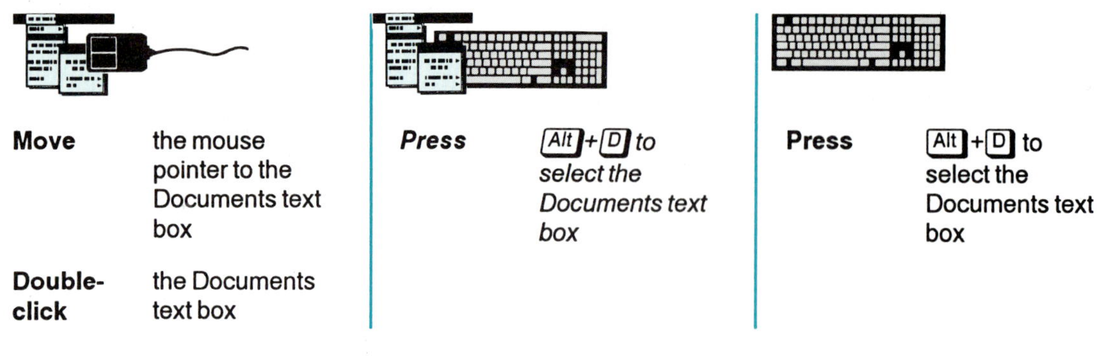

Move	the mouse pointer to the Documents text box	***Press***	*Alt+D to select the Documents text box*	**Press**	Alt+D to select the Documents text box
Double-click	the Documents text box				

To enter the drive and directory name:

Type	**a:\wpdocs**	***Type***	***a:\wpdocs***	**Type**	**a:\wpdocs**
Move	the mouse pointer to the OK command button	***Press***	*↵Enter to select the OK command button*	**Press**	↵Enter to select the OK command button
Click	the mouse button				

If you are not saving your document on a hard disk, you can proceed to the "Save Process" section.

Hard Disk

To change the default directory to the "wpdocs" directory you created on the C drive in Chapter 2:

Move	the mouse pointer to the File menu	***Press***	*Alt*	**Press**	Ctrl+Shift+F1
Click	the mouse button	***Press***	*→ to move to the File menu*		
Move	the mouse pointer to the Preferences option	***Press***	*↵Enter*		
Click	the mouse button	***Press***	*↓ to move to the Preferences option*		
		Press	*↵Enter*		
			or		
		Press	*Alt*		
		Type	*F for File*		
		Type	*E for Preferences*		

Your screen should look like Figure 3-8.

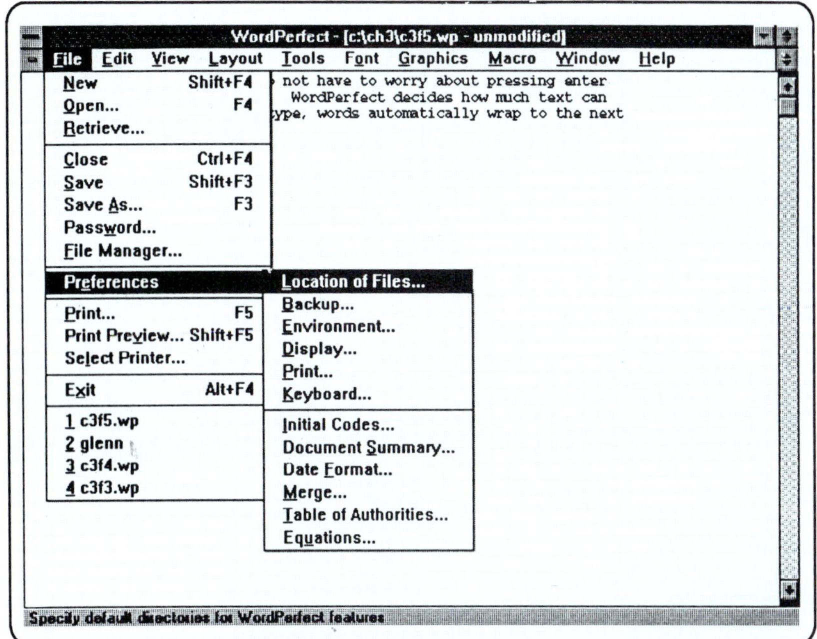

Figure 3-8

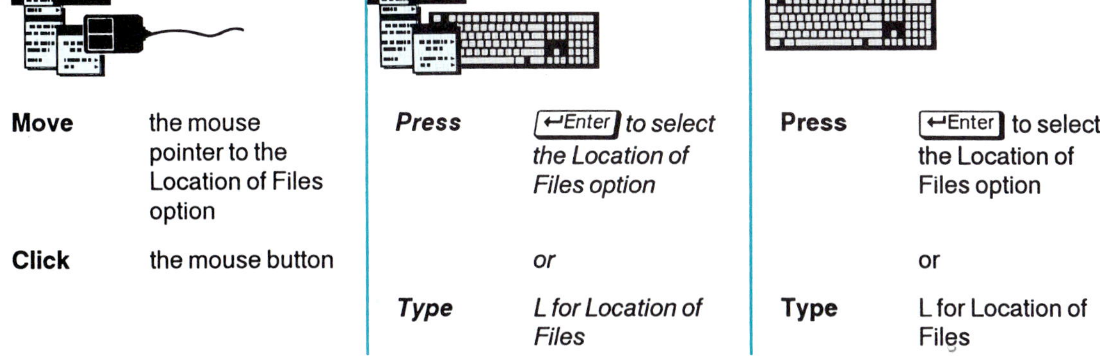

Move	the mouse pointer to the Location of Files option	***Press***	*↵Enter to select the Location of Files option*	**Press**	↵Enter to select the Location of Files option
Click	the mouse button		*or*		or
		Type	*L for Location of Files*	**Type**	L for Location of Files

Your screen should look like Figure 3-9.

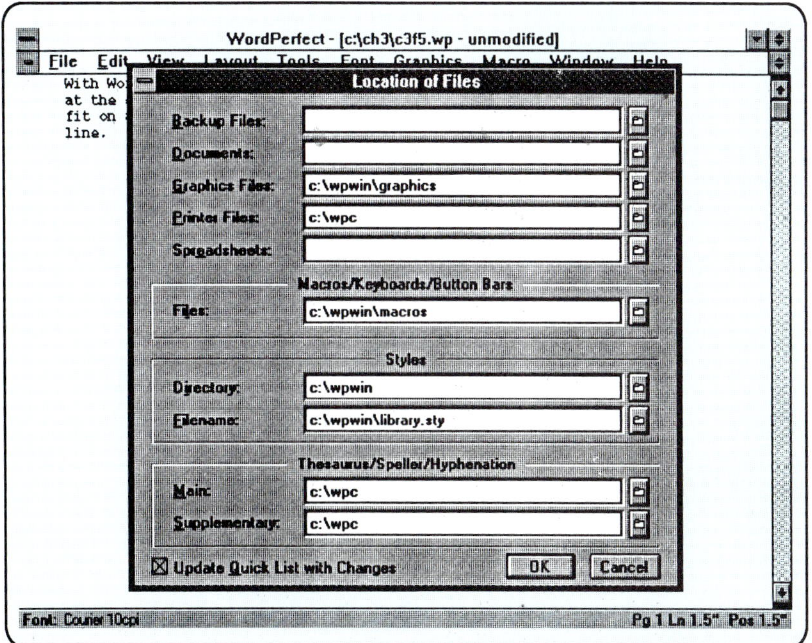

Figure 3-9

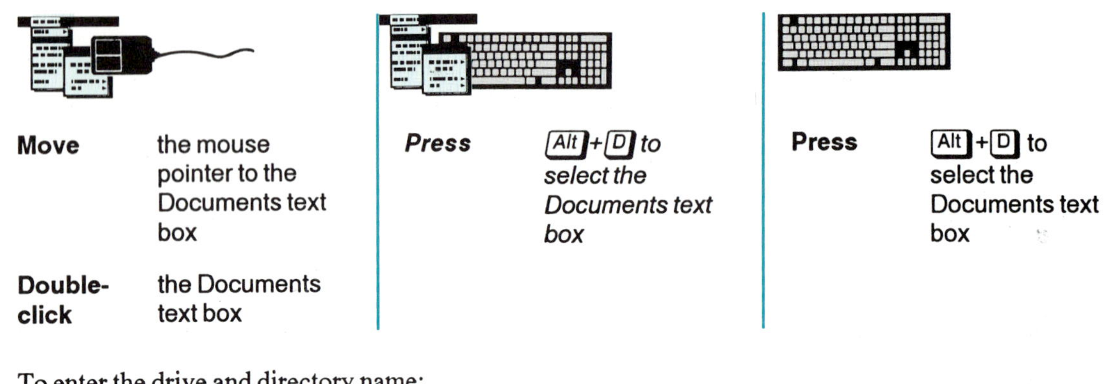

Move	the mouse pointer to the Documents text box	***Press***	*Alt+D to select the Documents text box*	**Press**	Alt+D to select the Documents text box
Double-click	the Documents text box				

To enter the drive and directory name:

Type	**c:\wpdocs**	***Type***	***c:/wpdocs***	**Type**	**c:\wpdocs**
Move	the mouse pointer to the OK command button	***Press***	*↵Enter to select the OK command button*	**Press**	↵Enter to select the OK command button
Click	the mouse button				

Save Process

Once you have specified the default directory for saving your documents, you can then continue with the save process. WordPerfect for Windows has two save commands: File Save As and File Save. The File Save As command allows you to change the document name or directory. Use the File Save As command the first time you save a file or any time that you want to change the file name.

The File Save command allows you to save a document under the same file name replacing the old document contents with the new document contents. Use the File Save command when you want to save the changes to a document, but you do not want to change the document name.

Since you have not saved this document yet, use the File Save As command to save the document using the filename "practice":

Move	the mouse pointer to the File menu	***Press***	*Alt*	**Press**	F3
Click	the mouse button	***Press***	*→ to select the File menu*		
Move	the mouse pointer to the Save As option	***Press***	*↵Enter*		
Click	the mouse button	***Press***	*↓ to select the Save As option*		
		Press	*↵Enter*		
			or		
		Press	*Alt*		
		Type	*F for File*		
		Type	*A for Save As*		

Your screen should look like Figure 3-10.

Figure 3-10

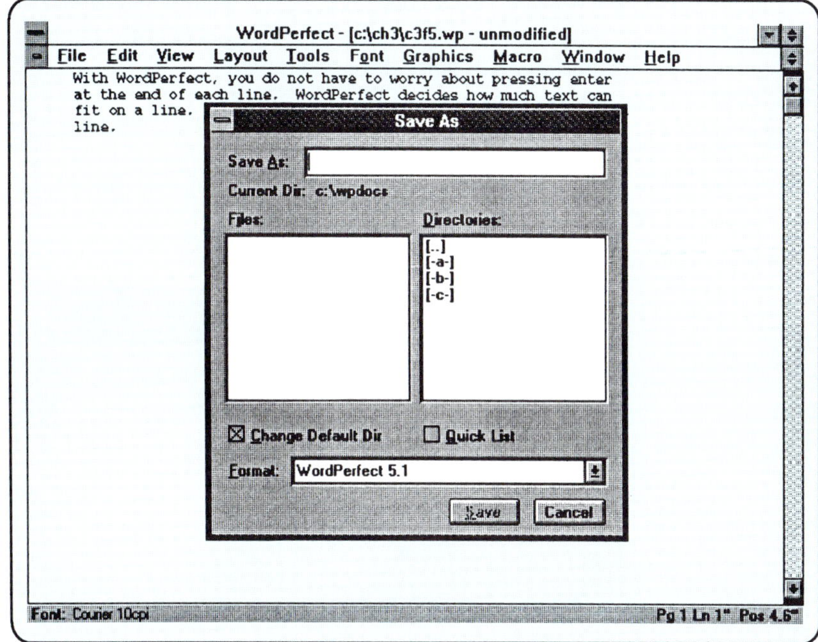

A dialog box appears on the screen with information about the File Save As command. Notice that the current directory appears under the Save As text box. This current directory is the same directory that you specified in the File Preferences, Location of Files command sequence.

To save the file as "practice":

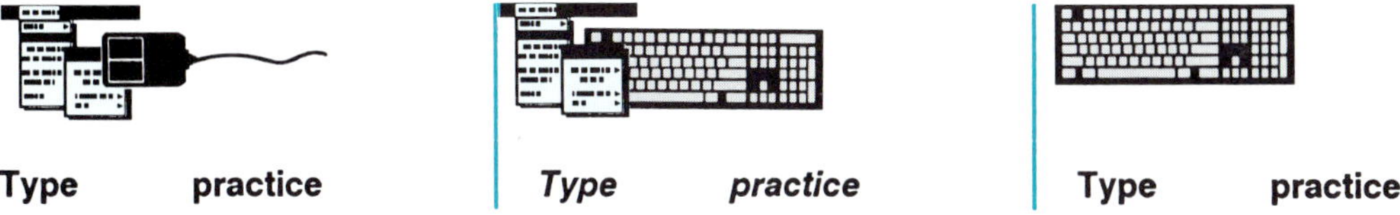

Type	**practice**	***Type***	***practice***	**Type**	**practice**

When you type a file name in WordPerfect for Windows, the file name appears in lowercase.

To accept the file name and return to your document:

Move	the mouse pointer to the Save command button	***Press***	*Alt+S to select the Save command button*	**Press**	Alt+S to select the Save command button
Click	the mouse button		*or*		or
		Press	*↵Enter*	**Press**	↵Enter

The top part of your screen should look like Figure 3-11.

Figure 3-11

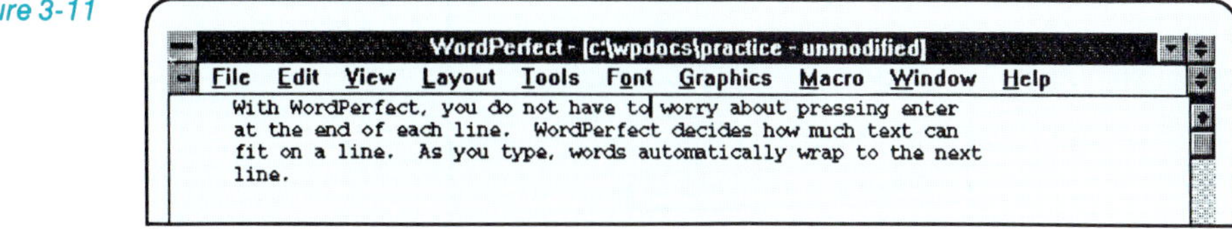

Notice that the document name appears in the title bar.

You will learn another method for saving a document in a later chapter.

If you are using a floppy disk, you will have "a:\wpdocs\practice" on the title bar If you are using a hard disk, "a:" will be replaced by "c:." Notice the word "unmodified" appears after the document name to indicate that the document has not been changed since it was last saved.

PRINTING THE DOCUMENT

After you create a document, you often print the document. Before printing a document, you can view the document to see what it will look like when it is printed.

To view the document as it will appear when you print it:

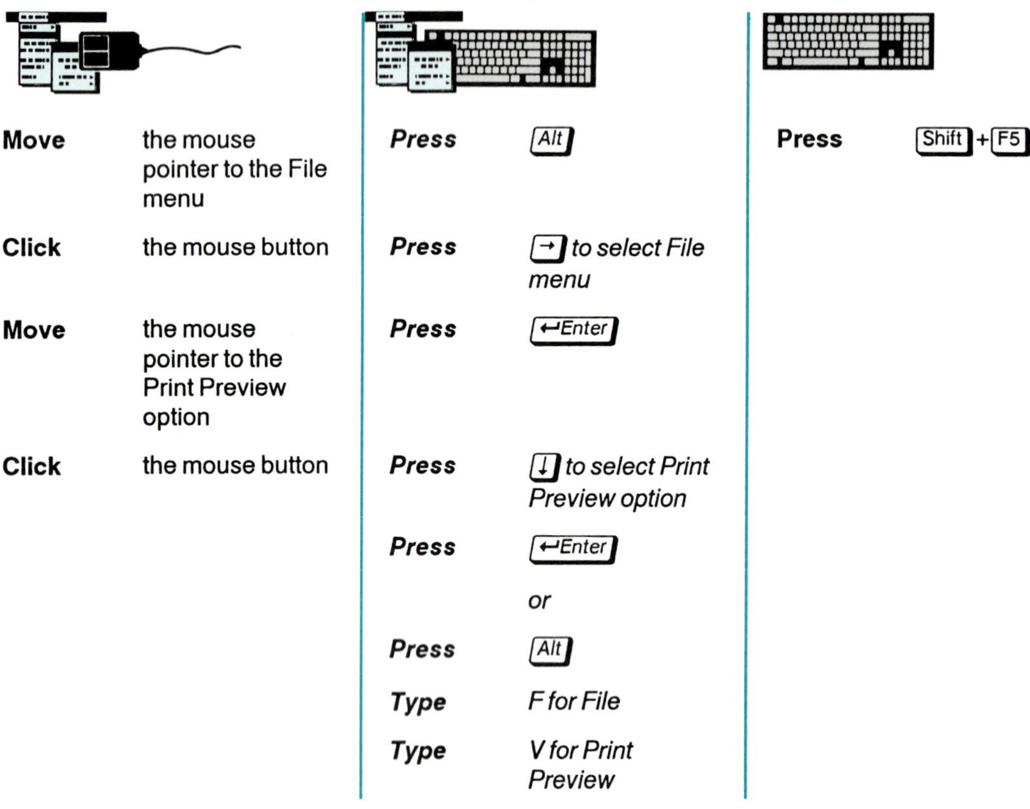

Mouse		Keyboard		Shortcut	
Move	the mouse pointer to the File menu	***Press***	*Alt*	**Press**	Shift + F5
Click	the mouse button	***Press***	*→ to select File menu*		
Move	the mouse pointer to the Print Preview option	***Press***	*↵Enter*		
Click	the mouse button	***Press***	*↓ to select Print Preview option*		
		Press	*↵Enter*		
			or		
		Press	*Alt*		
		Type	*F for File*		
		Type	*V for Print Preview*		

To view your document at 100%:

Mouse		Keyboard	
Move	the mouse pointer to the View menu	***Press***	*Alt*
Click	the mouse button	***Press***	*→ to select the View menu*
Move	the mouse pointer to the 100% option	***Press***	*↵Enter*
Click	the mouse button	***Press***	*↓ to select the 100% option*
		Press	*↵Enter*

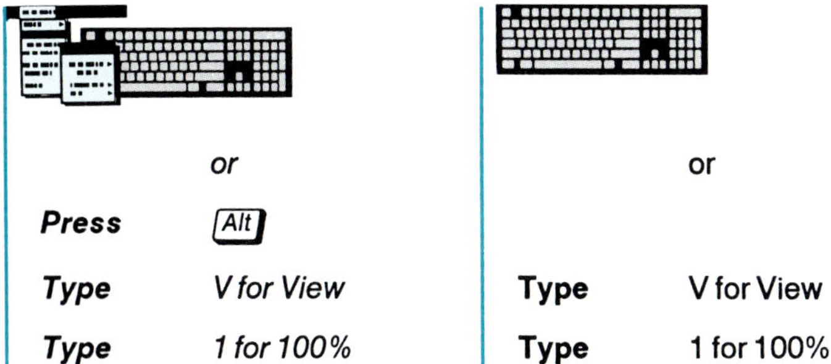

or
Press Alt
Type V for View
Type 1 for 100%
or
Type V for View
Type 1 for 100%

Your screen should look like Figure 3-12.

Figure 3-12

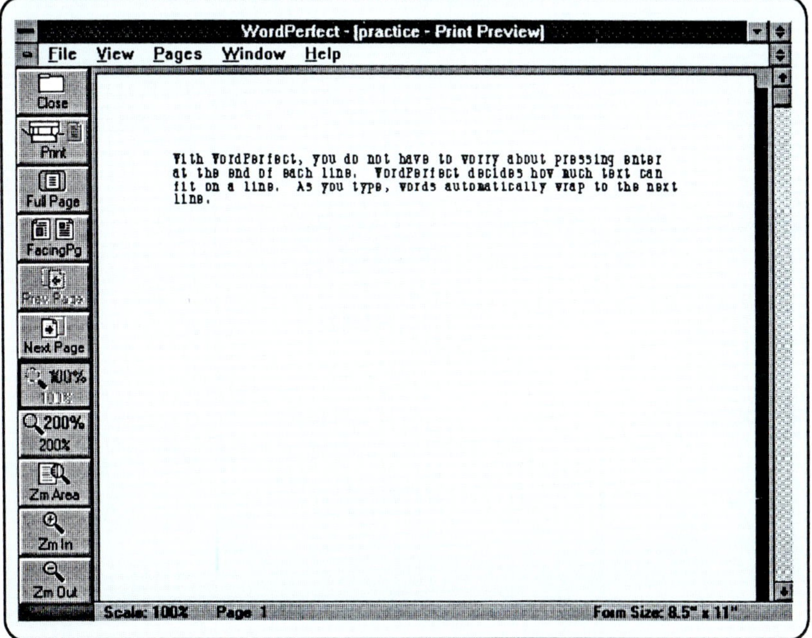

To return to your document:

Move	the mouse pointer to the File menu	***Press***	*Alt*	**Press**	Ctrl + F4
Click	the mouse button	***Press***	*→ to select the File menu*		
Move	the mouse pointer to the Close option	***Press***	*↵Enter*		
Click	the mouse button	***Press***	*↓ to select the Close option*		
		Press	*↵Enter*		

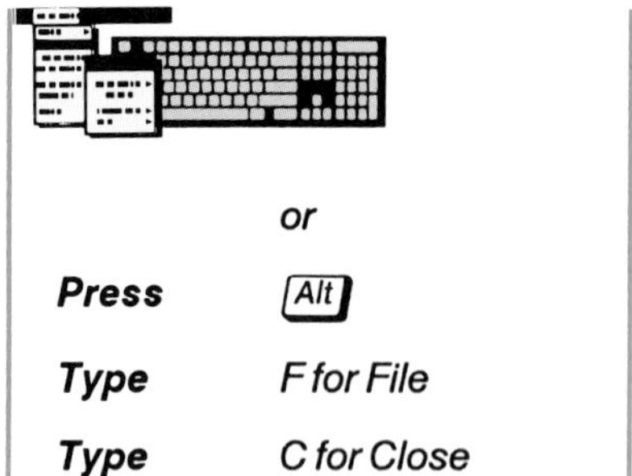	
	or
Press	Alt
Type	*F for File*
Type	*C for Close*

When you have finished viewing the document, you can then print it. You do not have to view the document before printing it. However, it is a good idea to see how the document appears before you print it.

To print the entire "practice" document:

Move	the mouse pointer to the File menu	***Press***	Alt	**Press**	F5
Click	the mouse button	***Press***	→ *to select the File menu*		
Move	the mouse pointer to the Print option	***Press***	↵Enter		
Click	the mouse button	***Press***	↓ *to select the Print option*		
		Press	↵Enter		
			or		
		Press	Alt		
		Type	*F for File*		
		Type	*P for Print*		

The Print dialog box should appear on your screen. Your screen should look like Figure 3-13.

Figure 3-13

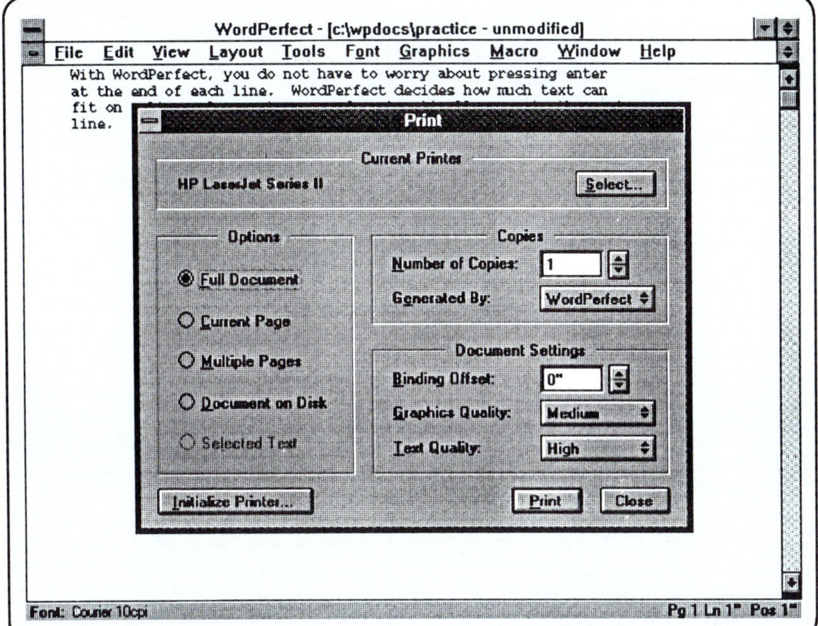

To print the document:

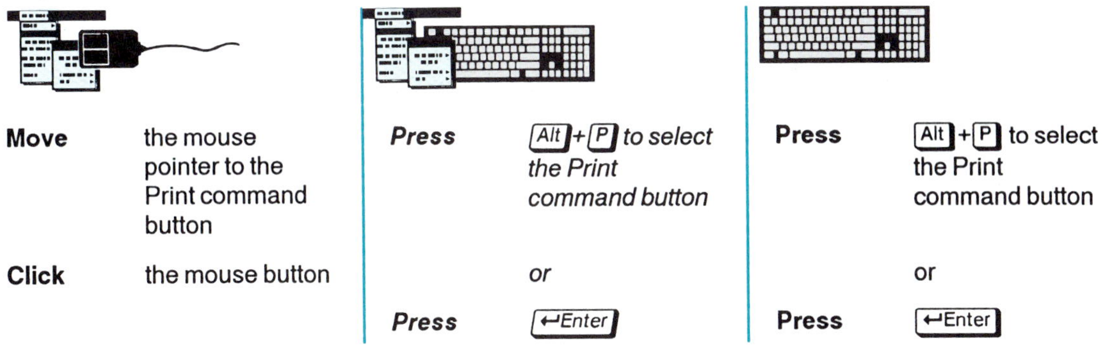

Move	the mouse pointer to the Print command button	***Press***	*Alt + P to select the Print command button*	**Press**	Alt + P to select the Print command button
Click	the mouse button		*or*		or
		Press	*↵Enter*	**Press**	↵Enter

Note that your document prints according to the default setting which is left justification. Additional printing features are presented in a later chapter.

■ CLOSING THE DOCUMENT

When you have finished working on a document, you should save it. You should also close the document before starting to work on another document. You can close a document by selecting Close from the File menu.

To close the document and clear the screen:

Move	the mouse pointer to the File menu	***Press***	*Alt*	**Press**	Ctrl + F4
Click	the mouse pointer	***Press***	*→ to select the File menu*		

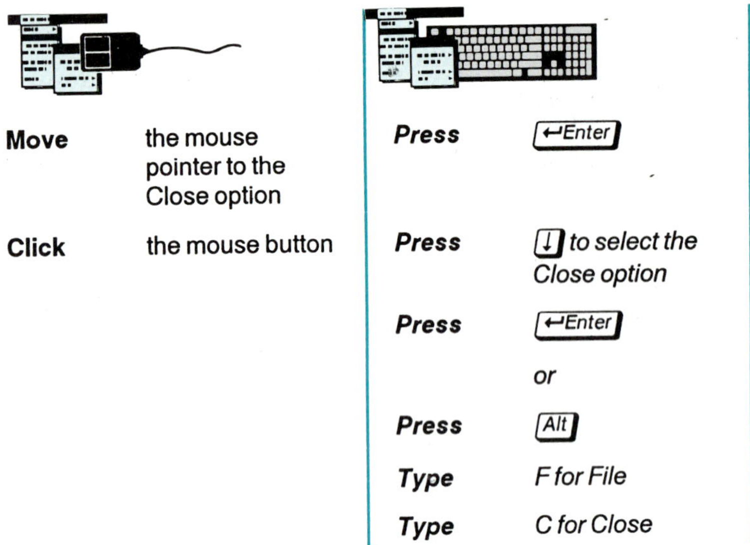

Your screen should look like Figure 3-14.

Figure 3-14

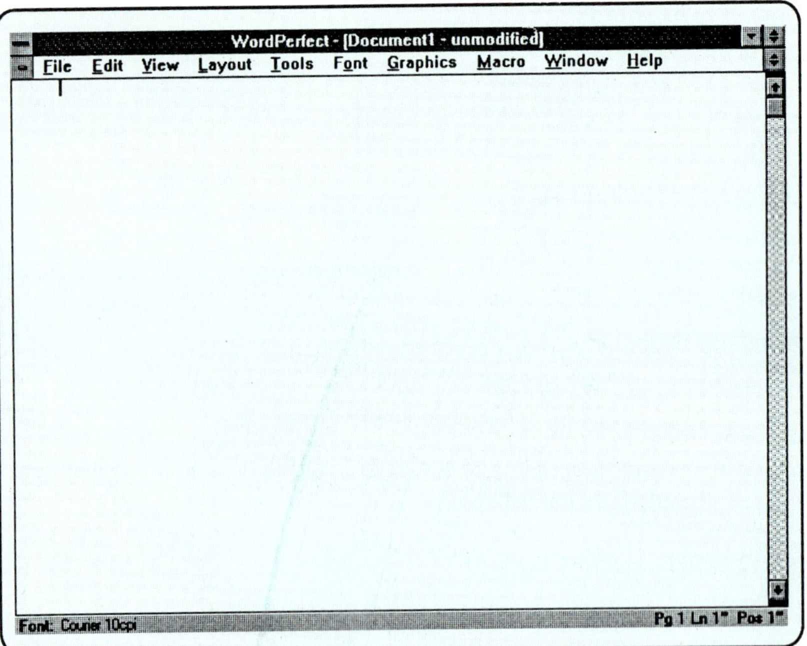

■ OPENING THE DOCUMENT

The documents you create in WordPerfect for Windows are saved in files. When you want to edit a document, you need to open a copy of the file from a disk and place it in the memory of your computer. A copy of the file appears on the computer screen.

The document is then active in your computer's memory and you can edit the document. However, the changes you make will affect only the document on the screen. They will not be recorded on the disk until you save them.

You can open a document from any directory. If the document is stored in the current directory, just enter the document name. If the document is stored in a different directory, you must include the drive and directory name before the document name.

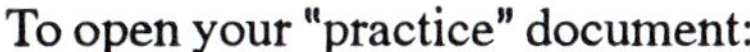

To open your "practice" document:

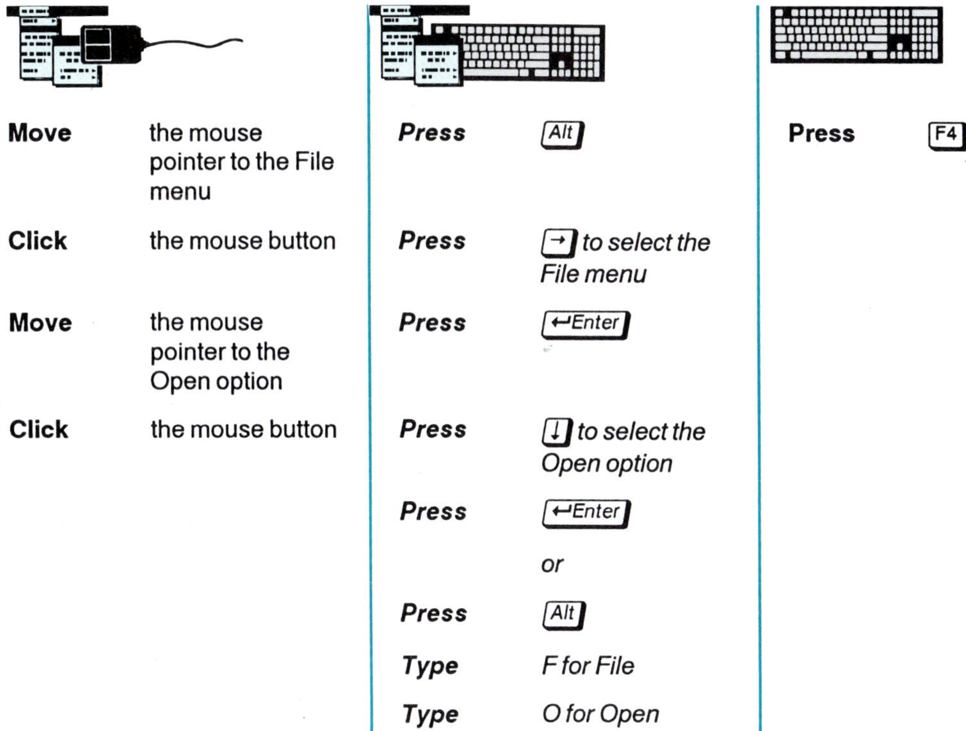

Mouse		Mouse and keyboard		Keyboard	
Move	the mouse pointer to the File menu	***Press***	*Alt*	**Press**	F4
Click	the mouse button	***Press***	*→ to select the File menu*		
Move	the mouse pointer to the Open option	***Press***	*↵Enter*		
Click	the mouse button	***Press***	*↓ to select the Open option*		
		Press	*↵Enter*		
			or		
		Press	*Alt*		
		Type	*F for File*		
		Type	*O for Open*		

Your screen should look like Figure 3-15.

Figure 3-15

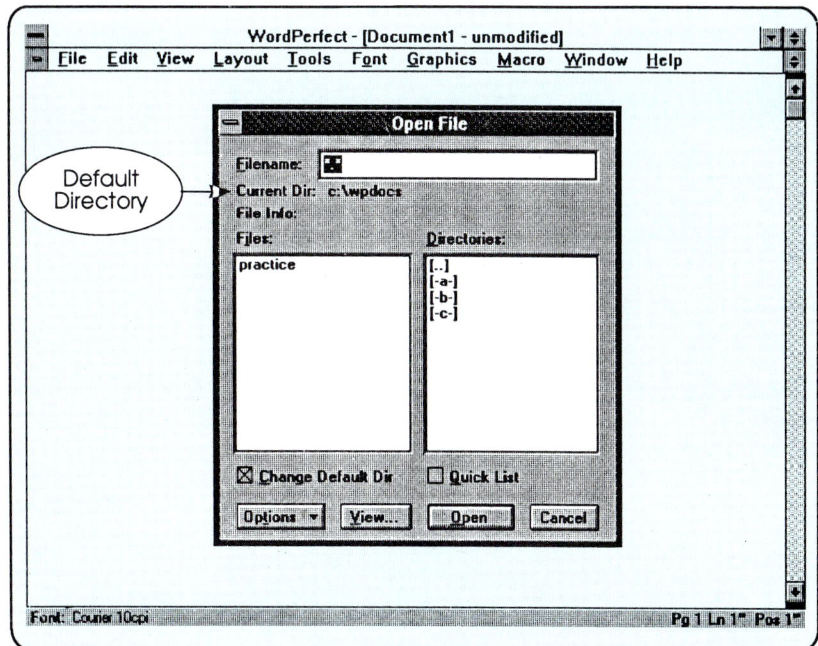

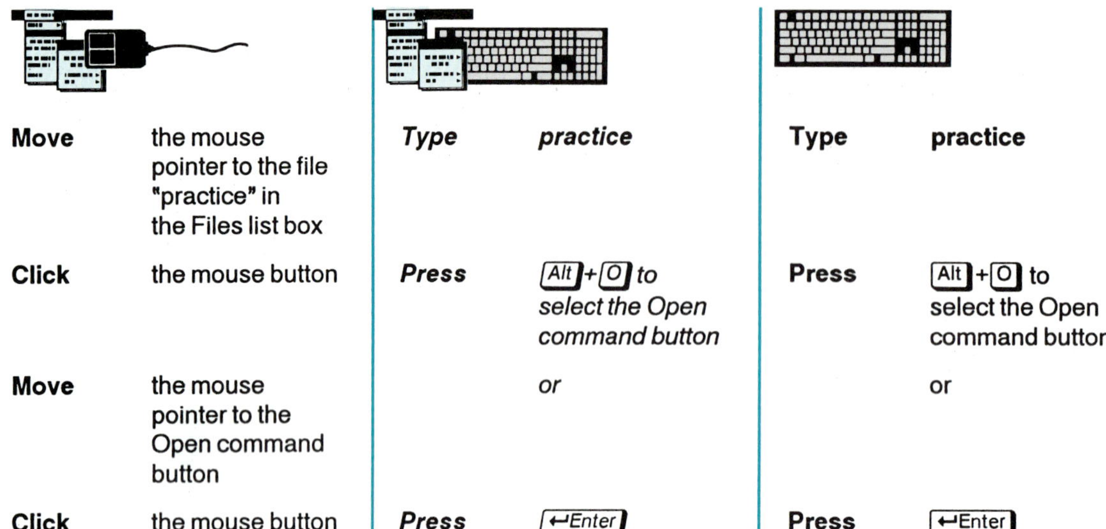

Mouse		Mouse and Keyboard		Keyboard	
Move	the mouse pointer to the file "practice" in the Files list box	***Type***	***practice***	**Type**	**practice**
Click	the mouse button	***Press***	*Alt+O to select the Open command button*	**Press**	Alt+O to select the Open command button
Move	the mouse pointer to the Open command button		*or*		or
Click	the mouse button	***Press***	*↵Enter*	**Press**	↵Enter

Your screen should look like Figure 3-16.

Figure 3-16

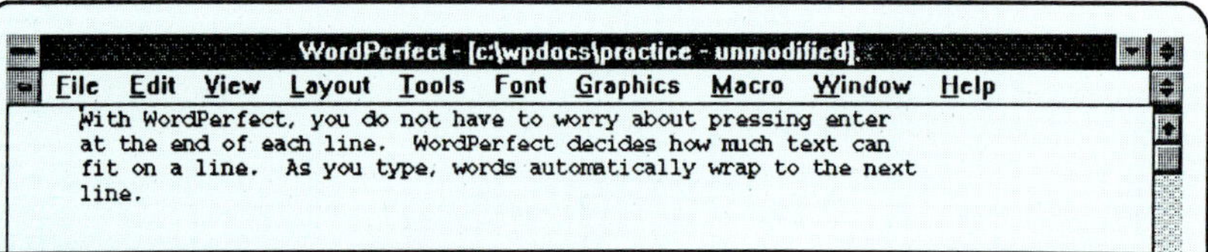

Now enter the additional text that appears in Figure 3-17.

Figure 3-17

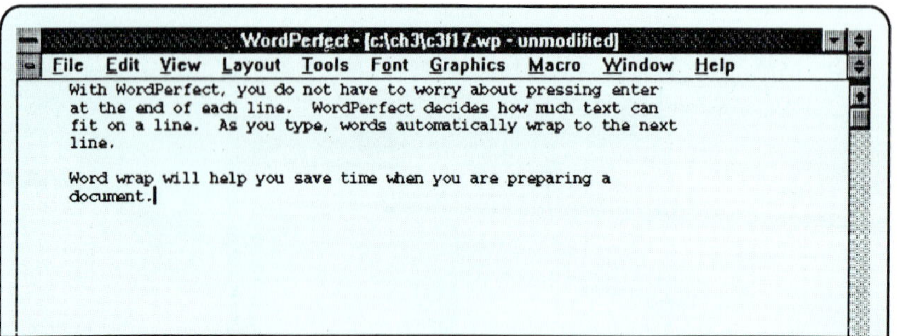

Move	the mouse pointer to the right of the last character in the document	***Move***	*the insertion point to the right of the last character in the document*	**Move**	the insertion point to the right of the last character in the document
Click	the mouse button	***Press***	*↵Enter twice*	**Press**	↵Enter twice

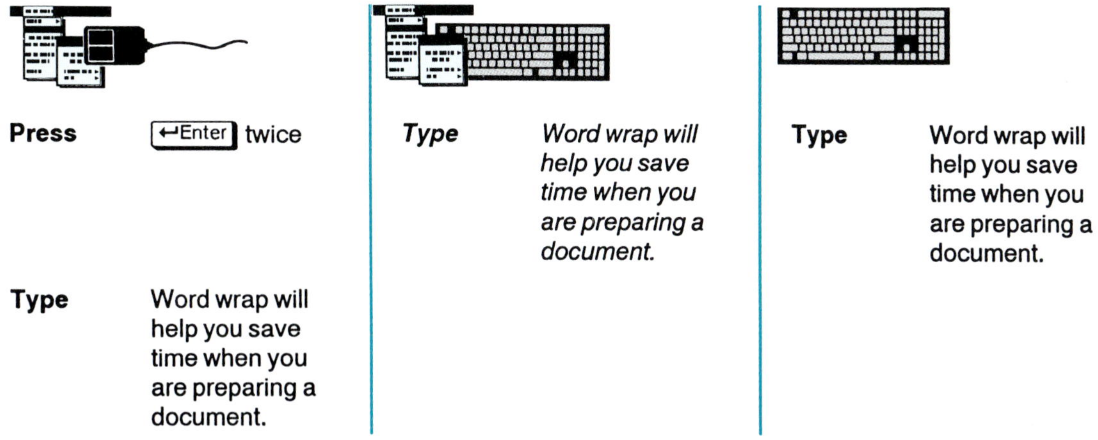

Press	↵Enter twice	***Type***	*Word wrap will help you save time when you are preparing a document.*	**Type**	Word wrap will help you save time when you are preparing a document.
Type	Word wrap will help you save time when you are preparing a document.				

After changing a document, you usually save it again using the same name for the document file. Since you have already named this file, you can use the File Save command. The File Save command saves the file under the same name and automatically replaces the old file.

To save the document with the same name:

Move	the mouse pointer to the File menu	***Press***	Alt	**Press**	Shift+F3
Click	the mouse button	***Press***	→ *to select the File menu*		
Move	the mouse pointer to the Save option	***Press***	↵Enter		
Click	the mouse button	***Press***	↓ *to select the Save option*		
		Press	↵Enter		
			or		
		Press	Alt		
		Type	*F for File*		
		Type	*S for Save*		

■ EXITING WORDPERFECT FOR WINDOWS

When you finish using WordPerfect for Windows, you will need to exit from the software.

To exit WordPerfect for Windows:

Move	the mouse pointer to the File menu	***Press***	Alt	**Press**	Alt+F4
Click	the mouse button	***Press***	→ *to select the File menu*		

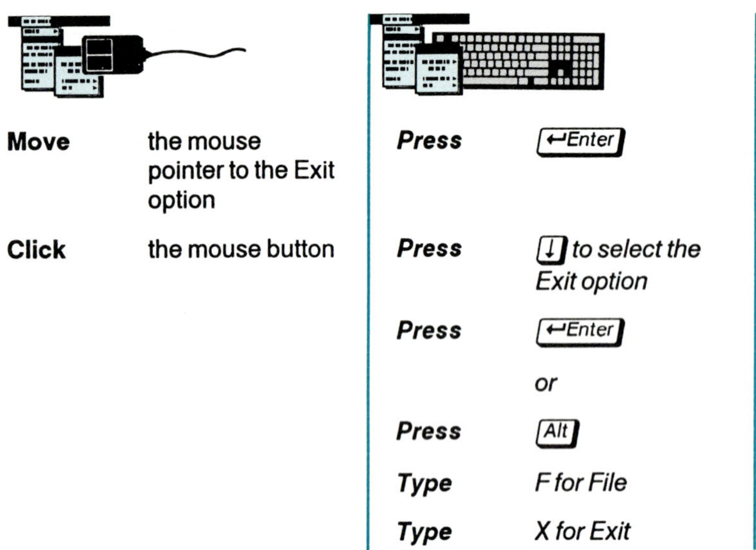

Move	the mouse pointer to the Exit option
Click	the mouse button

Press	*↵Enter*
Press	*↓ to select the Exit option*
Press	*↵Enter*
	or
Press	*Alt*
Type	*F for File*
Type	*X for Exit*

If you did not save your most recent changes, WordPerfect for Windows gives you a chance to save your current document before exiting the program. This feature can be very helpful if you have made some changes to your document and have not saved them, before entering your request to exit WordPerfect for Windows. In this example, we have already saved your last changes and therefore you are not prompted to save changes.

EXERCISE 1

INSTRUCTIONS: Define the following terms:

1. Insert ______________________________

   ____

2. Delete ______________________________

   ____

3. Word wrap ______________________________

   ____

4. Save As feature ______________________________

   ____

5. Exit feature ______________________________

   ____

6. Save feature ______________________________

   ____

7. Open feature ______________________________

____

8. Print feature ______________________________

____

9. Close feature ______________________________

____

EXERCISE 2

INSTRUCTIONS: Circle T if the statement is true and F if the statement is false.

T	F	1.	In WordPerfect for Windows, you do not need to press ↵Enter at the end of each line.
T	F	2.	When you are creating or editing a document, any changes you make are stored temporarily in your computer's memory.
T	F	3.	The Save feature saves a document and clears the screen.
T	F	4.	You can use letters, numbers, $, and - in a file name.
T	F	5.	A file is saved in your default directory.
T	F	6.	When you have finished working on a document, you should save it.
T	F	7.	It is necessary to close a document before starting to work on another document.
T	F	8.	When you want to edit a document, you need to open a copy of the file from a disk and place it in the memory of your computer so it will appear on your screen.
T	F	9.	You can open a document only if it is found in the default directory.
T	F	10.	When you finish using WordPerfect for Windows, you need to exit from the software.

In The Remaining Chapters of This Book

In the exercises, you are sometimes instructed to create a document. Your text may word wrap differently than the text in the illustration. Do not press ↵Enter at the end of a line of text to force it to wrap like the exercise illustration.

EXERCISE 3

INSTRUCTIONS:

1. Create the following document.
2. Save the document on a file using the name "ch03ex03."
3. Use the Print Preview feature to see how the document will appear when you print it.
4. Print the document.
5. Close the document

```
Word processing provides an individual with an effective and
efficient means of preparing documents.  You can create documents
and quickly make needed changes prior to printing the document.
The software allows your to save the document on a file for later
use.
```

EXERCISE 4

INSTRUCTIONS:

1. Open the file "ch03ex03."
2. Insert the word "software" on the first line between "processing" and "provides."
3. Delete the "r" in "your" on the fourth line.
4. Save the document with the same name.
5. Print the document.
6. Close the document.

EXERCISE 5

INSTRUCTIONS:

1. Create the following document.
2. Save the document to a file using the name "ch03ex05."
3. Use the Print Preview feature to see how the document will appear when you print it.
4. Print the document.
5. Close the document.

```
Thank you very much for attending our recent training class on
WordPerfect for Windows.  We hope you enjoyed the class and are
successfully using the software in your work.

Our company also provides training on products such as Lotus 1-2-3,
Microsoft Excel, dBASE IV, and Paradox.  A brochure is enclosed
that describes these courses and includes our class schedule for
the next months.  We look forward too having you attend some more
of our classes.
```

EXERCISE 6

INSTRUCTIONS:

1. Open the file "ch03ex05."
2. Insert the word "three" on the fourth line of the second paragraph between "next" and "months."
3. Delete the extra "o" in "too" on the fourth line of the second paragraph.
4. Save the document with the same name.
5. Print the document.
6. Close the document.

EXERCISE 7

INSTRUCTIONS:

1. Create the following document.
2. Save the document on a file using the name "ch03ex07."
3. Use the Print Preview feature to see how the document will appear when you print it.
4. Print the document.
5. Close the document.

```
The World Economic Summit will be held in Houston, Texas.  Rice
University will be the meeting site for the chiefs of state from
the industrialized nations of the worlds.  The conference will last
three days.

During the conference, the Rice University campus will be closed to
the public.  Professors and students will not be allowed on the
campus during the formal sessions.  Many of the buildings on the
campus will be used as temporary offices for the delegations from
the various countries.
```

EXERCISE 8

INSTRUCTIONS:

1. Open the file "ch03ex07."
2. Insert the words "this summer" at the end of the first sentence of paragraph one.
3. Delete the "s" in "worlds" on the third line of the first paragraph.
4. Save the document with the same name.
5. Print the document.
6. Close the document.

EXERCISE 9

INSTRUCTIONS:

1. Create the following document.
2. Save the document on a file using the name "ch03ex09."
3. Use the Print Preview feature to see how the document will appear when you print it.
4. Print the document.
5. Close the document.

```
Each year on July 4, people in the United States celebrate the
Independence Day holiday.  Many individuals have picnics with their
friends.  Often people watch fireworks displays.  In some cases,
people purchase their own fireworks and create their own shows.
Parades are held in many communities.

Sometimes people may take advantage of the day off to travel to the
beach for a day of sun and swimming.  Other individuals may travel
to a relative's house.  Family celebrations may include games,
fireworks, and preparation of special foods.
```

EXERCISE 10

INSTRUCTIONS:

1. Create the following document.
2. Save the document on a file using the name "ch03ex10."
3. Print the document.
4. Close the document.

```
I need information on the total number of graduates of full-time
students attending community colleges in the states of Illinois,
Florida, and California.

This information can probably be obtained from the U.S. Department of
Education.

Tuition and fees from these students affect the taxes of the above
states.  Can you find how it affects your state.
```

EXERCISE 11

INSTRUCTIONS:

1. Open the file "ch03ex10."
2. In the first line, delete "I need," and replace with "Find."
3. In the first sentence, delete the words "graduates of."
4. Also, in the first sentence insert "and part-time" after the words "full-time."
5. In the second paragraph delete the word "probably."
6. In the third paragraph, delete "Tuition and fees from," and capitalize the "T" in the word "these."

7. At the end of the third paragraph, change the period (".") to a question mark ("?").
8. Save the document on a file using the name "ch03ex11."
9. Close the document.

EXERCISE 12

INSTRUCTIONS:

1. Create the following document.
2. Save the document on a file using the name "ch03ex12."
3. Preview the document, then print it.
4. Close this document.
5. Open the file "ch03ex12."
6. In the first sentence after the word "their," insert the words "two-months" to the sentence.
7. In the second sentence of the first paragraph, delete the words "supervised by" and replace them with the phrase "under the supervision of."
8. In the third sentence of the first paragraph, change the word "learn" to "learned."
9. Also, in the third sentence of the first paragraph, insert "we follow" after the word "procedures" (place the insertion point before the comma and type the insert).
10. At the end of the second paragraph, insert two spaces after the period and insert the following text. "These trainees are very proficient in basic WordPerfect for Windows."
11. After making the changes, save the document with the same name.
12. Preview the document, then print it.
13. Close the document.

```
On September 1, four trainees will have finished their training and
will be ready to begin working on the regular staff.  They have
been supervised by T. James Crawford, our training director.  Each
person has learn the procedures, our company policies, and their
rights and responsibilities as a member of our company.

These people may be placed as soon as openings develop.  The
trainees are Sue Schneider, Betty Zilkowshi, Ryan Bradley, and
Scott Roberts.
```

CHAPTER FOUR

CREATING AND EDITING A DOCUMENT

OBJECTIVES

In this chapter, you will learn to:

- Enter the current date
- Use the mouse and pointer-movement techniques
- Insert, replace, delete, and undelete text

■ CHAPTER OVERVIEW

In the previous chapter, the basics of preparing, editing, saving, printing, and opening a document were presented. You mastered the use of these WordPerfect for Windows activities using the menus and keyboard methods. The processes for creating and editing documents are discussed in more detail in this chapter. Insertion point movement is explained for the mouse and keyboard methods. Methods for inserting, replacing, deleting, and undeleting text are described and illustrated. The Help feature is presented.

■ MOVEMENT TECHNIQUES

The insertion point is the blinking vertical bar on your screen. It marks the location where you enter text on the screen. You can quickly move to the top or bottom of the screen or to the top or bottom of your document. You can use either a mouse or the keyboard to move the insertion point through your document.

The insertion point can move only through text or lines that already exist in your document. When you reach a point where there are no text or blank lines, the insertion point stops moving.

Mouse Method

To position the insertion point using a mouse, move the mouse pointer to a specific location, then click the mouse button.

There are three basic mouse operations: clicking, double-clicking, and dragging. **Clicking** means to press the mouse button and then release it. **Double-clicking** means to press the mouse button twice quickly. **Dragging** means to press and hold down the mouse button while moving the mouse.

If you want to scroll to parts of the document that are not displayed, use the vertical and horizontal scroll bars to view different parts of your document. The vertical scroll bar is automatically displayed in WordPerfect for Windows. Use the vertical scroll bar to scroll up or down in your document.

The horizontal scroll bar allows you to scroll from the left side of the screen to the right side of the screen. By default, the horizontal scroll bar is not displayed. To view the horizontal scroll bar, choose Display from the Preferences option under the File menu. Turn on the Display Horizontal Scroll Bar check box by clicking the check box or pressing Alt+H until an X appears in the check box.

A scroll bar has two directional arrows. These arrows are separated by a gray shaded area containing a scroll box. The scroll box represents your position in the document. For example, if the vertical scroll box appears in the middle of the vertical scroll bar, you are viewing the middle of your document. Figure 4-1 illustrates the parts of the vertical scroll bar.

Figure 4-1

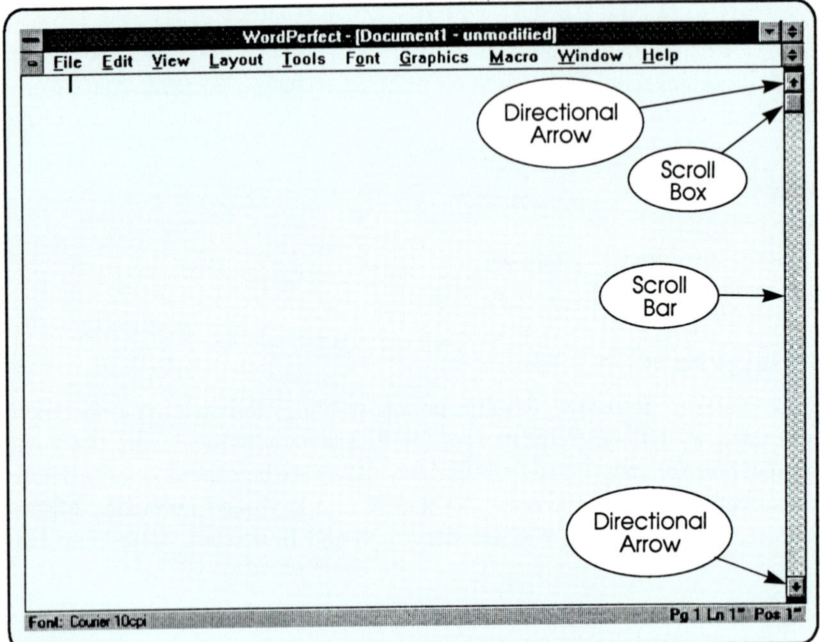

Using the scroll bar does not move the position of your insertion point. A scroll bar only changes your view of the document, not your position in the document. To move the insertion point with the mouse, you scroll to the new position, move your mouse pointer to the new position, and click the mouse button.

The following table lists the mouse techniques you can use to move the insertion point.

Movement	**Mouse Technique**
Up one line	Click the up scroll arrow
Down one line	Click the down scroll arrow
Up one page	Click the gray shaded area above the vertical scroll box
Down one page	Click the gray shaded area below the vertical scroll box
Beginning of a document	Drag the vertical scroll box to the top of the vertical scroll bar
End of a document	Drag the vertical scroll box to the bottom of the vertical scroll bar
Left side of screen	Click the left scroll arrow
Right side of screen	Click the right scroll arrow

Movement	Mouse Technique
Far left side of screen	Click the gray shaded area left of the horizontal scroll box
Far right of screen	Click the gray shaded area right of the horizontal scroll box

Keyboard Method

As you move the insertion point up or down through your document, the insertion point retains its current horizontal position, if possible. For example, if the insertion point is at position 5 inches on one line, it stays at position 5 inches in all the lines it moves through, unless they are shorter than 5 inches long, in which case the insertion point moves to the right edge of the line.

In This Book

In some situations, you will be asked to press several keys in succession to move the insertion point to a specific place on the screen. For example, you may be directed to move the insertion point to the left side of the screen by pressing the [Home] key and then the [Home] key again. This type of instruction will appear in the text as:

Press [Home], [Home]

The following table lists the keystrokes you can use to move the insertion point through the document.

Movement	Pointer-Movement Keys
Left one character	[←]
Right one character	[→]
Word left	[Ctrl]+[←]
Word right	[Ctrl]+[→]
Left side of screen (after any formatting codes)	[Home]
Left side of screen (before any formatting codes)	[Home],[Home]
Far right of line (even when the line extends beyond the right edge of the screen)	[End]
Left of screen	[Ctrl]+[PageUp]
Right of screen	[Ctrl]+[PageDown]
Up one line	[↑]
Down one line	[↓]
Top of screen	[PageUp]
Bottom of screen	[PageDown]

Movement	Pointer-Movement Keys
First line on the previous page	Alt+PageUp
First line on the following page	Alt+PageDown
Up one paragraph	Ctrl+↑
Down one paragraph	Ctrl+↓
Beginning of a document (after any formatting codes)	Ctrl+Home
Beginning of a document (before any formatting codes)	Ctrl+Home, Ctrl+Home
End of a document (after any formatting codes)	Ctrl+End

PREPARING A DOCUMENT

In This Book

When using a mouse, it is a common practice to choose an option from a menu by moving the mouse pointer to the desired option and clicking the mouse button. In the remaining portion of this book, you are instructed to simply *choose* a command rather than be given the set of instructions to move the mouse pointer to the menu or option and press or click the mouse button. Also, if you need to use a particular button like a command button in a dialog box, you are asked to click the button.

In selecting items from the menus using the keyboard, you are instructed to *select* the menu option rather than be told both methods for using the keyboard to select a menu option.

To save space, the symbols representing the mouse and the keyboard are omitted. The directions for the methods remain in the same columns. The directions in the left or first column are for the mouse method. They appear in normal type. The directions in the second or middle column are for using the menus with the keyboard. They appear in *italic* type. The directions in the right or third column are for the function key method. They appear in normal type.

You can mix the use of the mouse, keyboard, and function key methods.

At this point, change the default directory to "a:\wpdocs" or to "c:\wpdocs." Suppose you want to create the letter in Figure 4-2.

Figure 4-2

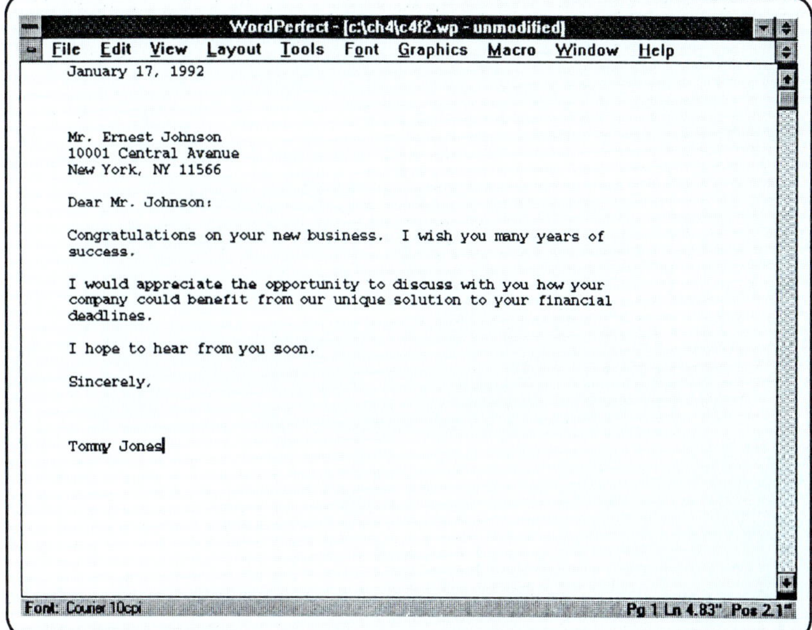

To insert the current date as text:

Move	the mouse pointer to the top of the document	***Move***	*the insertion point to the top of the document*
Click	the mouse button	***Press***	*Alt*
Choose	Tools	***Select***	*Tools*
Choose	Date	***Select***	*Date*
Choose	Format	***Select***	*Format*

In This Book

To this point in the book, the software has been referred to as WordPerfect for Windows. In most situations in the rest of the book, the software is simply called WordPerfect.

You can change the appearance of the date by selecting the Date Format option from the Tools menu. If you do not choose a date format, WordPerfect defaults to inserting the date using the month-day-year format.

Your screen should look like Figure 4-3.

Figure 4-3

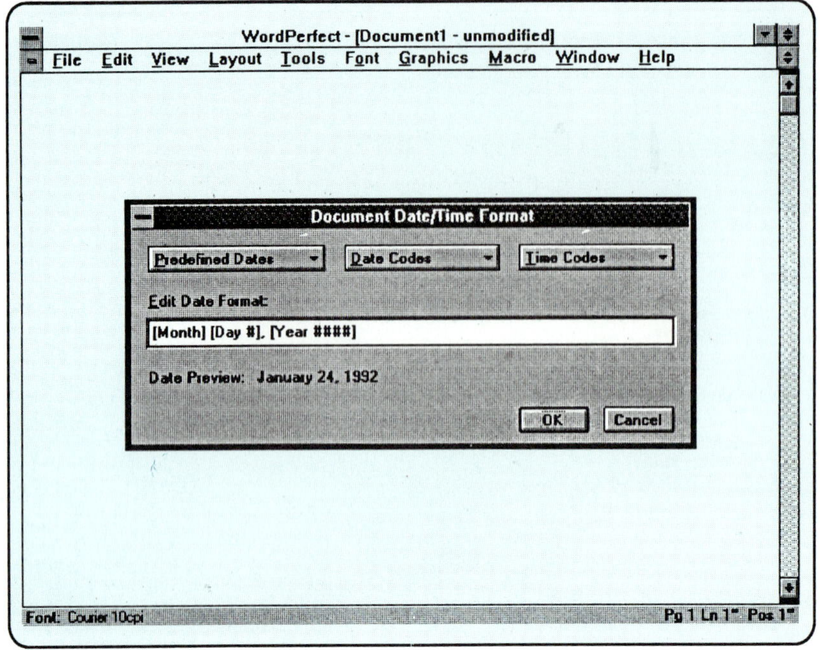

You can include words, spaces, and punctuation with the codes that appear in brackets to create your date format. The default date format ([Month] [Day #], [Year ####]) appears in the Edit Date Format text box as:

[Month]	month (word)
[Day #]	day of the month
,	,
[Year ####]	year (all four digits)

You can choose a predefined date format or create your own. To view the predefined date formats:

Click	the Predefined Dates pop-up list button	***Press***	*Alt+P to select the Predefined Dates pop-up list button*
Hold down	the mouse button to view the pop-up list	***Press***	*Alt+↓ to view the pop-up list*
Drag	the mouse pointer to select the format you desire	***Press***	*↑ or ↓ to select the format you desire*
Release	the mouse button		

To accept the default date format or the format you specify:

Click	the OK command button	***Press***	*↵Enter*

To insert the date as text:

Choose	Tools	***Press***	*Alt*	**Press**	Ctrl+F5
Choose	Date	***Select***	*Tools*		
Choose	Text	***Select***	*Date*		
		Select	*Text*		

The upper portion of your screen should look like Figure 4-4, except that you have a different date.

Figure 4-4

To leave three blank lines after the date:

Press	↵Enter four times	***Press***	*↵Enter four times*

Continue typing the letter in Figure 4-5, inserting blank lines as necessary. Save the document as "johnson.ltr". Your screen should look like Figure 4-5.

Figure 4-5

```
January 17, 1992



Mr. Ernest Johnson
10001 Central Avenue
New York, NY 11566

Dear Mr. Johnson:

Congratulations on your new business.  I wish you many years of
success.

I would appreciate the opportunity to discuss with you how your
company could benefit from our unique solution to your financial
deadlines.

I hope to hear from you soon.

Sincerely,



Tommy Jones
```

INSERTING AND REPLACING TEXT

After you enter a document you may need to edit it. For example, you may forget to include a word, or you may type a word incorrectly. You will now use WordPerfect options to change the letter you created in the previous section.

Insert Mode

WordPerfect automatically defaults to the Insert mode. When you are in the insert mode and enter new text, WordPerfect pushes forward any existing text and moves it to the right to make room for the new text. To add text to your document, move the insertion point to the location where you want to insert text and begin typing.

To insert the word "venture" at the end of the first sentence of your document:

Move	the mouse pointer before the period after the word "business"	***Move***	*the insertion point to some character in the word "Congrat-ulations"*
Click	the mouse button	***Press***	*Ctrl+→ four times*
		Press	*→ until the insertion point is before the period*

Your screen should look like Figure 4-6.

Figure 4-6

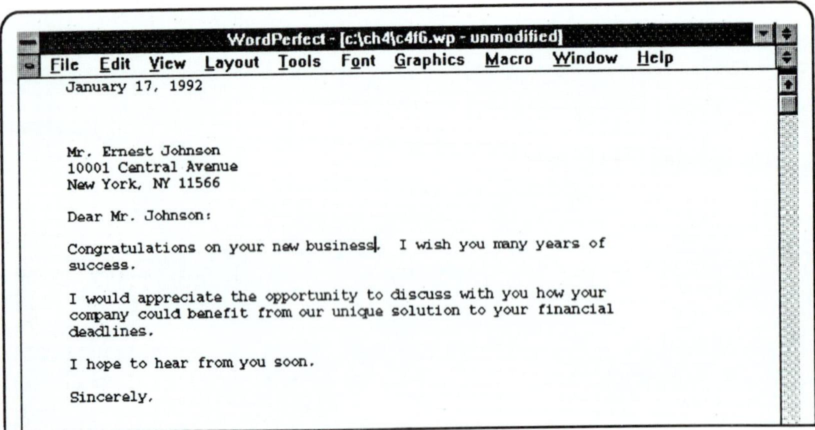

The insertion point is now before the period.

Press	Spacebar	***Press***	*Spacebar*
Type	venture	***Type***	*venture*

Your screen should look like Figure 4-7.

Figure 4-7

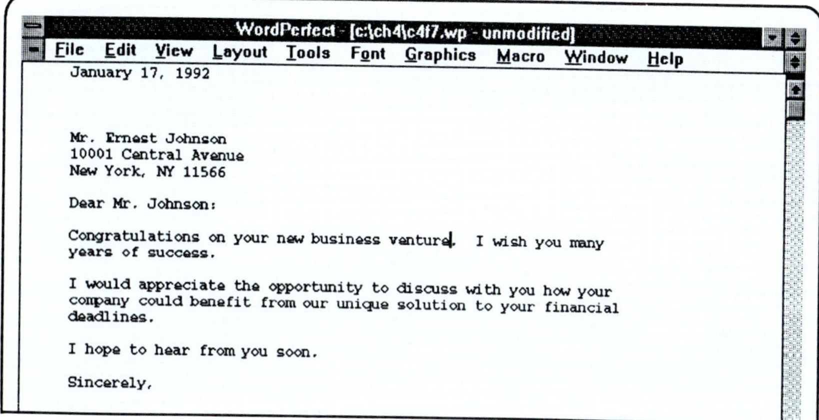

WordPerfect - [c:\ch4\c4f7.wp - unmodified]

File Edit View Layout Tools Font Graphics Macro Window Help

January 17, 1992

Mr. Ernest Johnson
10001 Central Avenue
New York, NY 11566

Dear Mr. Johnson:

Congratulations on your new business venture. I wish you many years of success.

I would appreciate the opportunity to discuss with you how your company could benefit from our unique solution to your financial deadlines.

I hope to hear from you soon.

Sincerely,

Typeover Mode

Typeover mode allows you to write over existing text with new text. The Insert key allows you to "toggle"--to change from Insert mode to Typeover mode and back again. To enter Typeover mode, press the Insert key. When you are in Typeover mode, any character you type replaces the character at the insertion point. As long as you are in typeover mode, the word "Typeover" appears at the left end of the status bar. When you want to return to Insert mode, press the Insert key again.

To replace the word "Avenue" with "Parkway" in the inside address of your document:

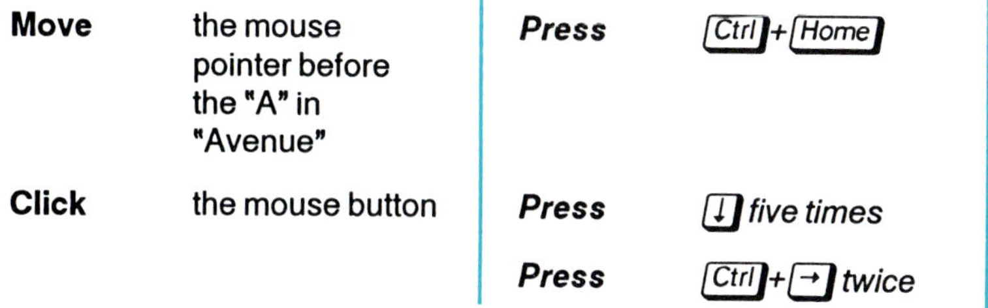

Move	the mouse pointer before the "A" in "Avenue"	***Press***	*Ctrl+Home*
Click	the mouse button	***Press***	*↓ five times*
		Press	*Ctrl+→ twice*

Your screen should look like Figure 4-8.

Figure 4-8

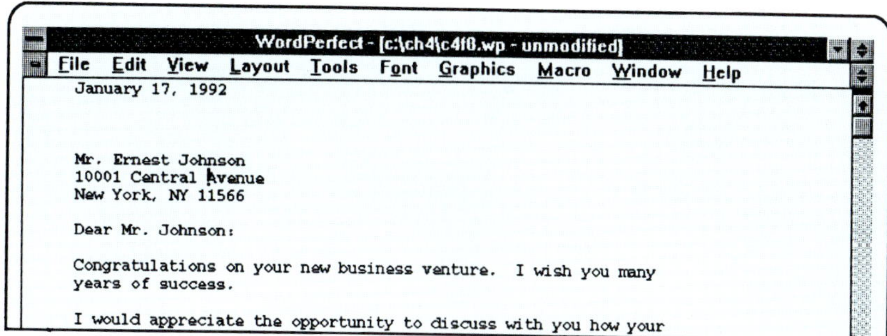

WordPerfect - [c:\ch4\c4f8.wp - unmodified]

File Edit View Layout Tools Font Graphics Macro Window Help

January 17, 1992

Mr. Ernest Johnson
10001 Central Avenue
New York, NY 11566

Dear Mr. Johnson:

Congratulations on your new business venture. I wish you many years of success.

I would appreciate the opportunity to discuss with you how your

To enter Typeover mode:

Press	Insert	***Press***	*Insert*
Type	Parkway	***Type***	*Parkway*

Your screen should look like Figure 4-9. Notice that the word "Typeover" appears on the status bar, indicating you are in the Typeover mode.

Figure 4-9

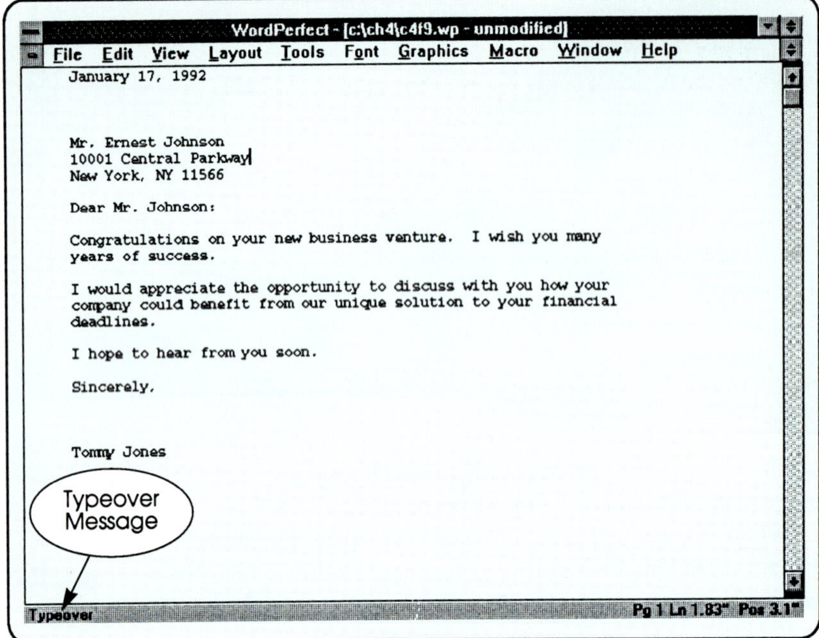

To return to Insert mode:

Press Insert

Press Insert

Your screen should look like Figure 4-10. Notice that the word "Typeover" no longer appears on the status bar. You are now in the Insert mode.

Figure 4-10

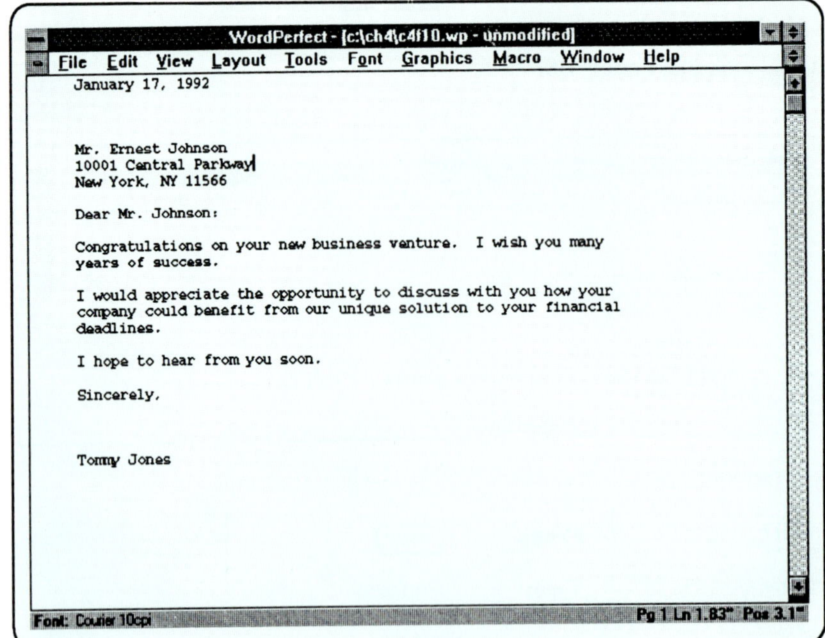

USING THE SELECT FEATURE

The Select feature is used to highlight text within your document. After you highlight text using the Select feature, you can apply many other WordPerfect features to the highlighted text. For example, you may want to underline all letters in a group of words. You first need to highlight the words using the Select feature. Then you can underline the words using the Underline feature available in WordPerfect.

Selecting Text with the Mouse

To select text with the mouse, you drag across the text. To drag, you click at the beginning of the text, hold down the mouse button, and move the mouse in the direction you want to highlight. When you have the text highlighted, release the mouse button.

WordPerfect also includes shortcuts for selecting certain text with the mouse. The following table lists the shortcuts for selecting a word, sentence, or paragraph with the mouse.

Select a word	Double-click on the word
Select a sentence	Triple-click on the sentence
Select a paragraph	Quadruple-click on the paragraph

To remove a selection or deselect text, click anywhere inside the document area.

Selecting Text with the Keyboard

You can select text from the keyboard by pressing [F8] and then pressing a pointer-movement key or by holding down the [Shift] key and pressing a pointer-movement key. Either method turns on the Select feature at the location of the insertion point. For example, if you wanted to highlight a word, move the insertion point to the beginning of the word, press [F8] to turn on the Select feature, and press [Ctrl]+[→] to highlight the word.

To remove a selection with the keyboard, press [F8] to turn the Select feature off.

To highlight the first paragraph of your document:

Move	the mouse pointer before the "C" in "Congrat-ulations"	***Move***	*the insertion point before the "C" in "Congrat-ulations"*
Click	the mouse button		

Your screen should look like Figure 4-11.

Figure 4-11

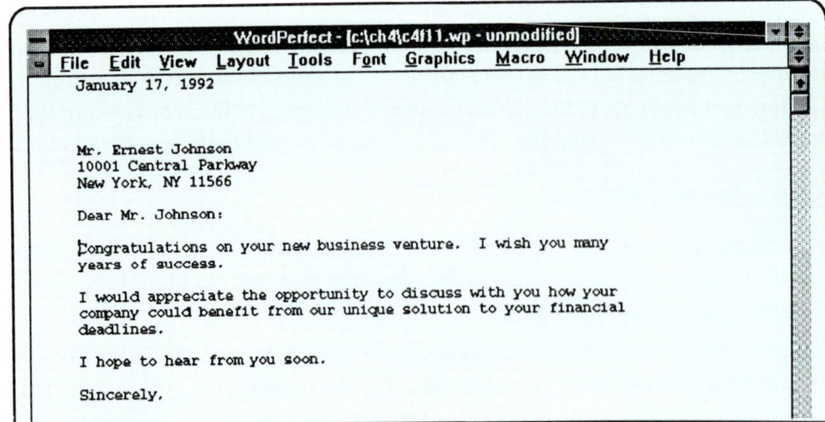

To select the first paragraph:

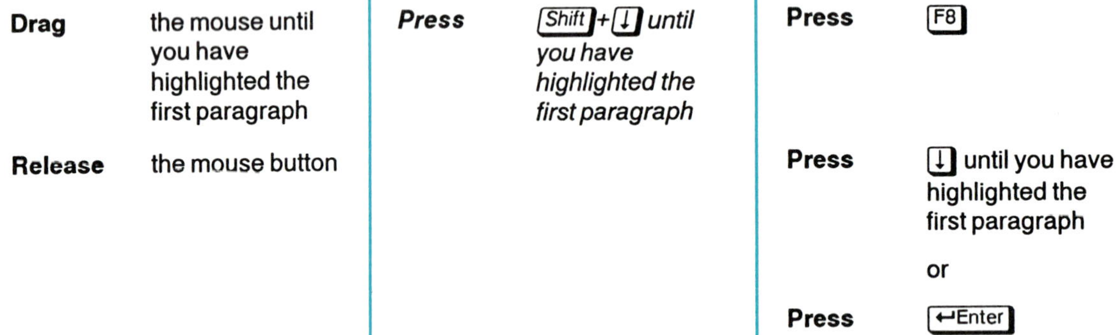

Drag	the mouse until you have highlighted the first paragraph	***Press***	*Shift+↓ until you have highlighted the first paragraph*	**Press**	F8
Release	the mouse button			**Press**	↓ until you have highlighted the first paragraph or
				Press	↵Enter

Your screen should look like Figure 4-12.

Figure 4-12

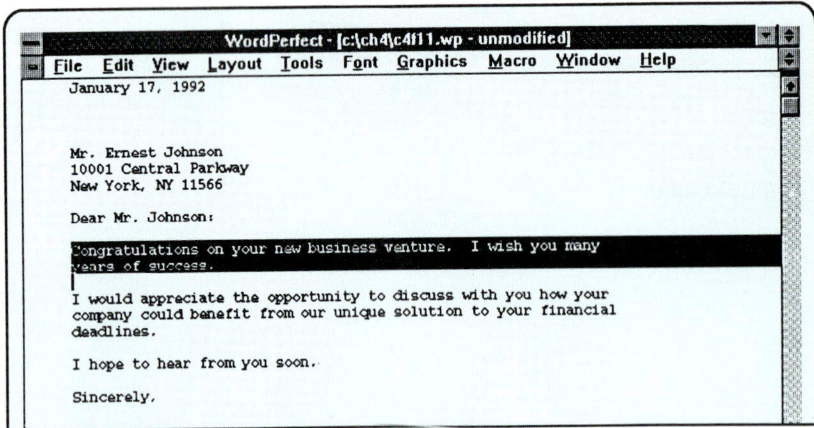

Notice that the text "Select On" or "Select Mode" appears on the status bar. The message "Select On" appears on the status bar if you use the mouse or the Shift key to select text. The message "Select Mode" appears on the status bar if you use the F8 key to select text.

You now can select another WordPerfect feature to apply to the selection. In some situations, you may need to stop using the Select feature. To turn off a selection without continuing with another WordPerfect feature:

Click	on the document area	***Press***	*a pointer-movement key*	**Press**	F8

Your screen should now display the current document prior to your use of the Select feature.

DELETING TEXT

There are many ways to delete text within your document. The following table lists the keystrokes to delete text.

Deletion	Keystrokes
Character to the left of the insertion point	[←Backspace]
Character at the insertion point	[Delete]
Word at the insertion point	[Ctrl]+[←Backspace]
From the insertion point to the end of the line	[Ctrl]+[Delete]
From the insertion point to the end of the page	[Shift]+[Ctrl]+[Delete]
Selected text	Select text, Press [Delete]

Suppose you need to delete the word "unique" from the second paragraph of your document. One method of deleting a word or group of words is to highlight the text using the Select feature and then press the [Delete] key. If you are deleting only one word, a more efficient method is to place the insertion point in the word and press [Ctrl]+[←Backspace].

To delete the word "unique" from the second paragraph of your document using the Select feature:

Move	the mouse pointer before the "u" in "unique"	***Move***	*the insertion point before the "u" in "unique"*	**Move**	the insertion point before the "u" in "unique"
Drag	the mouse until the word and the blank space after the word "unique" are highlighted	***Press***	*[Shift]+[→] until you have highlighted the word "unique" and the blank space after the word*	**Press**	[F8]
Release	the mouse button			**Press**	[→] until you have highlighted the word "unique" and the blank space after the word or
				Press	[Spacebar]

Your screen should look like Figure 4-13.

Figure 4-13

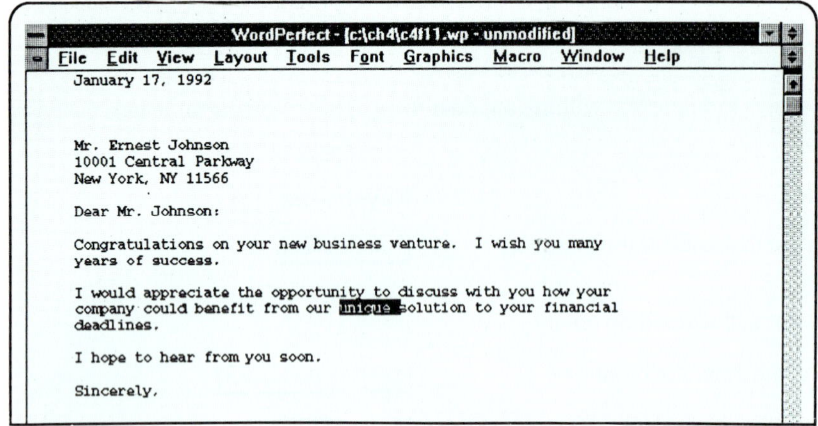

WordPerfect - [c:\ch4\c411.wp - unmodified]

File Edit View Layout Tools Font Graphics Macro Window Help

January 17, 1992

Mr. Ernest Johnson
10001 Central Parkway
New York, NY 11566

Dear Mr. Johnson:

Congratulations on your new business venture. I wish you many years of success.

I would appreciate the opportunity to discuss with you how your company could benefit from our unique solution to your financial deadlines.

I hope to hear from you soon.

Sincerely,

To delete the word "unique":

Press	Delete	***Press***	*Delete*	**Press**	Delete

The word "unique" and the blank space after it should now be removed from your document.

Another method for deleting the word "unique" is:

Move	the mouse pointer before the "u" in "unique"	***Move***	*the insertion point before the "u" in "unique"*	**Move**	the insertion point before the "u" in "unique"
Double-click	the word "unique"	***Press***	*Shift+Ctrl+→*	**Press**	Ctrl+ ←Backspace
Press	Delete	***Press***	*Delete*		

■ UNDELETING TEXT

If you mistakenly delete text, it is not lost at that moment. WordPerfect stores your last three text deletions. You can display them on your screen in reverse order at any time, and restore the deletion of your choice. The text is restored at the current location of the insertion point.

To restore the word "unique":

Move	the mouse pointer before the letter "s" in "solution"	***Move***	*the insertion point before the letter "s" in "solution"*	**Move**	the insertion point before the letter "s" in "solution"
Click	the mouse button	***Press***	*Alt*	**Press**	Alt+Shift+ ←Backspace
Choose	Edit	***Select***	*Edit*		
Choose	Undelete	***Select***	*Undelete*		

The Undelete dialog box appears. Your screen should look like Figure 4-14.

Figure 4-14

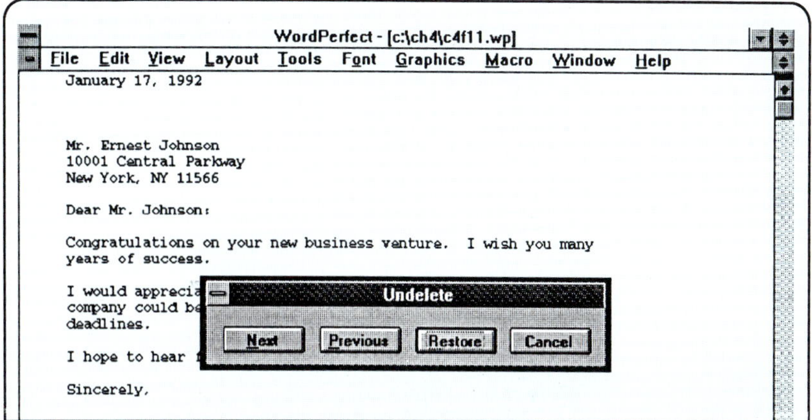

If the Undelete dialog box blocks your view of the text, you can move the box by dragging the title bar of the dialog box. If you are using the keyboard, you can move the dialog box by pressing Alt+Spacebar, selecting Move from the control menu, and using the pointer-movement keys to place the box. Press ↵Enter to select the new dialog box position. Further details of how to move windows are discussed in Chapter Fifteen.

To restore the highlighted text:

Click	the Restore command button	***Press***	*Alt+R to select the Restore command button*	**Press**	Alt+R to select the Restore command button

Your screen should look like Figure 4-15.

Figure 4-15

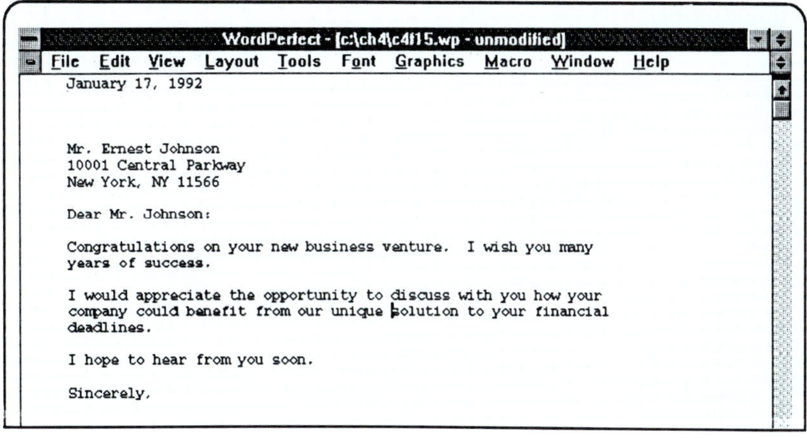

Save your document, replacing the old contents with the current document. Close the document.

■ USING THE HELP FEATURE

The Help feature allows you to learn more about WordPerfect quickly on your screen.

Use the Help feature to display any of these items on your screen:

An alphabetical listing of WordPerfect features and their keystrokes.

Descriptions of WordPerfect features and menu options.

Information about the current feature you are using.

To access the Help Index feature:

Choose Help

Choose Index

Click on any underlined topic that you need information about.

Press *Alt*

Select *Help*

Select *Index*

Use the Tab key to select any feature that you need information about.

Press F1

Use the Tab key to select any feature that you need information about.

Choosing Index from the Help menu or pressing the F1 key from the normal editing screen displays the main Help Index. You can then select any jump topic by clicking on it or by pressing the Tab key to select it. A jump topic moves you to a description of another feature. A jump topic is text that appears underlined and in a different color. In WordPerfect's Help Index, you can choose a letter to see an alphabetical listing of topics or choose a specific topic from the feature list.

If you cannot see all of the jump topics on the screen, use the scroll bars or the pointer-movement keys to view the additional topics.

Choosing Index from the Help menu or pressing F1 after you have initiated a WordPerfect feature provides a description of that particular feature. Help about a specific feature is called context-sensitive help.

To exit the Help feature:

Choose File

Choose Exit

Press *Alt*

Select *File*

Select *Exit*

Press Alt+F4

EXERCISE 1

INSTRUCTIONS: Define the following terms:

1. Insertion point ______________________________

____

2. Insert mode ____

____

3. Undeleting text ____

____

4. Movement techniques ____

____

5. Select feature ____

____

6. Date feature ____

____

7. Deleting text ____

____

8. Typeover mode ____

____

EXERCISE 2

INSTRUCTIONS: Circle T if the statement is true and F if the statement is false.

T F 1. When you are in the Insert mode and enter new text, WordPerfect pushes forward any existing text and moves it to the right to make room for the new text.

T F 2. WordPerfect defaults to inserting the date using the month-day-month format.

T F 3. Typeover mode allows you to replace old text with new text.

T F 4. To enter the Typeover mode, press [Insert].

T F 5. WordPerfect stores your last four deletions.

T F 6. The Select feature is used to highlight text within your document.

T F 7. The words "Select On" appear on the status bar to indicate you are using the Select option.

T F 8. You cannot restore text that has been deleted.

T F 9. The insertion point can move only through text that already exists in your document.

T F 10. WordPerfect automatically defaults to the Typeover mode.

EXERCISE 3

INSTRUCTIONS:

1. Create the following document. As you type the text, use the movement techniques and insert/delete functions available in WordPerfect to correct any errors.
2. Save the document on a file using the name "ch04ex03."
3. Use the Print Preview feature to see how the document will appear when you print it.
4. Print the document.
5. Close the document.

```
The company has changed a lot during the last year.  A new
president has been appointed.  The morale of most employees has
improved extensively with the addition of the new president.

The new product line introduced by the marketing department has
been a spectacular success.  Our customers have indicated the new
items are wonderful.  As a result of the new products, revenues for
the year are up 22% for the year.
```

EXERCISE 4

INSTRUCTIONS:

1. Open the file "ch04ex03."
2. Practice using the insertion point movement keys as follows:
   a. Move the insertion point to the end of the document using the Ctrl+End keys.
   b. Move the insertion point to the beginning of the document using the Ctrl+Home keys.
   c. Move the insertion point to the word "lot" in the first line of the first paragraph.
   d. Move the insertion point to the end of the first line of the first paragraph using the End key.
   e. Move the insertion point to the beginning of the first line of the first paragraph using the Home key.
   f. Move the insertion point to the second paragraph (down one paragraph) using the Ctrl+↓ keys.
   g. Move the insertion point to the first paragraph (up one paragraph) using the Ctrl+↑ keys.
   h. Move the insertion point to the top of the screen using the PageUp key.
3. Close the document.

EXERCISE 5

INSTRUCTIONS:

1. Create the following document. Insert the current date as text. As you type the letter, use the movement techniques and insert/delete functions available in WordPerfect to correct any errors.
2. Save the document on a file using the name "ch04ex05."
3. Use the Print Preview feature to see how the document will appear when you print it.
4. Print the document.
5. Close the document.

```
current date



FBN Software Company
2100 Skyview Way
Ventura, CA 91015

Dear Sir:

Please send by return mail all of your product brochures, technical
specifications and price list for your software related to
accounting for IBM PS/2 and IBM compatible personal computers.

Additionally, please add our name on your mailing list to update us
on any future changes in your product line.

Sincerely,



Jane Mitchell
```

EXERCISE 6

INSTRUCTIONS:

1. Open the file "ch04ex05."
2. Using the Typeover mode, replace the word "Way" in the inside address with "Avenue."
3. Using the Insert mode, insert the word "yours" after "Sincerely" in the complimentary closing.
4. Save the document on a file using the name "ch04ex06."
5. Print the document.
6. Close the document.

EXERCISE 7

INSTRUCTIONS:

1. Open the file "ch04ex06."
2. Using the Select feature, delete the words "IBM PS/2 and IBM compatible" in the first paragraph.
3. Delete the "s" in "computers" in the first paragraph.
4. Print the document.
5. Restore the words "IBM PS/2 and IBM compatible" in the first paragraph.
6. Restore the "s" in "computer" in the first paragraph.
7. Save the document on a file using the name "ch04ex07."
8. Print the document.
9. Close the document.

EXERCISE 8

INSTRUCTIONS:

1. Create the following document. Insert the current date as text. As you type the letter, use the movement techniques and insert/delete functions available in WordPerfect to correct any errors.
2. Save the document on a file using the name "ch04ex08."
3. Use the Print Preview feature to see how the document will appear when you print it.
4. Print the document.
5. Close the document.

Current date

Ms. T. J. Jackson
Travel Coordinator
Ace Travel Services
820 Gessner, Suite 1135
Houston, TX 77024

Dear Ms. Jackson:

Thank you for helping plan vacation trip to Europe this Summer. I am really looking forward to seeing England, Ireland and Scotland. Your courtesy is really appreciated. This is my first trip to Europe and you were quite patient in answering my questions.

Sincerely yours

Thomas Alexander

EXERCISE 9

INSTRUCTIONS:

1. Open the file "ch04ex08."
2. Make the corrections displayed below. The marks on the sheet are proofreader's marks. If you are not familiar with proofreader's marks, Appendix A contains a list of proofreader's marks and their meanings.
3. Save the document on a file using the name "ch04ex09."
4. Print the document.
5. Close the document.

```
current date


Ms. T. J. Jackson
Travel Coordinator
Ace Travel Service
820 Gessner, Suite 1135
Houston, TX 77024

Dear Ms. Jackson:
                me   my
Thank you for helping plan vacation trip to Europe this Summer.  I am really
looking forward to seeing England, Ireland and Scotland.  Your courtesy is
really appreciated. This is my first trip to Europe and you were quite
patient in answering my questions.

Sincerely yours


      W.
Thomas Alexander
```

EXERCISE 10

INSTRUCTIONS:

1. Create the following document. Insert the current date as text. As you type, use the movement techniques and insert/delete functions available in WordPerfect to correct errors.
2. Save the document on a file using the name "ch04ex10."
3. Use the Print Preview feature to see how the document will appear when you print it.
4. Print the document.
5. Close the document.

```
current date



Dr. George Mills
205 Wildwood Lane
Baton Rouge, LA 70806

Dear Dr. Mills:

It is my disagreeable job to remind you of your balance of $163.90.
You have been on time with your payments before; therefore, I find
it difficult to ask you to pay your balance promptly.  If you
cannot make your payments, please let me know.  I am always open to
the possibility of extending the time within reason.  Perhaps you
have overlooked this bill or maybe some crisis has occurred that
will not permit you to pay at this time.

Please phone me at my office 555-9812 and let me know your
situation.  I have enclosed a self-addressed envelope for your
convenience.  I await your phone call or your payment.

Most cordially yours,



John Rich
```

EXERCISE 11

INSTRUCTIONS:

1. Create the following document. Make the corrections shown. Refer to Appendix A for the Proofreader's Marks if you need help.
2. Insert the current date as text. As you type the letter, use the movement techniques and insert/delete functions available in WordPerfect to correct errors.
3. Save the document on a file using the name "ch04ex11."
4. Use the Print Preview feature to see how the document will appear when you print it.
5. Print the document.
6. Close the document.

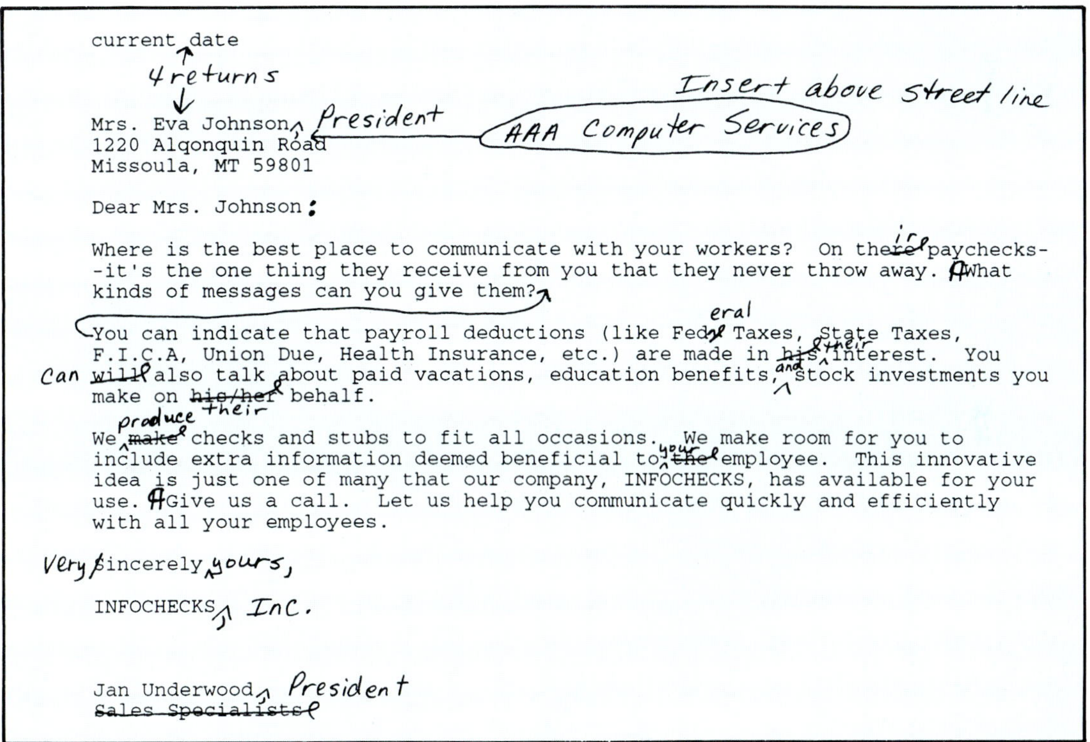

current date

Mrs. Eva Johnson
1220 Alqonquin Road
Missoula, MT 59801

Dear Mrs. Johnson:

Where is the best place to communicate with your workers? On there paychecks--it's the one thing they receive from you that they never throw away. What kinds of messages can you give them? You can indicate that payroll deductions (like Fed. Taxes, State Taxes, F.I.C.A, Union Due, Health Insurance, etc.) are made in his interest. You will also talk about paid vacations, education benefits, stock investments you make on his/her behalf.

We make checks and stubs to fit all occasions. We make room for you to include extra information deemed beneficial to the employee. This innovative idea is just one of many that our company, INFOCHECKS, has available for your use. Give us a call. Let us help you communicate quickly and efficiently with all your employees.

Sincerely

INFOCHECKS

Jan Underwood
Sales Specialists

EXERCISE 12

INSTRUCTIONS:

1. Open the file "ch04ex10."
2. Using the Typeover mode, replace the word "Lane" in the inside address to "Road."
3. Using the Select feature, delete the words "disagreeable job" in the first line of the message.
4. In the place of the words deleted in direction #3, insert "duty."
5. Create a new paragraph by adding two returns at the end of the second

sentence. The new paragraph will start "If you cannot... ."

6. Using the Select feature, delete the sentence "I am always open to the possibility of extending the time within reason."
7. In the last paragraph, first sentence, using the Select feature, delete "and let me know your situation."
8. In the last paragraph, first sentence, using the Insert mode after "555-9812" insert "and discuss the many options for payment available."
9. Save the document on a file using the name "ch04ex12."
10. Print the document.
11. Close the document.

CHAPTER FIVE

ADDITIONAL EDITING FEATURES

OBJECTIVES

In this chapter, you will learn to:

- Use the Reveal Codes
- Search and replace text
- Change the case of text
- Move and copy text

CHAPTER OVERVIEW

In this chapter, additional editing features are discussed. The Reveal Codes feature is introduced. The methods of searching and replacing text are described and illustrated. The process for changing letters from lowercase to uppercase and vice versa is also presented. Finally, the uses of the move and copy features are discussed.

REVEAL CODES

WordPerfect tries to show your document on the screen as it will appear when printed. This makes it easy for you to quickly see the results of any changes and improvements that you make.

But there is much happening "behind the scenes" in WordPerfect. Nearly every time that you use a feature to change the appearance of your document, a special code is placed into the document that you cannot see. These codes tell WordPerfect what to do when it is printing your document. For example, suppose you want to make a sentence stand out when printed. You could do this by formatting the sentence in bold letters (we will discuss exactly how to do this later). The sentence stands out on the screen in darker letters. But you have also inserted "bold on" and "bold off" codes before and after the sentence.

The Reveal Codes feature allows you to see these codes on the screen. When you select the Reveal Codes option from the View menu or press Alt+F3, the screen is split into two sections. The top section is the normal screen that you always see when you are editing.

The bottom part of the screen is the Reveal Codes section. The text is shown with the codes. As you move the mouse pointer or the insertion point through the codes and text in the Reveal Codes section, the insertion point also moves through the same text in the top section. You can edit the text in the Reveal Codes section just as you would in the top section. The menu and function keys can also be used. You can also delete a code if you wish.

At this point, change the default directory to "a:\wpdocs" or to "c:\wpdocs", then open your "johnson.ltr" document.

To display the codes for your document:

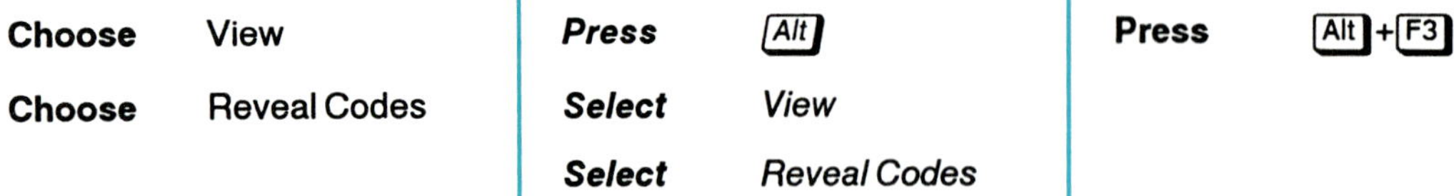

Choose	View	***Press***	*Alt*	**Press**	Alt+F3
Choose	Reveal Codes	***Select***	*View*		
		Select	*Reveal Codes*		

Your screen should look like Figure 5-1.

Figure 5-1

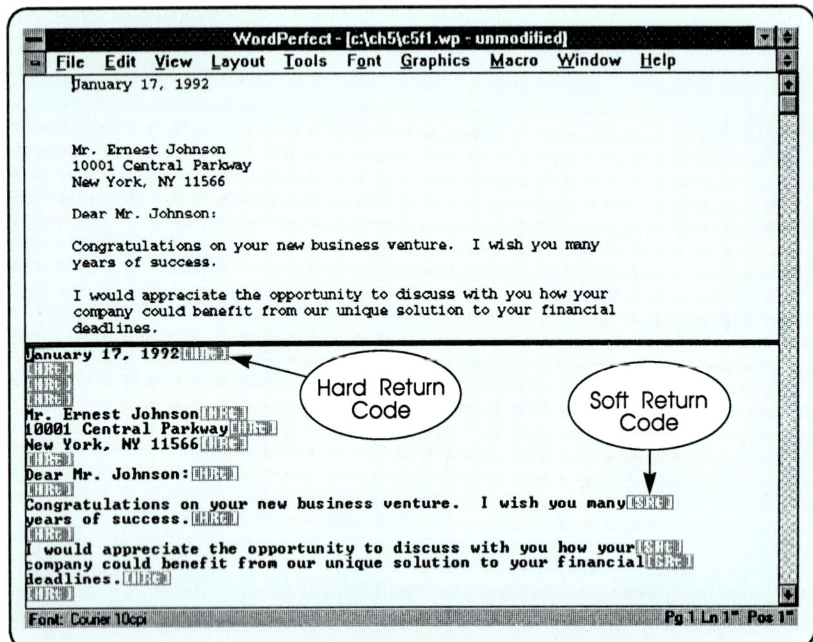

In the Reveal Codes section of your screen, the code [HRt] stands for a hard return. A hard return code is inserted whenever you press ↵Enter in the text. This causes the text following the insertion point to begin on a new line, and the insertion point is placed at the front of that line.

The code [SRt] stands for a soft return. A soft return code is inserted by WordPerfect at the end of every line where there is no hard return. This code allows WordPerfect to word wrap throughout the paragraph as you add or delete text. You can see a soft return code by moving the insertion point down so the body of the letter appears in the Reveal Codes section.

To remove the document codes from your screen using the Reveal Codes feature:

Choose	View	***Press***	*Alt*	**Press**	Alt+F3
Choose	Reveal Codes	***Select***	*View*		
		Select	*Reveal Codes*		

Your screen should now show the current document as it was before you used the Reveal Codes feature.

■ SEARCHING AND REPLACING TEXT

You can use the Search feature to locate specific text in your document. A Replace feature also exists to help you replace any text that is located with new text.

You can locate a word, phrase, or code each time it occurs in your document. You can search forward from your position in the document by selecting the Search option from the Edit menu or by pressing F2. You can search forward or backwards in your document by changing the direction option in the Search dialog box.

In the Search dialog box, you are asked to enter the text that WordPerfect should locate. This text is called a search string. If the search string contains only lowercase letters, then WordPerfect will look for matching text that is in lowercase and uppercase. If the search string contains one or more uppercase letters, then WordPerfect looks for an exact match on the uppercase letters. For example, if the search string is sum, then WordPerfect will find such words as sum, Sumaria, and resume. If the search string is Sum, then WordPerfect will only find Sumaria.

If your search string is a word, then put a space before and after the search string. In this way, only the word will be located, and no words containing the search string will be found. For example, if the search string is " sum ," then WordPerfect will not find Sumaria or resume. It will find sum.

> **In This Book**
>
> When using a mouse, it is common practice to move the insertion point in the document by moving the mouse pointer to the desired location and clicking the mouse button. In the remaining portion of this book, you are instructed to simply *click* at the appropriate location rather than be given the set of instructions to move the mouse pointer to the location and press or click the mouse button.

Searching Forward

To search forward for the word "your" in the document:

Click	at the beginning of the document	***Press***	*Ctrl+Home*	**Press**	Ctrl+Home
Choose	Edit	***Press***	*Alt*	**Press**	F2
Choose	Search	***Select***	*Edit*	**Press**	Spacebar
Press	Spacebar	***Select***	*Search*	**Type**	your
Type	your	***Press***	*Spacebar*	**Press**	Spacebar
Press	Spacebar	***Type***	*your*		
		Press	*Spacebar*		

The bottom portion of your screen should look like Figure 5-2.

Figure 5-2

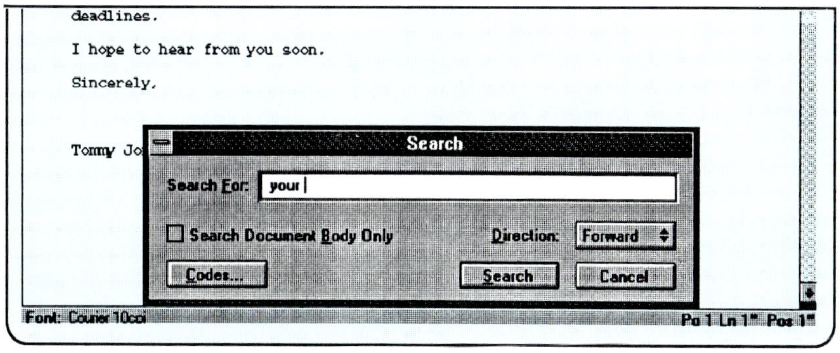

deadlines.

I hope to hear from you soon.

Sincerely,

Tommy Jo

Search

Search For: your

Search Document Body Only

Direction: Forward

Codes... Search Cancel

Font: Courier 10cpi Pg 1 Ln 1" Pos 1"

Notice that the Direction button is set for a forward search.

To begin the search:

Click	the Search command button	***Press***	*[↵Enter]*	**Press**	[↵Enter]

The upper portion of your screen should look like Figure 5-3.

Figure 5-3

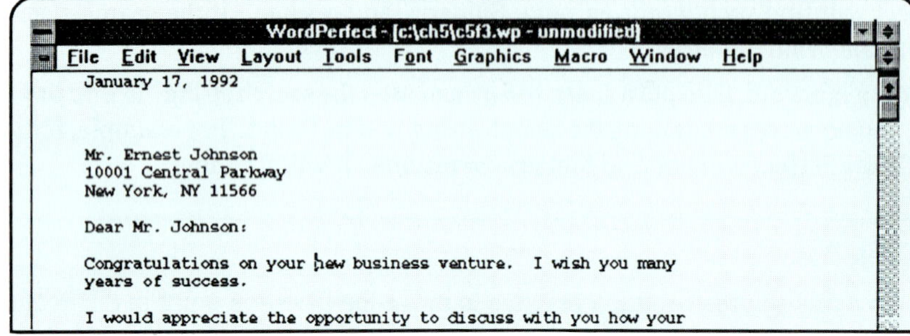

Notice the text that is being sought is always immediately before the location of the insertion point.

To continue searching for the same occurrence of the text:

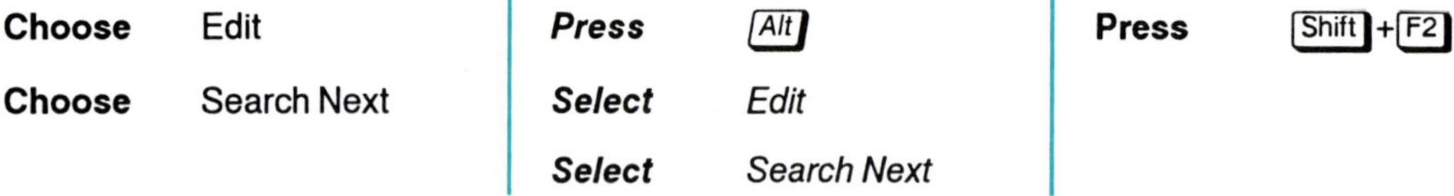

Choose	Edit	***Press***	*[Alt]*	**Press**	[Shift]+[F2]
Choose	Search Next	***Select***	*Edit*		
		Select	*Search Next*		

Continue repeating the process for finding the next occurrence of the text you specified. After you repeat the process twice, the message "String not found" will appear briefly on the status bar showing there are no more occurrences of that text.

Searching Backward

To search backward for the word "you" in the document, with the insertion point at the end of the document:

Click	at the end of the document	***Press***	*[Ctrl]+[End]*	**Press**	[Ctrl]+[End]
Choose	Edit	***Press***	*[Alt]*	**Press**	[F2]
Choose	Search	***Select***	*Edit*	**Press**	[Spacebar]
Press	[Spacebar]	***Select***	*Search*	**Type**	you
Type	you	***Press***	*[Spacebar]*	**Press**	[Spacebar]
Press	[Spacebar]	***Type***	*you*		
		Press	*[Spacebar]*		

To change the search direction to backward:

Click	the Direction pop-up list button	***Press***	*Alt+D to select the Direction pop-up list button*	**Press**	Alt+D to select the Direction pop-up list button
Hold down	the mouse button to view the Direction pop-up list	***Press***	*Alt+↓ to view the Direction pop-up list*	**Press**	Alt+↓ to view the Direction pop-up list
Choose	Backward	***Type***	*B for Backward*	**Type**	B for Backward

The bottom portion of your screen should look like Figure 5-4.

Figure 5-4

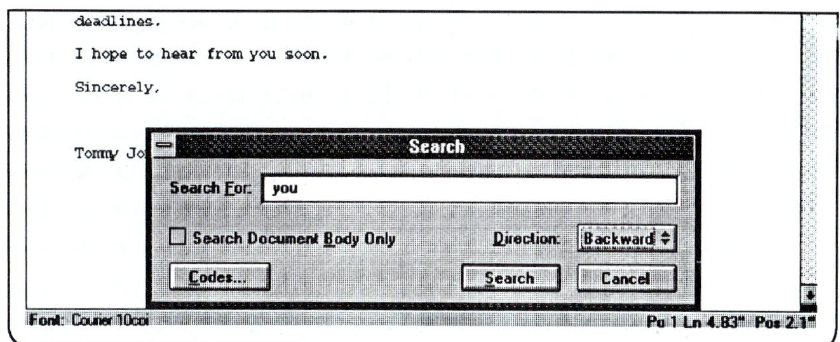

To begin the search:

Click	the Search command button	***Press***	*↵Enter*	**Press**	↵Enter

The bottom portion of your screen should look like Figure 5-5.

Figure 5-5

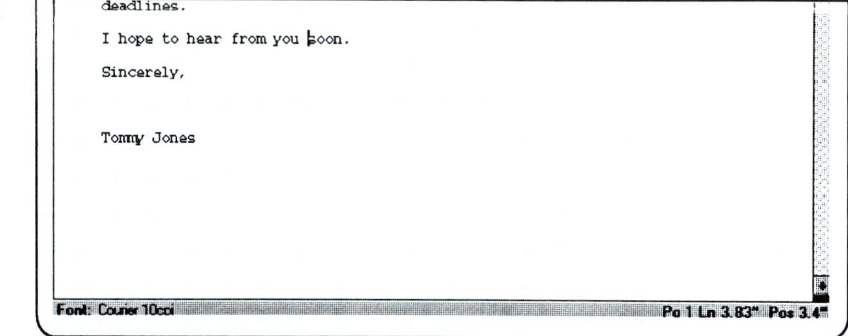

Notice the text that is being sought is just before the insertion point.

To continue searching for the word:

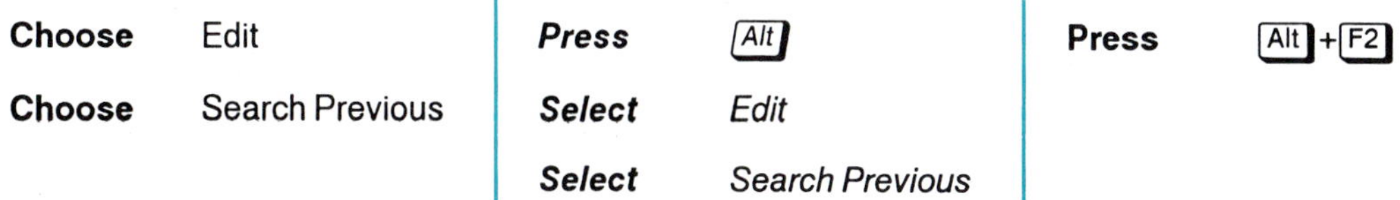

Choose	Edit	***Press***	*Alt*	**Press**	Alt+F2
Choose	Search Previous	***Select***	*Edit*		
		Select	*Search Previous*		

Repeat the process for finding the next occurrence of the search string. "String not found" is displayed on the status bar when no more matches exist.

Replacing Text

You can replace text by selecting the Replace option from the Edit menu or by pressing Ctrl+F2.

To replace "financial" with "accounting":

Click	at the beginning of the document	***Press***	*Ctrl+Home*	**Press**	Ctrl+Home
Choose	Edit	***Press***	*Alt*	**Press**	Ctrl+F2
Choose	Replace	***Select***	*Edit*		
		Select	*Replace*		

The bottom portion of your screen should look like Figure 5-6.

Figure 5-6

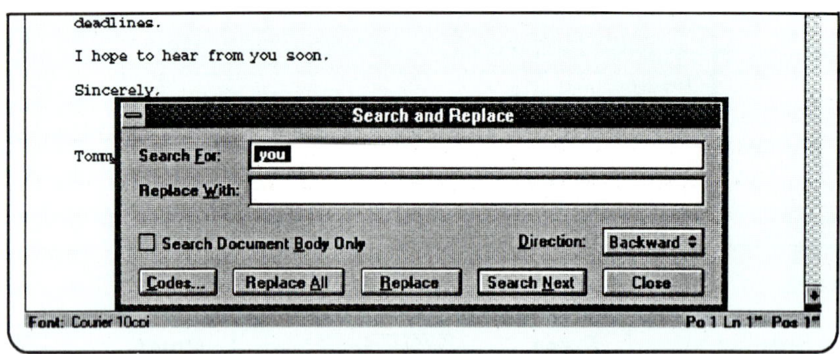

To specify you want to search for the word "financial":

Press	Spacebar	***Press***	*Spacebar*	**Press**	Spacebar
Type	financial	***Type***	*financial*	**Type**	financial
Press	Spacebar	***Press***	*Spacebar*	**Press**	Spacebar

The bottom portion of your screen should look like Figure 5-7.

Figure 5-7

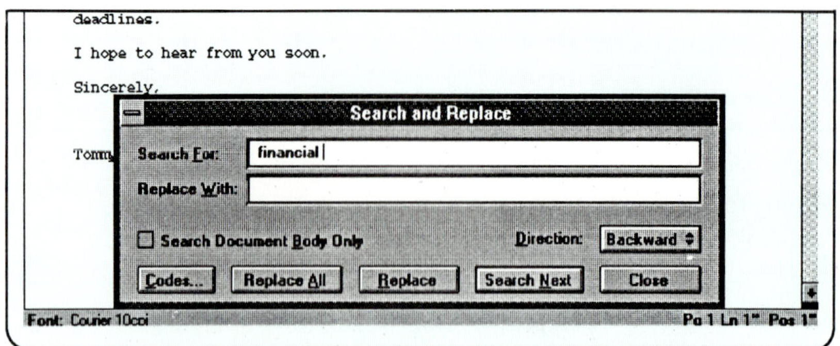

To replace the word "financial" with "accounting":

Click	the Replace With text box	***Press***	*Alt+W to select the Replace With text box*	**Press**	Alt+W to select the Replace With text box
Press	Spacebar	***Press***	*Spacebar*	**Press**	Spacebar
Type	accounting	***Type***	*accounting*	**Type**	accounting
Press	Spacebar	***Press***	*Spacebar*	**Press**	Spacebar

The bottom segment of your screen should look like Figure 5-8.

Figure 5-8

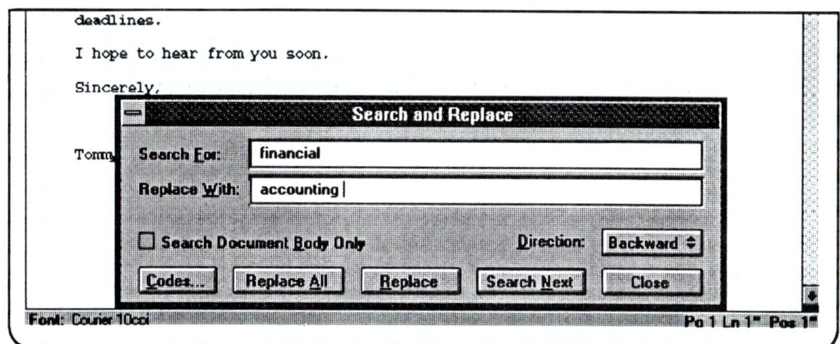

Notice that the Search feature remembers the last group of search settings. To change the direction of the search and replace to forward:

Click	the Direction pop-up list button	***Press***	*Alt+D to select the Direction pop-up list button*	**Press**	Alt+D to select the Direction pop-up list button
Hold down	the mouse button to view the Direction pop-up list	***Press***	*Alt+↓ to view the Direction pop-up list*	**Press**	Alt+↓ to view the Direction pop-up list
Choose	Forward	***Type***	*F for Forward*	**Type**	F for Forward

To replace the old text with the new text:

Click	the Replace command button	***Press***	*Alt+R to select the Replace command button*	**Press**	Alt+R to select the Replace command button

Your screen should look like Figure 5-9.

Figure 5-9

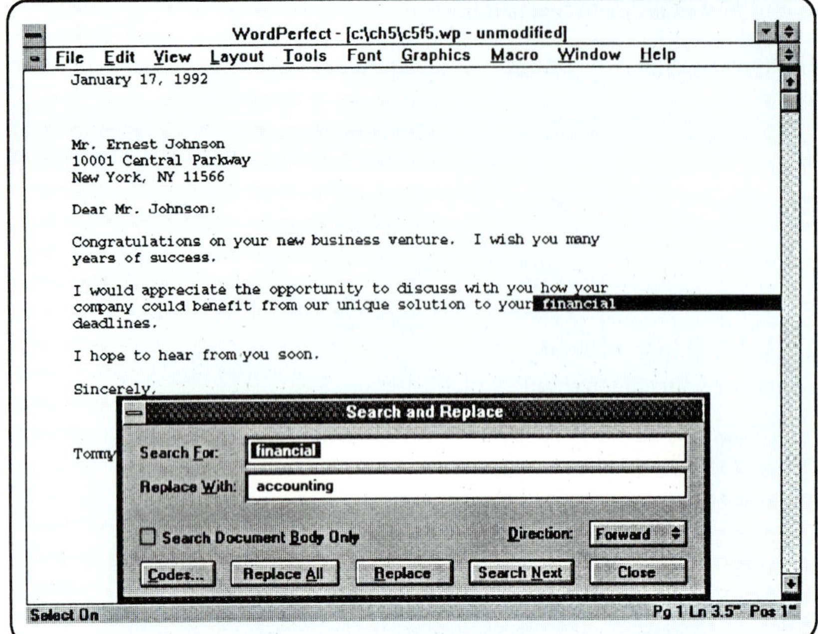

To confirm that you want to replace the old text and continue the search and replace routine:

Click	the Replace command button	***Press***	*Alt+R to select the Replace command button*	**Press**	Alt+R to select the Replace command button

If another match is found, you can replace it by choosing the Replace command button. When no more matches exist, close the Search and Replace dialog box.

If you do not want to replace text found with the Replace feature, choose the Search Next command button. The Search Next feature skips that occurrence of the search string.

If you want to replace every occurrence of a string, select the Replace All command button.

Your screen should look like Figure 5-10.

Figure 5-10

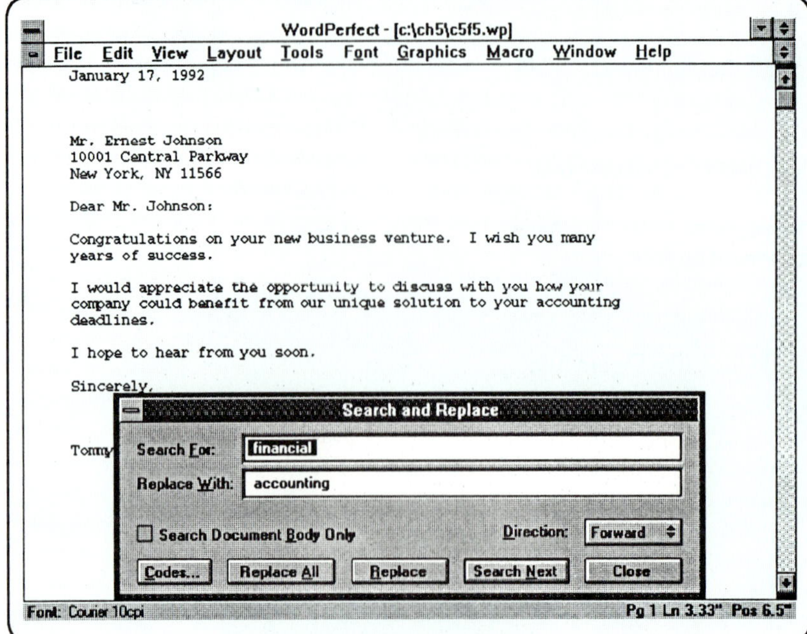

To close the Search and Replace dialog box:

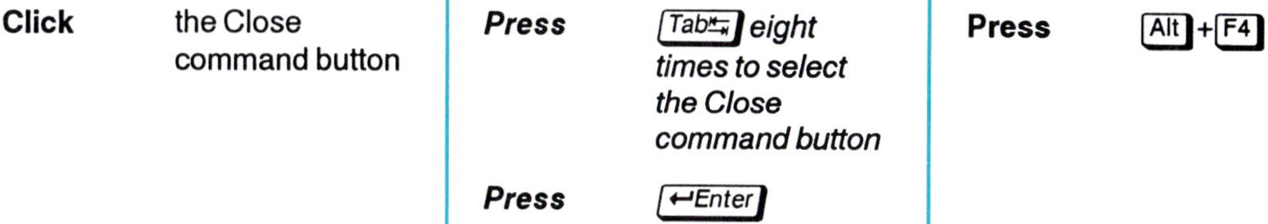

Click	the Close command button	***Press***	*Tab eight times to select the Close command button*	**Press**	Alt+F4
		Press	*↵Enter*		

Save your document. This action replaces the old contents of the file with the current document.

■ CHANGING THE CASE

The Convert Case feature lets you change letters from uppercase to lowercase, or from lowercase to uppercase. Select or highlight the text that you want to change. Then choose the Convert Case option from the Edit menu.

To change the word "Congratulations" in the first paragraph of your document to uppercase:

Double-click	the word "Congrat-ulations"	***Move***	*the insertion point before the "C" in the word "Congrat-ulations"*	**Move**	the insertion point before the "C" in the word "Congrat-ulations"
		Press	*Shift+Ctrl+→*	**Press**	F8
				Press	Ctrl+→

The top portion of your screen should look like Figure 5-11.

Figure 5-11

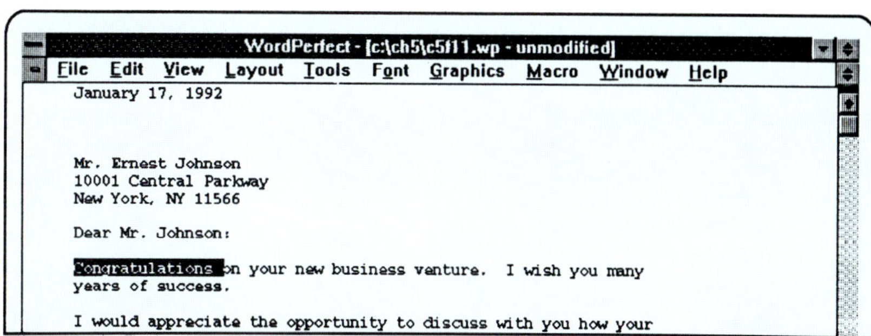

To switch to uppercase:

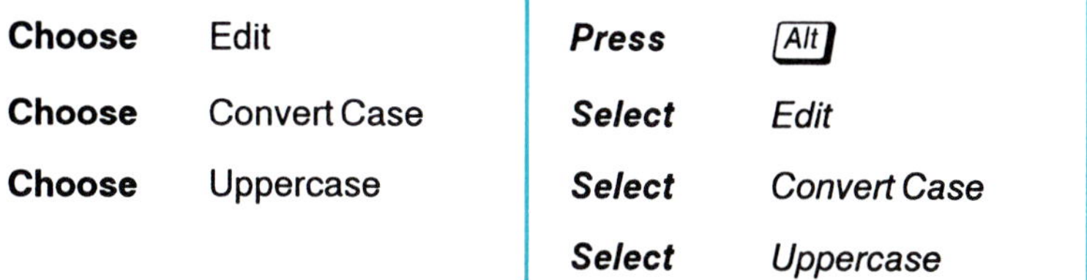

Choose	Edit	***Press***	*Alt*
Choose	Convert Case	***Select***	*Edit*
Choose	Uppercase	***Select***	*Convert Case*
		Select	*Uppercase*

The upper segment of your screen should look like Figure 5-12. All of the characters of the word "Congratulations" have been converted to uppercase.

Figure 5-12

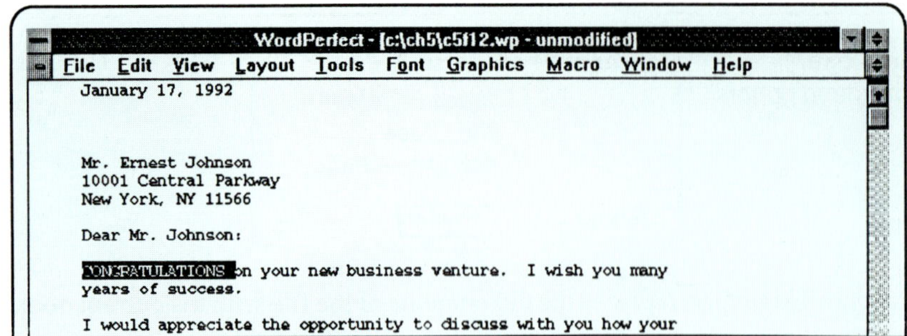

To deselect the word "Congratulations":

Click	in the document area	***Press***	*a pointer-movement key*	**Press**	F8

Save your document. This action replaces the old contents of the file with the current document.

■ MOVING AND COPYING TEXT

The Cut feature allows you to move text from one area of the document to another. The Copy feature lets you copy text from one area of the document to another. Cut and Copy are both located in the Edit menu.

To move or copy text, select the text that you wish to move or copy. Then choose Cut or Copy from the Edit menu. These commands move or copy text to the Windows Clipboard.

To place the cut or copied text in the document, move the insertion point to the desired location for the text and choose Paste from the Edit menu. The Edit Paste command places the text from the Clipboard into the document.

The Cut and Copy features do not have corresponding function keys. However, you may use accelerator keys. The Cut command can be performed by selecting the text and pressing Shift+Delete. The Copy command can be performed by selecting the text and pressing Ctrl+Insert. Shift+Insert performs the Edit Paste command.

To move the first paragraph of your current document and place it below the third paragraph:

Click	in the first paragraph	***Move***	*the insertion point before the first letter of the first paragraph*	**Move**	the insertion point before the first letter of the first paragraph
Quadruple-click	the paragraph	***Press***	*Shift+↓ three times to select the paragraph*	**Press**	F8
Choose	Edit	***Press***	*Alt*	**Press**	↓ three times
Choose	Cut	***Select***	*Edit*	**Press**	Shift+Delete
		Select	*Cut*		

The top portion of your screen should look like Figure 5-13.

Figure 5-13

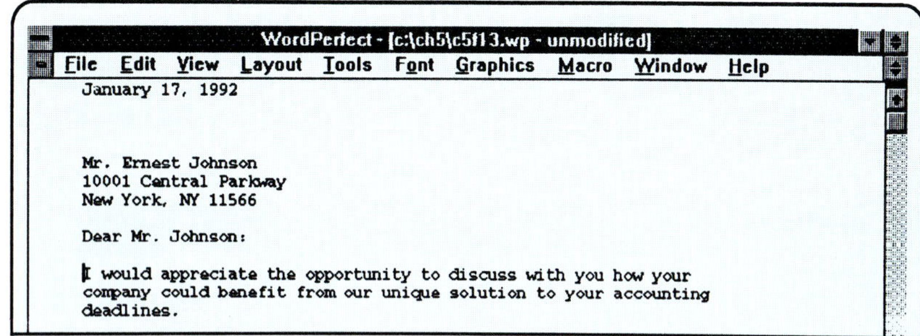

Notice that the first paragraph no longer appears in your document. The paragraph is in the Windows Clipboard.

To place the paragraph you removed at the proper location in your document:

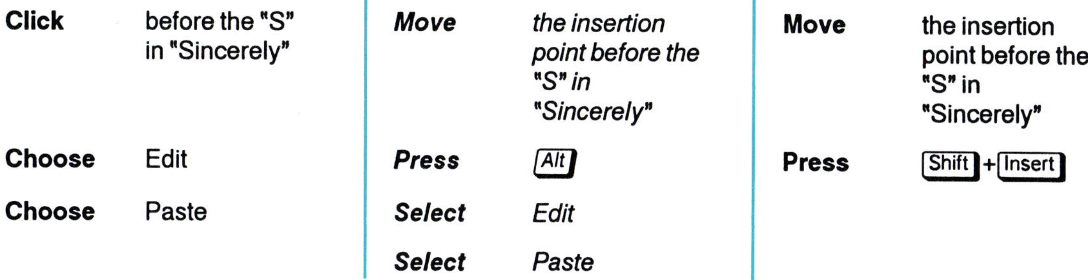

Click	before the "S" in "Sincerely"	***Move***	*the insertion point before the "S" in "Sincerely"*	**Move**	the insertion point before the "S" in "Sincerely"
Choose	Edit	***Press***	*Alt*	**Press**	Shift + Insert
Choose	Paste	***Select***	*Edit*		
		Select	*Paste*		

The bottom portion of your screen should look like Figure 5-14.

Figure 5-14

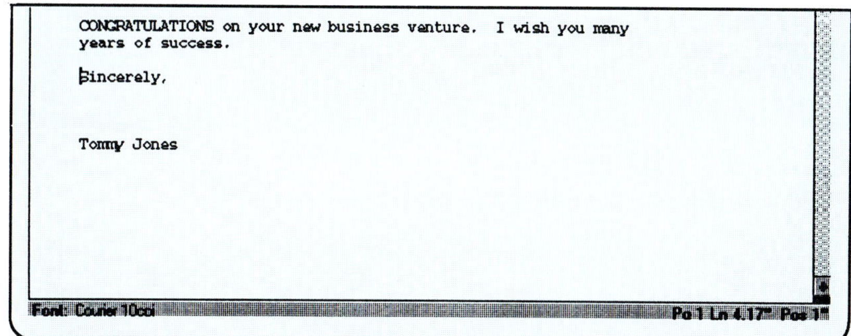

You can use the Select option under the Edit menu to quickly select a sentence or paragraph in your document.

To move the third paragraph using the Select feature and place it as the first paragraph again:

Click	before the "C" in "Congrat-ulations"	***Move***	*the insertion point before the "C" in "Congrat-ulations"*
Choose	Edit	***Press***	*Alt*
Choose	Select	***Select***	*Edit*

Choose	Paragraph	***Select***	*Select*
		Select	*Paragraph*

The bottom section of your screen should look like Figure 5-15.

Figure 5-15

To move the selected paragraph:

Choose	Edit	***Press***	Alt
Choose	Cut	***Select***	*Edit*
		Select	*Cut*

Your screen should look like Figure 5-16.

Figure 5-16

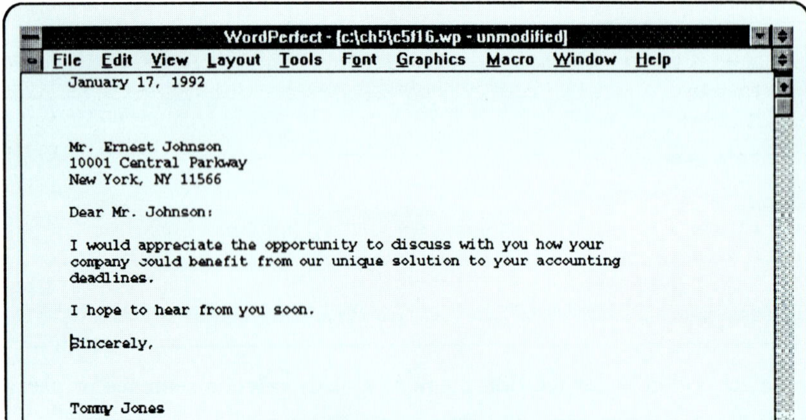

Click	before the "I" in the first paragraph	***Move***	*the insertion point before the "I" in the first paragraph*
Choose	Edit	***Press***	Alt
Choose	Paste	***Select***	*Edit*
		Select	*Paste*

Your screen should look like Figure 5-17.

Figure 5-17

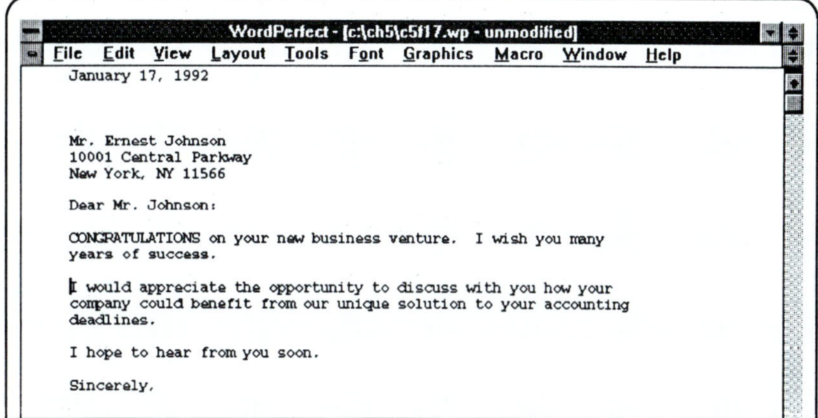

January 17, 1992

Mr. Ernest Johnson
10001 Central Parkway
New York, NY 11566

Dear Mr. Johnson:

CONGRATULATIONS on your new business venture. I wish you many years of success.

I would appreciate the opportunity to discuss with you how your company could benefit from our unique solution to your accounting deadlines.

I hope to hear from you soon.

Sincerely,

To copy the inside address using the Select feature and to place it at the end of the document:

Click	at the end of the document	***Press***	*Ctrl+End*	**Press**	Ctrl+End
Press	↵Enter twice to skip one line before copying the text to the end of the document	***Press***	*↵Enter twice to skip one line before copying the text to the end of the document*	**Press**	↵Enter twice to skip one line before copying the text to the end of the document
Click	before the "M" in "Mr." on the first line of the address	***Move***	*the insertion point before the "M" in "Mr." in the first line of the address*	**Move**	the insertion point before the "M" in "Mr." in the first line of the address
Drag	the mouse until you have highlighted the inside address	***Press***	*Shift+↓ until you have highlighted the inside address*	**Press**	F8
				Press	↓ until you have highlighted the inside address

The top portion of your screen should look like Figure 5-18.

Figure 5-18

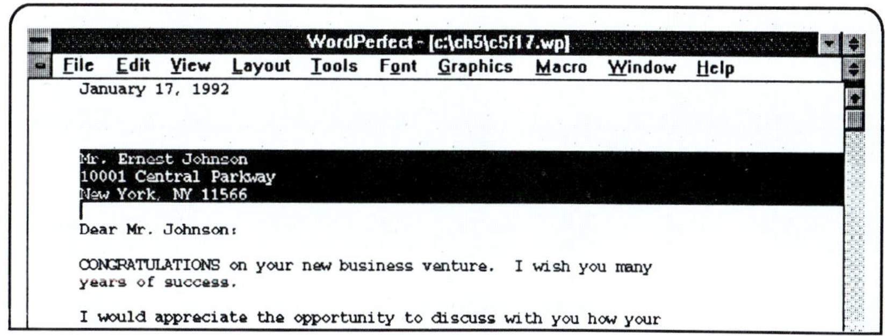

January 17, 1992

Mr. Ernest Johnson
10001 Central Parkway
New York, NY 11566

Dear Mr. Johnson:

CONGRATULATIONS on your new business venture. I wish you many years of success.

I would appreciate the opportunity to discuss with you how your

Choose	Edit	***Press***	*Alt*	**Press**	Ctrl+Insert
Choose	Copy	***Select***	*Edit*		
		Select	*Copy*		

To paste the address at the end of the letter:

Click	at the end of the document	***Move***	*the insertion point to the end of the document*	**Move**	the insertion point to the end of the document
Choose	Edit	***Press***	*Alt*	**Press**	Shift+Insert
Choose	Paste	***Select***	*Edit*		
		Select	*Paste*		

The lower part of your screen should look like Figure 5-19.

Figure 5-19

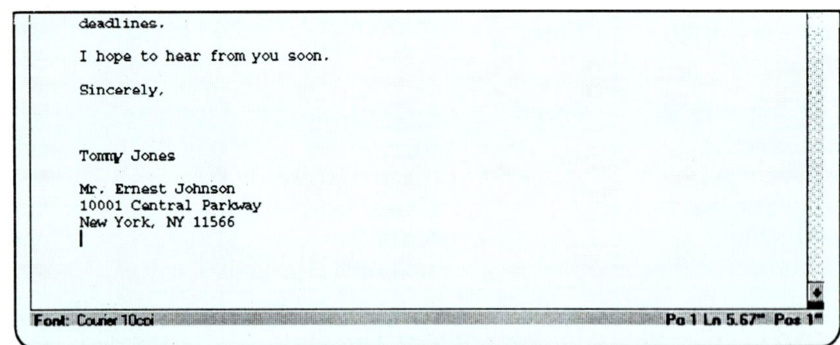

For more information on the various cut and copy options, see the WordPerfect Reference Manual. The Drag and Drop method for moving and copying text is discussed in Appendix D.

Close your document without saving the changes.

EXERCISE 1

INSTRUCTIONS: Define the following terms:

1. Replace feature ______________________________
____
2. Search feature ______________________________
____
3. Reveal codes ______________________________
____

4. Cut feature ______________________________

____

5. Select feature ______________________________

____

6. Hard return ______________________________

____

7. Soft return ______________________________

____

8. Convert Case feature ______________________________

____

9. Search string ______________________________

____

10. Replace string ______________________________

____

EXERCISE 2

INSTRUCTIONS: Circle T if the statement is true and F if the statement is false.

T F 1. The Replace feature allows you to locate a word, phrase, or code in a document and replace it with a word, phrase, or code.

T F 2. You can use the Copy feature to highlight a sentence, paragraph, or page of text.

T F 3. When you use the Search feature, you must be at the beginning of the document because you can only search from the insertion point forward.

T F 4. When you use the Cut feature, the text always stays on the screen.

T F 5. If the search string contains only lowercase letters, then WordPerfect will look for matching text that is in lowercase and uppercase.

T F 6. The Select feature is used to highlight text within your document.

T F 7. The codes that WordPerfect uses are not visible on your normal editing screen.

T F 8. When you press [↵Enter], a hard return is inserted into the document.

T F 9. The Convert Case feature allows text to be changed only from uppercase to lowercase.

EXERCISE 3

INSTRUCTIONS:

1. Create the following document.
2. Save the document on a file using the name "ch05ex03."
3. Display the document codes using the Reveal Codes feature. Notice the hard return [HRt] and the soft return [SRt] codes that appear in the document.
4. Close the document.

```
current date



Mr. T. J. Smith
11134 Moss Spring Street
Houston, TX 77881

Dear Mr. Smith:

Please remit your payment that is currently past due as soon as
possible.  Your prompt attention to this matter will be
appreciated.

We have sent you three letters advising you of the need to
complete payment for the furniture you purchased from us last
year.

If you need any additional information at this time, please
contact me at 672-1901.

Sincerely,


Nora Thompson
Accounts Receivable
```

EXERCISE 4

INSTRUCTIONS:

1. Create the following document.
2. Save the document on a file using the name "ch05ex04."
3. Display the document codes using the Reveal Codes feature. Notice the hard return [HRt] and the soft return [SRt] codes that appear in the document.
4. Close the document.

```
current date


Ms. S. K. Garza
Business Forms Company
2304 Gessner, Suite 798
Miami, FL 33533

Dear Ms. Garza:

Congratulations on your new job.  I know that you will enjoy
your position with Business Forms Company.

In your new position, you will have the responsibility for
preparing all documents that are distributed to our customers.
Please be careful as you create the materials you send to our
customers.

If you have any questions about your new position with Business
Forms Company, please contact your supervisor, Ms. Susan
Johnson at extension 7784.

Sincerely,


Mary K. Scanlan
Office Supervisor
```

EXERCISE 5

INSTRUCTIONS:

1. Open the file "ch05ex03."
2. Search the document from the beginning of the document forward to find each occurrence of the word "to."
3. Search the document from the end of the document backwards to find each occurrence of the word "you."
4. Search the document for the name "Smith" and replace it with "Jones."
5. Search the document for the word "furniture" and replace it with the word "appliances."
6. Save the document on a file using the name "ch05ex05."
7. Print the document.
8. Close the document.

EXERCISE 6

INSTRUCTIONS:

1. Open the file "ch05ex04."
2. Search the document from the beginning of the document forward to find each occurrence of the word "with."
3. Search the document from the end of the document backwards to find each occurrence of the word "your."
4. Search the document for the name "Business Forms" and replace it with "Graphics Art."
5. Search the document for the word "customers" and replace it with the word "clients."
6. Search the document for the words "new job" and replace the words with the word "promotion."
7. Save the document on a file using the name "ch05ex06."
8. Print the document.
9. Close the document.

EXERCISE 7

INSTRUCTIONS:

1. Create the following document.
2. Save the document on a file using the name "ch05ex07."
3. Print the document.
4. Change the case of the words "General Computer Corporation" to uppercase.
5. Change the case of the word "wonderful" to uppercase.
6. Change the case of the word "SUCCESS" to lowercase.
7. Change the case of the word "ME" to lowercase.
8. Print the document.
9. Save the document using the same file name.
10. Close the document.

```
current date


Dear Shirley,

Thank you for your recent letter regarding your new job at
General Computer Corporation.  I think the SUCCESS you are
enjoying is wonderful.

Please keep ME informed about your activities in your new
position.

With all my love,


Aunt Jan
```

EXERCISE 8

INSTRUCTIONS:

1. Create the following document. Note that you will move information around in the exercise so the document will make more sense.
2. Save the document on a file using the name "ch05ex08."
3. Print the document.
4. Move the third paragraph so it appears as the first paragraph in the document.
5. Move the first paragraph so it appears as the third paragraph in the document.
6. Print the document.
7. Save the document using the same name.
8. Close the document.

```
current date


Mr. A. J. Bohem
West Coast Production Company
11235 Anaheim Blvd.
Los Angeles, CA 90014

Dear A. J.:

Thanks again for your recent order from us.

We hope that you find our products to be the best quality
available.  Our employees work very diligently to make sure all
products meet the specifications of our customers.

Thank you for your recent letter in which you requested we send
you 10 of our best water pumps.  I am sure you will enjoy using
these fine products.

Sincerely,


T. J. Chin
```

EXERCISE 9

INSTRUCTIONS:

1. Create the following document. Note that you will move information around in the exercise so the document will make more sense.
2. Save the document on a file using the name "ch05ex09."
3. Print the document.
4. Move the third paragraph so it appears as the second paragraph in the document.
5. Create a fourth paragraph. Copy the contents of the first paragraph (FANTASTIC NEWS!!!) to the fourth paragraph.
6. Print the document.
7. Save the document using the same name.
8. Close the document.

```
current date


Mr. C. S. Baker
Midway Distribution Company
9225 Golden Arch Way
Chicago, IL 60606

Dear Carl:

FANTASTIC NEWS!!!

We will serve dinner for a maximum of four people any evening
between now and the end of the month.  Please call me at 758-
4700 so we can make arrangements for the dinner.

You have been selected as a winner in our special drawing for a
dinner.  Your name was selected from business cards left in our
restaurant.

Cordially,


Susan K. Thomas
Chicken Delight Restaurant
```

EXERCISE 10

INSTRUCTIONS:

1. Create the following document.
2. Save the document on a file using the name "ch05ex10."
3. Change the words "Global Marketing" to uppercase.
4. Change the word "newest" to uppercase.
5. Search the document for the word "teacher" and replace it with the word "professor."
6. Change words "Special Delivery" to uppercase.
7. Search the document from beginning to end for each occurrence of the word "the."
8. Move the second paragraph so it appears as the first paragraph in the document.
9. Change the case of the words "EXAMINATION COPY" to lowercase.
10. Print the document.
11. Save the document using the same name.
12. Close the document.

```
current date

Special Delivery

Dr. Don Sedik
William Rainey Harper College
1200 Algonquin Road
Palatine, IL 60067

Dear Dr. Sedik:

We would like to invite you to preview Global Marketing, the
newest text for the International Marketing Courses.  Global
Marketing will bring the European Common Market and the Asian
Markets right to your classroom.

Global Marketing is just off the press.  Global Marketing is
written by two professors who have studied global markets from
inside the Common Market.  William Zwilling, a teacher, from
the University of Switzerland and Fahad Faham, a teacher, from
Iraq World University have put real meaning into Global
Marketing.

Return the enclosed card to receive Global Marketing as an
EXAMINATION COPY.

Sincerely,



Mark Healy
Director of Marketing
```

EXERCISE 11

INSTRUCTIONS:

1. Create the following document.
2. Save the document on a file using the name "ch05ex11."
3. Print the document.
4. Move the third paragraph so it appears as the first paragraph.
5. Search the document from the beginning forward to find each occurrence of the word "your."
6. In the last paragraph, delete the words "future litigation" and insert "income tax fraud."
7. Search the document from the end of the document backwards and replace "Accountants Association" with "CPA'S."
8. In the first paragraph, insert "$100" after the word "enclosed."
9. Print Preview the document.
10. Save the document using the same name.

11. Print the document.
12. Close the document.

```
current date



Dr. Dan Danis
Dewey, Cheatum & Howe
616 North Michigan
Albuquerque, NM 87100

Dear Dr. Danis:

It was kind of you to address the Albuquerque Accountants
Association.  Your talk on white-collar fraud was very
informative and entertaining.

The Albuquerque Accountants Association will long remember your
talk and its implications for future litigation.

On behalf of the members of the Albuquerque Accountants
Association please accept the enclosed check for your March 25
speech.

Thank you,



Robert Held, President
Albuquerque Accountants Association
```

EXERCISE 12

INSTRUCTIONS:

1. Create the following document.
2. Save the document on a file using the name "ch05ex12."
3. Display the Reveal Codes. Notice the hard return [HRt] and the soft return [SRt] codes that appear in the document.
4. Print the document.
5. Delete the company name "ROSS, ANDERSON & COMPANY, INC." and replace it with the name "WORLDWIDE ACCOUNTING."
6. Move the first sentence of the first paragraph so it appears as the second sentence of the first paragraph in the document.
7. Search the document for the word "auditor" and replace it with "director of financial resources."
8. Change the case of the words "Certified Mail" to uppercase.

9. Print Preview and print the document.
10. Save the document using the same name.
11. Close the document.

```
current date

Certified Mail

Mrs. Rose Trunk
5999 North Meridian Street
Indianapolis, IN 46206

Dear Mrs. Trunk:

Your name has been suggested as a possible auditor for a
position that involves extensive foreign travel.  We are very
interested in an individual who is willing to travel in Europe,
the Far East, and Australia.

The position involves representing us as an auditor in areas
where we have operations, sales representative, and regional
offices.

The initial salary for an auditor is negotiable.  If you would
be interested in talking about this position further, contact
Mr. Charles Norris, Director of Financial Operations.

Very cordially yours,

ROSS, ANDERSON & COMPANY, INC.



James Seeck
Vice President
```

CHAPTER SIX

USING THE WORDPERFECT BUTTON BAR

OBJECTIVES

In this chapter you will learn to:

- View the Button Bar
- Use the Button Bar to create and edit a document
- Create a custom Button Bar
- Change the format of the Button Bar
- Select a different Button Bar

CHAPTER OVERVIEW

In this chapter, the WordPerfect Button Bar is discussed. The View Button Bar feature is introduced. The methods for using a Button Bar to create and edit a document are described and illustrated. Finally, the process for customizing and formatting the Button Bar are presented.

VIEWING THE BUTTON BAR

In this book, three methods for selecting features have been presented: using the mouse with the menus, selecting from the menu with the keyboard, and using the keyboard function keys. WordPerfect provides an alternative method to quickly access commands with the mouse. This feature is called the Button Bar.

The Button Bar is made up of buttons that represent commands. Each command has a predefined button. The most commonly used commands have been placed on the default Button Bar.

To view the default Button Bar:

Choose	View	***Press***	Alt	
Choose	Button Bar	***Select***	*View*	
		Select	*Button Bar*	

The top portion of your screen should look like Figure 6-1.

Figure 6-1

The Button Bar contains 10 buttons. The buttons can only be accessed using the mouse. Notice that some buttons may appear gray or shaded. When a button or command appears shaded, you cannot use the button at that time.

Notice that Close is one of the buttons on the bar. Rather than choose File Close from the menu or pressing Ctrl+F4, you can click the Close button to select the command.

■ PERFORMING TASKS WITH THE BUTTON BAR

You can use the Button Bar to perform tasks. This section demonstrates how to edit a document using the Button Bar. Alternative methods for performing these commands were discussed in previous chapters.

Opening a Document

You can open a document by using the Open button on the Button Bar. The Open button provides the same feature as choosing Open from the File menu or pressing F4.

If necessary, change the default directory to "a:\wpdocs" or "c:\wpdocs."

To open the "johnson.ltr" document using the Button Bar:

Click the Open button on the Button Bar

Click on the file "johnson.ltr" in the Files list box

Click the Open command button

Your screen should look like Figure 6-2.

Figure 6-2

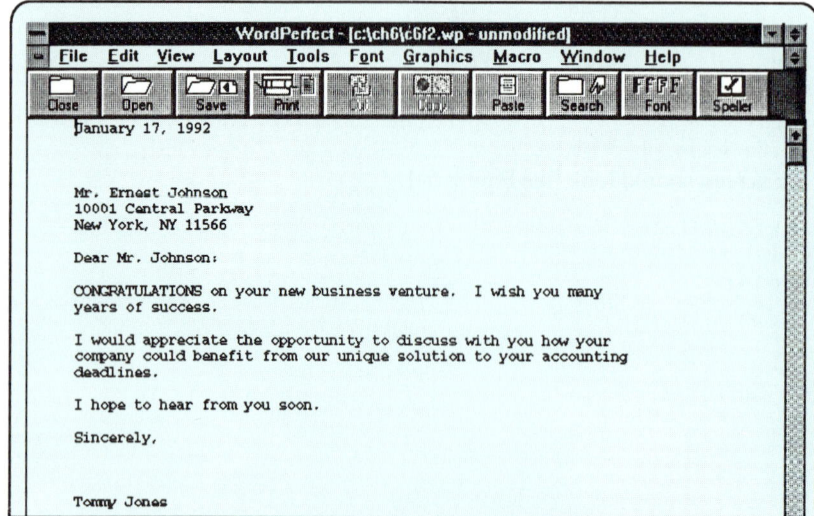

January 17, 1992

Mr. Ernest Johnson
10001 Central Parkway
New York, NY 11566

Dear Mr. Johnson:

CONGRATULATIONS on your new business venture. I wish you many years of success.

I would appreciate the opportunity to discuss with you how your company could benefit from our unique solution to your accounting deadlines.

I hope to hear from you soon.

Sincerely,

Tommy Jones

Searching a Document

You can use the Search button on the Button Bar to locate specific text in your document. The Search button provides the same feature as choosing Search from the Edit menu or pressing F2.

To search for the word "your" in the document:

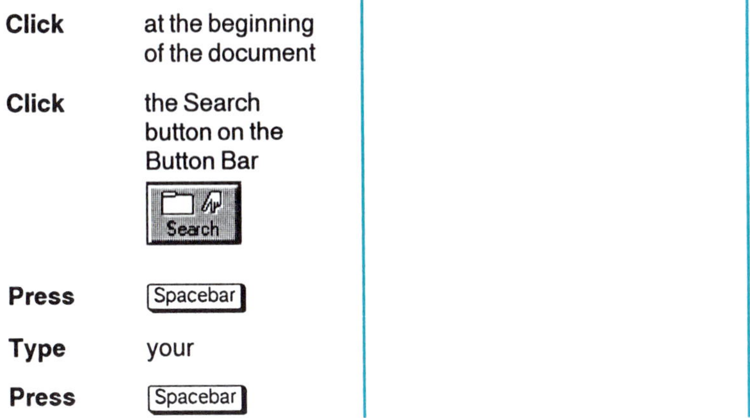

Click at the beginning of the document

Click the Search button on the Button Bar

Press Spacebar

Type your

Press Spacebar

The bottom portion of your screen should look like Figure 6-3.

Figure 6-3

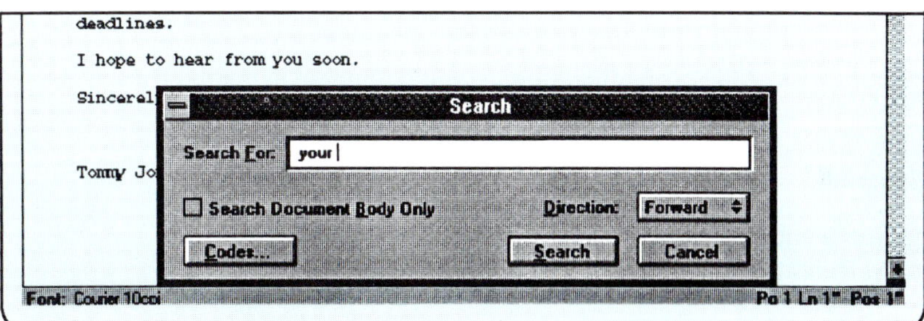

Notice that the search direction is set at Forward.

To begin the search:

Click the Search command button

Cutting and Pasting Text

The Cut feature allows you to cut or move text from the document. The Paste feature allows you to place the text in a new location in the document. You can use the Cut and Paste buttons on the Button Bar to perform these commands.

To move the first paragraph of your current document using the Button Bar:

Click in the first paragraph

Quadruple-click the first paragraph

Click the Cut button on the Button Bar

The top portion of your screen should look like Figure 6-4.

Figure 6-4

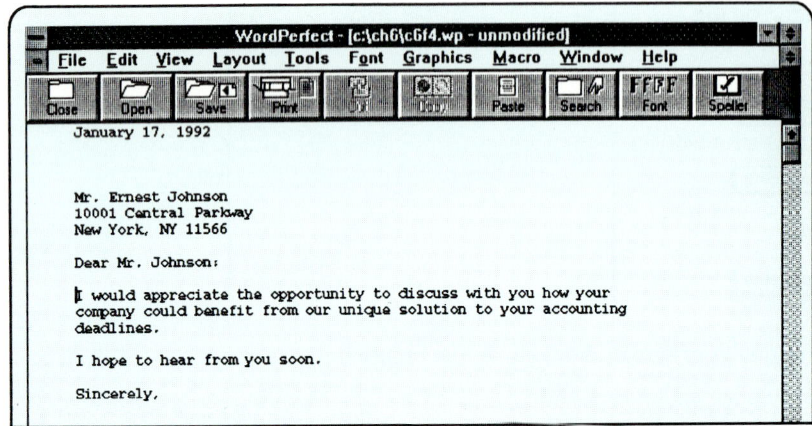

Notice that the first paragraph no longer appears in the document.

To place the cut paragraph at the proper location in your document using the Button Bar:

Click at the "S" in "Sincerely"

Click the Paste button on the Button Bar

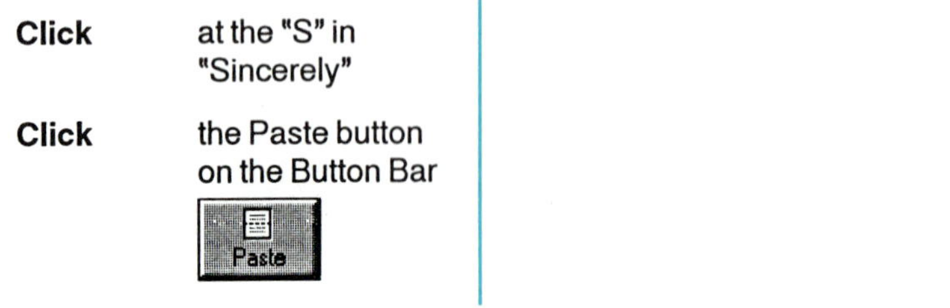

The bottom part of your screen should look like Figure 6-5.

Figure 6-5

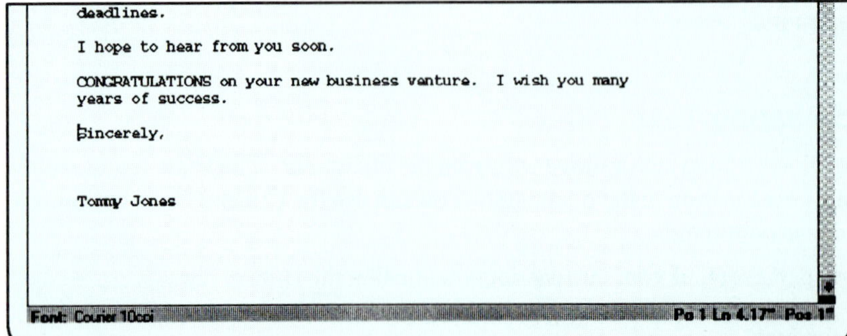

Copying and Pasting Text

You can copy text in the document using the Button Bar. To copy text, first select the text and then click the Copy button on the Button Bar. To place the copied text at the new location in the document, use the Paste button on the Button Bar.

To copy the inside address using the Button Bar:

Click at the end of the document

Press ↵Enter twice to add two blank lines at the end of the document

Click before the "M" in "Mr." on the first line of the address

Select the entire inside address

Click the Copy button on the Button Bar

The top portion of your screen should look like Figure 6-6.

Figure 6-6

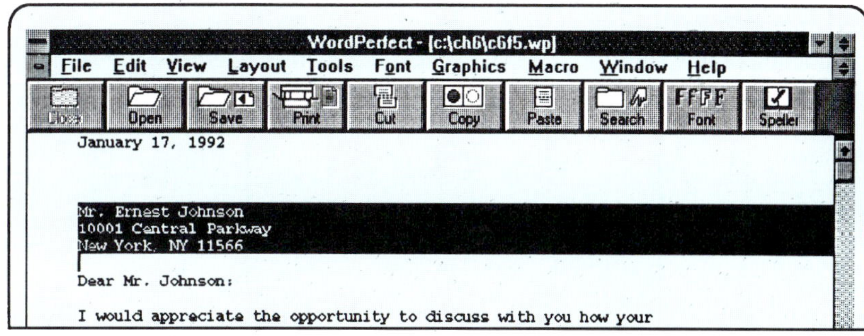

To place the address at the bottom of the document using the Button Bar:

Click at the bottom of the document

Click the Paste button on the Button Bar

The bottom portion of your screen should look like Figure 6-7.

Figure 6-7

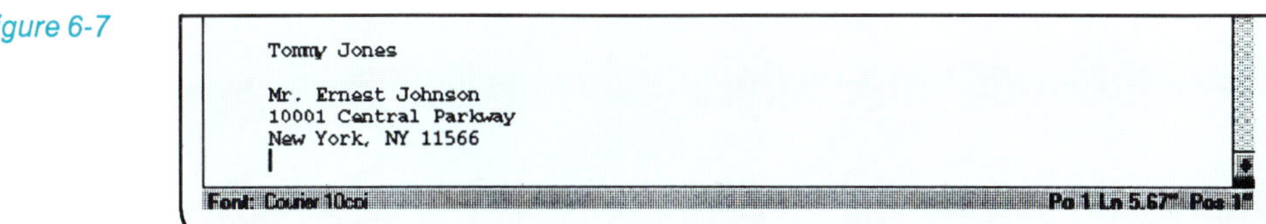

Printing a Document

You can print a document using the Button Bar. To print the current document:

Click	the Print button on the Button Bar		
Click	the Print command button		

Closing a Document

You can close a document using the Close button on the Button Bar. To close "johnson.ltr" without saving the changes:

Click	the Close button on the Button Bar		
Click	the No command button		

Removing the Button Bar

When you close a document, the Button Bar remains on the screen. To remove the Button Bar from the screen:

Choose	View	***Press***	*Alt*
Choose	Button Bar	***Select***	*View*
		Select	*Button Bar*

Your screen should look like Figure 6-8.

Figure 6-8

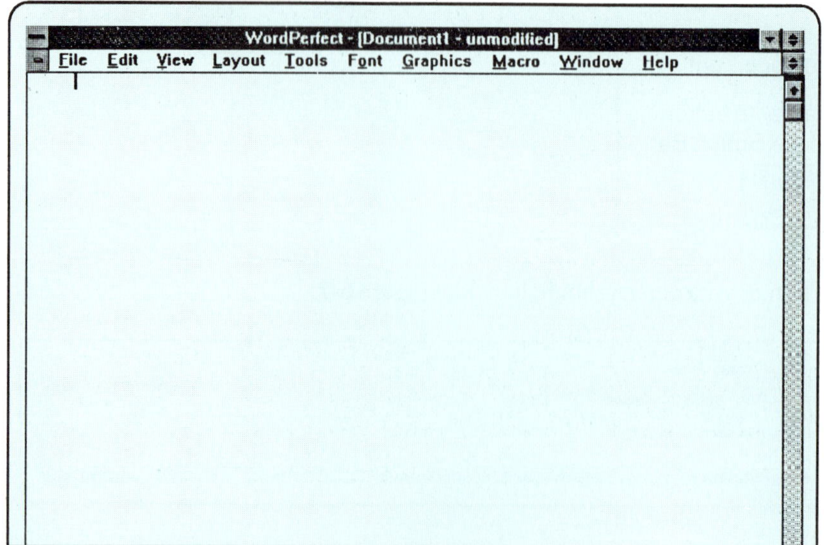

■ CREATING A BUTTON BAR

You might use different commands than those appearing on the default Button Bar. You can create your own Button Bar by selecting the Button Bar Setup, New command in the View menu.

To create a new Button Bar:

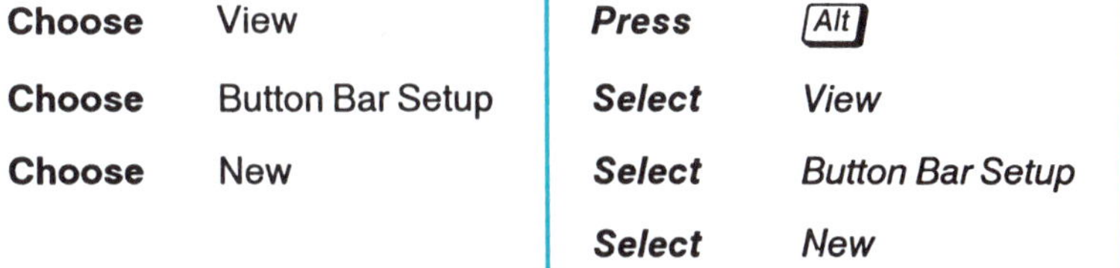

Choose	View	***Press***	Alt
Choose	Button Bar Setup	***Select***	*View*
Choose	New	***Select***	*Button Bar Setup*
		Select	*New*

Your screen should look like Figure 6-9.

Figure 6-9

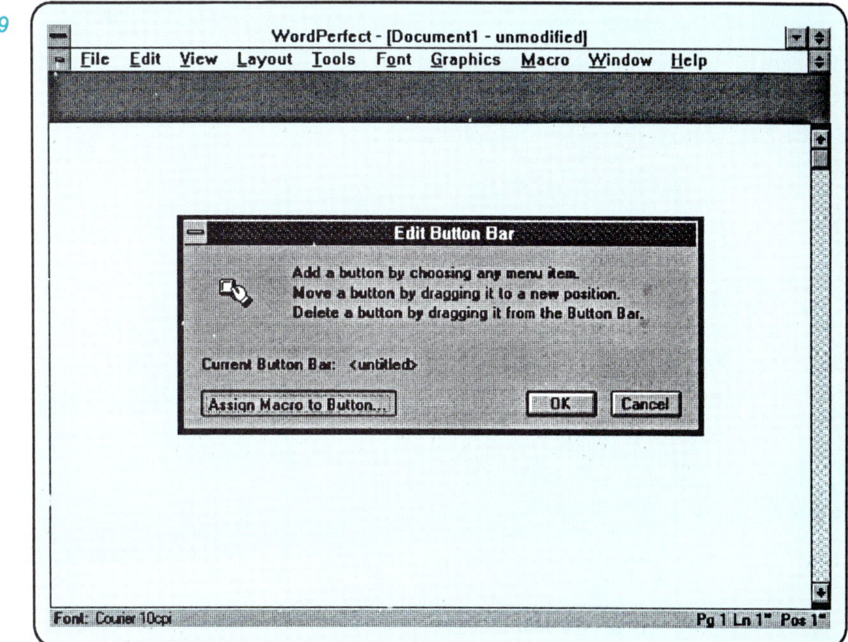

To add a command to the bar, choose the command from the menu. You must use the mouse to select items from the menu. You can not use the keyboard to create a Button Bar.

To add the File Open button to the Button Bar:

Choose	File
Choose	Open

The top portion of your screen should look like Figure 6-10.

Figure 6-10

Notice that when you point to the menu, the mouse pointer resembles a hand pressing a button. This icon indicates that you are choosing commands to be placed on the Button Bar.

The Open button appears at the beginning of the Button Bar. To add a File Close button:

Choose File

Choose Close

The top part of your screen should look like Figure 6-11.

Figure 6-11

The Close button appears in the second position on the Button Bar. Each button is placed on the bar in the order the command is chosen.

To complete the Button Bar, choose the following commands:

Choose File

Choose Save

Choose File

Choose Save As

Choose File

Choose Print

Choose Edit

Choose Undelete

Choose Edit

Choose Convert Case

Choose Uppercase

Choose Edit

Choose Convert Case

Choose Lowercase

Choose	Edit
Choose	Replace
Choose	View
Choose	Reveal Codes

The upper part of your screen should look like Figure 6-12.

Figure 6-12

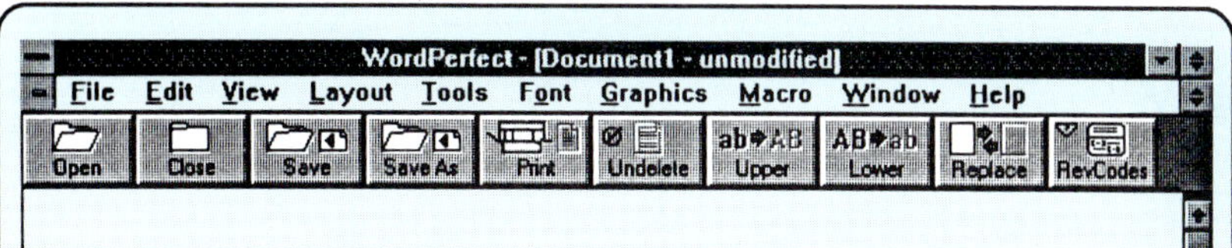

To accept the Button Bar you have created:

Click	the OK command button

Your screen should look like Figure 6-13.

Figure 6-13

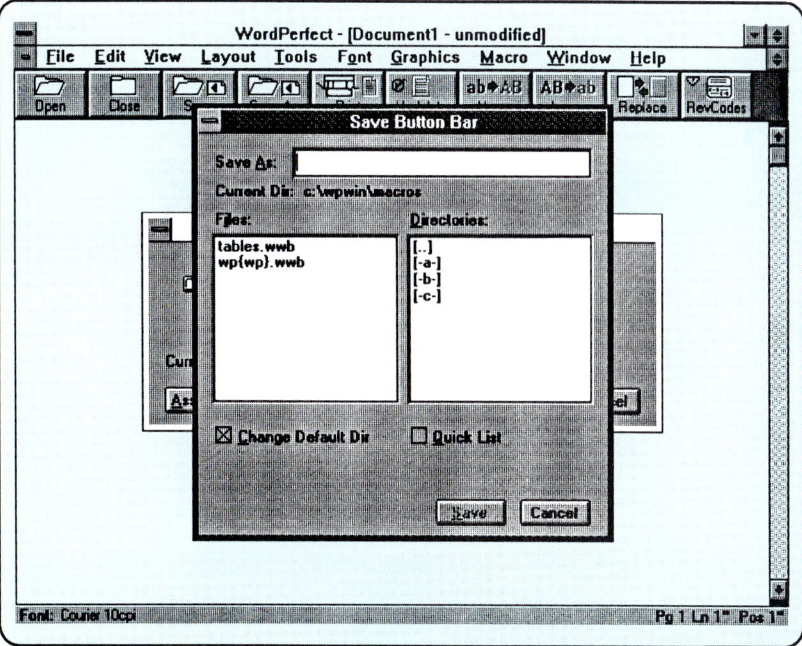

The Save Button Bar dialog box appears. A Button Bar can have a name with a maximum of eight characters and can not contain spaces. Button Bars are automatically saved with the extension ".wwb" to indicate that it is a WordPerfect for Windows Button Bar.

To save this bar as "letter.wwb":

Type	**letter** in the Save As text box

Click	the Save command button		

The Button Bar is saved as "letter.wwb" in the default macro directory. For the location of your macro directory, use the Preferences, Location of Files command from the File menu.

■ EDITING A BUTTON BAR

You can change a Button Bar that has already been created by using the Button Bar Setup, Edit command from the View menu. The Edit command allows you to delete buttons, add new buttons, and move buttons.

To change the "letter.wwb" Button Bar created in the previous exercise:

Choose	View	***Press***	Alt
Choose	Button Bar Setup	***Select***	*View*
Choose	Edit	***Select***	*Button Bar Setup*
		Select	*Edit*

Your screen should look like Figure 6-14.

Figure 6-14

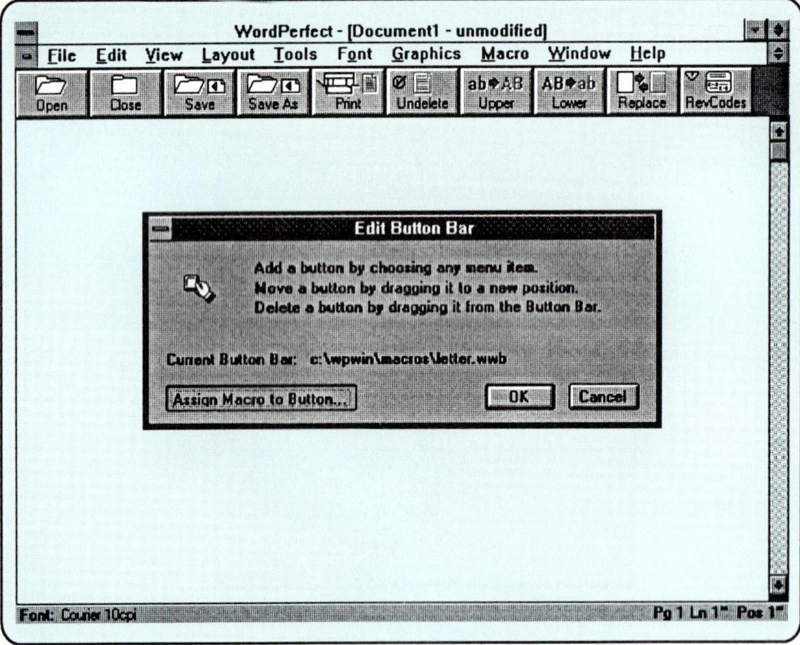

Suppose that you want to move the Save As button to the beginning of the bar. To move the Save As button:

Click	the Save As button		
Drag	the button to the first position on the bar		

The upper part of your screen should look like Figure 6-15.

Figure 6-15

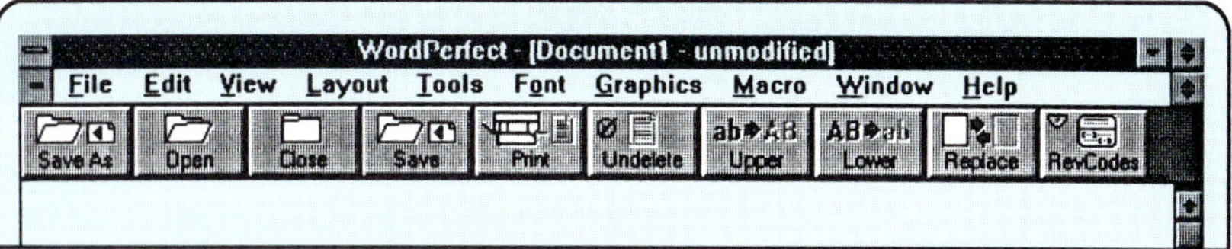

To delete a button, drag the button down off of the Button Bar. To delete the Replace button:

Click	the Replace button		
Drag	the Replace button down off of the Button Bar		

The top part of your screen should look like Figure 6-16.

Figure 6-16

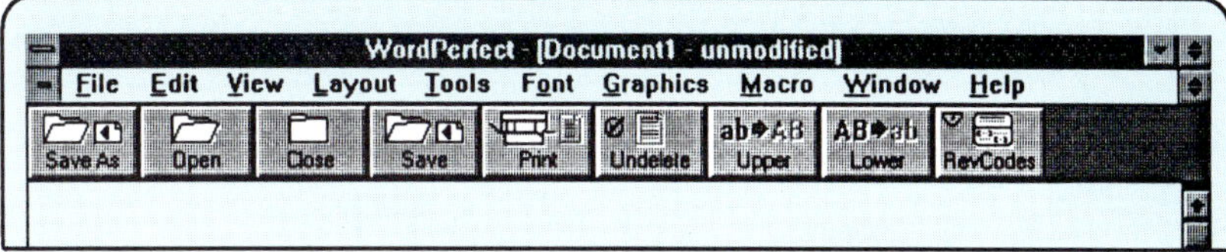

To accept the changes to the Button Bar:

Click	the OK command button		

The changes are automatically saved to the file "letter.wwb" in the macro directory.

■ FORMATTING THE BUTTON BAR

You can change the location of the Button Bar on the screen or the format of the buttons. Use the Button Bar Setup, Options command from the View menu to change the Button Bar format.

By default, the Button Bar appears at the top of the WordPerfect window. You can change the location of the Button Bar to any border of the window.

You can also change the format of the buttons. By default, the buttons appear with text and graphics. You can change the button format to text and graphics, text only, or graphics only.

To change the format of the "letter.wwb" created in the previous exercises:

Choose	View	***Press***	*Alt*
Choose	Button Bar Setup	***Select***	*View*
Choose	Options	***Select***	*Button Bar Setup*
		Select	*Options*

Your screen should look like Figure 6-17.

Figure 6-17

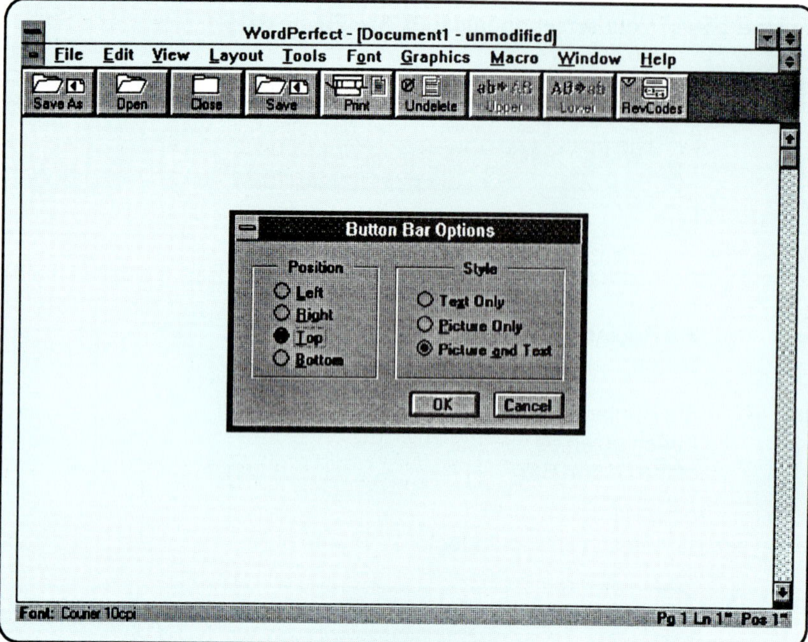

To change the position of the Button Bar to the right side of the window:

Click	the Right option button in the Position box	***Press***	*Alt+R to select the Right option button in the Position box*

Your screen should look like Figure 6-18.

Figure 6-18

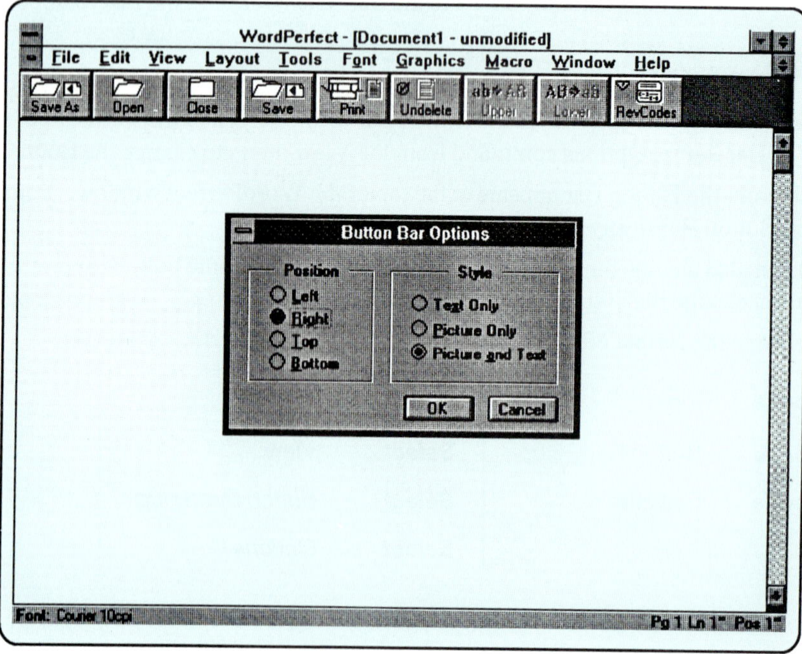

To change the style of the Button Bar to Picture only:

Click	the Picture Only option button in the Style box	***Press***	*Alt+P to select the Picture Only option button in the Style box*

To accept the changes to the Button Bar:

Click	the OK command button	***Press***	*↵Enter*

Your screen should look like Figure 6-19.

Figure 6-19

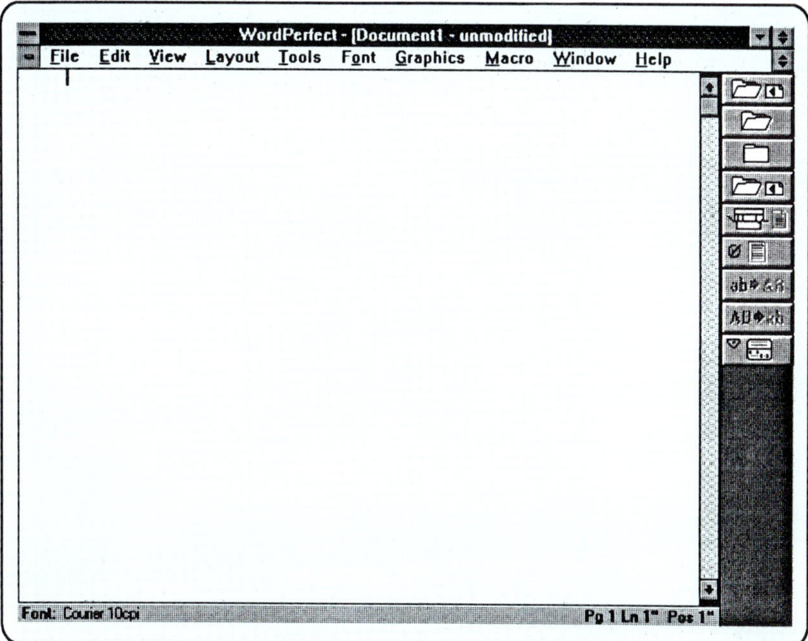

The Button Bar appears at the right of the window. Each button contains only the picture representing that command. The individual buttons are much smaller. The smaller buttons allow more buttons to be placed on the bar. However, without the text, some of the pictures are difficult to understand.

To change the Button Bar back to the defaults:

Choose	View	***Press***	*Alt*
Choose	Button Bar Setup	***Select***	*View*
Choose	Options	***Select***	*Button Bar Setup*
		Select	*Options*

To change the position and style settings:

Click	the Top option button in the Position box	***Press***	*Alt+T to select the Top option button in the Position box*
Click	the Picture and Text option button in the Style box	***Press***	*Alt+A to select the Picture and Text option button in the Style box*

Your screen should look like Figure 6-20.

Figure 6-20

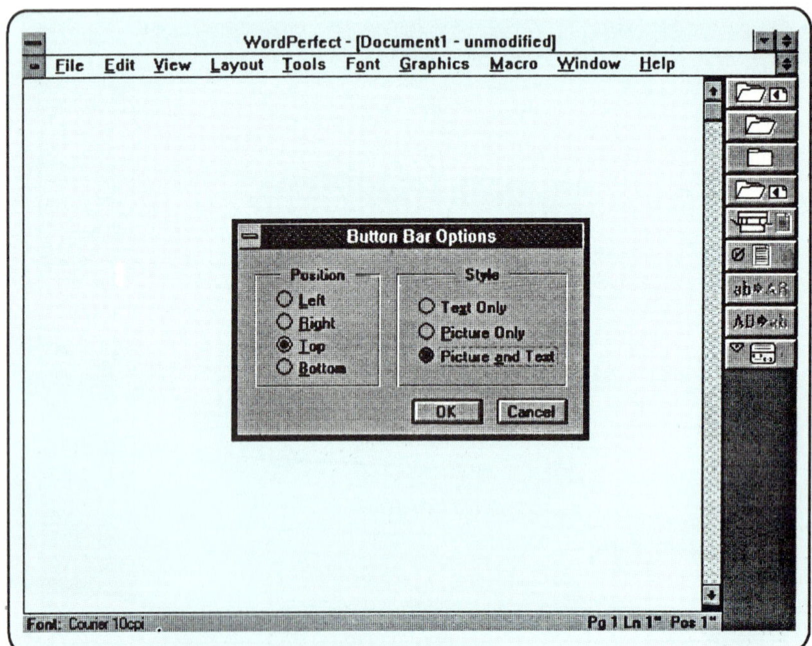

To accept the changes:

Click	the OK command button	***Press***	*↵Enter*

■ SELECTING A BUTTON BAR

You can create many different Button Bars in WordPerfect to meet your different document needs. Use the Button Bar Setup, Select command sequence from the View menu to choose a particular Button Bar.

You currently have the "letter.wwb" Button Bar on your screen. To select the default Button Bar "wp{wp}.wwb":

Choose	View	***Press***	*Alt*
Choose	Button Bar Setup	***Select***	*View*

Choose	Select	***Select***	*Button Bar Setup*
		Select	*Select*

Your screen should look like Figure 6-21.

Figure 6-21

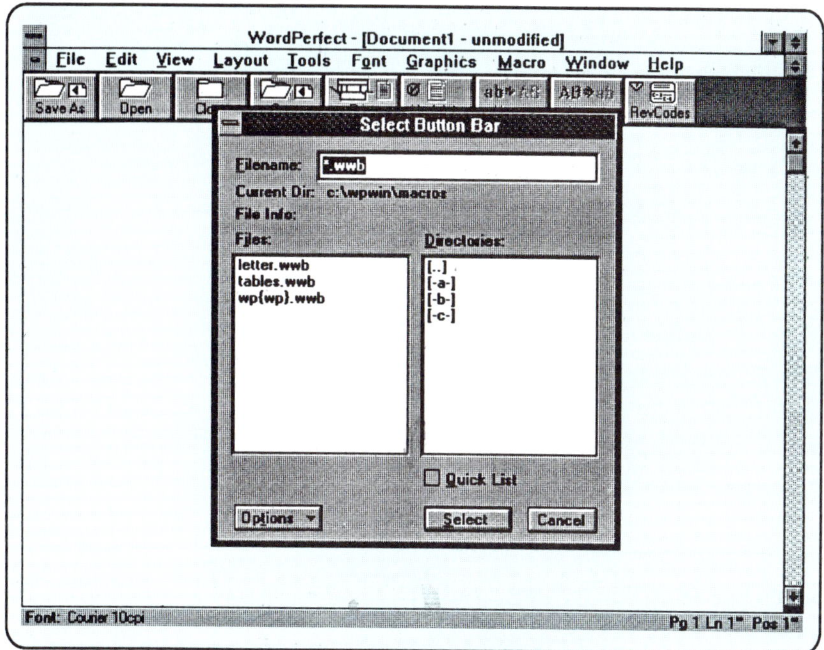

The Select Button Bar dialog box appears. The Button Bar files appear in the Files list box. Notice the Button Bar files are located in the "macros" directory within the "wpwin" directory. This is the default directory for macro and Button Bar files.

To select the "wp{wp}.wwb" Button Bar:

Click	on the file "wp{wp}.wwb" in the Files list box	***Type***	***wp{wp}.wwb*** *in the Filename text box*
Click	the Select command button	***Press***	*↵Enter*

The default Button Bar appears on your screen. The top part of your screen should look like Figure 6-22.

Figure 6-22

To remove the Button Bar from the screen:

Choose	View	***Press***	Alt
Choose	Button Bar	***Select***	*View*
		Select	*Button Bar*

The Button Bar disappears.

EXERCISE 1

INSTRUCTIONS: Define the following terms:

1. View Button Bar feature ______________________________

____

2. Button Bar Setup New feature ______________________________

____

3. Button Bar Setup Edit feature ______________________________

____

4. Button Bar Setup Options feature ______________________________

____

5. Button Bar Setup Select feature ______________________________

____

EXERCISE 2

INSTRUCTIONS: Circle T if the statement is true and F is the statement is False.

T F 1. The Button Bar feature allows you to perform commands quickly by clicking on buttons that represent commands.

T F 2. The default Button Bar is "wp{wp}.wwk."

T F 3. You can create your own Button Bars by using the View Button Bar command.

T F 4. The Print feature has a button on the default Button Bar.

T F 5. When you use the Button Bar Setup, Options command, you can move the buttons on the Button Bar.

T F 6. The Button Bar Setup Options command allows you to change the position of the Button Bar.

T F 7. Buttons can contain text, pictures, or text and pictures.

EXERCISE 3

INSTRUCTIONS:

1. Open the "johnson.ltr" file.
2. Display the default Button Bar.
3. Print the document using the Button Bar.
4. Close the document using the Button Bar.
5. Remove the Button Bar from the screen.

EXERCISE 4

INSTRUCTIONS:

1. Open the "johnson.ltr" file.
2. Display the default Button Bar.
3. Using the Button Bar, search the document for the word "business."
4. Using the Button Bar, move the first paragraph before the closing "Sincerely,."
5. Using the Button Bar, print the document.
6. Using the Button Bar, close the document. Do not save changes to the document.
7. Remove the Button Bar from the screen.

EXERCISE 5

INSTRUCTIONS:

1. Create a Button Bar that contains buttons to perform the following commands:

   File Save As
   File Open
   File Close
   Edit Replace
   Edit Copy
   Edit Paste
   Edit Undelete
2. Save the Button Bar as "ch06ex05.wwb."
3. Remove the Button Bar from the screen.

EXERCISE 6

INSTRUCTIONS:

1. View the "ch06ex05.wwb" Button Bar.
2. Using the Button Bar, open the "johnson.ltr" file.
3. Using the Button Bar, replace each occurrence of the word "Johnson" with the word "Smith."
4. Copy and paste the inside address to the bottom of the document, using the Button Bar.
5. Using the Button Bar, save the document as "ch06ex06."
6. Using the Button Bar, close the document.
7. Remove the Button Bar from the screen.

EXERCISE 7

INSTRUCTIONS:

1. Edit the "ch06ex05.wwb" Button Bar.
2. Delete the Undelete button.
3. Move the Open button to the first position on the Button Bar.
4. Add a File Save button to the Button Bar.
5. Move the Save As button to the end of the Button Bar.
6. Save the changes to the Button Bar.
7. Remove the Button Bar from the screen.

EXERCISE 8

INSTRUCTIONS:

1. Change the options for the "ch06ex05.wwb" Button Bar.
2. Place the Button Bar on the bottom of the screen.
3. Change the button style to text only.
4. Save the changes to the Button Bar.
5. Change the Button Bar position to the left of the screen.
6. Change the button style to picture only.
7. Save the changes to the Button Bar.
8. Remove the Button Bar from the screen.

CHAPTER SEVEN

ALTERNATIVE METHODS FOR OPENING AND SAVING A DOCUMENT

OBJECTIVES

In this chapter, you will learn to:

- Use alternative methods to open and save a document

CHAPTER OVERVIEW

In this chapter, alternative methods for opening and saving a document are shown.

FILE MANAGER

Document files that share a common trait should be organized and stored in the same directory. Think of a large file cabinet. In the cabinet, certain areas are dedicated to contain files concerning the same topic. On a computer, these areas are called directories. For example, all files concerning the same company, ABC Can Company, could be stored in a directory named "abccan."

On the computer, you can refer to a directory in two ways.

1. It can be the name of a disk drive. For example, A:.
2. It can be the name of another directory on a floppy or hard disk. For example, "\wpdocs."

The backslash (\) means a directory and a colon (:) means a disk drive. The full name of a file is specified as a drive letter, a colon, a backslash, the name of the directory if one is used, another backslash, and then the filename. The full name is also referred to as the "pathname." For example, if you save the "practice" document on drive A in the "wpdocs" directory, then the pathname for the document is "a:\wpdocs\practice."

Suppose you saved the "practice" document on a hard disk using the "wpdocs" directory. Then the pathname for using the "practice" document file is "c:\wpdocs\practice."

The File Manager feature lists the files stored in a directory. You can switch to different directories and view files stored in each one. Other abilities include opening, deleting, renaming, moving, printing, and copying files.

The File Manager screen is divided into two sections. The first section is the Navigator section. The Navigator allows you to see the different drives, directories, and files you have available. The first box in the Navigator displays the available drives. The current drive appears with a pointing hand next to it.

The second box in the Navigator displays the directories and files on that drive. The current directory or file appears with a pointing hand next to it.

The second section is the Viewer section. This section displays the contents of the file selected in the Navigator. If no file is selected, the Viewer is blank. If the selected file was not created in WordPerfect, odd characters may appear in the Viewer.

The status bar at the bottom of the File Manager indicates the number of files in the current directory and the number of bytes available on the drive. The top section of the File Manager displays a menu and a Button Bar. The menu and Button Bar can be used to perform commands in the File Manager. To perform most File Manager commands, select the file or directory that you want the command to affect, then choose the command from the menu or click the button on the Button Bar. Some function keys are available in the File Manager, but they are limited.

The following list describes the commands available on the File Manager Button Bar.

> **Open** displays the file in the normal editing screen. Here you can edit the document as usual. This button is equivalent to choosing Open from the File menu.
>
> **Copy** the current file to a new or existing file. You can also copy a file into another directory by specifying a different pathname. This button is equivalent to choosing Copy from the File menu or pressing Ctrl+C.
>
> **Move/Rename** allows you to move a file to a new directory, or to rename a file in the same directory. You are asked to enter a path and filename. This button is equivalent to the Move/Rename command under the File menu or pressing Ctrl+R.
>
> **Delete** the selected file or directory. Remember that a deletion is final; the file or directory will no longer exist. This button is equivalent to choosing Delete from the File menu or pressing Ctrl+D.
>
> **Find Word** in the files in a directory. This button is equivalent to the Find Words command under the Search menu.
>
> **Find Files** allows you to find a file by typing the filename or part of the filename. This button is equivalent to choosing Find Files from the Search menu.
>
> **File List** provides a list of files in a particular directory. File information such as file size and the date and time the file was last saved is displayed in the File List. This button is equivalent to the File List command from the View menu or pressing Ctrl+F.
>
> **Quick List** allows you to view a descriptive list of directory names rather than pathnames. Many of the descriptive names are borrowed from the File Preferences, Location of Files menu in WordPerfect. For example, the names Documents, Graphics, and Macros might appear in the Quick List just as they appear in the Location of Files dialog box. This button is equivalent to choosing Quick List from the View menu or pressing Ctrl+Q.
>
> **Edit QL** allows you to change the Quick List directories. This option allows you to add, edit, and delete items from the Quick List. This button is equivalent to choosing Edit Quick List from the View menu.

The File Manager also has the capability to run an application, print a file, or create a directory. These features can be accessed through the File Manager menu. For more information on any of the File Manager features, refer to your WordPerfect Reference Manual.

If you are using the A drive to store your documents, then change the default directory to "a:\wpdocs." If you are using the C drive, then change the default directory to "c:\wpdocs."

To open your "practice" document using the File Manager feature:

Choose	File	***Press***	*Alt*
Choose	File Manager	***Select***	*File*
		Select	*File Manager*

Your screen should look similar to Figure 7-1.

Figure 7-1

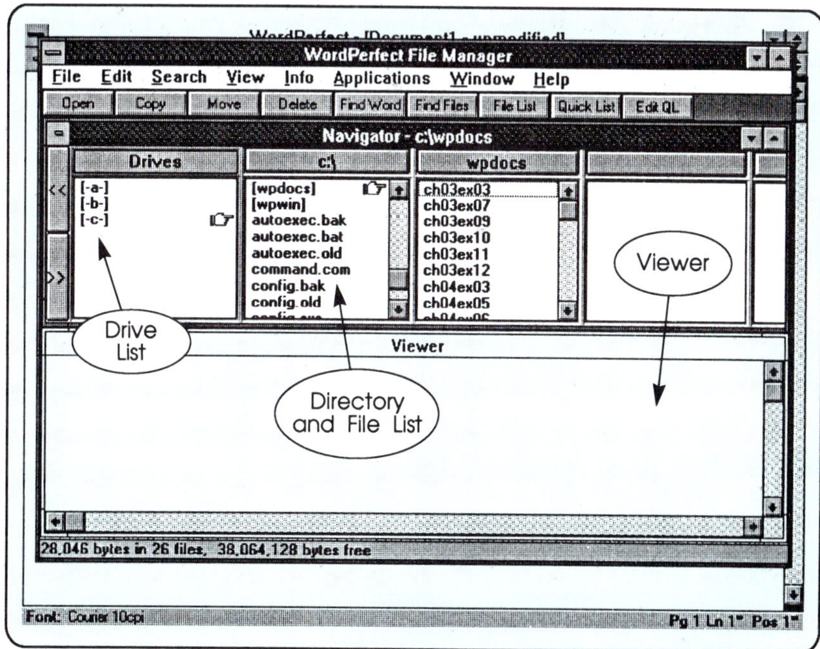

The first box in the Navigator displays the drives available. The second box in the Navigator displays the files or directories on the current drive. The third box displays the next level of directories or files on the current drive. You should be viewing the "c:\wpdocs" or "a:\wpdocs" directory.

To open your "practice" document:

Click	on the file "practice" in the third box of the Navigator	***Press***	*↓ to select the "practice" file in the third box of the Navigator*

Your screen should look like Figure 7-2.

Figure 7-2

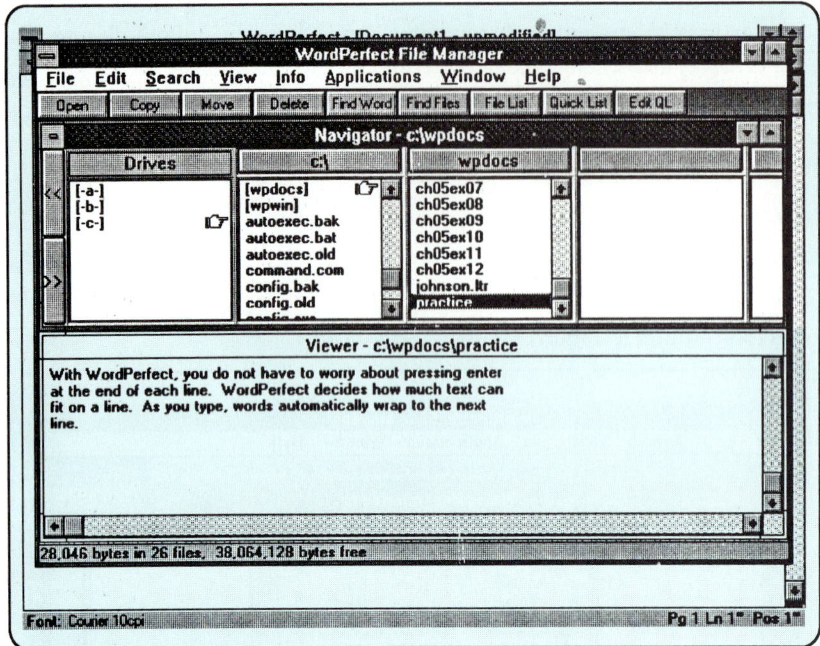

Notice that the Viewer displays the document.

Click	the Open button on the Button Bar	***Press***	*Alt*	
Click	the Open command button in the File Open dialog box	***Select***	*File*	
		Select	*Open*	
		Press	*↵Enter*	

The "practice" document now appears on your screen and the File Manager is closed.

■ SAVING A FILE USING THE CLOSE FEATURE

When you choose Close from the File menu or press Ctrl+F4, you can save your current document, if you so desire, and then clear the screen so you can begin another document. When you use the Close feature to save a document, the document is saved with the same name in the same directory.

To add a sentence to the "practice" file:

Click	at the end of the document	***Press***	*Ctrl+End*	**Press**	Ctrl+End
Press	↵Enter twice	***Press***	*↵Enter twice*	**Press**	↵Enter twice

Type	When you finish, you can use the Close feature to save and close your document at the same time.	***Type***	*When you finish, you can use the Close feature to save and close your document at the same time.*	**Type**	When you finish, you can use the Close feature to save and close your document at the same time.

To save your "practice" document and clear the screen:

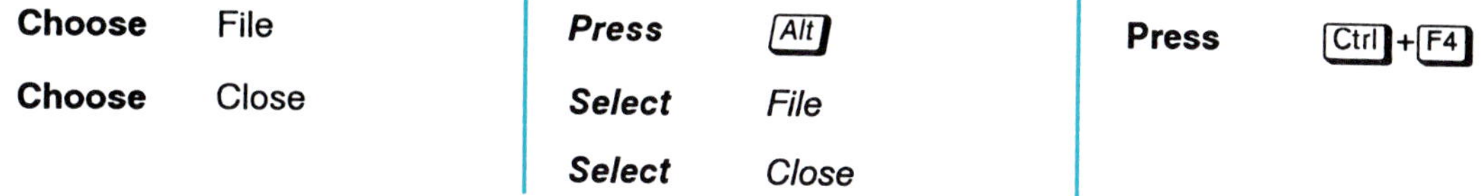

Choose	File	***Press***	*Alt*	**Press**	Ctrl+F4
Choose	Close	***Select***	*File*		
		Select	*Close*		

Your screen should look like Figure 7-3.

Figure 7-3

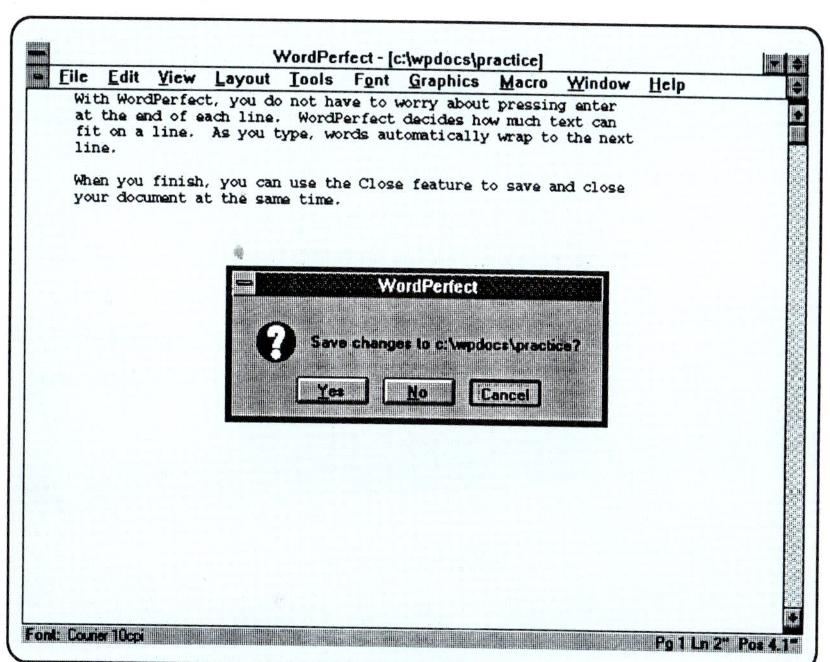

To save the present document:

Click	the Yes command button	***Press***	*Alt+Y to select the Yes command button*	**Press**	Alt+Y to select the Yes command button

If you select the No command button, your file will not be saved.

You should have a clear screen.

EXERCISE 1

INSTRUCTIONS: Define the following terms:

1. File Manager feature ______________________________

 ____

2. Close feature ______________________________

 ____

3. Pathname ______________________________

 ____

EXERCISE 2

INSTRUCTIONS: Circle T if the statement is true and F if the statement is false.

T F 1. Document files are stored in directories.

T F 2. A correct example of the pathname of a file is "c:\research\wpfile."

T F 3. You cannot delete a file using the File Manager feature.

T F 4. The File Manager feature lets you open a document for editing.

T F 5. The Close feature allows you to save your document and clear the screen so you can begin another document.

EXERCISE 3

INSTRUCTIONS:

1. Use the standard method to open the document file "johnson.ltr."
2. Save the document using the standard method. Close the file.
3. Open the document file "johnson.ltr" using the File Manager feature.
4. Save the document using the Close feature.

EXERCISE 4

INSTRUCTIONS:

1. Use the standard method to open the document file "practice."
2. Save the document using the standard method. Close the file.
3. Open the document file "practice" using the File Manager feature.
4. Move to the end of the document and type the sentence "You can open a document using the File Manager feature."
5. Save the document using the Close feature.

EXERCISE 5

INSTRUCTIONS:

1. List the files in the default directory by using the File Manager feature.
2. Print a document that you created for Chapter 3 ("ch03ex03") by choosing Print from the File menu or by pressing [Ctrl]+[P].
3. Close the File Manager feature by choosing Exit from File the menu or by pressing [Alt]+[F4].

EXERCISE 6

INSTRUCTIONS:

1. List the files in the default directory by using the File Manager feature.
2. Select a document that you created for Chapter 4 ("ch04ex06").
3. Click on the Viewer window or choose Viewer from the Window menu to access a display of the document. Use the scroll bars or the pointer-movement keys to view the rest of the document.
4. Select another document from the Navigator. Switch to viewer and scroll through the document.
5. Close the File Manager by choosing Exit from the File menu or by pressing [Alt]+[F4].

EXERCISE 7

INSTRUCTIONS:

1. Use the standard method to open a document that you created in Chapter 5 ("ch05ex08").
2. Save the document using the standard method. Close the document.
3. Open the same document using the File Manager feature.
4. Move to the bottom of the document and type the sentence "You can save a document using the File Close feature."
5. Save the document using the Close feature.

EXERCISE 8

INSTRUCTIONS:

1. List the files in the default directory using the File Manager.
2. Select the document "johnson.ltr."
3. Look at the document using the Viewer.
4. Print "johnson.ltr" by choosing Print from the File menu or by pressing Ctrl+P.
5. Exit the File Manager by choosing Exit from the File menu or by pressing Alt+F4.

CHAPTER EIGHT

SPELLER AND THESAURUS FEATURES

OBJECTIVES

In this chapter, you will learn to:

- Use the Speller feature
- Use the Thesaurus feature

■ CHAPTER OVERVIEW

In this chapter, the Speller and Thesaurus features are discussed.

■ SPELLER

You can use the Speller feature to check for spelling errors in your document. The Speller can also find repeated words, words that contain numbers, and words with capitalization problems.

To access the Speller feature, select the Speller option from the Tools menu or press Ctrl+F1. The Speller dialog box displays options for checking a document, to the end of a document, a page, to the end of a page, or selected text.

When WordPerfect finds a word that it does not recognize, it tries to find all the possible words that you could have meant to write. These words are displayed in the Suggestions list box, and you can select one to replace the word in your text. You can also edit the unrecognized word, or you can choose to ignore the Speller and continue with the spell check.

Change the default directory to the "a:\wpdocs" or to the "c:\wpdocs" directory. Then open your "johnson.ltr" document.

To show the use of the Speller feature, you need to change the spelling of some words in your document. You will now intentionally misspell three words for this purpose.

To misspell the word "business":

Click	before the "i" in "business"	***Move***	*the insertion point before the "i" in "business"*
Press	Delete	***Press***	Delete

To misspell the word "appreciate" in the second paragraph:

Click	before the first "p" in "appreciate"	***Move***	*the insertion point before the first "p" in "appreciate"*
Press	Delete	***Press***	Delete

To misspell the word "solution" in the second paragraph:

Click	before the first "o" in "solution"	***Move***	*the insertion point before the first "o" in "solution"*
Press	Delete	***Press***	Delete

Your screen should look like Figure 8-1.

Figure 8-1

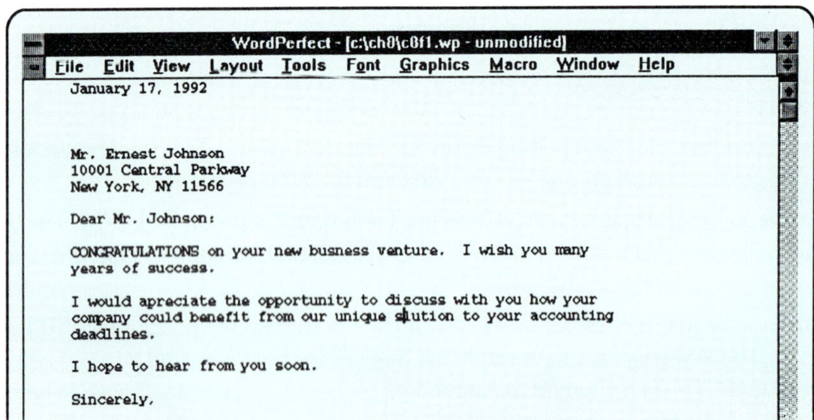

January 17, 1992

Mr. Ernest Johnson
10001 Central Parkway
New York, NY 11566

Dear Mr. Johnson:

CONGRATULATIONS on your new busness venture. I wish you many years of success.

I would apreciate the opportunity to discuss with you how your company could benefit from our unique slution to your accounting deadlines.

I hope to hear from you soon.

Sincerely,

To start the Spell Check feature:

Choose	Tools	***Press***	Alt	**Press**	Ctrl+F1
Choose	Speller	***Select***	*Tools*		
		Select	*Speller*		

The bottom portion of your screen should look like Figure 8-2.

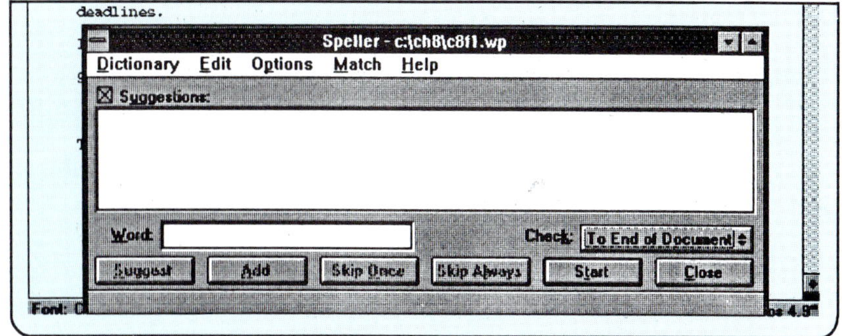

Figure 8-2

The Speller dialog box appears on the screen.

The Speller dialog box menu options are described below:

> **Dictionary** - Specify a dictionary for the Speller. You can use the main dictionary or a supplementary dictionary. You can create your own personal dictionaries that can be used in addition to the main dictionary. See the "Speller, Dictionaries" section in the WordPerfect Reference Manual for more information.
>
> **Edit** - Allows you to cut, copy, or paste words between the Windows Clipboard and the Word text box in the Speller feature.
>
> **Options** - Set your Speller options. You can choose to look for words with numbers, duplicate words, and irregular capitalization as well as incorrect spelling. You can also use the Options menu to move the speller box to the bottom of the screen so that you can see as much of your document as possible while running the spell check.
>
> **Match** - Looks up words based on a pattern. You may omit one character or multiple characters from the word. The match menu replaces the character or characters with the appropriate wildcard.

To use the menu defaults, no changes or settings need to be made.

The Check pop-up list is used to specify what part of the file you would like checked for spelling. To check the entire document:

Click	the Check pop-up list button	***Press***	*Alt+K to select the Check pop-up list button*	**Press**	Alt+K to select the Check pop-up list button
Hold down	the mouse button to view the pop-up list	***Press***	*Alt+↓ to view the pop-up list*	**Press**	Alt+↓ to view the pop-up list

The bottom portion of your screen should look like Figure 8-3.

Figure 8-3

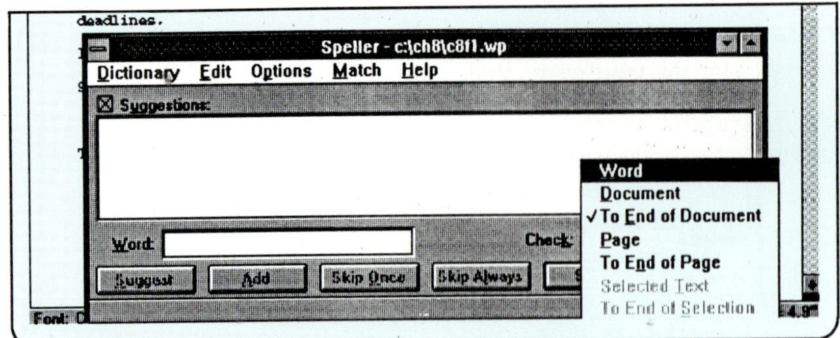

The Check pop-up list is displayed. You may select from the choices described below:

Word - Spell check the word in which the insertion point is located

Document - Spell check the entire document in which the insertion point is located

To End of Document - Spell check from the insertion point to the end of the document

Page - Spell check the page on which the insertion point is located

To End of Page - Spell check from the insertion point to the end of the page

Selected Text - Spell check the selected text in the document

To End of Selection - Spell check to the end of the selected text

To check the entire document:

Click	the Document option	***Type***	*D for Document*	**Type**	D for Document

To start the Speller:

Click	the Start command button	***Press***	*↵Enter*	**Press**	↵Enter

When a word is not found by the Speller feature, it is highlighted in the document and a list of possible choices are displayed in the Suggestions list box.

The text "Not Found" appears in the bottom left-hand corner of the Speller dialog box. The commands you may use to continue the Speller feature are described below:

Add - Add this word to the dictionary so that it is valid for every document that you spell check.

Skip Once - WordPerfect has found a word that it does not know. This option allows you to tell WordPerfect to skip this occurrence of the word, and continue with the spell check.

Skip Always - This option allows you to tell WordPerfect not only to skip this one word, but to skip this word every time it occurs in the rest of the document.

Replace - Replaces the incorrect word in the document with the text that appears in the Word text box of the Speller.

To select the correct spelling of "business":

Click	the word "business" in the Suggestions list box	***Press***	*the pointer-movement keys to highlight the word "business" in the Suggestions list box*	**Press**	the pointer-movement keys to highlight the word "business" in the Suggestions list box
Click	the Replace command button	***Press***	*[↵Enter] to select the Replace command button*	**Press**	[↵Enter] to select the Replace command button

The word "business" is now spelled correctly.

To select the proper spelling of "appreciate" and then "solution":

Click	the word "appreciate" in the Suggestions list box	***Press***	*the pointer-movement keys to select the word "appreciate" in the Suggestions list box*	**Press**	the pointer-movement keys to select the word "appreciate" in the Suggestions list box
Click	the Replace command button	***Press***	*[↵Enter] to select the Replace command button*	**Press**	[↵Enter] to select the Replace command button
Click	the word "solution" in the Suggestions list box	***Press***	*the pointer-movement keys to select the word "solution" in the Suggestions list box*	**Press**	the pointer-movement keys to select the word "solution" in the Suggestions list box
Click	the Replace command button	***Press***	*[↵Enter] to select the Replace command button*	**Press**	[↵Enter] to select the Replace command button

The name "Tommy" is now highlighted, because it is a proper name. The Speller feature does not recognize proper names as words.

To indicate "Tommy" is spelled correctly:

Click	the Skip Once command button	***Press***	*Alt+O to select the Skip Once command button*	**Press**	Alt+O to select the Skip Once command button

Your screen should look like Figure 8-4.

Figure 8-4

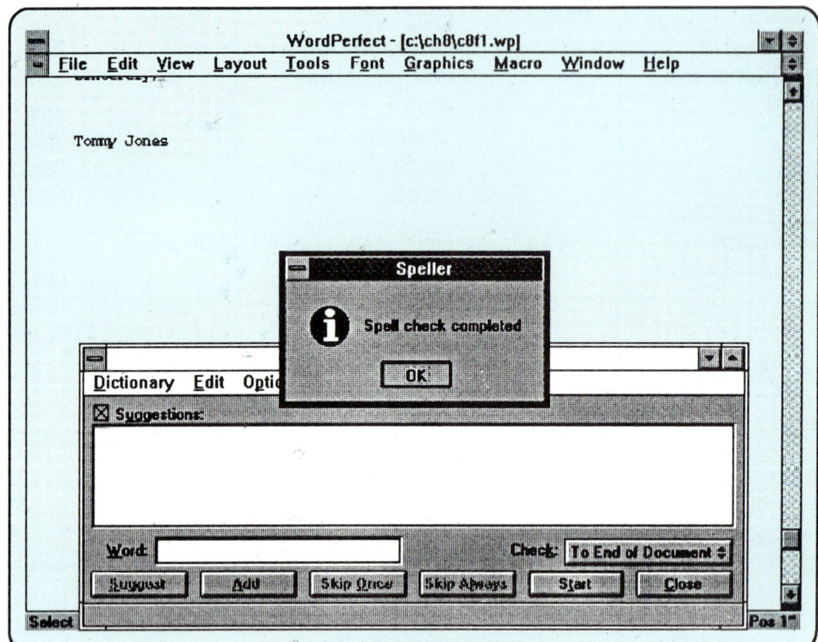

A dialog box is displayed with the message "Spell check completed."

To close the dialog box:

Click	the OK command button	***Press***	*↵Enter*	**Press**	↵Enter

To close the Speller dialog box:

Click	the Close button	***Press***	*Alt+C*	**Press**	Alt+C

■ THESAURUS

The Thesaurus feature displays words with the same or very similar meaning as that of the word at the insertion point.

To show a list of words that mean the same as "benefit" in the second paragraph:

Click	on the word "benefit"	***Move***	*the insertion point to the word "benefit"*	**Move**	the insertion point to the word "benefit"
Choose	Tools	***Press***	*Alt*	**Press**	Alt+F1

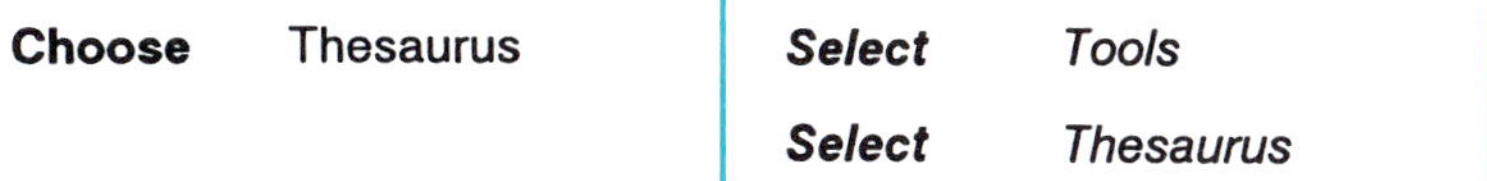

Choose	Thesaurus	***Select***	*Tools*	
		Select	*Thesaurus*	

Your screen should look like Figure 8-5.

Figure 8-5

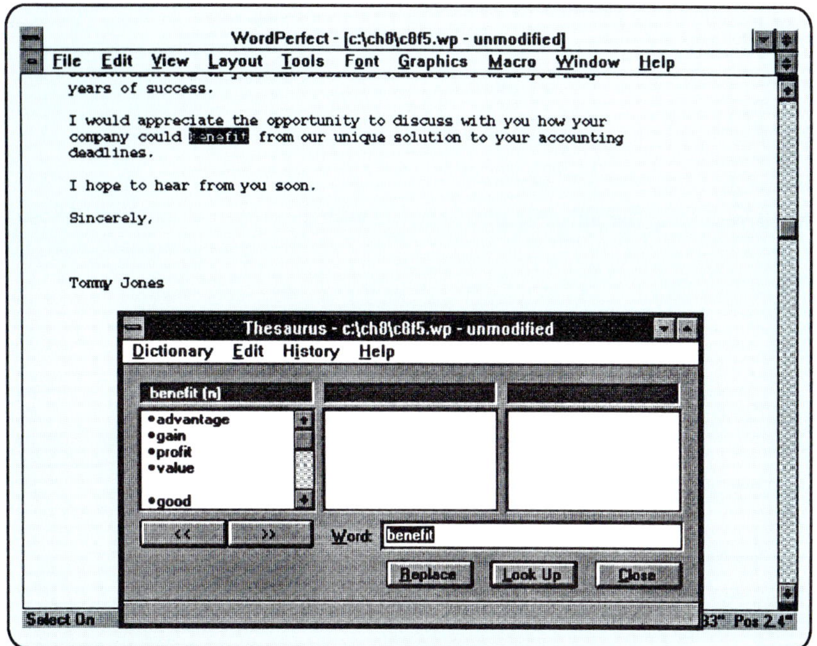

To replace "benefit" with "profit":

Click	on the word "profit" in the benefit box	***Press***	*Tab until the highlight appears in the benefit box*	**Press**	Tab until the highlight appears in the benefit box
Click	the Replace command button	***Press***	*the pointer-movement keys to select "profit"*	**Press**	the pointer-movement keys to select "profit"
		Press	*Alt+R to select the Replace command button*	**Press**	Alt+R to select the Replace command button

The top portion of your screen should look like Figure 8-6.

Figure 8-6

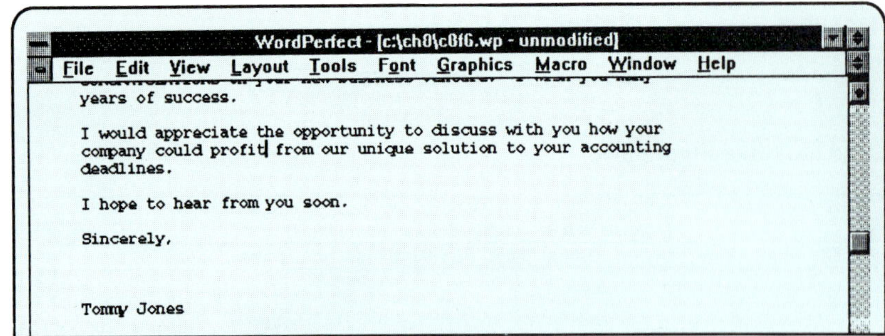

The word "benefit" is now replaced by "profit."

Save your document, replacing the old contents of the file with the current document. Close the document.

EXERCISE 1

INSTRUCTIONS: Define the following terms:

1. Speller feature ______________________________

   ____

2. Thesaurus feature ______________________________

   ____

EXERCISE 2

INSTRUCTIONS: Circle T if the statement is true and F if the statement is false.

T F 1. The WordPerfect Speller feature only checks for spelling errors in your document.

T F 2. The Speller feature can only spell check a word or page.

T F 3. When a word is not found by the Speller feature, it is highlighted and a list of possible choices is displayed.

T F 4. The Speller feature recognizes proper names as words.

T F 5. When a spell check is complete, a count of the number of words is shown at the bottom left of the screen.

T F 6. The Thesaurus feature displays words with the same or very similar meaning as that of the word at the insertion point.

EXERCISE 3

INSTRUCTIONS:

1. Create the following document. Prepare the document exactly as it appears. You will make corrections for the errors using the Speller feature.
2. Correct the spelling errors using the Speller feature.
3. Use the Thesaurus feature to select another word for "comparing" in the first paragraph.
4. Use the Thesaurus feature to choose another word for "approach" in the second paragraph.
5. Use the Thesaurus feature to pick another word for "purchase" in the second paragraph.
6. Save the document on a file using the name "ch08ex03."
7. Print the document.
8. Close the document.

```
current date


Ms. Betty Smith
3457 Tanglewood Drive
Seattle, WA 99703-4596

Dear Ms. Smith:

I recently read your article comparing wrd processing software
packages in a personal computer magazine.

As I read through the article, I really appreciated the ojeciv
approach you took in preparin the materials.  It helped me
decide to purchase WordPerfect for Windows.

Cordially,



Thomas J. Tucker
```

EXERCISE 4

INSTRUCTIONS:

1. Create the following document. Prepare the document exactly as it appears. You will make corrections for the errors using the Speller feature.
2. Correct the spelling errors using the Speller feature.
3. Use the Thesaurus feature to select another word for "document" in the first paragraph.

4. Use the Thesaurus feature to choose another word for "contact" in the third paragraph.
5. Save the document on a file using the name "ch08ex04."
6. Print the document.
7. Close the document.

```
current date


Ms. Jo Ann Garza
1717 W. 43rd St.
Seattle, WA 93712

Dear Ms. Garza:

Per our conversation, enclosed is a credit application for our
departent stor.  Please complete all qustions and return the
document to me at yore ealiest convenince.

We are sure that yu will enjy using our credet card.

If you have any questions concernng the credit application,
please contact me.

Sincerely yours,


T. W. House
```

EXERCISE 5

INSTRUCTIONS:

1. Create the following document. Prepare the document exactly as it appears. You will make corrections for errors using the Speller feature.
2. Correct the spelling errors using the Speller feature.
3. Use the Thesaurus feature to select another word for "occurred" in the first paragraph.
4. Use the Thesaurus feature to select another word for "inconvenience" in the third paragraph.
5. Save the document using the name "ch08ex05."
6. Print the document.
7. Close the document.

```
current date


Mrs. Barbara Radebaugh
243 Missisippi Avenue
Richmond, VA 23200

Dear Mrs. Radebaugh:

Has it ever occured to you that our recomendation for your
credit card has long been delaid.

Please axcept our appology for this.  We enadvertently sent
your file to Washinton D.C.

We will reemburse you for any inconveneince this may have
caused.

Sincerely yours,


Lawrence King
```

EXERCISE 6

INSTRUCTIONS:

1. Create the following document. Prepare the document exactly as it appears. You will make corrections for errors using the Speller feature.
2. Correct the spelling errors by using the Speller feature. ("Eva" is spelled correctly.)
3. Use the Thesaurus feature to select another word for "fantastic" in the first paragraph.
4. Use the Thesaurus feature to select another word for "freakish" in the first paragraph.
5. Use the Thesaurus feature to select another word for "praised" in the second paragraph.
6. Save the document in a file using the name "ch08ex06."
7. Print the document.
8. Close the document.

```
current date


Mrs. Eva Groft
249 Sentree Avenue
Charllotte, NC 28214

Dear Mrs. Groft:

You realise, of course, that the sale of your new book are
seting fantactic records.  HOT WINDS is a well-docummented
story of freskish summer storms.

Congradulations on the reseption your book is recieving.  I am
sure it gives you great satisfation to have your book praeised
by many readers.

Sincerly,


Edith Hagan
```

EXERCISE 7

INSTRUCTIONS:

1. Create the following document. Prepare the document exactly as it appears. You will make corrections for errors using the Speller feature.
2. Check for proper spelling by using the Speller feature.
3. Use the Thesaurus feature to select another word for "information" in the first paragraph.
4. Use the Thesaurus feature to select another word for "treatment" in the second paragraph.
5. Use the Thesaurus feature to select another word for "happy" in the second paragraph.
6. Use the Thesaurus feature to select another word for "greatly" in the first paragraph.
7. Save the document in a file using the name "ch08ex07."
8. Print the document.
9. Close the document.

```
current date


Dr. Georgia Miller
Brown County Pike
Buffalo, NY 14210

Dear Dr. Miller:

We would greatley appresiate recieving any information you can
give us about the diagnose, treatment, and progress the patient
(Mr. Wayne Goebert) maide in the hospital.

If you have any other pertenint information about this patient
that would help us in his treatment, we should be most happy to
recieve it.

Sincerely yours,



Xi Se Chung, M.D.
```

EXERCISE 8

INSTRUCTIONS:

1. Create the following document. Prepare the document exactly as it appears. You will make corrections for errors using the Speller feature.
2. Correct the spelling errors using the Speller feature.
3. Use the Thesaurus feature to change "beautiful" in the first paragraph.
4. Change the words "Registered Mail" to all uppercase letters.
5. Use the Thesaurus feature to change the word "parties" in the second paragraph.
6. At the end of the first paragraph, delete the semicolon and the remainder of the line. Replace the semicolon with a period.
7. Search and replace "$10,000" with "$12,500."
8. Save the document in the file "ch08ex08."
9. Print the document.
10. Close the document.

current date

Registered Mail

Mrs. Halina Polakowski
12600 Review Drive
Portland, OR 97203

Dear Mrs. Polakowski:

The Carney Company which you recomended to me has done a beuatiful job on our covered patio. The outdoor custom brick has been layed smoothley, and the grass was not hurt with all the diging and traffic. When we first talked to Pat Carney, the owner, we were somewhat apprehinsive about the estimate given for doing th work; but the total bill was very fair.

We can hopefuly treat big partys on our spaceious, covered patio. Thank you for your loan of $10,000 to cover the cost of building the patio and your advice.

Our check to repay you the $10,000 is inclosed.

Sincerely,

Barb Bednarz
Executive Vice President

CHAPTER NINE

FORMATTING A DOCUMENT

OBJECTIVES

In this chapter, you will learn to:

- Change the initial font
- Set margins, tabs, line spacing, and text justification
- Use the hyphenation feature
- Use the indent feature

CHAPTER OVERVIEW

In this chapter, the procedures for formatting a document are discussed. The procedure for changing the base font is explained. Methods for setting margins, tabs, line spacing, and text justification are described and illustrated. The indent and hyphenation features are demonstrated.

DEFAULT SETTINGS

WordPerfect has default settings for several of the most commonly used formatting features. These default settings are already defined when you begin preparing a document.

Some of WordPerfect's default settings for a document are:

Feature	**Initial Setting**
Footers	None
Headers	None
Hyphenation	No
Justification	Left
Line Spacing	1
Margins	
Top Margin	1″
Bottom Margin	1″

Feature	Initial Setting
Left Margin	1″
Right Margin	1″
Page Numbers	No Page Numbers
Tabs	Relative to Left Margin, every 0.5″
Unit of Measure	Inches (″)

If necessary, change the default directory to "a:\wpdocs" or to "c:\wpdocs."

Create the document in the figure below using the default settings. Press the Tab key before typing the first line of each paragraph to indent the first line of that paragraph. Save the document as "report.ltr."

Figure 9-1

```
   Two chapters recently have hired executive secretaries to
support growing activities.  The Northwest and the South Coast
chapters are the first to take advantage of the newly revised
Chapter Assistance Program.
   Alice Jones began duties as executive secretary of the
Northwest Chapter on August 16.  She has over 14 years experience
in bookkeeping and secretarial services.  For the past five
years, Jones has conducted a home bookkeeping service.
Presently, she services two civic clubs, an insurance
association, and 32 other private accounts.
   Michael Scott became the South Coast executive secretary on
November 5.  Owner of Scott Business Services, a marketing
management company, Scott brings to the chapter position a wide
range of business and community experience.  With Scott's
support, the chapter hopes to develop CPE programs and later
expand to other areas.
   The new mailing addresses of the Northwest and South Coast
chapters are as follows:
Alice Jones
Executive Secretary
Northwest Chapter
P.O. Box 11111
Phoenix, TX 78908
Michael Scott
Executive Secretary
South Coast Chapter
P.O. 22222
Orange, TX 89876
```

■ FONTS

Fonts are sets of printed characters with the same size and appearance. A font can be described in four ways: typeface, weight, style, and point size.

1. **Typeface** refers to the design and appearance of printed characters on a page. Examples of typeface are:

Times Roman	Helvetica
Courier	Century Schoolbook

2. **Weight** refers to bold, medium, or light print density or darkness of the characters. Normal print is in medium weight. **This is bold print.**
3. **Style** refers to upright or italic print. Normal print is upright. *This is italic.*
4. **Point size** refers to the size of the printed characters.

11 point	12 point
14 point	8 point

Your printer comes with the capability to print in at least one font.

The font that is used for normal printing is called the initial font. The initial font depends on the fonts in your printer and what your printer can do with those fonts. Whenever your printer has only one font available, then any text that you print uses this font.

Your printer has a specific font that it uses initially. If you are using an appropriate printer, there are several ways that you can change the base font selection.

One way you can set the initial font is to choose Select Printer from the File menu. Instructions on how to set the initial font using this method are discussed in Chapter 14. Another way you can set the initial font is to select Document from the Layout Menu or press Ctrl+Shift+F9.

In this section, it is assumed that your computer is connected to a Hewlett Packard LaserJet Series II with a Microsoft Z1A font cartridge. Even if you do not have such a printer setup, you can go through the following steps and make selections that you consider appropriate for your printer.

To change the document font:

Choose	Layout	***Press***	*Alt*	**Press**	Ctrl+Shift+F9
Choose	Document	***Select***	*Layout*		
		Select	*Document*		

The top part of your screen should look like Figure 9-2.

Figure 9-2

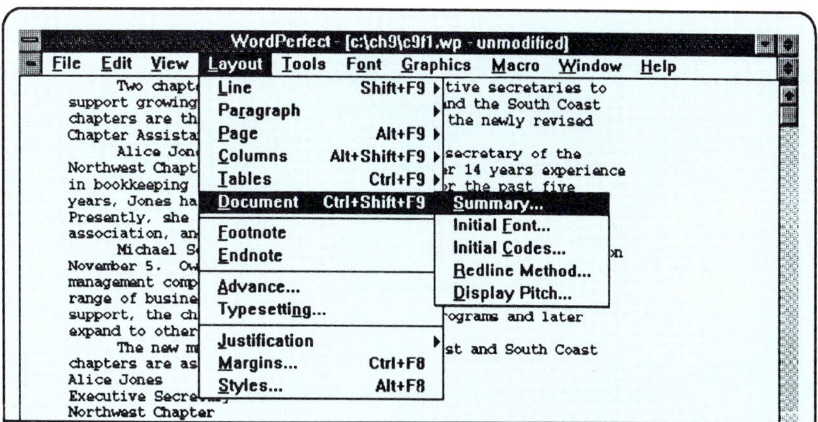

To select Initial Font:

Choose	Initial Font	***Select***	*Initial Font*	**Select**	Initial Font

Your screen should look similar to Figure 9-3.

Figure 9-3

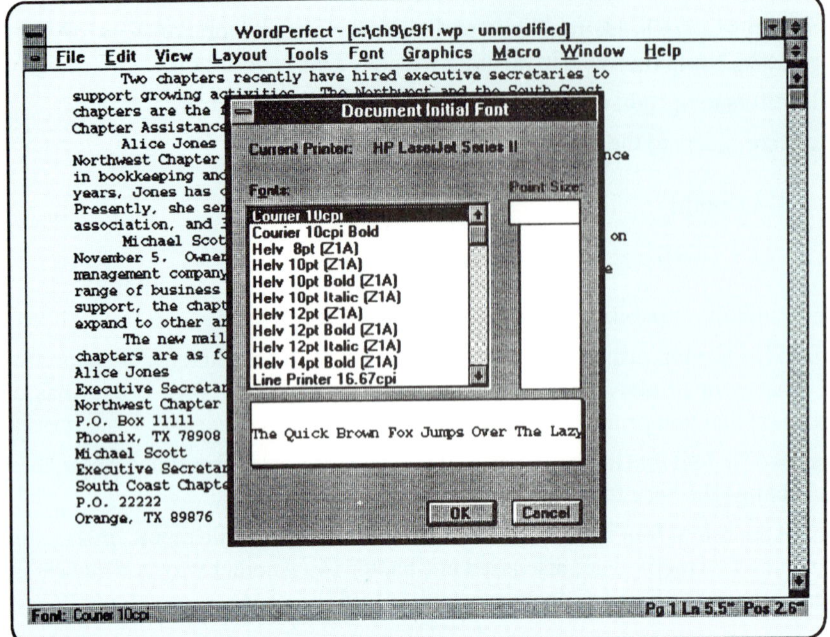

To specify Times Roman 10pt as the initial font:

Click	the TmsRmn 10pt (Z1A) option in the Fonts list box	***Press***	*↑ or ↓ to select the TmsRmn 10pt (Z1A) option from the Fonts list box*	**Press**	↑ or ↓ to select the TmsRmn 10pt (Z1A) option from the Fonts list box

Your screen should look like Figure 9-4.

Figure 9-4

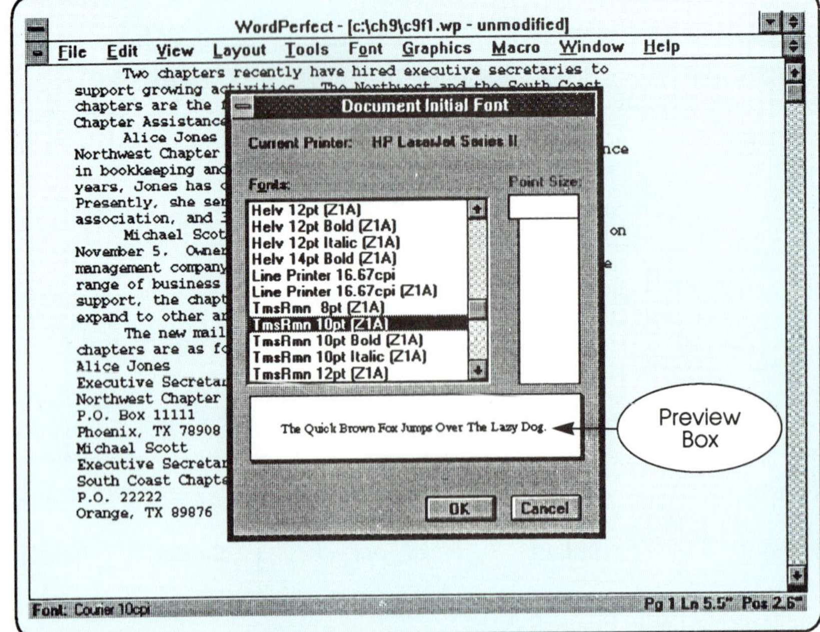

Notice that a sample of the font and size of the text appears at the bottom of the dialog box.

To accept TmsRmn 10pt as the initial font:

Click	the OK command button	***Press***	*↵Enter*	**Press**	↵Enter

Notice that the text TmsRmn 10pt (Z1A) now appears on the status bar next to the font indicator.

To use the Courier 10cpi font again:

Choose	Layout	***Press***	*Alt*	**Press**	Ctrl+Shift+F9
Choose	Document	***Select***	*Layout*	**Select**	Initial Font
Choose	Initial Font	***Select***	*Document*	**Press**	↓ or ↑ to select the Courier 10cpi option from the Fonts list box
Click	the Courier 10cpi option in the Fonts list box	***Select***	*Initial Font*		
		Press	*↓ or ↑ to select the Courier 10cpi option from the Fonts list box*		

The initial font on your screen should be Courier 10cpi again.

To accept the initial font and return to your document:

Click	the OK command button	***Press***	*↵Enter*	**Press**	↵Enter

A third way you can select the font is to select Font from the Font menu or press F9. When this option is used, a code is inserted and the font is changed to a new one. The new font is used from the current insertion point location forward in your document. Instructions on how to set fonts using this method are discussed in Chapter 13.

■ MARGINS

Margins refer to the distance from the top, bottom, left, and right sides of the page. All text in a document appears within the margins you specify. The initial setting specified by WordPerfect for the top, bottom, left, and right margins is 1″ from each edge of the page.

Whenever you modify the margins, a code is placed in the document. The new settings for the margins affect all text entered after the location of the code. The text in the document that appears before the code uses whatever margin settings that were previously defined.

To change the left and right margins to 1 1/2″:

Click	at the beginning of the document	***Move***	*the insertion point to the beginning of the document*	**Move**	the insertion point to the beginning of the document

To change the margins for this document:

Choose	Layout	***Press***	*Alt*	**Press**	Ctrl+F8
Choose	Margins	***Select***	*Layout*		
		Select	*Margins*		

Your screen should look like Figure 9-5.

Figure 9-5

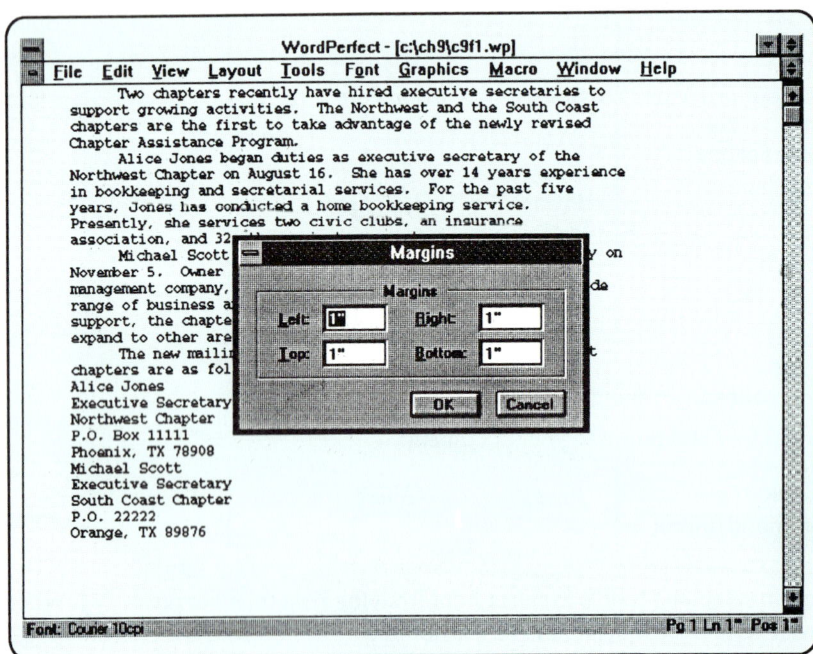

Notice that the 1″ associated with the left margin is highlighted in the Margins dialog box.

You can enter either a fraction or a decimal number as the new value for a margin. For example, you can enter 1.75 or 1 3/4 to change the margin to 1.75 inches. If you use a fraction, it will be converted to the decimal equivalent for the number.

To change the left margin to 1 1/2″:

Type	1.5 or 1 1/2	***Type***	*1.5 or 1 1/2*	**Type**	1.5 or 1 1/2

To change the right margin to 1 1/2″:

Double-click	the Right text box	***Press***	*Alt+R to select the Right text box*	**Press**	Alt+R to select the Right text box
Type	1.5 or 1 1/2	***Type***	*1.5 or 1 1/2*	**Type**	1.5 or 1 1/2

Your screen should look like Figure 9-6.

Figure 9-6

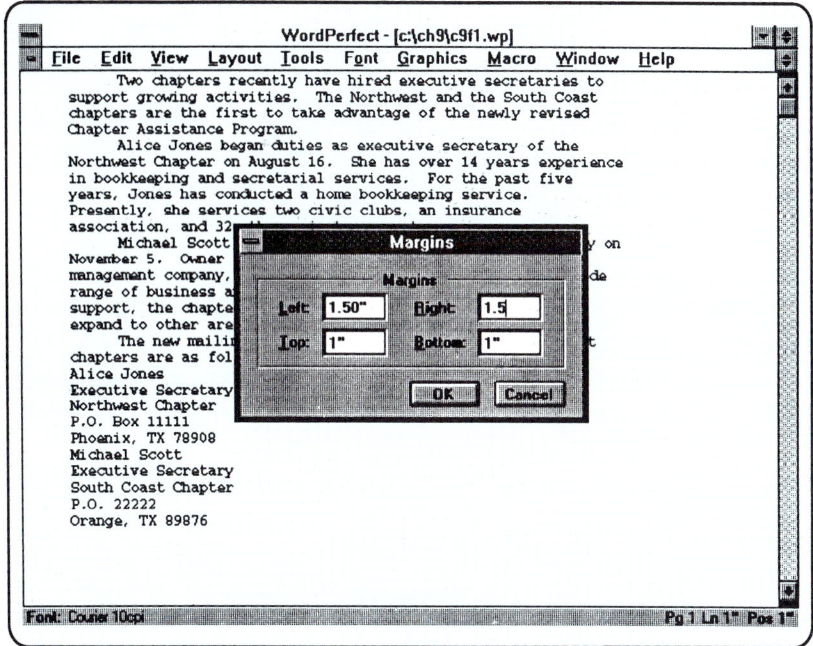

To change the top margin to 1 1/2":

Double-click	the Top text box	***Press***	*Alt+T to select the Top text box*	**Press**	Alt+T to select the Top text box
Type	1.5 or 1 1/2	***Type***	*1.5 or 1 1/2*	**Type**	1.5 or 1 1/2

Your screen should look like Figure 9-7.

Figure 9-7

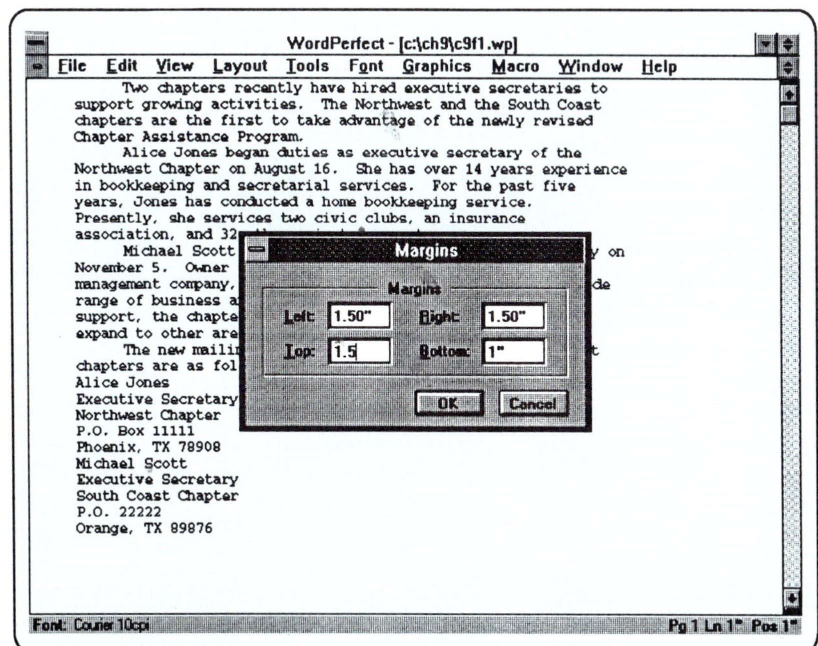

To return to your document:

Click	the OK command button	***Press***	*Enter*	**Press**	Enter

Notice the change in Ln from 1" to 1.5" in the status bar indicating the top margin is now 1.5". Notice the change in Pos from 1" to 1.5" in the status bar indicating that the left margin is now 1.5".

TABS

Tabs are used to move text a certain number of spaces in a document. Tabs are also used to keep columns of text straight and ordered. You can define where each tab should occur on the page and how much space is defined for each one.

WordPerfect has four types of tab settings: Left, Center, Right, and Decimal. When you press the Tab key to move to a new location, the type of tab used at that location depends on whatever tab code was specified.

The following table lists the type of tab stop settings available in WordPerfect.

Selection	Type of Tab Stop Setting
Left	Text is left-aligned at the tab stop.
Center	Text is centered over the tab setting.
Right	Text is right-aligned at the tab stop.
Decimal	Text is aligned at the align character.

One method for changing the type of tab, and the position of a tab, is to use the Tab Set feature. The Tab Set feature changes the tab settings from the insertion point forward in the document.

Another way to insert a new tab setting is through the use of the hard tabs. A hard tab sets a tab for one line, not the entire document. For example, if you want to create a center tab at 5" for one line, you would use the Line, Special Codes option from the Layout menu.

When you change the position and type of tab, the text in the document reflects the change immediately.

Left Margin Tabs

Left margin tabs are set relative to the left margin. You can change the left margin any number of times, but the tabs will always remain the same distance from the left margin. For example, if the left margin is 1" (inch) and you set the first tab at 0.5", then the tab will be located at 0.5 inches to the right of the left margin or 1.5" from the left edge of the page. If you change the left margin to 2", your tab setting will still be 0.5 inches to the right of the new left margin or 2.5" from the left edge of the page.

To change the current tab settings:

Click	at the beginning of the document	***Move***	*the insertion point to the beginning of the document*	**Move**	the insertion point to the beginning of the document
Choose	Layout	***Press***	*Alt*	**Press**	Shift+F9
Choose	Line	***Select***	*Layout*	**Select**	Tab Set
Choose	Tab Set	***Select***	*Line*		
		Select	*Tab Set*		

Your screen should look like Figure 9-8.

Figure 9-8

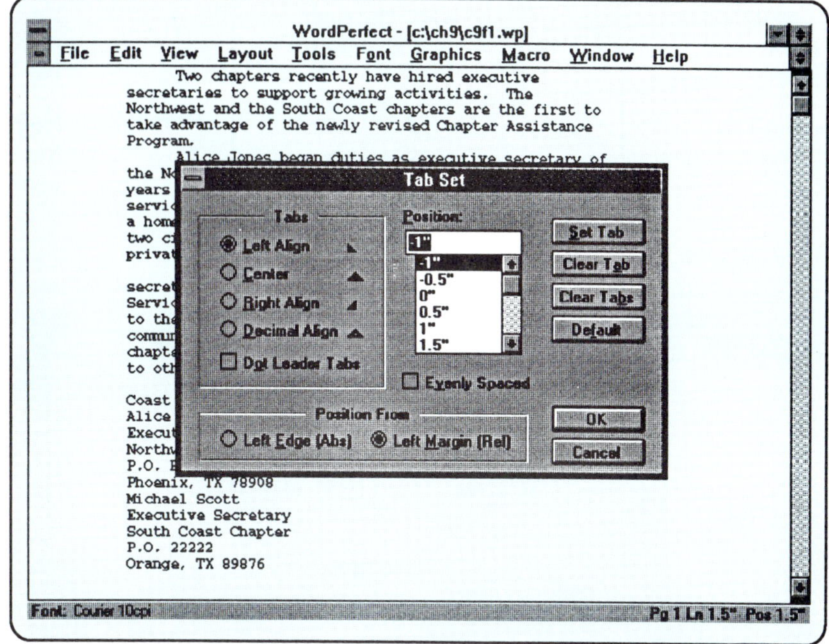

The Tab Set dialog box appears. Notice that the Left Align option button is chosen from the Tabs box and your current tab positions appear in the Position list box.

To delete all existing tabs from the current location of the insertion point forward:

Click	the Clear Tabs command button	***Press***	*[Alt]+[B] to select the Clear Tabs command button*	**Press**	[Alt]+[B] to select the Clear Tabs command button

All of the tab settings in the Positions list box have been removed.

To set a left tab at 2″:

Type	2	***Type***	*2*	**Type**	2
Click	the Set Tab command button	***Press***	*[Alt]+[S] to select the Set Tab command button*	**Press**	[Alt]+[S] to select the Set Tab command button

2″ appears in the Position list box. Notice that the Left Align option button is selected in the Tabs box. By default, tabs are set as left aligned tabs.

To specify a particular type of tab setting, you must first type the tab position and then select the tab type.

For example, to set a right tab at 3″:

Double-click	the Position text box	***Press***	*[Alt]+[P] to select the Position text box*	**Press**	[Alt]+[P] to select the Position text box
Type	3	***Type***	*3*	**Type**	3

Click	the Right Align option button in the Tabs box	***Press***	*Alt+R to select the Right Align option button in the Tabs box*	**Press**	Alt+R to select the Right Align option button in the Tabs box
Click	the Set Tab command button	***Press***	*Alt+S to select the Set Tab command button*	**Press**	Alt+S to select the Set Tab command button

Your screen should look like Figure 9-9.

Figure 9-9

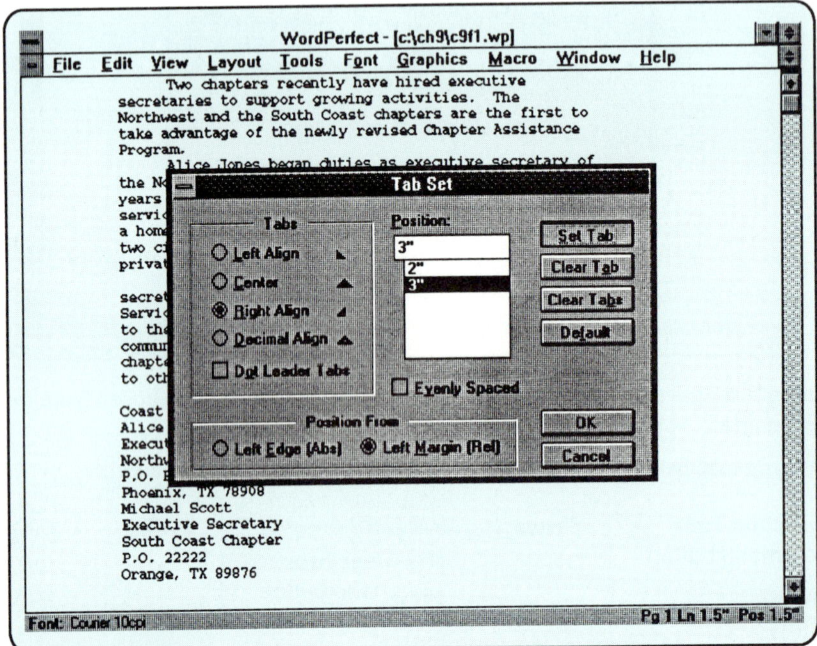

Left Edge of Page Tabs

At times you may want to place tabs a specific distance from the left edge of the page. When a left edge tab is used, current margin settings are ignored. For example, if you set a left edge tab at 2″ (inches), then the tab will be 2″ from the left edge of the page. Note that the current left margin does not affect the location of the left edge tab.

To change to left edge tabs:

Click	the Left Edge option button in the Position From box	***Press***	*Alt+E to select the Left Edge option button in the Position From box*	**Press**	Alt+E to select the Left Edge option button in the Position From box

Your screen should look like Figure 9-10.

Figure 9-10

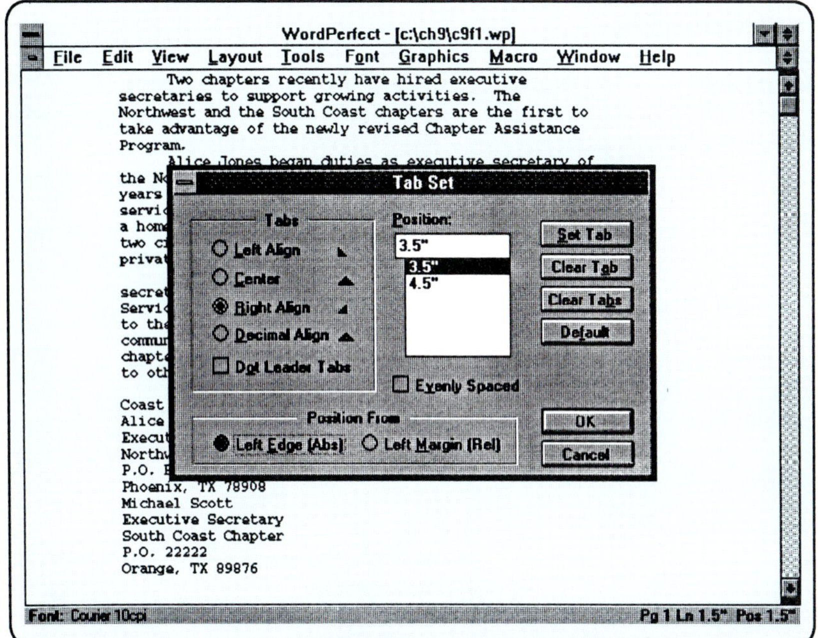

Notice that your tab positions automatically adjusted by 1.5″ or the amount of the left margin.

To clear the current tabs:

Click	the Clear Tabs command button	***Press***	*Alt+B to select the Clear Tabs command button*	**Press**	Alt+B to select the Clear Tabs command button

Evenly Spaced Tabs

By default WordPerfect documents have tabs set at every 1/2″. To set your own evenly spaced tabs, you can use the evenly spaced option in the Tab Set dialog box.

To select the Evenly Spaced feature:

Click	the Evenly Spaced check box until an X appears	***Press***	*Alt+V until an X appears in the Evenly Spaced text box*	**Press**	Alt+V until an X appears in the Evenly Spaced text box

To set tabs every 1/4″ beginning at position 0″:

Type	0 in the Position text box	***Type***	*0 in the Position text box*	**Type**	0 in the Position text box
Double-click	the Repeat Every text box	***Press***	*Alt+T to select the Repeat Every text box*	**Press**	Alt+T to select the Repeat Every text box
Type	.25 or 1/4	***Type***	*.25 or 1/4*	**Type**	.25 or 1/4

To change back to left margin tabs:

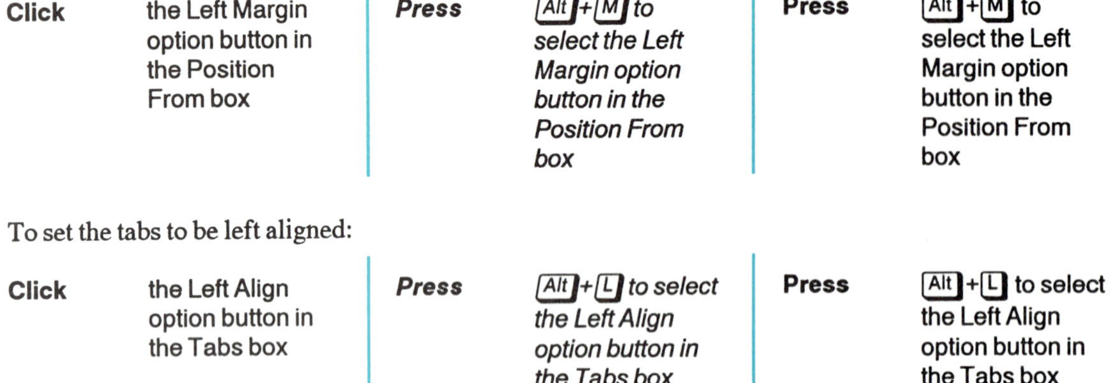

Click	the Left Margin option button in the Position From box	***Press***	*Alt+M to select the Left Margin option button in the Position From box*	**Press**	Alt+M to select the Left Margin option button in the Position From box

To set the tabs to be left aligned:

Click	the Left Align option button in the Tabs box	***Press***	*Alt+L to select the Left Align option button in the Tabs box*	**Press**	Alt+L to select the Left Align option button in the Tabs box

Your screen should look like Figure 9-11.

Figure 9-11

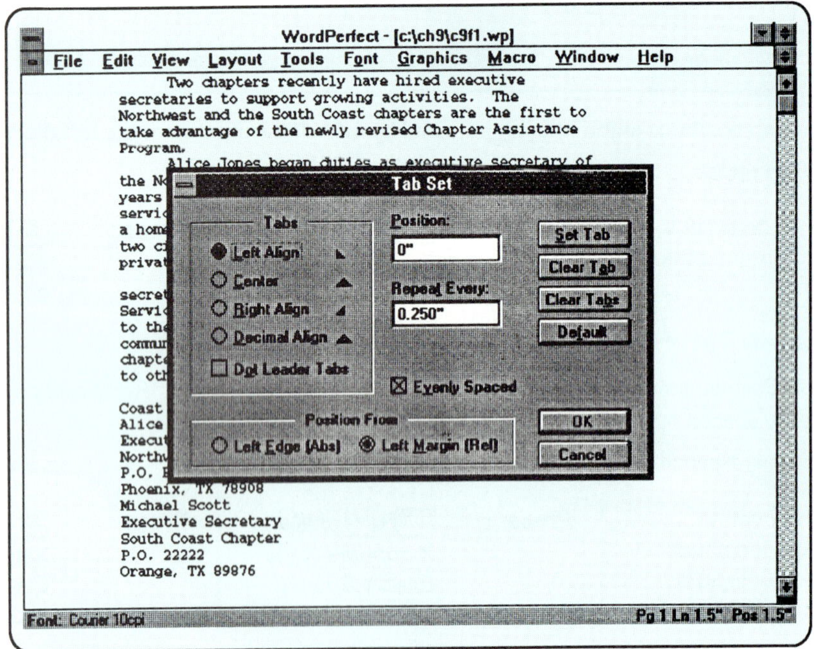

To return to your document:

Click	the OK command button	***Press***	*↵Enter*	**Press**	↵Enter

■ LINE SPACING

The Line Spacing feature is used to specify the number of lines to move down each time WordPerfect word wraps to a new line or the ↵Enter key is pressed. The default setting for line spacing in WordPerfect is single spacing.

Assume that you are using single line spacing. Each time WordPerfect wraps to a new line, a Soft Return code [SRt] is placed in the document prior to moving to a new line. When the ↵Enter key is pressed, a Hard Return code [HRt] is placed in the document before moving to a new line. If double spacing is used, then two Soft Return codes or Hard Return codes are placed in the document.

Whenever you change the line spacing in a document, the text that is entered following the location of the change will be affected. Any text appearing before the point in the document where you change the line spacing will not be modified.

To change the line spacing in your document:

Click	at the beginning of the document	***Move***	*the insertion point to the beginning of the document*	**Move**	the insertion point to the beginning of the document
Choose	Layout	***Press***	*Alt*	**Press**	Shift + F9
Choose	Line	***Select***	*Layout*		
		Select	*Line*		

To select Line Spacing:

Choose	Spacing	***Select***	*Spacing*	**Select**	Spacing

You can enter any number or fraction to change the line spacing.

To change the Line Spacing to 2:

Type	2	***Type***	*2*	**Type**	2
	or		*or*		or
Click	the up triangle button twice	***Press***	*↑ twice*	**Press**	↑ twice

Your screen should look like Figure 9-12.

Figure 9-12

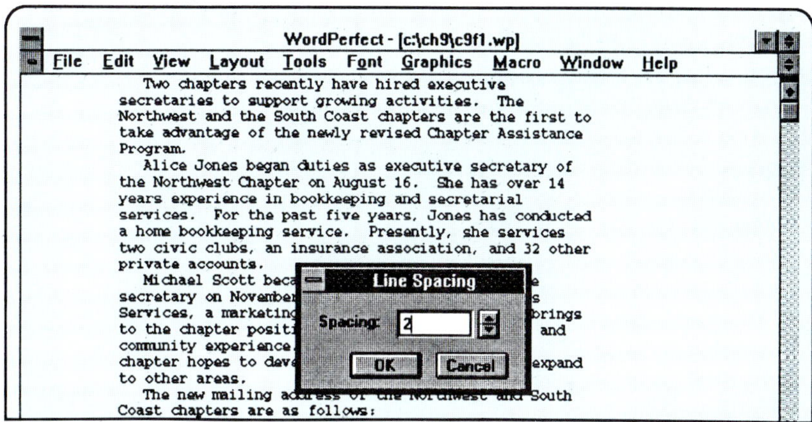

To return to your document:

Click	the OK command button	***Press***	*↵Enter*	**Press**	↵Enter

Your screen should look like Figure 9-13.

Figure 9-13

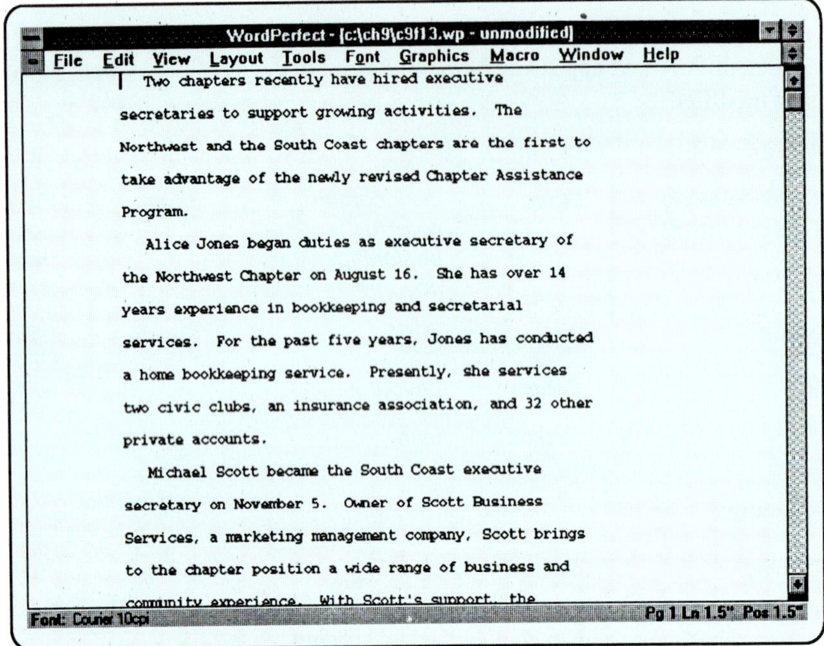

Notice that the spacing between each line of text has increased to two lines.

JUSTIFICATION

Text can be aligned to your requirements by using the Justification feature. There are four types of justification. They are left, right, full, and center.

When Left justification is used, your text is aligned along the left margin and the result is a ragged right margin. Similarly, when Right justification is specified, text is aligned along the right margin and a ragged left margin appears on your screen. If you use Center justification, the text is centered.

When you use Full justification, the text is aligned along both the left and right margins. The paragraphs in this book use Full justification. Spaces among words are compressed or expanded so the text is spread appropriately between the left and right margins.

To specify the justification, you can choose the type from the Justification option in the Layout menu or use the accelerator keys. The four accelerator keys are listed below.

Justification	Accelerator Keys
Left	Ctrl+L
Right	Ctrl+R
Center	Ctrl+J
Full	Ctrl+F

To change Justification to Full:

Click	at the beginning of the document	***Move***	*the insertion point to the beginning of the document*	**Move**	the insertion point to the beginning of the document
Choose	Layout	***Press***	*Alt*		
		Select	*Layout*		

To select the Justification option:

Choose	Justification	***Select***	*Justification*

Your screen should look like Figure 9-14.

Figure 9-14

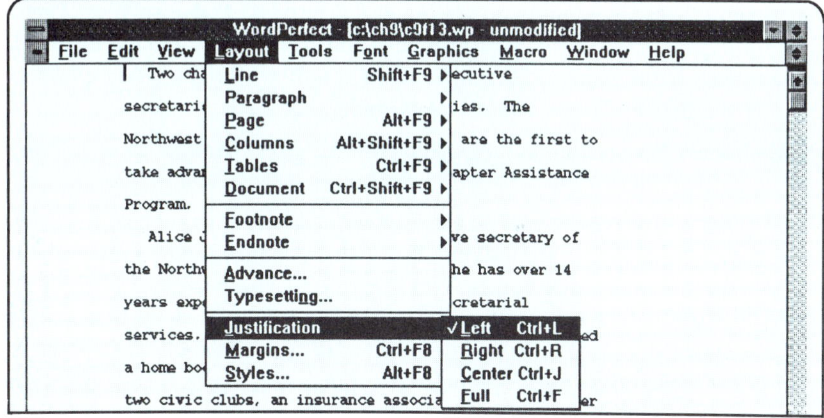

Notice that a check mark appears next to the Left option. This indicates that the current justification is Left.

To change the Justification to full:

Choose	Full	***Select***	*Full*	**Press**	Ctrl+F

Notice that the Justification selection is now Full.

If you want Right, Left, or Center justification, you can specify the new justification by choosing the appropriate option from the Justification option under the Layout menu.

Your screen should look similar to Figure 9-15.

Figure 9-15

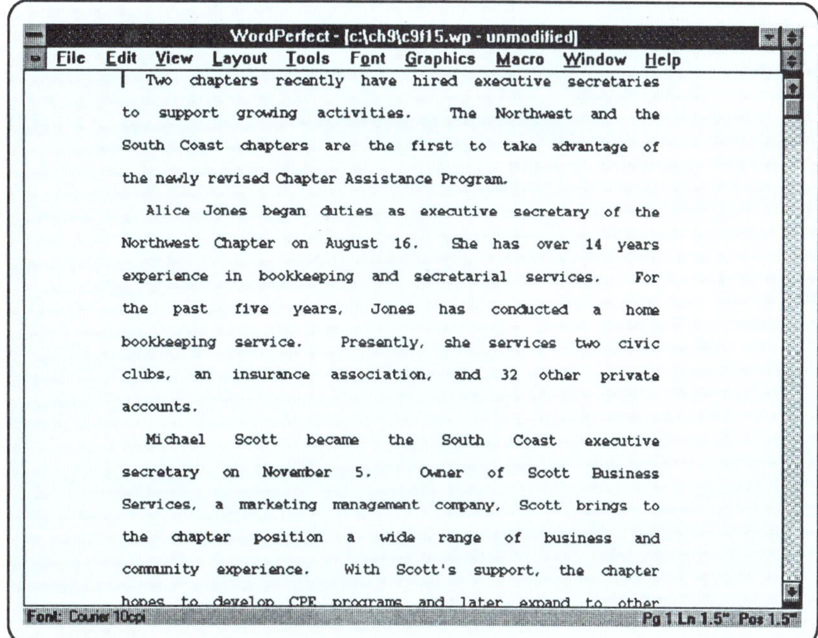

HYPHENATION

WordPerfect uses the word wrap feature to move a word to the next line whenever the word would appear beyond the right margin. The Hyphenation feature allows you to hyphenate these words in your document.

Three items must be considered when the Hyphenation feature is used. The elements include: the hyphenation zone, the hyphenation dictionary, and the hyphenation prompt option.

The hyphenation zone is a special area that WordPerfect uses to test whether a word should be hyphenated. This test is done "behind-the-scenes" and you are never aware of it. Suppose WordPerfect finds a word that is a candidate for hyphenation. If the word fits into this special area, the hyphenation zone, then the word is not hyphenated. If the word does not fit, then it is hyphenated. You can set the size of the hyphenation zone. If you make it larger, fewer words are hyphenated.

The hyphenation dictionary is a special dictionary that WordPerfect uses to "look up" words and find out where a word can contain hyphens.

The Hyphenation Prompt option tells WordPerfect whether it should ask you how to hyphenate a word, or use the special hyphenation dictionary to find out where the hyphen should be placed. The three options available for the hyphenation prompt are Never, When Required, and Always. "Never" tells WordPerfect to always use the hyphenation dictionary. "When Required" tells WordPerfect to first use the hyphenation dictionary, but if the word does not exist in the dictionary, then WordPerfect asks you what to do. "Always" tells WordPerfect to always ask you how to hyphenate a word. The Hyphenation Prompt and Hyphenation dictionary features can be changed by choosing Preferences, Environment from the File menu. By default, WordPerfect prompts for hyphenation when required.

To use the Hyphenation feature:

Click	at the beginning of the document	***Move***	*the insertion point to the beginning of the document*	**Move**	the insertion point to the beginning of the document
Choose	Layout	***Press***	*Alt*	**Press**	Shift+F9
Choose	Line	***Select***	*Layout*		
		Select	*Line*		

To select Hyphenation:

Choose	Hyphenation	***Select***	*Hyphenation*	**Select**	Hyphenation

Your screen should look like Figure 9-16.

Figure 9-16

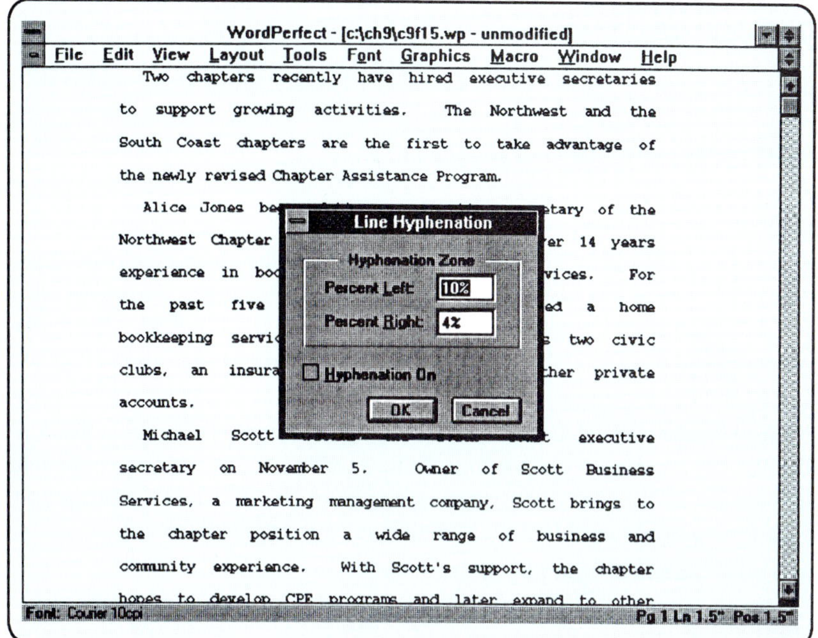

To use the Hyphenation feature:

Click	the Hyphenation On check box until an X appears	***Press***	*Alt+H until an X appears in the Hyphenation On check box*	**Press**	Alt+H until an X appears in the Hyphenation On check box

To return to your document:

Click	the OK command button	***Press***	*↵Enter*	**Press**	↵Enter

Your screen should look like Figure 9-17.

Figure 9-17

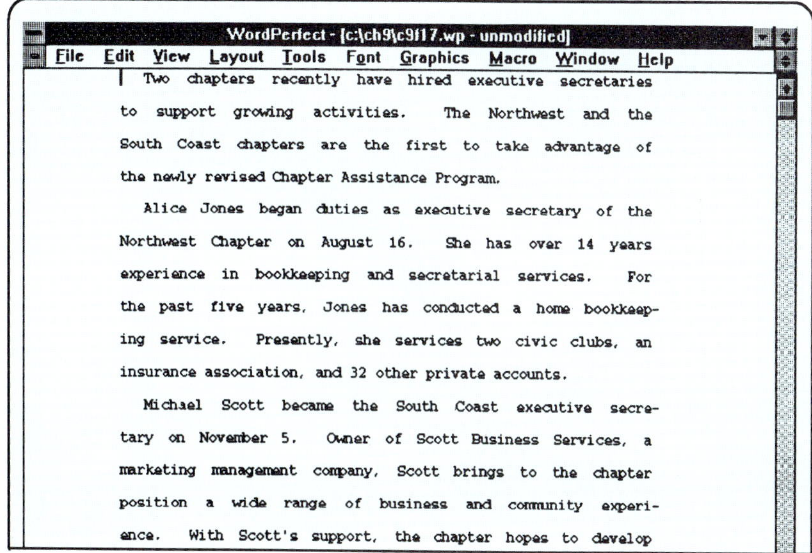

Notice that several words are now hyphenated.

INDENT

Whenever you need to move a complete paragraph a specific number of spaces, you can use the Indent feature.

A tab and an indent are very different formatting features.

If you press the [Tab] key, WordPerfect moves one line of text to the next tab setting. If you use the Indent feature, it appears as if a new left margin is set at the next tab setting. However, this margin is not permanent. Any text entered after the indent is aligned at the next tab setting. The indent is terminated whenever you press [↵Enter]. The Indent feature uses whatever existing tab settings are present in the document.

There are three types of indents: Left, Double, and Hanging Indent. In a left indent, the lines in a paragraph are indented from the left margin. A double indent allows you to indent text an equal distance from both the left and right margins. Whenever you use a hanging indent, the first line of a paragraph is placed at the left margin and the remaining lines of text are indented using the next tab setting.

To remove the tab code from the beginning of the second paragraph:

Click	at the left margin at the beginning of the second paragraph	***Move***	*the insertion point to the left margin at the beginning of the second paragraph*	**Move**	the insertion point to the left margin at the beginning of the second paragraph
Press	[Delete]	***Press***	*[Delete]*	**Press**	[Delete]

To left indent the second paragraph in your document at the first tab stop from the left margin:

Choose	Layout	***Press***	*[Alt]*	**Press**	[F7]
Choose	Paragraph	***Select***	*Layout*		
Choose	Indent	***Select***	*Paragraph*		
		Select	*Indent*		

Your screen should look like Figure 9-18.

Figure 9-18

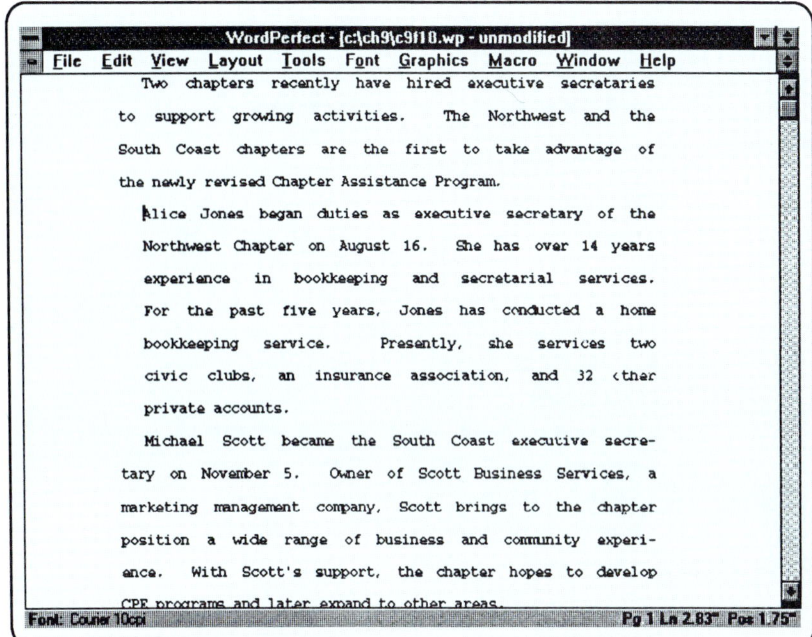

Notice that only the second paragraph is indented. An indent code indents text from the insertion point to the next hard return or [HRt] code.

To double indent the third paragraph to the second tab stop from both margins:

Click	at the left margin at the beginning of the third paragraph	***Move***	*the insertion point to the left margin at the beginning of the third paragraph*	**Move**	the insertion point to the left margin at the beginning of the third paragraph
Press	Delete	***Press***	*Delete*	**Press**	Delete
Choose	Layout	***Press***	*Alt*	**Press**	Ctrl+Shift+F7
Choose	Paragraph	***Select***	*Layout*	**Press**	Ctrl+Shift+F7
Choose	Double Indent	***Select***	*Paragraph*		
Choose	Layout	***Select***	*Double Indent*		
Choose	Paragraph	***Press***	*Alt*		
Choose	Double Indent	***Select***	*Layout*		
		Select	*Paragraph*		
		Select	*Double Indent*		

Your screen should look like Figure 9-19.

Figure 9-19

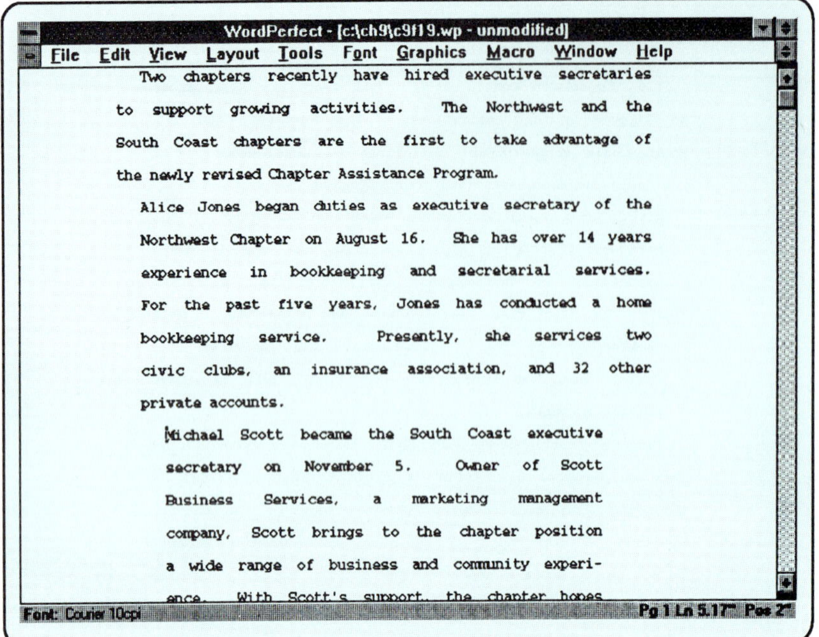

WordPerfect - [c:\ch9\c9f19.wp - unmodified]

File Edit View Layout Tools Font Graphics Macro Window Help

Two chapters recently have hired executive secretaries to support growing activities. The Northwest and the South Coast chapters are the first to take advantage of the newly revised Chapter Assistance Program.

Alice Jones began duties as executive secretary of the Northwest Chapter on August 16. She has over 14 years experience in bookkeeping and secretarial services. For the past five years, Jones has conducted a home bookkeeping service. Presently, she services two civic clubs, an insurance association, and 32 other private accounts.

Michael Scott became the South Coast executive secretary on November 5. Owner of Scott Business Services, a marketing management company, Scott brings to the chapter position a wide range of business and community experi-ence. With Scott's support, the chapter hopes

Font: Courier 10cpi Pg 1 Ln 5.17" Pos 2"

Save the document as "report1.ltr." Close the document.

EXERCISE 1

INSTRUCTIONS: Define the following terms:

1. Indent ______________________________

2. Justification ______________________________

3. Fonts ______________________________

4. Hyphenation ______________________________

5. Line spacing ______________________________

6. Default settings ______________________________

7. Tabs ____

____

8. Margins ____

____

EXERCISE 2

INSTRUCTIONS: Circle T if the statement is true and F if the statement is false.

T F 1. A font typeface is the design and appearance of printed characters on the page.

T F 2. A font consists of four elements: typeface, pound, style, and point size.

T F 3. The default setting for margins in WordPerfect is 1 1/2″.

T F 4. Current margin settings are ignored when using left edge tabs.

T F 5. Left, Center, Right, Decimal, and Dollar are the five types of tab settings available in WordPerfect.

T F 6. A left margin tab is one that is set relative to the left edge of the page.

T F 7. Default tab settings are pre-set at one-half inch intervals.

T F 8. WordPerfect double spaces your document unless you change the line spacing.

T F 9. Full justification means that text is aligned with the right margin of the document.

T F 10. When you use the Indent feature, you have to press TAB to indent each line of text.

EXERCISE 3

INSTRUCTIONS: 1. Create the following document. The format settings for the document are listed below:

Initial Font:	Helvetica 10 pt (Z1A)
Margins:	
Left	1.5″
Right	1.0″
Top	2.0″
Bottom	1.0″
Left Margin tabs:	0.5″, 1.0″ and 2.0″ left aligned tabs
Line spacing:	Double. Use single line spacing for the paragraph listing the stores.

Justification: Full
Hyphenation: None
Enter the information about each store at the 2″ tab stop.

2. Preview the document.
3. Save the document on a file using the name "ch09ex03."
4. Print the document.
5. Close the document.

> As you already know, sales in District A were level from last November to March of this year, and have started to decline since March. A research group was created in late April to study the situation in District A. The group consists of Maria Alvares, Senior Market Analyst, Jennifer Chang, Financial Advisor to the HQ Sales Department, and Sharon Jackson, Senior Sales Analyst for the Southern Division.
>
> There are five stores in District A. The five stores and their locations are listed below:
>
> Store A1, Bering Street
> Store A2, Bookman Avenue
> Store A3, Taft Street
> Store A4, Howard Street
> Store A5, Oliver Boulevard
>
> This district is managed by Howard Smith who has been with the company for 35 years. Mr. Smith has been the manager of District A for ten years.

EXERCISE 4

INSTRUCTIONS:

1. Create the memo shown below.

The format settings for the document are listed below:

Initial Font:	Courier 10cpi
Margins:	
Left	1.5″
Right	1.0″
Top	2.0″
Bottom	0.5″
Left Edge tabs:	2.2″ and 3.25″ left aligned tabs
Justification:	Full
Line spacing:	Single
Hyphenation:	Yes

2. Preview the document.
3. Save the document on a file using the name "ch09ex04."
4. Print the document.
5. Close the document.

```
TO:      J. Chang
         S. Jackson
         M. Alvarez

FROM:    Hector Garcia
         Division Manager

DATE:    January 22, 1992

RE:      Meeting on District A


There will be a meeting on June 11 at 8:30 am in Conference Room
1109.  At this time, you will present the results of your preliminary
study on District A sales problems.  Approximate meeting time will be
1 1/2 hours.

Present at this meeting will be Robert Chambers, Regional Manager,
Marla Johnson, HQ Sales Manager, James Gonzalez, Personnel Manager
and myself.

You will each have 20 minutes to present each of your topics.  Topics
are assigned in the following manner:

         Alvarez   Market Analysis for District A; include comparison
                   with other districts.

         Chang     Financial analysis for District A; include graphs
                   with your spreadsheets.

         Jackson   Sales analysis for District A; also present possible
                   cause(s) of sales problems.

If you have any questions, please contact me at Ext. 8099.
```

EXERCISE 5

INSTRUCTIONS:

1. Open the document in file "ch09ex04."
2. Make the left and right margins 1.0″ for the entire document.
3. Change the first tab setting to 1.7″.

4. Change the line spacing to 2 beginning with the first sentence of the first paragraph below the memo headings. Delete the extra [HRt] codes at the end of the memo text paragraphs.
5. Make the three paragraphs concerning the topic assignments for Alvarez, Chang, and Jackson single-spaced.
6. Make the entire document left justified.
7. Change the second tab setting to 2.75″.
8. Preview the document.
9. Save the document on a file using the name "ch09ex05."
10. Print the memo.
11. Close the document.

EXERCISE 6

INSTRUCTIONS:

1. Create the document shown below. The format settings for the document are listed below:

Initial Font:	Courier 10cpi
Margins:	
Left	1.5″
Right	1.0″
Top	1.5″
Bottom	1.0″
Justification:	Left
Hyphenation:	None
Line spacing:	Single
Tabs:	Set your own tabs. The column titles, "1988," "1989," and "1990(est.)" should be centered over each column. The dollar amounts should be right-aligned in each column.

2. Preview the document.
3. Save the document on a file using the name "ch09ex06."
4. Print the document.
5. Close the document.

	1988	1989	1990(est)
District A	$150,000	$151,000	$90,000
District B	209,000	215,000	218,000
District C	80,000	90,000	95,000
District D	92,000	98,000	102,000
District E	180,000	187,000	197,000

EXERCISE 7

INSTRUCTIONS:

1. Create the following document. The format settings for the document are listed below:

Initial Font:	Helvetica 10 pt (Z1A)
Margins:	
Left	1.5″
Right	1.0″
Top	2.0″
Bottom	1.0″
Left Margin tabs:	0.5″, 1.0″ and 2.0″ left aligned tabs
Line spacing:	Double. Use single line spacing for the paragraphs that are numbered 1 and 2.
Justification:	Full
Hyphenation:	None

2. Preview the document.
3. Be sure that the paragraphs numbered 1 and 2 are single-spaced. All other paragraphs should be double-spaced.
4. Note that the paragraphs numbered 1 and 2 are indented from both margins.
5. Save the document on a file using the name "ch09ex07."
6. Print the document.
7. Close the document.

Various investigative tools were used to study the stores in District A. Extensive interviews were conducted by myself and the staff. We interviewed the store managers and various sales personnel. A marketing research firm, Sanchez and Locken, was contracted to interview repeat customers. Customers were queried about service and product satisfaction. A private retail investigator, Sam Malone of Malone Investigations, was contracted to secretly observe store activities. This investigation was done before we arrived to audit the stores. The accounting firm, Jackson, Johnson & James, was hired to perform a full audit on the district. This audit is still in progress and is expected to be complete in four weeks.

The results of the preliminary study indicate two possible causes for the sales decline in District A:

1. Surveys and interviews with customers indicate that service has declined in the past months. Customers cite instances where sales personnel were unwilling to solve problems with products, or assist customers at the desk. Telephone support has also declined. Numerous complaints concerned poor telephone support. Stores A3 and A5 were especially lapse in these areas.

2. Customers and the retail investigator noticed the shoddy appearance of the stores. Products were in disarray on the shelves while sales personnel "loafed in back." Parking lots were strewn with trash in some cases. Stores A2, A3, and A5 needed building repairs. The investigator noted a ceiling leak in Store A5.

However, customer comments and investigative reports indicate that Store A4 may be an exception to the problems listed above. Several compliments were given concerning this store, and the investigators thought this store to be adequately organized. However, it is recommended that all stores be thoroughly inspected by company personnel.

EXERCISE 8

INSTRUCTIONS:

1. Create the document shown below. Define your own format settings. However, you must define the initial font to be Helvetica 10pt (Z1A).
2. The items in column "Size Type 1" are decimal aligned. The items in column "Size Type 2" are right aligned. In the third column, the items are left aligned. In the last column, they are centered. The headings of each column are centered.
3. Preview the document.
4. Save the document on a file using the name "ch09ex08."

5. Print the document.
6. Close the document.

Please fill out the information below using a pencil. Please print legibly.

NAME:

ADDRESS:

TELEPHONE NUMBER: AGE: SEX:

Please circle the sizes desired:

Size Type 1	Size Type 2	Size Type 3	Size Type 4
1,200.34	150	Octagon	One
299.11	2,900	Square	Round
25.09	10	Triangle	Parallel
7.1	2	Box	3-D

EXERCISE 9

INSTRUCTIONS:

1. Create the document shown below using the following format settings:

Initial Font:	Helvetica 12 pt (Z1A)
Margins:	
Left	1.5″
Right	1.5″
Top	1.75″
Bottom	1.75″
Left Edge tabs:	2.5″ and 5.5″ left aligned tabs
Line spacing:	Double spacing for the table only. Then change back to single spacing.
Justification:	Left
Hyphenation:	On

2. Spell check the document.

3. Preview the document.
4. Save the document in file "ch09ex09."
5. Print the document.
6. Close the document.

current date

Mr. Charles Harrington
119 Ferndale Road
Atlanta, GA 30327

Dear Mr. Harrington:

I have just seen your current picture "Skyway Paradise." As a result of this startling film, I would like to invite you to participate in a Senior Film Seminar to be held November 15, at the Oak Street Theater in Chicago. During this seminar, we would discuss the following films you have made:

"Date with Desire"	1960
"Remembering Africa"	1970
"Chicago Byline"	1980
"Moonbeam"	1989

At this seminar, you will be expected to present some remarks comparing and contrasting your changes in cinematic style. Of course, questions from the audience will be accepted. The whole program will last only two hours. During this time you may wish to comment about your latest releases.

Sincerely.

John Muchmore
Film Critic

EXERCISE 10

INSTRUCTIONS:

1. Create the document shown below. Use the following format settings:

Initial Font:	Courier 10cpi
Margins:	
Left	1.5″
Right	1.5″
Top	0.75″
Bottom	0.75″
Line spacing:	Change to double spacing for the first and last paragraphs only.
Left Margin tabs:	.25″, .625″, .94″ left aligned
Justification:	Left
Hyphenation:	On

2. Press the [Tab] key before typing the numbers.
3. Use a left indent after typing the numbers.
4. Use a left indent after the a, b, and c items.
5. Spell check the document.
6. Save the document in file "ch09ex10."
7. Print the document.

Division of words at the end of a line should be avoided, but when it is unavoidable in order to have as even a right margin as possible, the following rules are presented:

1. WordPerfect for Windows will frequently present hyphenated words that you must not hyphenate if you are to follow the rules. A word of six or more letters containing two or more syllables may be divided between syllables, provided such division does not violate other standard word division rules or guides. The division is indicated by a hyphen at the correct point of division at the end of the line.
2. A Word Division Guide book should be consulted if there is any doubt about the point of division.
3. One-syllable words, such as wrapped, through, planned, height, or strolled, must not be divided.
4. Do NOT separate from the remainder of the word:
    a. A one-letter syllable at the beginning of a word, such as abandon, enough, or enormous.
    b. A one- or two-letter syllable at the end of a word, such as already, mighty, or teacher.
    c. A syllable that does not contain a vowel, such as the contraction, doesn't.
5. Avoid dividing proper names, abbreviations, and numbers. A date may, if necessary, be divided between the day and the year (the hyphen is not used).
6. Avoid the division of words at the end of two or more successive lines, or the final word on a page, or the word at the end of the last complete line of a paragraph.

More guides for dividing words properly can be found in any Word Division Guide book found in bookstores.

CHAPTER TEN

FORMATTING WITH THE RULER

OBJECTIVES

In this chapter, you will learn to:

- View the Ruler
- Set margins, tabs, line spacing, and text justification using the Ruler
- Remove the Ruler from display

CHAPTER OVERVIEW

In this chapter, the procedures for formatting a document using the Ruler are discussed. Methods for setting left and right margins, tabs, line spacing, and text justification are described and illustrated using the WordPerfect Ruler.

VIEWING THE RULER

WordPerfect allows you to quickly format your document using the Ruler. The Ruler is made up of three parts: the margin marker, the tab marker, and the format buttons.

Figure 10-1 illustrates the parts of the Ruler.

Figure 10-1

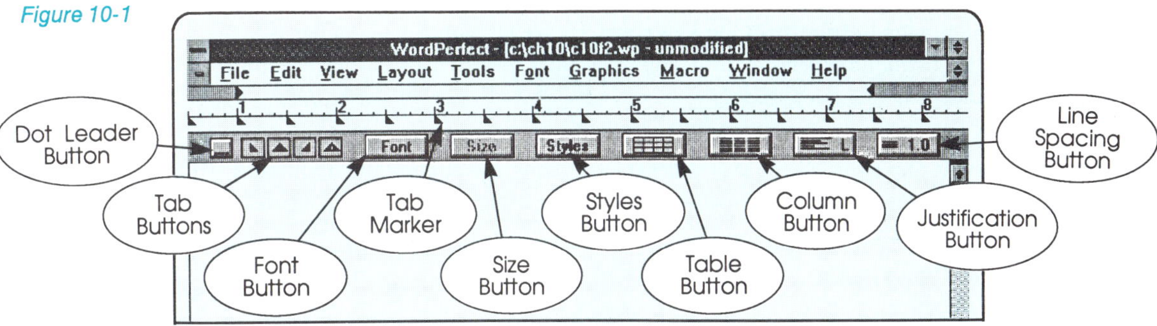

The Font, Size, Styles, Tables, and Columns buttons will be discussed in later chapters.

To view the Ruler:

Choose	View	***Press***	Alt	**Press**	Alt + Shift + F3
Choose	Ruler	***Select***	*View*		
		Select	*Ruler*		

The top portion of your screen should look like Figure 10-1.

The Ruler appears at the top of the document window.

Change the default directory to "a:\wpdocs" or "c:\wpdocs." Create the document in Figure 10-2. Separate each memo heading from the following text by pressing the Tab key once.

Save the document as "ruler.ltr."

Figure 10-2

```
TO:  All Department Managers

FROM:   James Smith

DATE:   January 22, 1992

RE:  Staff Meeting

We will be having a staff meeting on Friday, January 24, 1992 at
10:00 a.m. in the conference room.  We will be discussing our
long and short term goals.  Please prepare long and short term
goals for your department.
```

■ USING THE RULER TO FORMAT

You can view the Ruler using the mouse or the keyboard. However, you can only access the Ruler features using the mouse. In the formatting section of this chapter, only mouse instructions are given.

Margins

You can change the left and right margins of a document using the Ruler. The document "ruler.ltr" was created using the default margin settings. Notice that the left and right margin markers display a 1″ margin from the left and right edges of the page.

To change the left and right margins to 1 1/2″:

Click	at the beginning of the document		

To change the left margin to 1 1/2″:

Click the left margin marker

Drag the margin marker to position 1.5 on the Ruler

To change the right margin to 1 1/2″:

Click the Right margin marker

Drag the margin marker to position 7

Your screen should look like Figure 10-3.

Figure 10-3

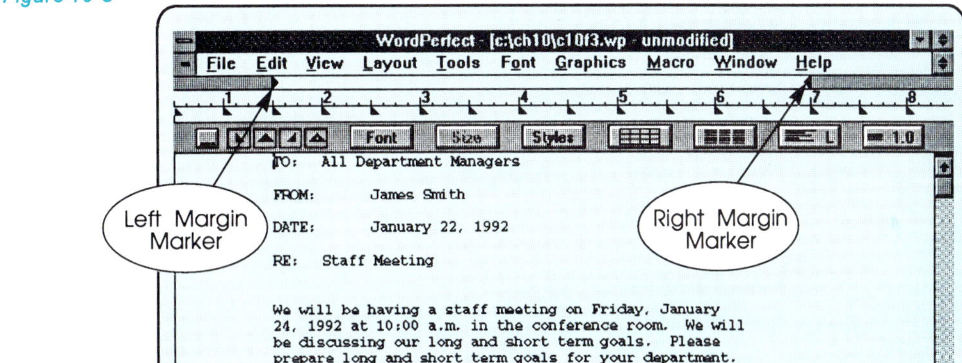

Notice the change in Pos from 1″ to 1.5″ on the status bar indicating the left margin is now 1.5″.

Tabs

Tabs are easy to set with the Ruler. The tab marker displays a left aligned tab at every 1/2″. The left aligned tabs are represented by triangles that slant from the left to the right.

The left, center, right, and decimal tabs can be set by clicking on the appropriate tab button and dragging the icon to the tab setting on the ruler. For example, if you want a right aligned tab at 5″, click on the right tab button and drag the icon to the 5″ position on the ruler.

You can create dot leader tabs by clicking the dot leader button before you select the tab button. A dot leader tab places dots between the tab stops.

To change the location of a tab marker already on the Ruler, drag the tab marker to a new setting. For example, to move the tab marker from 4″ to 4.25″, click the 4″ tab marker and drag the marker to position 4.25″.

To delete a tab marker from the Ruler, drag the tab marker down, off the Ruler.

The memo headings in "ruler.ltr" are not aligned correctly. To change the tab settings for "ruler.ltr":

Click at the top of the document

To delete the tab marker from the 2″ position:

Click the left tab marker at position 2

Drag the marker down off the ruler

Your screen should look like Figure 10-4.

Figure 10-4

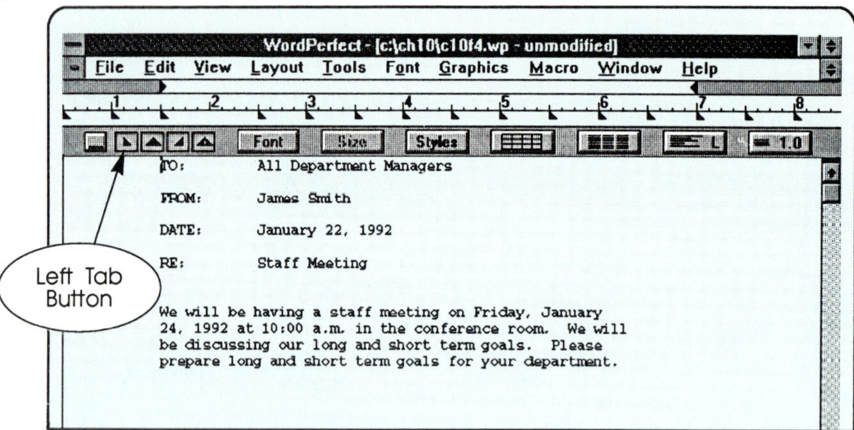

To create a new tab marker at position 2 1/4″:

Click the left tab button on the Ruler

Drag the left tab icon to position 2 1/4

Your screen should look like Figure 10-5.

Figure 10-5

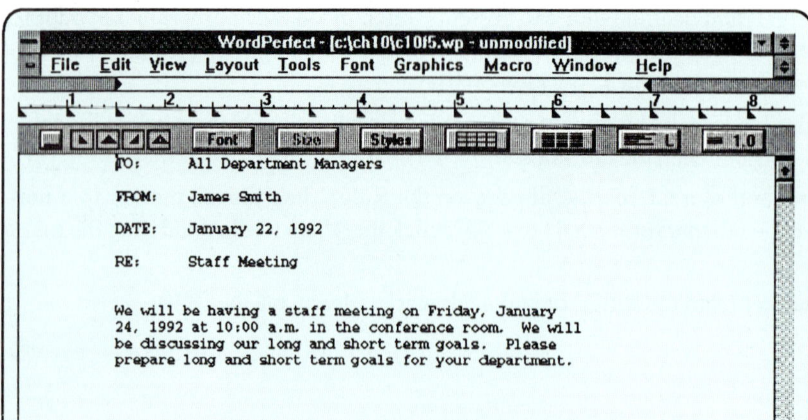

You also could have moved the tab marker from 2″ to position 2 1/4″.

Line Spacing

You can change the line spacing in your document using the Ruler. The Ruler allows you to set line spacing for 1.0, 1.5, and 2.0. For other line spacing options, you should use the Line, Spacing feature under the Layout menu.

To change the line spacing in your document:

Click	at the beginning of the document

To change the Line Spacing to 1.5:

Click	the Line Spacing pop-up list button ≡ 1.0
Hold down	the button to view the Line Spacing pop-up list
Choose	1.5

Your screen should look like Figure 10-6.

Figure 10-6

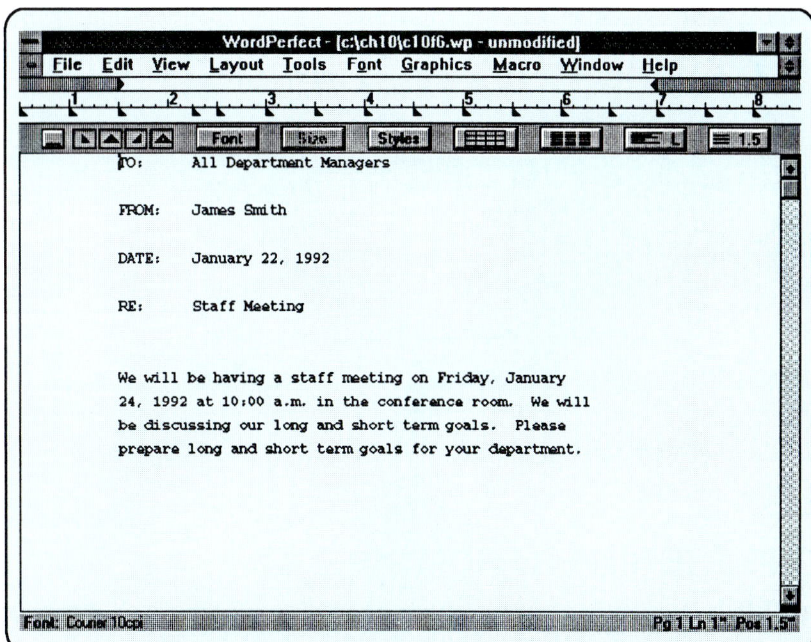

Notice that the Line Spacing button now displays 1.5 to represent the new line spacing.

Justification

You can use the Justification button on the Ruler to change the justification to Left, Right, Center, or Full. The justification option changes the document justification from the insertion point forward.

To change Justification to Full:

Click at the beginning of the document

Click the Justification pop-up list button [≡ L]

Hold down the Justification button to view the pop-up list

To change the Justification to Full:

Choose Full

Your screen should look like Figure 10-7.

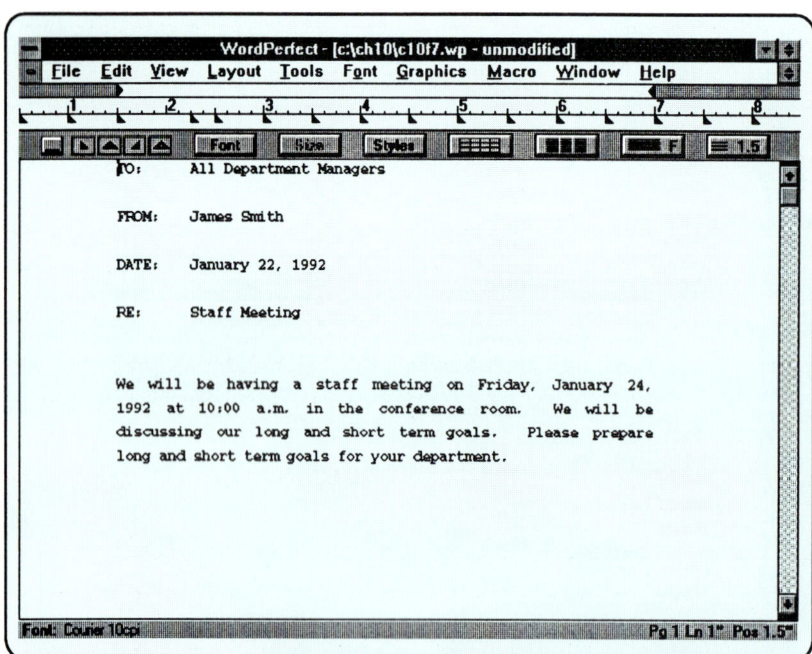

Figure 10-7

Notice that the Justification button now displays an F to represent Full justification.

Save your document as "ruler.ltr."

■ REMOVING THE RULER FROM DISPLAY

The Ruler is automatically removed from the screen when you close a document. You can also remove the Ruler by choosing Ruler from the View menu or by pressing [Alt]+[Shift]+[F3].

To close the "ruler.ltr" document and remove the Ruler from the screen:

Choose	File	***Press***	*[Alt]*	**Press**	[Ctrl]+[F4]
Choose	Close	***Select***	*File*		
		Select	*Close*		

Notice that the Ruler is no longer displayed when you close a document. To have the Ruler automatically displayed at all times, select the Automatic Ruler Display option from the Preferences, Environment option under the File menu.

EXERCISE 1

INSTRUCTIONS: Define the following terms:

1. Ruler ______________________________

____

2. Margin marker ______________________________

____

3. Tab marker ______________________________

____

EXERCISE 2

INSTRUCTIONS: Circle T if the statement is true and F if the statement is false.

T F 1. The Ruler remains on the screen after you close a document.

T F 2. You can use the Ruler to change the left, right, top, and bottom margins of a document.

T F 3. You can delete a tab stop from the Ruler by dragging the tab marker off the Ruler.

T F 4. The Columns feature is not represented on the Ruler.

T F 5. Only 1.0, 1.5, and 2.0 line spacings are available from the Ruler.

EXERCISE 3

INSTRUCTIONS: 1. Create the following document. The format settings for the document are listed below:

Margins:	
Left	1.5″
Right	1.0″
Tabs:	Delete the tabs at 2.5″ and 3″
Line spacing:	Double. Use single line spacing for the paragraph listing the stores.
Justification:	Full

Enter the information about each store at the 3.5″ tab stop.

2. Preview the document.
3. Save the document on a file using the name "ch10ex03."
4. Print the document.
5. Close the document.

```
     As you already know, sales in District A were level from last
November to March of this year, and have started to decline since
March.  A research group was created in late April to study the
situation in District A.  The group consists of Maria Alvares, Senior
Market Analyst, Jennifer Chang, Financial Advisor to the HQ Sales
Department, and Sharon Jackson, Senior Sales Analyst for the Southern
Division.
     There are five stores in District A.  The five stores and their
locations are listed below:

               Store A1, Bering Street
               Store A2, Bookman Avenue
               Store A3, Taft Street
               Store A4, Howard Street
               Store A5, Oliver Boulevard

     This district is managed by Howard Smith who has been with the
company for 35 years.  Mr. Smith has been the manager of District A
for ten years.
```

EXERCISE 4

INSTRUCTIONS:

1. Create the memo shown below.

   The format settings for the document are listed below:

   Margins:

Left	1.5″
Right	1.0″
Tabs:	Set left-aligned tabs at 2.25″ and 3.25″. Delete the tabs at 2.5″ and 3″.
Justification:	Full
Line spacing:	Single

2. Preview the document.
3. Save the document on a file using the name "ch10ex04."
4. Print the document.
5. Close the document.

```
TO:     J. Chang
        S. Jackson
        M. Alvarez

FROM:   Hector Garcia
        Division Manager

DATE:   current date

RE:     Meeting on District A

There will be a meeting on June 11 at 8:30 am in Conference Room
1109.  At this time, you will present the results of your preliminary
study on District A sales problems.  Approximate meeting time will be
1 1/2 hours.

Present at this meeting will be Robert Chambers, Regional Manager,
Marla Johnson, HQ Sales Manager, James Gonzalez, Personnel Manager
and myself.

You will each have 20 minutes to present each of your topics.  Topics
are assigned in the following manner:

        Alvarez  Market Analysis for District A; include comparison
                 with other districts.

        Chang    Financial analysis for District A; include graphs
                 with your spreadsheets.

        Jackson  Sales analysis for District A; also present possible
                 cause(s) of sales problems.

If you have any questions, please contact me at Ext. 8099.
```

EXERCISE 5

INSTRUCTIONS:

1. Open the document in file "ch10ex04."
2. Make the left and right margins 1.0″ for the entire document.
3. Change the line spacing to 2 beginning with the first sentence of the first paragraph below the memo headings. Delete the extra [HRt] codes at the end of the memo text paragraphs.
4. Make the three paragraphs concerning the topic assignments for Alvarez, Chang, and Jackson single-spaced.
5. Make the entire document left justified.
6. Preview the document.
7. Save the document on a file using the name "ch10ex05."
8. Print the memo.
9. Close the document.

EXERCISE 6

INSTRUCTIONS:

1. Create the document shown below. The format settings for the document are listed below:

   Margins:

Left	1.5″
Right	1.0″
Justification:	Left
Line spacing:	Single
Tabs:	Set your own tabs. The column titles, "1988," "1989," and "1990(est.)" should be centered over each column. The dollar amounts should be right-aligned in each column.

2. Preview the document.
3. Save the document on a file using the name "ch10ex06."
4. Print the document.
5. Close the document.

	1988	1989	1990(est)
District A	$150,000	$151,000	$90,000
District B	209,000	215,000	218,000
District C	80,000	90,000	95,000
District D	92,000	98,000	102,000
District E	180,000	187,000	197,000

EXERCISE 7

INSTRUCTIONS:

1. Create the following document.
2. The format settings for the document are listed below:

   Margins:

Left	1.5″
Right	1.0″
Line spacing:	Double. Use single line spacing for the paragraphs that are numbered 1 and 2.
Justification:	Full

3. Preview the document.
4. Be sure that the paragraphs numbered 1 and 2 are single-spaced. All other paragraphs should be double-spaced.

5. Note that the paragraphs numbered 1 and 2 are indented from both margins.
6. Save the document on a file using the name "ch10ex07."
7. Print the document.
8. Close the document.

Various investigative tools were used to study the stores in District A. Extensive interviews were conducted by myself and the staff. We interviewed the store managers and various sales personnel. A marketing research firm, Sanchez and Locken, was contracted to interview repeat customers. Customers were queried about service and product satisfaction. A private retail investigator, Sam Malone of Malone Investigations, was contracted to secretly observe store activities. This investigation was done before we arrived to audit the stores. The accounting firm, Jackson, Johnson & James, was hired to perform a full audit on the district. This audit is still in progress and is expected to be complete in four weeks.

The results of the preliminary study indicate two possible causes for the sales decline in District A:

1. Surveys and interviews with customers indicate that service has declined in the past months. Customers cite instances where sales personnel were unwilling to solve problems with products, or assist customers at the desk. Telephone support has also declined. Numerous complaints concerned poor telephone support. Stores A3 and A5 were especially lapse in these areas.

2. Customers and the retail investigator noticed the shoddy appearance of the stores. Products were in disarray on the shelves while sales personnel "loafed in back." Parking lots were strewn with trash in some cases. Stores A2, A3, and A5 needed building repairs. The investigator noted a ceiling leak in Store A5.

However, customer comments and investigative reports indicate that Store A4 may be an exception to the problems listed above. Several compliments were given concerning this store, and the investigators thought this store to be adequately organized. However, it is recommended that all stores be thoroughly inspected by company personnel.

EXERCISE 8

INSTRUCTIONS:

1. Create the document shown below. Define your own format settings.
2. The items in column "Size Type 1" are decimal aligned. The items in column "Size Type 2" are right aligned. In the third column, the items are left aligned. In the last column, they are centered. The headings of each column are centered.

3. Preview the document.
4. Save the document on a file using the name "ch10ex08."
5. Print the document.
6. Close the document.

```
Please fill out the information below using a pencil.  Please print
legibly.

NAME:


ADDRESS:



TELEPHONE NUMBER:                  AGE:        SEX:


Please circle the sizes desired:

 Size Type 1      Size Type 2          Size Type 3       Size Type 4

    1,200.34            150              Octagon              One
      299.11          2,900              Square              Round
       25.09             10              Triangle           Parallel
        7.1               2              Box                  3-D
```

EXERCISE 9

INSTRUCTIONS:

1. Create the document shown below using the following format settings:

   Margins:

Left	1.5″
Right	1.5″
Tabs:	Delete the tabs at 2.5″, 3″, 3.5″, and 4″
Line spacing:	Double spacing for the table only. Then change back to single spacing.
Justification:	Left

2. Spell check the document.
3. Preview the document.
4. Save the document in file "ch10ex09."
5. Print the document.
6. Close the document.

```
current date


Mr. Charles Harrington
119 Ferndale Road
Atlanta, GA 30327

Dear Mr. Harrington:

I have just seen your current picture "Skyway Paradise."  As a
result of this startling film, I would like to invite you to
participate in a Senior Film Seminar to be held November 15, at the
Oak Street Theater in Chicago.  During this seminar, we would
discuss the following films you have made:

      "Date with Desire"       1960
      "Remembering Africa"     1970
      "Chicago Byline"         1980
      "Moonbeam"               1989

At this seminar, you will be expected to present some remarks
comparing and contrasting your changes in cinematic style.  Of
course, questions from the audience will be accepted.  The whole
program will last only two hours.  During this time you may wish to
comment about your latest releases.

Sincerely.



John Muchmore
Film Critic
```

EXERCISE 10

INSTRUCTIONS:

1. Create the following document. Use the following format settings:

   Margins:

Left	1.5″
Right	1.5″
Line spacing:	Change to double spacing for the first and last paragraphs only.
Tabs:	Set left aligned tabs at 1.75″, 2.25″, and 2.75″. Delete the tabs at 2″ and 2.5″.
Justification:	Left

2. Press the [Tab] key before typing the numbers.
3. Use a left indent after typing the numbers.
4. Use a left indent after the a, b, and c items.

5. Spell check the document.
6. Save the document in file "ch10ex10."
7. Print the document.
8. Close the document.

Division of words at the end of a line should be avoided, but when it is unavoidable in order to have as even a right margin as possible, the following rules are presented:

1. WordPerfect for Windows will frequently present hyphenated words that you must not hyphenate if you are to follow the rules. A word of six or more letters containing two or more syllables may be divided between syllables, provided such division does not violate other standard word division rules or guides. The division is indicated by a hyphen at the correct point of division at the end of the line.

2. A Word Division Guide book should be consulted if there is any doubt about the point of division.

3. One-syllable words, such as wrapped, through, planned, height, or strolled, must not be divided.

4. Do NOT separate from the remainder of the word:

   a. A one-letter syllable at the beginning of a word, such as abandon, enough, or enormous.

   b. A one- or two-letter syllable at the end of a word, such as already, mighty, or teacher.

   c. A syllable that does not contain a vowel, such as the contraction, doesn't.

5. Avoid dividing proper names, abbreviations, and numbers. A date may, if necessary, be divided between the day and the year (the hyphen is not used).

6. Avoid the division of words at the end of two or more successive lines, or the final word on a page, or the word at the end of the last complete line of a paragraph.

More guides for dividing words properly can be found in any Word Division Guide book found in bookstores.

CHAPTER ELEVEN

ADDITIONAL FORMATTING FEATURES

OBJECTIVES

In this chapter, you will learn to:

- Create headers and footers
- Create page numbers
- Create page breaks

■ CHAPTER OVERVIEW

This chapter discusses how to create headers, footers, page numbers, and page breaks.

■ HEADERS AND FOOTERS

Headers and footers allow text to appear on every page of a document. Headers appear at the top of each page. Footers appear at the bottom of each page. A blank line separates them from the main body of the text. You can adjust the placement of headers and footers on the page by adjusting the top and bottom margins.

Headers and footers are created only once for a document. You can tell WordPerfect if you want headers or footers to print only on certain pages. For example, if you want headers and footers printed on every page, define a header code and a footer code at the top of the first page.

If you want a header to print from page 10 to the end of your document, define the header code at the top of page 10. If you want a footer to print from page 10 to page 20, define a footer code at the top of page 10, and discontinue the code on page 21.

You can also suppress header and footer codes for certain pages. This is helpful when you are creating a report with a cover letter. You do not want headers or footers on the cover letter. Suppress the headers and footers for page 1.

Change the default directory to the "a:\wpdocs" or to "c:\wpdocs." Then open your "report1.ltr" document.

To create a header in the "report1.ltr" document:

Click	at the beginning of the document	***Move***	*the insertion point to the beginning of the document*	**Move**	the insertion point to the beginning of the document
Choose	Layout	***Press***	*Alt*	**Press**	Alt + F9
Choose	Page	***Select***	*Layout*		
		Select	*Page*		

Your screen should look like Figure 11-1.

Figure 11-1

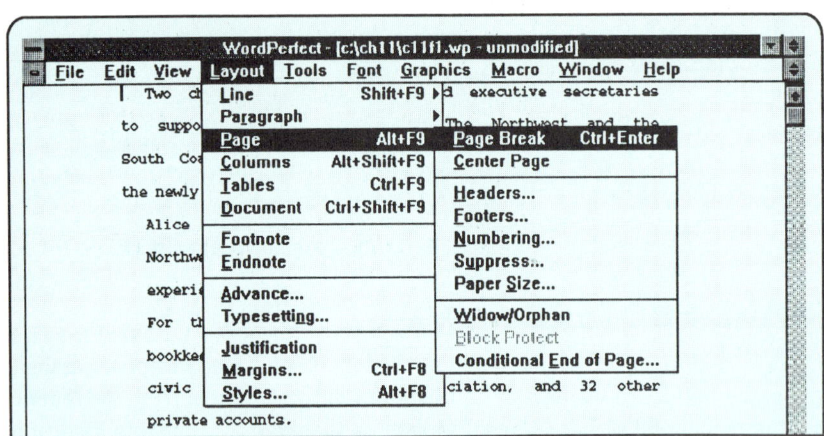

To select Headers:

Choose	Headers	***Select***	*Headers*	**Select**	Headers

You can create two different headers or footers on each page (Header A and Header B).

To select Header A:

Click	the Header A option button	***Press***	*Alt + A to select the Header A option button*	**Press**	Alt + A to select the Header A option button

To create the Header:

Click	the Create command button	***Press***	*↵Enter to select the Create command button*	**Press**	↵Enter to select the Create command button

The top portion of your screen should look like Figure 11-2.

Figure 11-2

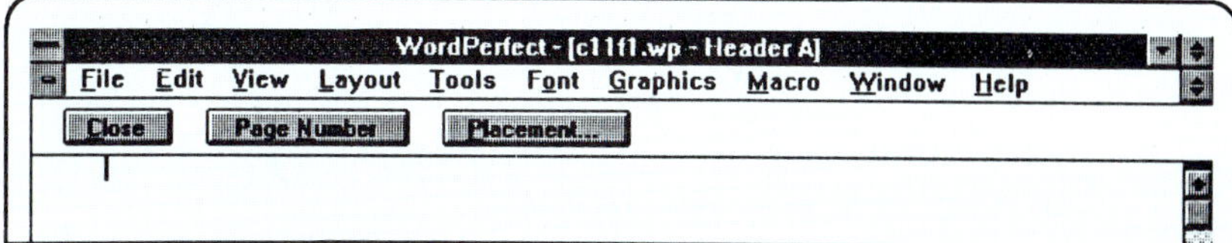

Notice that "Header A" appears in the title bar.

Type	State Financial Society	***Type***	*State Financial Society*	**Type**	State Financial Society
Press	↵Enter	***Press***	*↵Enter*	**Press**	↵Enter

The top portion of your screen should look like Figure 11-3.

Figure 11-3

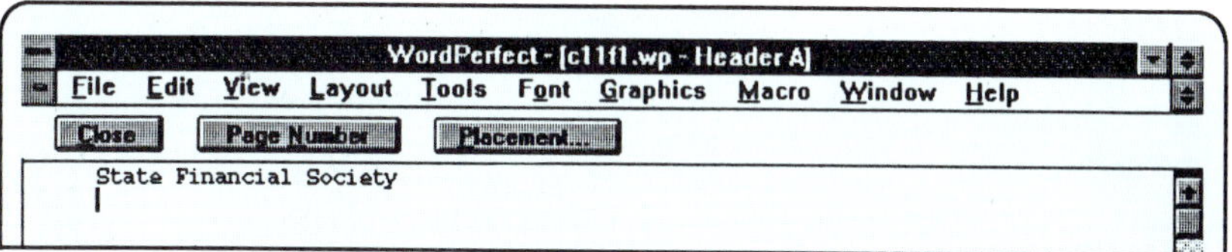

To place the header on every page:

Click	the Placement command button	***Press***	*Alt+P to select the Placement command button*	**Press**	Alt+P to select the Placement command button
Click	the Every Page option button	***Type***	*E to select the Every Page option button*	**Type**	E to select the Every Page option button
Click	the OK command button	***Press***	*↵Enter*	**Press**	↵Enter

To close the Header:

Click	the Close command button	***Press***	*Alt+C to select the Close command button*	**Press**	Alt+C to select the Close command button

You cannot see the headers or footers on the screen when you are editing your document. But you can see them if you use the Print Preview feature.

To view your Header:

Choose	File	***Press***	*Alt*	**Press**	Shift+F5
Choose	Print Preview	***Select***	*File*		
		Select	*Print Preview*		

To view the document at 100%:

Click	the 100% button on the Button Bar	***Press***	*Alt*		

Select	*View*
Select	*100%*

Your screen should look like Figure 11-4.

Figure 11-4

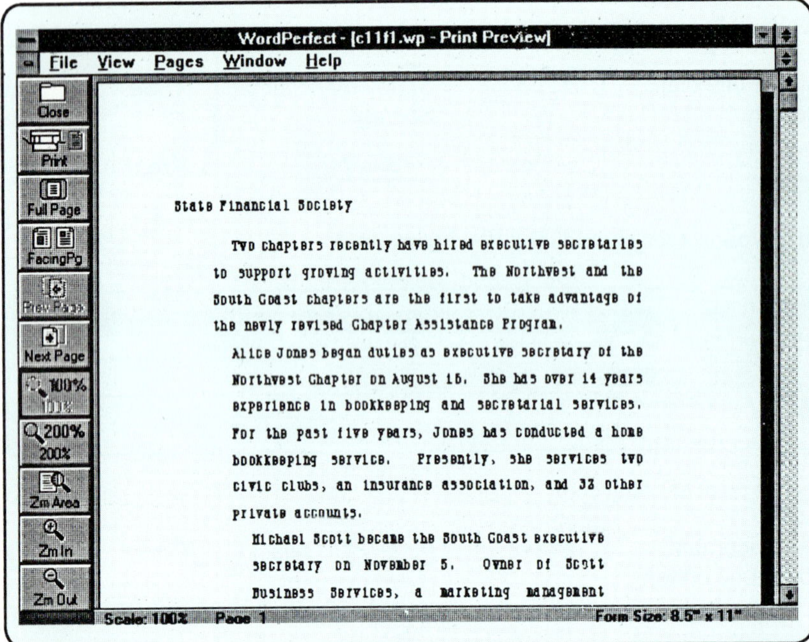

To return to your document:

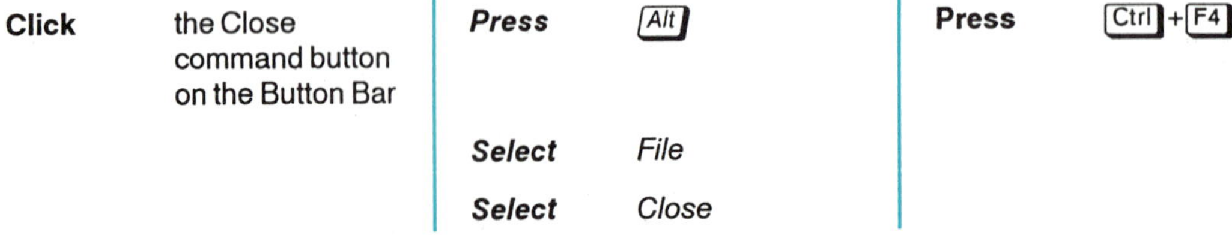

Click	the Close command button on the Button Bar	***Press***	Alt	**Press**	Ctrl+F4
		Select	*File*		
		Select	*Close*		

Save your document. Replace the old contents of the file with the current document.

■ PAGE NUMBERING

The Page Numbering feature lets you attach page numbers to each page in your document. The page numbers can be one of three formats: Arabic (1, 2, 3 ...), lowercase Roman numerals (i, ii, iii...), and uppercase Roman numerals (I, II, III...).

To insert a page number at the bottom center of every page:

Click	at the beginning of the document	***Move***	*the insertion point to the beginning of the document*	**Move**	the insertion point to the beginning of the document
Choose	Layout	***Press***	Alt	**Press**	Alt+F9
Choose	Page	***Select***	*Layout*		
		Select	*Page*		

To select Page Numbering:

Choose	Numbering	***Select***	*Numbering*	**Select**	Numbering

Your screen should look like Figure 11-5.

Figure 11-5

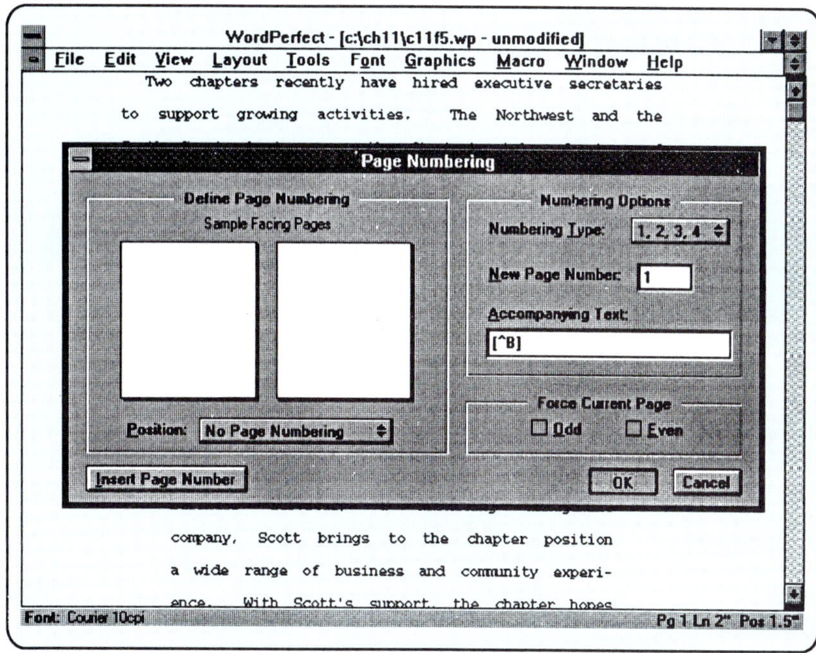

You must also tell WordPerfect where you would like the page numbers to appear on the page. WordPerfect shows you eight possible locations for the page number, and you must choose one.

To select the Page Number Position:

Click	the Position pop-up list button	***Press***	*Alt+P to select the Position pop-up list button*	**Press**	Alt+P to select the Position pop-up list button
Hold down	the mouse button to view the Position pop-up list	***Press***	*Alt+↑ to view the Position pop-up list*	**Press**	Alt+↑ to view the Position pop-up list

To have the page number appear at the bottom center of each page:

Select	the Bottom Center option	***Type***	*O*	**Type**	O

Your screen should look like Figure 11-6.

Figure 11-6

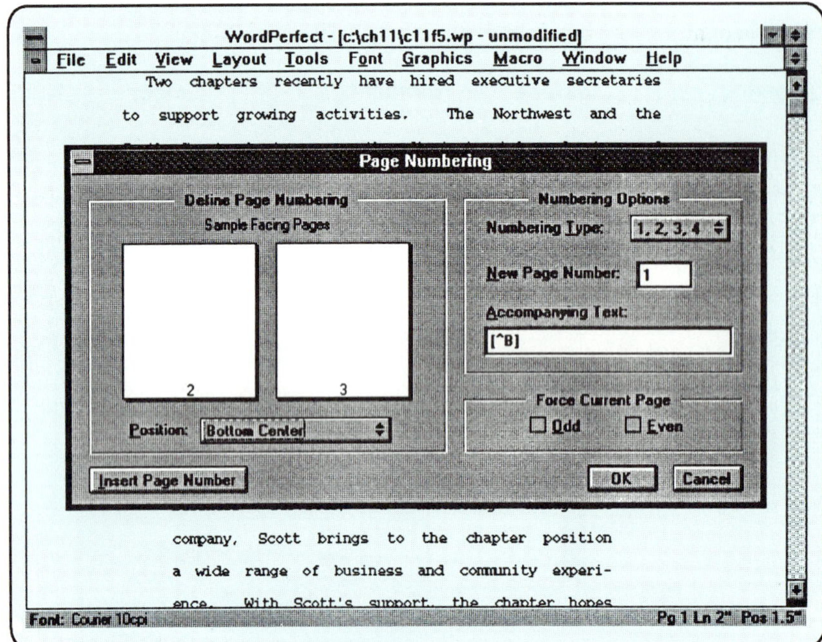

Notice the page numbers appear in the bottom center of the sample facing pages.

To return to your document:

Click
the OK command button
Press
Enter
Press
Enter

You do not need to worry about keeping the page numbers in order when you are editing your document. WordPerfect manages it all for you.

You cannot see the page numbers on the screen when you are editing your document. If you wish to see them, you must use the Print Preview feature.

To see the page number use the Print Preview feature. Use the scroll bars or the pointer-movement keys to scroll to the bottom of the page and view the page number. You also can click the Full Page button on the Button Bar or choose Full Page from the Page menu to view the page number.

Your screen should look like Figure 11-7.

Figure 11-7

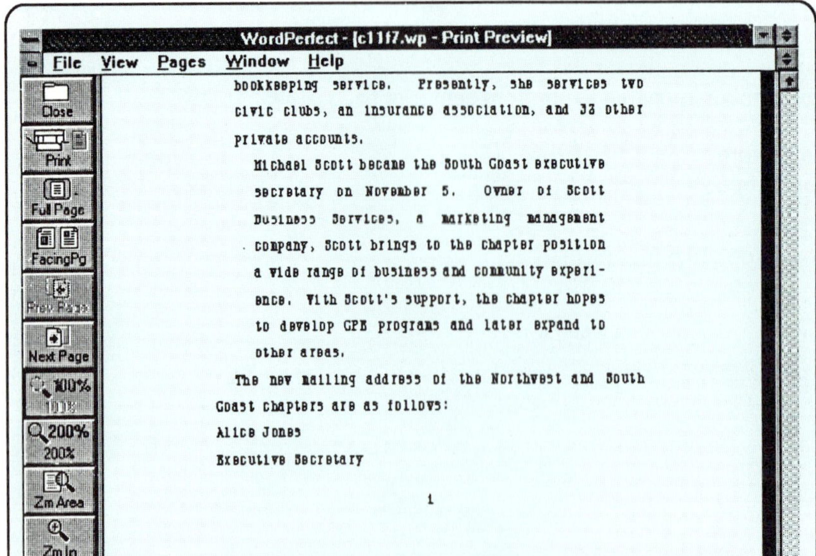

Return to your document and save your document using the filename "report2.ltr."

■ PAGE BREAKS

A page break is a code that tells WordPerfect where one page ends and another begins. There are two types of page breaks in WordPerfect: a soft page break ([SPg]) and a hard page break ([HPg]). The program inserts the soft page break. You insert the hard page break.

WordPerfect calculates when the text has filled a page and inserts a soft page break code into the document. You can identify a soft page break by a single line that appears in your document. As you make changes to your document, WordPerfect is always coordinating the position of the soft page break codes with each page of text. You have no control over a soft page break. These codes cannot be edited.

However, you do have control over hard page break codes. Whenever you want to force a page break in your document, you can place a hard page break into the text. You can identify a hard page break in your document by a double line that appears. You can easily delete this code as well.

To insert a hard page break:

Click	at the left margin of the fourth paragraph	***Move***	*the insertion point to the left margin of the fourth paragraph*	**Move**	the insertion point to the left margin of the fourth paragraph
Choose	Layout	***Press***	*Alt*	**Press**	Ctrl + ↵Enter
Choose	Page	***Select***	*Layout*		
Choose	Page Break	***Select***	*Page*		
		Select	*Page Break*		

Your screen should look like Figure 11-8.

Figure 11-8

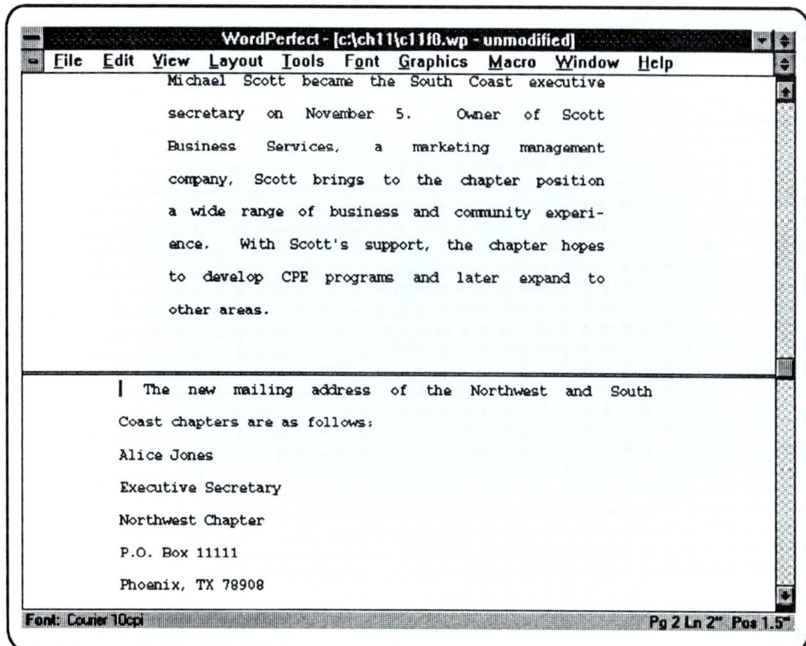

Notice that a double line appears above the fourth paragraph indicating a hard page break. The page indicator in the status bar now displays Pg 2.

To delete a hard page break using the Reveal Codes feature:

Click	above the double line	***Move***	*the insertion point above the double line*	**Move**	the insertion point above the double line
Choose	View	***Press***	*Alt*	**Press**	Alt+F3
Choose	Reveal Codes	***Select***	*View*	**Press**	Delete
Press	Delete	***Select***	*Reveal Codes*		
		Press	*Delete*		

To remove the document codes using the Reveal Codes feature:

Choose	View	***Press***	*Alt*	**Press**	Alt+F3
Choose	Reveal Codes	***Select***	*View*		
		Select	*Reveal Codes*		

You can also delete a hard page break from the normal editing screen. If you want to delete a hard page break from the normal editing screen:

Click	above the double line	***Move***	*the insertion point above the double line*	**Move**	the insertion point above the double line
Press	Delete	***Press***	*Delete*	**Press**	Delete

To insert a hard page break in the document again before you save it:

Click	at the left margin of the fourth paragraph	***Move***	*the insertion point to the left margin of the fourth paragraph*	**Move**	the insertion point to the left margin of the fourth paragraph
Choose	Layout	***Press***	*Alt*	**Press**	Ctrl+↵Enter
Choose	Page	***Select***	*Layout*		
Choose	Page Break	***Select***	*Page*		
		Select	*Page Break*		

Your screen should look like Figure 11-8.

Save your document. Replace the old contents of the file with the current document. Close the file.

EXERCISE 1

INSTRUCTIONS: Define the following terms:

1. Soft page break ______________________________
____
2. Hard page break ______________________________
____
3. Headers and footers ______________________________
____
4. Page break ______________________________
____
5. Page numbering ______________________________
____

EXERCISE 2

INSTRUCTIONS: Circle T if the statement is true and F if the statement is false.

T F 1. Headers appear at the bottom of a page, and footers appear at the top of a page.

T F 2. The Page Numbering feature allows you to select where you want the page number to appear on the page.

T F 3. You can add or delete soft page breaks.

T F 4. A hard page break is used when you want to force a page to end and another to begin at a certain location in a document.

T F 5. Once you define a header in your document, you cannot stop the header from printing on every page.

T F 6. If you look closely, you can see the tiny footer on the screen when you are editing your document.

T F 7. You can identify a soft page break by a single line that appears in the document.

T F 8. When using the Page Numbering feature, you can choose between Arabic, Egyptian, and Roman numerals.

T F 9. WordPerfect manages the order of the page numbers when you are editing your document.

T F 10. You cannot see a hard page break on the screen. You must use the Reveal Codes feature to see it.

EXERCISE 3

INSTRUCTIONS:

1. Create the following document.
2. Use the format settings listed below:

Initial Font:	Helvetica 12 pt (Z1A)
Margins:	
Left	1.0″
Right	1.0″
Top	1.0″
Bottom	0.5″
Left Margin tabs:	Use your own discretion.
Line spacing:	Single space questions. Double space between questions.

3. Double space the software types in question 3. Place 3 hard returns after "Other."
4. Copy the software types in question 3 to question 4.
5. Place 20 hard returns after question 7.
6. Place a page break after question 3, question 6, and question 8.
7. Place a page number at the bottom center of every page.
8. Place a Header A against the left margin. The first and only line should say "ABC CAN COMPANY."
9. Place a Header B against the left margin. The first line should be a hard return code and the second line should be the current date.
10. Place one footer against the left margin. It should say "Survey #1577."
11. Preview the document.
12. Save the document on a file using the name "ch11ex03."
13. Print the document.
14. Close the document

NAME: ID#:

JOB TITLE: EXT:

ADDRESS:

1. How long have you been with ABC Can Company?
2. How long have you been in your present job?
3. Indicate the number of hours you spend per week using the following types of software packages:

   Word Processing
   Spreadsheet Analysis
   Graphics
   Operating System
   Electronic Mail
   Calendaring
   Desktop Publishing
   Communications
   Database
   Other - please list below.

4. Circle the type of software package you would like to learn:
5. Do you know how to type?
6. Would you like to improve your typing skills by using a special software package that teaches typing?
7. Briefly describe two or three critical tasks in your position.
8. Are there specific applications of information technology that need to be considered in your work area? If so, then please specify them; otherwise, proceed to the next question.
9. Are there ways information technology can be used to improve your individual efficiency and effectiveness as an employee? If so, then please specify them.

EXERCISE 4

INSTRUCTIONS:

1. Open the document file "ch11ex03."
2. Place a hard return after "ABC CAN COMPANY" in Header A.
3. Delete Header B.

4. Edit Footer A to say "Survey: MP8-4."
5. Move the page number to the bottom right corner of every page.
6. Preview the document.
7. Save the document on a file using the name "ch11ex04."
8. Print the document.
9. Close the document.

EXERCISE 5

INSTRUCTIONS:

1. Create the following document. Prepare the document exactly as it appears.
2. Place the text "Chapter 11, Exercise 5 Solution" and a hard return in Header A.
3. Place a footer at the left side of the page. Use your first and last name, followed by a comma and the word "typist" i.e., "Ann Student, typist."
4. Page break after each paragraph.
5. Double space the entire document.
6. Number the pages at the top right corner of each page.
7. Suppress Header A, Footer A, and the page numbers on the first page.
8. Spell check the document.
9. Preview the document.
10. Save the document in a file using the name "ch11ex05."
11. Print the document.
12. Close the document.

I have been involved with three deliberations with the members of the Program Committee to make plans for the forthcoming yearly meeting to which all supervisors will be summoned. This is the result of the discussions held by the Executive Committee. Each of the meetings proved to be significantly interesting and profitable.

The unanimity of the group approved an outline including a variety of endeavors only two of which would be a prescribed talk by some persons considered outstanding in the field of supervision. The meeting will take place at our Northwest Facilities and last all day. Lunch will be catered by the Four French Chefs.

I want you to study the proposed program and let me know at your earliest convenience whether or not you think the suggestions are suitable.

At this meeting, we will map plans for the new products we plan to introduce to the public and the ad campaigns to accompany them.

EXERCISE 6

INSTRUCTIONS:

1. Create the following list of client names, addresses, and paragraph numbers to be used for form letters.
2. Page break after each paragraph listing. Do not page break after the last one.
3. Place a header entitled "Client letters."
4. Place page numbers at the top center of each page.
5. Use your name as the footer.
6. Spell check the document.
7. Preview the document.
8. Print the document.
9. Save the document in a file using the name "ch11ex06."
10. Close the document.

Bridgette O'Connor
84 Bristol Place
Farmingdale, NY 11735

Paragraphs 1, 3, 15, 14

Kent R. Burnham
582 San Ysidro Road
Shippenburg, PA 17257

Paragraphs 12, 10, 2

Pat Dickey-Olson
1026 Highmont Road
Cheney, WA 99004

Paragraphs 8, 5, 9, 13, 3

Jan Charbaulski
429 Sulgrave Drive
St. Louis, MO 63153

Paragraphs 16, 7, 11, 14, 9, 13

Claudis Orr
512 Mariposa Avenue
Rio Piedras, CA 90012

Paragraphs 6,2

EXERCISE 7

INSTRUCTIONS:

1. Open the document in file "ch11ex06."
2. Delete the page breaks, footer, header, and page numbering codes from the document.
3. Double space the entire document.
4. Preview the document.
5. Print the document.
6. Save the document in a file using the name "ch11ex07."
7. Close the document.

EXERCISE 8

INSTRUCTIONS:

1. Create the following document. Prepare the document exactly as it appears.
2. Use Full justification in the document.
3. Double space the document.
4. Place the header "Investment Paragraphs" in the document.
5. Number the pages at the bottom center of each page.
6. Use your name as the footer.
7. Place a page break after each paragraph.
8. Suppress the header on the first page.
9. Spell check the document.
10. Preview the document.
11. Print the document.
12. Save the document in a file using the name "ch11ex08."
13. Close the document.

This is an excellent time for you to take a close look at the income you are receiving from the tax exempt bonds in your portfolio. When you bought the bonds, did you buy fixed income or lifetime maturation?

Essentially any person can earn funds today, but only an informed person will know how to correctly invest her extra money to gain utmost safety of principal and gain the greatest growth in investment appreciation.

To many investors, earnings is the most important purpose of their investment program. It is their maintenance income, their retirement plan, their self-insurance for children and grandchildren, as well as their trust for charities.

CHAPTER TWELVE

TEXT ENHANCEMENTS

OBJECTIVES

In this chapter, you will learn to:

- Center new and existing text; remove centering
- Bold new and existing text; remove bolding
- Underline new and existing text; remove underlining

■ CHAPTER OVERVIEW

In this chapter, the processes for enhancing text are discussed. Centering, bolding, and underlining text capabilities are described and illustrated.

■ CENTERING TEXT

The Center feature allows you to place text in the center of a line in your document. The text can be centered between the left and right margins.

A [Center] code is placed before the text to be centered. To turn on the Center feature, select Center under the Line option from the Layout menu or press Shift+F7. After entering the text, press ↵Enter to end the Center feature. A Hard Return code [HRt] is placed in the document after the words to be centered.

New Text

Before starting this section, make sure you have a clear screen. Change the default directory to "a:\wpdocs" or to "c:\wpdocs."

To center the text "LIBRARY BULLETIN" between the left and right margins:

Click	at the beginning of the document	***Move***	*the insertion point to the beginning of the document*	**Move**	the mouse pointer to the beginning of the document
Choose	Layout	***Press***	*Alt*	**Press**	Shift+F7
Choose	Line	***Select***	*Layout*		

Choose	Center	***Select***	*Line*		
		Select	*Center*		

Notice that the insertion point is now in the center of the first line on your screen.

Type	LIBRARY BULLETIN	***Type***	*LIBRARY BULLETIN*	**Type**	LIBRARY BULLETIN

To end the Center feature:

Press	↵Enter	***Press***	*↵Enter*	**Press**	↵Enter

The top part of your screen should look like Figure 12-1.

Figure 12-1

To insert a blank line:

Press	↵Enter	***Press***	*↵Enter*	**Press**	↵Enter

Removing the Code

You can remove centering by deleting the Center code [Center] using the Reveal Codes feature.

Display the document codes using the Reveal Codes feature.

The lower portion of your screen should look like Figure 12-2.

Figure 12-2

To delete the [Center] code:

Click	on the [Center] code	***Move***	*the insertion point on the [Center] code*	**Move**	the insertion point on the [Center] code
Press	Delete	***Press***	*Delete*	**Press**	Delete

Note that the text is no longer centered.

Remove the document codes from your screen using the Reveal Codes feature.

Existing Text

To use the Center feature on existing text, select the text and then choose Center from the Line option under the Layout menu or press Shift+F7. Another way to center existing text is to move the insertion point before the first character you want centered, and then choose Center from the Line option under the Layout menu or press Shift+F7.

To center the existing text "LIBRARY BULLETIN":

Select	the text "LIBRARY BULLETIN"	***Select***	*the text "LIBRARY BULLETIN"*	**Select**	the text "LIBRARY BULLETIN"
Choose	Layout	***Press***	*Alt*	**Press**	Shift+F7
Choose	Line	***Select***	*Layout*		
Choose	Center	***Select***	*Line*		
		Select	*Center*		

Notice that the text "LIBRARY BULLETIN" is centered again.

You can also use the Ruler to center text by selecting the text and choosing the Center option from the Justification button on the Ruler.

BOLDING TEXT

The Bold feature lets you print text that is darker than the rest so that it will attract attention on the page. When you use the Bold feature, WordPerfect inserts a [Bold On] and a [Bold Off] code around the selected text in your document.

New Text

To use the Bold feature:

Click	at the bottom of the document	***Move***	*the insertion point to the bottom of the document*	**Move**	the insertion point to the bottom of the document
Choose	Font	***Press***	*Alt*	**Press**	Ctrl+B
Choose	Bold	***Select***	*Font*	**Type**	New Additions to the Research Library:
Type	New Additions to the Research Library:	***Select***	*Bold*		
		Type	*New Additions to the Research Library:*		

The top part of your screen should look like Figure 12-3.

Figure 12-3

Notice the change in the appearance of the Font indicator on the status bar. It is darker since bold is activated.

To exit the Bold feature:

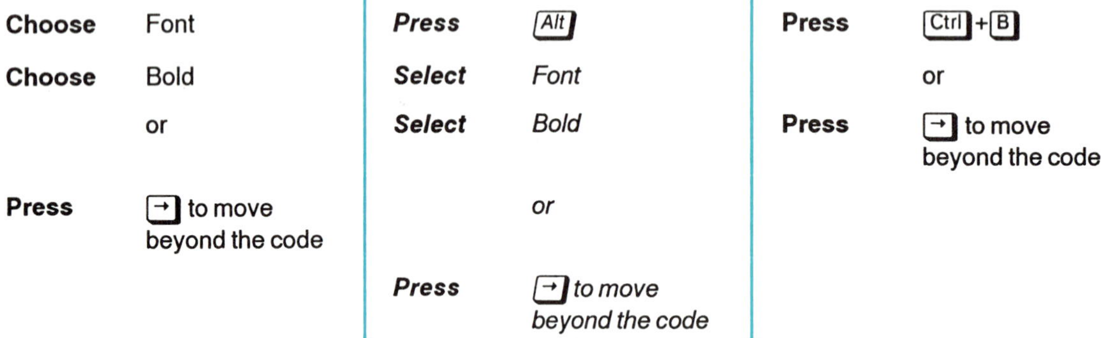

Choose	Font	***Press***	*Alt*	**Press**	Ctrl+B
Choose	Bold	***Select***	*Font*		or
	or	***Select***	*Bold*	**Press**	→ to move beyond the code
Press	→ to move beyond the code		*or*		
		Press	*→ to move beyond the code*		

Notice the change in the appearance of the Font indicator on the status bar. The intensity has changed back to normal, since bold is no longer active.

To insert two blank lines:

Press	↵Enter twice	***Press***	*↵Enter twice*	**Press**	↵Enter twice

Removing the Code

As indicated earlier, WordPerfect inserts a [Bold On] and [Bold Off] code in your document. You can remove bold enhancement from the text by deleting the [Bold On] or [Bold Off] code using the Reveal Codes feature.

Display the document codes using the Reveal Codes feature.

The bottom part of your screen should look like Figure 12-4.

Figure 12-4

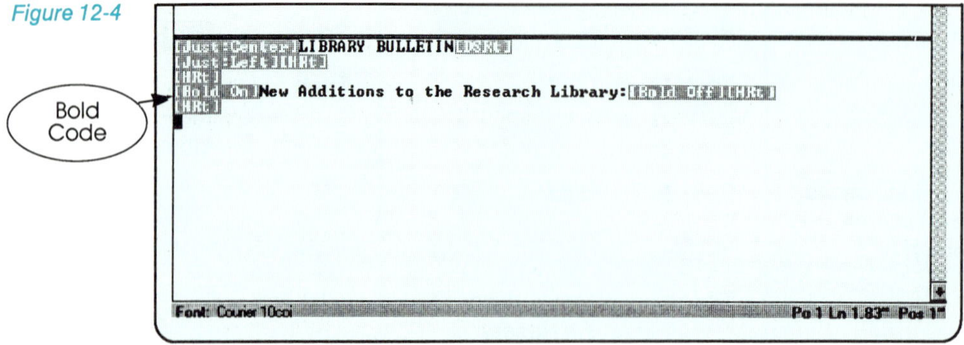

To remove the Bold feature:

Click	on the [Bold On] code	***Move***	*the insertion point on the [Bold On] code*	**Move**	the insertion point on the [Bold On] code
Press	Delete	***Press***	*Delete*	**Press**	Delete

Notice that the text is no longer bold.

Remove the document codes from your screen using the Reveal Codes feature.

Existing Text

To use the Bold feature on existing text, you must first select the text and then choose Bold from the Font menu or press Ctrl+B.

To illustrate the process for using the Bold feature on existing text:

Select	the text "New Additions to the Research Library:"	***Select***	*the text "New Additions to the Research Library:"*	**Select**	the text "New Additions to the Research Library:"

To bold the text:

Choose	Font	***Press***	*Alt*	**Press**	Ctrl+B
Choose	Bold	***Select***	*Font*		
		Select	*Bold*		

The text "New Additions to the Research Library" is now bold again.

UNDERLINING TEXT

The Underline feature allows you to emphasize text by placing a line under the text. You can choose between underlining just the words or the words with the spaces between them. The default is to underline words with the spaces.

When you use the Underline feature, an [Und On] code is inserted at the front of the text and an [Und Off] code is inserted at the end of the underlined text in your document.

New Text

Move the insertion point to the bottom of the document and type the last line displayed in Figure 12-5.

Figure 12-5

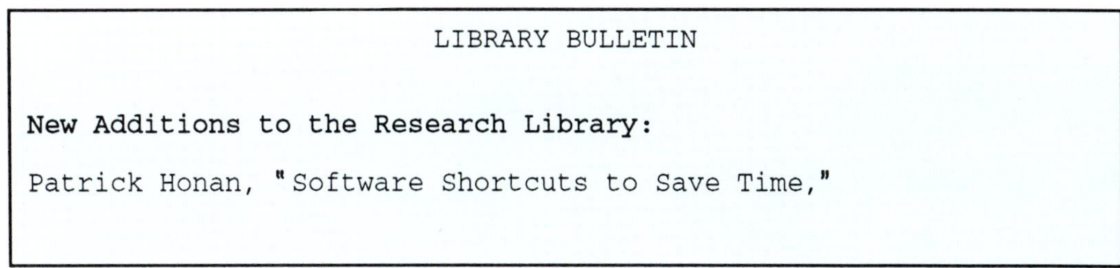
LIBRARY BULLETIN

New Additions to the Research Library:

Patrick Honan, "Software Shortcuts to Save Time,"

To use the Underline feature:

Choose	Font	***Press***	*Alt*	**Press**	Ctrl+U
Choose	Underline	***Select***	*Font*		
		Select	*Underline*		

Notice the change in the appearance of the Font indicator on the status bar. An underline appears to show that the Underline feature is active.

Type	Personal Computing	***Type***	*Personal Computing*	**Type**	Personal Computing

Your screen should look like Figure 12-6.

Figure 12-6

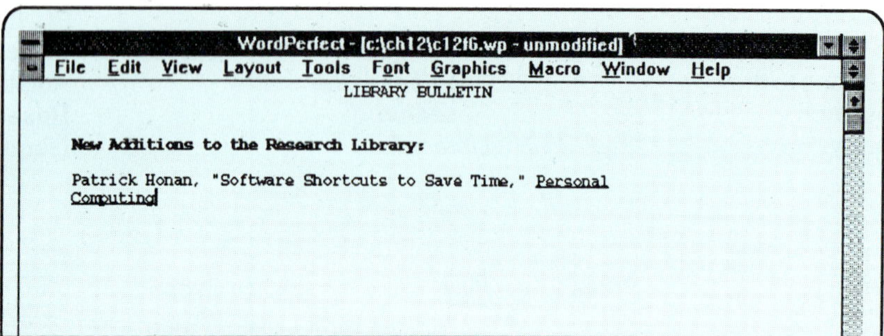

To stop using the Underline feature:

Choose	Font	***Press***	*Alt*	**Press**	Ctrl+U
Choose	Underline	***Select***	*Font*		or
	or	***Select***	*Underline*	**Press**	→ to move beyond the code
Press	→ to move beyond the code		*or*		
		Press	*→ to move beyond the code*		

Notice the change in the appearance of the Font indicator on the status bar. The Underline feature is no longer active.

Continue typing the remainder of the document as displayed in Figure 12-7.

Figure 12-7

LIBRARY BULLETIN

New Additions to the Research Library:

Patrick Honan, "Software Shortcuts to Save Time," Personal Computing (December 1989) pp. 111-114.

Removing the Code

As mentioned earlier, WordPerfect inserts [Und On] and [Und Off] codes around the underlined text in your document.

You can remove underlining by deleting the [Und On] or [Und Off] code using the Reveal Codes feature.

View the document codes using the Reveal Codes feature.

The bottom part of your screen should look like Figure 12-8.

Figure 12-8

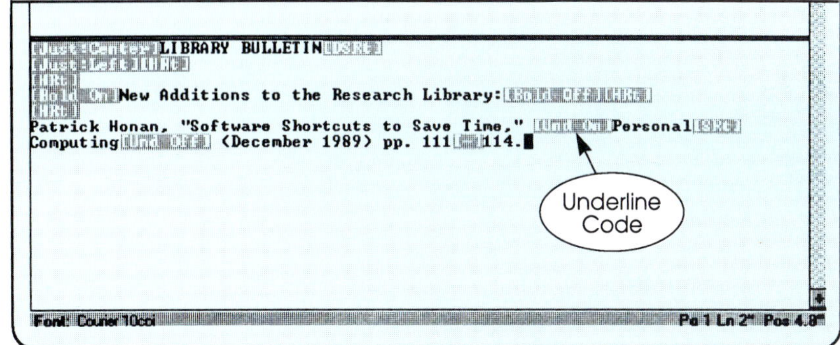

To remove the underlining:

Click	on the [Und On] code	***Move***	*the insertion point on the [Und On] code*	**Move**	the insertion point on the [Und On] code
Press	[Delete]	***Press***	*[Delete]*	**Press**	[Delete]

The text is no longer underlined.

Existing Text

To underline existing text, you must first select the text and then choose Underline from the Font menu or press [Ctrl]+[U].

To underline the text:

Select	the text "Personal Computing"	***Select***	*the text "Personal Computing"*	**Select**	the text "Personal Computing"
Choose	Font	***Press***	*[Alt]*	**Press**	[Ctrl]+[U]
Choose	Underline	***Select***	*Font*		
		Select	*Underline*		

The text "Personal Computing" is underlined again.

Remove the document codes from your screen using the Reveal Codes feature.

Finish typing the text displayed in Figure 12-9.

Figure 12-9

LIBRARY BULLETIN

New Additions to the Research Library:

Patrick Honan, "Software Shortcuts to Save Time," Personal Computing (December 1989) pp. 111-114.

Eric Knorr, "Software's Next Wave: Putting the User First," PC World (January 1990) pp. 134-143.

Bruce Brown and Kellyn Betts, "Input Devices Wanted: More Than Just a Replacement," PC Magazine (December 12, 1989) pp. 225-251.

Whenever you desire, please help yourself to these articles in the Research Library. There is only one requirement: **Please remember to return them to the library.**

Save the document as "library.ltr." Close the document.

EXERCISE 1

INSTRUCTIONS: Define the following terms:

1. Bold ____________________

   ____

2. Center ____________________

   ____

3. Underline ____________________

   ____

EXERCISE 2

INSTRUCTIONS: Circle T if the statement is true and F if the statement is false.

T F 1. You can center text between the margins.

T F 2. Pressing [↵Enter] ends centering.

T	F	3.	You can remove all text enhancements by deleting the appropriate code in Reveal Codes.
T	F	4.	The Bold feature allows you to create text that prints lighter than the rest of the text.
T	F	5.	The Font indicator on the status bar changes when you use the bold feature.
T	F	6.	You can remove bolding by selecting the text.
T	F	7.	Press Alt + F7 to center text.
T	F	8.	WordPerfect defaults to underlining words and spaces.
T	F	9.	The line number on the status bar changes when you use the Underline feature.
T	F	10.	Pressing ↵Enter ends bolding.

EXERCISE 3

INSTRUCTIONS:

1. Create the following document.
2. Center the text "LIBRARY ANNOUNCEMENT."
3. Bold the text "New Additions to the Reference Library:."
4. Underline the titles of each book.
5. Spell check your document.
6. Preview the document.
7. Save the document on a file using the name "ch12ex03."
8. Close the document.

LIBRARY ANNOUNCEMENT

New Additions to the Reference Library:

Mastering and Using WordPerfect for Windows, by H. Albert Napier and Philip J. Judd.

Mastering and Using Lotus 1-2-3 Release 3.0, by H. Albert Napier and Philip J. Judd.

Mastering and Using Lotus 1-2-3 Release 2.3, by H. Albert Napier and Philip J. Judd.

EXERCISE 4

INSTRUCTIONS:

1. Open the "ch12ex03" document.
2. Remove the center, bold, and underline codes.
3. Save the document on a file using the name "ch12ex04."
4. Close the document.

EXERCISE 5

INSTRUCTIONS:

1. Create the following document.
2. Center the last line of the notice.
3. Underline the sentence beginning with "All halls and labs."
4. Bold the words "Mr. Michael Nguyen" and "ext. 5622."
5. Preview the document.
6. Save the document on a file using the name "ch12ex05."
7. Print the document.
8. Close the document.

```
                    DANGER! DANGER! DANGER!

                  ONLY AUTHORIZED PERSONNEL

                MAY PROCEED BEYOND THIS POINT


This area is restricted due to sensitive chemical experiments in
process.  You must have security clearance level 7 or higher to
enter this level.  All halls and labs are monitored by surveillance
cameras and security guards.  If you require assistance, then
please contact Mr. Michael Nguyen at ext. 5622.


ABC Can Company, R&D Division, Policy #125
```

EXERCISE 6

INSTRUCTIONS:

1. Create the following document.
2. Spell check the document and make the necessary corrections.
3. Use Full justification in the document.

4. Add the title "WORDPERFECT FOR WINDOWS AND OTHER SOFTWARE PACKAGES." Center and bold the title. Place two blank lines between the title and the text.
5. Bold the words "WordPerfect for Windows" in the entire document.
6. Underline every sentence that refers to "WordPerfect for Windows."
7. Preview the document.
8. Save the document on a file using the name "ch12ex06."
9. Print the document.
10. Close the document

There are thousands of software packages available for the personal computer. These packages can be divided into many different categories. Three of these categories are word processing, spreadsheets and graphics. WordPerfect for Windows can communicate closely with packages in each of these categories.

Word processing software allows you to create and print documents. The word processing packages on the market today have varying levels of sophistication. Of course, WordPerfect for Windows is one of the most sophisticated word processors available. WordPerfect for Windows can also read documents created in other word processors. It uses the special Convert Program feature to change a non-WordPerfect for Windows document into one that it can edit.

Spreadsheets are tables of data usually filled with numbers. All accountants use spreadsheets, and nearly all accountants use a spreadsheet software program. With spreadsheet software, you can easily compute numbers and organize massive amounts of numeric information. WordPerfect for Windows can **import or receive spreadsheets** from the most popular spreadsheet packages directly into a document. WordPerfect for Windows can also **link into a spreadsheet** so that whenever a number changes in the spreadsheet, it automatically changes in the document.

Graphics software is used to create graphic images or pictures on your computer. Since WordPerfect for Windows is an advanced word processing package, it can **combine text and graphic images** created in many different graphics packages into one document.

EXERCISE 7

INSTRUCTIONS:

1. Open the document file "ch12ex06."
2. Move the title to the left margin. Make sure the title is not bold.
3. Remove the underlines.
4. Make the words "WordPerfect for Windows" normal type in the entire document.
5. Preview the document.

6. Save the document on a file using the name "ch12ex07."
7. Print the document.
8. Close the document.

EXERCISE 8

INSTRUCTIONS:

1. Create the following document.
2. Use Full justification in the document.
3. Center, bold, and underline the titles and words as indicated.
4. Use a 2″ top margin.
5. Spell check the document.
6. Preview the document.
7. Print the document.
8. Save the document in a file using the name "ch12ex08."
9. Close the document.

HARPER COLLEGE

PRESENTS

BUSINESS INFORMATION MANAGEMENT

A Listing of Fall Courses

BIM 170 <u>Intro to Information Applications and Technologies</u>

Provides an overview of business information applications -- technology, people, and procedures within organizational and environmental contexts.

BIM 175 <u>Enterprise-Wide Information Analysis</u>

Collecting and analyzing organizational needs, utilizing planning tools, and collecting data for assessing the impact of change upon work groups and teams.

BIM 250 <u>Multi-Media Business Presentations</u>

Effective transparencies, slides, and computer presentations using a Storyboard. This course will be taught by an outstanding educational television producer.

Sign Up Now!

For more information, contact:

<u>COORDINATOR, BUSINESS INFORMATION MANAGEMENT</u>

<u>HARPER COLLEGE</u>

EXERCISE 9

INSTRUCTIONS:

1. Create the following document.
2. Use Full justification in the document.
3. Bold, underline, and center text as indicated.
4. Set the top and bottom margins to 1.5″.
5. Spell check the document.
6. Preview the document.
7. Print the document.
8. Save the document in a file using the name "ch12ex09."
9. Close the document.

ANNOUNCING A COMMONSENSE SOLUTION TO TODAY'S HEALTH INSURANCE COSTS: THE $5,000,000 LIFETIME MEDICAL BENEFIT

Dear Anne Mohr:

I think you will find this letter very interesting, since it explains how you will be able to reduce your health insurance costs <u>and save yourself hundreds of dollars a year!</u>

NOW, HERE'S HOW THE MAJOR MEDICAL PLAN CAN SAVE YOU MONEY...

You select the amount of deductible you would like from the enclosed table ($250, $500, $1,000). Our plan will pay up to 90% of all eligible costs up to $12,000. If your bill is in excess of $12,000, the plan will pay 100% of all eligible costs for the remainder of the one year to a maximum lifetime benefit of $5,000,000.

<u>You should compare this plan with other group plans or any health insurance policy you have now or may be considering.</u>

A higher deductible will mean you may have to spend more money at the beginning of your illness, but this will also result in significant premium savings.

IT'S EASY TO APPLY

<u>Return the enclosed card with your Application so it can be personally embossed.</u> It provides answers to basic questions the medical team needs before treating you.

Most sincerely yours,

Robert Hardig
Managing Director

EXERCISE 10

INSTRUCTIONS:

1. Open document "ch12ex09."
2. Underline the top two centered lines that are in bold.
3. Remove the underline from the text at the end of the first paragraph. Bold the text.
4. Remove the bold from the entire line that begins "NOW, HERE'S HOW. . .."
5. Bold all the amounts of money in the second paragraph.
6. Remove the underline on the centered lines following the second paragraph.
7. Underline the entire third paragraph that starts with "A higher deductible. . .."
8. Print the document.
9. Save the document in a file using the name "ch12ex10."
10. Close the document.

CHAPTER THIRTEEN

ADDITIONAL TEXT ENHANCEMENTS

OBJECTIVES

In this chapter, you will learn to:

- Flush right new and existing text; remove flush right
- Superscript and subscript new and existing text; remove superscripts and subscripts
- Change the font size of new and existing text; remove font sizes
- Change the font appearance of new and existing text; remove font appearances

■ CHAPTER OVERVIEW

In this chapter, additional text enhancements are discussed. The Flush Right feature is introduced. Procedures for inserting superscripts and subscripts as well as changing font size and appearance are discussed.

■ FLUSH RIGHT

With the Flush Right feature, you can quickly adjust text so that it is placed against the right margin. The Flush Right feature can be used to adjust a word, part of a line, or a group of lines.

The Flush Right feature is activated by choosing Flush Right from the Line option under the Layout menu or by pressing Alt+F7. A Flush Right code [Flsh Rgt] is placed before the adjusted text. Flush Right is turned off by pressing ↵Enter. A Hard Return code [HRt] is inserted at the end of the line and the insertion point is placed at the beginning of the next line.

New Text

Before starting this section, change the default directory to "a:\wpdocs" or to "c:\wpdocs." Then open your "library.ltr" document.

To insert the date at the top of the page at the right margin:

Click	at the left margin at the top of the document	***Move***	*the insertion point to the left margin at the top of the document*	**Move**	the insertion point to the left margin at the top of the document

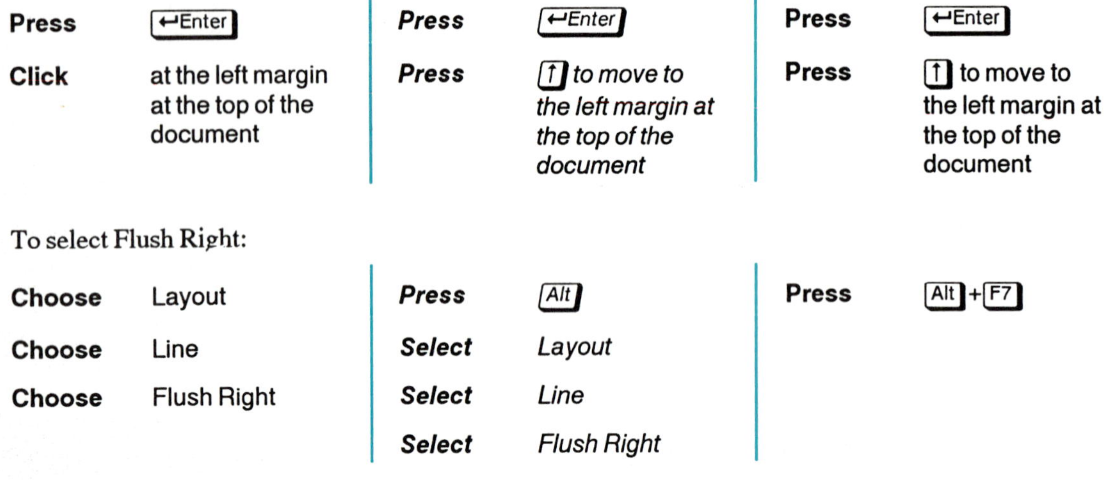

Press	↵Enter	***Press***	*↵Enter*	**Press**	↵Enter
Click	at the left margin at the top of the document	***Press***	*↑ to move to the left margin at the top of the document*	**Press**	↑ to move to the left margin at the top of the document

To select Flush Right:

Choose	Layout	***Press***	*Alt*	**Press**	Alt+F7
Choose	Line	***Select***	*Layout*		
Choose	Flush Right	***Select***	*Line*		
		Select	*Flush Right*		

Notice the insertion point moves to the right margin.

To insert the current date as text:

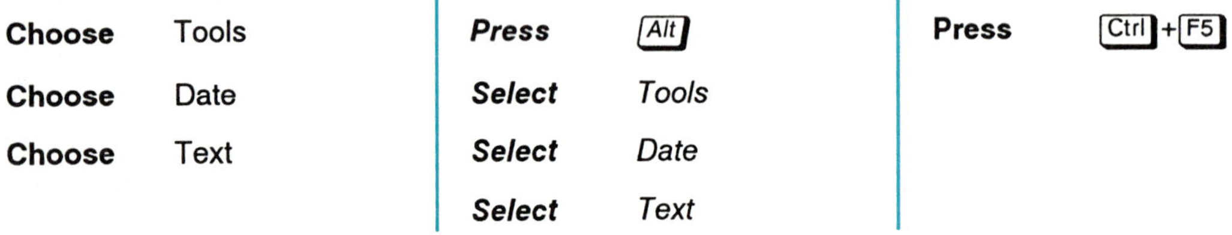

Choose	Tools	***Press***	*Alt*	**Press**	Ctrl+F5
Choose	Date	***Select***	*Tools*		
Choose	Text	***Select***	*Date*		
		Select	*Text*		

Except for a different date, the top part of your screen should look like Figure 13-1.

Figure 13-1

To end the Flush Right feature:

Press	↵Enter	***Press***	*↵Enter*	**Press**	↵Enter

Removing the Code

You can remove the Flush Right feature by deleting the Flush Right code [Flsh Rgt]. To remove the Flush Right code, use the Reveal Codes feature to display the document codes on your screen. The [Flsh Rgt] code is the first code shown in the Reveal Codes section of the screen.

The bottom portion of your screen should look like Figure 13-2.

Figure 13-2

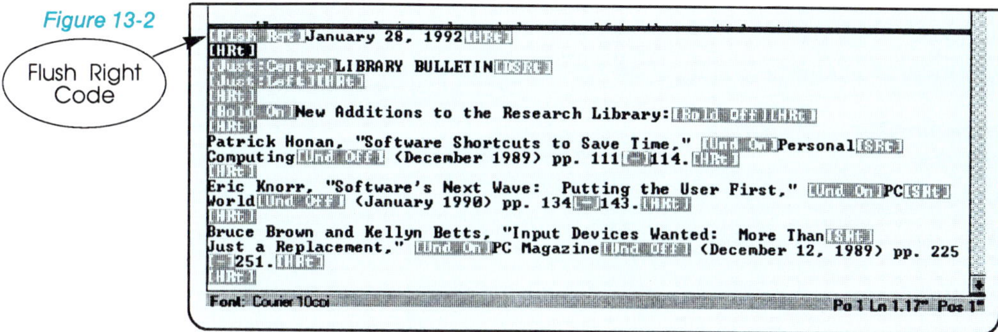

To delete the [Flsh Rgt] code:

Click	on the [Flsh Rgt] code	***Move***	*the insertion point on the [Flsh Rgt] code*	**Move**	the insertion point on the [Flsh Rgt] code
Press	Delete	***Press***	*Delete*	**Press**	Delete

The [Flsh Rgt] code has been deleted. The date is now flush to the left which is the default setting.

Remove the document codes from your screen using the Reveal Codes feature.

Existing Text

To align existing text flush against the right margin, select the text and then choose the Flush Right feature or press Alt+F7. Another way to align existing text flush against the right margin is to move the insertion point before the first character you want flush right, and then choose the Flush Right feature or press Alt+F7.

To Flush Right the current date:

Select	the date text	***Select***	*the date text*	**Select**	the date text
Choose	Layout	***Press***	*Alt*	**Press**	Alt+F7
Choose	Line	***Select***	*Layout*		
Choose	Flush Right	***Select***	*Line*		
		Select	*Flush Right*		

The date is now flush to the right margin again. Deselect the text by clicking on the document or moving the insertion point. Save the document as "library.ltr."

■ SUPERSCRIPTS AND SUBSCRIPTS

The Superscript feature places text slightly above a line of normal printed text. The Subscript feature places text slightly below a line of normal printed text. This is ^{superscript}, and this is $_{\text{subscript}}$.

WordPerfect inserts a [Suprscpt On] and [Suprscpt Off] code around the text that is raised by the Superscript feature. A [Subscpt On] and [Subscpt Off] code is placed around the text that is lowered by the Subscript feature.

New Text

To Superscript the number 1 at the beginning of the first magazine article:

Click	before the "P" in Patrick	***Move***	*the insertion point before the "P" in Patrick*
Choose	Font	***Press***	*Alt*
Choose	Superscript	***Select***	*Font*
Type	1	***Select***	*Superscript*
		Type	*1*

The top part of your screen should look like Figure 13-3.

Figure 13-3

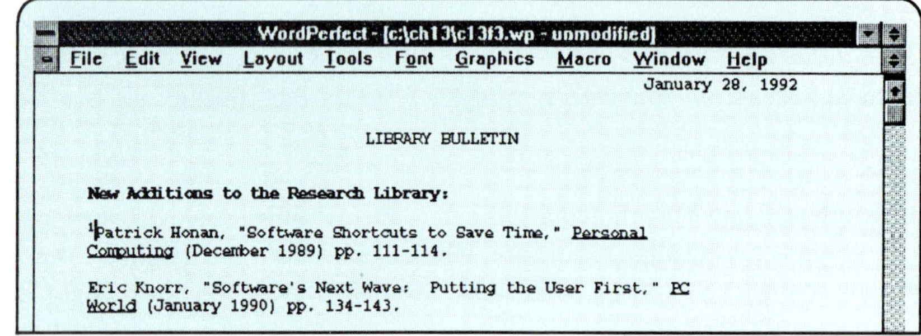

To stop using the Superscript feature:

Choose	Font	***Press***	*Alt*
Choose	Superscript	***Select***	*Font*
	or	***Select***	*Superscript*
Choose	Font		*or*
Choose	Normal	***Press***	*Alt*
	or	***Select***	*Font*
Press	→ to move beyond the code	***Select***	*Normal*
			or
		Press	*→ to move beyond the code*

To Subscript the number 2 at the beginning of the second magazine article:

Click	before the "E" in Eric	***Move***	*the insertion point before the "E" in Eric*

Choose	Font	***Press***	*Alt*
Choose	Subscript	***Select***	*Font*
Type	2	***Select***	*Subscript*
		Type	*2*

The top part of your screen should look like Figure 13-4.

Figure 13-4

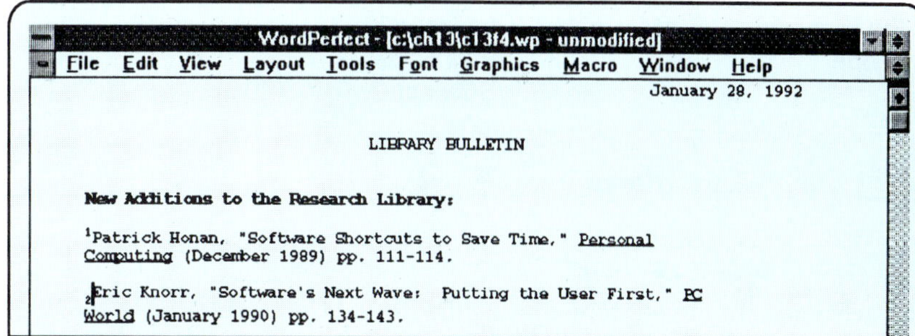

To stop using the Subscript feature:

Choose	Font	***Press***	*Alt*
Choose	Subscript	***Select***	*Font*
	or	***Select***	*Subscript*
Choose	Font		*or*
Choose	Normal	***Press***	*Alt*
	or	***Select***	*Font*
Press	→ to move beyond the code	***Select***	*Normal*
			or
		Press	*→ to move beyond the code*

Removing the Code

You can remove superscripts and subscripts by deleting the [Suprscpt] and [Subscript] codes. To remove the Superscript and Subscript codes, display the document codes on your screen using the Reveal Codes feature.

The bottom portion of your screen should look like Figure 13-5.

Figure 13-5

To delete the [Suprscpt] code:

Click	on the [Suprscpt On] code	***Move***	*the insertion point on the [Suprscpt On] code*
Press	Delete	***Press***	Delete

To delete the [Subscpt] code:

Click	on the [Subscpt On] code	***Move***	*the insertion point on the [Subscpt On] code*
Press	Delete	***Press***	Delete

The superscript and subscript codes no longer appear on your screen.

Remove the document codes from your screen using the Reveal Codes feature.

Existing Text

To add superscripts and subscripts to existing text, you must first select the text and then choose superscript or subscript.

To Superscript the number "1" next to Patrick:

Select	the "1" before Patrick	***Select***	*the "1" before Patrick*
Choose	Font	***Press***	Alt
Choose	Superscript	***Select***	*Font*
		Select	*Superscript*

To subscript the number "2" next to Eric:

Select	the "2" before Eric	***Select***	*the "2" before Eric*
Choose	Font	***Press***	Alt
Choose	Subscript	***Select***	*Font*
		Select	*Subscript*

The superscript and subscript should now appear in your document again. Deselect the "2" by clicking in the document area or moving the insertion point.

Save the document as "library.ltr."

■ CHANGING FONT SIZE

You can use the Font Size feature to change the size of printed characters and the spacing between characters on a line. This feature can be used as an alternative to changing the Font every time you want to place text in a new font size.

The Font Size selections are Fine, Small, Large, Very Large, or Extra Large. These selections are available by choosing the Size option from the Font menu or by pressing [Ctrl]+[S].

The program adjusts the point sizes of the Fine, Small, Large, Very Large, and Extra Large font sizes depending on the setting for the initial font. The font sizes available to you are limited to the fonts contained in your printer.

For example, if your printer contains Times Roman 10 point and Times Roman 12 point, your document will print only in those two sizes. If your initial font is Times Roman 12 point, then selecting a Very Large Font Size will still result in Times Roman 12 point text.

Additional information on printing is included in Chapter 14.

New Text

To show the process of changing the Font Size:

Click	at the left margin at the beginning of the document	***Move***	*the insertion point to the left margin at the beginning of the document*	**Move**	the insertion point to the left margin at the beginning of the document

To insert a blank line:

Press	[↵Enter]	***Press***	*[↵Enter]*	**Press**	[↵Enter]

To change the Font Size to very large:

Click	at the beginning of the document	***Press***	[↑]	**Press**	[↑]
Choose	Font	***Press***	[Alt]	**Press**	[Ctrl]+[S]
Choose	Size	***Select***	*Font*	**Select**	Very Large
Choose	Very Large	***Select***	*Size*	**Type**	NAPIER & JUDD, INC.
Type	NAPIER & JUDD, INC.	***Select***	*Very Large*		
		Type	*NAPIER & JUDD, INC.*		

To stop using the Font Size option:

Choose	Font	***Press***	[Alt]	**Press**	[Ctrl]+[N]
Choose	Normal	***Select***	*Font*		or
	or	***Select***	*Normal*	**Press**	[→] to move beyond the code
Press	[→] to move beyond the code		*or*		
		Press	*[→] to move beyond the code*		

The top portion of your screen should look like Figure 13-6.

Figure 13-6

Removing the Code

You can remove the Font Size code by deleting the [Vry Large On] or [Vry Large Off] code. To remove the Very Large code, display the document codes on your screen using the Reveal Codes feature.

The bottom section of your screen should look like Figure 13-7.

Figure 13-7

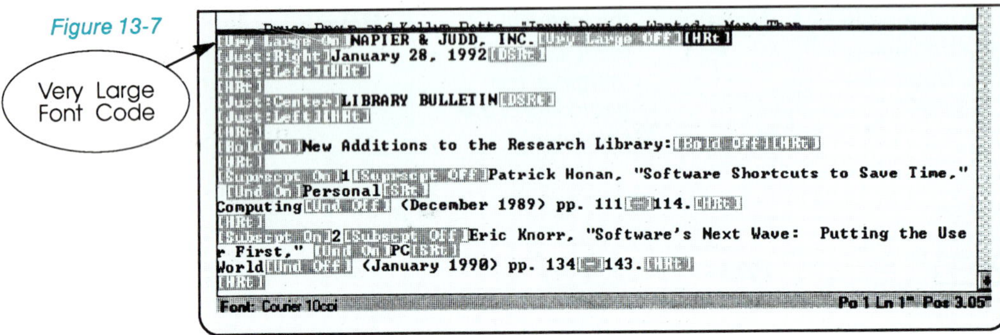

To delete the [Vry Large] code:

Click	on the [Vry Large On] code	***Move***	*the insertion point on the [Vry Large On] code*	**Move**	the insertion point on the [Vry Large On] code
Press	Delete	***Press***	*Delete*	**Press**	Delete

The [Vry Large] code has been deleted. Remove the document codes from your screen using the Reveal Codes feature.

Existing Text

To change the Font Size of existing text, you must first select the text and then choose the Font Size or press Ctrl+S.

To change the Font Size of "NAPIER & JUDD, INC.":

Select	the text "NAPIER & JUDD, INC."	***Select***	*the text "NAPIER & JUDD, INC."*	**Select**	the text "NAPIER & JUDD, INC."
Choose	Font	***Press***	*Alt*	**Press**	Ctrl+S
Choose	Size	***Select***	*Font*	**Select**	Very Large
Choose	Very Large	***Select***	*Size*		
		Select	*Very Large*		

The text "NAPIER & JUDD, INC." appears using the Very Large option. Deselect the text by clicking on the document or moving the insertion point.

Save the document as "library.ltr."

■ CHANGING FONT APPEARANCE

With the Font feature, you can change the font, point size, appearance, or size of text. You can change the appearance of text to italics, bold, underline, double underline, small caps, strikeout, outline, shadow, or redline. You can activate a font appearance by choosing Font from the Font menu or by pressing F9.

Some appearance features can be selected directly from the Font menu. For example, you can select bold, italic, underline, double underline, redline, and strikeout without accessing the Font dialog box. However, to view all of the font appearance features, you should use the Font dialog box.

New Text

To show the process of changing the Font Appearance:

Click	at the bottom of the document	***Move***	*the insertion point to the bottom of the document*	**Move**	the insertion point to the bottom of the document
Press	Spacebar twice	***Press***	*Spacebar twice*	**Press**	Spacebar twice

To access the Font dialog box:

Choose	Font	***Press***	*Alt*	**Press**	F9
Choose	Font	***Select***	*Font*		
		Select	*Font*		

Your screen should look like Figure 13-8.

Figure 13-8

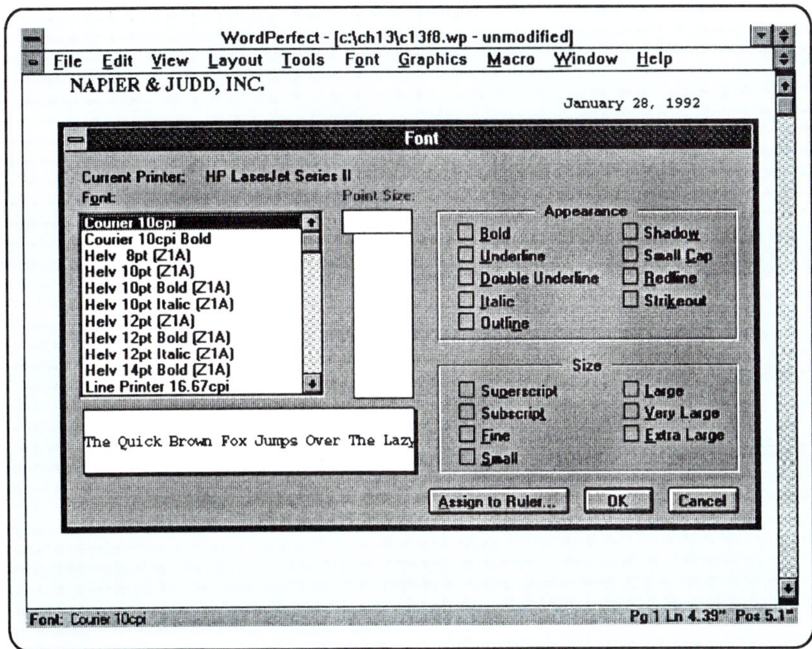

To change the Font Appearance to italic:

Click	the Italic check box until an X appears	***Press***	*Alt+I until an X appears in the Italic check box*	**Press**	Alt+I until an X appears in the Italic check box
Click	the OK command button	***Press***	*↵Enter*	**Press**	↵Enter
Type	The next library bulletin will be printed next month.	***Type***	*The next library bulletin will be printed next month.*	**Type**	The next library bulletin will be printed next month.

The bottom portion of your screen should look like Figure 13-9.

Figure 13-9

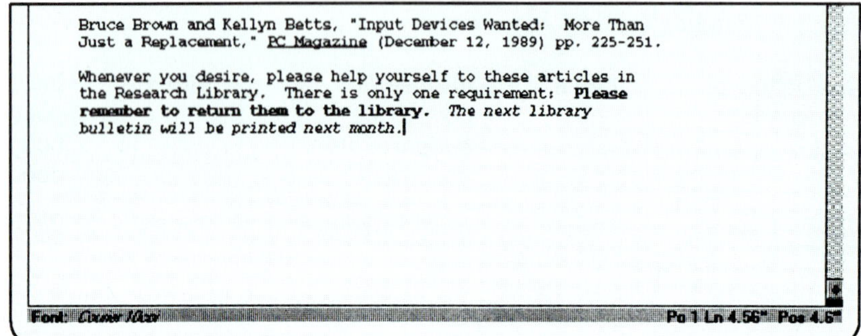
Bruce Brown and Kellyn Betts, "Input Devices Wanted: More Than Just a Replacement," PC Magazine (December 12, 1989) pp. 225-251.

Whenever you desire, please help yourself to these articles in the Research Library. There is only one requirement: **Please remember to return them to the library.** *The next library bulletin will be printed next month.*

Font: Courier Italic Pg 1 Ln 4.56" Pos 4.6"

To stop using italics:

Choose	Font	***Press***	*Alt*	**Press**	Ctrl+N
Choose	Normal	***Select***	*Font*		or
	or	***Select***	*Normal*	**Press**	→ to move beyond the code
Press	→ to move beyond the code		*or*		
		Press	*→ to move beyond the code*		

Because italic is a common Font Appearance it appears directly on the Font menu. To italicize text, you can choose Font Italic or press Ctrl+I rather than accessing the Font dialog box.

Removing the Code

You can remove the Font Appearance code by deleting the [Italc] code. Display the document codes using the Reveal Codes feature.

The bottom section of your screen should look like Figure 13-10.

Figure 13-10

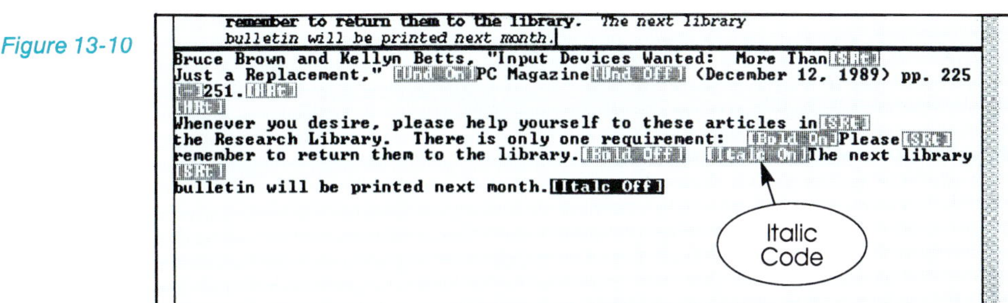

To delete the [Italc] code:

Click	on the [Italc On] code	***Move***	*the insertion point on the [Italc On] code*	**Move**	the insertion point on the [Italc On] code
Press	Delete	***Press***	*Delete*	**Press**	Delete

The [Italc] code has been deleted. Use the Reveal Codes feature to remove the document codes from your screen.

Existing Text

To add a Font Appearance code to existing text, you must first select the text and then choose the Font feature from the Font menu or press F9.

To change the Font Appearance of the last sentence in the document:

Select	the last sentence	***Select***	*the last sentence*	**Select**	the last sentence
Choose	Font	***Press***	*Alt*	**Press**	F9
Choose	Font	***Select***	*Font*	**Press**	Alt+I until an X appears in the Italic check box
Click	the Italic check box until an X appears	***Select***	*Font*	**Press**	↵Enter
Click	the OK command button	***Press***	*Alt+I until an X appears in the Italic check box*		
		Press	*↵Enter*		

Deselect the text by clicking in the document or moving the insertion point. Save the document as "library.ltr." Close the document.

EXERCISE 1

INSTRUCTIONS: Define the following terms:

1. Font size ______________________________

____

2. Superscript ______________________________

____

3. Font appearance ______________________________

____

4. Flush right ______________________________

____

5. Subscript ______________________________

____

EXERCISE 2

INSTRUCTIONS: Circle T if the statement is true and F if the statement is false.

T	F	1.	The Flush Right feature aligns text against the left margin.
T	F	2.	The Superscript feature places text slightly below a line of normal printed text.
T	F	3.	The Subscript feature places text slightly above a line of normal printed text.
T	F	4.	The Font Size selections are Fine, Small, Medium, Very Large, and Extra Large.
T	F	5.	The Font Appearance selections are Bold, Underline, Double Underline, Flush Right, Italic, Outline, Shadow, Small Caps, Redline, or Strikeout.
T	F	6.	When using the Flush Right feature, you can adjust only a word or part of a line.
T	F	7.	The Flush Right feature is turned off by pressing [↵Enter].
T	F	8.	You can remove a small font size by deleting its code from the document.

EXERCISE 3

INSTRUCTIONS:

1. Create the following document. Read the instructions in steps 2 and 3 before you enter the text.

   The format settings for the document are listed below:

Initial Font:	Helvetica 10pt (Z1A)
Margins:	
Left	1.0″
Right	1.0″
Top	1.0″
Bottom	1.0″
Tabs:	Set at your discretion.
Justification:	Full
Line spacing:	Single
Hyphenation:	None

2. As you type in the document, flush right "example" in the third paragraph.
3. As you type the document, flush right the phrase "is an example using several words" in the fourth paragraph.
4. Use the Flush Right feature on the fifth paragraph.
5. Change the last sentence in the fifth paragraph, "It's really quite simple!," to shadow text.
6. Preview the document.
7. Save the document on a file using the name "ch13ex03."
8. Print the document.
9. Close the document.

TO: Jack Fontana
Accounting Department

FROM: Donna Kainer
Micro User Support Team (MUST)

DATE: current date

RE: Flush Right Question

Jack, I want to follow up on your WordPerfect question from yesterday. If you have a word, phrase or paragraph that you want "pushed" to the right margin, then the Flush Right feature is the one to use. You are only creating more work for yourself if you create a right tab at or near the right margin.

You can use the Flush Right feature by pressing the Alt+F7 keys. For example, if you want a word at the right margin, then press Alt+F7, type the word, and then press the Enter key to end the Flush Right feature.

Here is an example.

Here is an example using several words.

You can flush right an entire paragraph by blocking the paragraph first. Then press the Alt+F7 keys to move it. I entered this paragraph in the normal manner - flush against the *left* margin. Then I made it flush right. It's really quite simple!

The Flush Right feature is especially useful in headers and footers, too.

I hope that I have been of help to you. Please call me at Ext. 1500 if you have any more questions.

EXERCISE 4

INSTRUCTIONS:

1. Create the following document.

   The format settings for the document are listed below:

Initial Font:	Helvetica 12pt (Z1A)
Margins:	
Left	1.5″
Right	1.5″
Top	1.0″
Bottom	1.0″

Tabs:	Set at your discretion.
Justification:	Full
Line spacing:	Double
Hyphenation:	None

2. The title of the document is bold, centered, and in a Large font size.
3. Change the underlined sentences to double underlines.
4. Bold the first sentence of paragraph five, "As a result of . . .." Then change the text to small caps.
5. Preview the document.
6. Save the document on a file using the name "ch13ex04."
7. Print the document.
8. Close the document.

RESULTS OF
COMPUTER SKILL INVENTORY

Last month, the Micro User Support Team (MUST) conducted a survey of ABC Can Company personnel. This survey asked users about their computer skills. The results of this survey have been computed and are listed below.

The type of software that is used by the greatest number of people at ABC Can Company is electronic mail. 87% of ABC personnel use electronic mail (E-main). Users spend an average of 3.2 hours per week sending and receiving messages on E-mail. Since MUST installed E-mail at ABC only a year ago, this statistic is considered quite significant. Second and third in this category are word processing and graphics software.

ABC users spend the most time on word processing software. Average usage time is 22.5 hours per week. Users requested word processing the most as the type of software package that they wanted to learn. 80% of the requests for more training in word processing specified WordPerfect as the package to learn. Second and third in this category are spreadsheet and graphics software.

A small number of users want to learn or improve their typing skills. 9% of the respondents to the survey said that they are interested in learning through a typing software program. 3% of the respondents want a course with a teacher.

As a result of the computer skills survey, MUST is in the process of evaluating the computer training program at ABC Can Company. We are creating new courses and updating old courses to meet ABC's computer needs. We are also hiring an outside training firm, Napier & Judd, Inc., to help us meet the demand for more training.

The Training Services Department will send a notice and schedule of classes in three weeks to all ABC personnel.

EXERCISE 5

INSTRUCTIONS:

1. Create the following document.
2. Use the Center feature for your return address.
3. Use Full justification for the remainder of the document.
4. Use Times Roman 12 point for the vacation site lines.
5. Spell check the document.
6. Preview the document.
7. Print the document.
8. Save the document in a file using the name "ch13ex05."
9. Close the document.

Student's Street Address
Student's City, State, and Zip Code

current date

Mr. Jay DeCook
7880 Kiawa Road
St. Louis, MO 63135

Dear Mr. DeCook:

I would like to invite you to select one of the following free vacation spots.

BELIZE
CAYMAN ISLANDS
JAMAICA
AUSTRALIA

If you can answer correctly the questions on the enclosed card, you may be one of the lucky winners to the vacation spot of your choice mentioned above.

Hurry, time is limited. If you answer all questions correctly, your name will be placed on a computer list of all those who have also answered correctly. The computer will be programmed to randomly select a winner of a seven day, six night stay at the Vacationland Hotel. (Meals, airfare, and incidental expenses **not included.**)

Yours for the vacation of a lifetime,

VACATIONLAND HOTELS, INC.

Dave Ecternaught, Managing Director

EXERCISE 6

INSTRUCTIONS:

1. Open document "ch13ex05."
2. Use an italic font for the sentence enclosed in parentheses at the end of the third paragraph.
3. Use double underline under the word "free" in the first paragraph.
4. Use the "shadow" Font Appearance feature for the company name in the closing.
5. Change the name and title in the closing to Small Caps.
6. Add a Superscript 1 after the word "VACATIONLAND" in the closing.
7. Return four times after "Managing Director" and add the following sentence starting with the Superscript 1: "Not affiliated with Vacationland, USA."
8. Spell check the document.
9. Preview the document.
10. Print the document.
11. Save the document in a file using the name "ch13ex06."
12. Close the document.

EXERCISE 7

INSTRUCTIONS:

1. Create the following document using the font changes as indicated.
2. Use Full justification in the document.
3. Spell check the document.
4. Preview the document.
5. Print the document.
6. Save the document in a file using the name "ch13ex07."
7. Close the document.

current date

Mr. William Trunk
1408 Redbud Lane
Bloomington, IN 47401

Dear Mr. Trunk:

DON'T WAIT TILL NEXT YEAR!

Now that the dreaded tax season has passed, start reorganizing your files now. FILE IT RIGHT, TAXES LESS is our **new book just off the press**.

FILE IT RIGHT, TAXES LESS tries to bring every step of the process in preparing your taxes down to its lowest and easiest level. We have been selling this philosophy for years. If 5,000,000 customers use this book, that tells you **we must be on to something worthwhile.**

Remember what the Director of Internal Revenue said about doing your taxes. "File early, keep good records." **Don't be late again with your taxes.** Send in your order NOW! The cost of this book is only $10.95, a small price to pay.

Very sincerely yours,

ORGANIZATION UNLIMITED

Rupert James McGrath, Publisher

EXERCISE 8

INSTRUCTIONS:

1. Open document "ch13ex07."
2. Delete all bold codes from the document.
3. Single underline the book title.
4. Change all font sizes to the default font size.
5. Preview the document.
6. Print the document.
7. Save the document in a file using the name "ch13ex08."
8. Close the document.

EXERCISE 9

INSTRUCTIONS:

1. Create the following document.
2. Use Full justification in the document.
3. Spell check the document.
4. Preview the document.
5. Print the document.
6. Save the document in a file using the name "ch13ex09."
7. Close the document.

Student's Street Address
Student's City, State, and Zip Code

current date

Mr. Bill Liskowske
1776 Freedom Road
Boston, MA 02109

Dear Mr. Liskowske:

"A little knowledge is a dangerous thing."[1]

Since you are in the education business, you must realize that the above quote is a serious problem. Millions of high school students drop out of school every day with only a little knowledge.

INTERACTIVE VIDEO

This is not a buzz word. It is a whole new concept in teaching. It combines computers, video, instant replay, and testing on almost any topic you would like[2].

For a demonstration and complete discussion of how this works, and how it has improved the education of some misguided students, CALL 1-800-555-9090.

WE BELIEVE that everyone should be able to reach their greatest potential for self fulfillment and have the necessary skills to start some type of career.

DON'T HESITATE! This opportunity is only for a short time. Remember "Live every day as if it were your last."[3] Make sure this quote can be your students' dream and your legacy.

Most sincerely yours,

INTERACTIVE LEARNING CORPORATION

Gary Jacobs, Vice President for Sales

[1]Alexander Pope, *An Essay on Criticism, Part II, line 15.*
[2]Read our book *Education for the Masses.*
[3]Marcus Aurelis (121-180 A.D.)

CHAPTER FOURTEEN

PRINTING FEATURES

OBJECTIVES

In this chapter, you will learn to:

- Print a document from the screen
- Print a document from a disk
- Set printer options
- View a document

CHAPTER OVERVIEW

In this chapter, the processes for printing a document are discussed. The methods for printing a document from the screen or disk, setting printer options, and viewing a document are described and illustrated.

PRINTING A DOCUMENT ON SCREEN

The Print feature allows you to print the document that is currently displayed on the screen. By choosing the Print option from the File menu or pressing F5, the Print dialog box is displayed on the screen.

There are three options for printing a document that appears on the screen. The Full Document option prints the entire document. The Current Page option prints only the page on which the insertion point is located. The Multiple Pages option prints selected pages of the document.

Before starting this section, be sure you have a clear screen. Change the default directory to "a:\wpdocs" or to "c:\wpdocs." Then, open the document "report2.ltr."

To print the entire document:

Choose	File	***Press***	*Alt*	**Press**	F5
Choose	Print	***Select***	*File*		
		Select	*Print*		

Your screen should look like Figure 14-1.

Figure 14-1

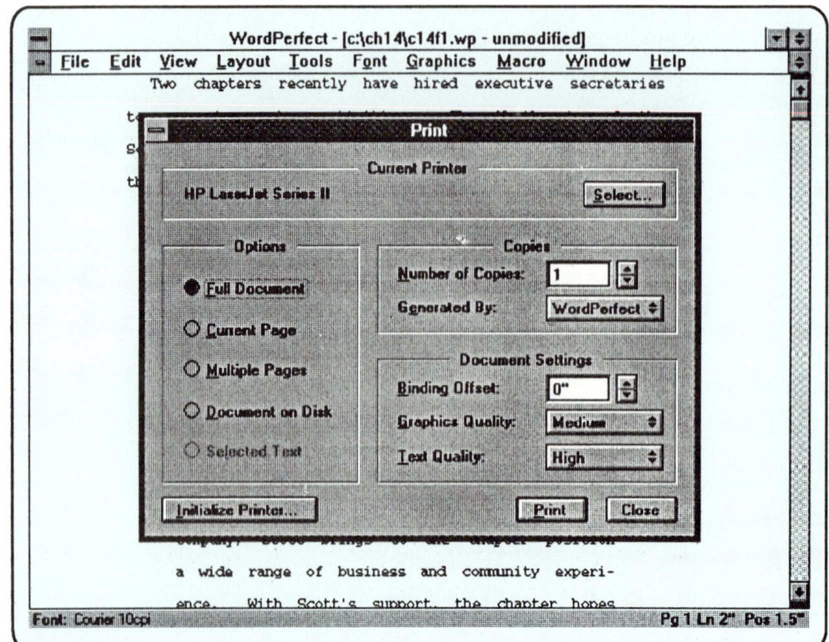

To select Full Document:

Click	the Full Document option button in the Options box	***Press***	*Alt+F to select the Full Document option button in the Options box*	**Press**	Alt+F to select the Full Document option button in the Options box
Click	the Print command button	***Press***	*↵Enter to select the Print command button*	**Press**	↵Enter to select the Print command button

The Current Print Job dialog box appears and the document is printed.

To print the page on which the insertion point is located:

Choose	File	***Press***	*Alt*	**Press**	F5
Choose	Print	***Select***	*File*		
		Select	*Print*		

To select Page:

Click	the Current Page option button in the Options box	***Press***	*Alt+C to select the Current Page option button in the Options box*	**Press**	Alt+C to select the Current Page option button in the Options box
Click	the Print command button	***Press***	*↵Enter to select the Print command button*	**Press**	↵Enter to select the Print command button

The Current Print Job dialog box appears, and then the page is printed.

To print only page 2:

Choose	File
Choose	Print
Click	the Multiple Pages option button in the Options box
Click	the Print command button

Press	*Alt*
Select	*File*
Select	*Print*
Press	*Alt+M to select the Multiple Pages option button in the Options box*
Press	*↵Enter to select the Print command button*

Press	F5
Press	Alt+M to select the Multiple Pages option button in the Options box
Press	↵Enter to select the Print command button

The Multiple Pages dialog box appears. Your screen should look like Figure 14-2.

Figure 14-2

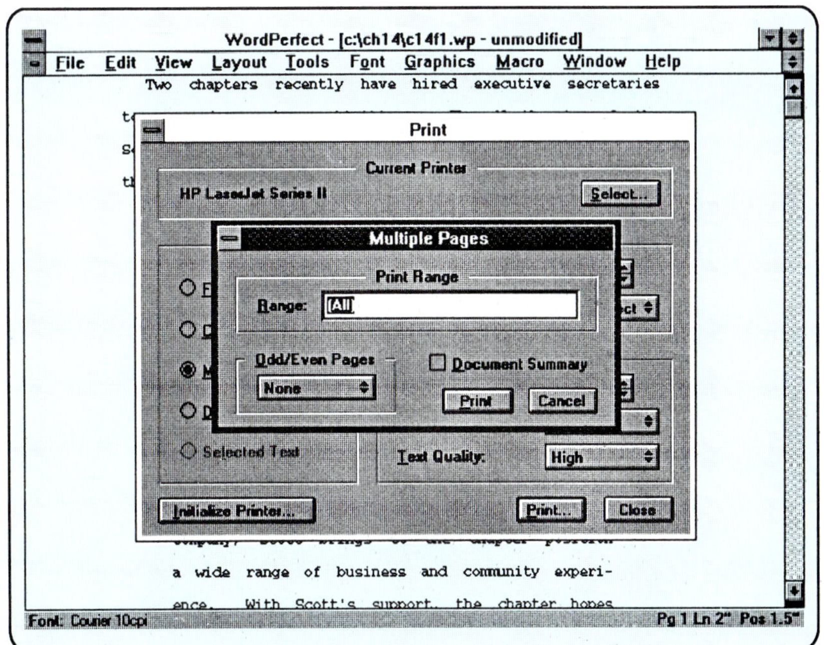

You can specify individual pages or groups of pages to be printed by using the examples presented in the following list:

Page(s)	**Pages Printed**
1	Page 1
1,2	Pages 1 and 2
1 2	Pages 1 and 2
1-	Page 1 through the end of the document
1-3	Pages 1 through 3
-5	The beginning of the document through page 5

To print only page 2:

Type	2 in the Print Range text box	***Type***	*2 in the Print Range text box*	**Type**	2 in the Print Range text box

Your screen should look like Figure 14-3.

Figure 14-3

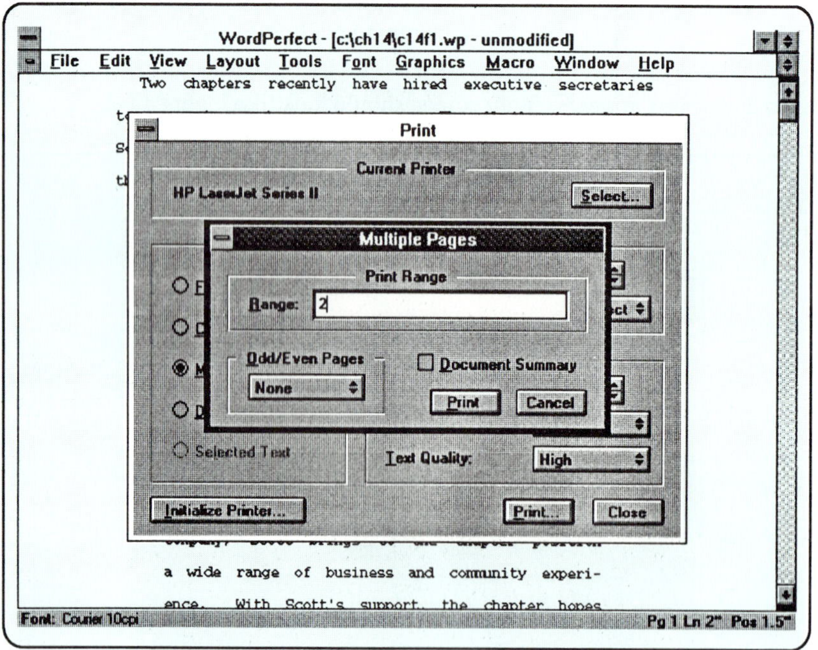

To begin printing:

Click	the Print command button	***Press***	*↵Enter to select the Print command button*	**Press**	↵Enter to select the Print command button

Close the document.

PRINTING A DOCUMENT ON DISK

The Print Document on Disk feature allows you to print a document that is not currently displayed on your screen. Instead, the document was created in a previous editing session and saved on disk. You can print part or all of a document.

To print a document on disk:

Choose	File	***Press***	*Alt*	**Press**	F5
Choose	Print	***Select***	*File*	**Press**	Alt+D to select the Document on Disk option button in the Options box
Click	the Document on Disk option button in the Options box	***Select***	*Print*	**Press**	↵Enter to select the Print command button
Click	the Print command button	***Press***	*Alt+D to select the Document on Disk option button in the Options box*		
		Press	*↵Enter to select the Print command button*		

Your screen should look like Figure 14-4.

Figure 14-4

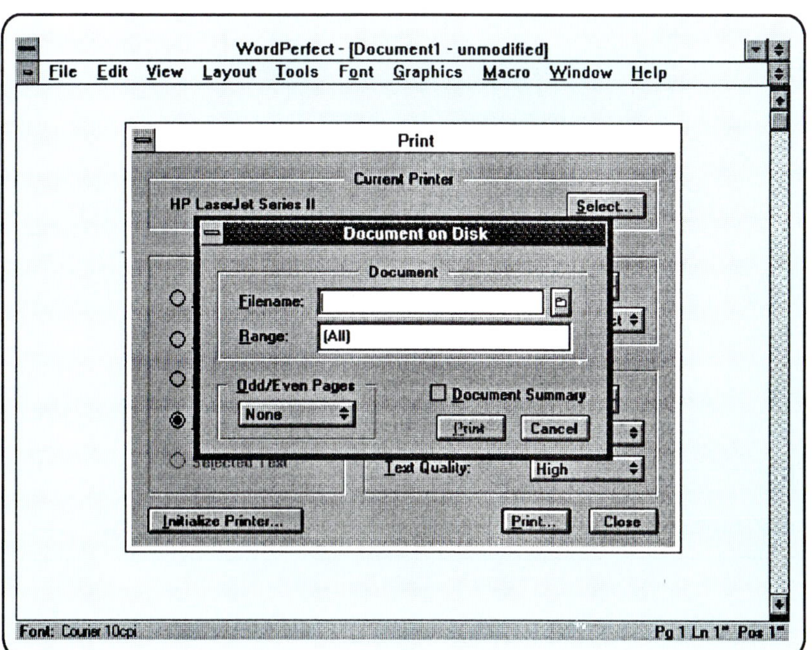

To print the document "report2.ltr":

Type	**report2.ltr**	***Type***	***report2.ltr***	**Type**	**report2.ltr**

You can specify individual pages or groups of pages to be printed by using the examples presented in the following list:

Page(s)	**Pages Printed**
1	Page 1
1,2	Pages 1 and 2
1 2	Pages 1 and 2
1-	Page 1 through the end of the document
1-3	Pages 1 through 3
-5	The beginning of the document through page 5

To print pages 1 and 2:

Double-click	the Range text box	***Press***	*Alt+R to select the Range text box*	**Press**	Alt+R to select the Range text box
Type	1-2	***Type***	*1-2*	**Type**	1-2

Your screen should look like Figure 14-5.

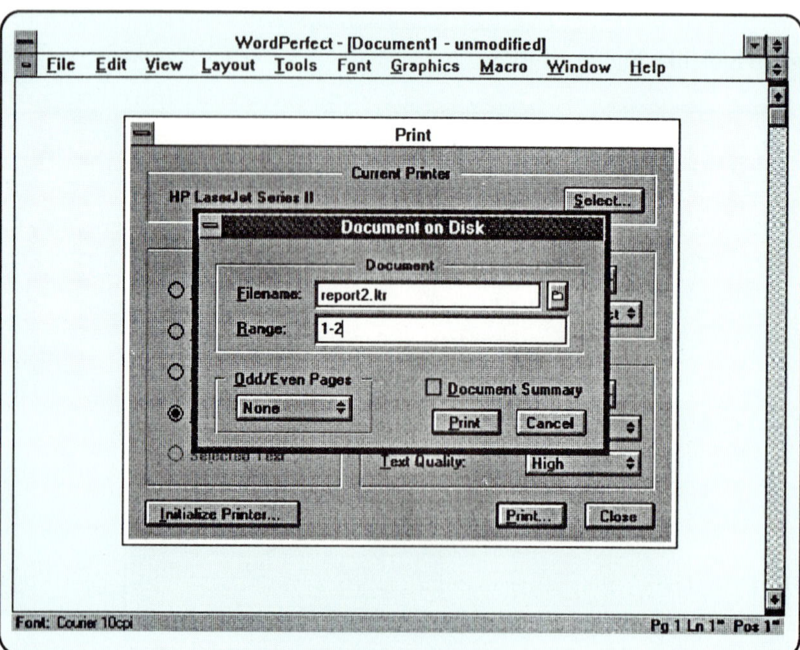

Figure 14-5

To begin printing:

Click	the Print command button	***Press***	*[↵Enter] to select the Print command button*	**Press**	[↵Enter] to select the Print command button

The Current Print Job dialog box appears, and then the pages are printed.

Since the document contains only two pages, you did not have to specify a print range and could have accepted the (All) range by clicking the Print command button or pressing [↵Enter].

■ INITIALIZING THE PRINTER

The Initialize Printer option allows you to download soft fonts to your printer. Soft fonts are special software that contain the design of certain fonts.

You can use this option if you have a printer that supports soft fonts. Choose File Print or press [F5] and select the Initialize Printer command button. WordPerfect loads these fonts into your printer. This option should be run each time you power up your printer if you plan to use the soft fonts. For more information on initializing the printer see the "Print" section in your WordPerfect Reference manual.

■ PRINTER OPTIONS

The Print dialog box contains several features that you can use to alter printing. These options are described in the following pages. All of these options, except the number of copies option, are saved with your document and only affect the current document.

To display the printer options:

Choose	File	***Press***	*[Alt]*	**Press**	[F5]
Choose	Print	***Select***	*File*		
		Select	*Print*		

Selecting a Printer

The Current Printer box identifies the current printer being used and lets you select a new printer and change your printer settings. A list of available printers is shown from which to choose. If your printer is not shown, then you may need to run the WordPerfect Installation program again to copy more printer files to your WordPerfect directory.

To display the Select Printer options:

Click	the Select command button in the Current Printer box	***Press***	*[Alt]+[S] to select the Select command button in the Current Printer box*	**Press**	[Alt]+[S] to select the Select command button in the Current Printer box

Except for the printer name(s),which may be different, your screen should look like Figure 14-6.

Figure 14-6

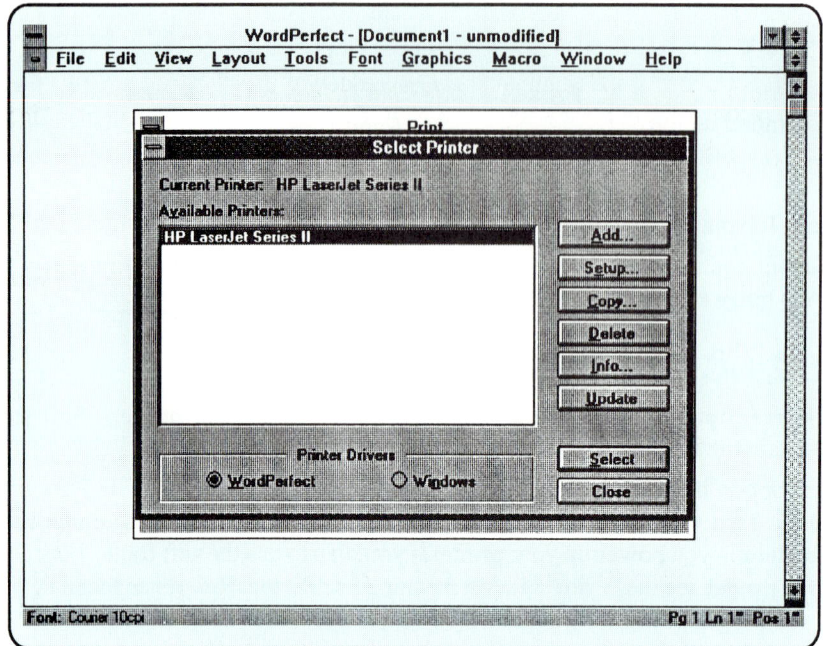

Using the Select command button in the Select Printer dialog box is the same as the Select Printer option under the File menu. For additional information on selecting a printer, see "Printer, Select" in the WordPerfect Reference Manual.

To return to the Print dialog box:

Click	the Close command button	***Press***	*Shift+Tab to select the Close command button*	**Press**	Shift+Tab to select the Close command button
		Press	*Enter*	**Press**	Enter

Number of Copies

The Number of Copies option in the Copies box allows you to enter the number of copies you want printed. To change the number of copies printed, click the up or down triangle button next to the Number of Copies text box to increase or decrease the number of copies. You can also type the number of desired copies in the Number of Copies text box.

Copies Generated By

The Generated By option in the Copies box specifies whether WordPerfect or the printer should make the extra copies.

When WordPerfect creates the copies, the print time is slower. However, the copies are collated. When the printer makes the copies, WordPerfect needs to send only one copy to the printer, and the printer does the extra work. However, the copies are not collated.

Note that your printer may not support this feature.

Binding Offset

The Binding Offset option in the Document Settings box allows you to move printed text to one side so that the document may be bound. This option will shift text correctly for even- and odd-numbered pages.

Graphics Quality

The Graphics Quality option in the Document Settings box determines the print quality of graphics within a document. These settings affect the clarity of the printed document that contains graphic images.

To display the Graphics Quality options:

Click	the Graphics Quality pop-up list button	***Press***	*Alt+G to select the Graphic Quality pop-up list button*	**Press**	Alt+G to select the Graphic Quality pop-up list button
Hold down	the mouse button to view the pop-up list	***Press***	*Alt+↑ to view the pop-up list*	**Press**	Alt+↑ to view the pop-up list

Your screen should look like Figure 14-7.

Figure 14-7

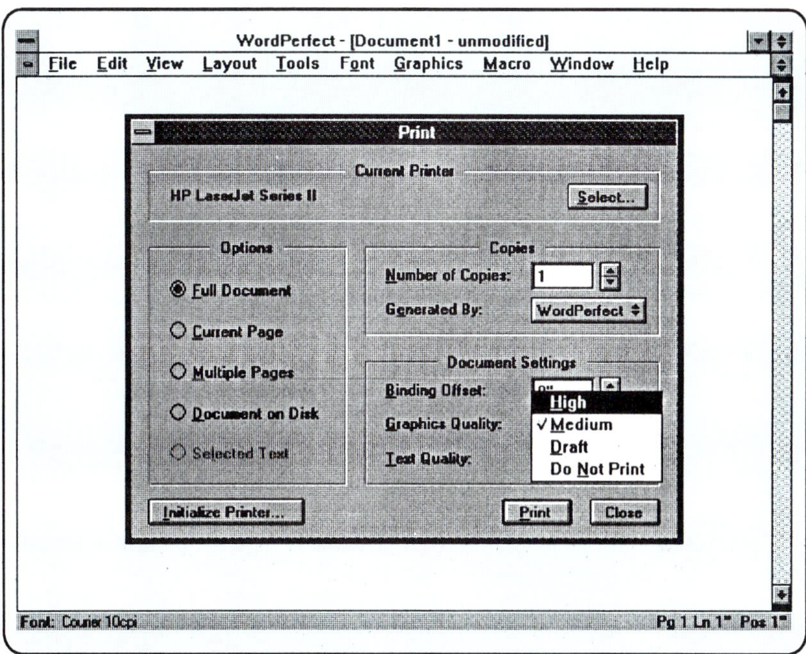

The pop-up list displays the options available for graphics quality. For additional information on the Graphics Quality options, see the WordPerfect Reference Manual.

To close the pop-up list:

Release	the mouse button	***Press***	*Alt*	**Press**	Alt

Text Quality

The Text Quality option in the Document Settings box sets the print quality of text within a document. These settings affect the clarity of the printed characters in a document.

To display the Text Quality options:

Click	the Text Quality pop-up list button	***Press***	*Alt+T to select the Text Quality pop-up list button*	**Press**	Alt+T to select the Text Quality pop-up list button
Hold down	the mouse button to view the pop-up list	***Press***	*Alt+↑ to view the pop-up list*	**Press**	Alt+↑ to view the pop-up list

Your screen should look like Figure 14-8.

Figure 14-8

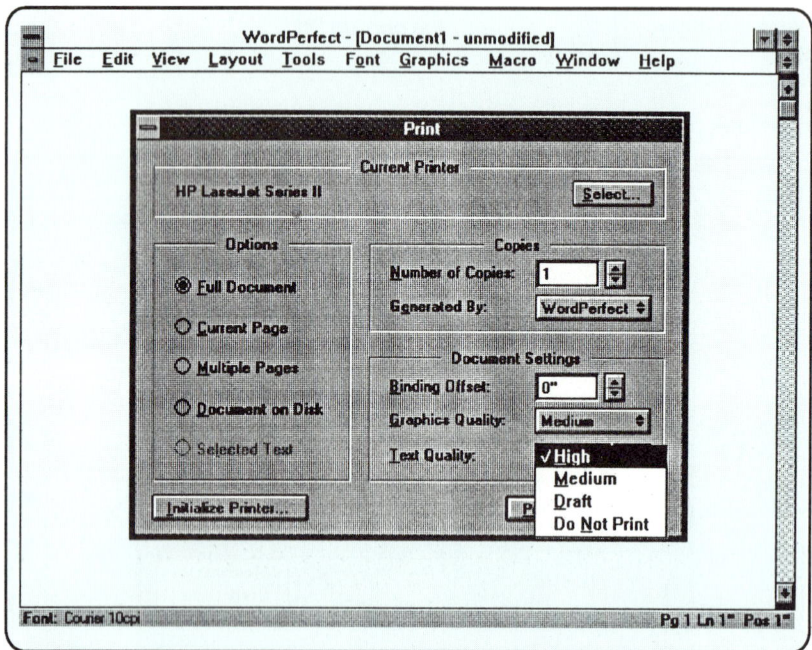

The pop-up lists displays the options available for text quality. For additional information on the Text Quality options, see the WordPerfect reference manual.

To close the pop-up list:

Release	the mouse button	***Press***	*Alt*	**Press**	Alt

To close the Print dialog box:

Click	the Close command button	***Press***	*Esc*	**Press**	Esc

■ PREVIEWING A DOCUMENT

With the Print Preview feature, you can see on the screen how a document will look when it is printed. Headers, footers, margins, page numbers, text, and graphics are shown on the screen. WordPerfect tries to duplicate the printed page on the screen as closely as possible. You cannot edit your document while using the Print Preview feature.

There are several options on the Print Preview menu. To view the normal size of the document, select 100% from the View menu. Select 200% from the View menu to view the document at twice its normal size. You can use the scroll bars or the pointer-movement keys to move around the screen.

The Full Page option under the Pages menu lets you view the entire page. The Facing Pages option under the Pages menu displays even-numbered and odd-numbered pages on one screen.

Use the Next Page and Previous Page options under the Pages menu to move between pages in your document.

To view a document:

Open	the document "report2.ltr"	***Open***	*the document "report2.ltr"*	**Open**	the document "report2.ltr"
Choose	File	***Press***	Alt	**Press**	Shift+F5
Choose	Print Preview	***Select***	*File*		
		Select	*Print Preview*		

Your screen should look like Figure 14-9.

Figure 14-9

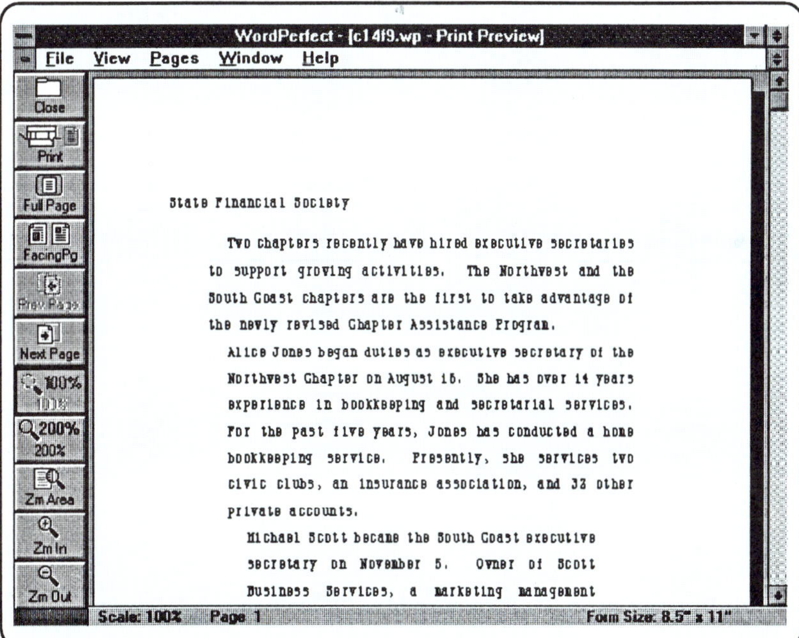

You can use the menu or the Print Preview Button Bar to perform tasks.

To view your document at 100%:

Click	the 100% button on the Button Bar	***Press***	Alt
		Select	*View*
		Select	*100%*

To view your document at 200%:

Click	the 200% button on the Button Bar	***Press***	Alt		
		Select	*View*		
		Select	*200%*		

To view your document with the Full Page option:

Click	the Full Page button on the Button Bar	***Press***	Alt		
		Select	*Pages*		
		Select	*Full Page*		

To return to your document:

Click	the Close button on the Button Bar	***Press***	Alt	**Press**	Ctrl + F4
		Select	*File*		
		Select	*Close*		

You can use the Zoom feature in the normal editing screen to also change your view of the document. The Zoom feature is discussed in Appendix D. Close the document "report2.ltr" without saving changes.

EXERCISE 1

INSTRUCTIONS: Define the following terms:

1. Document on disk ______________________________

   ____

2. Print Preview ______________________________

   ____

3. Multiple pages ______________________________

   ____

4. Full document ______________________________

   ____

5. Page ______________________________

   ____

6. Binding offset ____

____

7. Graphics quality ____

____

8. Text quality ____

____

EXERCISE 2

INSTRUCTIONS: Circle T if the statement is true and F if the statement is false.

T F 1. To print the page containing the insertion point, you would select the Current Page option from the Print dialog box.

T F 2. To print the entire document that you are currently editing, you would select the Full Document option from the Print dialog box.

T F 3. When printing multiple pages, if you specify -20 at the Multiple Pages dialog box, WordPerfect prints from page 20 to the end of the document.

T F 4. The Document on Disk feature allows you to print the document that you are currently editing to a file on your hard disk.

T F 5. The Document on Disk feature allows you to print a document without having to open it first.

T F 6. Through the Print Preview feature, WordPerfect tries to duplicate the printed page on the screen as closely as possible.

T F 7. You can make last-minute changes to your document through the Print Preview feature.

T F 8. You can actually see the document codes when you select the 200% option from the Print Preview screen.

T F 9. The Binding Offset option allows you to move printed text to one side so that the document may be bound.

T F 10. You can start and stop your printer by using the Initialize Printer option.

T F 11. The Generated By option specifies whether WordPerfect or the printer should make the extra copies.

T F 12. The Graphics Quality option determines the print quality of text.

EXERCISE 3

INSTRUCTIONS:

1. Create the following document.
2. Preview the document.
3. Print the document.
4. Save the document in a file using the name "ch14ex03."
5. Close the document.
6. Print the document without opening it.
7. Open document "ch14ex03."
8. Place a page break before the word "Sincerely."
9. Preview the document.
10. Print the second page of the document.
11. Save the document.
12. Close the document.
13. Print the second page of the document without opening the document.

current date

Mr. Thomas D. Little
3434 Lakeland Drive
Princeton, NJ 02234

Dear Mr. Little:

It has been six months since you had your last dental examination.

Research studies show that with regular checkups and professional teeth cleaning, you can reduce the incidents of serious dental problems. Of course, proper brushing and flossing of your teeth between your office visits help to lessen the likelihood of any dental problems.

Please call Darlene at 876-4300 to make an appointment.

Sincerely yours,

Dr. A. Lanham Johnson, D.D.S.

EXERCISE 4

INSTRUCTIONS:

1. Open document "ch11ex06." If you have not yet created it, then do so at this time.
2. Print pages 3 and 4 only using the Multiple Pages option from the Print dialog box.
3. Close the document.

EXERCISE 5

INSTRUCTIONS:

1. Open document "ch12ex09." If you have not yet created it, then do so at this time.
2. Preview the document at full page.
3. Preview the document at 100%. Scroll down through the document to the bottom.
4. Preview the document at 200%. Scroll to the right margin. Scroll down to the bottom of the document along the right margin.
5. Close the preview screen. Close the document.

EXERCISE 6

INSTRUCTIONS:

1. Open document "ch11ex08." If you have not yet created it, then do so at this time.
2. Preview page 2 of the document at 100%.
3. Preview page 3 of the document at 200%.
4. Print only pages 2 and 3 of this document.
5. Close the document.

EXERCISE 7

INSTRUCTIONS:

1. Create the following document using Full justification.
2. Save this document in a file using the name "ch14ex07."
3. Print three copies of this document. Use the Number of Copies option.

```
current date


Mr. John Mogab
1800 Roscoe Lane
Pasadena, TX 77199

Dear Mr. Mogab:

                    YOU ARE OUR NUMBER ONE CUSTOMER!

I am sure that you were wondering why I asked for your address last
Friday evening.  Now you know.

I have been the manager of Casa Adobe for the past six years.  Never
have I seen a customer enjoy our restaurant more than you.  It seems
that I never fail to see you in our restaurant at least two or three
times a week.  Of course, you are a "regular" on Friday evenings.
Moreover, you bring at least ten or twenty people with you!

Thank you so much for your support!  As a gesture of our
appreciation, Casa Adobe would like to send you to Cozumel for one
week at our expense.

Let's discuss this over lunch (my treat, of course).  Please call me
at 888-9090.

Sincerely.



Ms. Cynthia Harlowe
Manager, Casa Adobe
```

EXERCISE 8

INSTRUCTIONS:

1. Open document "ch14ex07."
2. Change the Text Quality to draft.
3. Print one copy of the document.
4. Change the Binding Offset to 0.5″.
5. Print one copy of the document.
6. Compare the two copies.
7. Close the document.

EXERCISE 9

INSTRUCTIONS:

1. Create the following document using Full justification.
2. Change the Text Quality to draft.
3. Change the Binding Offset to 1″.
4. Print five copies.
5. Save this document in a file using the name "ch14ex09."
6. Close the document.

```
current date


Mr. Jerry Underwood
4422 Woodburn Road
Bowling Green, KY 42101

Dear Mr. Underwood:

This is an example of using WordPerfect for Windows to illustrate how
to use the printer options feature.

This copy was set for a 1-inch binding, with a text quality of DRAFT,
with five copies being made from one command.

Sincerely,



Marge Braun
```

EXERCISE 10

INSTRUCTIONS:

1. Create the following document using Full justification.
2. Change the Text Quality to draft.
3. Change the Binding Offset to 0.25″.
4. If your computer is connected to two printers, then select the second printer.
5. Print three copies.
6. Save the document in a file using the name "ch14ex10."

current date

Ms. Sonny Drake
300 Jay Street
Upper Montclair, NJ 07043

Dear Ms. Drake:

Your former students are planning an early retirement party for you on May 25. We know that you will be having many retirement parties and want to be sure to get on your calendar.

The party will be held at the Kelsey Road House in the Tea Room at 2 p.m. I think it's only fair to tell you that this group will be giving you and your spouse a two-week trip to Europe. You may pick the date.

Most respectfully yours,

Michelle Keller

CHAPTER FIFTEEN

USING MULTIPLE WINDOWS

OBJECTIVES

In this chapter, you will learn to:

- Open more than one document
- View more than one document window
- Size a window
- Move a window
- Move a dialog box

CHAPTER OVERVIEW

In this chapter, the process for using multiple document windows is described and illustrated.

OPENING MORE THAN ONE DOCUMENT

In WordPerfect, you can have a maximum of nine documents open at the same time. Each file appears in a separate window on your screen. When more than one document window is open, you can use the same WordPerfect features that are available when only one document is open.

You can open documents using the Open feature or create new documents using the New feature. The Open feature allows you to open a document saved on a diskette or hard disk. To open a document, choose Open from the File menu or press [F4].

The New feature allows you to create a blank document. The first blank document is called "Document1." When no other documents are open, "Document1" automatically appears on the screen. Any following documents that are created are numbered "Document2," "Document3," and so on. To create a blank document, choose New from the File menu or press [Shift]+[F4].

Before starting this section, be sure you have a clear screen. Change the default directory to "a:\wpdocs" or to "c:\wpdocs."

Open the document "johnson.ltr." Your screen should look like Figure 15-1.

Figure 15-1

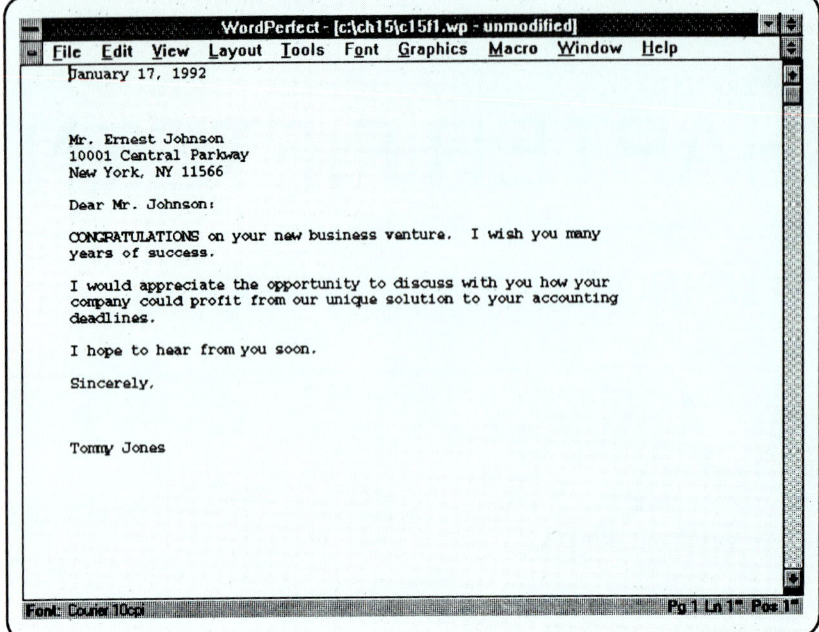

January 17, 1992

Mr. Ernest Johnson
10001 Central Parkway
New York, NY 11566

Dear Mr. Johnson:

CONGRATULATIONS on your new business venture. I wish you many years of success.

I would appreciate the opportunity to discuss with you how your company could profit from our unique solution to your accounting deadlines.

I hope to hear from you soon.

Sincerely,

Tommy Jones

To create a blank document while "johnson.ltr" is on the screen, choose New from the File menu or press Shift + F4.

To create a blank document:

Choose File
Choose New
Press Alt
Select File
Select New
Press Shift + F4

Your screen should look like Figure 15-2.

Figure 15-2

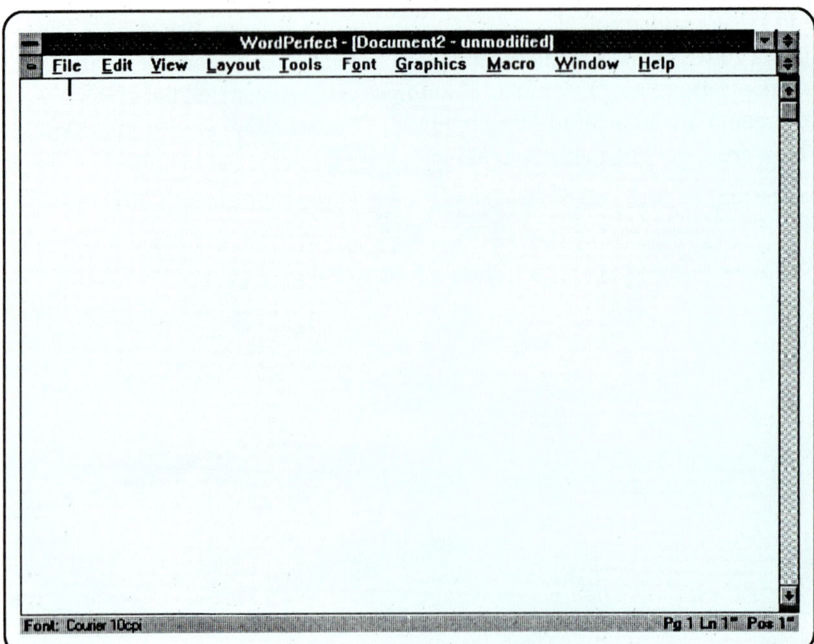

Since each document is maximized, only "Document2" is visible on the screen.

■ VIEWING MORE THAN ONE DOCUMENT

With WordPerfect, you can have up to nine documents open at one time; however, you may not be able to see each document. You can use the Window Tile command or the Window Cascade command to view part of each open document.

Tiling Windows

The Window Tile command allows you to see all of your open documents by dividing the screen into equal parts.

To split the screen so that you can see both of your documents:

Choose	Window	***Press***	*Alt*
Choose	Tile	***Select***	*Window*
		Select	*Tile*

Your screen should look like Figure 15-3.

Figure 15-3

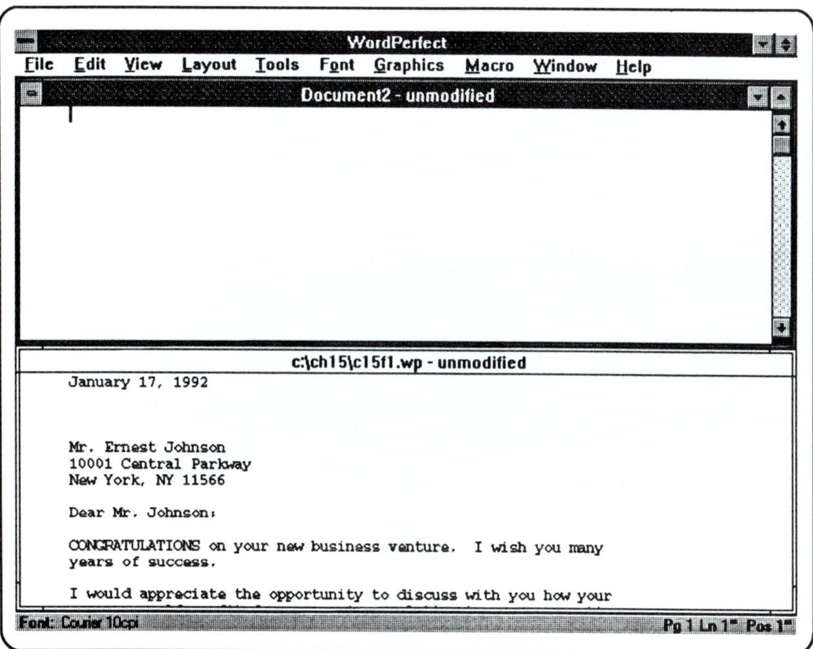

Notice that "Document2" appears on the top portion of the screen. The active document, when the Window Tile command is chosen, appears in the top left window. You can make another document the active document by clicking on the window or pressing Ctrl+F6.

To make "johnson.ltr" the active window:

Click	on the "johnson.ltr" window	***Press***	*Alt*	**Press**	Ctrl+F6 until the "johnson.ltr" window becomes the active window

Select	*Window*
Select	*johnson.ltr*

Your screen should look like Figure 15-4.

Figure 15-4

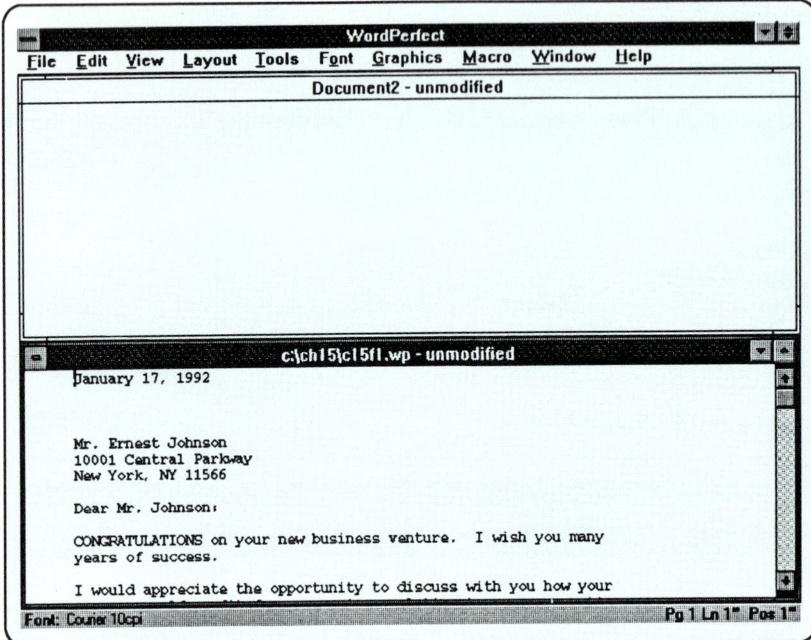

When a window is active, you can see the insertion point in the document. The window title bar should appear in a different color when the window is active.

Cascading Windows

You can also view multiple documents by using the Window Cascade command. When you cascade windows, you can see the title bar of each window. The active window is placed before the other open documents allowing you to see the contents of the active document.

To view "Document2" and "johnson.ltr" files using the Cascade command:

Choose	Window	***Press***	Alt
Choose	Cascade	***Select***	*Window*
		Select	*Cascade*

Your screen should look like Figure 15-5.

Figure 15-5

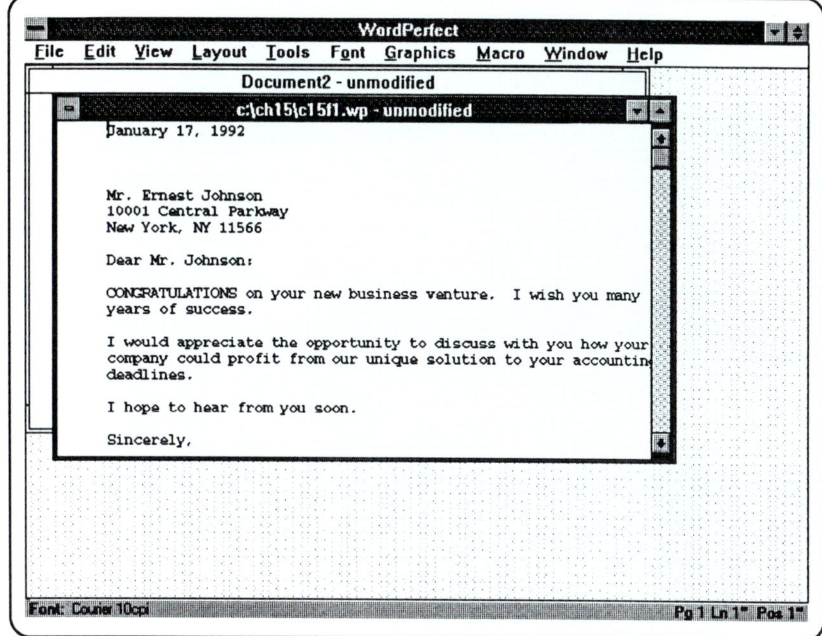

Notice that the active document, "johnson.ltr", is placed before "Document2." Close "johnson.ltr" and "Document2." Do not save any changes.

■ SIZING A WINDOW

You can change the size of a window by changing the size of the window frame. Open the document "practice."

Notice that, by default, the document is maximized and is displayed as a full screen. When a document is maximized, you cannot see the window frame. To make the window smaller, click the document Restore button shown in Figure 15-6 or use the document control menu also identified in Figure 15-6.

Figure 15-6

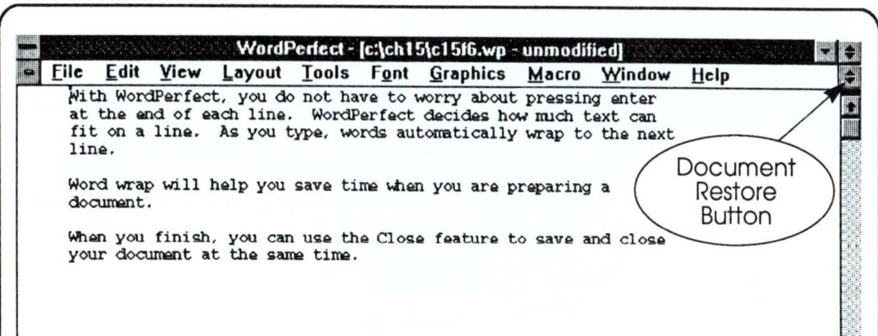

To restore "practice" to a smaller size:

Click	the document Restore button	***Press***	*Alt+- to open the document control menu*
		Select	*Restore*

Your screen should look like Figure 15-7.

Figure 15-7

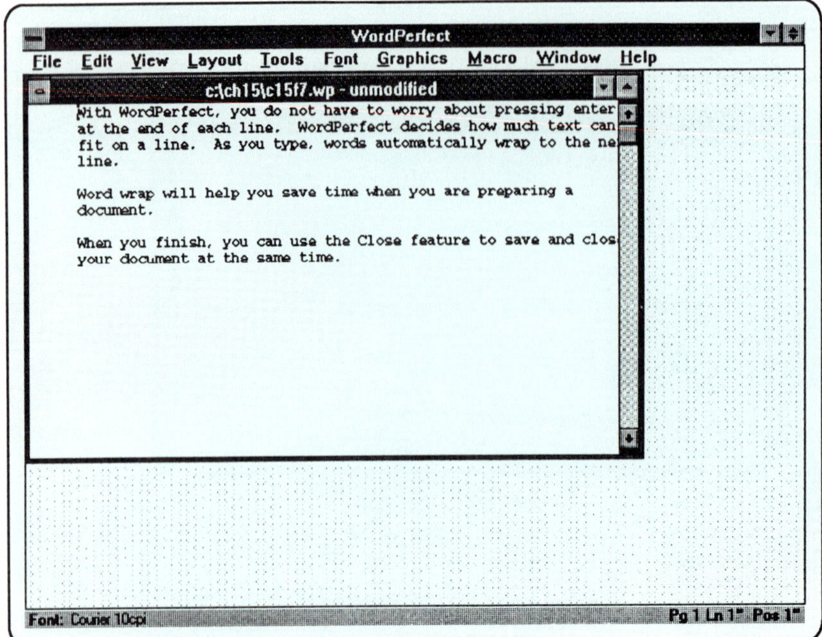

Notice that you can now see the window frame of the "practice" window.

In order to change the size of the window, drag the window frame or choose Size from the control menu. To change the size of the "practice" window:

Move	the mouse pointer to the bottom of the "practice" window until it becomes a double pointing arrow	***Press***	*[Alt]+[-] to open the control menu*
Click	on the bottom frame and drag the frame up to make the window smaller	***Select***	*Size*
Release	the mouse button to accept the window size	***Press***	*[↓] to select the bottom window frame as the border to size*
		Press	*[↑] to make the window smaller*
		Press	*[↵Enter] to accept the new window size*

Your screen should look similar to Figure 15-8.

Figure 15-8

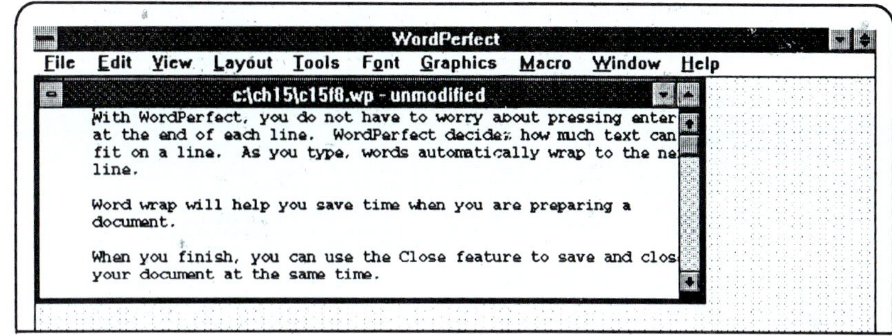

Any one of the four frame sides can be used to change the window size. If you move to a corner of the window frame, you can size the window proportionally.

MOVING A WINDOW

At times, you may want to move a window. To move a window, you can drag the window title bar or choose Move from the document control menu.

To move the "practice" window to the middle of the WordPerfect window:

Move	the mouse pointer to the "practice" title bar	***Press***	*Alt+- to open the document control menu*
Drag	the title bar toward the middle of the screen	***Select***	*Move*
Release	the mouse button to accept the new window position	***Press***	*↓ and → to move the "practice" window to the middle of the screen*
		Press	*↵Enter to accept the new window position*

Your screen should look similar to Figure 15-9.

Figure 15-9

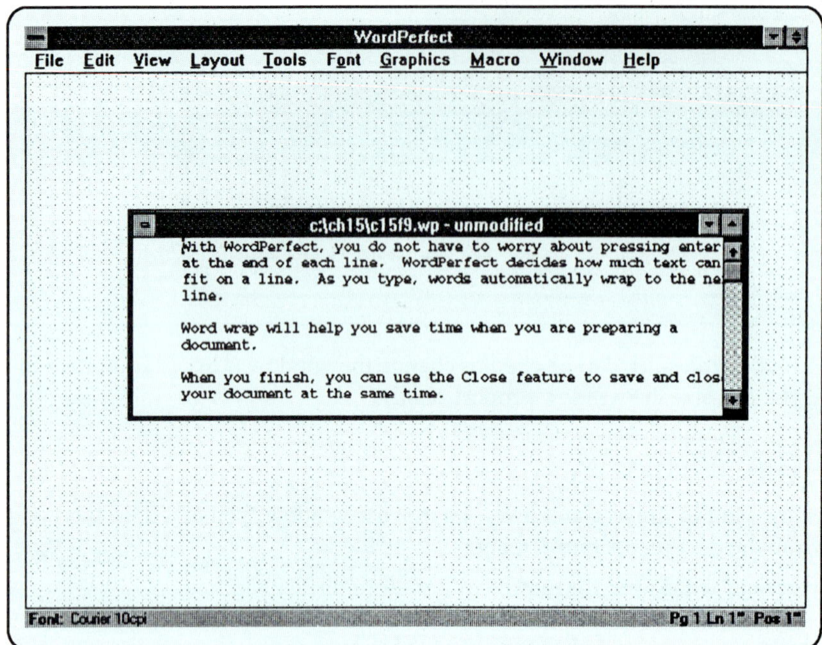

■ MOVING A DIALOG BOX

You can move a dialog box in the same way that you move a window. First, a dialog box must be active. To view the File Save As dialog box:

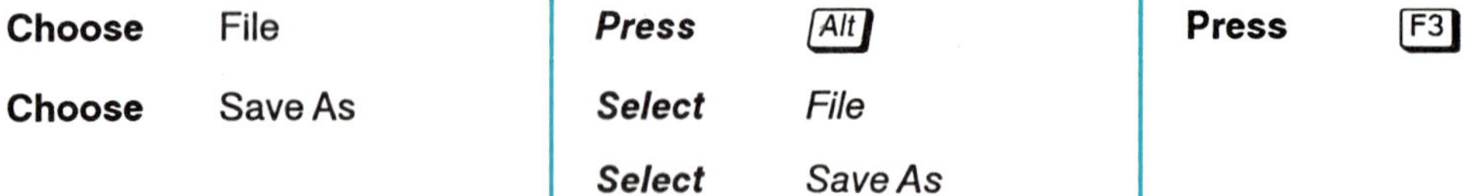

Choose	File	***Press***	*Alt*	**Press**	F3
Choose	Save As	***Select***	*File*		
		Select	*Save As*		

The dialog box covers the document. To move the dialog box:

Move	the mouse pointer to the Save As title bar	***Press***	*Alt+Spacebar to select the dialog box control menu*
Drag	the dialog box until you see the text in the "practice" document	***Select***	*Move*
Release	the mouse button to accept the new window position	***Press***	*the pointer-movement keys until you can see the text in the "practice" document*
		Press	*↵Enter to accept the new window position*

Your screen should look similar to Figure 15-10.

Figure 15-10

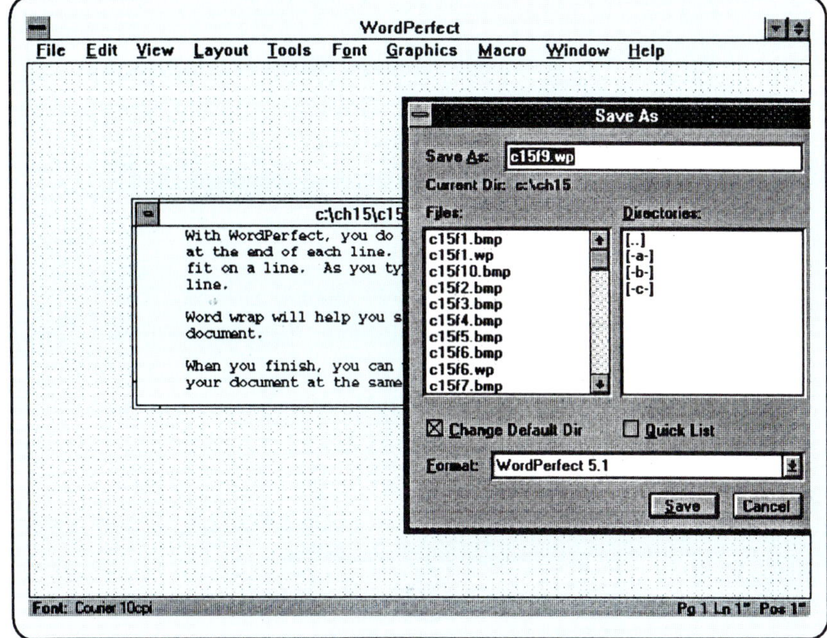

To close the dialog box and cancel the File Save As command:

Click	the Cancel command button	***Press***	*Esc*

Close the "practice" document without saving any changes.

EXERCISE 1

INSTRUCTIONS: Define the following terms:

1. File New feature ______________________________

____

2. Window Tile feature ______________________________

____

3. Window Cascade feature ______________________________

____

4. Window Move feature ______________________________

____

5. Window Size feature ______________________________

____

EXERCISE 2

INSTRUCTIONS: Circle T if the statement is true and F if the statement is false.

T F 1. The Window Tile feature allows you to display more than one document on the same screen at the same time.

T F 2. Each window contains a separate document.

T F 3. While using the Window Cascade feature, you can use only certain WordPerfect features.

T F 4. You can only size a window using the mouse.

T F 5. WordPerfect allows you to have a maximum of three documents open at one time.

T F 6. You can move a window in WordPerfect, but you cannot move a dialog box.

T F 7. The File New feature allows you to open a file saved on a diskette or a hard disk.

T F 8. The Cascade feature allows you to see all of your open documents by dividing the screen into equal parts.

EXERCISE 3

INSTRUCTIONS: 1. Create the following document.

```
This is a perfect example of changing from one document to another.
You can look at both screens at the same time and make corrections
or additions to two documents.  This is particularly valuable if
both documents are related to each other.  Another valuable benefit
of using multiple windows is that it provides some security for
your document from prying eyes.
```

2. Create a new document.
3. Enter the following text in the new document.

```
You can use multiple windows to copy and paste information between
documents.  If you need information in one document and the text
already exists in another document, you can copy and paste the data
using multiple windows.  Multiple windows allow you to see what you
are copying in the first document, and where you want to place the
copied text in the second document.
```

4. Preview and print "Document1."
5. Preview and print "Document2."
6. Add to "Document1" the sentence "Document security during preparation is very important in many offices."
7. Add to "Document2" the sentence "Copying and pasting are just two of the features that are enhanced with multiple windows."
8. Save "Document1" using the name "ch15ex03.01."
9. Save "Document2" using the name "ch15ex03.02."
10. Close both documents.

EXERCISE 4

INSTRUCTIONS:

1. Create the following document.

```
current date


Ms. Anna Marie Brummett
507 Burning Tree Lane
Dover, DE 19901

Dear Ms. Brummett:

Enclosed with this letter you will find your contract for
submitting ideas that were used by our company.  We would like to
keep you on a retainer.  We have never had anyone as prolific with
ideas as you are.
```

2. Create a blank document.
3. Enter the following text in the blank document.

```
                              MEMO


TO:        Beth Adams
FROM:      Eileen Bannon, Manager
DATE:      current date
SUBJECT: NEW PROMOTION

Beth, let me be the first to congratulate you.  I am promoting you
to Administrative Assistant for Susan O'Brien.  You have shown
excellent work habits, extreme dedication to the job, and the
necessary sense of humor.

Good luck in your new position.   I will tell payroll of your new
increase in salary.



xx
```

4. Spell check the memo.
5. Preview and print the memo.
6. Save the memo in a file using the name "ch15ex04.02."
7. Continue with the first document adding the following text.

```
According to our Research and Development department, you have come
up with some very exciting ideas for future development.

Keep up the good work.  We are happy to be able to offer you the
retainer.

Sincerely,



Deborah Cook
Vice President



xx
```

8. Spell check the letter.
9. Preview and print the letter.
10. Save the letter in a file using the name "ch15ex04.01."
11. Close both documents.

EXERCISE 5

INSTRUCTIONS: 1. Create the following document.

```
When you use the multiple windows feature of WordPerfect, you are
giving yourself the advantage of being able to do two things
simultaneously.  If you are interrupted by the telephone, you can
switch to a different document and take the message down in
WordPerfect.
```

2. Create a new document.
3. Enter the following text in the new document.

```
You can use multiple windows to hide confidential documents from
people who shouldn't see them.  For example, you can have two
documents open and quickly maximize the non-confidential document
so that it is the only document displayed on the screen.  This
prevents a visitor at your desk from seeing something confidential
or sensitive in nature.
```

4. Save "Document1" in a file using the name "ch15ex05.01."
5. Save "Document2" in a file using the name "ch15ex05.02."
6. Print both documents.
7. Close both documents.

EXERCISE 6

INSTRUCTIONS: 1. Create the following document.

```
current date



Ms. Sharon Perroni
645 Thornwood Court
Naples, FL 33962

Dear Ms. Perroni:

You have been a customer of ours for over 15 years.  In that time
you have always paid your charges on time.

Because you are a good customer
```

2. Create a new document.
3. Enter the following text in the blank document.

```
                              MEMORANDUM


TO:       TIRSH DOSTALEK, Manager, Store 14001
FROM:     JANES SUEFERT, CUSTOMER SERVICES
DATE:     current date
SUBJECT: TOO MANY UNSATISFIED CUSTOMERS

Please stop in to see me as soon as possible.  Your office has
received its fourth complaint this week.  What is going on?

I know that "off" locations have their problems, but four
complaints in one week is too many.  Is it because your workers did
not receive the proper indoctrination?


xx
```

4. Spell check the memo.
5. Preview and print the memo.
6. Save the memo in a file using the name "ch15ex06.02."
7. Continue with the first document adding the following text.

```
we want to give you a 25 percent off coupon to use the next time
you are in our store.  We really appreciate your patronage.

Sincerely,



Linda Breuer, Store Manager



xx
```

8. Spell check the letter.
9. Preview and print the letter.
10. Save the letter in a file using the name "ch15ex06.01."
11. Close both documents.

EXERCISE 7

INSTRUCTIONS:

1. Open the document "ch15ex04.01."
2. Open the document "ch15ex06.02."
3. Delete the first paragraph from "ch15ex04.01."
4. Delete the second paragraph from "ch15ex06.02."
5. Print both documents.
6. Print document "ch15ex05.02" without opening it.
7. Close both documents without saving changes.

EXERCISE 8

INSTRUCTIONS:

1. Open the document "ch15ex04.01."
2. Open the document "ch15ex05.02."
3. Open the document "ch15ex03.02."
4. Tile the documents.
5. Create a new document.
6. Cascade the documents.
7. Size the "Document4" window so that it appears very small.
8. Move the "Document4" window to the bottom, left corner of the screen.
9. Close all of the documents without saving changes.

EXERCISE 9

INSTRUCTIONS:

1. Open the document "ch12ex03." If you have not created the document yet, do so at this time.
2. Open the document "ch11ex03." If you have not created the document yet, do so at this time.
3. Create a new document.
4. Cascade the documents.
5. Tile the documents.
6. Print the document "ch12ex03."

7. Spell check the document "ch11ex03."
8. Type the following text in "Document3."

```
The July 24th meeting has been cancelled.  Please reschedule any
appointments as necessary.

Please advise all staff of the schedule change.
```

9. Save the note as "ch15ex09."
10. Close all the documents without saving changes.

CHAPTER SIXTEEN

MERGING DOCUMENTS

OBJECTIVES

In this chapter, you will learn to:

- Create a primary file
- Create a secondary file
- Merge a primary and secondary file

CHAPTER OVERVIEW

In this chapter, the processes for merging documents and for printing merged documents are described and illustrated.

CREATING A PRIMARY FILE

A document merge is a procedure in which text is combined from several documents and printed. Some applications of document merge are mass-produced form letters, mailing labels, and contracts. Merges are useful when the same text is repeated in many documents. For example, suppose the same letter must be sent to ABC Can Company's 1,000 customers. The only difference between one letter and the next is the customer's name, address, and salutation. You can work very hard and create 1,000 separate documents.

Or you can work very smart by creating only two documents! One document contains the repeated text and special merge codes that take the place of the customer's name, address, and salutation. A second document contains only the text that corresponds to the merge codes in the first document; i.e., the names, addresses, and salutations of each customer. You then use the Merge feature to merge these two documents to print 1,000 letters.

The document that contains the merge codes and any repeated text is called the primary file. This file manages the entire merge operation. The merge codes in the primary file call for text to be inserted where each code resides. This text can be supplied from three sources. One source is a secondary file. This file is a WordPerfect document that contains text to be merged, like the document in the example above that contains the names, addresses, and salutations.

Another source for text to be inserted into the primary file is the keyboard. As the merge is operating, you can enter data (i.e., names and addresses) from the keyboard. The third source is a DOS delimited text file. This source is useful when you are getting the data from a program other than WordPerfect.

One of the merge codes in the primary file that calls for text to be inserted in its place is the {FIELD} merge code. A field is a data item or piece of text, like name, address, salutation, or phone number. In the primary file, there can be many field merge codes throughout the document. In the secondary file, there is a corresponding field of text for each field merge code. All fields in the secondary file make up a record.

The following example shows how to create a primary file and insert the {FIELD} codes into the document. The next section will show you how to create a secondary file with text to correspond with each {FIELD} code.

Before starting this section, close any documents on the screen. Change the default directory to "a:\wpdocs" or to "c:\wpdocs."

To display the Merge Codes screen:

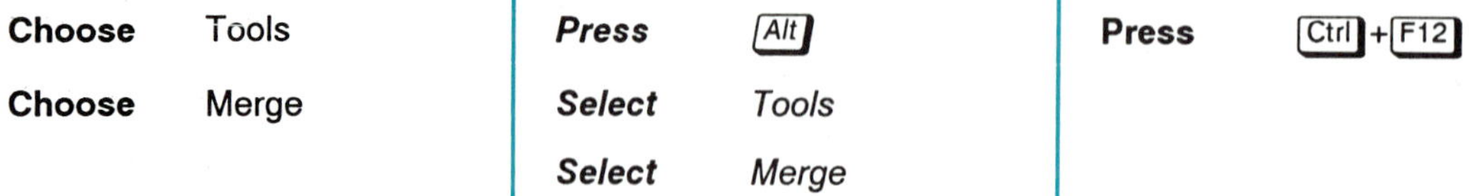

Choose	Tools	***Press***	*Alt*	**Press**	Ctrl+F12
Choose	Merge	***Select***	*Tools*		
		Select	*Merge*		

Your screen should look like Figure 16-1.

Figure 16-1

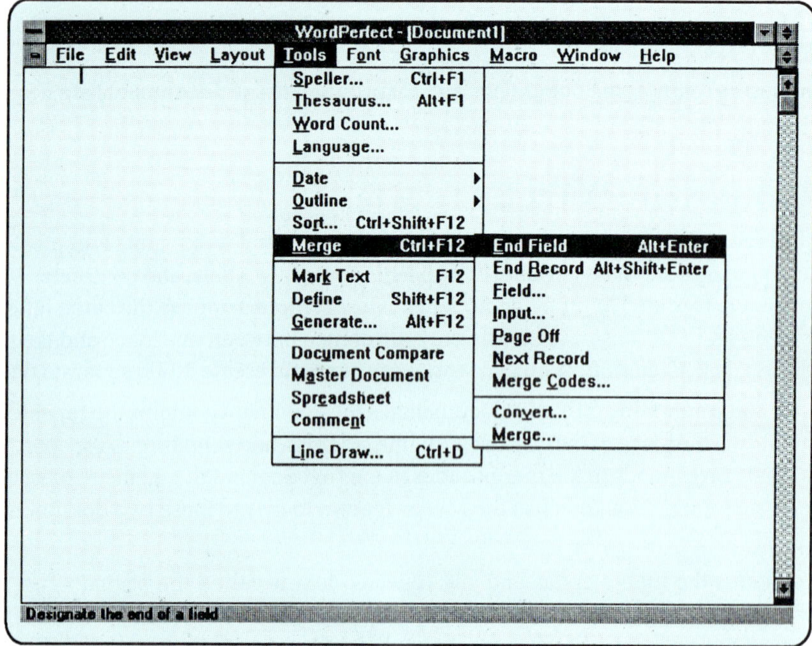

The menu items are described below:

The **End Field** merge code indicates the end of a secondary field. A field is a data item or piece of text, like name, address, or phone number.

The **End Record** merge code indicates the end of a secondary file record. A record contains all of the fields for an individual entry in a secondary file. For example, one record can contain the name field, address field and salutation field.

The **Field** merge code indicates which field from the secondary file you would like inserted at the current position in the primary file. You will be prompted for the field name or number.

The **Input** merge code stops the merge and waits for you to input information from the keyboard.

The **Page Off** merge code tells WordPerfect not to place each printed merge document on a new page.

The **Next Record** merge code instructs the merge process to move ahead to the next record in the secondary file.

The **Merge Codes** option allows you to select other merge codes. A dialog box appears containing a list of various merge codes. You can use the scroll bars or pointer-movement keys to scroll through the list. For additional information on the list of merge codes, see the WordPerfect Reference Manual.

To insert the merge code for the current date in our primary file example:

Choose	Merge Codes	***Select***	*Merge Codes*	**Select**	Merge Codes

Your screen should look like Figure 16-2.

Figure 16-2

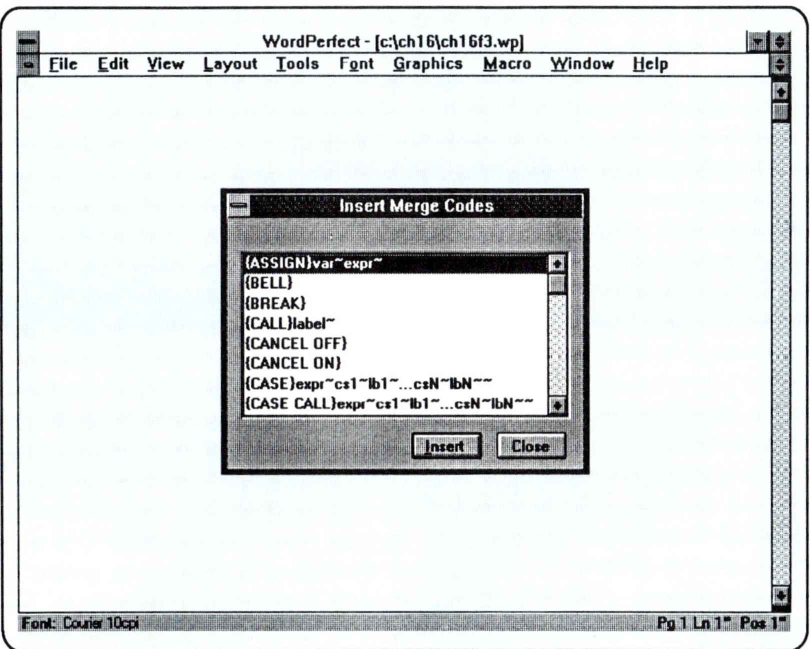

Notice the Insert Merge Codes dialog box appears on your screen.

To select the {DATE} merge code:

Click	the down scroll arrow until the {DATE} option is visible	***Type***	*D*	**Type**	D
Click	on the {DATE} option		*or*		or

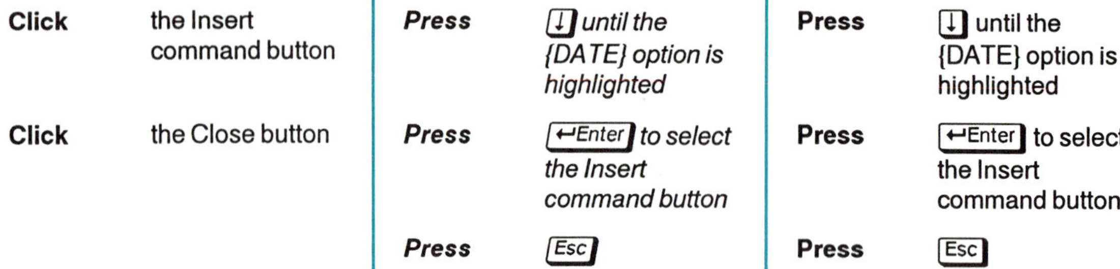

Click	the Insert command button	***Press***	*[↓] until the {DATE} option is highlighted*	**Press**	[↓] until the {DATE} option is highlighted
Click	the Close button	***Press***	*[↵Enter] to select the Insert command button*	**Press**	[↵Enter] to select the Insert command button
		Press	*[Esc]*	**Press**	[Esc]

The top part of your screen should look like Figure 16-3.

Figure 16-3

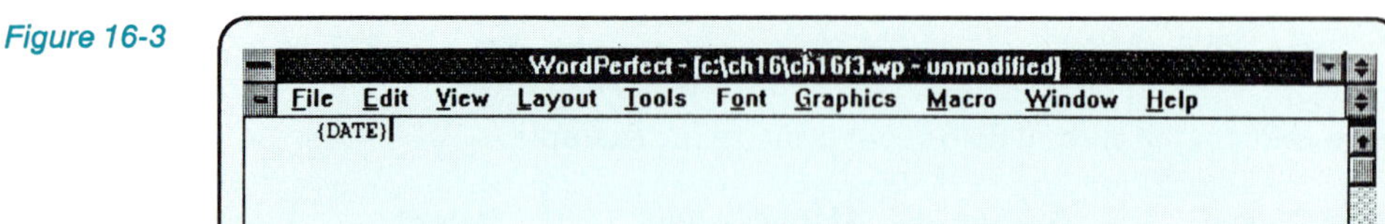

To insert three blank lines:

Press	[↵Enter] four times	***Press***	*[↵Enter] four times*	**Press**	[↵Enter] four times

The Field code indicates which field in the secondary file you want to insert at the current position in the primary file. You are prompted for the field name or number.

To insert a field code:

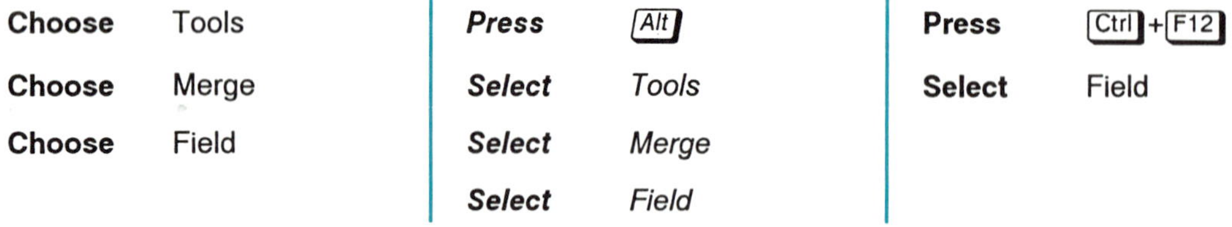

Choose	Tools	***Press***	*[Alt]*	**Press**	[Ctrl]+[F12]
Choose	Merge	***Select***	*Tools*	**Select**	Field
Choose	Field	***Select***	*Merge*		
		Select	*Field*		

A field can be a name or a number.

To identify the first field as "Title":

Type	Title	***Type***	*Title*	**Type**	Title
Click	the OK command button	***Press***	*[↵Enter]*	**Press**	[↵Enter]

Your screen should look like Figure 16-4.

Figure 16-4

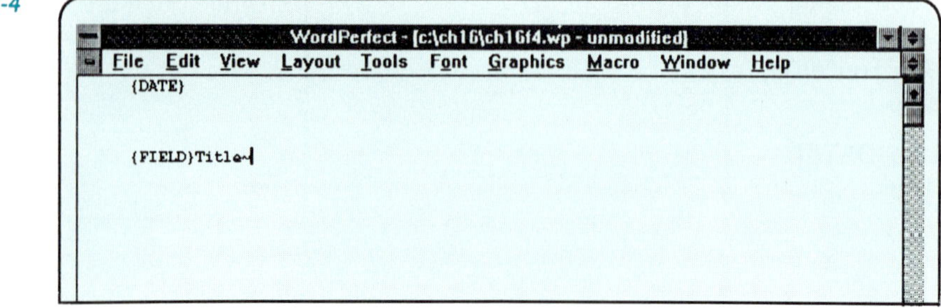

Notice that WordPerfect places a tilde (~) after the field name "Title" to mark the end of the merge code.

To insert a space between fields:

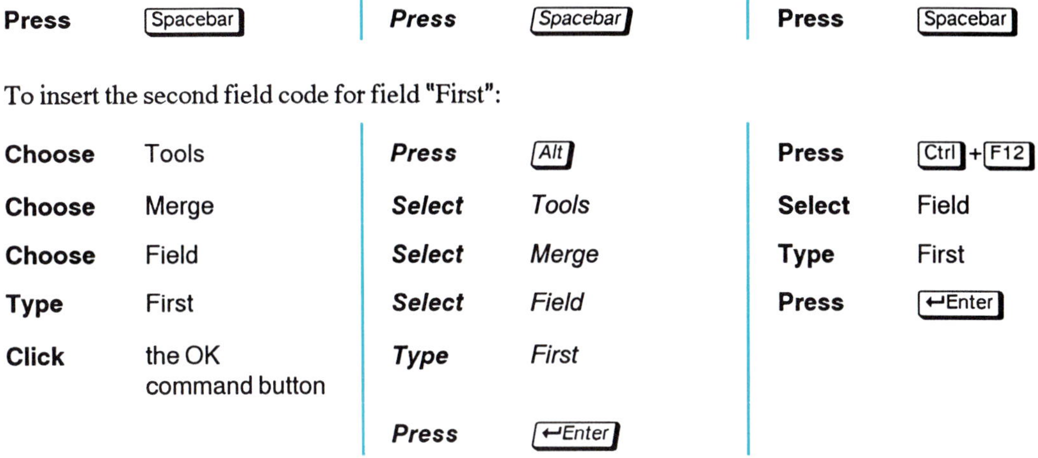

Press	Spacebar	***Press***	*Spacebar*	**Press**	Spacebar

To insert the second field code for field "First":

Choose	Tools	***Press***	*Alt*	**Press**	Ctrl + F12
Choose	Merge	***Select***	*Tools*	**Select**	Field
Choose	Field	***Select***	*Merge*	**Type**	First
Type	First	***Select***	*Field*	**Press**	↵Enter
Click	the OK command button	***Type***	*First*		
		Press	*↵Enter*		

The upper part of your screen should look like Figure 16-5.

Figure 16-5

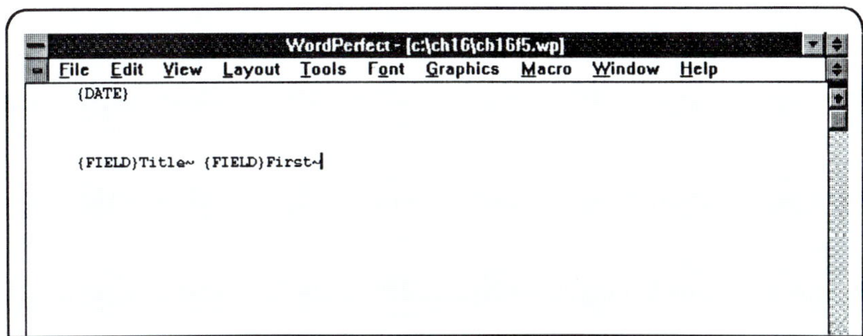

To insert a space between fields:

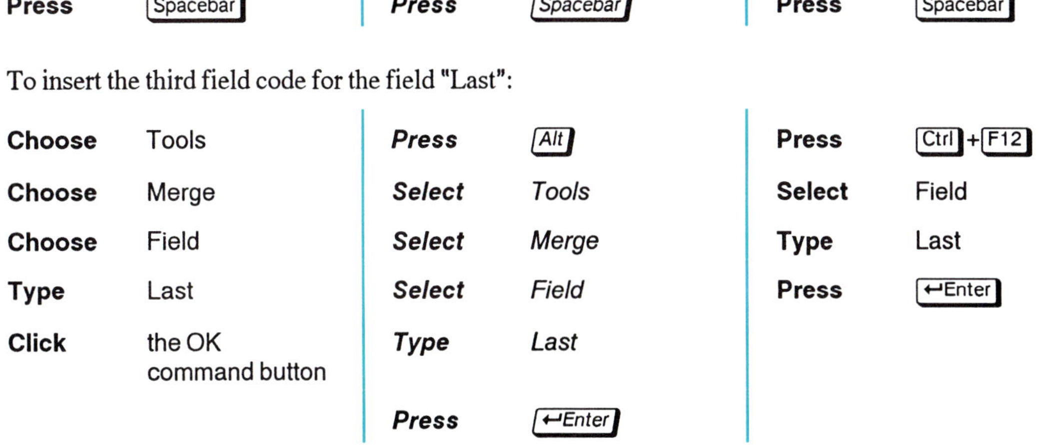

Press	Spacebar	***Press***	*Spacebar*	**Press**	Spacebar

To insert the third field code for the field "Last":

Choose	Tools	***Press***	*Alt*	**Press**	Ctrl + F12
Choose	Merge	***Select***	*Tools*	**Select**	Field
Choose	Field	***Select***	*Merge*	**Type**	Last
Type	Last	***Select***	*Field*	**Press**	↵Enter
Click	the OK command button	***Type***	*Last*		
		Press	*↵Enter*		

The top segment of your screen should look like Figure 16-6.

Figure 16-6

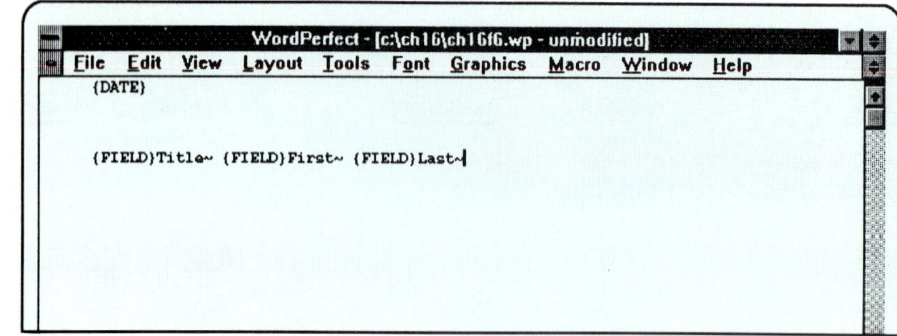

To move to the next line:

Press	↵Enter	***Press***	*↵Enter*	**Press**	↵Enter

To insert the fourth field code for field "Company":

Choose	Tools	***Press***	*Alt*	**Press**	Ctrl+F12
Choose	Merge	***Select***	*Tools*	**Select**	Field
Choose	Field	***Select***	*Merge*		
		Select	*Field*		

If one or more fields do not contain text in the secondary file, spaces or blank lines are printed in the resulting document. You can place a "?" after the field name to avoid blank lines or spaces. When the primary and secondary files are merged, fields in the secondary file that do not contain text are ignored.

There are a few records that do not include a company name. To avoid blank lines in the merged document:

Type	Company?	***Type***	*Company?*	**Type**	Company?
Click	the OK command button	***Press***	*↵Enter*	**Press**	↵Enter

To move to the next line:

Press	↵Enter	***Press***	*↵Enter*	**Press**	↵Enter

To insert the fifth field code for field "Address":

Choose	Tools	***Press***	*Alt*	**Press**	Ctrl+F12
Choose	Merge	***Select***	*Tools*	**Select**	Field
Choose	Field	***Select***	*Merge*	**Type**	Address
Type	Address	***Select***	*Field*	**Press**	↵Enter
Click	the OK command button	***Type***	*Address*		
		Press	*↵Enter*		

The top part of your screen should look like Figure 16-7.

Figure 16-7

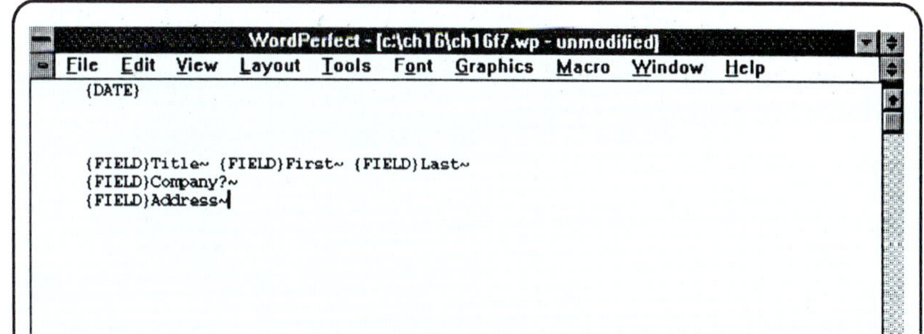

To insert one blank line:

Press	↵Enter twice	***Press***	*↵Enter twice*	**Press**	↵Enter twice

To insert the salutation text:

Type	Dear	***Type***	*Dear*	**Type**	Dear
Press	Spacebar	***Press***	*Spacebar*	**Press**	Spacebar

You can repeat fields in a primary file.

To repeat the "Title" field code in the salutation:

Choose	Tools	***Press***	*Alt*	**Press**	Ctrl+F12
Choose	Merge	***Select***	*Tools*	**Select**	Field
Choose	Field	***Select***	*Merge*	**Type**	Title
Type	Title	***Select***	*Field*	**Press**	↵Enter
Click	the OK command button	***Type***	*Title*		
		Press	*↵Enter*		

To insert a space between fields:

Press	Spacebar	***Press***	*Spacebar*	**Press**	Spacebar

To repeat the "Last" field code in the salutation, add a colon, and skip one line before starting the letter:

Choose	Tools	***Press***	*Alt*	**Press**	Ctrl+F12
Choose	Merge	***Select***	*Tools*	**Select**	Field
Choose	Field	***Select***	*Merge*	**Type**	Last
Type	Last	***Select***	*Field*	**Press**	↵Enter
Click	the OK command button	***Type***	*Last*	**Type**	:

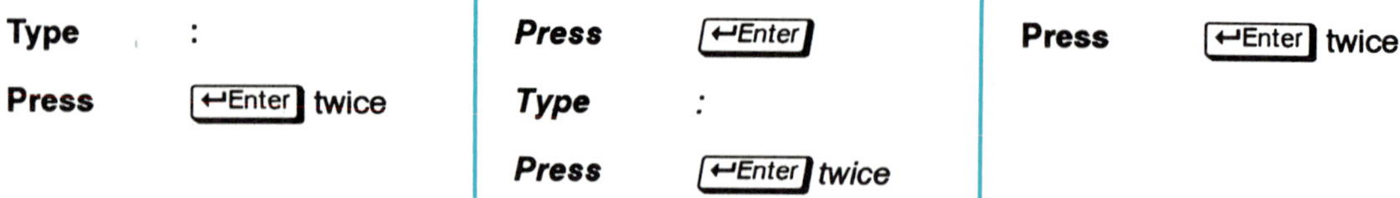

Type :
Press ↵Enter twice

Press ↵Enter
Type :
Press ↵Enter twice

Press ↵Enter twice

The upper part of your screen should look like Figure 16-8.

Figure 16-8

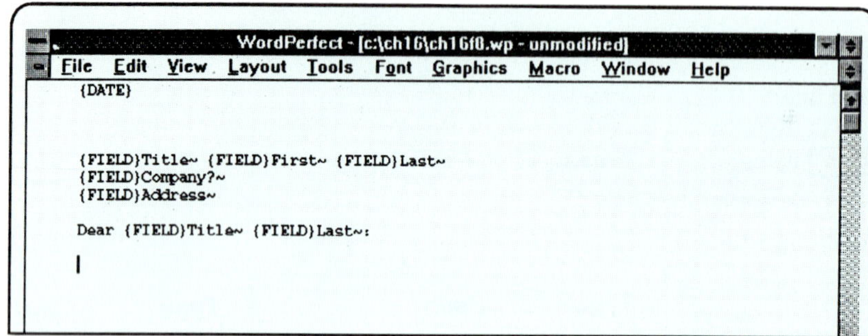

Complete the letter as shown in Figure 16-9.

Figure 16-9

```
Congratulations on your new business venture.  I wish you many
years of success.

My firm is a full service CPA firm.  We are committed to serving
our clients' needs efficiently and effectively.  We offer all
types of accounting and auditing services, as well as tax
counseling and tax return preparation.  Additionally, we also
provide pickup and delivery service.

I would appreciate the opportunity to discuss with you how your
company could benefit from our unique solution to your financial
deadlines.

I hope to hear from you soon.

Sincerely,



Michael Roberts
```

Save the document as "letter.ltr."

To view the beginning of the document:

Click	at the left margin at the top of the document	***Move***	*the insertion point to the left margin at the top of the document*	**Move**	the insertion point to the left margin at the top of the document

■ CREATING A SECONDARY FILE

The secondary file is a WordPerfect document that contains the text that is inserted at each field merge code in the primary file. A field is an item of data or text, such as name, address, or title. All fields in a merge document make up a record. A record is a set of related data or text.

In the secondary file, you first define the record and the fields that make up the record. There is no limit to the number of fields in a record. The primary file does not have to use all the fields defined in a record. During the merge operation, the primary file will select only the fields it needs to complete the merge document.

You may enter as much data or text for each record as you want. Every field must be represented in each record. The field can contain text or be empty, but the field must exist. For example, suppose a record has fields for name, company, and address. However, not everyone may have a company. When entering text into the secondary file, everyone must have a field designated for the company. But some of the people will have no text in the company field.

Each field can have varying lines of text. For example, you might have two lines in the address field of one record and three lines in the address field of another record.

You need a blank document to create your secondary file. To create a blank document:

Choose	File	***Press***	*Alt*	**Press**	Shift+F4
Choose	New	***Select***	*File*		
		Select	*New*		

Your screen should look like Figure 16-10.

Figure 16-10

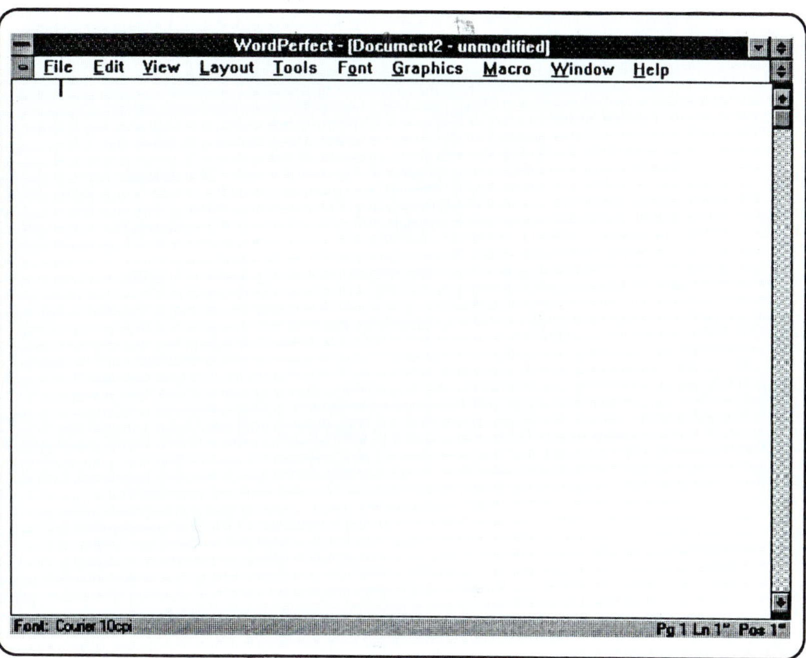

Notice that you cannot see the document "letter.ltr" when the blank document is open.

To arrange the documents so that you can see both:

Choose	Window	***Press***	*Alt*
Choose	Tile	***Select***	*Window*
		Select	*Tile*

Your screen should look like Figure 16-11.

Figure 16-11

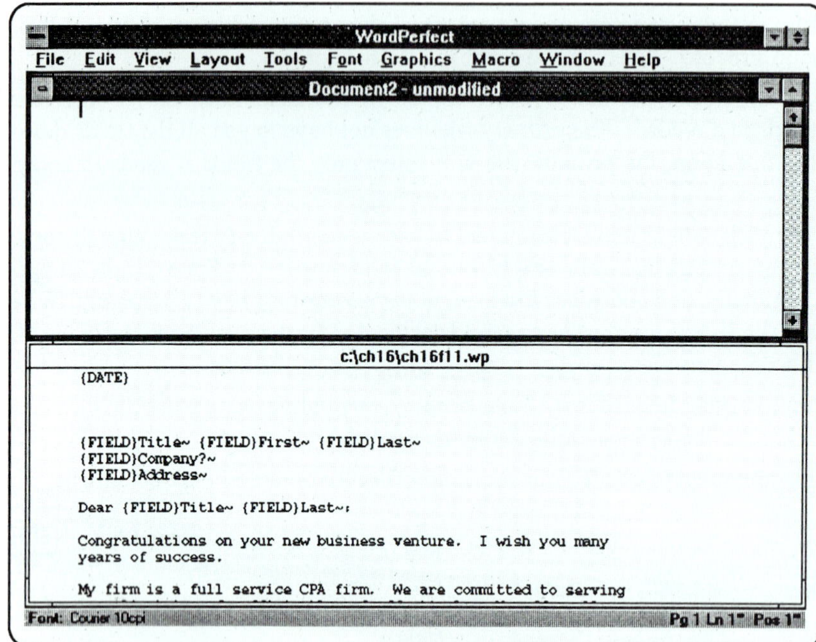

Notice that "Document2" is the active window. Any commands that are performed or text that is entered will affect "Document2."

The first merge code in the secondary file should be the {FIELD NAMES} code. This code defines the names of the fields and sets their order in the record. The names of the fields must match the names defined in the primary file. This code should be the first line of the secondary file.

To name the fields in the secondary file:

Choose	Tools	***Press***	*Alt*	**Press**	Ctrl+F12
Choose	Merge	***Select***	*Tools*	**Select**	Merge Codes
Choose	Merge Codes	***Select***	*Merge*	**Type**	F
Click	the down scroll arrow until the option {FIELD NAMES}name1~ ...nameN~~ is visible	***Select***	*Merge Codes*	**Press**	↓ to select the option {FIELD NAMES}name1~ ...nameN~~

Click	on the {FIELD NAMES}name1~ ...nameN~~ option	***Type***	*F*	**Press**	[↵Enter] to select the Insert command button
Click	the Insert command button	***Press***	*[↓] to select the option {FIELD NAMES}name1~ ...nameN~~*		
		Press	*[↵Enter] to select the Insert command button*		

The Merge Field Name(s) dialog box appears. Your screen should look like Figure 16-12.

Figure 16-12

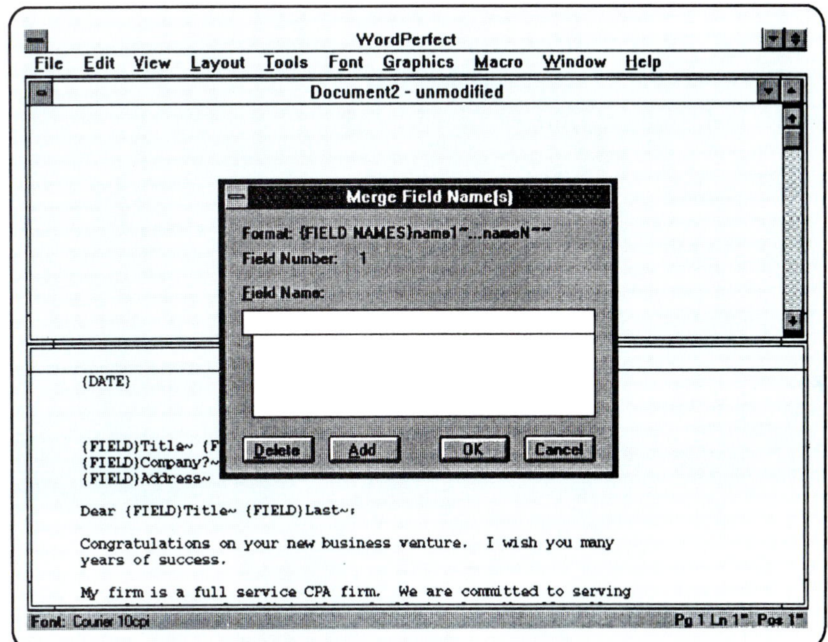

Notice that you are prompted to enter the name for Field Number 1 in the dialog box.

To enter the name:

Type	Title	***Type***	*Title*	**Type**	Title
Click	the Add command button	***Press***	*[Alt]+[A] to select the Add command button*	**Press**	[Alt]+[A] to select the Add command button

To enter the name for Field Number 2:

Type	First	***Type***	*First*	**Type**	First
Click	the Add command button	***Press***	*[Alt]+[A] to select the Add command button*	**Press**	[Alt]+[A] to select the Add command button

To enter the name for Field Number 3:

Type	Last	***Type***	*Last*	**Type**	Last
Click	the Add command button	***Press***	*Alt+A to select the Add command button*	**Press**	Alt+A to select the Add command button

To enter the name for Field Number 4:

Type	Company	***Type***	*Company*	**Type**	Company
Click	the Add command button	***Press***	*Alt+A to select the Add command button*	**Press**	Alt+A to select the Add command button

Notice that the "?" is not part of the "Company" field name. The "?" is a variable to be entered in the primary file only. Do not use the "?" in the secondary file.

To enter the name for Field Number 5, the last field in the record:

Type	Address	***Type***	*Address*	**Type**	Address
Click	the Add command button	***Press***	*Alt+A to select the Add command button*	**Press**	Alt+A to select the Add command button

To end naming the fields:

Click	the OK command button	***Press***	*Tab to select the OK command button*	**Press**	Tab to select the OK command button
		Press	*↵Enter*	**Press**	↵Enter

To close the Merge Codes dialog box:

Click	the Close command button	***Press***	*Esc*	**Press**	Esc

Notice that an {END RECORD} code is placed at the end of the line to tell WordPerfect that this is the end of the record definition. This code is inserted between each record in the secondary file.

The top section of your screen should look like Figure 16-13.

Figure 16-13

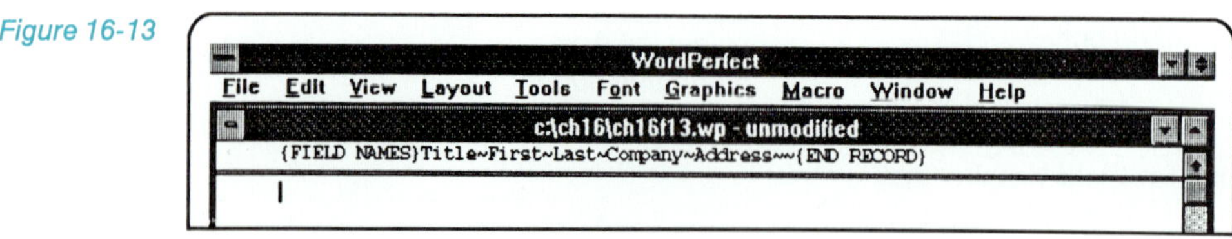

To enter the data for the first field "Title" of record 1:

Type	Mr.	***Type***	*Mr.*	**Type**	Mr.

Fields in each record are separated by the {END FIELD} code and a hard return.

To end the "Title" field:

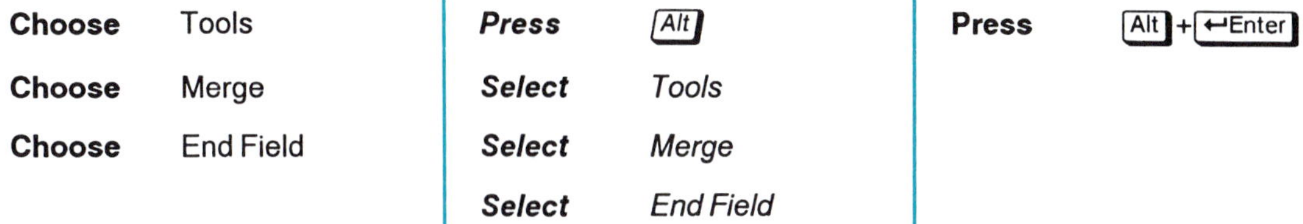

Choose	Tools	***Press***	*Alt*	**Press**	Alt + ↵Enter
Choose	Merge	***Select***	*Tools*		
Choose	End Field	***Select***	*Merge*		
		Select	*End Field*		

Your screen should look like Figure 16-14.

Figure 16-14

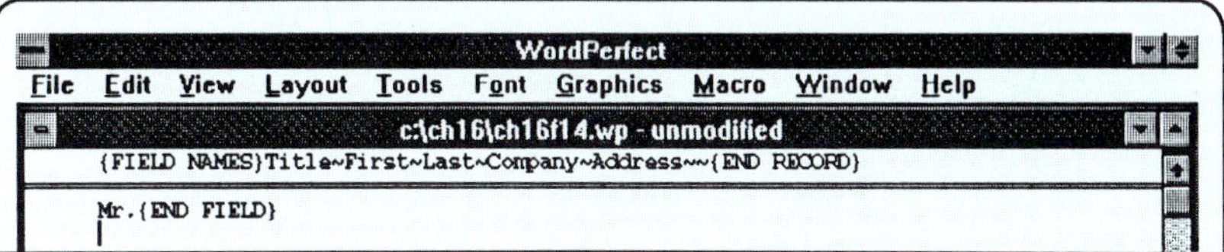

Notice that the next field name appears on the status bar at the bottom of the screen.

To enter the data for the second field "First" of record 1:

Type	John	***Type***	*John*	**Type**	John

To end the "First" field:

Choose	Tools	***Press***	*Alt*	**Press**	Alt + ↵Enter
Choose	Merge	***Select***	*Tools*		
Choose	End Field	***Select***	*Merge*		
		Select	*End Field*		

To enter the data for the third field "Last" of record 1:

Type	Brown	***Type***	*Brown*	**Type**	Brown

To end the "Last" field:

Choose	Tools	***Press***	*Alt*	**Press**	Alt + ↵Enter
Choose	Merge	***Select***	*Tools*		
Choose	End Field	***Select***	*Merge*		
		Select	*End Field*		

If a field is empty, the field still needs an {END FIELD} code.

To enter the code for the empty fourth field "Company" of record 1:

Choose	Tools	***Press***	*Alt*	**Press**	Alt + ↵Enter
Choose	Merge	***Select***	*Tools*		

Choose	End Field	***Select***	*Merge*		
		Select	*End Field*		

To enter the two-line data for the fifth field "Address" of record 1:

Type	1900 West Road	***Type***	*1900 West Road*	**Type**	1900 West Road
Press	[↵Enter]	***Press***	*[↵Enter]*	**Press**	[↵Enter]
Type	Houston, TX 77088	***Type***	*Houston, TX 77088*	**Type**	Houston, TX 77088

To end the "Address" field:

Choose	Tools	***Press***	*[Alt]*	**Press**	[Alt]+[↵Enter]
Choose	Merge	***Select***	*Tools*		
Choose	End Field	***Select***	*Merge*		
		Select	*End Field*		

Records are separated by the {END RECORD} merge code followed by a hard page break [HPg]. To end record 1:

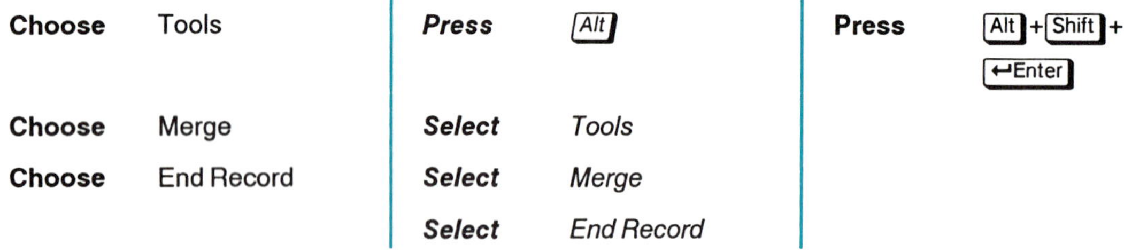

Choose	Tools	***Press***	*[Alt]*	**Press**	[Alt]+[Shift]+[↵Enter]
Choose	Merge	***Select***	*Tools*		
Choose	End Record	***Select***	*Merge*		
		Select	*End Record*		

Your screen should look like Figure 16-15.

Figure 16-15

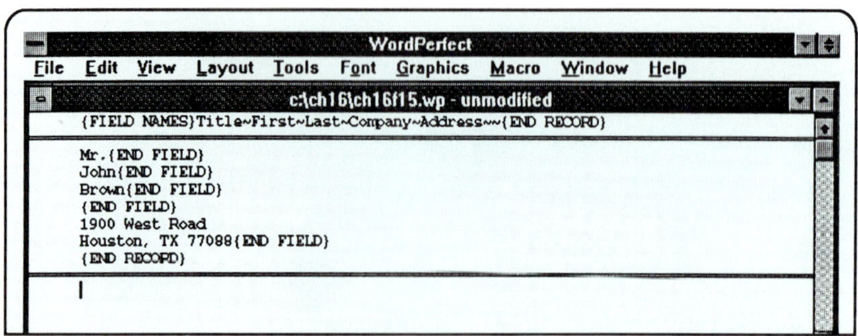

Complete records 2 and 3 as displayed in Figure 16-16.

Figure 16-16

```
Mr.{END FIELD}
George{END FIELD}
Johnson{END FIELD}
ABC Company{END FIELD}
3305 West University
Houston, TX 77098{END FIELD}
{END RECORD}
===========================================
Ms.{END FIELD}
Elsa{END FIELD}
Moreland{END FIELD}
XYZ Company{END FIELD}
1301 Washington
Houston, TX 77004{END FIELD}
{END RECORD}
===========================================
```

Save the document as "address.ltr." Close both documents.

■ MERGING PRIMARY AND SECONDARY FILES

During the merge operation, the text from the primary file is combined with the fields of text from the secondary file. Each merged document is separated from the next with a hard page break [HPg].

The merged documents produced are first displayed on the screen. You can save this document or print it.

To perform a merge:

Choose	Tools	***Press***	*Alt*	**Press**	Ctrl+F12
Choose	Merge	***Select***	*Tools*	**Select**	Merge
Choose	Merge	***Select***	*Merge*		
		Select	*Merge*		

Your screen should look like Figure 16-17.

Figure 16-17

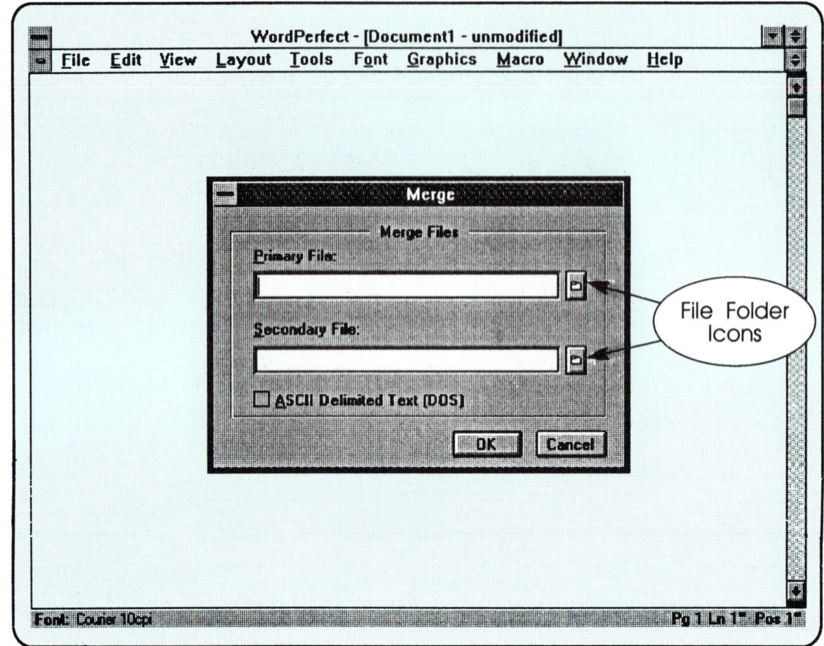

You can either type in the file name for the primary or secondary file or use a list of files by clicking on the file folder icon. When you find the file you want, choose Select.

To enter the name of the primary file:

Type	**letter.ltr**	***Type***	***letter.ltr***	**Type**	**letter.ltr**

To enter the name of the secondary file:

Double-click	the Secondary File text box	***Press***	*Alt+S to select the Secondary File text box*	**Press**	Alt+S to select the Secondary File text box
Type	**address.ltr**	***Type***	***address.ltr***	**Type**	**address.ltr**
Click	the OK command button	***Press***	*↵Enter*	**Press**	↵Enter

The message "Merging" appears on the status bar briefly while the documents are being merged. After the merge is completed:

Click	at the beginning of the document	***Move***	*the insertion point to the beginning of the document*	**Move**	the insertion point to the beginning of the document

Except for the date, your screen should look like Figure 16-18.

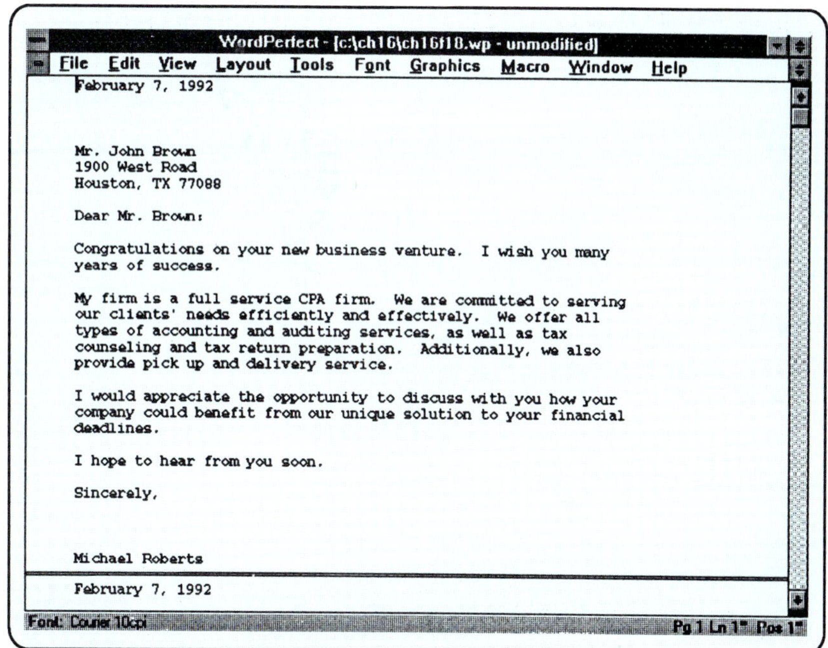

Figure 16-18

You may have an extra page at the bottom of the document that only includes the current date. This extra page is created if you have an extra hard return at the end of your secondary file. You can delete the extra page from your merge document using normal editing techniques. To avoid merging an extra page in the future, remove the extra hard return from your secondary file.

If you want, select the Print feature to print the merged documents.

You do not need to save the merged documents since you can perform the merge again at any time. Close the document without saving changes.

EXERCISE 1

INSTRUCTIONS: Define the following terms:

1. Document merge ______________________________

   ____

2. Primary file ______________________________

   ____

3. Merge codes ______________________________

   ____

4. Secondary file ______________________________

   ____

5. Record ____

____

6. Field ____

____

7. Field merge code ____

____

8. End Record merge code ____

____

9. End Field merge code ____

____

EXERCISE 2

INSTRUCTIONS: Circle T if the statement is true and F if the statement is false.

T F 1. A document merge is a procedure in which text from several documents is appended into one document.

T F 2. The primary file manages the entire merge operation.

T F 3. Three sources of data for the document merge are secondary files, DOS delimited text files, and the keyboard.

T F 4. In the primary file, there can be only one field merge code in the document.

T F 5. In the secondary file, there is a corresponding field of text for each field merge code.

T F 6. A tilde (~) after the field name marks the beginning of the merge code.

T F 7. When inserting field merge codes in the primary file, you can place a "?" after the field name to avoid blank lines or spaces for fields that do not contain text.

T F 8. You cannot repeat the fields in a primary file.

T F 9. The first merge code in the secondary file should be the {FIELD NAMES} code.

T F 10. When defining the record in the secondary file, you can enter a maximum of five fields.

EXERCISE 3

INSTRUCTIONS:

1. Create the following documents.
2. Spell check each document.
3. Save the letter in a primary file using the name "ch16ex03.pri."
4. Save the address list in a secondary file using the name "ch16ex03.sec."
5. Print the primary file and the secondary file.
6. Close both documents.
7. Merge the two documents.
8. Print the merge document.
9. Save the merge document in a file using the name "ch16ex03.mrg."
10. Close the document.

PRIMARY FILE

```
{DATE}


{FIELD}Title~ {FIELD}First~ {FIELD}Middle~ {FIELD}Last~
{FIELD}Address~

Dear {FIELD}First~:

As a preferred customer, you are invited to our special pre-July
4th sale.  It will be held on July 1-3 at all locations in town.

We will have all of our summer clothing on sale at 50% off regular
prices.  For the best selection, be sure and get to one of our
stores early.

We look forward to seeing you!

Sincerely yours,



Tom Jackson
President
```

SECONDARY FILE

```
{FIELD NAMES}Title~First~Middle~Last~Address~~{END RECORD}
====================================================================
Ms.{END FIELD}
Susan{END FIELD}
K.{END FIELD}
Jackson{END FIELD}
1643 Main Street
St. Louis, MO  64072{END FIELD}
{END RECORD}
====================================================================
Mr.{END FIELD}
William{END FIELD}
A.{END FIELD}
Batsell{END FIELD}
P.O. Box 2299
St. Louis, MO  64033-2099{END FIELD}
{END RECORD}
====================================================================
```

EXERCISE 4

INSTRUCTIONS:

1. Create the following documents.
2. Spell check each document.
3. Save the letter in a primary file using the name "ch16ex04.pri."
4. Save the address list in a secondary file using the name "ch16ex04.sec."
5. Print the primary and secondary files.
6. Close both documents.
7. Merge the two documents.
8. Print the merge document.
9. Save the merge document in a file using the name "ch16ex04.mrg."
10. Close the document.

PRIMARY FILE

```
{DATE}


{FIELD}Title~ {FIELD}First~ {FIELD}Last~
{FIELD}Address~

Dear {FIELD}Title~ {FIELD}Last~:

We would like your help in contributing to the Annual Save the
Mongoose Fund.  You have helped many causes in the past.  We know
that once you read the enclosed information you will give
generously.

This is a new cause, and we will not bother you again if you do not
want to help.  Just return the enclosed envelope and mark "No."

Sincerely,



George Voegel
Chairman

Enclosures
```

SECONDARY FILE

```
{FIELD NAMES}Title~First~Last~Address~~{END RECORD}
========================================================
Ms.{END FIELD}
Kelli{END FIELD}
McKinnon{END FIELD}
2467 California Avenue
Huntsville, AL  35804{END FIELD}
{END RECORD}
========================================================
Mrs.{END FIELD}
Victoria{END FIELD}
Prestia{END FIELD}
9204 Sunset Drive
Flagstaff, AZ  86001{END FIELD}
{END RECORD}
========================================================
Ms.{END FIELD}
Jennifer{END FIELD}
Price{END FIELD}
3829 Cherry Court
Little Rock, AR  72201{END FIELD}
{END RECORD}
========================================================
Ms.{END FIELD}
Debbie{END FIELD}
Janezick{END FIELD}
212 Mountview Road
Durango, CO  81301{END FIELD}
{END RECORD}
========================================================
```

EXERCISE 5

INSTRUCTIONS:

1. Create the following documents.
2. Spell check each document.
3. Save the letter in a primary file using the name "ch16ex05.pri."
4. Save the address list in a secondary file using the name "ch16ex05.sec."
5. Print the primary and secondary files.
6. Close both documents.

PRIMARY FILE

```
{DATE}


{FIELD}Title~ {FIELD}First~ {FIELD}Last~
{FIELD}Pos?~
{FIELD}Company?~
{FIELD}Address~

Dear {FIELD}First~,

As a long-time customer, you must be aware that we have been having
some financial difficulties.

The problems have gotten worse, and we will be forced to close our
doors for good at the end of May.  We thank you for your past
patronage.

Sincerely,


Zigmund Zachary

xx
```

SECONDARY FILE

```
{FIELD NAMES}Title~First~Last~Pos~Company~Address~~{END RECORD}
================================================================
Mr.{END FIELD}
James{END FIELD}
Washington{END FIELD}
Director of Sales{END FIELD}
Nevada Lumber{END FIELD}
1177 Wickshire Lane
Reno, NV  89501{END FIELD}
{END RECORD}
================================================================
Ms.{END FIELD}
Debbie{END FIELD}
Murphy{END FIELD}
{END FIELD}
{END FIELD}
300 Shadow Bend Road
Aztec, NM  87101{END FIELD}
{END RECORD}
================================================================
Mr.{END FIELD}
Steve{END FIELD}
Gobert{END FIELD}
{END FIELD}
{END FIELD}
174 York Street
Columbus, IN  47201{END FIELD}
{END RECORD}
================================================================
Ms.{END FIELD}
Jennifer{END FIELD}
Gartner{END FIELD}
Purchasing Agent{END FIELD}
AAA Kitchen & Bath{END FIELD}
2020 Smith Rd.
Amherst, MA  03031{END FIELD}
{END RECORD}
================================================================
Dr.{END FIELD}
Michael{END FIELD}
Ellasser{END FIELD}
{END FIELD}
{END FIELD}
348 East Main Street
Asheboro, NC  27203{END FIELD}
{END RECORD}
================================================================
```

EXERCISE 6

INSTRUCTIONS:

1. Add the following names and addresses to "ch16ex05.sec."
2. Save the secondary file using the same name.
3. Merge the document with "ch16ex05.pri."
4. Preview the merge document.
5. Print the merge document.
6. Close the document without saving changes.

```
Mr.{END FIELD}
Anthony{END FIELD}
Cacaccio{END FIELD}
Sales Agent{END FIELD}
{END FIELD}
914 Lawndale
Kansas City, KS  66110{END FIELD}
{END RECORD}
```

```
Ms.{END FIELD}
Laura{END FIELD}
Sundberiage{END FIELD}
{END FIELD}
Barrington Lumber Company{END FIELD}
1022 Pepper Road
Barrington, IL  60010{END FIELD}
{END RECORD}
```

```
Mr.{END FIELD}
Kevin{END FIELD}
Martins{END FIELD}
Regional Manager{END FIELD}
Park Lumber Company{END FIELD}
865 Skyline Drive
Laramie, WY  82070{END FIELD}
{END RECORD}
```

EXERCISE 7

INSTRUCTIONS:

1. Create the following documents.
2. Spell check each document.
3. Save the letter in a primary file using the name "ch16ex07.pri."
4. Save the address list in a secondary file using the name "ch16ex07.sec."
5. Close the two documents.
6. Merge the two documents.
7. Print the merge document.
8. Close the merge document without saving changes.

PRIMARY FILE

```
{DATE}


{FIELD}First?~ {FIELD}Last?~
{FIELD}Pos?~
{FIELD}School?~
{FIELD}Address?~

Dear {FIELD}Last~:

The Fall Conference for the National Business Teachers is just
around the corner.  It will be held this year at the Hilton Head,
South Carolina, November 10, 11, and 12.

I hope that you are planning to attend.  The meetings sound
exciting and the exhibitions will be better than ever.

Read the enclosed brochure for all the details.

Sincerely,



Richard Dyer
President

xx
```

SECONDARY FILE

```
{FIELD NAMES}First~Last~Pos~School~Address~~{END RECORD}
================================================================
Richard{END FIELD}
Cardinali{END FIELD}
Department Chairman{END FIELD}
Central High School{END FIELD}
Madison, WI  53701{END FIELD}
{END RECORD}
================================================================
Mark{END FIELD}
Hale{END FIELD}
Department Chairman{END FIELD}
Lincoln Community College{END FIELD}
Tacoma, WA  98402{END FIELD}
{END RECORD}
================================================================
Jim{END FIELD}
Godell{END FIELD}
{END FIELD}
Washington High School{END FIELD}
233 Randolf Street
Wheeling, WV  26003{END FIELD}
{END RECORD}
================================================================
Ms. Courtney S.{END FIELD}
Fergusen{END FIELD}
Secretarial Science Dept.{END FIELD}
Bayside Community College{END FIELD}
1200 East Coast Road
McLean, VA  22101{END FIELD}
{END RECORD}
================================================================
```

EXERCISE 8

INSTRUCTIONS:

1. Create the following documents.
2. Spell check each document.
3. Save the letter in a primary file using the name "ch16ex08.pri."
4. Save the address list in a secondary file using the name "ch16ex08.sec."
5. Close both documents.
6. Merge the two documents.
7. Print the merge document.
8. Close the merge document without saving changes.

PRIMARY FILE

```
{DATE)


{FIELD}Title~ {FIELD}First~ {FIELD}Last~
{FIELD}Address~

Dear {FIELD}Title~ {FIELD}Last~:

This is to confirm your reservations to stay in the lodge during
the family conference this August.  You will be staying in room
{FIELD}Room number~.  You may arrive as early as 4:00 on Friday
afternoon, the 12th, and we ask that you clear the room before you
go to lunch on Sunday.

If you have any questions please feel free to contact me.  We hope
that you and your family will enjoy your stay.

Sincerely,


Oran Miller
Retreat Director
```

SECONDARY FILE

```
{FIELD NAMES}Title~First~Last~Address~Room number~~{END RECORD}
================================================================
Mr.{END FIELD}
Andrew{END FIELD}
Gibson{END FIELD}
11300 Sinclair
San Marcos, TX 78134{END FIELD}
#B-109{END FIELD}
{END RECORD}
================================================================
Mr.{END FIELD}
Benjamin{END FIELD}
Horwitz{END FIELD}
2901 Lark Meadow
Bandera, TX 78078{END FIELD}
#A-114{END FIELD}
{END RECORD}
{END RECORD}
================================================================
Ms.{END FIELD}
Melody{END FIELD}
Jackson{END FIELD}
8611 Pine Ridge
New Braunfels, TX 78189{END FIELD}
#A-120{END FIELD}
{END RECORD}
================================================================
Dr.{END FIELD}
Steve{END FIELD}
Knight{END FIELD}
358 Spring Ridge
San Antonio, TX 78243{END FIELD}
#B-115{END FIELD}
{END RECORD}
================================================================
```

EXERCISE 9

INSTRUCTIONS:

1. Create the following documents.
2. Save the letter in a primary file using the name "ch16ex09.pri."
3. Save the address list in a secondary file using the name "ch16ex09.sec."
4. Print both documents.
5. Close both documents.
6. Merge the two documents.
7. Print the merge document.
8. Close the merge document without saving changes.

PRIMARY FILE

```
{DATE}


{FIELD}Title~ {FIELD}First~ {FIELD}Last~
{FIELD}Position~
{FIELD}Address~

Dear {FIELD}Title~ {FIELD}Last~:

This is to inform you that the sales promotion for next year will
be announced next week at your area meeting.  You will be receiving
a video tape the day of the meeting.  The tape contains a message
from Edward in which he explains the new product line and all the
new promotions for the coming year.

Along with the video tape you will also receive a meeting agenda.
This will explain how the tape should be used at your meeting for
maximum effectiveness.

You know how important promotions are in motivating sales, so
please make sure that all your people attend.

Thank you and I know this is going to be a great new year!

Sincerely,


Mark Seymour
Southwest Regional Sales Manager
```

SECONDARY FILE

```
{FIELD NAMES}Title~First~Last~Position~Address~~{END RECORD}
==========================================================
Mr.{END FIELD}
Brian{END FIELD}
Gilbert{END FIELD}
Houston Area Sales Manager{END FIELD}
7392 Southwest Frwy.
Houston, TX 77088{END FIELD}
{END RECORD}
==========================================================
Mr.{END FIELD}
Lloyd{END FIELD}
Jones{END FIELD}
San Antonio Area Sales Manager{END FIELD}
1708 Point Park Dr.
San Antonio, TX 78243{END FIELD}
{END RECORD}
==========================================================
Mr.{END FIELD}
Ben{END FIELD}
Madison{END FIELD}
Austin Area Sales Manager{END FIELD}
306 Ridgeway
Austin, TX 78765{END FIELD}
{END RECORD}
{END RECORD}
==========================================================
Ms.{END FIELD}
Ann{END FIELD}
Maddox{END FIELD}
Dallas Area Sales Manager{END FIELD}
822 Greenridge
Dallas, Texas 75297{END FIELD}
{END RECORD}
==========================================================
```

CHAPTER SEVENTEEN

ADVANCED MERGING TECHNIQUES

OBJECTIVES

In this chapter, you will learn to:

- Merge from the keyboard
- Merge a document as a list of items

CHAPTER OVERVIEW

In this chapter, the processes for merging a document from the keyboard are described and illustrated. The process for creating a list of items with the merge feature is also demonstrated.

MERGING FROM THE KEYBOARD

Although you always need a primary file for a merge, you do not always need a secondary file. You can enter merge data directly from the keyboard. This means that you can type the text during the merge. This type of merge is useful when you need to create only one form letter from a primary file.

Two merge codes can be used to enter data from the keyboard: {INPUT} and {KEYBOARD}. The {INPUT} merge code pauses the merge and prompts you with a message, while the {KEYBOARD} merge code just pauses the merge. The use of both codes is illustrated in this section.

Before starting this section, close any documents on screen. Change the default document directory to "a:\wpdocs" or "c:\wpdocs."

The {INPUT} Merge Code

The {INPUT} merge code pauses the merge and prompts you for data. The prompt appears in a dialog box at the bottom of your screen. The {INPUT} message displays in your document, but does not print.

The following example creates a primary file to illustrate the {INPUT} keyboard merge. To insert the {DATE} merge code:

Choose	Tools	***Press***	*Alt*	**Press**	Ctrl+F12
Choose	Merge	***Select***	*Tools*	**Select**	Merge Codes

Choose	Merge Codes	***Select***	*Merge*	**Type**	D
Click	the down scroll arrow until the {DATE} code appears	***Select***	*Merge Codes*	**Press**	↵Enter to select the Insert command button
Click	on the {DATE} code	***Type***	*D*	**Press**	Esc
Click	the Insert command button	***Press***	*↵Enter to select the Insert command button*		
Click	the Close command button	***Press***	*Esc*		

To insert three blank lines:

Press	↵Enter four times	***Press***	*↵Enter four times*	**Press**	↵Enter four times

The Input merge code is used to stop the merge so that you can enter text from the keyboard. To insert an {INPUT} merge code for the addressee's name:

Choose	Tools	***Press***	*Alt*	**Press**	Ctrl+F12
Choose	Merge	***Select***	*Tools*	**Select**	Input
Choose	Input	***Select***	*Merge*		
		Select	*Input*		

The Insert Merge Code dialog box appears. Your screen should look like Figure 17-1.

Figure 17-1

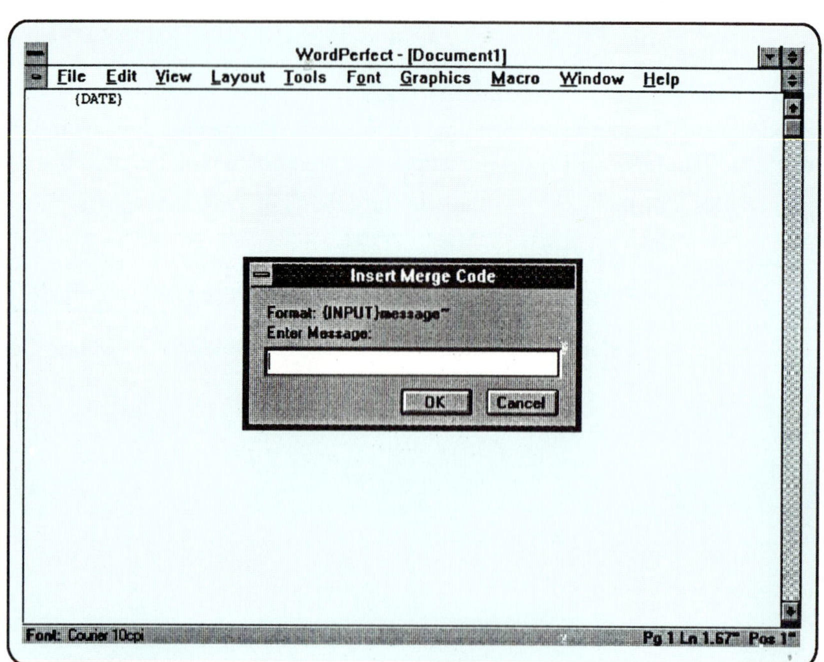

With the {INPUT} merge code, you can enter a message to prompt you for the proper merge information. The message appears in a dialog box near the bottom of the screen.

To enter the message:

Type	Enter the person's name	***Type***	*Enter the person's name*	**Type**	Enter the person's name
Click	the OK command button	***Press***	*[↵Enter] twice*	**Press**	[↵Enter] twice
Press	[↵Enter]				

Your screen should look like Figure 17-2.

Figure 17-2

To insert an {INPUT} merge code for the address:

Choose	Tools	***Press***	*[Alt]*	**Press**	[Ctrl]+[F12]
Choose	Merge	***Select***	*Tools*	**Select**	Input
Choose	Input	***Select***	*Merge*		
		Select	*Input*		

To enter the prompt message:

Type	Enter the address	***Type***	*Enter the address*	**Type**	Enter the address
Click	the OK command button	***Press***	*[↵Enter] three times*	**Press**	[↵Enter] three times
Press	[↵Enter] twice				

The top part of your screen should look like Figure 17-3.

Figure 17-3

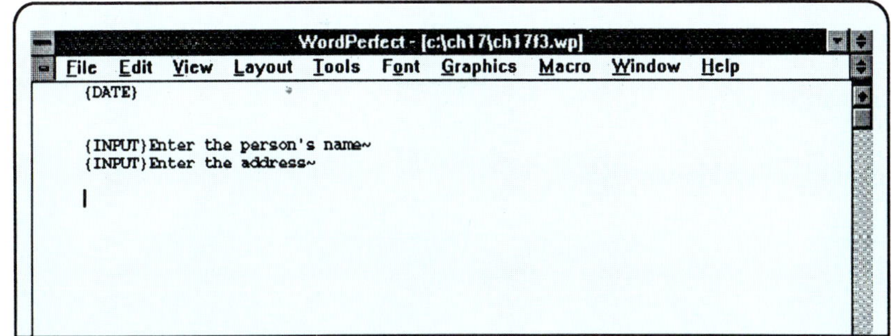

Type in the text shown in Figure 17-4.

Figure 17-4

```
Dear Sir or Madam:

As a valued customer of the Tasty Gourmet Food Services Company,
you are invited to enjoy a free dinner for two at Brandon's -  a
four star restaurant specializing in Southwestern cuisine.
Enclosed is a certificate that you must present to the waiter
after your meal.

All of us at Tasty Gourmet would like to say . . . Thank you!

Sincerely,



Mr. Doug Travis
President
```

Save the document as "prize.ltr" and close the document.

To illustrate a keyboard merge using the {INPUT} merge code:

Choose	Tools	***Press***	*Alt*	**Press**	Ctrl+F12
Choose	Merge	***Select***	*Tools*	**Select**	Merge
Choose	Merge	***Select***	*Merge*		
		Select	*Merge*		

You can either type in the file name for the primary or secondary file or click the file folder button next to the text box to search for the file.

To enter the primary file:

Type	**prize.ltr**	***Type***	***prize.ltr***	**Type**	**prize.ltr**

Since a keyboard merge only needs a primary file, click the OK command button or press ↵Enter to bypass the secondary file name.

To bypass the secondary file:

Click	the OK command button	***Press***	*↵Enter*	**Press**	↵Enter

Your screen should look like Figure 17-5.

Figure 17-5

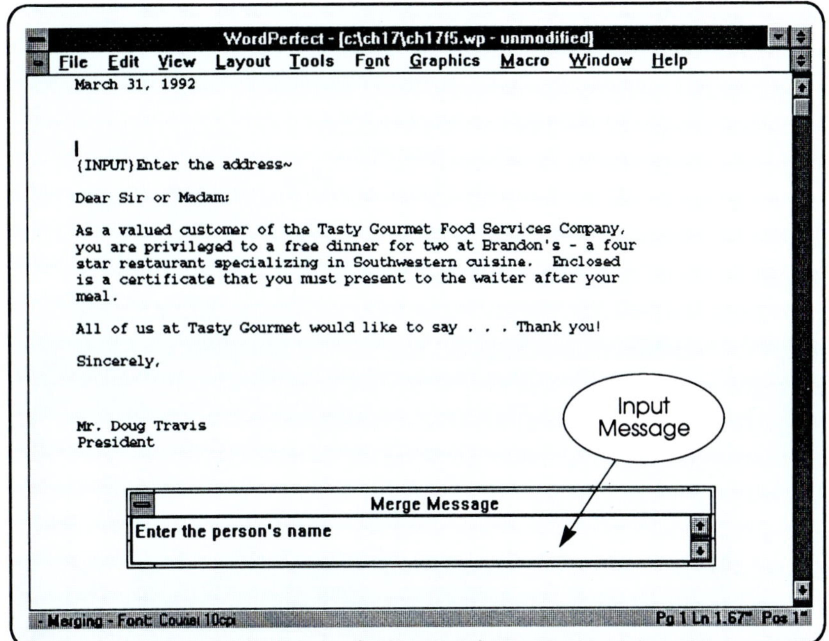

The primary file text appears on the screen and the insertion point is placed at the first pause for the addressee's name. The message that you entered appears in the dialog box at the bottom of the screen.

To enter the addressee's name:

Type	Ms. Linda Chesser	***Type***	*Ms. Linda Chesser*	**Type**	Ms. Linda Chesser

To continue the merge process:

Choose	Tools	***Press***	*Alt*	**Press**	Alt+↵Enter
Choose	Merge	***Select***	*Merge*		
Choose	End Field	***Select***	*End Field*		

To enter the address:

Type	1211 Lakewood Drive	***Type***	*1211 Lakewood Drive*	**Type**	1211 Lakewood Drive
Press	↵Enter	***Press***	*↵Enter*	**Press**	↵Enter
Type	Houston, TX 77099	***Type***	*Houston, TX 77099*	**Type**	Houston, TX 77099
Choose	Tools	***Press***	*Alt*	**Press**	Alt+↵Enter
Choose	Merge	***Select***	*Tools*	**Move**	the insertion point to the beginning of the document
Choose	End Field	***Select***	*Merge*		

Click	at the beginning of the document	***Select***	*End Field*		
		Move	*the insertion point to the beginning of the document*		

Except for the date, your screen should look like Figure 17-6.

Figure 17-6

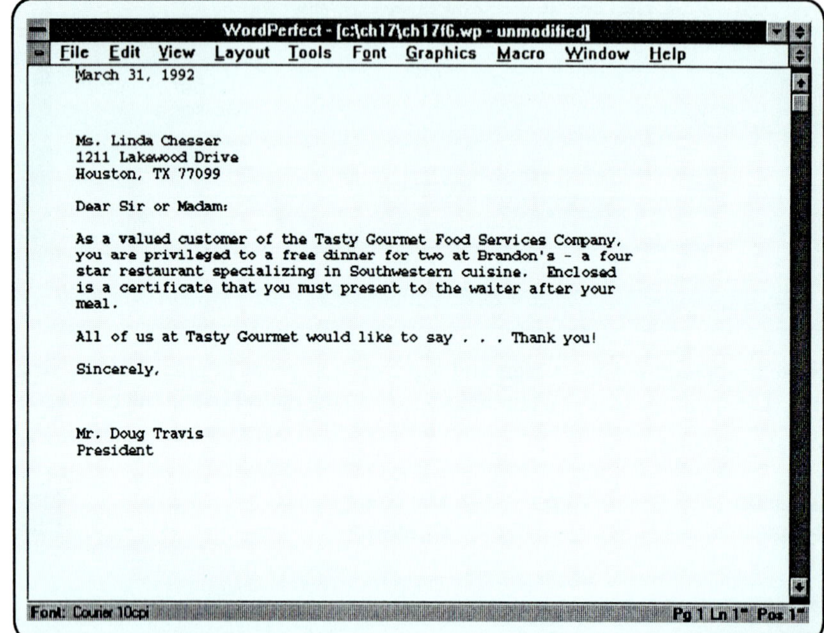

Close the document without saving changes.

The {KEYBOARD} Merge Code

In the previous example, a message prompted you for specific information. This prompt may not always be necessary.

The {KEYBOARD} merge code pauses the merge so that you can enter data, but does not provide a message on the screen. In the following example, you create a memo form using the {KEYBOARD} merge code.

To begin the memo:

Type	To:	***Type***	*To:*	**Type**	To:
Press	Tab twice	***Press***	*Tab twice*	**Press**	Tab twice

To insert the {KEYBOARD} merge code:

Choose	Tools	***Press***	*Alt*	**Press**	Ctrl+F12
Choose	Merge	***Select***	*Tools*	**Select**	Merge Codes
Choose	Merge Codes	***Select***	*Merge*	**Type**	K

Click	the down scroll arrow until the {KEYBOARD} code appears	***Select***	*Merge Codes*	**Press**	↵Enter to select the Insert command button
Click	on the {KEYBOARD} code	***Type***	*K*	**Press**	Esc
Click	the Insert command button	***Press***	*↵Enter to select the Insert command button*		
Click	the Close command button	***Press***	*Esc*		

To create a blank line:

Press	↵Enter twice	***Press***	*↵Enter twice*	**Press**	↵Enter twice

To create the second line of the memo:

Type	From:	***Type***	*From:*	**Type**	From:
Press	Tab	***Press***	*Tab*	**Press**	Tab
Choose	Tools	***Press***	*Alt*	**Press**	Ctrl+F12
Choose	Merge	***Select***	*Tools*	**Select**	Merge Codes
Choose	Merge Codes	***Select***	*Merge*	**Type**	K
Click	the down scroll arrow until the {KEYBOARD} code appears	***Select***	*Merge Codes*	**Press**	↵Enter to select the Insert command button
Click	on the {KEYBOARD} code	***Type***	*K*	**Press**	Esc
Click	the Insert command button	***Press***	*↵Enter to select the Insert command button*	**Press**	↵Enter twice
Click	the Close command button	***Press***	*Esc*		
Press	↵Enter twice	***Press***	*↵Enter twice*		

To create the Date line of the memo:

Type	Date:	***Type***	*Date:*	**Type**	Date:
Press	Tab	***Press***	*Tab*	**Press**	Tab
Choose	Tools	***Press***	*Alt*	**Press**	Ctrl+F12

Choose	Merge	***Select***	*Tools*	**Select**	Merge Codes
Choose	Merge Codes	***Select***	*Merge*	**Type**	D
Click	the down scroll arrow until the {DATE} code appears	***Select***	*Merge Codes*	**Press**	[↵Enter] to select the Insert command button
Click	on the {DATE} code	***Type***	*D*	**Press**	[Esc]
Click	the Insert command button	***Press***	*[↵Enter] to select the Insert command button*	**Press**	[↵Enter] twice
Click	the Close command button	***Press***	*[Esc]*		
Press	[↵Enter] twice	***Press***	*[↵Enter] twice*		

To create the Subject line:

Type	Subject:	***Type***	*Subject:*	**Type**	Subject:
Press	[Tab]	***Press***	*[Tab]*	**Press**	[Tab]
Choose	Tools	***Press***	*[Alt]*	**Press**	[Ctrl]+[F12]
Choose	Merge	***Select***	*Tools*	**Select**	Merge Codes
Choose	Merge Codes	***Select***	*Merge*	**Type**	K
Click	the down scroll arrow until the {KEYBOARD} code appears	***Select***	*Merge Codes*	**Press**	[↵Enter] to select the Insert command button
Click	on the {KEYBOARD} code	***Type***	*K*	**Press**	[Esc]
Click	the Insert command button	***Press***	*[↵Enter] to select the Insert command button*	**Press**	[↵Enter] twice
Click	the Close command button	***Press***	*[Esc]*		
Press	[↵Enter] twice	***Press***	*[↵Enter] twice*		

The top portion of your screen should look like Figure 17-7.

Figure 17-7

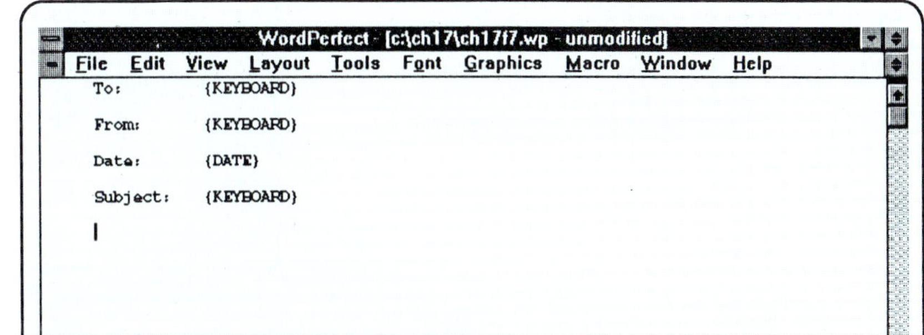

Save the document as "memo.ltr." Close the document.

To illustrate a merge using the {KEYBOARD} code:

Choose	Tools	***Press***	*Alt*	**Press**	Ctrl + F12
Choose	Merge	***Select***	*Tools*	**Select**	Merge
Choose	Merge	***Select***	*Merge*		
		Select	*Merge*		

You can type the primary file name or click the file folder button to search for the file. To enter the primary file name:

Type	**memo.ltr**	***Type***	***memo.ltr***	**Type**	**memo.ltr**

In a {KEYBOARD} merge the secondary file information is provided from the keyboard. To bypass the secondary file name, click the OK command button or press ↵Enter.

To bypass the secondary file name:

Click	the OK command button	***Press***	*↵Enter*	**Press**	↵Enter

The top half of your screen should look like Figure 17-8.

Figure 17-8

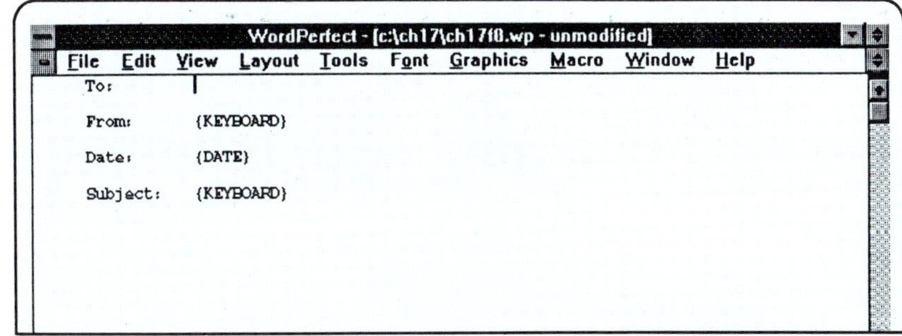

The primary file text appears on the screen and the insertion point is placed at the first pause for the recipient's name.

To enter the recipient's name:

Type	Michael Roberts	***Type***	*Michael Roberts*	**Type**	Michael Roberts
Choose	Tools	***Press***	*Alt*	**Press**	Alt + ↵Enter

Choose	Merge	***Select***	*Tools*		
Choose	End Field	***Select***	*Merge*		
		Select	*End Field*		

The top portion of your screen should look like Figure 17-9.

Figure 17-9

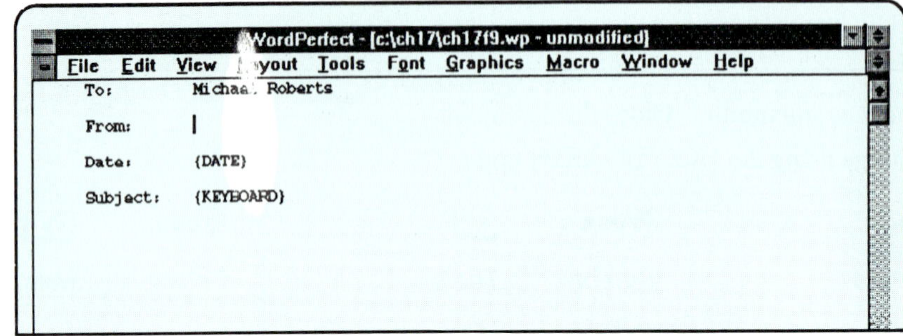

To continue the merge:

Type	Doug Travis	***Type***	*Doug Travis*	**Type**	Doug Travis
Choose	Tools	***Press***	*Alt*	**Press**	Alt+↵Enter
Choose	Merge	***Select***	*Tools*	**Type**	Sales Figures
Choose	End Field	***Select***	*Merge*	**Press**	Alt+↵Enter
Type	Sales Figures	***Select***	*End Field*		
Choose	Tools	***Type***	*Sales Figures*		
Choose	Merge	***Press***	*Alt*		
Choose	End Field	***Select***	*Tools*		
		Select	*Merge*		
		Select	*End Field*		

Except for the date, the top half of your screen should look like Figure 17-10.

Figure 17-10

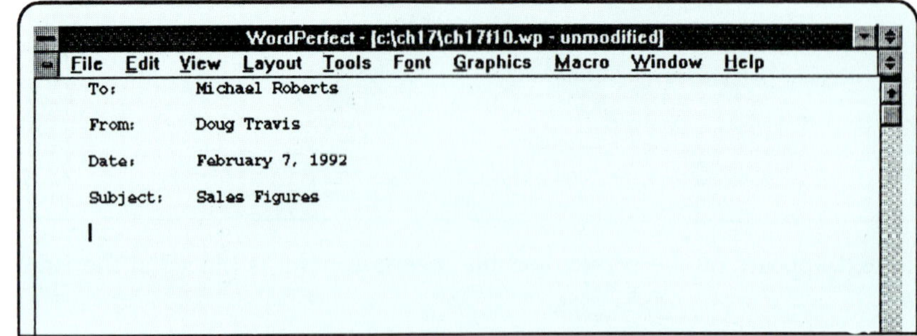

Close the document without saving changes.

CREATING A MERGED LIST

You can create a list of data using the Merge feature. When you create a secondary file, a hard page code [HPg] is placed between each record. This hard page code places each record on a separate page when you merge the primary and secondary files.

When you create a list, you do not want each record on a separate page. To combine information in a list format, you use the {PAGE OFF} code in your primary file. The {PAGE OFF} code allows you to remove the hard page code and place more than one record on a page.

To create a list of data, you first create a primary file containing the fields that you want in your list. Suppose that you want a list of individuals and addresses from your "address.ltr" secondary file. You will create a primary file with the field names "Title," "First," "Last," and "Address." You do not want the company name in the list, so you exclude it from the primary file.

To create the primary file:

Choose	Tools	***Press***	*Alt*	**Press**	Ctrl+F12
Choose	Merge	***Select***	*Tools*	**Select**	Field
Choose	Field	***Select***	*Merge*	**Type**	Title
Type	Title	***Select***	*Field*	**Press**	↵Enter
Click	the OK command button	***Type***	*Title*		
		Press	*↵Enter*		

To enter the "First" field:

Press	Spacebar	***Press***	*Spacebar*	**Press**	Spacebar
Choose	Tools	***Press***	*Alt*	**Press**	Ctrl+F12
Choose	Merge	***Select***	*Tools*	**Select**	Field
Choose	Field	***Select***	*Merge*	**Type**	First
Type	First	***Select***	*Field*	**Press**	↵Enter
Click	the OK command button	***Type***	*First*	**Press**	Spacebar
Press	Spacebar	***Press***	*↵Enter*		
		Press	*Spacebar*		

To create the "Last" field:

Choose	Tools	***Press***	*Alt*	**Press**	Ctrl+F12
Choose	Merge	***Select***	*Tools*	**Select**	Field
Choose	Field	***Select***	*Merge*	**Type**	Last
Type	Last	***Select***	*Field*	**Press**	↵Enter twice
Click	the OK command button	***Type***	*Last*		
Press	↵Enter	***Press***	*↵Enter twice*		

To create the "Address" field:

Choose	Tools	***Press***	*Alt*	**Press**	Ctrl+F12
Choose	Merge	***Select***	*Tools*	**Select**	Field
Choose	Field	***Select***	*Merge*	**Type**	Address
Type	Address	***Select***	*Field*	**Press**	↵Enter
Click	the OK command button	***Type***	*Address*		
		Press	*↵Enter*		

Your screen should look like Figure 17-11.

Figure 17-11

To place a blank line between each record:

Press	↵Enter twice	***Press***	*↵Enter twice*	**Press**	↵Enter twice

To remove the hard page code from each record:

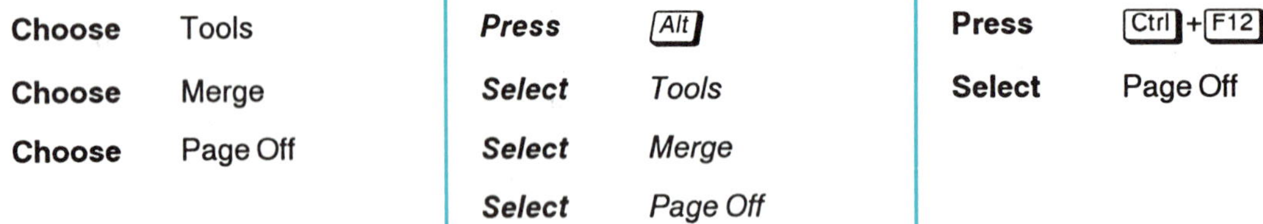

Choose	Tools	***Press***	*Alt*	**Press**	Ctrl+F12
Choose	Merge	***Select***	*Tools*	**Select**	Page Off
Choose	Page Off	***Select***	*Merge*		
		Select	*Page Off*		

Your screen should look like Figure 17-12.

Figure 17-12

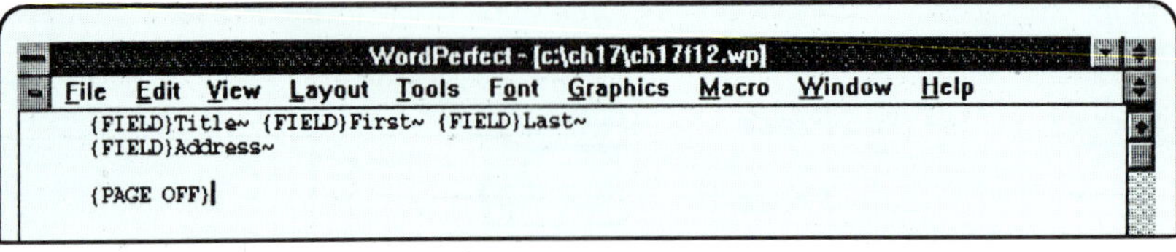

Save the document as "list.ltr." Close the document.

To merge the list:

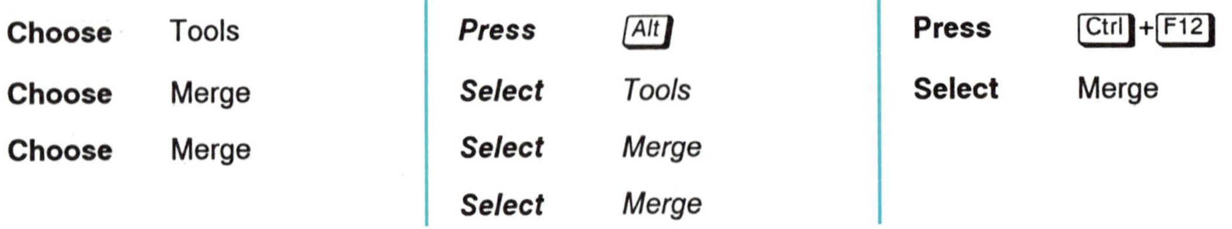

Choose	Tools	***Press***	*Alt*	**Press**	Ctrl+F12
Choose	Merge	***Select***	*Tools*	**Select**	Merge
Choose	Merge	***Select***	*Merge*		
		Select	*Merge*		

To enter the primary file name:

Type	**list.ltr**	***Type***	***list.ltr***	**Type**	**list.ltr**

To enter the secondary file name and execute the merge:

Double-click	the Secondary File text box	***Press***	*Alt+S to select the Secondary File text box*	**Press**	Alt+S to select the Secondary File text box
Type	**address.ltr**	***Type***	***address.ltr***	**Type**	**address.ltr**
Click	the OK command button	***Press***	*↵Enter*	**Press**	↵Enter

Your screen should look like Figure 17-13.

Figure 17-13

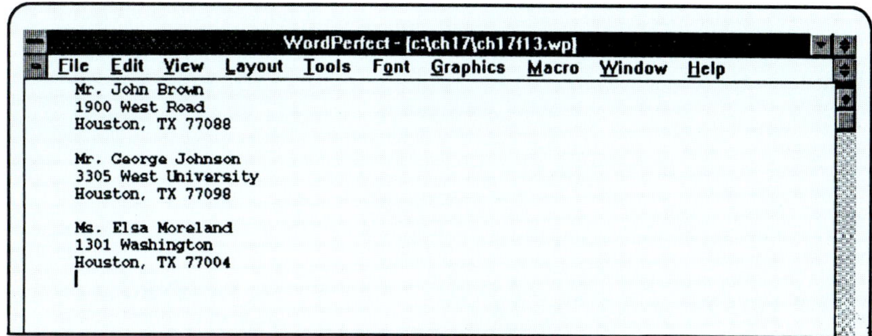

Close the file without saving changes.

EXERCISE 1

INSTRUCTIONS: Define the following terms.

1. Keyboard merge ______________________________

2. {INPUT} merge code ______________________________

3. {KEYBOARD} merge code ______________________________

4. {PAGE OFF} merge code ______________________________

EXERCISE 2

INSTRUCTIONS: Circle T if the statement is true and F if the statement is false.

T F 1. The {KEYBOARD} merge code pauses the merge so that you can enter text from the keyboard and prompts you with a message.

T F 2. By default, each record is placed on a separate page when you perform a merge.

T F 3. The {INPUT} merge code pauses the merge so that you can enter text from the keyboard and prompts you with a message.

T F 4. Secondary records can be combined in a list by using the {END RECORD} merge code.

T F 5. The {INPUT} merge code prompts you with a message that appears on the status bar.

T F 6. The {PAGE OFF} merge code tells WordPerfect not to place a hard page code after each record.

EXERCISE 3

INSTRUCTIONS:

1. Create the following document using the {INPUT} merge code to prompt you for the addressee's name and team ID.
2. Spell check the document.
3. Save the document as "ch17ex03.pri." Close the document.
4. Send the memo to the following individuals.

   Mr. Jack Rather
   Supervisor, South Team 10

   Ms. Mary Ann Turbell
   Supervisor, North Team 9

5. Save each memo as a separate file. Save the Rather memo as "ch17ex03.01." Save the Turbell memo as "ch17ex03.02."
6. Print both documents.
7. Close both documents.

```
                         MEMORANDUM

TO:    {INPUT}Addressee's name~
       {INPUT}Addressee's team ID~

FROM: Howard J. Dalrymple, Village Manager

DATE: {DATE}

RE:    Waste Recycling

Our community is about to undergo a severe test.  We will be asking
all residents to recycle paper, glass, and compostable materials.

You, as a supervisor of a Public Works team, must make sure that
your employees make a good effort to collect all materials and
separate them into the proper bins on the new trucks.  This is an
important event for our community and our country.  Please ask all
employees to make an extra effort during the first few weeks to
help the residents place the correct materials in the right
container.
```

EXERCISE 4

INSTRUCTIONS:

1. Create the following document using the {INPUT} merge code to prompt you for the addressee and address data.
2. Spell check the document.
3. Save the document as "ch17ex04.pri."
4. Close the document.
5. Merge the document with the address information below.
6. Save each letter. Save the White letter as "ch17ex04.01." Save the Brunner letter as "ch17ex04.02."
7. Print each document.
8. Close each document.

PRIMARY FILE

```
{DATE}


{INPUT}Addressee's name~
{INPUT}Address~

Dear {INPUT}Addressee's first name~:

There will be several Real Estate Property Law seminars at the next
State Convention.  As a member of the real estate division of your
law firm, I want to encourage your attendance.

One seminar in particular, "Keeping Up With Property Law," should
be very rewarding.  The speaker, Mr. Bill Anderson, is excellent
and he will be reviewing pertinent changes for the last year.

Please read over the Bar Convention brochure for more information
about this and the many other fine seminars at this year's
convention.

Sincerely,



Ronald O'Connor
Director, Continuing Legal Education
```

ADDRESSES

```
Ms. Judy White
383 Parkway, Suite 34
Dallas, Texas 75223

Mr. Stephen Brunner
765-B Commerce,
San Antonio, Texas 78213
```

EXERCISE 5

INSTRUCTIONS:

1. Create the following document using the {INPUT} merge code to prompt you for the addressee and address data.
2. Spell check the document.
3. Save the document as "ch17ex05.pri."
4. Close the document.
5. Merge the document with the address information below.
6. Save each letter. Save the Armstrong letter as "ch17ex05.01." Save the James letter as "ch17ex05.02." Save the Johnson letter as "ch17ex05.03." Save the McBrady letter as "ch17ex05.04."
7. Print each document.
8. Close each document.

PRIMARY FILE

```
{DATE}


{INPUT}Addressee's name~
{INPUT}Address~

Dear {INPUT}Addressee's first name~:

As a valued customer, you have earned a 10% discount on your next
purchase.  I also want to let you know that we have received
shipment of the newest Harold Jackson novel.  It has been given
wonderful reviews and I know you will want to add this book to your
library.

Most exciting of all, Mr. Jackson will be at our location on August
15th to personally autograph your copy.  He is a delightful
gentleman and you won't want to miss this chance to meet him!

Sincerely,



Bob Greenburg
Owner, The Little Bookstore
```

ADDRESSES

```
Mr. Allen Armstrong
1234 Broadway
Houston, Texas 77055

Mr. Mark James
12959 Oak Tree Way
Houston, Texas 77245

Ms. Christina Johnson
6135 Archway
Houston, Texas 77057

Ms. Lynn McBrady
1212 Talley Road
Houston, Texas 77198
```

EXERCISE 6

INSTRUCTIONS:

1. Create the following document using the {KEYBOARD} merge code to pause the merge.
2. Spell check the document.
3. Save the document as "ch17ex06.pri."
4. Close the document.
5. Merge the document with the names and suite numbers listed below.
6. Save each memo. Save the Brown memo as "ch17ex06.01." Save the Roodman memo as "ch17ex06.02." Save the Carter memo as "ch17ex06.03." Save the Williams memo as "ch17ex06.04."
7. Print each document.
8. Close each document.

PRIMARY FILE

```
                         MEMORANDUM

TO:          {KEYBOARD}

SUITE:       {KEYBOARD}

FROM:        Madeline Howard, Head Office Manager

DATE:        {DATE}

SUBJECT:     Break Rooms

It has been brought to my attention that everyone is not doing his
part to keep the break rooms in good condition.

Also please keep track of what you leave in the refrigerators.  The
refrigerators are intended to give you a place to keep your food
during the day, not overnight.  It is your responsibility to remove
any uneaten food at the end of the day.

Thank you for your attention in this matter.
```

RECIPIENTS

```
Henry Brown
Suite 245

Elizabeth Roodman
Suite 249

Barbara Carter
Suite 353

Frank Williams
Suite 359
```

EXERCISE 7

INSTRUCTIONS:

1. Create the following primary file to merge a list of items.
2. Save the document as "ch17ex07.pri."
3. Close the document.
4. Create a secondary file using the addresses listed below.
5. Save the document as "ch17ex07.sec." Close the document.
6. Merge the two documents.
7. Print the list.
8. Close the document without saving changes.

PRIMARY FILE

```
{FIELD}First~ {FIELD}Last~
{FIELD}Address~

{PAGE OFF}
```

SECONDARY FILE

```
{FIELD NAMES}First~Last~Address~~{END RECORD}
================================================
Charles{END FIELD}
Edwards{END FIELD}
11226 Timbercraft Drive
San Antonio, Texas 78244{END FIELD}
{END RECORD}
================================================
Robert{END FIELD}
Garcia{END FIELD}
4735 Valley Lane
Houston, Texas 77077{END FIELD}
{END RECORD}
================================================
Philip{END FIELD}
Howle{END FIELD}
700 N.W. 34th St.
Austin, Texas 78749{END FIELD}
{END RECORD}
================================================
Arthur{END FIELD}
Jordan{END FIELD}
17209 Longwood
Dallas, Texas 75387{END FIELD}
{END RECORD}
================================================
Thomas{END FIELD}
McDonald{END FIELD}
4414 Bellbrook
San Antonio, Texas 78253{END FIELD}
{END RECORD}
================================================
Karen{END FIELD}
Ho{END FIELD}
7812 Windchase Drive
Ft. Worth, Texas 75213{END FIELD}
{END RECORD}
================================================
```

EXERCISE 8

INSTRUCTIONS:

1. Create the following primary file to merge a list of items.
2. Save the document as "ch17ex08.pri."
3. Close the document.
4. Create a secondary file using the addresses listed below.
5. Save the document as "ch17ex08.sec." Close the document.
6. Merge the two documents.

7. Print the list.
8. Close the document without saving changes.

PRIMARY FILE

```
{FIELD}Title~ {FIELD}Last~
{FIELD}Company?~
{FIELD}Address~

{PAGE OFF}
```

SECONDARY FILE

```
{FIELD NAMES}Title~First~Last~Company~Address~~{END RECORD}
================================================================
Mr.{END FIELD}
Donald{END FIELD}
Roberts{END FIELD}
Acme Company{END FIELD}
209 West Avenue
Rochester, New York 14699{END FIELD}
{END RECORD}
================================================================
Ms.{END FIELD}
Joan{END FIELD}
Robinson{END FIELD}
{END FIELD}
8871 Business Park Blvd.
Plano, Texas 75077{END FIELD}
{END RECORD}
================================================================
Mr.{END FIELD}
Allen{END FIELD}
Winters{END FIELD}
All Rite Paints. Inc.{END FIELD}
4332 S. Bonham
Orem, Utah 84194{END FIELD}
{END RECORD}
================================================================
Mr.{END FIELD}
John{END FIELD}
Welch{END FIELD}
Long Construction Company{END FIELD}
18773 NW 45th Street
Redmond, Washington 98001{END FIELD}
{END RECORD}
================================================================
```

CHAPTER EIGHTEEN

MACROS

OBJECTIVES

In this chapter, you will learn to:

- Create a macro
- Use a macro
- Assign a macro to a menu
- Edit a macro
- Create an interactive macro
- Delete a macro

■ CHAPTER OVERVIEW

In this chapter, the procedures for creating, using, editing, and deleting a macro are described and illustrated.

■ CREATING A MACRO

A macro is a set of recorded actions in WordPerfect. The macro commands represent the actions exactly as they are executed when you choose them from the various menus, enter text, or move the insertion point.

Macros are especially useful when performing detailed, repetitive tasks. For example, you can use a macro to format many documents the same way. A macro can insert an entire memo heading at the top of a document at the touch of a key. Or you can use a macro to add the same closing for most letters that you prepare. Rather than enter the same keystrokes each time you want to perform the same task, you can create a macro to do the work for you.

You can create a macro by using the Macro Record feature. To begin recording a macro, choose Record from the Macro menu or press Ctrl+F10. You will be asked to enter a name for the macro. Each macro is stored in a file using the name you specified. WordPerfect adds a ".wcm" extension to all macro names and stores the macros in the "macros" directory in the "wpwin" directory. You can change the macro directory by using the File Preferences, Location of Files command.

There are two ways to name a macro. One way is to enter a name between one and eight characters long. The characters in a macro name should be either letters or numbers. You cannot use spaces in a macro name.

Another way to define a macro name is to hold down the Ctrl or the Ctrl+Shift keys and type a letter from A to Z or a number 0 through 9. The advantage of naming a macro in this way is that to use the macro, you simply press Ctrl or Ctrl+Shift and the letter or number.

You should be careful when using the Ctrl+letter method for naming a macro. Many WordPerfect commands can also be accessed by pressing Ctrl and a letter. For example, if you name a macro Ctrl+B, the macro will replace the accelerator keys for the Bold feature which are also Ctrl+B. To avoid this conflict, you might use the Ctrl+Shift method for naming macros.

If necessary, change the default document directory to "a:\wpdocs" or to "c:\wpdocs."

Suppose a memo is sent every week to the same department. You can create a macro that inserts the memo heading at the top of the document.

To record a macro that inserts a memo heading into a document using a name of one to eight characters:

Choose	Macro	***Press***	*Alt*	**Press**	Ctrl+F10
Choose	Record	***Select***	*Macro*		
		Select	*Record*		

To enter the name for the macro:

Type	**sales**	***Type***	***sales***	**Type**	**sales**

To enter a description of the macro:

Double-click	the Descriptive Name text box	***Press***	*Alt+D to select the Descriptive Name text box*	**Press**	Alt+D to select the Descriptive Name text box
Type	Weekly Sales Memo	***Type***	*Weekly Sales Memo*	**Type**	Weekly Sales Memo

Your screen should look like Figure 18-1.

Figure 18-1

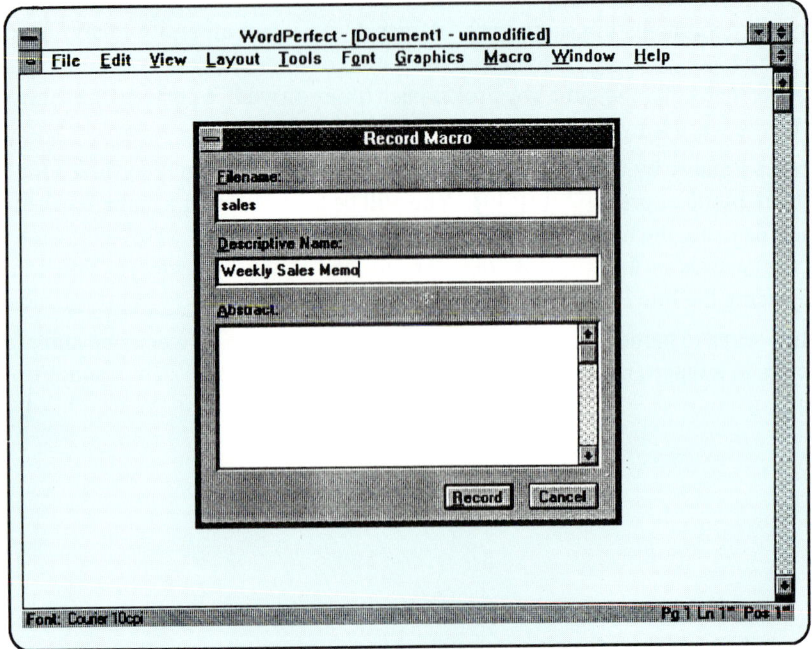

An abstract provides a detailed description of the macro. To create the abstract:

Double-click	the Abstract text box	***Press***	*Alt+A to select the Abstract text box*	**Press**	Alt+A to select the Abstract text box
Type	Create a memo for the Weekly Sales report	***Type***	*Create a memo for the Weekly Sales report*	**Type**	Create a memo for the Weekly Sales report

Your screen should look like Figure 18-2.

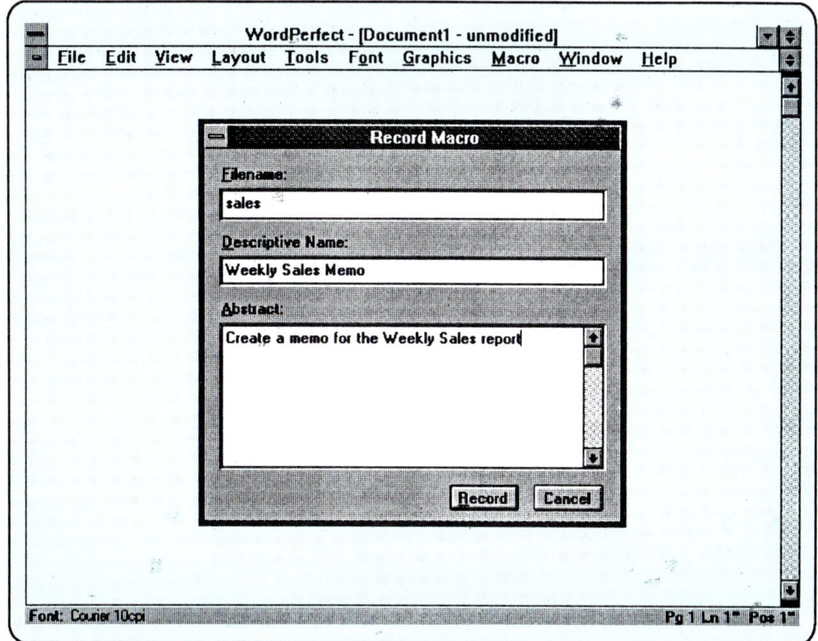

Figure 18-2

To begin recording the macro:

Click	the Record command button	***Press***	*Enter to select the Record command button*	**Press**	Enter to select the Record command button

The lower part of your screen should look like Figure 18-3. Notice that the message "Recording Macro" appears on the status bar, indicating that WordPerfect is recording your actions.

Figure 18-3

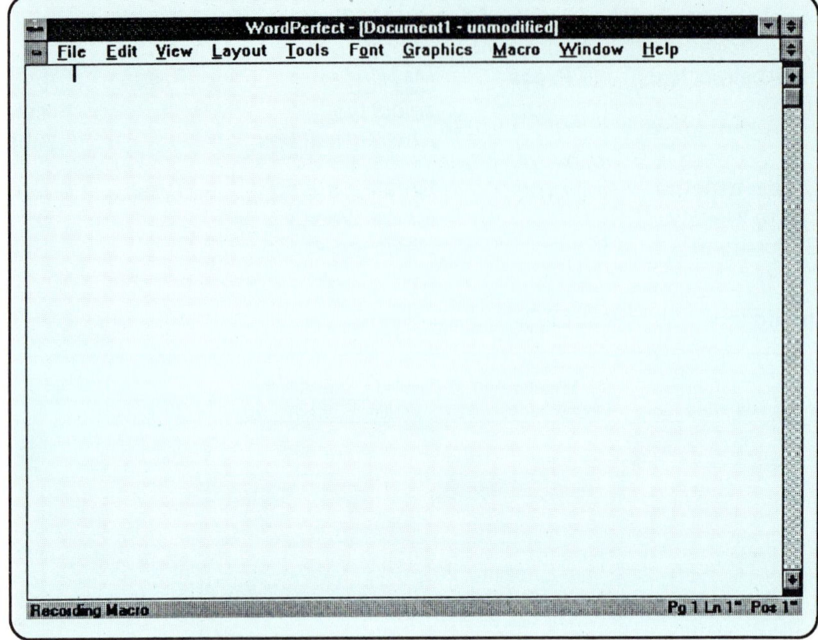

You can use the mouse to access menus while recording a macro. However, you cannot use the mouse to move the insertion point while recording a macro. If you move the mouse pointer into the document area while the macro is recording, the mouse pointer appears as a "no" symbol (⃠) indicating that the mouse cannot be used for movement. You must use the pointer-movement keys to move through the document while recording a macro.

Create the document shown in Figure 18-4. Use the Code option from the Date option under the Tools menu or press Ctrl+Shift+F5. Set a left-aligned tab at 0.7″ at the beginning of the document.

Figure 18-4

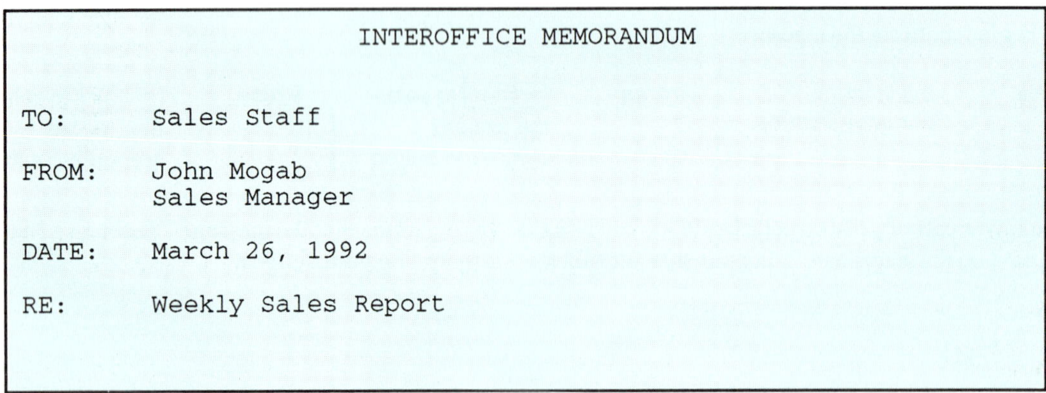

INTEROFFICE MEMORANDUM

TO: Sales Staff

FROM: John Mogab
Sales Manager

DATE: March 26, 1992

RE: Weekly Sales Report

To stop recording keystrokes:

Choose	Macro	***Press***	*Alt*	**Press**	Ctrl+Shift+F10
Choose	Stop	***Select***	*Macro*		
		Select	*Stop*		

Notice that the message "Recording Macro" no longer appears on the status bar, indicating that WordPerfect is no longer recording your actions. Your macro has been saved in the "c:\wpwin\macros" directory under the name "sales.wcm."

Close your document. Do not save any changes.

Suppose you want to create a macro that sets a standard format for a letter. This standard format sets a 1.5″ left margin, a 2.5″ top margin to allow space for the letterhead, full justification, left-aligned tabs and a Helvetica 12pt initial font.

To record a macro to format a letter:

Choose	Macro	***Press***	*Alt*	**Press**	Ctrl+F10
Choose	Record	***Select***	*Macro*		
		Select	*Record*		

To enter the name, description, and abstract for the macro:

Type	**formdoc**	***Type***	***formdoc***	**Type**	**formdoc**
Double-click	the Descriptive Name text box	***Press***	*Alt+D to select the Descriptive Name text box*	**Press**	Alt+D to select the Descriptive Name text box
Type	Format for a letter	***Type***	*Format for a letter*	**Type**	Format for a letter
Double-click	the Abstract text box	***Press***	*Alt+A to select the Abstract text box*	**Press**	Alt+A to select the Abstract text box
Type	Set margins, tabs, justification, and initial font for a letter	***Type***	*Set margins, tabs, justification, and initial font for a letter*	**Type**	Set margins, tabs, justification, and initial font for a letter
Click	the Record command button	***Press***	*↵Enter to select the Record command button*	**Press**	↵Enter to select the Record command button

You are now ready to select all of the format options for your letter. If you make an error, continue the process for creating the macro. You will learn how to edit or modify a macro in a later section.

To define the margins for the letter:

Choose	Layout	***Press***	*Alt*	**Press**	Ctrl+F8
Choose	Margins	***Select***	*Layout*	**Set**	the left margin to 1.5"
Set	the left margin to 1.5"	***Select***	*Margins*	**Set**	the top margin to 2.5"
Set	the top margin to 2.5"	***Set***	*the left margin to 1.5"*	**Press**	↵Enter

Click	the OK command button	***Set***	*the top margin to 2.5"*		
		Press	*↵Enter*		

To set the letter justification:

Choose	Layout	***Press***	*Alt*	**Press**	Ctrl+F
Choose	Justification	***Select***	*Layout*		
Choose	Full	***Select***	*Justification*		
		Select	*Full*		

To set the letter tabs:

Choose	Layout	***Press***	*Alt*	**Press**	Shift+F9
Choose	Line	***Select***	*Layout*	**Select**	Tab Set
Select	Tab Set	***Select***	*Line*	**Set**	left aligned tabs at .5", .1", 1.5", and 2.0"
Set	left aligned tabs at .5", 1", 1.5", and 2.0"	***Select***	*Tab Set*	**Press**	↵Enter
Click	the OK command button	***Set***	*left aligned tabs at .5", 1", 1.5", and 2.0"*		
		Press	*↵Enter*		

To set the initial font:

Choose	Layout	***Press***	*Alt*	**Press**	Ctrl+Shift+F9
Choose	Document	***Select***	*Layout*	**Select**	Initial Font
Choose	Initial Font	***Select***	*Document*	**Select**	Helvetica 12pt (Z1A)
Choose	Helvetica 12pt (Z1A)	***Select***	*Initial Font*	**Press**	↵Enter
Click	the OK command button	***Select***	*Helvetica 12pt (Z1A)*		
		Press	*↵Enter*		

The bottom portion of your screen should look like Figure 18-5. Notice the change in the Pos indicator from 1″ to 1.5″ on the status bar, indicating the left margin is now 1.5″. Also, the Ln value is now 2.5″ corresponding to the top margin of 2.5″.

Figure 18-5

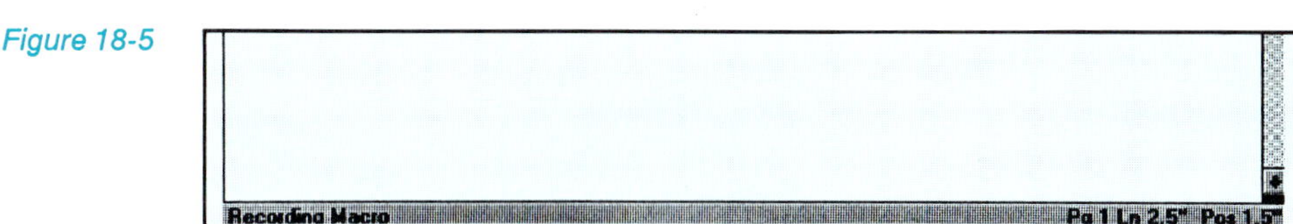

To stop recording keystrokes:

Choose	Macro	***Press***	*Alt*	**Press**	Ctrl+Shift+F10
Choose	Stop	***Select***	*Macro*		
		Select	*Stop*		

Notice that the message "Macro Recording" no longer appears on the status bar, indicating that WordPerfect is no longer recording your actions. Your macro has been saved in the "c:\wpwin\macros" directory in the file "formdoc.wcm."

Close your document without saving changes.

Often, you may use the same closing for a letter. Suppose you want to record a macro that creates the closing for you and you want to name it by holding down the Ctrl+Shift keys and selecting a letter.

To begin recording the macro:

Choose	Macro	***Press***	*Alt*	**Press**	Ctrl+F10
Choose	Record	***Select***	*Macro*	**Press**	Ctrl+Shift+C to create the macro name
Press	Ctrl+Shift+C to create the macro name	***Select***	*Record*	**Press**	Alt+D to select the Descriptive Name text box
Double-click	the Descriptive Name text box	***Press***	*Ctrl+Shift+C to create the macro name*	**Type**	Closing for a letter
Type	Closing for a letter	***Press***	*Alt+D to select the Descriptive Name text box*	**Press**	Alt+A to select the Abstract text box
Double-click	the Abstract text box	***Type***	*Closing for a letter*	**Type**	Closing for Joseph Carson - includes Enclosure statement
Type	Closing for Joseph Carson - includes Enclosure statement	***Press***	*Alt+A to select the Abstract text box*	**Press**	↵Enter to select the Record command button

Click	the Record command button	***Type***	*Closing for Joseph Carson - includes Enclosure statement*		
		Press	*[↵Enter] to select the Record command button*		

To enter the closing:

Type	Sincerely,	***Type***	*Sincerely,*	**Type**	Sincerely,
Press	[↵Enter] four times	***Press***	*[↵Enter] four times*	**Press**	[↵Enter] four times
Type	Joseph Carson	***Type***	*Joseph Carson*	**Type**	Joseph Carson
Press	[↵Enter] twice	***Press***	*[↵Enter] twice*	**Press**	[↵Enter] twice
Type	Enclosure	***Type***	*Enclosure*	**Type**	Enclosure

The top part of your screen should look like Figure 18-6.

Figure 18-6

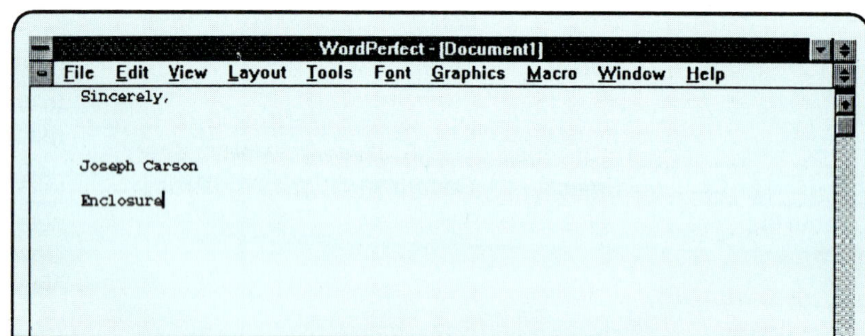

To stop recording keystrokes:

Choose	Macro	***Press***	*[Alt]*	**Press**	[Ctrl]+[Shift]+[F10]
Choose	Stop	***Select***	*Macro*		
		Select	*Stop*		

Notice that the message "Macro Recording" no longer appears on the status bar, indicating that WordPerfect is no longer recording your actions. The macro has been saved in the "c:\wpwin\macros" directory using the name "ctrlsftc.wcm."

Close the document without saving changes.

■ USING A MACRO

The instructions for using or executing a macro depend on the name you gave the macro when you created it. If you need to cancel the execution of the macro while it is processing, press the [Esc] key.

To use or execute your "sales" macro:

Choose	Macro	***Press***	*Alt*	**Press**	Alt+F10
Choose	Play	***Select***	*Macro*		
		Select	*Play*		

Your screen should look like Figure 18-7.

Figure 18-7

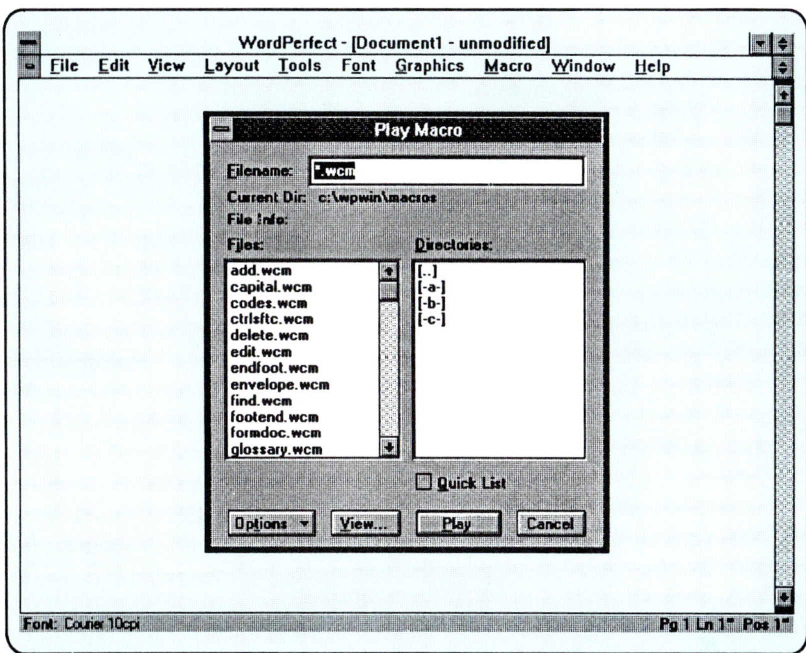

To enter the name of the macro:

Click	the down scroll arrow until the "sales.wcm" file appears	***Type***	***sales***	**Type**	**sales**
Click	on the file "sales.wcm"	*When you enter the macro name, you do not have to include the .wcm extension. WordPerfect automatically adds the extension to the file name.*		When you enter the macro name, you do not have to include the .wcm extension. WordPerfect automatically adds the extension to the file name.	
Click	the Play command button	***Press***	*↵Enter to select the Play command button*	**Press**	↵Enter to select the Play command button

When you play a macro for the first time after you create or edit it, WordPerfect must compile, or assemble, the macro. The message "Compiling macro" will appear on the status bar. The next time you play the macro, the steps will begin immediately. The top part of your screen should look like Figure 18-8.

Figure 18-8

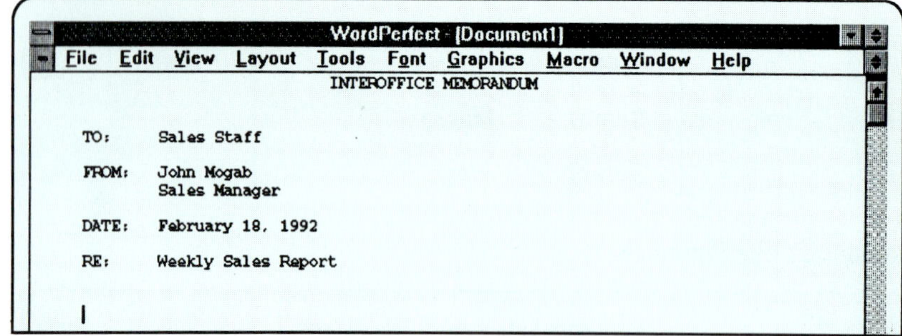

Close the document without saving changes.

To play your "formdoc" macro:

Choose	Macro	***Press***	*Alt*	**Press**	Alt+F10
Choose	Play	***Select***	*Macro*	**Type**	**formdoc**
Click	the down scroll arrow until the "formdoc.wcm" file appears	***Select***	*Play*	**Press**	↵Enter to select the Play command button
Click	on the "formdoc.wcm" file	***Type***	***formdoc***		
Click	the Play command button	***Press***	*↵Enter to select the Play command button*		

To see the format settings inserted by the "formdoc" macro:

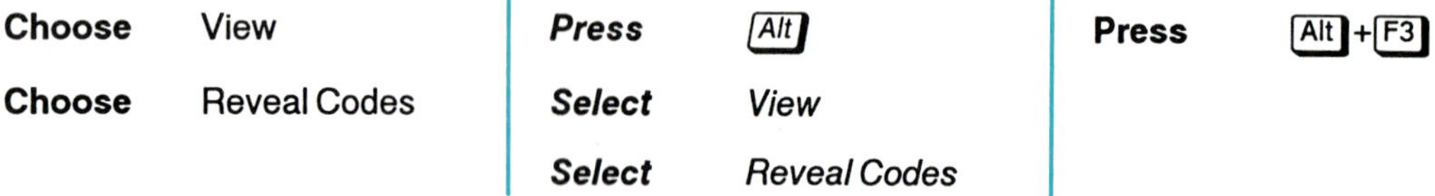

Choose	View	***Press***	*Alt*	**Press**	Alt+F3
Choose	Reveal Codes	***Select***	*View*		
		Select	*Reveal Codes*		

The bottom part of your screen should look like Figure 18-9.

Figure 18-9

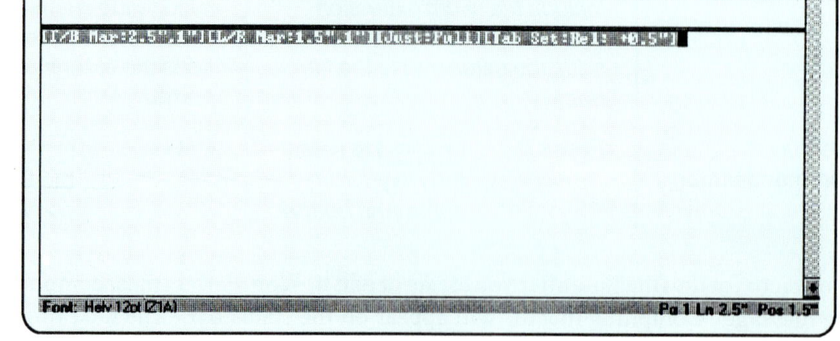

Turn off the Reveal Codes feature.

Type the text appearing in Figure 18-10. Use the Code option from the Date option under the Tools menu for the current date. Place two hard returns after the last line of the letter.

Figure 18-10

April 2, 1992

Dr. Joel Fleischman
Huberot University
P.O. 1822
Allentown, AZ 90012-1822

Dear Dr. Fleischman:

I thoroughly enjoyed the executive seminar "Gaining the Competitive Edge with Information Technology" that you presented at Huberot University last week. The information that you presented was most enlightening.

As CEO of ABC Can Company, I am concerned with finding new ways to gain competitive advantage. I now view my company in a new way. Your comments about global economy were especially interesting.

Thank you for a wonderful seminar! Enclosed is my business card. Please let me know whenever you present other executive seminars.

To play your Ctrl+Shift+C macro to place a standard closing on a letter:

Click	at the end of the document	***Move***	*the insertion point to the end of the document*	**Move**	the insertion point to the end of the document
Press	Ctrl+Shift+C	***Press***	*Ctrl+Shift+C*	**Press**	Ctrl+Shift+C

Your screen should look like Figure 18-11.

Figure 18-11

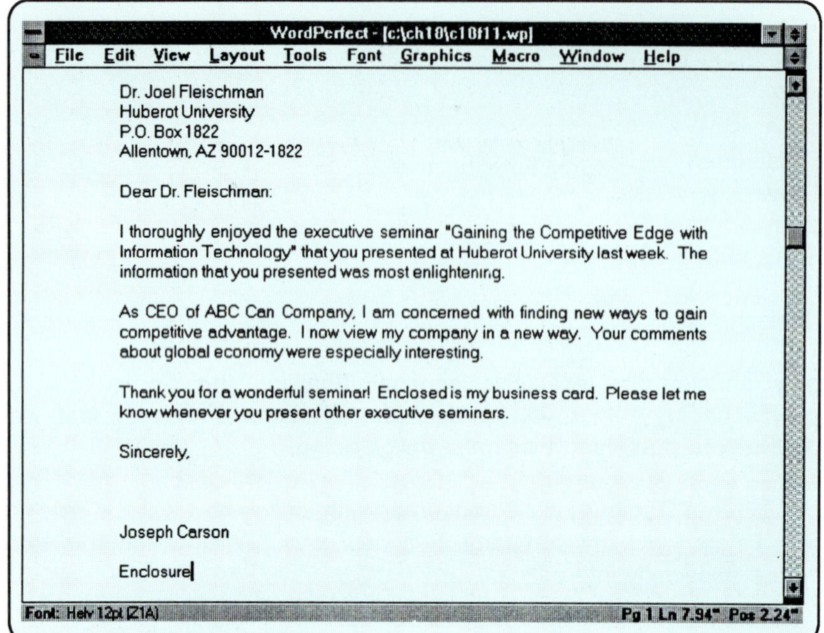

Dr. Joel Fleischman
Huberot University
P.O. Box 1822
Allentown, AZ 90012-1822

Dear Dr. Fleischman:

I thoroughly enjoyed the executive seminar "Gaining the Competitive Edge with Information Technology" that you presented at Huberot University last week. The information that you presented was most enlightening.

As CEO of ABC Can Company, I am concerned with finding new ways to gain competitive advantage. I now view my company in a new way. Your comments about global economy were especially interesting.

Thank you for a wonderful seminar! Enclosed is my business card. Please let me know whenever you present other executive seminars.

Sincerely,

Joseph Carson

Enclosure

Close your document without saving changes.

■ ASSIGNING A MACRO TO A MENU

You may use certain macros quite frequently. Rather than having to access the Macro Play feature each time you want to execute a macro, you can assign a macro to a menu.

You use the Assign to Menu option under the Macro menu to place a macro on a menu. Each macro that you select is assigned to the Macro menu.

Suppose that you want to access the "formdoc.wcm" macro frequently. To add the macro to the Macro menu:

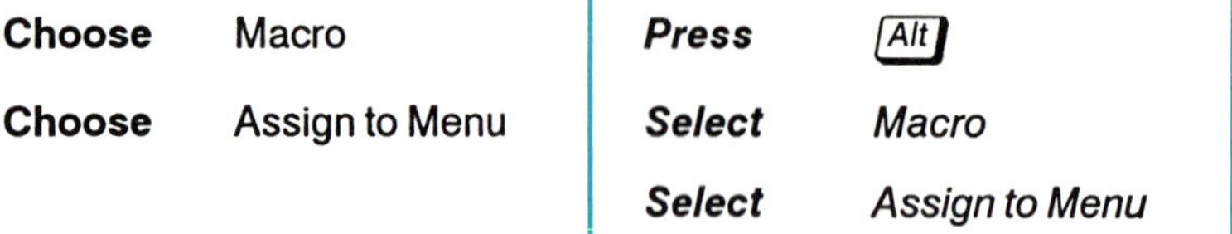

Choose	Macro	***Press***	Alt
Choose	Assign to Menu	***Select***	*Macro*
		Select	*Assign to Menu*

Your screen should look like Figure 18-12.

Figure 18-12

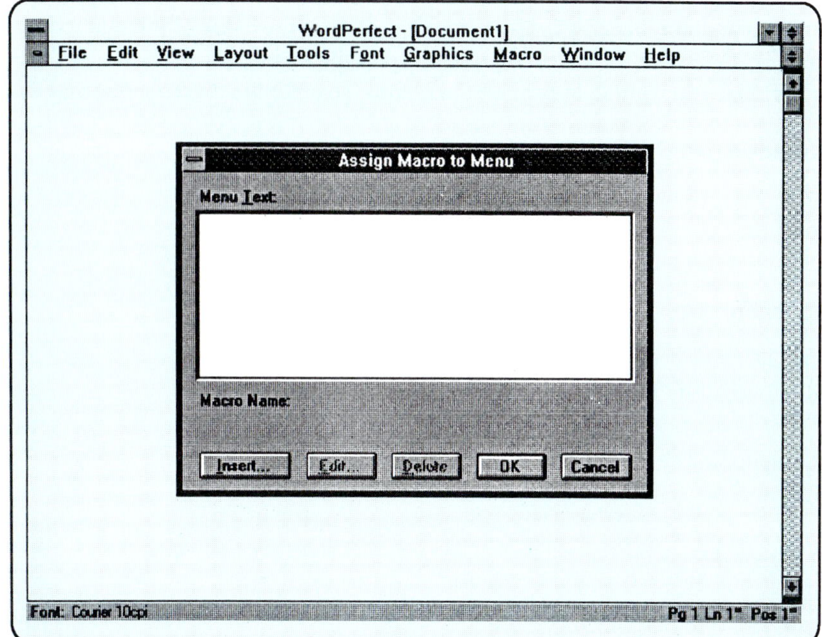

The Assign Macro to Menu dialog box appears. Notice that the Menu Text list box is blank indicating that no macros have been assigned to a menu yet.

To add the "formdoc" macro:

Click	the Insert command button	***Press***	*Alt+I to select the Insert command button*

Your screen should look like Figure 18-13.

Figure 18-13

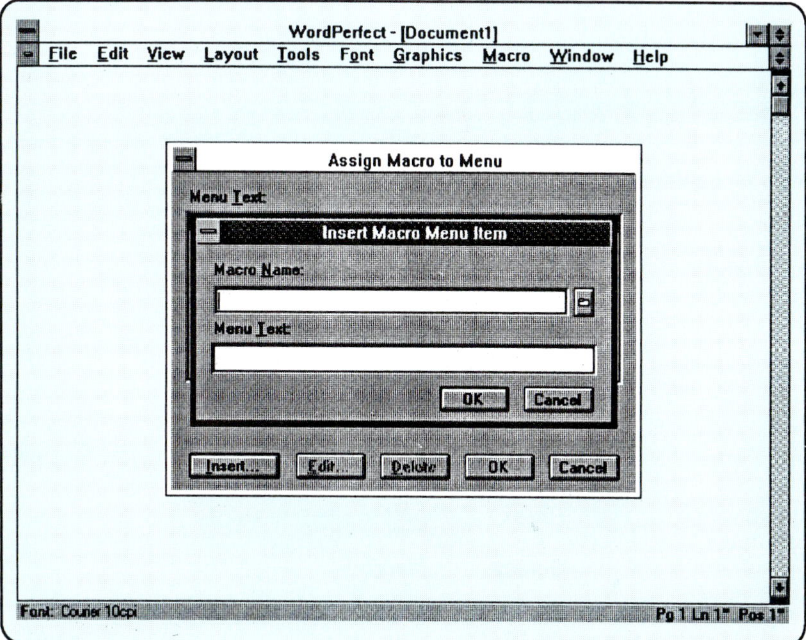

The Insert Macro Menu Item dialog box appears. You can type the name of the macro in the Macro Name box or you can click on the file folder button to search for the macro file. The Menu Text text box allows you to type the text that you want to appear on the menu. To enter the macro name and the menu text:

Type	**formdoc**	***Type***	***formdoc***
Double-click	on the Menu Text text box	***Press***	*Alt+T to select the Menu Text text box*
Type	Letter Format	***Type***	*Letter Format*
Click	the OK command button	***Press***	*↵Enter*

Your screen should look like Figure 18-14.

Figure 18-14

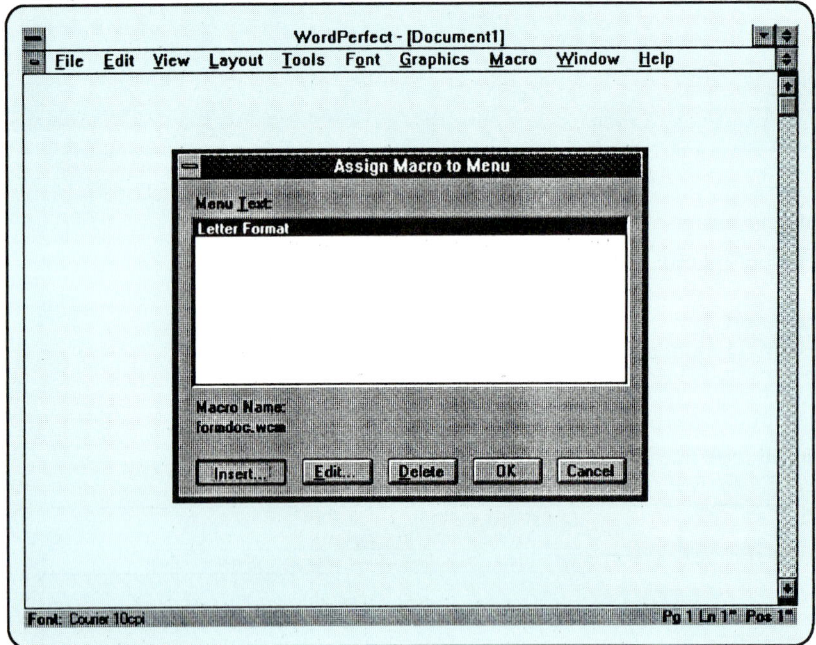

To accept the new menu item:

Click	the OK command button	***Press***	*Tab three times to highlight the OK command button*
		Press	*↵Enter*

The option Letter Format has been added to the end of the Macro menu. To view the new option:

Choose	Macro	***Press***	*Alt*
		Select	*Macro*

Your screen should look like Figure 18-15.

Figure 18-15

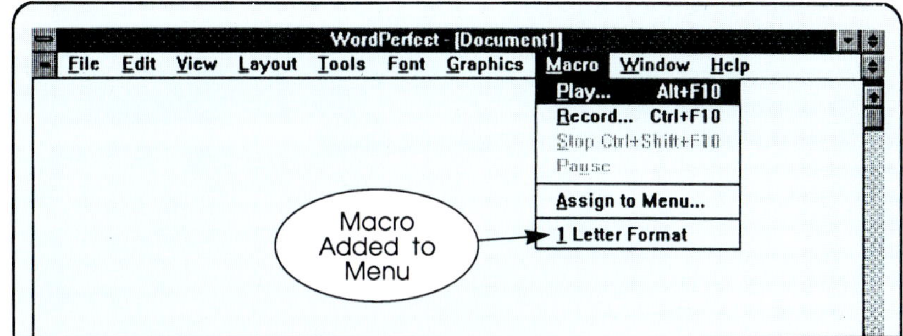

To run a macro that has been assigned to the menu, you select the menu option. To run the Letter Format macro:

Choose	1 Letter Format	***Select***	*1 Letter Format*

View the Reveal Codes to ensure that the macro executed properly.

Remove the document codes from the screen using the Reveal Codes feature.

You also use the Macro Assign to Menu feature to delete a macro from a menu. To delete the Letter Format option from the Macro menu:

Choose	Macro	***Press***	*Alt*
Choose	Assign to Menu	***Select***	*Macro*
Click	on the Letter Format text in the Menu Text list box	***Select***	*Assign to Menu*
Click	the Delete command button	***Press***	*the pointer-movement keys to highlight the Letter Format text in the Menu Text list box*
Click	the OK command button	***Press***	*Alt+D to select the Delete command button*
		Press	*Tab to highlight the OK command button*
		Press	*↵Enter*

The Letter Format option has been deleted from the Macro menu. Choose Macro from the menu and notice that Letter Format is no longer an option on the menu.

Your screen should look like Figure 18-16.

Figure 18-16

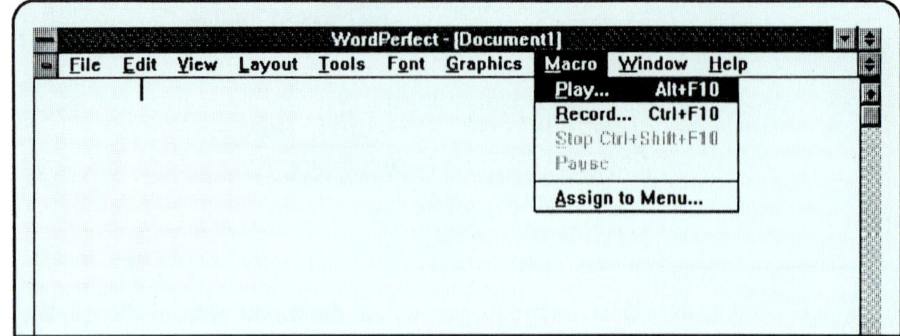

Close the document without saving changes.

■ EDITING A MACRO

In some situations you may need to edit or change a macro that you created. For instance, it may be necessary to add some text or commands. You may also need to delete text or incorrect commands that exist in a macro.

You can open a macro file to modify the existing macro. Macro files are made up of a series of commands called functions. Every WordPerfect command has a corresponding function.

Most functions have a similar format. The typical function format is the function name followed by conditions that appear in parentheses. Each function has a different name and a different set of conditions. For more detailed information about the different macro commands and functions, see the "Macro" section of your WordPerfect Reference Manual.

Suppose you forgot to include the title "Chief Executive Officer" for Mr. Carson in the letter closing. You can change the closing macro to include the title.

To open the "ctrlsftc.wcm" file:

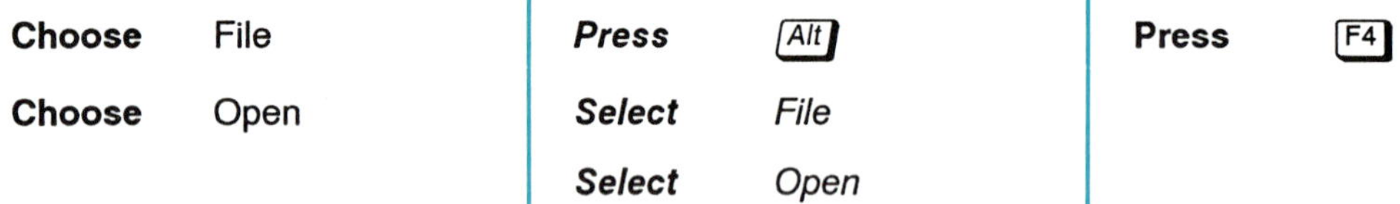

Choose	File	***Press***	*Alt*	**Press**	F4
Choose	Open	***Select***	*File*		
		Select	*Open*		

The current directory is the "c:\wpdocs" or the "a:\wpdocs" directory. To quickly access the macros directory, you can use the Quick List feature. The Quick List provides an easy way to move to directories that are used frequently. The Quick List items refer directly to the options listed in the Location of Files dialog box under the File Preferences menu. If you have a macros directory designated in the Location of Files feature, a "Macros" Quick List item will be available.

To turn on the Quick List feature:

Click	the Quick List check box until an X appears	***Press***	*Alt+Q until an X appears in the Quick List check box*	**Press**	Alt+Q until an X appears in the Quick List check box

Your screen should look similar to Figure 18-17.

Figure 18-17

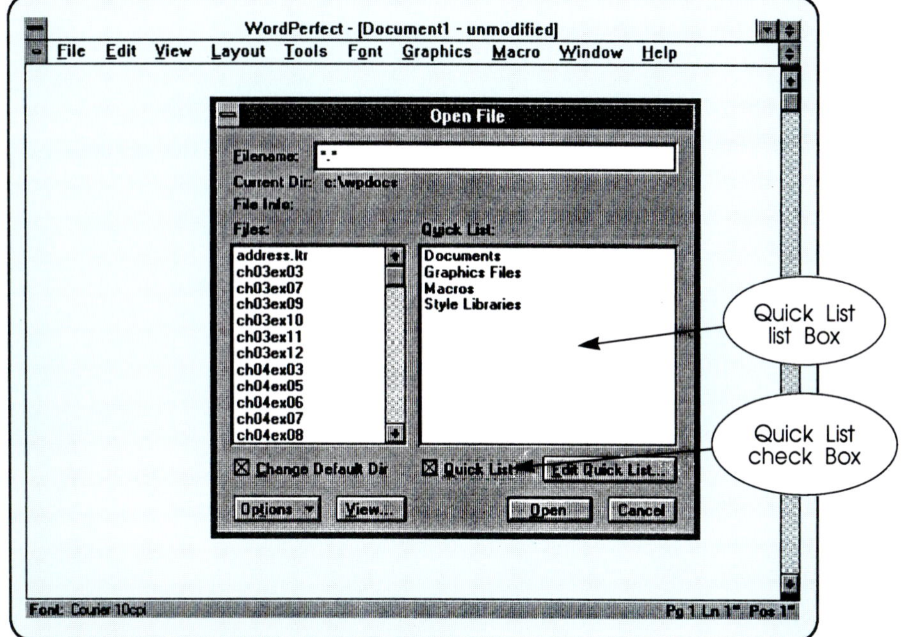

The names appearing in the Quick List list box correspond with the file locations in the Location of Files feature under the Preferences option of the File menu. To select the "Macros" item in the Quick List list box:

Double-Click	on the Macros text in the Quick List list box	***Press***	*Alt+U to select the Quick List list box*	**Press**	Alt+U to select the Quick List list box
		Press	*↓ to highlight the Macros text*	**Press**	↓ to select the Macros text
		Press	*↵Enter*	**Press**	↵Enter

Your screen should look like Figure 18-18.

Figure 18-18

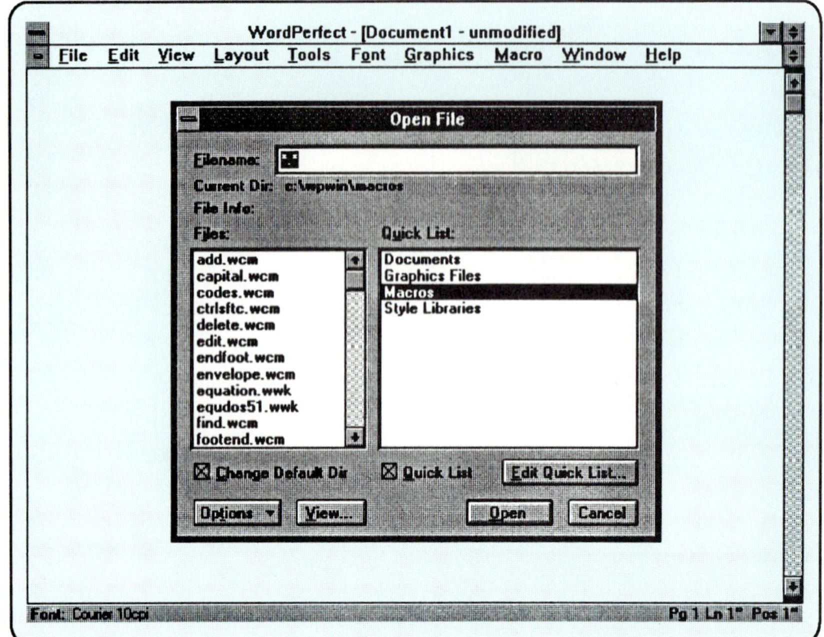

Notice the macro files are listed in the Files list box. To remove the Quick List:

Click	the Quick List check box until the X disappears	***Press***	*Alt+Q until the X disappears from the Quick List check box*	**Press**	Alt+Q until the X disappears from the Quick List check box

To open the "ctrlsftc.wcm" file:

Click	on the "ctrlsftc.wcm" file	***Press***	*Alt+I to select the Files list box*	**Press**	Alt+I to select the Files list box
Click	the Open command button	***Press***	*↓ to select the "ctrlsftc.wcm" file*	**Press**	↓ to select the "ctrlsftc.wcm" file
		Press	*↵Enter to select the Open command button*	**Press**	↵Enter to select the Open command button

Your screen should look like Figure 18-19.

Figure 18-19

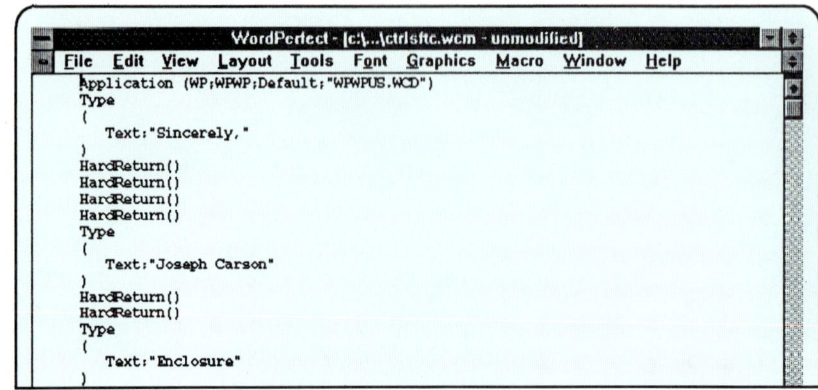

Notice that there are three functions in this macro. The Application function tells the macro to perform each command in WordPerfect rather than some other software program. Each macro begins with an Application function.

The Type function allows you to enter text as part of a macro. Notice that the Type function is placed on several lines in the macro document so that it is easier to read. The argument for the Type function begins "Text:" followed by the string of text that you want the macro to insert in your document. The string of text should appear in quotation marks.

The HardReturn function places a hard return in your document during macro execution. Each time you press ↵Enter as you record the macro, the HardReturn function is placed in your macro. Notice that the HardReturn function does not have a specific condition.

To insert the title "Chief Executive Officer" on the line immediately below the words "Joseph Carson," you must insert a HardReturn function to move to the line immediately below "Joseph Carson."

To insert the HardReturn function:

Click	after the ")" following the Type function for the text "Joseph Carson"	***Move***	*the insertion point after the ")" following the Type function for the text "Joseph Carson"*	**Move**	the insertion point after the ")" following the Type command for the text "Joseph Carson"

Your screen should look like Figure 18-20.

Figure 18-20

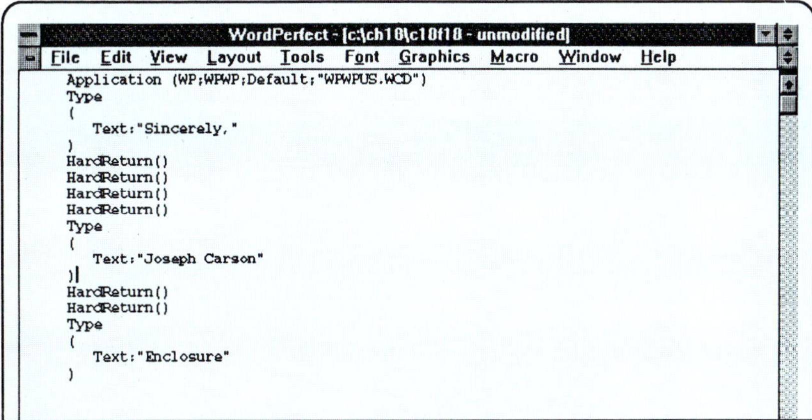

Press	↵Enter to add a blank line	***Press***	*↵Enter to add a blank line*	**Press**	↵Enter to add a blank line
Type	HardReturn()	***Type***	*HardReturn()*	**Type**	HardReturn()

Your screen should look like Figure 18-21.

Figure 18-21

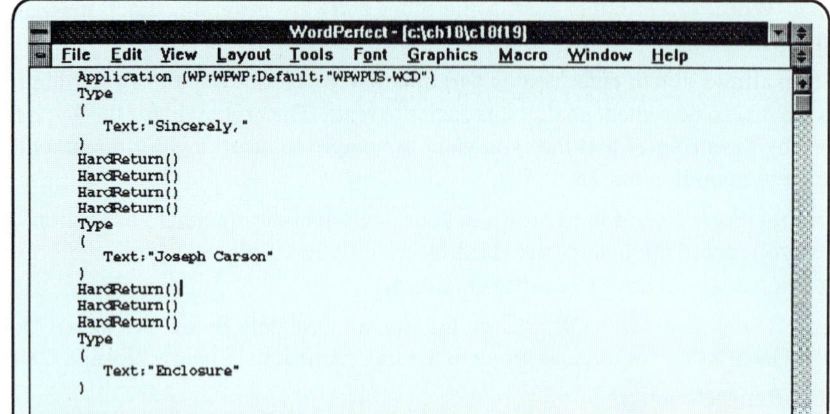

To add the text "Chief Executive Officer" after the HardReturn function, you use the Type function. To insert the Type function:

Press	Enter	***Press***	*Enter*	**Press**	Enter
Type	Type(Text: "Chief Executive Officer")	***Type***	*Type(Text: "Chief Executive Officer")*	**Type**	Type(Text: "Chief Executive Officer")

Your screen should look like Figure 18-22.

Figure 18-22

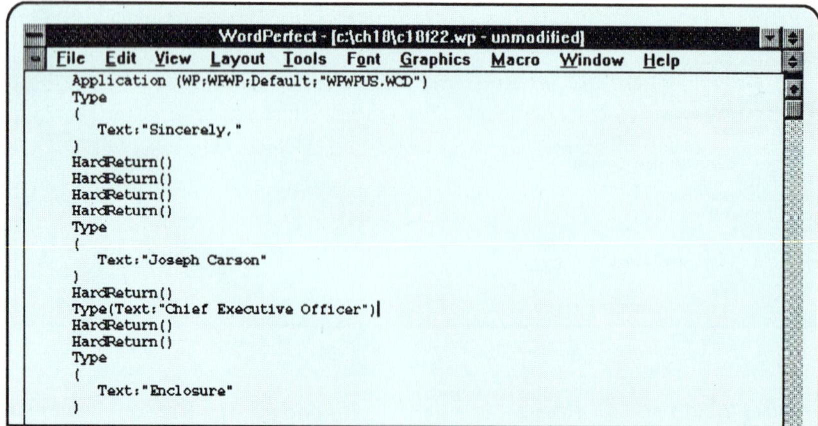

Save your macro document and close the file.

To test the changes to the macro:

Press	Ctrl+Shift+C	***Press***	*Ctrl+Shift+C*	**Press**	Ctrl+Shift+C

Your screen should look like Figure 18-23.

Figure 18-23

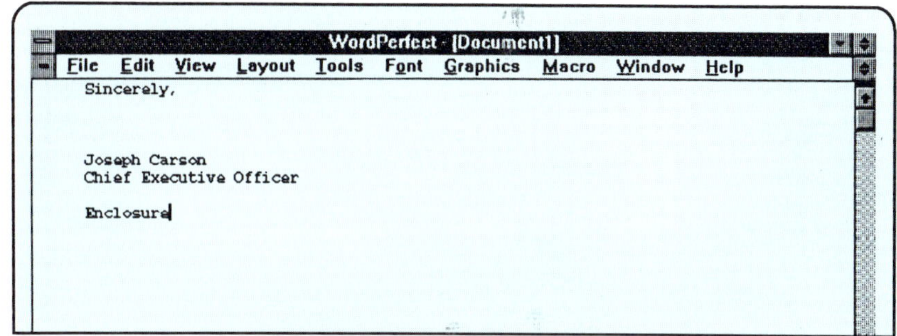

Close the document without saving changes.

CREATING AN INTERACTIVE MACRO

The "sales.wcm" macro creates a weekly sales memo. The memo is always addressed to the sales staff and sent from John Mogab, the sales manager.

Sometimes, you might want to enter different data in the memo headings. You can use macro programming commands to create an interactive macro.

The PauseKey macro command allows you to pause the macro until you press a specified key. While the macro is paused, you can access WordPerfect features as if no macro were running.

The PauseKey command has the following syntax: PauseKey(Key,Character). The Key condition is the key that you want to end the pausing of the macro. You can use the ↵Enter key, the Esc key, the Ctrl+F4 keys, or any single character key. If the Key condition is Enter!, then you press the ↵Enter key to resume the macro. If the Key condition is Cancel!, then you press the Esc to continue the macro. If the Key condition is Close!, then you press Ctrl+F4 to continue the macro. If the Key condition is Character!, then you press the character specified in the Character condition to resume the macro.

The Character condition is only used when the Key condition is Character!. The Character condition specifies the single key that continues the macro. For example, if the Key condition is Character!, you can set the Character condition to P. In this example, pressing the P key continues the macro.

To add the PauseKey macro command to a macro, you edit the macro. To edit the "sales.wcm" macro, open the "sales.wcm" file from the "c:\wpwin\macros" directory.

Your screen should look like Figure 18-24.

Figure 18-24

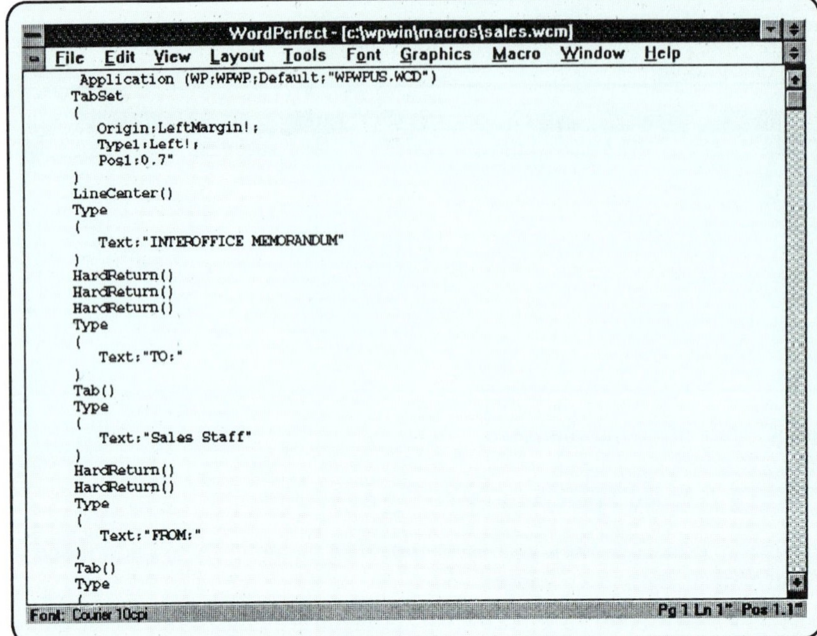

Suppose you want the macro to pause after each of the memo headings except the date. You need to replace the Type function that enters the text after the memo heading with a PauseKey command.

To replace the third Type function with a PauseKey command:

Click	at the left margin of the third Type function	***Move***	*the insertion point to the left margin of the third Type function*	**Move**	the insertion point to the left margin of the third Type function

Your screen should look like Figure 18-25.

Figure 18-25

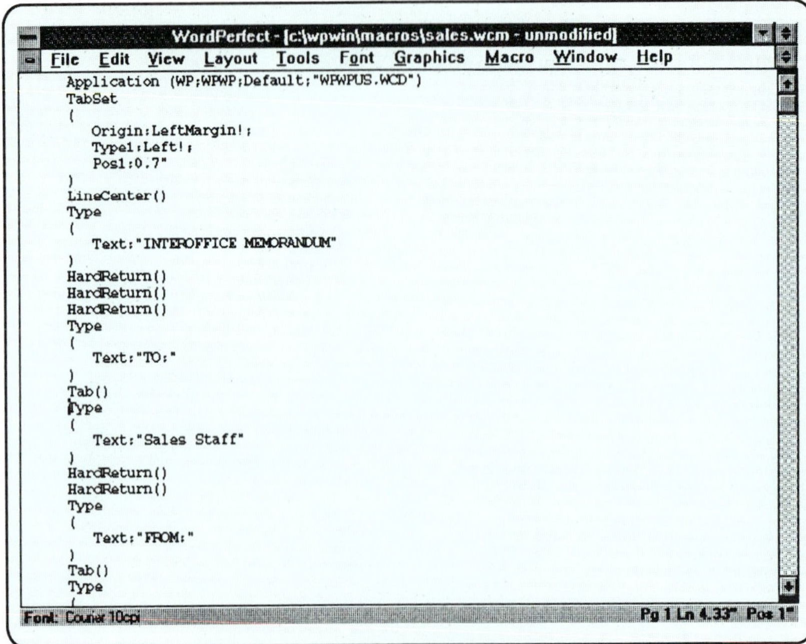

Select	the four lines of the Type function	***Select***	*the four lines of the Type function*	**Select**	the four lines of the Type function
Press	Delete	***Press***	*Delete*	**Press**	Delete

Your screen should look like Figure 18-26.

Figure 18-26

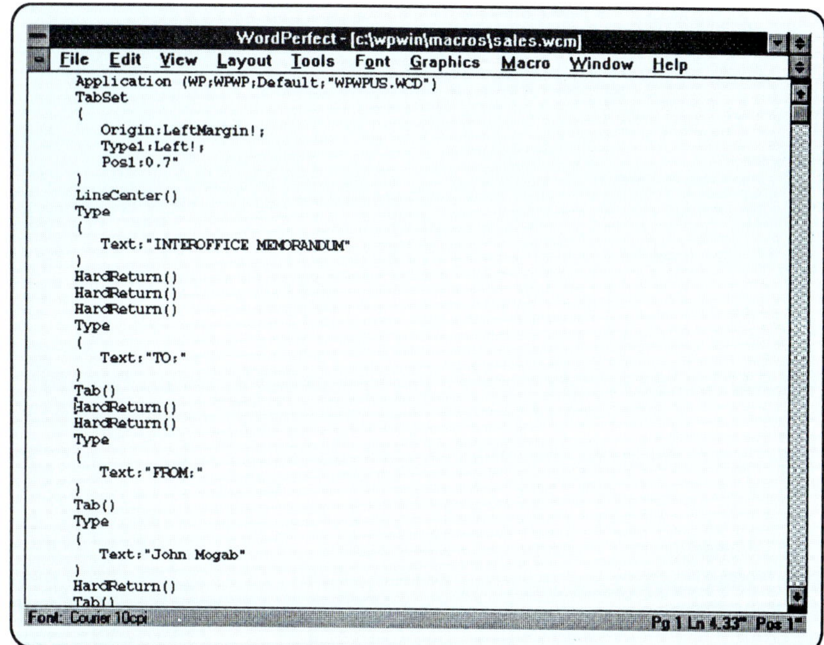

To add a PauseKey command that pauses the macro until the ↵Enter key is pressed:

Type	PauseKey(Key: Enter!)	***Type***	*PauseKey(Key: Enter!)*	**Type**	PauseKey(Key: Enter!)
Press	↵Enter	***Press***	*↵Enter*	**Press**	↵Enter

Your screen should look like Figure 18-27.

Figure 18-27

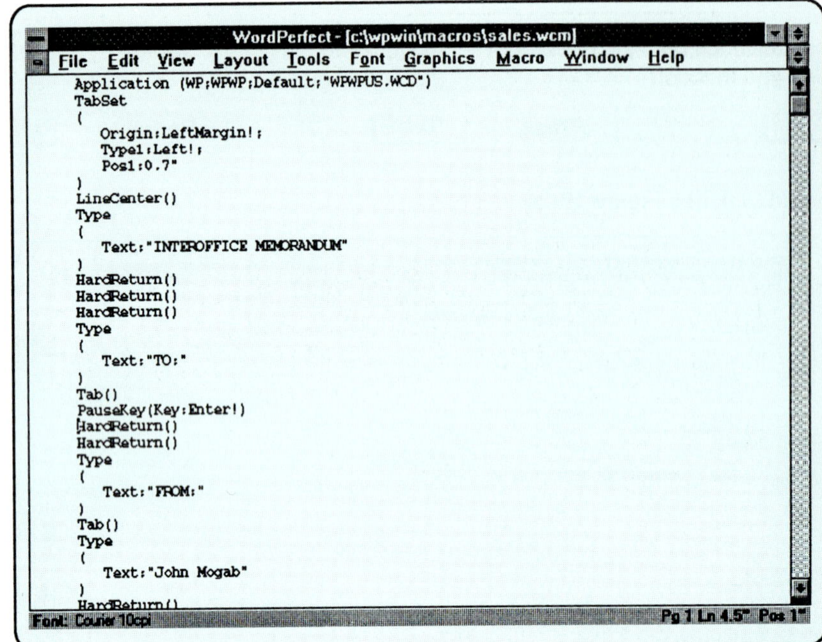

To replace the Type command for the text "John Mogab" and the title "Sales Manager" with a PauseKey command:

Click	at the left margin of the Type command for the text "John Mogab"	***Move***	*the insertion point to the left margin of the Type command for the text "John Mogab"*	**Move**	the insertion point to the left margin of the Type command for the text "John Mogab"
Select	the line and the following nine lines	***Select***	*the line and the following nine lines*	**Select**	the line and the following nine lines

Your screen should look similar to Figure 18-28.

Figure 18-28

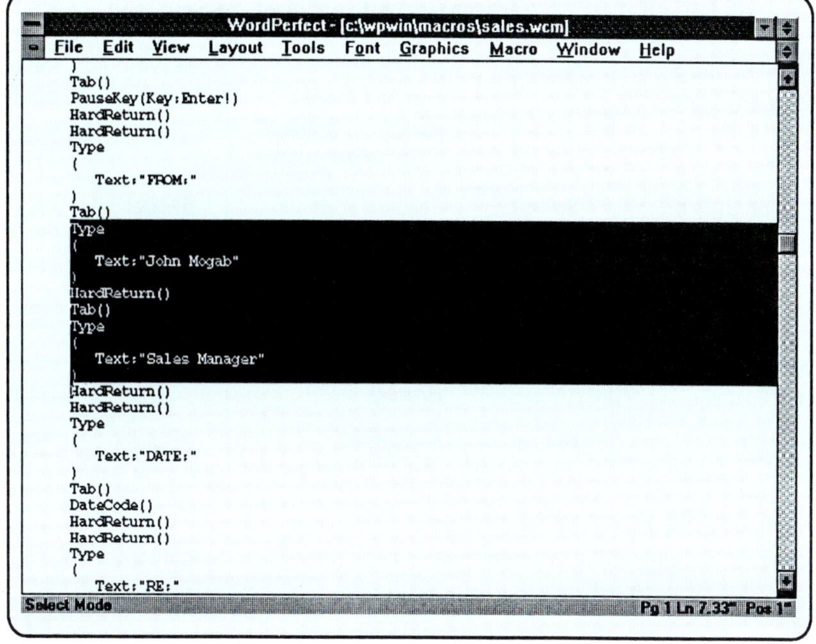

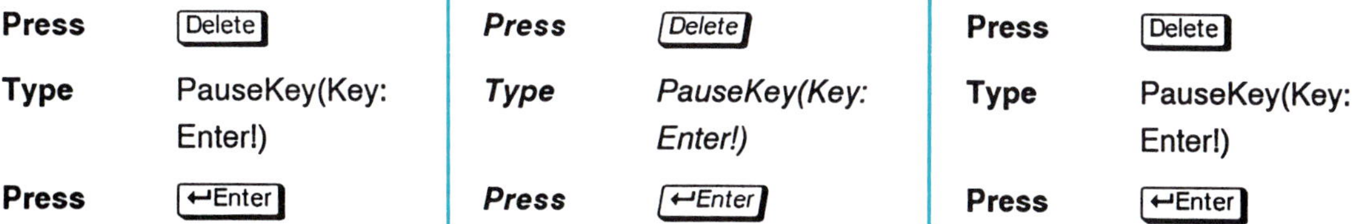

Press Delete

Type PauseKey(Key: Enter!)

Press ↵Enter

Press *Delete*

Type *PauseKey(Key: Enter!)*

Press *↵Enter*

Press Delete

Type PauseKey(Key: Enter!)

Press ↵Enter

Your screen should look like Figure 18-29.

Figure 18-29

```
WordPerfect - [c:\wpwin\macros\sales.wcm]
File Edit View Layout Tools Font Graphics Macro Window Help
)
Tab()
PauseKey(Key:Enter!)
HardReturn()
HardReturn()
Type
(
   Text:"FROM:"
)
Tab()
PauseKey(Key:Enter!)
HardReturn()
HardReturn()
Type
(
   Text:"DATE:"
)
Tab()
DateCode()
HardReturn()
HardReturn()
Type
(
   Text:"RE:"
)
Tab()
Type
(
   Text:"Weekly Sales Report"
)
HardReturn()
HardReturn()
HardReturn()
Font: Courier 10cpi                                   Pg 1 Ln 5.83" Pos 1"
```

To replace the "Weekly Sales Report" Type command with a PauseKey command:

Click	at the left margin of the last Type command	***Move***	*the insertion point to the left margin of the last Type command*	**Move**	the insertion point to the left margin of the last Type command
Select	the four lines of the Type command	***Select***	*the four lines of the Type command*	**Select**	the four lines of the Type command
Press	Delete	***Press***	*Delete*	**Press**	Delete
Type	PauseKey(Key: Enter!)	***Type***	*PauseKey(Key: Enter!)*	**Type**	PauseKey(Key: Enter!)
Press	↵Enter	***Press***	*↵Enter*	**Press**	↵Enter

Your screen should look like Figure 18-30.

Figure 18-30

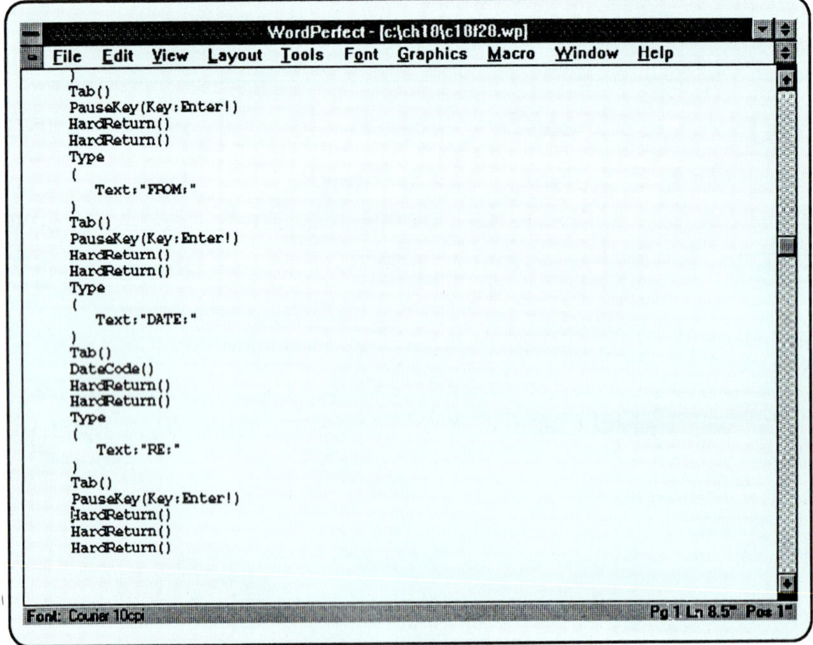

To save the macro under a different name:

Choose	File	***Press***	*Alt*	**Press**	F3
Choose	Save As	***Select***	*File*	**Type**	**memos.wcm**
Type	**memos.wcm**	***Select***	*Save As*	**Press**	↵Enter to select the Save command button
Click	the Save command button	***Type***	***memos.wcm***		

		Press	*↵Enter to select the Save command button*		

Close the document.

To run the interactive macro:

Choose	Macro	***Press***	*Alt*	**Press**	Alt+F10
Choose	Play	***Select***	*Macro*	**Type**	**memos**
Click	the down scroll arrow until the "memos.wcm" file appears	***Select***	*Play*	**Press**	↵Enter to select the Play command button
Click	on the "memos.wcm" file	***Type***	***memos***		
Click	the Play command button	***Press***	*↵Enter to select the Play command button*		

Your screen should look like Figure 18-31.

Figure 18-31

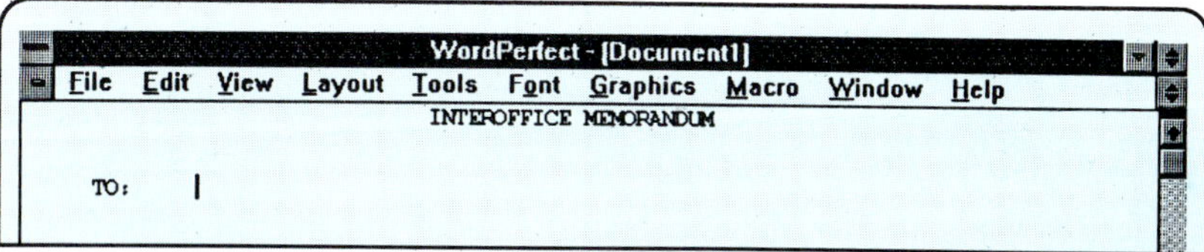

When the macro pauses, you can enter data and use WordPerfect commands. When you press the ↵Enter key, the macro continues. To create a blank line while the macro is paused, press Shift+↵Enter rather than ↵Enter.

To enter the addressee's name:

Type	Paula Jones	***Type***	*Paula Jones*	**Type**	Paula Jones
Press	↵Enter	***Press***	*↵Enter*	**Press**	↵Enter

To enter the sales manager's name and title:

Type	John Wylie	***Type***	*John Wylie*	**Type**	John Wylie

To create a blank line during the pause and enter the title:

Press	Shift+↵Enter	***Press***	*Shift+↵Enter*	**Press**	Shift+↵Enter
Press	Tab	***Press***	*Tab*	**Press**	Tab
Type	Sales Manager	***Type***	*Sales Manager*	**Type**	Sales Manager
Press	↵Enter	***Press***	*↵Enter*	**Press**	↵Enter

To enter the subject text:

Type	Monthly Sales Meeting	***Type***	*Monthly Sales Meeting*	**Type**	Monthly Sales Meeting
Press	↵Enter	***Press***	*↵Enter*	**Press**	↵Enter

The macro ends and your screen should look like Figure 18-32.

Figure 18-32

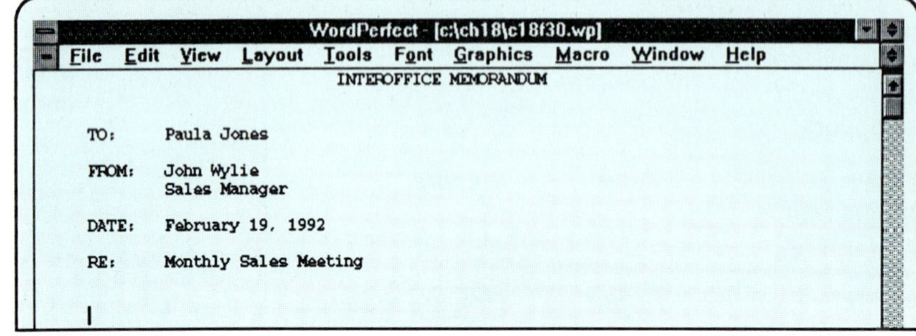

Close the document without saving changes.

WordPerfect also has a Pause macro command. The Pause command pauses the macro until you choose Pause from the Macro menu. The Pause command does not have any conditions.

For more information on the various macro commands, contact the WordPerfect Corporation for a Macros Manual.

■ DELETING A MACRO

You can delete a macro by using the File Manager feature and deleting the macro file from the list. Recall that a macro file has an extension of ".wcm."

First, you must locate the directory where all macro files are stored. By default, all macros are stored in the "c:\wpwin\macros" directory. You can check the location of your macro files by using the File Preferences, Location of Files command.

To select the File Manager feature:

Choose	File	***Press***	*Alt*
Choose	File Manager	***Select***	*File*
		Select	*File Manager*

Your screen should look similar to Figure 18-33.

Figure 18-33

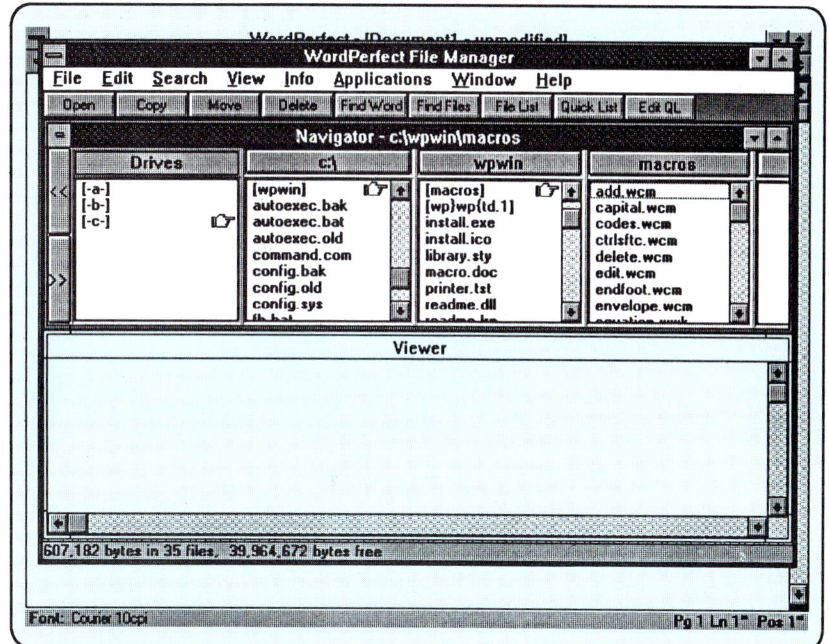

Notice that the current directory is "c:\wpwin\macros."

To delete the macro file for Ctrl+Shift+C:

Click	on the file "ctrlsftc.wcm"	***Press***	*↓ to select the "ctrlsftc.wcm" file*	**Press**	↓ to select the "ctrlsftc.wcm" file
Choose	File	***Press***	*Alt*	**Press**	Ctrl+D
Choose	Delete	***Select***	*File*	**Press**	↵Enter to select the Delete command button
Click	the Delete command button	***Select***	*Delete*		
		Press	*↵Enter to select the Delete command button*		

The file no longer appears in the Navigator window.

To close the File Manager:

Choose	File	***Press***	*Alt*	**Press**	Alt+F4
Choose	Exit	***Select***	*File*		
		Select	*Exit*		

EXERCISE 1

INSTRUCTIONS: Discuss the following items briefly:

1. Macro feature ______________________________

2. The process for recording a macro ______________________________

3. The steps for playing a macro ______________________________

4. The process for editing a macro ______________________________

5. The steps for deleting a macro ______________________________

6. The process for assigning a macro to a menu ______________________________

7. The process for pausing a macro ______________________________

EXERCISE 2

INSTRUCTIONS: Circle T if the statement is true and F if the statement is false.

T	F	1.	A macro is a set of recorded actions in WordPerfect.
T	F	2.	All macros must be named using a Ctrl + Shift key combination.
T	F	3.	WordPerfect adds a ".wcm" extension to all macro names.
T	F	4.	"Macro Recording" appears in the status bar when you are recording actions.
T	F	5.	"Weekly sales demo.wcm" is a valid macro name.
T	F	6.	You can press the Esc key to stop the execution of a macro.
T	F	7.	You can edit the macro by opening the file.
T	F	8.	Every menu command has a corresponding macro function.
T	F	9.	The HardReturn() function places a hard page break in your document.
T	F	10.	When you add a macro to the menu, the macro appears under the File option.

EXERCISE 3

INSTRUCTIONS:

1. Create a macro to prepare the following heading and date for letters that are prepared on a routine basis. Bold and center the heading. The name of the macro should be "company."
2. Execute the macro.
3. Print the document after the macro is executed.
4. Close the document without saving changes.

```
                Jackson, Kemp & Garza
             Certified Public Accountants
              829 Gessner Road, Suite 430
                 Richmond, VA 23489



April 2, 1992
```

EXERCISE 4

INSTRUCTIONS:

1. Create a macro to include the following information needed at the closing of all letters for your firm. Name the macro using the Ctrl+Shift+A keys.
2. Execute the macro.
3. Print the document after the macro is executed.
4. Close the document.

```
Cordially,



Susan K. Scanlan
Attorney at Law

SKS/df
```

EXERCISE 5

INSTRUCTIONS:

1. Create a heading for a letter. The heading macro should create the letter heading shown below. This heading includes the current date, four returns, the inside address, and the salutation.
2. Name this macro Ctrl+Shift+B.
3. Close the document and do not save changes.

```
February 7, 1992



President George Bush
The White House
1600 Pennsylvania Avenue
Washington, D.C. 20013

Dear President Bush:
```

EXERCISE 6

INSTRUCTIONS:

1. Create the following macro for the beginning paragraph of letters. Name this macro Ctrl + Shift + R.
2. After creating the macro, use it in the letter shown below.
3. Print the letter.
4. Save the letter in a file using the name "ch18ex06."
5. Close the letter.

MACRO

```
Thank you for your letter of inquiry regarding a position at our
company.  At this time, we do not have any openings for someone
with your background.
```

LETTER

Date

Mr. Mark Robinson
1090 West Roslyn Road
Irvine, CA 92711

Dear Mr. Robinson:

Use Macro Ctrl + Shift + R

Your background in Chemical Analysis could be of value to us in the near future. We are considering opening a Research and Development department within the next year. We will call you after this department is given permission to exist.

Thank you for your interest in our company.

Sincerely

ADAMS SOLVENTS

Marshall Smith
Director of Personnel

EXERCISE 7

INSTRUCTIONS:

1. Assign the Ctrl+Shift+R to the Macro menu. Use the text "No Openings" as the menu text.
2. Type the following letter using the No Openings option on the Macro menu as the first paragraph.
3. Spell check the letter.
4. Preview the letter.
5. Print the letter.
6. Save the letter in a file using the name "ch18ex07."
7. Close the document.

```
April 2, 1992

Mrs. Theo Reid
1647 Portage
River Edge, NJ 07661

Dear Mrs. Reid:

Ctrl+Shift+R

If anything does develop in your area of expertise, Survey
Developer, in the next six months, we will contact you to see if
you are still interested in pursuing a position with our company.

Thank you again for your interest in our company.

Very truly yours,



James Stutesman, Manager
Quantitative Measuring
```

EXERCISE 8

INSTRUCTIONS:

1. Create a macro for the full heading of the memorandum shown below. Bold and center "MEMORANDUM." Use a 2″ top margin. Place the insertion point so that you are ready to start typing.
2. Name this macro "memo."
3. Execute the macro.
4. Print the document after executing the macro.
5. Assign the macro to the menu using the text "President Memos" as the menu text.
6. Close the document and do not save changes.

MEMORANDUM

```
TO:

FROM:     Samuel E. Beckett

DATE:     April 16, 1992

SUBJECT:
```

EXERCISE 9

INSTRUCTIONS:

1. Edit the "memo" macro.
2. After "Beckett," add a comma (,) and the word "President."
3. Execute the macro.
4. Print the document after executing the macro.
5. Close the document without saving changes.

EXERCISE 10

INSTRUCTIONS:

1. Edit the "memo" macro.
2. Add a PauseKey command at the To: and Subject: lines to pause the macro until the ↵Enter key is pressed.
3. Execute the macro.
4. Address the memo to Maria Campbell. The subject of the memo is New Products. Add the following text to the memo after the macro executes.
5. Print the memo.
6. Save the memo as "ch18ex10."
7. Close the document.

```
The Fall product line is being announced July 22nd at B & J's
department store in Los Angeles.  Please notify all staff members
of the announcement date and location.

Invitations to the Fall line introduction will be distributed at a
later date.
```

CHAPTER NINETEEN

ENVELOPES AND LABELS

OBJECTIVES

In this chapter, you will learn to:

- Create envelopes
- Create labels
- Create labels using a macro

CHAPTER OVERVIEW

In this chapter, the Paper Size feature is discussed. The process for creating envelope and label paper sizes is illustrated. The use of macros to create label forms is also illustrated.

PAPER SIZE

The Paper Size feature in WordPerfect enables you to define a printer form for special sizes of paper that you wish to use when printing your document. Your "document" can be an address for an envelope or label, an invitation on 5″ x 7″ cards, or any printed material that requires special paper. You can also define a printer form so that the printer handles paper a certain way.

You can use the Paper Size feature by selecting the Page option from the Layout menu or by pressing [Alt]+[F9]. The existing forms are listed in the Paper Size dialog box. WordPerfect has already created the standard 8.5″ x 11″ form for you. Depending on the type of printer that you selected, there may be other forms already defined for you. Most laser printers include a form for business envelopes. You will see all of the existing forms in the Paper Type list box. To use a new paper type, select the desired form from the Paper Type list box and click the Select command button. Once you select a form, a Paper Size code is inserted into your document.

The Paper Size feature enables you to create custom forms by adding new forms or editing existing forms. To add a new form, click the Add command button in the Paper Size dialog box. To edit an existing form, select the paper type from the Paper Type list box and click the Edit command button. If you are using the Windows print drivers, your ability to change the paper size is limited. Refer to the WordPerfect Reference manual for more information on how to use the Paper Size feature with the Windows printer drivers.

When defining a form through the Paper Size feature, you can specify the following attributes:

Size of the paper

The orientation of the font. A portrait font type is shown on this page where the text is printed down the length of the page. A rotated or landscape font type is used when text is printed across the length of the page. (Some printers may not be able to print landscape if they do not contain fonts for landscape printing.)

Continuous or manual (by hand) paper feed by your printer

Whether WordPerfect should prompt you to load the new form when printing

Double-sided printing. (Some printers may not be able to print on both sides of the page.)

Whether the form is a label

You can also copy a form in the Paper Size feature. The Copy command button allows you to copy the settings of one paper type so that you can use them in a new paper type.

The Delete command button deletes a paper type from the Paper Size dialog box. Once you delete a paper type, it is no longer available for any new documents that you create.

■ ENVELOPES

Printing addresses on envelopes is a word processing task that almost everyone must perform at one time or another. You can print on envelopes one at a time as needed. You can also print many addresses on envelopes by using a secondary file containing addresses. Either way, WordPerfect can do the job for you.

Envelopes do not use the standard 8.5″ x 11″ paper upon which you normally print letters and reports. A standard business envelope is 9.5″ x 4″, and a standard short envelope is 6.5″ x 3.5″.

Before starting this section, be sure all documents are closed. Change the default directory to "a:\wpdocs" or to "c:\wpdocs."

Creating an Envelope Form

Suppose you want to create an envelope to accompany the "johnson.ltr" letter. You use 6.5″ x 3.5″ envelopes for which WordPerfect does not include a standard form. If you want to print small envelopes using the address for the "johnson.ltr" letter, you need to create the paper size for the 6.5″ x 3.5″ envelope form.

To select the Paper Size feature:

Choose	Layout	***Press***	*Alt*	**Press**	Alt+F9
Choose	Page	***Select***	*Layout*	**Select**	Paper Size
Choose	Paper Size	***Select***	*Page*		
		Select	*Paper Size*		

The Paper Size dialog box appears. A list of paper types is displayed in the Paper Type list box. The paper types in the Paper Type list box depend on the printer that you have selected. Assuming you have selected the HP LaserJet Series II printer, your screen should look like Figure 19-1.

Figure 19-1

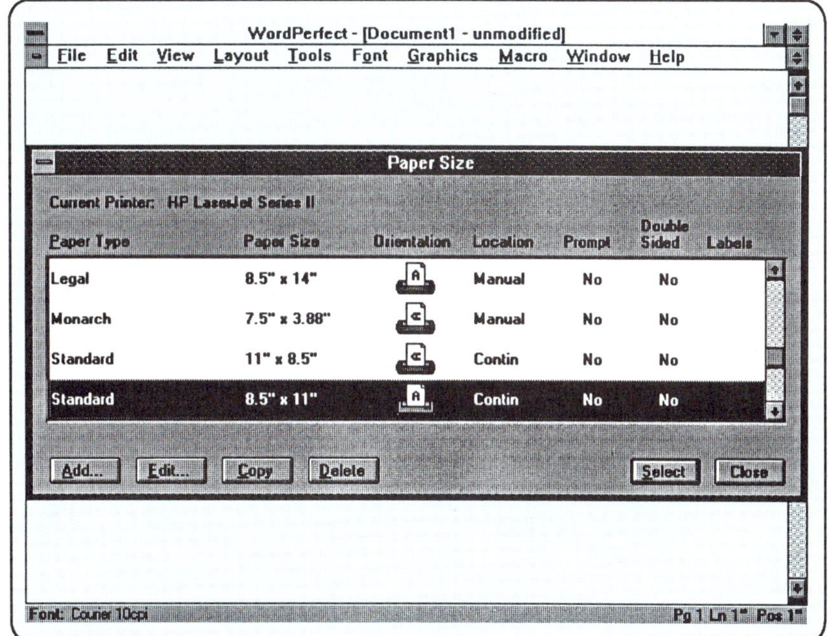

To create a new paper type for the small envelope and add it to the list:

Click	the Add command button	***Press***	*Alt+A to select the Add command button*	**Press**	Alt+A to select the Add command button

The Add Paper Size dialog box appears. Your screen should look like Figure 19-2.

Figure 19-2

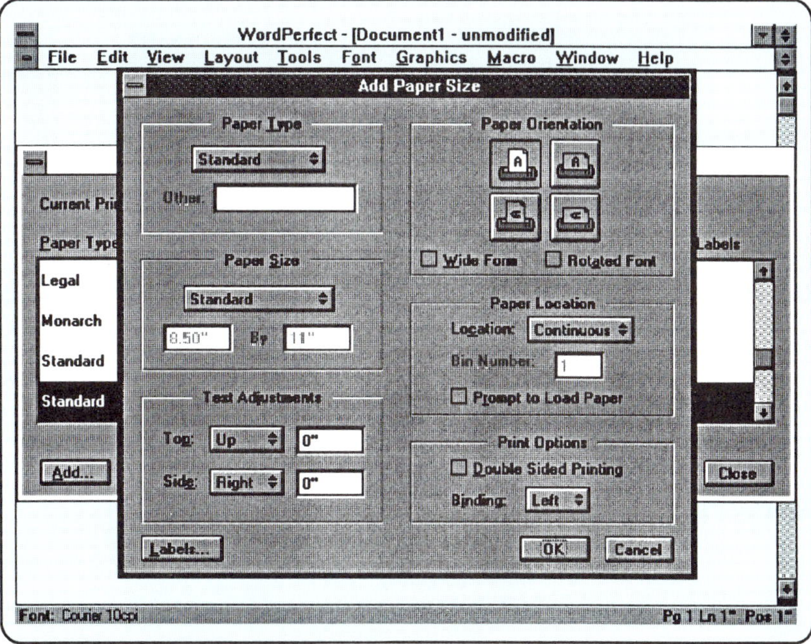

You can select from various types of paper to define your form. "Standard" paper type is the paper you normally would have loaded in your printer. If you do not find the type that you want, then select the option "Other."

To define envelopes:

Click	the Paper Type pop-up list button	***Press***	*Alt+T to select the Paper Type pop-up list button*	**Press**	Alt+T to select the Paper Type pop-up list button
Hold down	the mouse button to view the pop-up list	***Press***	*Alt+↑ to view the pop-up list*	**Press**	Alt+↑ to view the pop-up list
Choose	Envelope	***Type***	*V to select Envelope*	**Type**	V to select Envelope

Your screen should look like Figure 19-3.

Figure 19-3

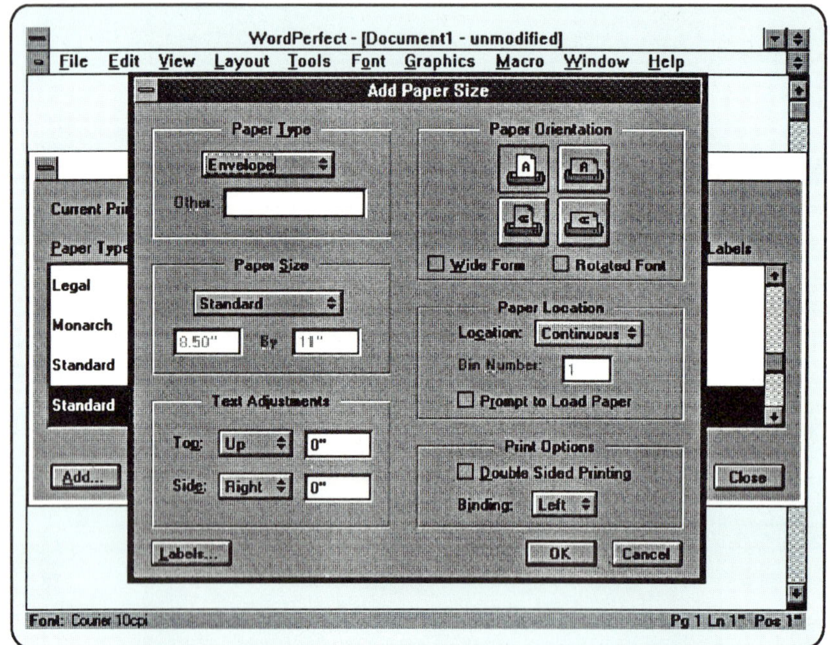

To change the paper size to that of a small envelope:

Click	the Paper Size pop-up list button	***Press***	*Alt+S to select the Paper Size pop-up list button*	**Press**	Alt+S to select the Paper Size pop-up list button
Hold down	the mouse button to view the pop-up list	***Press***	*Alt+↑ to view the pop-up list*	**Press**	Alt+↑ to view the pop-up list

Your screen should look like Figure 19-4.

Figure 19-4

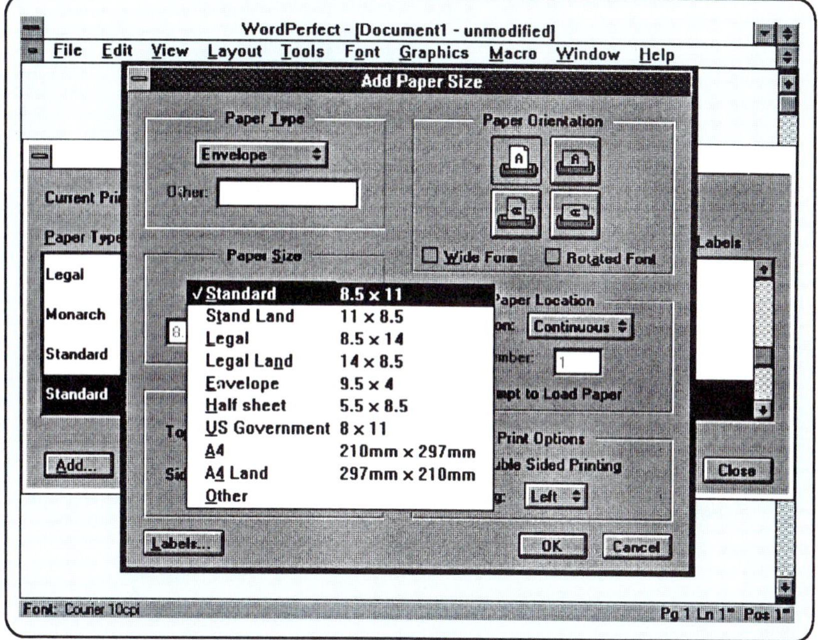

Notice that 6.5″ x 3.5″ is not listed. You must select "Other" to define a custom size. You are prompted to enter the width (6.5″) and height (3.5″) of the new form.

Choose	Other	***Type***	*O to select Other*	**Type**	O to select Other
Double-click	the left Paper Size text box	***Press***	*Tab to select the left Paper Size text box*	**Press**	Tab to select the left Paper Size text box
Type	6.5	***Type***	*6.5*	**Type**	6.5
Double-click	the right Paper Size text box	***Press***	*Tab to select the right Paper Size text box*	**Press**	Tab to select the right Paper Size text box
Type	3.5	***Press***	*Delete until the current number is deleted*	**Press**	Delete until the current number is deleted
		Type	*3.5*	**Type**	3.5

Your screen should look like Figure 19-5.

Figure 19-5

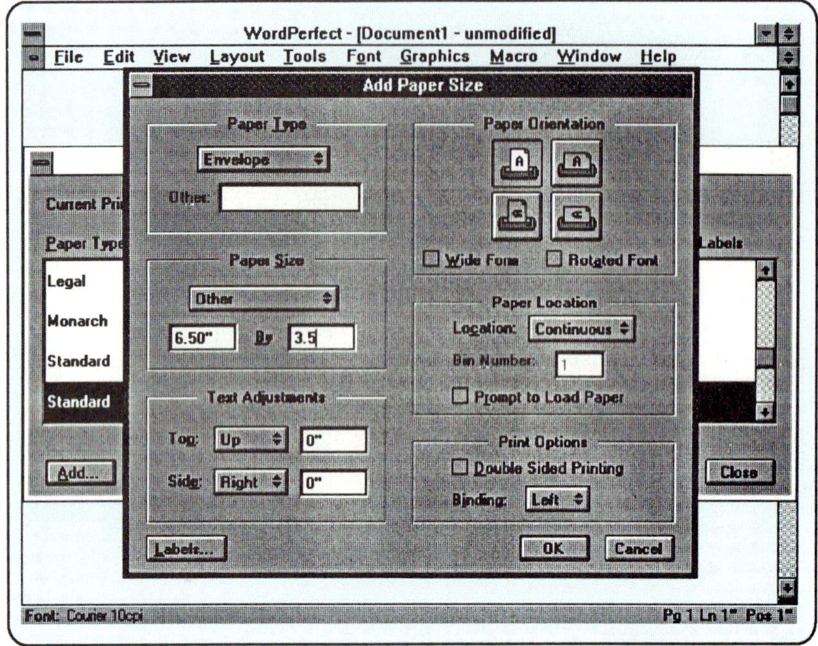

You must also specify a font orientation in the Paper Orientation box. You can choose between a portrait or rotated font type. A portrait font type is shown on this page where the text is printed down the length of the page. A rotated font type is used when text is printed across the length of the page. (Some printers may not be able to print rotated fonts if they do not contain fonts for rotated or landscape printing.)

Whether to choose a rotated or portrait font depends on how the envelope is fed into the printer. If the long side of the envelope is fed first, then choose a portrait font type. If the short side is fed first, then choose a rotated font type.

In this example, the envelope will be fed short side first into a laser printer. To specify a rotated font type:

Click	the Rotated Font check box until an X appears	***Press***	*Alt+A until an X appears in the Rotated Font check box*	**Press**	Alt+A until an X appears in the Rotated Font check box

Notice that the Wide Form check box has been checked in the Paper Orientation box. Whenever the width is greater than the height in the paper size, then the Wide Form check box is turned on in the Paper Orientation box.

When you are using an HP Laserjet Series II, you do not want this form to print wide since you feed the narrow end of the envelope into the printer. With this type of printer the envelopes are fed into the printer short side first. To turn the Wide Form option off:

Click	the Wide Form check box until the X disappears	**Press**	Alt+W until the X disappears in the Wide Form check box	Press	Alt+W until the X disappears in the Wide Form check box

Your screen should look like Figure 19-6.

Figure 19-6

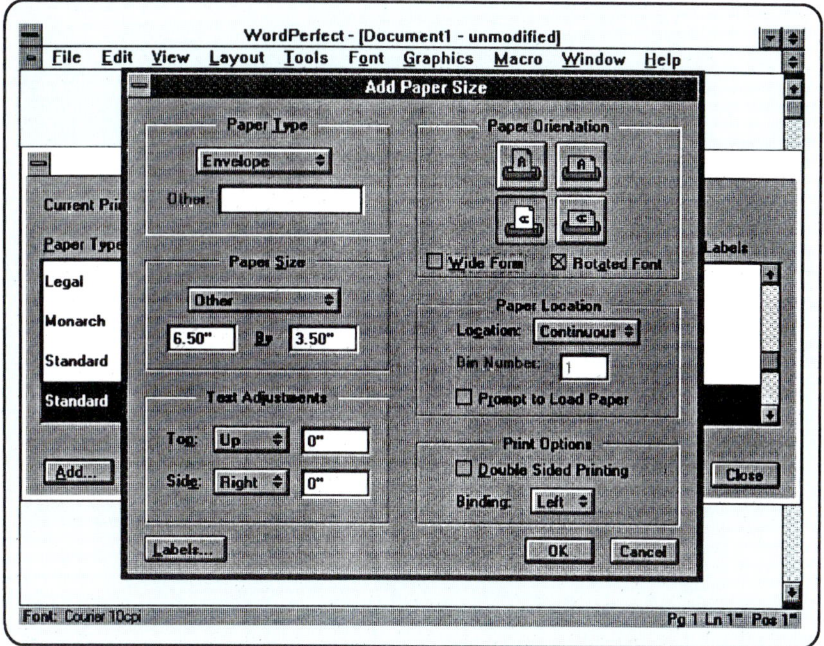

The Paper Location option in the Add Paper Size dialog box tells the printer where it should look for the paper. A Manual selection tells the printer that it should look in the manual paper feed slot for the paper. This means that you will hand feed each envelope into the printer. A Continuous selection indicates that paper is fed continuously into the printer either by a tractor feeder on a dot matrix printer or by a sheet feeder on a laser printer. However, if you have a laser printer with a sheet feeder that has several bins or trays for different types of paper, then select the Bin Number option.

To indicate that the envelope will be fed manually or by hand into the printer:

Click	the Location pop-up list button	***Press***	*Alt+C to select the Location pop-up list button*	**Press**	Alt+C to select the Location pop-up list button
Hold down	the mouse button to view the pop-up list	***Press***	*Alt+↑ to view the pop-up list*	**Press**	Alt+↑ to view the pop-up list
Choose	Manual	***Type***	*M to select Manual*	**Type**	M to select Manual

Your screen should look like Figure 19-7.

Figure 19-7

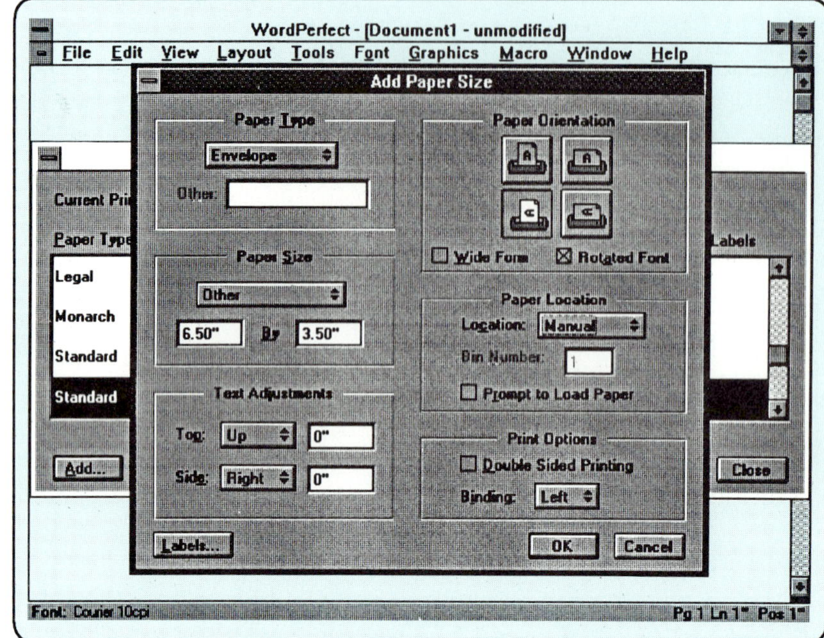

For additional information on the Add Paper Size options, see the "Paper Size" section in the WordPerfect Reference Manual.

To return to the list of paper types:

Click	the OK command button	**Press**	↵Enter	Press	↵Enter

Your screen should look like Figure 19-8.

Figure 19-8

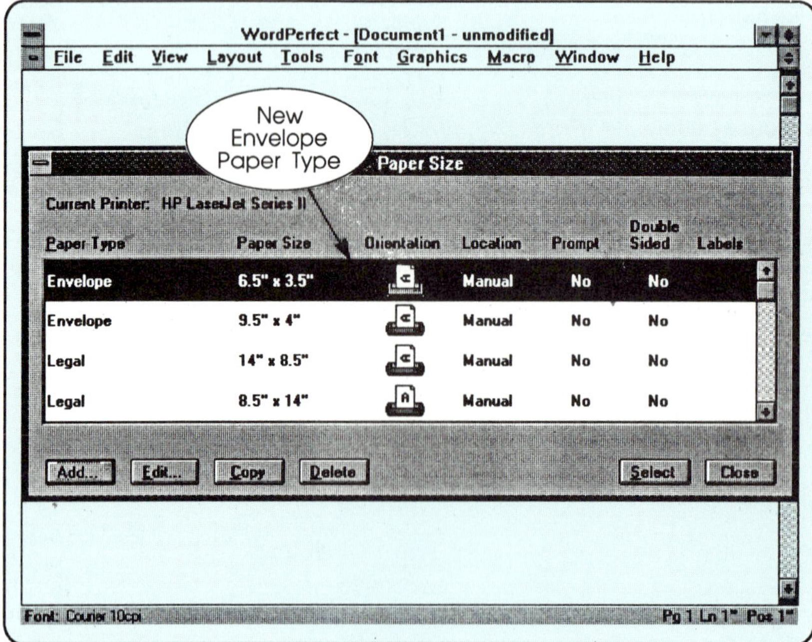

The new form definition that you created for small envelopes is highlighted in the list.

Using an Envelope Form

When using an envelope paper size, you can use any of the WordPerfect features you would in other documents, just on smaller paper. In this example, you will create a single envelope. However, you could create several envelopes by separating each address with a hard page break [HPg]. You could also merge envelopes by adding field codes to your envelope document and merging it with a secondary file.

To choose the envelope definition that you created:

Click	the Select command button	***Press***	*Alt+S to select the Select command button*	**Press**	Alt+S to select the Select command button

Now that the envelope form is selected, you can create your envelope document. When using small envelopes that are 6.5″ x 3.5″, the first line of the address is 2.5″ from the left edge of the envelope and 1.75″ below the top edge of the envelope. This means that the left margin is set to 2.5″. The right margin is 0″. The top and bottom margin should be set to 0″. When entering text into the primary document, hard returns are inserted so that the first line of the address is approximately 1.5″ from the top. This is done instead of setting a top margin, because some printers have trouble advancing pages correctly.

Certain printers require a minimum margin on each side of the page. If you try to type in a value smaller than the minimum value, WordPerfect warns you that the specified value is invalid and adjusts the margins for you. For example, you cannot have a 0″ margin on a laser printer. Most laser printers require a small margin on the edges of the page.

Assuming you have selected the HP LaserJet Series II printer, the minimum left margin is .24″. The minimum right margin is .21″. The minimum top margin is .195″. The minimum bottom margin is .32″.

To change the margins, choose Margins from the Layout menu or press Ctrl+F8:

Type	2.5	***Type***	*2.5*	**Type**	2.5
Double-click	the Right text box	***Press***	*Alt+R to select the Right text box*	**Press**	Alt+R to select the Right text box
Type	.21	***Type***	*.21*	**Type**	.21
Double-click	the Top text box	***Press***	*Alt+T to select the Top text box*	**Press**	Alt+T to select the Top text box
Type	.195	***Type***	*.195*	**Type**	.195
Double-click	the Bottom text box	***Press***	*Alt+B to select the Bottom text box*	**Press**	Alt+B to select the Bottom text box
Type	.32	***Type***	*.32*	**Type**	.32
Click	the OK command button	***Press***	*↵Enter*	**Press**	↵Enter

To move down the screen 1.53″:

Press	↵Enter until the Ln indicator approximates 1.53"	***Press***	*↵Enter until the Ln indicator approximates 1.53"*	**Press**	↵Enter until the Ln indicator approximates 1.53"

To enter the address information:

Type	Mr. Ernest Johnson
Press	↵Enter
Type	10001 Central Parkway
Press	↵Enter
Type	New York, NY 11566

Type	*Mr. Ernest Johnson*
Press	*↵Enter*
Type	*10001 Central Parkway*
Press	*↵Enter*
Type	*New York, NY 11566*

Type	Mr. Ernest Johnson
Press	↵Enter
Type	10001 Central Parkway
Press	↵Enter
Type	New York, NY 11566

The top part of your screen should look like Figure 19-9.

Figure 19-9

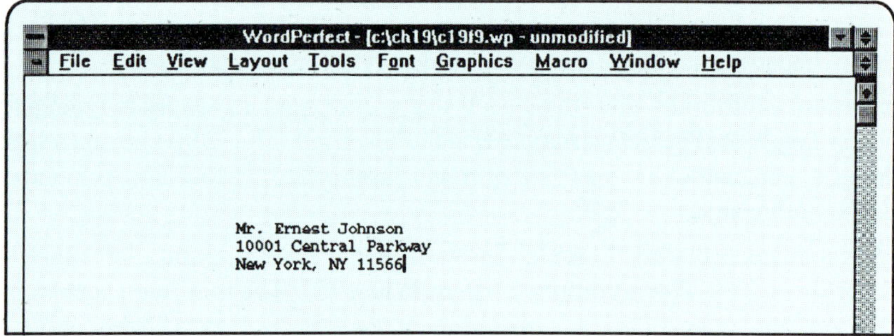

Preview the document so you can see a small envelope with the address properly placed on it. Your screen should look like Figure 19-10 if you use the Full Page option.

Figure 19-10

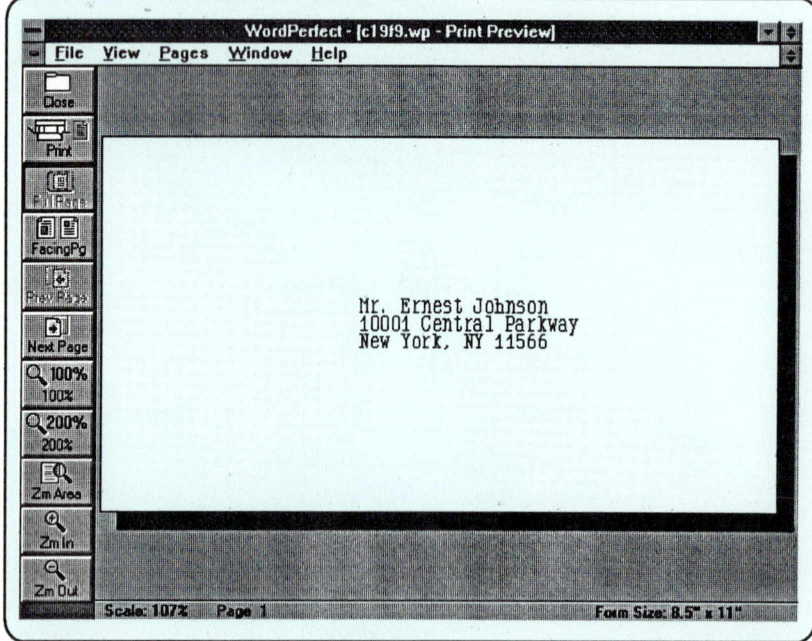

Return to the normal editing screen by clicking the Close button on the Button Bar, choosing Close from the File menu, or pressing Ctrl+F4.

Save the document as "johnson.env."

Printing Envelopes

To print the envelope:

Choose	File	***Press***	*Alt*	**Press**	F5
Choose	Print	***Select***	*File*	**Press**	↵Enter to select the Print command button
Click	the Print command button	***Select***	*Print*		
		Press	*↵Enter to select the Print command button*		

WordPerfect returns you to your document. Since you set the location to manual, your printer will not actually print the envelope until you manually feed it into the printer. Insert the envelope into the manual paper feed slot on the printer. It may take a few seconds for your printer to respond.

Sometimes you might want WordPerfect to prompt you to load the paper manually. In order to receive a prompt to load the paper, edit the small envelope paper type and place an X in the Prompt to Load Paper check box.

When the Prompt to Load Paper option is on, you will hear a beep after you issue the print command. WordPerfect is prompting you to load the envelope into the printer. To see the prompt, you must access the Windows Print Manager. To access the Print Manager:

Click	the Program control menu box	***Press***	*Alt+Spacebar to select the Program control menu box*	**Press**	Ctrl+Esc to view the Windows Task List
Choose	Switch To	***Select***	*Switch To*	**Select**	Print Manager from the Task List list box
Click	Print Manager in the Task List list box	***Select***	*Print Manager from the Task List list box*	**Press**	Alt+S to select the Switch To command button
Click	the Switch To command button	***Press***	*Alt+S to select the Switch To command button*		

In the Print Manager the message "Load Paper: envelope 3.5″ x 6.5″" appears. Insert an envelope in the manual paper feed slot on the printer and choose the OK command button. Continue this process until each of your envelopes is printed.

Close the "johnson.env" document.

■ LABELS

If you need to print many addresses for envelopes, it is quicker to print them on labels. There are many different sizes of labels. Dot matrix printers use labels that pass through by tractor feed. Laser printers use labels on sheets that enter the printer through the sheet feeder. Be sure to buy labels specifically made for laser printers. Using labels made for a copier in a laser printer may damage your printer.

Labels can have many different sizes. You must tell WordPerfect when it is printing with paper that is not standard 8.5″ x 11″ paper. In this section, creating a label paper type manually and with a macro is demonstrated.

Creating a Label Paper Type with the Paper Size Feature

Like envelopes, labels also require a custom paper type. However, label paper types are more complex to define than envelopes. With label paper types, you must define numerous size specifications. These will be explained as you work through the example.

To create a label form for 4″ x 1.5″ labels:

Choose	Layout	***Press***	*Alt*	**Press**	Alt+F9
Choose	Page	***Select***	*Layout*	**Select**	Paper Size
Choose	Paper Size	***Select***	*Page*	**Press**	Alt+A to select the Add command button
Click	the Add command button	***Select***	*Paper Size*		
		Press	*Alt+A to select the Add command button*		

Note that the Paper Size option defines the size of each sheet of labels and not the size of one label. The size of each label is defined in the Edit Labels dialog box.

To display the Edit Labels dialog box:

Click	the Labels command button	***Press***	*Alt+L to select the Labels command button*	**Press**	Alt+L to select the Labels command button

Your screen should look like Figure 19-11.

Figure 19-11

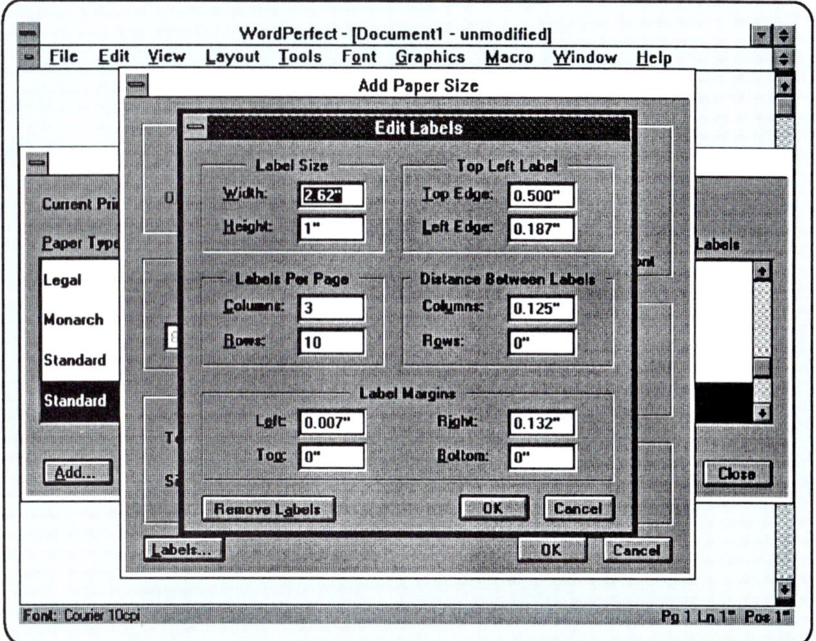

The Edit Labels dialog box appears on your screen. The options in this dialog box are used to define how each label looks on the page. Various brands of labels are placed differently on the page. You must tell WordPerfect how many labels are on a page, the size of each label, and exactly where each one is placed on the page. Each dialog box option is explained below:

Label Size - Define the width and height of one label. You can get the exact size from the cover of the box of labels. The default size is 2.62″ x 1″.

Labels Per Page - Define the number of columns of labels across the page and the number of rows of labels down the page.

Top Left Label - Define the distance from the edge of the page to the top left corner of the first label on the page. Measure the distance from the top of the page to the label, and then the distance from the left of the page to the label.

Distance Between Labels - Some manufacturers of labels place a small amount of space between labels. This option records the distance between rows and columns of labels.

Label Margins - Define the top, bottom, left, and right margins inside the label.

The default settings on the menu are for the most commonly used 2.62″ x 1″ labels with 3 columns and 10 rows on an 8.5″ x 11″ sheet.

Rather than use the standard size label, assume that your sheet of labels has 2 columns, 7 rows, and a label size of 4″ x 1.5″.

By default the Width text box in the Label Size box is automatically selected. To change the Label Size option to 4″ by 1.5″:

Type	4	***Type***	*4*	**Type**	4
Double-click	the Height text box in the Label Size box	***Press***	*Alt+H to select the Height text box in the Label Size box*	**Press**	Alt+H to select the Height text box in the Label Size box
Type	1.5	***Type***	*1.5*	**Type**	1.5

To change the Labels Per Page option to 2 columns and 7 rows:

Double-click	the Columns text box in the Labels Per Page box	***Press***	*Alt+C to select the Columns text box in the Labels Per Page box*	**Press**	Alt+C to select the Columns text box in the Labels Per Page box
Type	2	***Type***	*2*	**Type**	2
Double-click	the Rows text box in the Labels Per Page box	***Press***	*Alt+R to select the Rows text box in the Labels Per Page box*	**Press**	Alt+R to select the Rows text box in the Labels Per Page box
Type	7	***Type***	*7*	**Type**	7

To change the Top Left Label option to 0.25″ for top and 0.125″ for left:

Double-click	the Top Edge text box in the Top Left Label box	***Press***	*Alt+T to select the Top Edge text box in the Top Left Label box*	**Press**	Alt+T to select the Top Edge text box in the Top Left Label box
Type	.25	***Type***	*.25*	**Type**	.25
Double-click	the Left Edge text box in the Top Left Label box	***Press***	*Alt+L to select the Left Edge text box in the Top Left Label box*	**Press**	Alt+L to select the Left Edge text box in the Top Left Label box
Type	.125	***Type***	*.125*	**Type**	.125

To change the Distance Between Labels option to 0.25″ for columns:

Double-click	the Columns text box in the Distance Between Labels box	***Press***	*Alt+U to select the Columns text box in the Distance Between Labels Box*	**Press**	Alt+U to select the Columns text box in the Distance Between Labels Box
Type	.25	***Type***	*.25*	**Type**	.25

The row value does not need to be changed.

To change the Label Margins option for the left, right, and top margins:

Double-click	the Left text box in the Label Margins box	***Press***	*Alt+E to select the Left text box in the Label Margins box*	**Press**	Alt+E to select the Left text box in the Label Margins box
Type	.165	***Type***	*.165*	**Type**	.165
Double-click	the Right text box in the Label Margins box	***Press***	*Alt+I to select the Right text box in the Label Margins box*	**Press**	Alt+I to select the Right text box in the Label Margins box
Type	.185	***Type***	*.185*	**Type**	.185
Double-click	the Top text box in the Label Margins box	***Press***	*Alt+P to select the Top text box in the Label Margins box*	**Press**	Alt+P to select the Top text box in the Label Margins box
Type	.125	***Type***	*.125*	**Type**	.125

The bottom margin does not need to be changed.

Your screen should look like Figure 19-12.

Figure 19-12

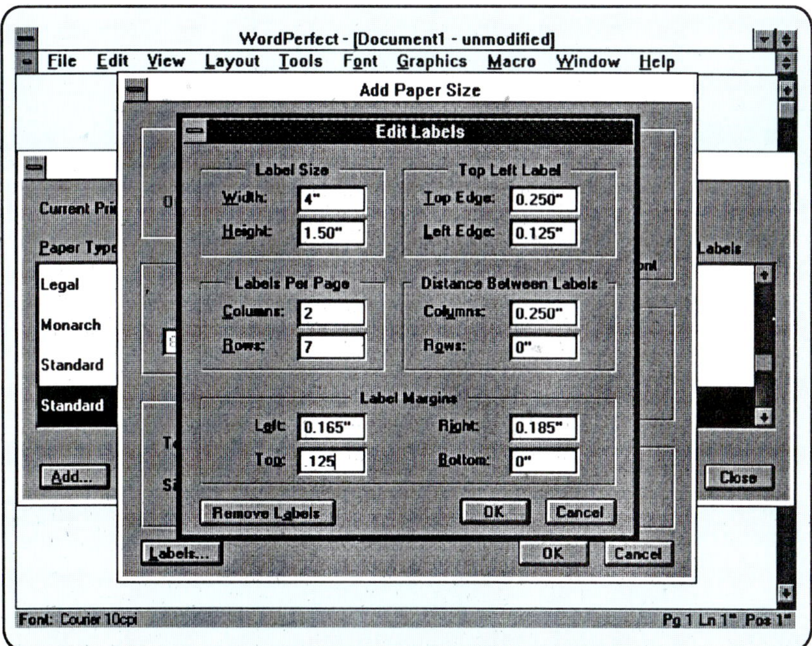

To return to the Add Paper Size dialog box:

Click	the OK command button	***Press***	*Enter*	**Press**	Enter

For additional information on the Paper Size options, see the "Paper Size" section in the WordPerfect Reference Manual.

To return to the list of forms:

Click	the OK command button	***Press***	*Tab to select the OK command button*	**Press**	Tab to select the OK command button
		Press	*↵Enter*	**Press**	↵Enter

Your screen should look like Figure 19-13.

Figure 19-13

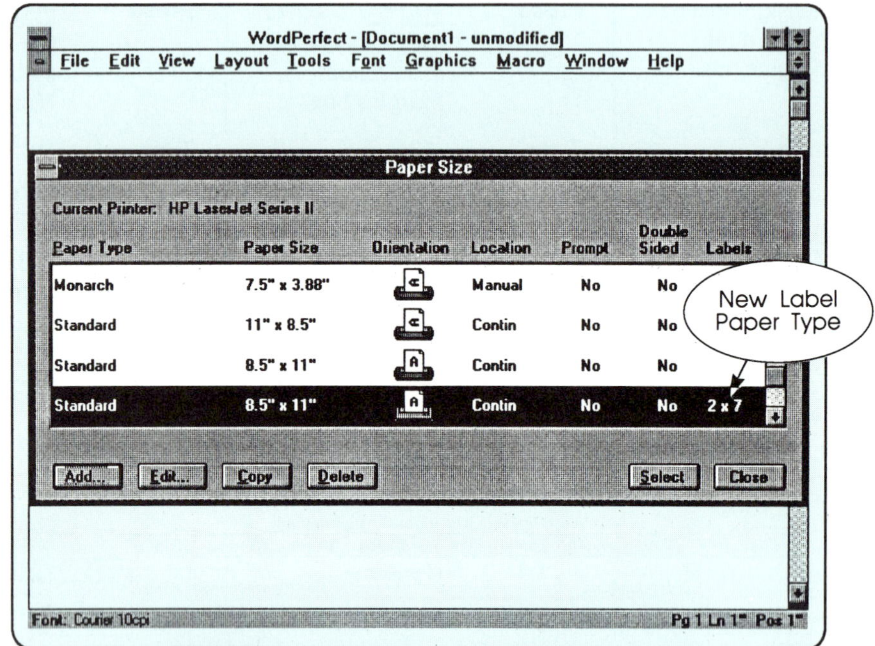

The new definition that you created for 4″ x 1.5″ labels is highlighted.

Using a Label Paper Type

When using a label paper type, you can use any of the WordPerfect features you would use in other documents, just on a small label. You could create a single label or create several labels by separating each address with a hard page break [HPg]. In this example, you will merge the labels with the secondary file "address.ltr" by adding field codes to your labels document.

To select the Labels paper type for your document:

Click	the Select command button	***Press***	*Alt+S to select the Select command button*	**Press**	Alt+S to select the Select command button

The bottom part of your screen should look like Figure 19-14.

Figure 19-14

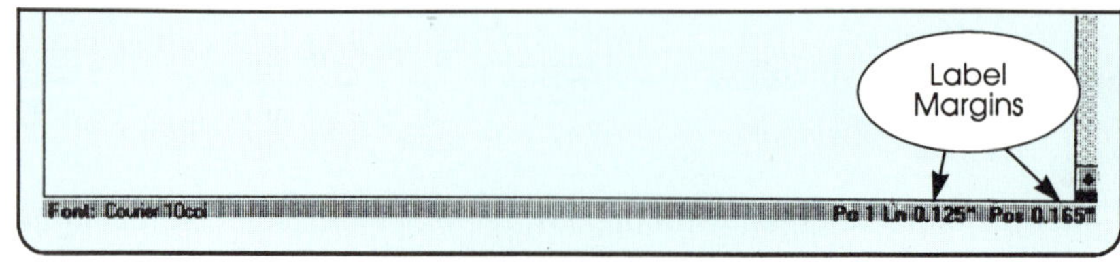

Notice that the "Ln" and "Pos" indicators in the status bar have changed to reflect the margins defined in the labels paper type.

You are now ready to enter the field merge codes into the primary file that you are creating. You will use the "address.ltr" document as the secondary file. The fields in "address.ltr" are: Title, First, Last, Company, and Address.

To enter the "Title" field merge code into the primary file:

Choose	Tools	***Press***	*Alt*	**Press**	Ctrl+F12
Choose	Merge	***Select***	*Tools*	**Select**	Field
Choose	Field	***Select***	*Merge*	**Type**	Title
Type	Title	***Select***	*Field*	**Press**	↵Enter
Click	the OK command button	***Type***	*Title*		
		Press	*↵Enter*		

To enter the "First" field merge code into the primary file:

Press	Spacebar	***Press***	*Spacebar*	**Press**	Spacebar
Choose	Tools	***Press***	*Alt*	**Press**	Ctrl+F12
Choose	Merge	***Select***	*Tools*	**Select**	Field
Choose	Field	***Select***	*Merge*	**Type**	First
Type	First	***Select***	*Field*	**Press**	↵Enter
Click	the OK command button	***Type***	*First*		
		Press	*↵Enter*		

To enter the "Last" field merge code:

Press	Spacebar	***Press***	*Spacebar*	**Press**	Spacebar
Choose	Tools	***Press***	*Alt*	**Press**	Ctrl+F12
Choose	Merge	***Select***	*Tools*	**Select**	Field
Choose	Field	***Select***	*Merge*	**Type**	Last
Type	Last	***Select***	*Field*	**Press**	↵Enter
Click	the OK command button	***Type***	*Last*		
		Press	*↵Enter*		

To enter the "Company" field merge code on a new line and avoid blank lines in the document if the Company field is empty:

Press	↵Enter	***Press***	*↵Enter*	**Press**	↵Enter
Choose	Tools	***Press***	*Alt*	**Press**	Ctrl+F12

Choose	Merge	***Select***	*Tools*	**Select**	Field
Choose	Field	***Select***	*Merge*	**Type**	Company?
Type	Company?	***Select***	*Field*	**Press**	↵Enter
Click	the OK command button	***Type***	*Company?*		
		Press	↵Enter		

To enter the "Address" field on a new line:

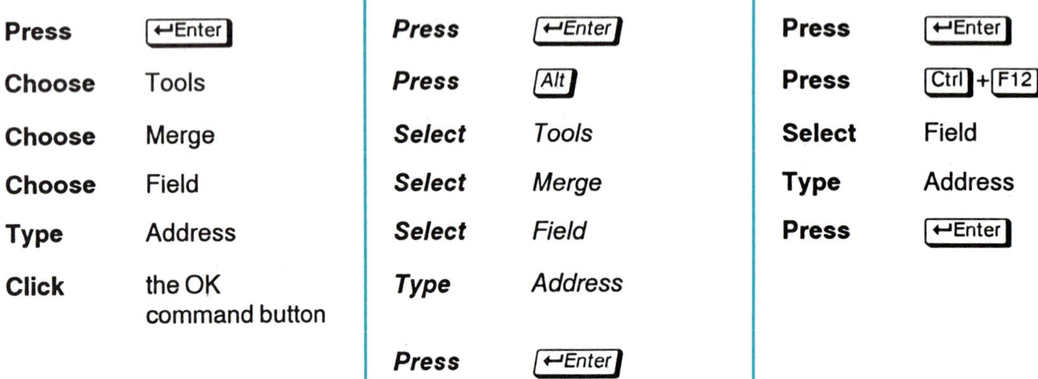

Press	↵Enter	***Press***	↵Enter	**Press**	↵Enter
Choose	Tools	***Press***	Alt	**Press**	Ctrl+F12
Choose	Merge	***Select***	*Tools*	**Select**	Field
Choose	Field	***Select***	*Merge*	**Type**	Address
Type	Address	***Select***	*Field*	**Press**	↵Enter
Click	the OK command button	***Type***	*Address*		
		Press	↵Enter		

The top part of your screen should look like Figure 19-15.

Figure 19-15

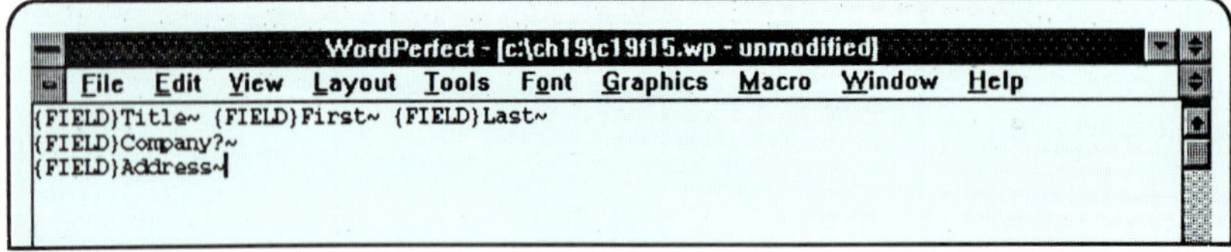

Save the document as "lab4x15.doc." Close the document.

Merge the "lab4x15.doc" (Primary File) and "address.ltr" (Secondary File) files together. Move your insertion point to the beginning of the document.

The top part of your screen should look like Figure 19-16.

Figure 19-16

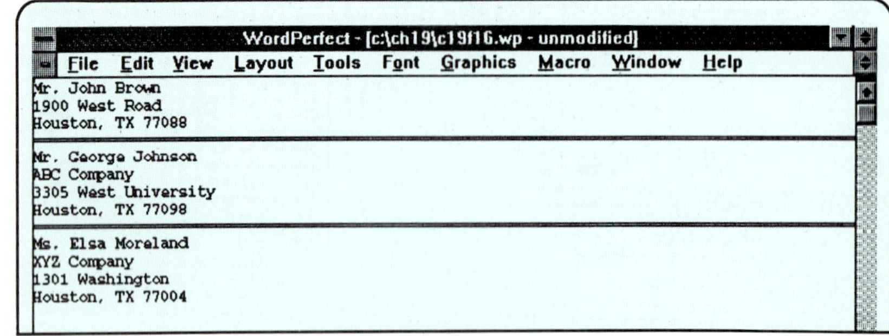

A hard page break is used to separate each address label. When the insertion point is moved from one label to another, the page number in the status bar changes.

Use the Print Preview feature to see the layout of the labels on the page. Select the Full Page option.

Your screen should look like Figure 19-17.

Figure 19-17

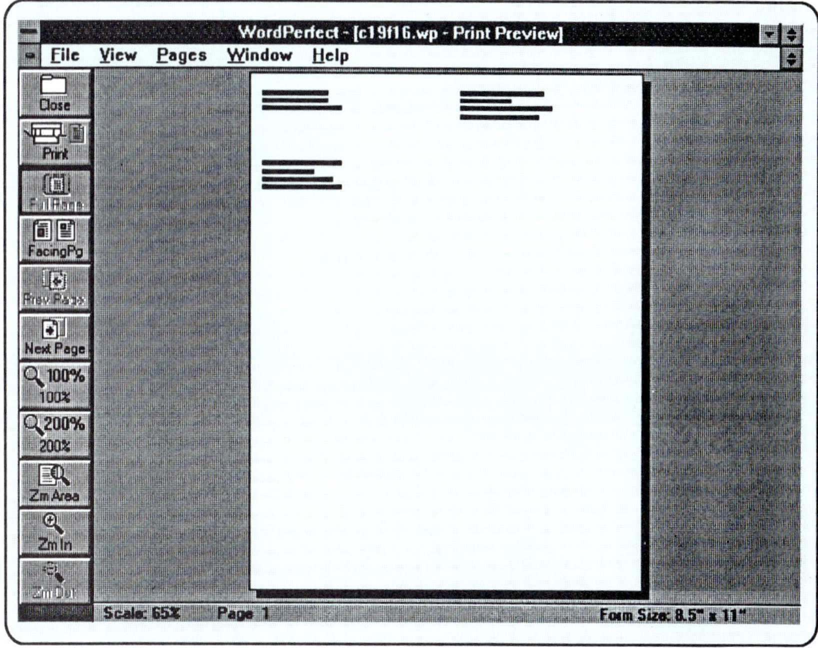

Printing Labels

Load the labels into your printer, or leave standard 8.5" x 11" paper in your printer if you want to print the labels on paper. To print the entire merge document:

Click	the Print button on the Button Bar	***Press***	*Alt*	**Press**	F5
Click	the Print command button	***Select***	*File*	**Press**	↵Enter to select the Print command button
		Select	*Print*		
		Press	*↵Enter to select the Print command button*		

WordPerfect returns you to your document. Close the document without saving the merge document.

Creating a Label Paper Type Using a Macro

Label paper types require many changes in the Paper Size feature. Because labels are difficult to create manually, WordPerfect provides a macro that allows you to select the type of label you are using and automatically creates the paper type for you. The macro is named "labels.wcm" and is located in the directory "c:\wpwin\macros." This macro is quite large and takes several minutes to complete.

To create a label paper type using the macro:

Choose	Macro	***Press***	*Alt*	**Press**	Alt+F10
Choose	Play	***Select***	*Macro*	**Type**	**labels**

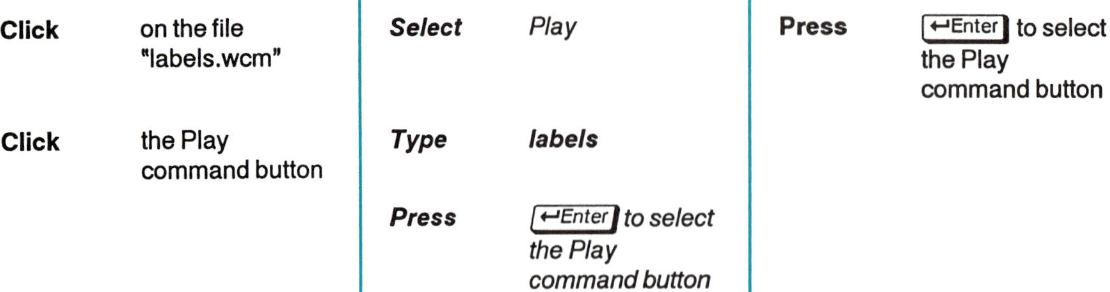

Click	on the file "labels.wcm"	***Select***	*Play*	**Press**	↵Enter to select the Play command button
Click	the Play command button	***Type***	***labels***		
		Press	*↵Enter to select the Play command button*		

Your screen should look like Figure 19-18.

Figure 19-18

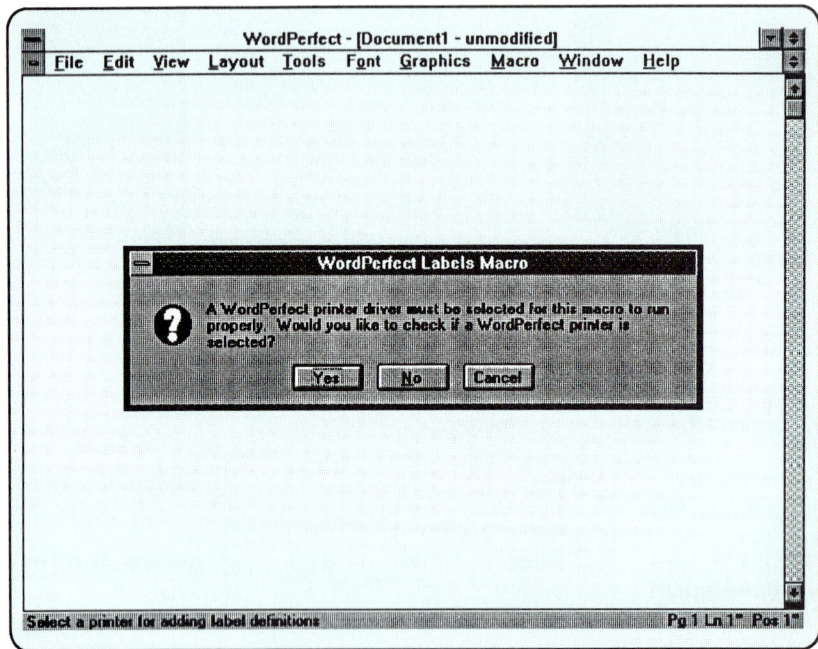

The macro first checks to see if you have a WordPerfect print driver selected. If you already have a WordPerfect printer selected, choose No. If you are not sure which printer you are using or if you are using a Windows printer, choose Yes.

In this exercise, it is assumed that you are already using a WordPerfect printer. To accept the current printer selection:

Click	the No command button	***Press***	*Alt+N to select the No command button*	**Press**	Alt+N to select the No command button

WordPerfect prompts you for the type of labels you will be using. The Page option allows you to print labels using a laserjet printer. The Tractor feed option allows you to print labels using a dot matrix printer.

To create Page labels:

Click	the Page option button	***Press***	*Alt+P to select the Page option button*	**Press**	Alt+P to select the Page option button

Click	the OK command button	***Press***	*↵Enter*	**Press**	↵Enter

Your screen should look like Figure 19-19.

Figure 19-19

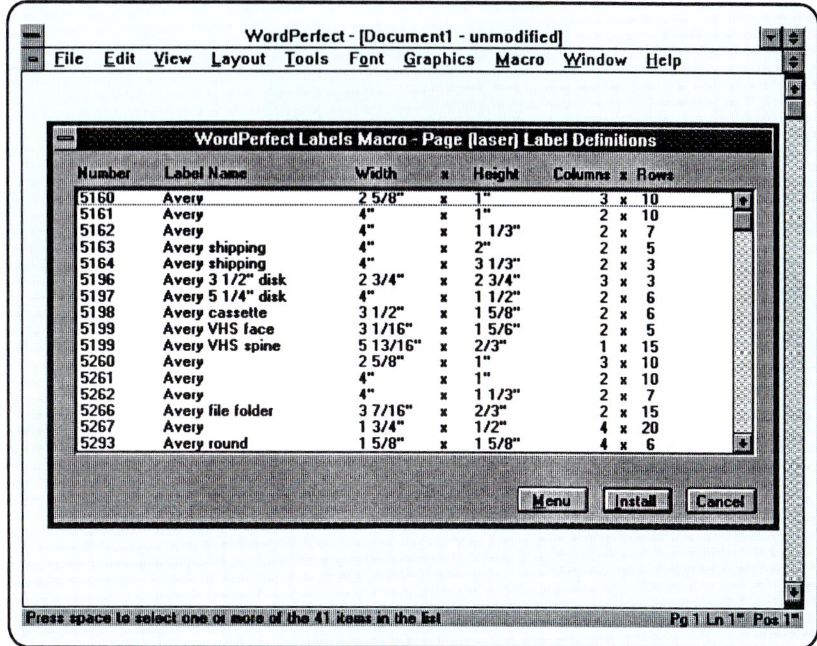

Number	Label Name	Width	x	Height	Columns	x	Rows
5160	Avery	2 5/8"	x	1"	3	x	10
5161	Avery	4"	x	1"	2	x	10
5162	Avery	4"	x	1 1/3"	2	x	7
5163	Avery shipping	4"	x	2"	2	x	5
5164	Avery shipping	4"	x	3 1/3"	2	x	3
5196	Avery 3 1/2" disk	2 3/4"	x	2 3/4"	3	x	3
5197	Avery 5 1/4" disk	4"	x	1 1/2"	2	x	6
5198	Avery cassette	3 1/2"	x	1 5/8"	2	x	6
5199	Avery VHS face	3 1/16"	x	1 5/6"	2	x	5
5199	Avery VHS spine	5 13/16"	x	2/3"	1	x	15
5260	Avery	2 5/8"	x	1"	3	x	10
5261	Avery	4"	x	1"	2	x	10
5262	Avery	4"	x	1 1/3"	2	x	7
5266	Avery file folder	3 7/16"	x	2/3"	2	x	15
5267	Avery	1 3/4"	x	1/2"	4	x	20
5293	Avery round	1 5/8"	x	1 5/8"	4	x	6

The WordPerfect Labels Macro dialog box appears. This dialog box provides you with a definition for most Avery and 3M brand labels. To select a label paper type, click on the paper type or highlight the paper type using the pointer-movement keys and press the Spacebar to select the paper type. You can select as many label paper types as you desire. Once you have all of the label paper types you need highlighted, choose Install. If you need to return to a previous dialog box, choose the Menu button.

To install Avery label number 5160:

Click	the 5160 paper type	***Press***	*the pointer-movement keys to highlight the 5160 paper type*	**Press**	the pointer-movement keys to highlight the 5160 paper type
Click	the Install command button	***Press***	*Spacebar*	**Press**	Spacebar
		Press	*↵Enter to select the Install command button*	**Press**	↵Enter to select the Install command button

Your screen should look like Figure 19-20.

Figure 19-20

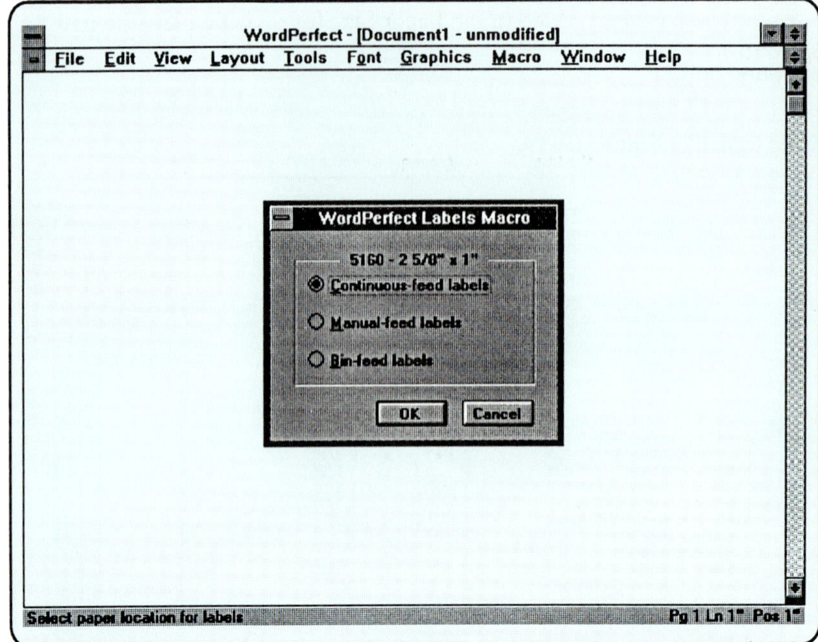

WordPerfect prompts you for the location of the labels. To use manual feed labels:

Click	the Manual-feed labels option button	***Press***	*Alt+M to select the Manual-feed labels option button*	**Press**	Alt+M to select the Manual-feed labels option button
Click	the OK command button	***Press***	*↵Enter*	**Press**	↵Enter

A dialog box appears asking if you want WordPerfect to prompt you to load the label 5160 when you print. To set the prompt to load option to No:

Click	the No command button	***Press***	*Alt+N to select the No command button*	**Press**	Alt+N to select the No command button

The message "Installing 5160-2 5/8" x1" Paper Size/Type Definition.." appears on the status bar. When the paper type is installed, WordPerfect allows you to select the new paper type to use in your current document. If you would like to select the paper type, choose Yes. To return to your document without selecting the new paper type, choose No.

To bypass selecting the new paper type:

Click	the No command button	***Press***	*Alt+N to select the No command button*	**Press**	Alt+N to select the No command button

A final message appears to inform you that the macro is finished. Click the OK command button or press ↵Enter to remove the dialog box from the screen.

The Avery 5160 paper type has been added to the Paper Size feature. To view the new paper type in the Paper Size dialog box:

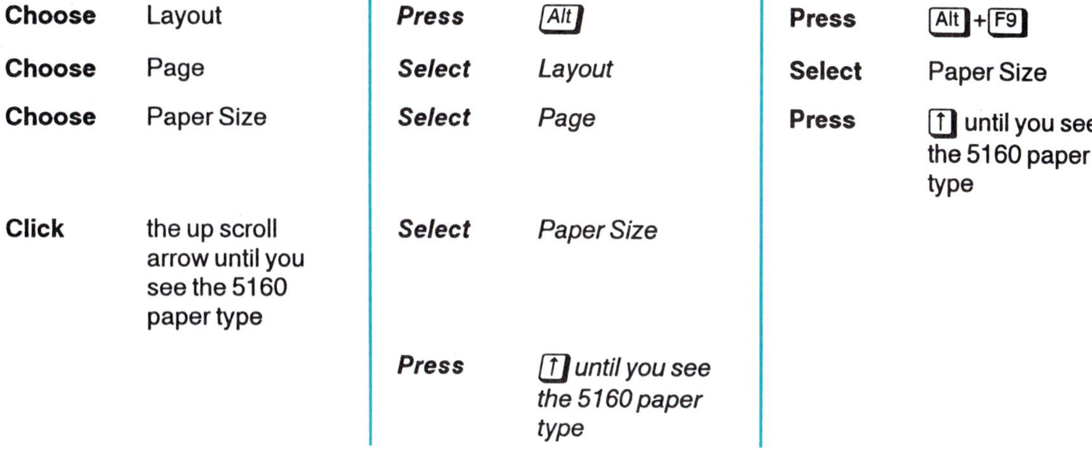

Choose	Layout	***Press***	*Alt*	**Press**	Alt+F9
Choose	Page	***Select***	*Layout*	**Select**	Paper Size
Choose	Paper Size	***Select***	*Page*	**Press**	↑ until you see the 5160 paper type
Click	the up scroll arrow until you see the 5160 paper type	***Select***	*Paper Size*		
		Press	*↑ until you see the 5160 paper type*		

Your screen should look like Figure 19-21.

Figure 19-21

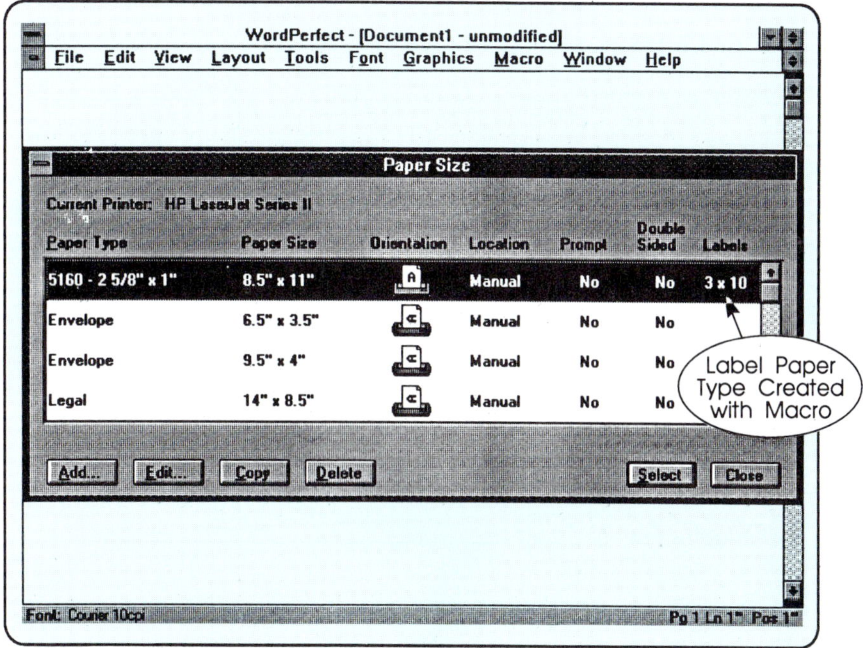

Click the Close button or press Esc to close the dialog box.

EXERCISE 1

INSTRUCTIONS: Define the following terms:

1. Paper type ______________________________
2. Paper Size feature ______________________________
3. Paper location option ______________________________
4. Paper orientation option ______________________________
5. Rotated font option ______________________________
6. Labels per page option ______________________________
7. Label size option ______________________________
8. Top left label option ______________________________
9. Distance between labels option ______________________________
10. Label margins option ______________________________

EXERCISE 2

INSTRUCTIONS: Circle T if the statement is true and F if the statement is false.

T F 1. The Paper Size feature allows you to create paper types for special sizes of paper and to handle special printer instructions.

T F 2. A Manual Location selection in the Add Paper Sizes dialog box tells WordPerfect that you are feeding the paper into the printer by hand.

T F 3. A Rotated Font Type selection causes the text to be printed across the length of the page.

T F 4. Some printers may not be able to print rotated fonts if they do not contain fonts for rotated or landscape printing.

T F 5. When defining a label paper type, the Paper Size option on the Add Paper Size dialog box refers to the size of each label.

T F 6. The Top Left Label option in the Edit Labels dialog box defines the distance from the edge of the page to the top left corner of the first label on the page.

T F 7. The Distance Within Labels option allows you to enter the left, right, top, and bottom margins you want for each label.

T F 8. The Labels Per Page option tells WordPerfect how many labels your printer can print at one moment in time.

T F 9. Once you have created a paper type, you cannot edit it. You must delete the form, and then add a new one.

T F 10. You cannot use envelopes or labels to create primary files for a merge document.

EXERCISE 3

INSTRUCTIONS:

1. Create a document using the 9.5″ x 4″ standard business envelopes paper type.
2. The address should start 2″ from the top edge of the envelope and 4.5″ from the left edge of the envelope.
3. Create an envelope for each of the following addresses. Separate each address with a hard page break.
4. Preview the envelopes.
5. Print the envelopes.
6. Save the document as "ch19ex03."
7. Close the document.

```
Ms. Felice Avila            Mrs. Audree Walsh
Zurich Products Company     Sunrise Breakfast Company
616 West Main Street        1045 Collins Avenue
Houston, TX  77013          Miami, FL  33152

Mr. Ray Devery              Dr. Paul Thompson
Liberty Foundation          Super Visions Corporation
234 Park Avenue             8990 Roselle Road
New York, NY  10001         Schaumburg, IL  60172

Ms. Joan Young
Publications Press
4515 Harbor Lane
Saginaw, MI  48605
```

EXERCISE 4

INSTRUCTIONS:

1. Create the following mailing list as a secondary file. Save the file using the name "ch19ex04.sec."
2. Create a small envelope paper type for a 6.5″ x 3.5″ envelope. The Wide Form option should be off, the Rotated Font option should be on, and set the location to continuous.
3. Create a primary file using the small envelope paper type and the field names in the secondary file "ch19ex04.sec."
4. Save the file as "ch19ex04.pri." Close the document.
5. Merge the two documents.
6. Preview the merge document.
7. Print the Murphy envelope only.
8. Save the merge document in a file using the name "ch19ex04.env."
9. Close the document.

```
Ms. Gerry Goncher      Ms. Geetha Murthy
Traffic Programmer     Lab Assistant
Semper Corporation     Computer Wizards
888 West Wayne         6321 North Route 37
Omaha, NB 66108        Louisville, KY 40201

Mr. Jack Carroll       Ms. Debbie Murphy
Finer Lawn Products    International Products
2288 North Holland     1401 Frontage Road
Concord, NH  03301     New Orleans, LA  70113
```

EXERCISE 5

INSTRUCTIONS:

1. Create the following mailing list as a secondary file. Save the file using the name "ch19ex05.sec." Close the document.
2. Merge the mailing list with a primary file for standard business envelopes. The name of the primary file should be "ch19ex05.pri."
3. Preview the merge document.
4. Print the envelopes using plain paper inserted manually.
5. Save the merge document in a file using the name "ch19ex05.env."
6. Close the document.

```
Mr. Larry Haffner               Ms. Dolores Samson
247 Einstein Street             620 Braintree Lane
Anchorage, AK  99502            Brookline, MA  02146

Mr. William Neuwmann            Mr. Michael Oester
Engineering and Maintenance     Canonsburg Chemical Company
Absolute Corporation            639 Newton Boulevard
135 Pecos Circle Drive          Canonsburg, PA  15317
Escanaba, MI  49829
```

EXERCISE 6

INSTRUCTIONS:

1. Create a label form for 2.62″ x 1″ labels. This is the default label size. Use all of the default measurements in the Edit Labels dialog box. These defaults are listed below:

Label Size	Width = 2.62″, Height = 1″
No. of Labels	3 columns by 10 rows
Top Left Corner	Top = 1/2″, Left = 3/16″
Distance Between Labels	Column = 1/8″, Row = 0″
Label Margins	Left = 1/3″, Right = 0.123″
	Top and Bottom = 0″

2. Create a primary file for labels to merge with "ch19ex04.sec." The primary file name should be "ch19ex06.pri."
3. Close the document.
4. Merge the documents to create labels.
5. Preview the document.
6. Print the labels.
7. Do not save the merge document.

EXERCISE 7

INSTRUCTIONS:

1. Create the following mailing list as a secondary file using the name "ch19ex07.sec." Close the document.
2. Create a primary file with the following letter. The name of the primary file should be "ch19ex07.pri." Close the document.
3. Merge the two documents.
4. Print the merged letters.
5. Save the merged letters in a file using the name "ch19ex07.ltr."
6. Create a primary file for the addresses on standard 2.63″ x 1″ labels. Save the file as "ch19ex07.lab." Close the document.
7. Merge the labels and the secondary file. Print the labels on a sheet of paper.
8. Close the document.

```
Ms. Faith Anderson          Mr. Stewart Straka
635 Bothwell Drive          Personnel Specialist
Tuscaloosa, AZ  35401       Moraine Empire Steel
                            2278 W. Highland Avenue
                            Jackson, MS  39205

Mr. William Mahaffey        Mr. Kent Barron
University Press            Personnel Consultant
Parkland University         234 West Park Avenue
Iron Mountain, MI  49801    Cleveland, OH  44101
```

Date

Inside Address

Dear (title and last name):

The Executive Board of the Nationwide Personnel Association will have its monthly meeting at Iron Mountain, Michigan. As usual the meeting will be held the last weekend of this month.

I hope that you have received the material dealing with "Termination." We all have problems when someone is fired. One of the outcomes of our meeting will be to develop a seminar to be presented around the country.

Bring your ideas for someone who could conduct this seminar. We also need to develop a marketing plan for the seminar.

See you at the end of the month.

Very truly yours,

Martin Q. Ryan
President N.P.A.

xx

EXERCISE 8

INSTRUCTIONS:

1. You have just purchased a box of laser labels. You have never used this size of labels with WordPerfect before, so you must create a paper type for them.

   The top of the box says:

   100 Sheets/8.5 x 11 inches
   Label Size: 4 x 2 inches
   10 labels per page
   Reorder No. 5163

   There is no distance between labels. There is no distance between the edge of the paper and any label on the sheet. Assume no interior margins for the labels. The labels are page labels and are manual fed into the printer. You do not want WordPerfect to prompt you for each page.

2. Use the "labels.wcm" macro to create the label form.
3. Create a primary file using the new label paper type for the addresses in the secondary file "ch19ex04.sec." The primary filename should be "ch19ex08.pri."
4. Merge the two documents.
5. Preview the merged labels.
6. Print the labels on a sheet of paper.
7. Save the merged labels in a file using the name "ch19ex08.lab."
8. Close the file.

EXERCISE 9

INSTRUCTIONS:

1. You have purchased a box of 3M labels. The product number is 7721. Create a labels paper type for these new labels using the "labels.wcm" macro. The labels are page labels that are manually fed into the printer. You do not want WordPerfect to prompt you to load the paper.
2. Create a primary file using the new label type for the addresses in the secondary file "ch19ex07.sec." Save the primary file as "ch19ex09.pri." Close the document.
3. Merge the two documents.
4. Preview the merged labels.
5. Print the labels on a sheet of paper.
6. Save the merged labels in a file using the name "ch19ex09.lab." Close the document.

CHAPTER TWENTY

SORTING AND SELECTING

OBJECTIVES

In this chapter, you will learn to:

- Sort by lines and paragraphs
- Sort with more than one key
- Sort a portion of a document
- Sort a secondary (merge) file
- Select specific records from a secondary file

CHAPTER OVERVIEW

With the Sort feature, you can sort lines or paragraphs in a WordPerfect document. You can also sort secondary merge files or part of a document. This chapter covers sorting lines and paragraphs in a document, portions of a document, and secondary files.

You can also use the Sort feature to select records from a list of items or a secondary file. This chapter illustrates the process for selecting records using the Sort feature.

Change the default directory to "a:\wpdocs" or to "c:\wpdocs." Then create the document in Figure 20-1. This document contains the last name, first name, city, state, and zip code of each individual. Before entering the text, delete all existing tabs. Then set left tabs at 2″, 3.5″, 5″, and 6″.

Figure 20-1

```
Adams        Joseph     New York      NY   10014
Konkel       Joel       Santa Cruz    CA   12100
Aaron        Sandra     San Antonio   TX   78221
Adams        Jennifer   New York      NY   10061
Fernandez    Jose       Miami         FL   33471
Nguyen       Alfred     San Antonio   TX   78201
Kainer       Donna      Newark        NJ   90122
Adams        Charles    San Antonio   TX   78216
Cernosky     Elena      Miami         FL   33201
Mogab        John       New York      NY   10042
Travis       Doug       New Haven     CT   50088
Chesser      Linda      San Jose      CA   12001
Aguilar      Maria      Provo         UT   01155
```

Save the document as "sortinp." You should *always save* your document before sorting.

■ LINE AND PARAGRAPH SORT

Suppose you want to sort the "sortinp" document by city. To rearrange the"sortinp" document by city:

Choose	Tools	***Press***	*Alt*	**Press**	Ctrl + Shift + F12
Choose	Sort	***Select***	*Tools*		
		Select	*Sort*		

The Sort dialog box appears. Your screen should look like Figure 20-2.

Figure 20-2

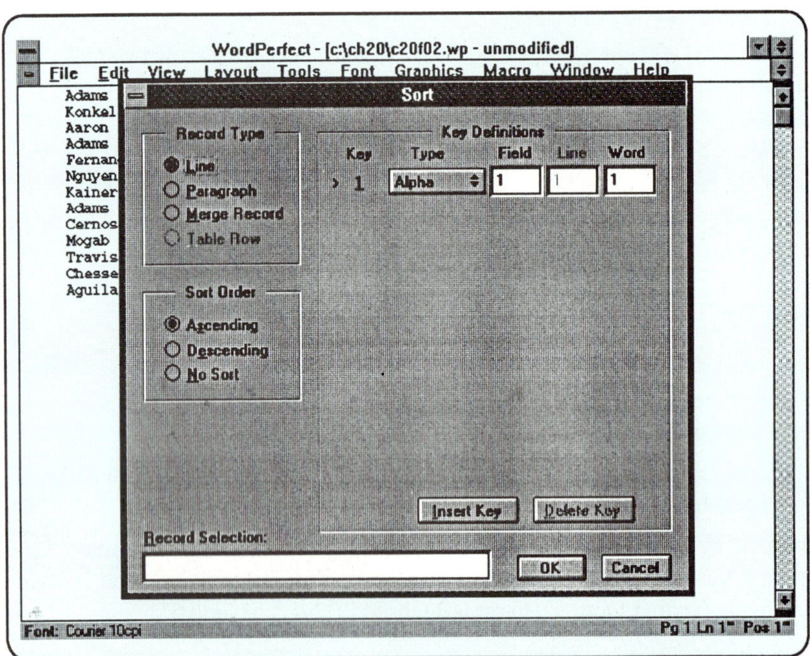

The Sort dialog box appears. By default, the Line option is selected. The Sort feature in WordPerfect allows you to sort lines and paragraphs in a document. For example, you can sort the entire "sortinp" document by last name, city, or zip code. Since there are no blank lines between lines of text, you can use the line option to sort the document. If there is a blank line between lines of text, use the paragraph option to sort the document. You can also sort a segment of a document by highlighting part of the document before choosing the Sort feature.

Keys are fields, words, or phrases by which a document is sorted. For example, suppose you want to sort a document by the city in which people live. The sort key is the city.

When sorting, you must create a key that identifies the field that is to be sorted, like city in the example above. This is done by counting the fields from left to right. In the current document, city is field 3. This number is entered into the Field text box in the Key Definitions box. In line and paragraph sorts, fields are separated by tabs.

Also associated with each key definition is the type of data that appears in the key field. Text in the field can be alphanumeric (contains both letters and numbers) or numeric (only numbers). This selection is chosen from the Type pop-up list in the Key Definition box.

The location of a word in the key field is also needed for the sort. If the key field contains more than one word, then you must select one of those words by which to sort the document. This number is positive if you count from left to right in the field. The number is negative if you count from right to left, from the end of the field to the beginning. In line and paragraph sorts, words are separated by spaces.

If you would like to sort by dates, you treat each part of the date as a separate word in a field. For the sort to work properly the parts of the date must be separated by slashes (1/1/92) or dashes (1-1-92). To insert the dash character, choose the Hyphen option button from the Special Codes feature under the Line option on the Layout menu. If the date is separated by pressing just the [-] key, WordPerfect will not recognize the numbers as a date.

In the "sortinp" document, there are five fields: last name, first name, city, state abbreviation, and zip code. Each field has one or two words in it. All of the fields are alphanumeric (can contain alphabetic or numeric characters), except for the zip code which is numeric. Note that you can consider the zip code an alphanumeric field if you so desire.

The Record Selection option in the Sort feature dialog box lets you define a subset of the document to be sorted. This option is covered later in this chapter.

The default Sort Order for the Sort feature shows that the document is to be sorted in ascending order. This setting appears in the Sort Order box.

Suppose you want to sort the "sortinp" document by city only.

To change key 1 to sort by city:

Double-click	the Field text box for Key 1	***Press***	*[Alt]+[1] to select Key 1*	**Press**	[Alt]+[1] to select Key 1
		Press	*[Tab] to select the Field text box for Key 1*	**Press**	[Tab] to select the Field text box for Key 1

Your screen should look like Figure 20-3.

Figure 20-3

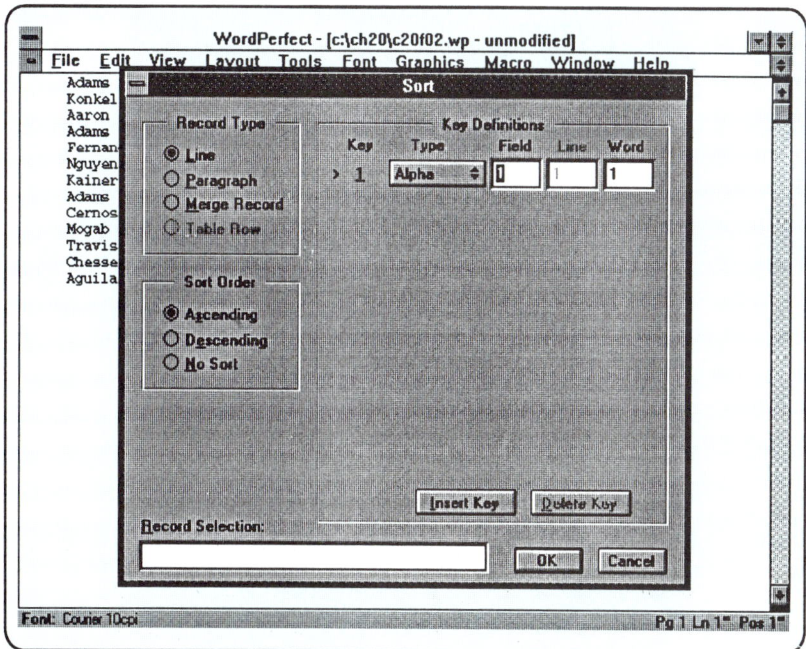

The type of field is already alphanumeric. To change the field of key 1 to identify city, which is the third field in the document:

Type	3	***Type***	*3*	**Type**	3

You do not need to change the Word setting since you will sort by the first word only in the city field. Your screen should look like Figure 20-4.

Figure 20-4

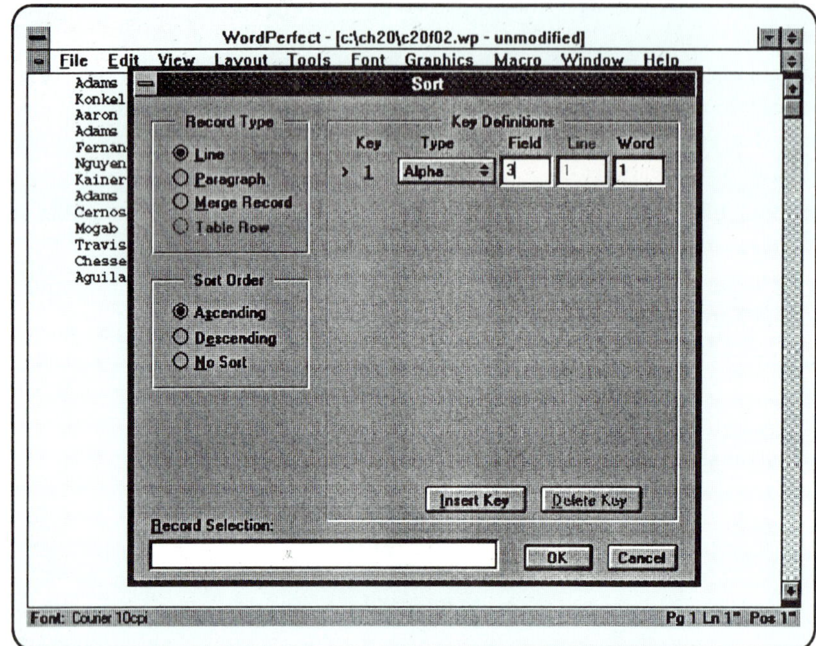

To begin the sort process:

Click	the OK command button	***Press***	*↵Enter*	**Press**	↵Enter

Your screen should look like Figure 20-5.

Figure 20-5

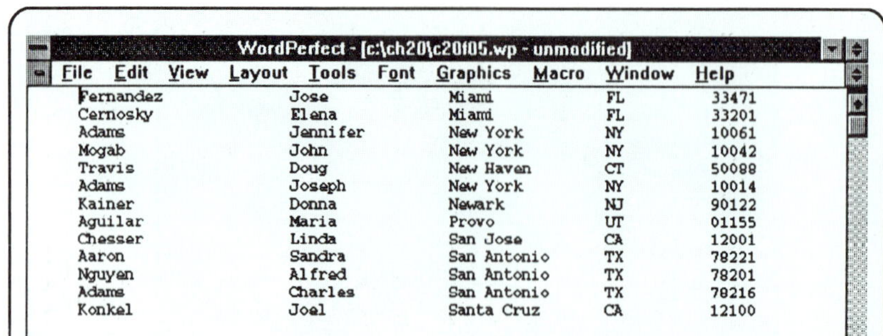

Notice that the third column, which is the city, is now in alphabetical order by the first word only. However, problems exist when the city is two words. This problem is solved in the next section.

■ SORTING WITH MORE THAN ONE KEY

There are times when you need to sort a document using more than one key. The example in the previous section where the document was sorted by city is such a case. Since some names of cities contain more than one word, two keys must be defined to sort the document. The first key should sort by the first word in the city field, and the second key should sort by the second word.

To sort the "sortinp" document by the first and then the second words of the city:

Choose	Tools	***Press***	*Alt*	**Press**	Ctrl+Shift+ F12
Choose	Sort	***Select***	*Tools*		
		Select	*Sort*		

To add a second key:

Click	the Insert Key command button	***Press***	*Alt+I to select the Insert Key command button*	**Press**	Alt+I to select the Insert Key command button

A second key appears.

To define key 1 as the first word of the city field:

Double-click	the Field text box for Key 1	***Press***	*Alt+1 to select Key 1*	**Press**	Alt+1 to select Key 1
Type	3	***Press***	*Tab to select the Field text box for Key 1*	**Press**	Tab to select the Field text box for Key 1
		Type	*3*	**Type**	3

To define a key for the second word in the city field:

Double-click	the Field text box for Key 2	***Press***	*Alt+2 to select Key 2*	**Press**	Alt+2 to select Key 2
Type	3	***Press***	*Tab to select the Field text box for Key 2*	**Press**	Tab to select the Field text box for Key 2
Double-click	the Word text box for Key 2	***Type***	*3*	**Type**	3
Type	2	***Press***	*Tab to select the Word text box for Key 2*	**Press**	Tab to select the Word text box for Key 2
		Type	*2*	**Type**	2

To begin the sort process:

Click	the OK command button	***Press***	*↵Enter*	**Press**	↵Enter

The top part of your screen should look like Figure 20-6.

Figure 20-6

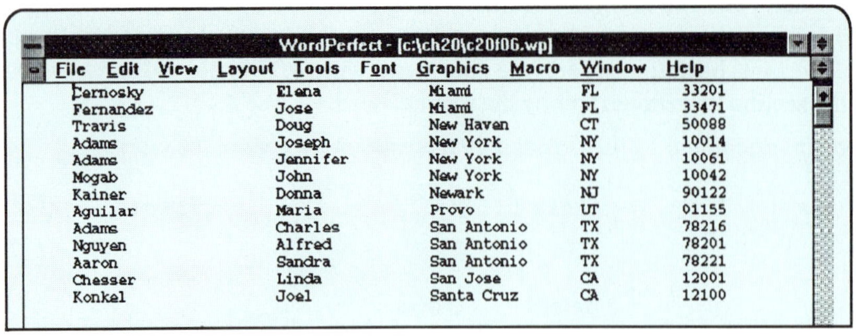

WordPerfect - [c:\ch20\c20f06.wp]

File Edit View Layout Tools Font Graphics Macro Window Help

Cernosky	Elena	Miami	FL	33201
Fernandez	Jose	Miami	FL	33471
Travis	Doug	New Haven	CT	50088
Adams	Joseph	New York	NY	10014
Adams	Jennifer	New York	NY	10061
Mogab	John	New York	NY	10042
Kainer	Donna	Newark	NJ	90122
Aguilar	Maria	Provo	UT	01155
Adams	Charles	San Antonio	TX	78216
Nguyen	Alfred	San Antonio	TX	78201
Aaron	Sandra	San Antonio	TX	78221
Chesser	Linda	San Jose	CA	12001
Konkel	Joel	Santa Cruz	CA	12100

Notice that the city column is sorted correctly.

Suppose you want to sort the lines in the document by last name and then by first name. To sort the "sortinp" document by last name and then first name:

Choose	Tools	***Press***	*Alt*	**Press**	Ctrl + Shift + F12
Choose	Sort	***Select***	*Tools*		
		Select	*Sort*		

To change the field of key 1 to sort by last name (field 1):

Double-click	the Field text box for Key 1	***Press***	*Alt + 1 to select Key 1*	**Press**	Alt + 1 to select Key 1
Type	1	***Press***	*Tab to select the Field text box for Key 1*	**Press**	Tab to select the Field text box for Key 1
		Type	*1*	**Type**	1

To change the field of key 2 to sort by first name (field 2) and first word:

Double-click	the Field text box for Key 2	***Press***	*Alt + 2 to select Key 2*	**Press**	Alt + 2 to select Key 2
Type	2	***Press***	*Tab to select the Field text box for Key 2*	**Press**	Tab to select the Field text box for Key 2
Double-click	the Word text box for Key 2	***Type***	*2*	**Type**	2
Type	1	***Press***	*Tab to select the Word text box*	**Press**	Tab to select the Word text box
		Type	*1*	**Type**	1

Your screen should look like Figure 20-7.

Figure 20-7

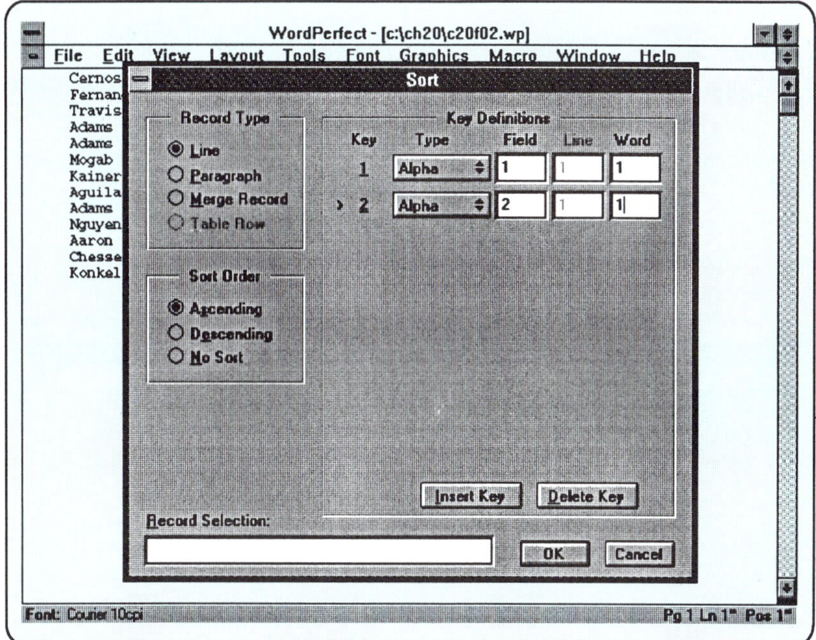

To begin the sort process:

Click	the OK command button	***Press***	↵Enter	**Press**	↵Enter

The top part of your screen should look like Figure 20-8.

Figure 20-8

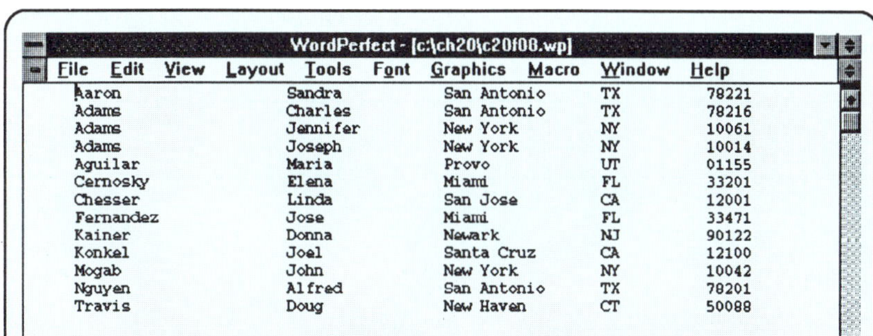

Notice that field 1 is in alphabetical order. Since there are several individuals with the same last name "Adams," WordPerfect then alphabetized by first name, which is field 2.

Save your document using the name "sortout."

■ SORTING A PORTION OF A DOCUMENT

You can also sort a portion or subset of a document by highlighting the records before choosing the Sort feature. The following example shows this process.

Suppose you want to sort the addresses for those individuals whose last names begin with "A" in ascending order by zip code.

To highlight those individuals whose last names begin with "A":

Click	before the "A" in "Aaron"	***Move***	*the insertion point before the "A" in "Aaron"*	**Move**	the insertion point before the "A" in "Aaron"
Select	the first five records	***Select***	*the first five records*	**Select**	the first five records

The top portion of your screen should look like Figure 20-9.

Figure 20-9

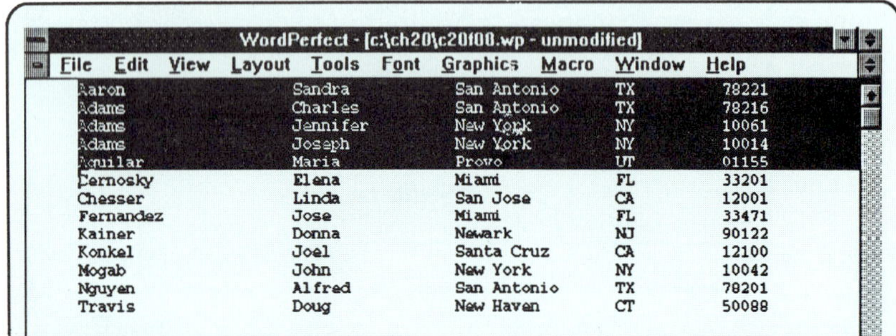

To sort the selected lines in ascending order by zip code:

Choose	Tools	***Press***	*Alt*	**Press**	Ctrl + Shift + F12
Choose	Sort	***Select***	*Tools*		
		Select	*Sort*		

Your screen should look like Figure 20-10.

Figure 20-10

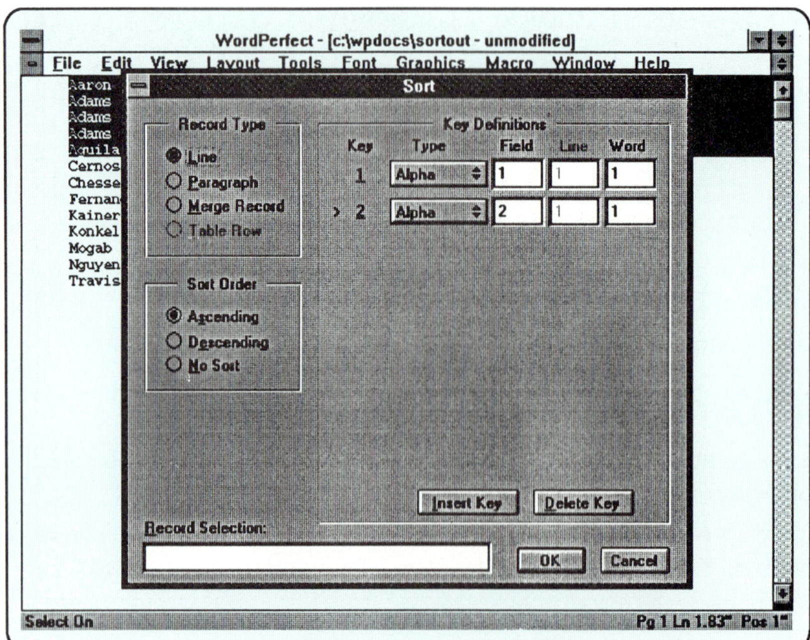

Two sort keys appear in the Key Definitions box. For this sort, only one key is needed. The Delete Key command button deletes the last sort key. In this example, key 2 is the last sort key. To delete the second sort key:

Click	the Delete Key command button	***Press***	*Alt+D to select the Delete Key command button*	**Press**	Alt+D to select the Delete Key command button

To change the type of key 1 to numeric:

Click	the Type pop-up list button for Key 1	***Press***	*Alt+1 to select Key 1*	**Press**	Alt+1 to select Key 1
Hold down	the Type pop-up list button	***Press***	*Alt+↑ to view the Type pop-up list for Key 1*	**Press**	Alt+↑ to view the Type pop-up list for Key 1
Choose	Numeric	***Type***	*N to select Numeric*	**Type**	N to select Numeric

To change the field of key 1 to sort by zip code, which is the fifth field:

Double-click	the Field text box for Key 1	***Press***	*Tab to select the Field text box for Key 1*	**Press**	Tab to select the Field text box for Key 1
Type	5	***Type***	*5*	**Type**	5

Your screen should look like Figure 20-11.

Figure 20-11

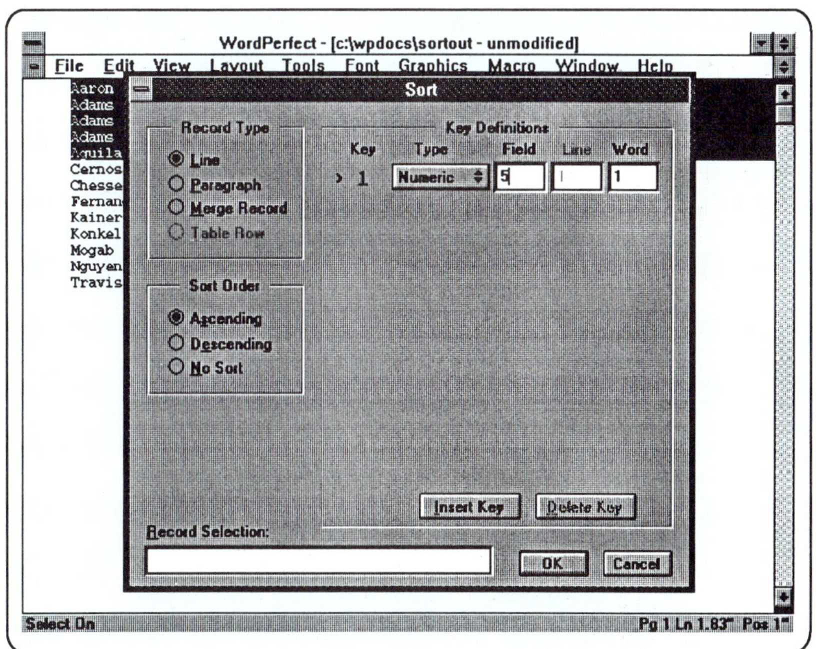

To begin the sort process:

Click	the OK command button	***Press***	*↵Enter*	**Press**	↵Enter

The upper portion of your screen should look like Figure 20-12.

Figure 20-12

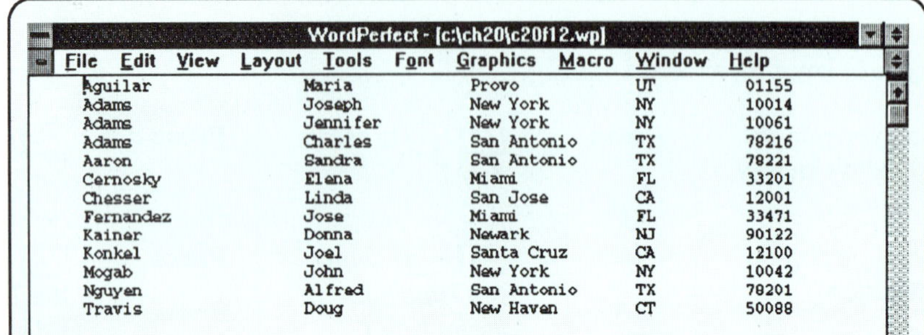

Notice that the zip codes are now in ascending order for those people who have a last name starting with the letter "A."

Save your document using the name "sortport." Close the document.

■ SORTING A SECONDARY (MERGE) FILE

The Sort feature in WordPerfect can also be used to sort information in a secondary merge file.

Open the document "address.ltr" that you created in Chapter 16. Your screen should look like Figure 20-13.

Figure 20-13

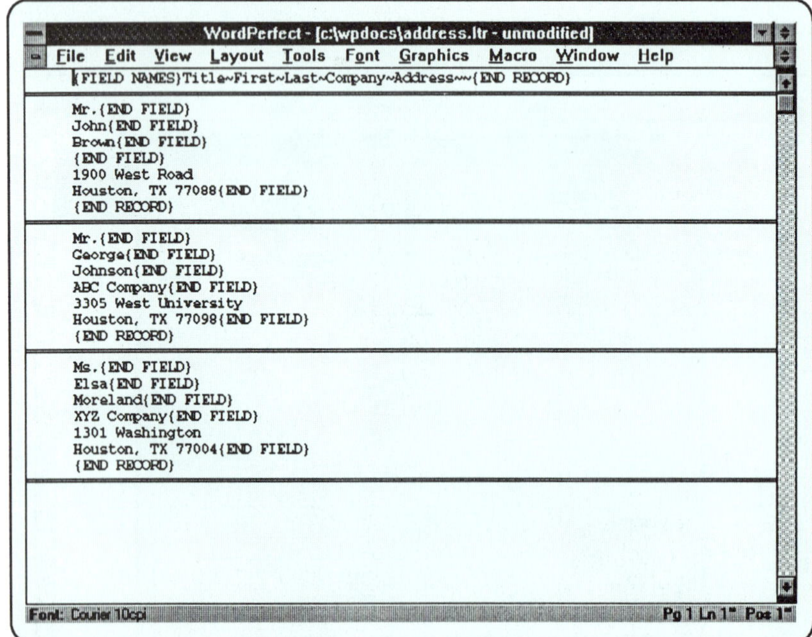

To change the name of the city where George Johnson lives into a two-word name:

Click	at the beginning of the record for George Johnson	***Move***	*to the record for George Johnson*	**Move**	to the record for George Johnson
Change	"Houston" to "San Antonio"	***Change***	*"Houston" to "San Antonio"*	**Change**	"Houston" to "San Antonio"

Suppose you want to sort the addresses in ascending order by zip code.

To sort by zip code:

Click	at the beginning of the document	***Move***	*the insertion point to the beginning of the document*	**Move**	the insertion point to the beginning of the document
Choose	Tools	***Press***	*Alt*	**Press**	Ctrl + Shift + F12
Choose	Sort	***Select***	*Tools*		
		Select	*Sort*		

Since you are sorting a secondary file, change the record type to merge record:

Click	the Merge Record option button in the Record Type box	***Press***	*Alt + M to select the Merge Record option button in the Record Type box*	**Press**	Alt + M to select the Merge Record option button in the Record Type box

Your screen should look like Figure 20-14.

Figure 20-14

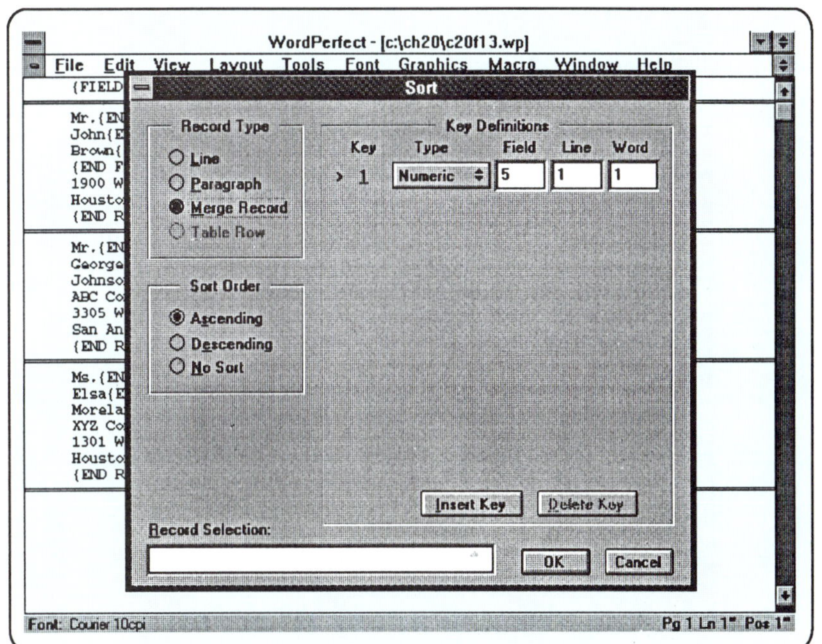

Notice that the Line text box is no longer shaded in the Keys Definition box. In a secondary file, each field is separated by an {END FIELD} code. A field can have more than one line in it. For example, the address field has two lines of text. You must enter the number of the line in the Line text box in the dialog box. The line number is positive if you count from the top of the field down to the bottom. The line number is negative if you count from the bottom of the field to the top. For example, if you want the last line of the field, the line number is -1. The second to last line number is -2.

It is possible that an address can be more than two lines. It is also possible that the name of a city can be more than one word. Therefore, it is difficult to know the exact line number and word number of the zip code. However, you do know that the zip code is always last in an address. Therefore, the zip code is on the last line, so the line number is -1. The zip code is also the last word in the last line, so the word number is also -1.

To change key 1 to sort by zip code in the address field (field 5):

Double-click	the Field text box for Key 1	***Press***	*Alt+1 to select Key 1*	**Press**	Alt+1 to select Key 1
Type	5	***Press***	*Tab to select the Field text box for Key 1*	**Press**	Tab to select the Field text box for Key 1
Double-click	the Line text box for Key 1	***Type***	*5*	**Type**	5
Type	-1	***Press***	*Tab to select the Line text box for Key 1*	**Press**	Tab to select the Line text box for Key 1
Double-click	the Word text box for Key 1	***Type***	*-1*	**Type**	-1
Type	-1	***Press***	*Tab to select the Word text box for Key 1*	**Press**	Tab to select the Word text box for Key 1
		Type	*-1*	**Type**	-1

Your screen should look like Figure 20-15.

Figure 20-15

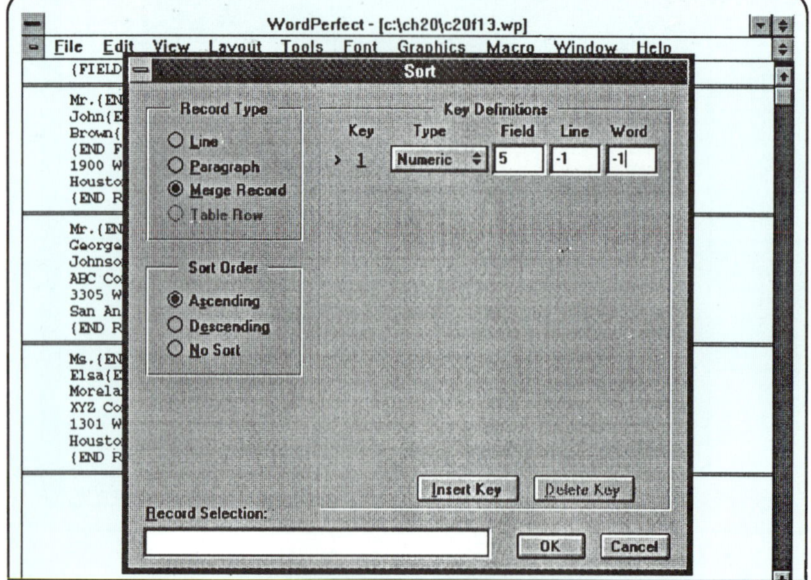

To begin the sort process:

Click	the OK command button	***Press***	*[↵Enter]*	**Press**	[↵Enter]

Scroll through the document. Notice that the zip codes are now in ascending order. Scroll to the end of the document. Your screen should look like Figure 20-16.

Figure 20-16

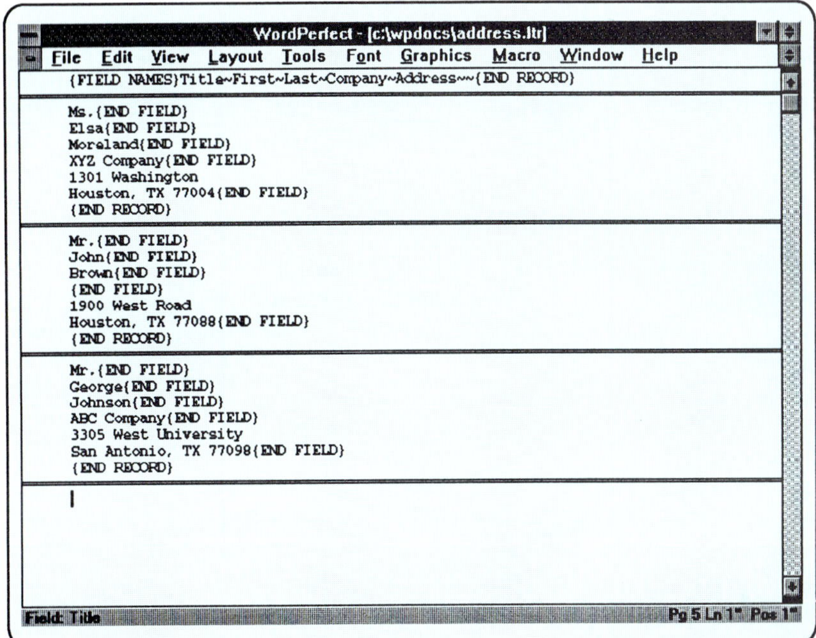

Save the document as "sortmrg."

■ SELECTING RECORDS

Some of your lists or secondary merge files might be quite large. At times, you may want to select only some of the records in that list or secondary file. The Record Selection feature in the Sort command allows you to select records based on certain criteria.

Suppose you want to select the records of the people who live in Houston from the document "sortmrg."

To select by city:

Click	at the beginning of the document	***Move***	*the insertion point to the beginning of the document*	**Move**	the insertion point to the beginning of the document
Choose	Tools	***Press***	*[Alt]*	**Press**	[Ctrl]+[Shift]+[F12]
Choose	Sort	***Select***	*Tools*		
		Select	*Sort*		

Notice that the Record Type is set for Merge Record and the Sort Order is Ascending.

To select records, you first define the key by which you want to select and sort your records. For example, to select the city Houston, the first key should be Field 5, Line -1, Word 1. To define the first key as city:

Click	the Type pop-up list button for Key 1	***Press***	*Alt+1 to select Key 1*	**Press**	Alt+1 to select Key 1
Hold down	the mouse button to view the Type pop-up list	***Press***	*Alt+↑ to view the Type pop-up list for Key 1*	**Press**	Alt+↑ to view the Type pop-up list for Key 1
Choose	Alpha	***Type***	*A to select Alpha*	**Type**	A to select Alpha
Double-click	the Field text box for Key 1	***Press***	*Tab to select the Field text box for Key 1*	**Press**	Tab to select the Field text box for Key 1
Type	5	***Type***	*5*	**Type**	5
Double-click	the Line text box for Key 1	***Press***	*Tab to select the Line text box for Key 1*	**Press**	Tab to select the Line text box for Key 1
Type	-1	***Type***	*-1*	**Type**	-1
Double-click	the Word text box for Key 1	***Press***	*Tab to select the Word text box for Key 1*	**Press**	Tab to select the Word text box for Key 1
Type	1	***Type***	*1*	**Type**	1

Your screen should look like Figure 20-17.

Figure 20-17

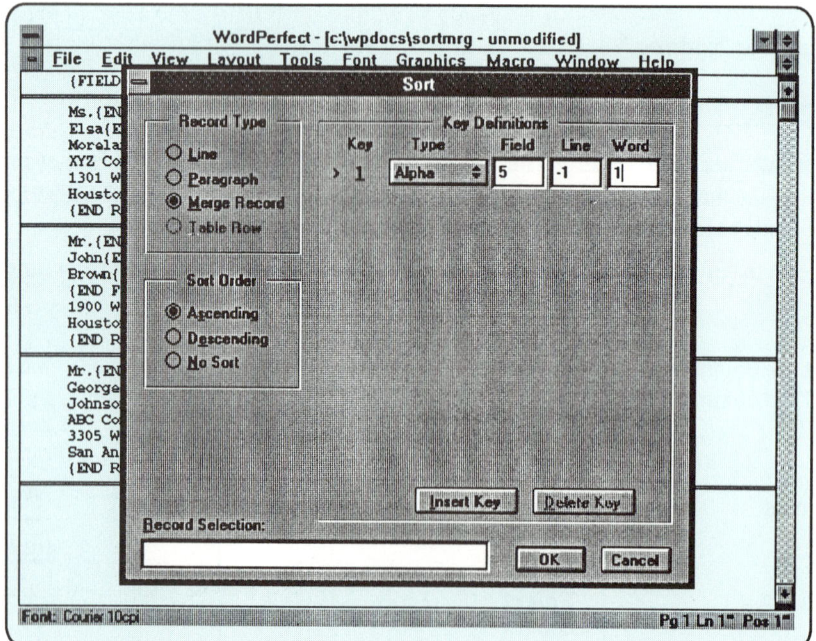

The Record Selection statement allows you to specify which records you want to select. The selection statement consists of the key number and the criteria, or data you want to select.

The key number is entered as text "key1" through "key9." You can also use a global key. A global key lets you specify text that may appear anywhere in the record. For example, if you are looking for records that contain the word "Houston" anywhere in the record, then you would use a global key. The global key is specified as "keyg" in a selection statement. If you use a global key, you do not have to define a key in the Keys Definition box.

After you enter the key number in the selection statement, you need to enter an operator or symbol. The following operators can be used as part of your selection statement.

Symbol	**Description**
=	Specifies records with the same value. For example, key1=Houston searches for records that contain the text "Houston" in key1.
+ (OR)	Allows you to select records that meet any of several conditions. For example, key1=Houston+key1=Dallas searches for records containing the text "Houston" or "Dallas" in key1.
* (AND)	Allows you to select records that must meet several conditions. For example, key1=Houston*key2=77024 searches for records containing the text "Houston" in key1 and the number "77024" in key2.
<>	Specifies records that do not match the following criteria. For example, key1<>Houston selects records that do not contain the text "Houston" in key1.
>	Specifies records that are greater than the criteria. For example, key1>77024 selects records with a numeric value greater than "77024" in key1. If the criteria were a word rather than a number, the > operator searches for records that are alphabetically greater than the word in the criteria.
<	Specifies records that are less than the criteria. For example, key1<77024 selects records with a numeric value less than "77024" in key1. If the criteria were a word rather than a number, the < operator searches for records that are alphabetically less than the word in the criteria.
>=	Specifies records that are greater than or equal to the criteria. For example, key1>=77024 selects records with a numeric value greater than or equal to "77024" in key1. If the criteria were a word rather than a number, the >= operator searches for records that are alphabetically greater than or equal to the word in the criteria.
<=	Specifies records that are less than or equal to the criteria. For example, key1<=77024 selects records with a numeric value less than or equal to "77024" in key1. If the criteria were a word rather than a number, the <= operator searches for records that are alphabetically less than or equal to the word in the criteria.

You want to select the records whose city is Houston. To create the Record Selection statement:

Double-click	the Record Selection text box	***Press***	*Alt+R to select the Record Selection text box*	**Press**	Alt+R to select the Record Selection text box

Your screen should look like Figure 20-18.

Figure 20-18

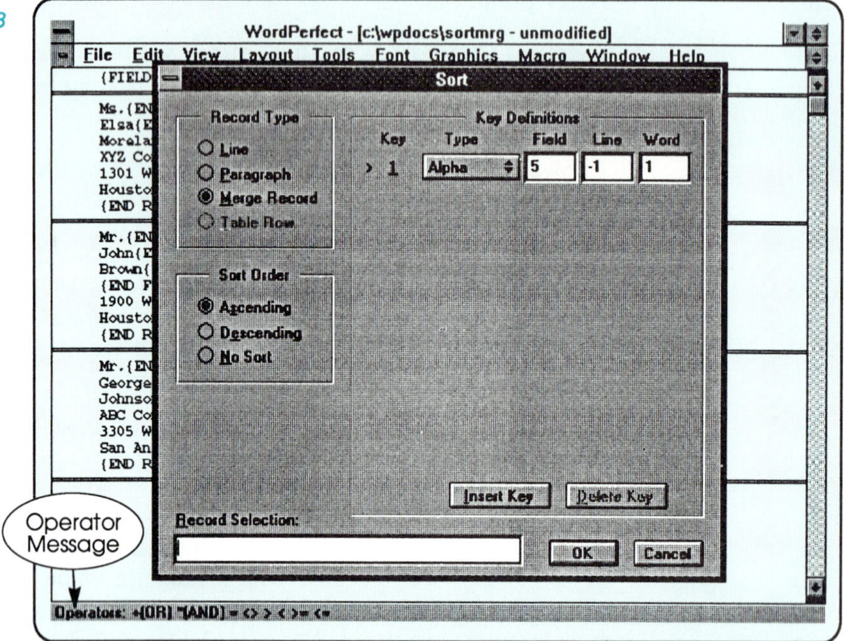

Notice the "Operators" message that appears on the status bar displaying the various operators that can be used in your selection statement.

To enter the selection statement:

Type	key1=Houston	***Type***	*key1=Houston*	**Type**	key1=Houston

The select statement is not case sensitive. You can use uppercase or lowercase letters when entering your selection statement. Your screen should look like Figure 20-19.

Figure 20-19

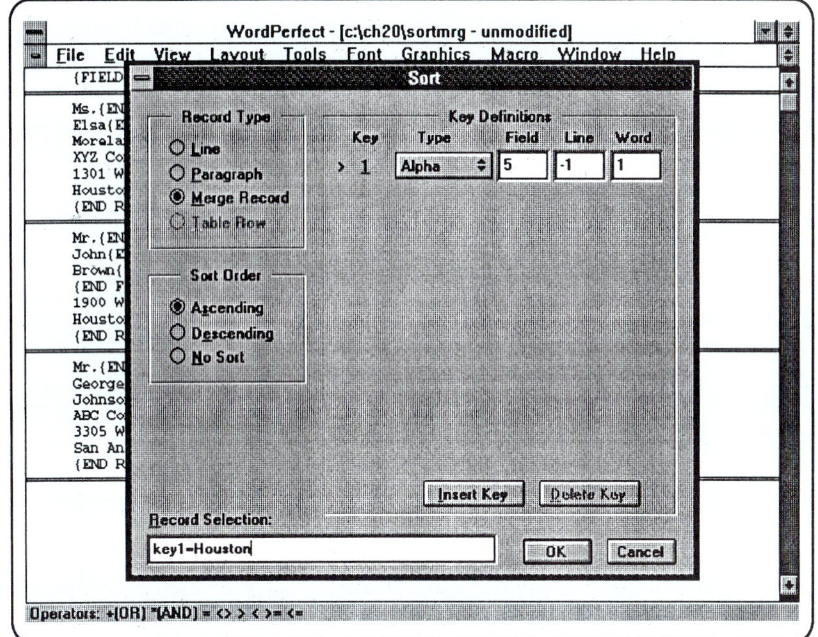

To select and sort the records:

Click	the OK command button	***Press***	*↵Enter*	**Press**	↵Enter

Your screen should look like Figure 20-20.

Figure 20-20

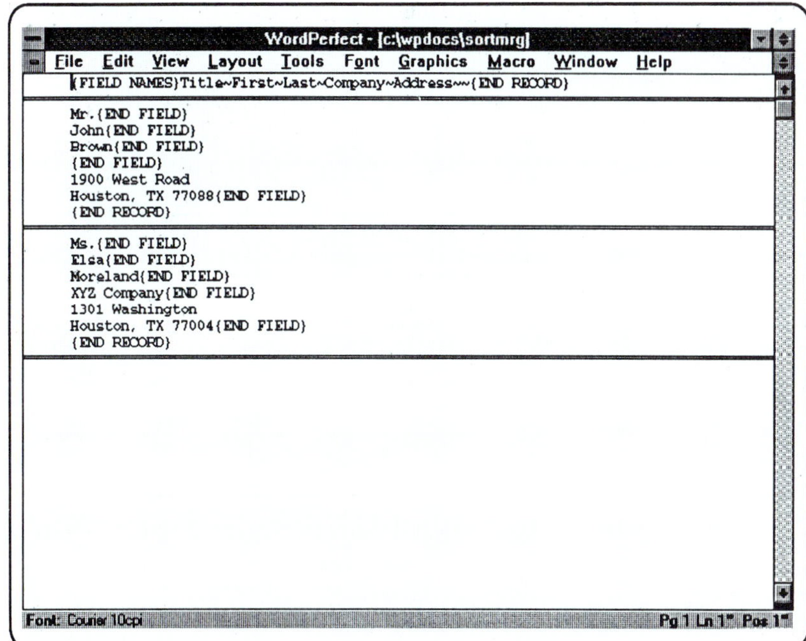

The field names code and the two records with Houston addresses are left in the file. The record with a San Antonio address is deleted. Notice that the document still has the name "sortmrg." Do not save the file with the same name or your old document will be replaced. To save the file with a new name, use the Save As option under the File menu.

Save the document as "sortcity." Close the document.

EXERCISE 1

INSTRUCTIONS: Define the following terms:

1. Sort feature ______________________________
____
2. Line sort ______________________________
____
3. Paragraph sort ______________________________
____
4. Keys ______________________________
____
5. Fields ______________________________
____
6. Words ______________________________
____
7. Merge Record sort ______________________________
____
8. Record selection ______________________________
____
9. Record selection operators ______________________________
____
____

EXERCISE 2

INSTRUCTIONS: Circle T if the statement is true and F if the statement is false.

T F 1. With the Sort feature, you can sort lines, paragraphs, secondary merge files, or selected text.

T F 2. You can perform a line sort if there are no blank lines between the text.

T F 3. You cannot perform a paragraph sort if there are blank lines between the text.

T F 4. You should always save your document before sorting.

T F 5. Keys are words, fields, or phrases by which a document is sorted.

T F 6. Numeric keys are made up of letters or numbers.

T F 7. If you want to sort by the last word in a field of a secondary merge file, then the word number of the key should be -1.

T F 8. If the key occurs in the second to last line of a field in a secondary merge file, then the line number should be -2.

T F 9. When you use the Record Selection feature, you have to define a key and create a selection statement.

T F 10. The * operator in a Record Selection statement indicates that either of two conditions can be met for the record to be selected.

EXERCISE 3

INSTRUCTIONS:

1. Create the following document. You will need to set left-aligned tabs at 1.5", 3.0", 3.5", 5.0", and 6.0". The order of the data in the columns is last name, first name, middle initial, city, state, and zip code.
2. Save the document in a file using the name "ch20ex03."
3. Sort the document by state abbreviation.
4. Print the document.
5. Sort the document in descending order by zip code.
6. Print the document.
7. Sort the document by last name, first name, and middle initial.
8. Print the document.
9. Sort the document by city within each state. Make sure that the zip codes are in ascending order within each city.
10. Print the document.
11. Sort the individuals that live in California by last name, first name, and middle initial.
12. Print the document.
13. Close the document without saving changes.

Smith	Albert	D	Seattle	WA	93006
Thompson	Sally	W	Minneapolis	MN	55455
Jackson	Thomas	C	Omaha	NE	65532
Smith	Albert	B	San Francisco	CA	95476
James	Susan	W	Chicago	IL	60672
Garcia	Mary	L	Laredo	TX	76549
Baker	Dave	M	Dallas	TX	75543
Yee	Teresa	M	Oxnard	CA	93321
Allen	William	X	San Francisco	CA	75436
Jackson	Mary	D	Durham	NC	23498
Baker	Dale	T	New Bern	NC	23653
Martinez	Anna	B	Del Rio	TX	78890

EXERCISE 4

INSTRUCTIONS:

1. Create the following document. Use left-aligned tabs set at 2″, 3.5″, 5″, and 5.5″.
2. Print the document.
3. Sort the document by last names.
4. Print the document.
5. Save the document in a file using the name "ch20ex04."
6. Close the document.

MONTHLY SALES REPORT

Walters	Phil	Rockford	IL	3,432
Koch	Victor	Elgin	IL	4,372
McFarland	Marilyn	DeKalb	IL	6,175
Kohlmeyer	Paulette	Indianapolis	IN	5,329
Zwerger	William	Evansville	IN	3,778
Wyrwicz	Norbert	Plymouth	IN	4,309
Paskalides	James	LaPorte	IN	2,909
Tkemetarovic	Joseph	Ames	IA	4,588
Hijjawi	Syed	Ottumwa	IA	5,272
Fatah	Renee	Des Moines	IA	6,377
Sherrell	Wilhelmina	Lewiston	ID	5,440
Bishop	Robert	Moscow	ID	3,970

EXERCISE 5

INSTRUCTIONS:

1. Open the document "ch20ex04."
2. Sort the amount column in descending order.
3. Print the document.
4. Save the document in a file using the name "ch20ex05."

EXERCISE 6

INSTRUCTIONS:

1. Create the following document. Use left-aligned tabs set at 2″, 4″, 5.3″, and 5.8″.
2. Sort the document by zip code.
3. Add the title **"SELECTED SALES PERSONNEL"** to the top of the document. Make the title two lines above the first line of the list.
4. Print the document.
5. Save the document in a file using the name "ch20ex06."
6. Close the document.

Irwin	Tom	Albany	GA	31701
Jorandy	Gwen	Moline	IL	61265
Lorek	Austin	Albany	GA	31702
Nix	Madie	Albany	GA	31701
Rau	John	Albany	GA	31701
Cassidy	Ian	Moline	IL	61265
Shapiro	Robert	Portland	ME	04101
Cloyd	Johan	Albany	GA	31702
Kahle	Jerry	Portland	ME	04102
Peterman	Tim	Chicago	IL	60616
Panagakis	Angela	Moline	IL	61265

EXERCISE 7

INSTRUCTIONS:

1. Create the following document. Set left-aligned tabs at 2″, 3.5″, and 5.8″.
2. Sort by country and then by year in descending order.
3. Print the document.
4. Save the document in a file using the name "ch20ex07."

5. Sort by last name and then first name in ascending order.
6. Print the document.
7. Close the document.

SELECTED OLYMPIC GOLD MEDAL WINNERS

(Name, Year, Event and Country Represented)

Carl Lewis	1988	100-Meters	USA
Volker Beck	1980	400-Meters	GDR
Sergi Bubka	1988	Pole Vault	USSR
John Walker	1976	1,500-Meters	NZ
Carl Lewis	1988	Long Jump	USA
Tapio Korjus	1988	Javelin	FIN
Lasse Viren	1976	5,000-Meters	FIN
Steve Lewis	1988	400-Meters	USA
Sergei Litinov	1988	Hammer Throw	USSR
Mark Todd	1988	Equestrian	NZ

EXERCISE 8

INSTRUCTIONS:

1. Create a secondary merge file using the mailing list shown below. Name the file "ch20ex08.sec."
2. Sort the secondary file by zip code in ascending order.
3. Print the document.
4. Save the document in a file using the name "ch20ex08."
5. Close the document.

```
Ms. Geri Bitting
1122 Inverrary
High Point, NC  27260

Mr. William Komarek
Director of Financial Planning
101 Bar Harbor Road
Charlotte, NC  28202

Mr. Mike Isermann
Decision Support Manager
1520 South Belmont
High Point, NC  27261

Mrs. Margaret Brinkman
Director of Marketing
347 Pleasant Hill
Durham, NC  27701

Mr. Delmar Cotes
1216 Houbolt Avenue
Durham, NC  27702

Ms. Gina Sterr
Vice President
Flood Enterprises
Asheville, NC  28801

Ms. Norma Aguilar
Chief Financial Officer
9911 South San Felipe Drive
San Louis Obispo, CA  02211
```

EXERCISE 9

INSTRUCTIONS:

1. Create the following secondary merge file. Name the file "ch20ex09.sec." The fields should be Name, Department, and Magazine. Each field corresponds to one line.
2. Sort the document by date of magazine in descending order.
3. Print the document.
4. Sort the document by department in ascending order.
5. Print the document.
6. Sort the document by last name and then first name in ascending order.
7. Print the document.
8. Close the document without saving changes.

```
Janet Harborow
Marketing Department
PC Magazine, 7/1/88

John Mogab
Internal Auditing
Computers in Accounting, 6/1/88

Joel Konkel
Information Systems
InfoWorld, 4/30/90

Linda Chesser
Accounting Department
PC World, 5/1/90

Donna Gail Kainer
Information Systems
ComputerWorld, 4/22/90

Doug Travis
Research & Development
Communications of the ACM, 6/1/90
```

EXERCISE 10

INSTRUCTIONS:

1. Open the file "ch20ex08.sec."
2. Select only the records from Durham, N.C.
3. Save the file as "ch20ex10."
4. Print the file.
5. Close the file.

EXERCISE 11

INSTRUCTIONS:

1. Open the file "ch20ex08.sec."
2. Select the records for people from Durham or from High Point.
3. Save the file as "ch20ex11."
4. Print the file.
5. Close the file.

CHAPTER TWENTY-ONE

CREATING AND USING COLUMNS

OBJECTIVES

In this chapter, you will learn to:

- Create newspaper-style columns
- Create newspaper-style columns with the Ruler
- Create parallel columns

CHAPTER OVERVIEW

There may be times when you want to include columns in a document. WordPerfect allows you to have parallel and newspaper-style columns. This chapter illustrates the process for creating these types of columns using the Columns feature.

NEWSPAPER-STYLE COLUMNS

In WordPerfect you can create newspaper-style columns where text continues from column to column. To create columns, you choose Definition from the Columns option under the Layout menu or press Alt + Shift + F9 and select Definition.

Whenever you want to use columns in a document, you need to define:

1. The number of columns
2. The type of column
3. The column options
4. The left and right margins for each of the columns
5. The distance between each column

A Column Definition code is placed in your document with the values for each of these attributes. The definition continues in effect until another column definition is specified. You can mix regular text paragraphs with columns in one document.

Change the default directory to "a:\wpdocs" or to "c:\wpdocs."

To show the use of newspaper-style columns, suppose the State Financial Society needs to prepare a story for a newsletter to announce two job appointments.

Center and bold the words "CHAPTERS ADD ASSISTANTS" and press [↵Enter] twice. The top part of your screen should look like Figure 21-1.

Figure 21-1

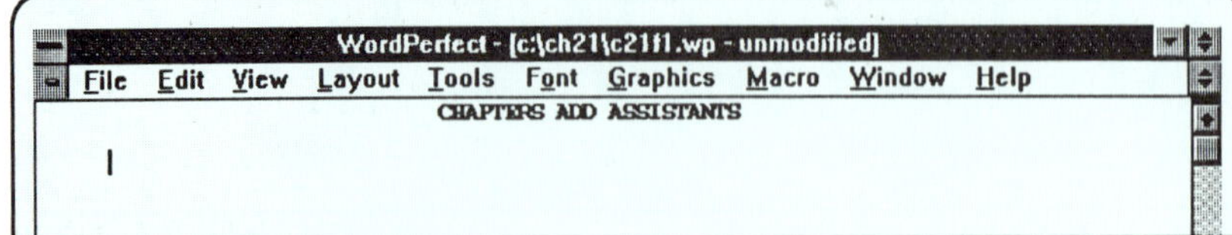

To define the characteristics for the columns:

Choose	Layout	***Press***	*[Alt]*	**Press**	[Shift]+[Alt]+[F9]
Choose	Columns	***Select***	*Layout*	**Select**	Define
Choose	Define	***Select***	*Columns*		
		Select	*Define*		

The Define Columns dialog box appears. Your screen should look like Figure 21-2.

Figure 21-2

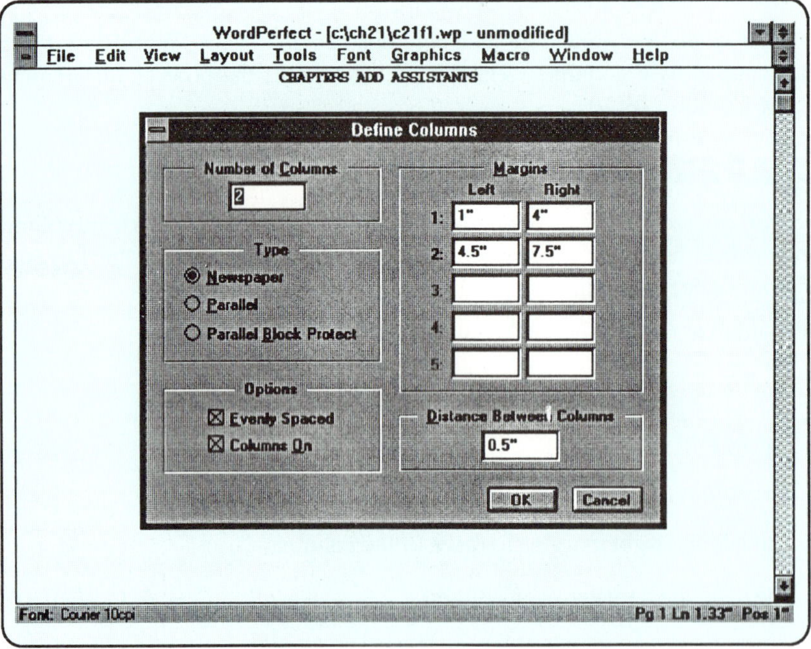

Note that the default settings for columns in WordPerfect are newspaper-style columns and two columns to a page. Unless you change the distance between columns, WordPerfect assumes a value of approximately one-half inch. You can have a maximum of 24 columns in a document.

To change the number of columns to three columns:

Double-click	the Number of Columns text box	***Press***	*Alt+C to select the Number of Columns text box*	**Press**	Alt+C to select the Number of Columns text box
Type	3	***Type***	*3*	**Type**	3

Your screen should look like Figure 21-3.

Figure 21-3

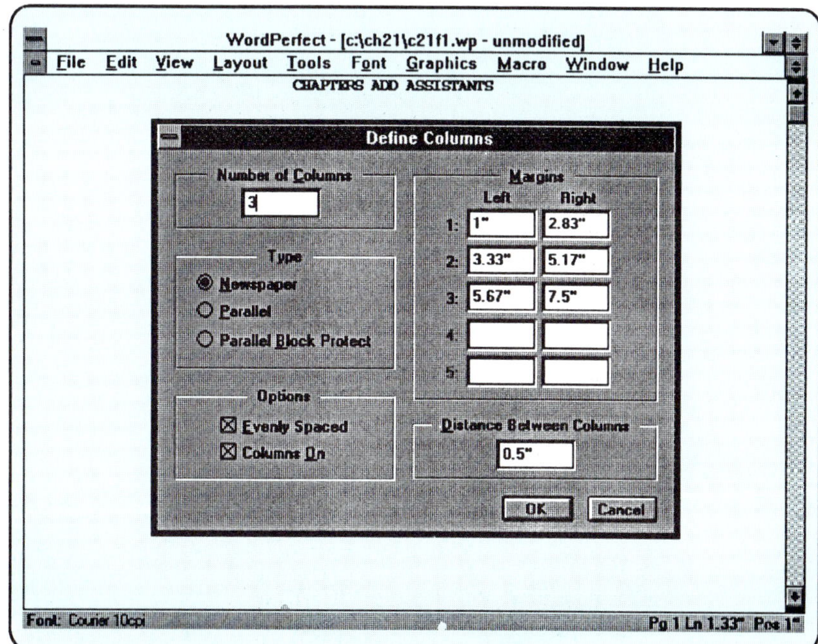

The left and right margin settings for each column are based on the number of columns that you defined and the current margins for the document. You can change the margins for each column in this dialog box. Select the appropriate Margins text box and enter the new settings.

You should not set the column margins out of the bounds of the document margins. To avoid confusion, you should set the first column's left margin to that of the document's left margin. And you should also set the last column's right margin to that of the document's right margin.

Notice that you now have three equally spaced columns.

To change the Number of Columns option to two columns again:

Double-click	the Number of Columns text box	***Press***	*Alt+C to select the Number of Columns text box*	**Press**	Alt+C to select the Number of Columns text box
Type	2	***Type***	*2*	**Type**	2

Notice that you now have two equally spaced columns.

The Distance Between Columns option is calculated for you at approximately one-half inch. But you can change the value by selecting the Distance Between Columns text box.

To return to your document:

Click	the OK command button	***Press***	*↵Enter*	**Press**	↵Enter

Once you have defined the columns, you can enter text using the Columns feature. By default, the columns are turned on when you choose OK from the Define Columns dialog box.

The bottom section of your screen should look like Figure 21-4.

Figure 21-4

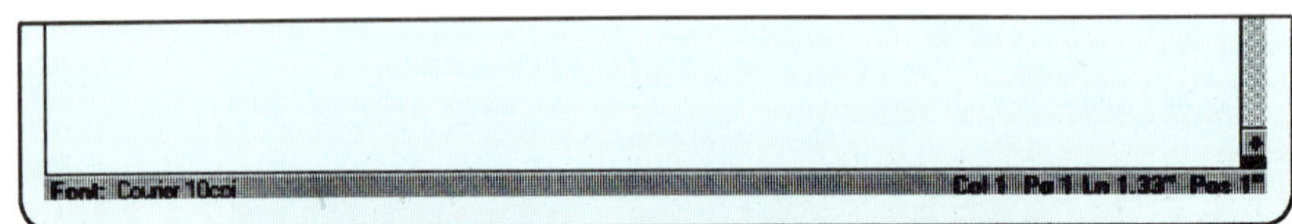

Notice that a "Col" indicator is displayed before the page indicator on the status bar.

Enter the text in Figure 21-5 in your document.

Figure 21-5

Two chapters recently have hired executive secretaries to support growing activities. The Southwest and the Southeast Texas chapters are the first to take advantage of the newly revised Chapter Assistance Program.

Susan Jones began duties as executive secretary of the Southwest Chapter on June 1. She has over 14 years experience in bookkeeping and secretarial services. For the past five years, Jones has conducted a home bookkeeping service. Presently, she services two civic clubs, an insurance association, and 22 other private accounts.

In her eight-month tenure with the chapter, Jones has concentrated her efforts in the area of CPE and dues billing. She says she is working on transferring the chapter records to a computer.

Doris Brown became the Southeast Texas executive secretary on November 10. Owner of Brown Business Services, a marketing-management company, Brown brings to the chapter position a wide range of business and community experience.

Brown also has been associated for more than 15 years with the Greater Orange Area Chamber of Commerce. She has served on the Chamber Board of Directors Committee, the Executive Committee, the Civic Affairs Division, and the Convention Visitors Bureau.

With Brown's support, the chapter hopes to develop CPE programs and later expand to other areas.

Once you have typed text in the columns, you can move the insertion point to a column by moving the mouse pointer to that column and clicking or by pressing Alt+→ to move right one column or Alt+← to move left one column.

Your screen should look like Figure 21-6.

Figure 21-6

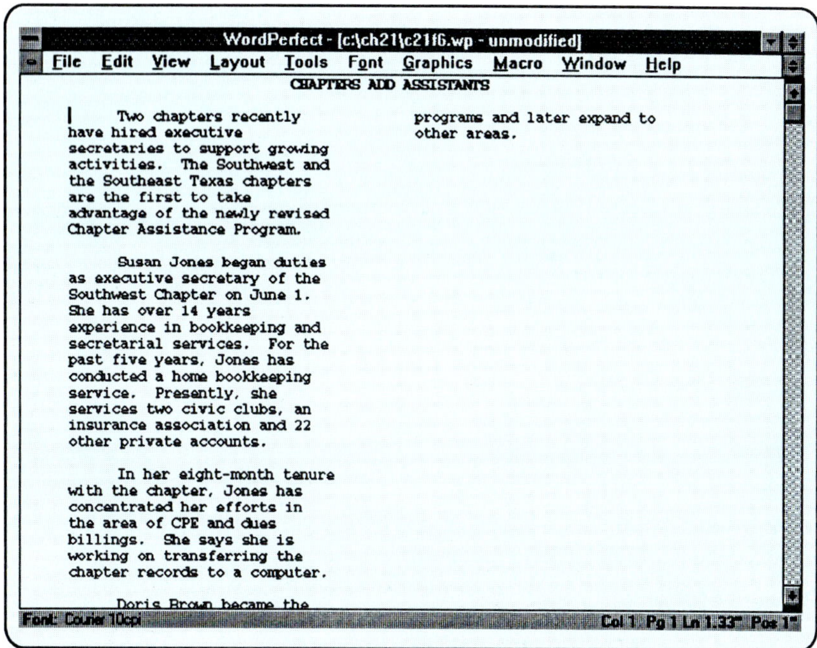

A Soft Page break code [SPg] is placed in the document when you enter text beyond a column. The insertion point is placed at the top of the next column. You can break a column by inserting a page break. To insert a page break, choose Page Break from the Page option under the Layout menu or press Ctrl+↵Enter. The text will move to the next column.

To move the fourth paragraph beginning with "Doris Brown" to the top of column two:

Click	at the left margin of the fourth paragraph	***Move***	*the insertion point to the left margin of the fourth paragraph*	**Move**	the insertion point to the left margin of the fourth paragraph
Choose	Layout	***Press***	*Alt*	**Press**	Ctrl+↵Enter
Choose	Page	***Select***	*Layout*		
Choose	Page Break	***Select***	*Page*		
		Select	*Page Break*		

Your screen should look like Figure 21-7.

Figure 21-7

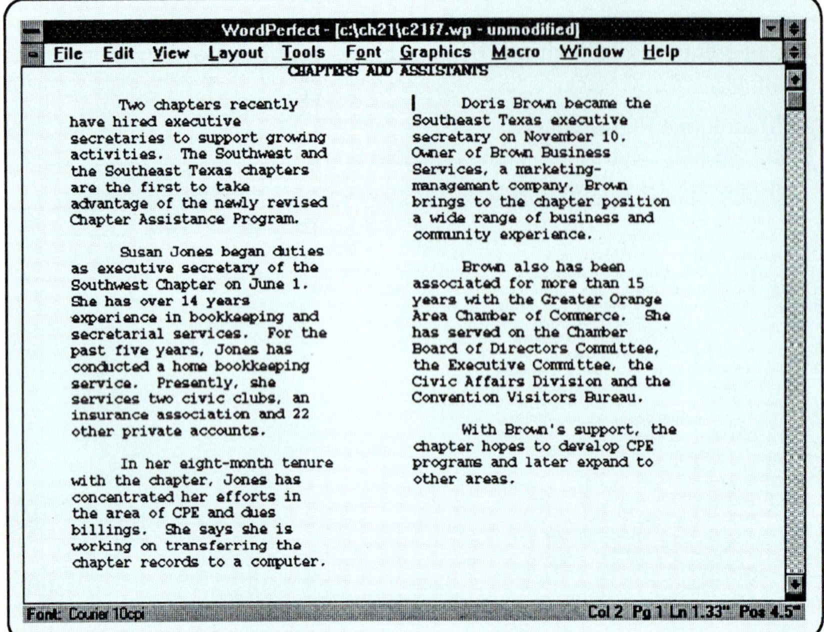

You must move the insertion point below the columns before you turn off the Columns feature. This step places a Column Off code [Col Off] in the document.

To turn off the Columns feature:

Click	at the bottom of Column 2	***Move***	*the insertion point to the bottom of Column 2*	**Move**	the insertion point to the bottom of Column 2
Choose	Layout	***Press***	*Alt*	**Press**	Alt + Shift + F9
Choose	Columns	***Select***	*Layout*	**Select**	Columns Off
Choose	Columns Off	***Select***	*Columns*		
		Select	*Columns Off*		

Your screen should look like Figure 21-8.

Figure 21-8

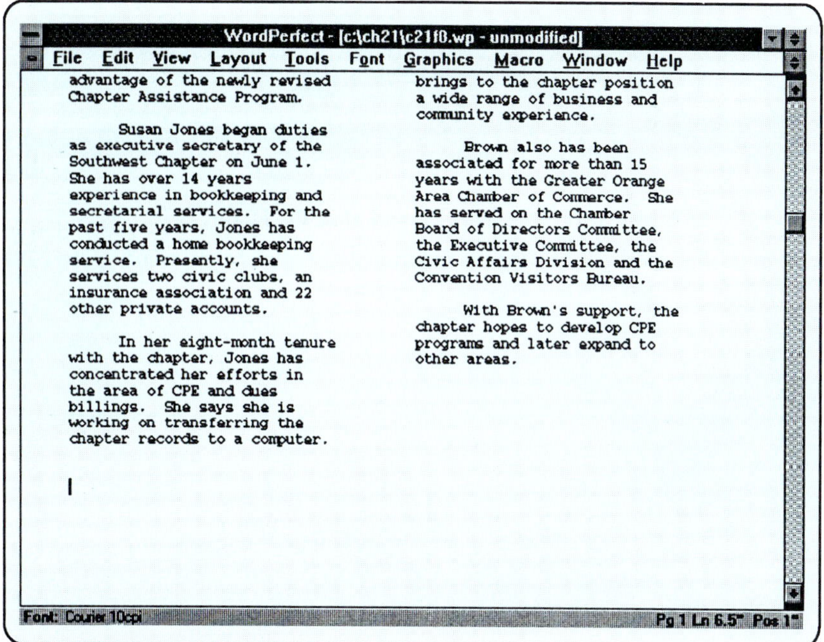

Notice that the "Col" indicator no longer appears on the status bar.

Save the document as "newscol" and close the document.

■ CREATING NEWSPAPER-STYLE COLUMNS WITH THE RULER

You can easily create newspaper-style columns with the mouse by using the Ruler.

To view the Ruler:

Choose	View	***Press***	*Alt*	**Press**	Alt + Shift + F3
Choose	Ruler	***Select***	*View*		
		Select	*Ruler*		

The Columns button on the Ruler allows you to use the default settings for newspaper-style columns. You can select from two, three, four, or five evenly spaced newspaper-style columns.

To create three newspaper-style columns:

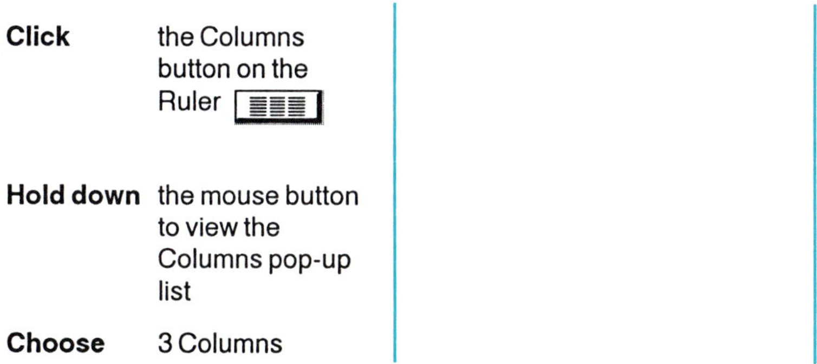

Click	the Columns button on the Ruler
Hold down	the mouse button to view the Columns pop-up list
Choose	3 Columns

The top portion of your screen should look like Figure 21-9.

Figure 21-9

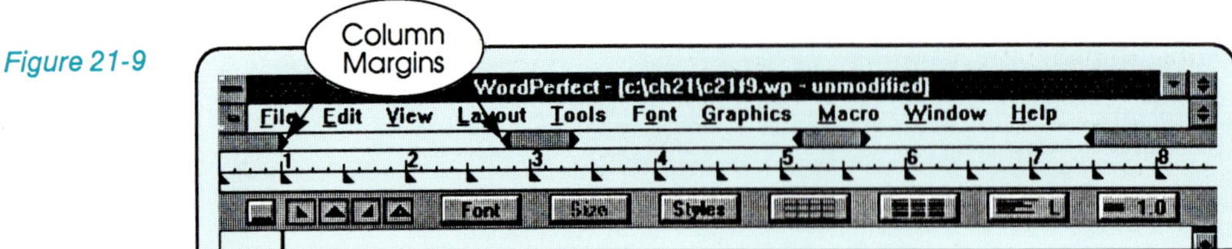

Notice the column margins displayed on the margin marker of the Ruler.

Create the document in Figure 21-10. Force the columns to break as shown in Figure 21-11 by inserting page breaks.

Figure 21-10

Garage Sale

The employee-sponsored garage sale will be held on November 12. If you have any donations, please bring them in one of the appropriate containers.

Alex Newberry has donated his 1965 Mustang convertible to be auctioned off.

All proceeds will be donated to the Saint Mary Orphanage.

Volunteers for the garage sale can sign up with Denise Newcastle. Several times are available in the morning.

Refreshments will be provided for volunteers by Chez Tim - Bakery and Cafe.

Volunteer Hours

Our company has volunteered 700 hours so far this year.

If you do volunteer work and would like someone in the company to match your hours, please turn in the name of the organization and the time that you serve. Libby Street coordinates all volunteer hours.

Keep up the good work!

Your screen should look like Figure 21-11.

Figure 21-11

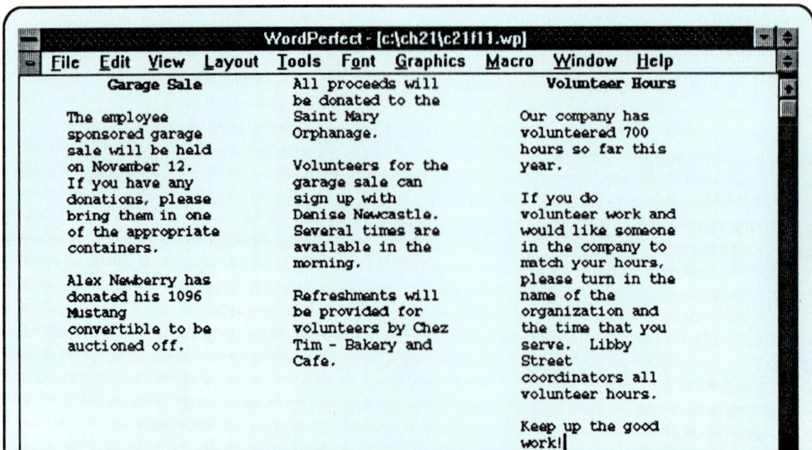

To turn the columns off using the Ruler:

Click	at the end of the document
Click	the Columns button on the Ruler
Hold down	the mouse button to view the Columns pop-up list
Choose	Columns Off

Save the document as "rulercol.ltr." Close the document.

■ PARALLEL COLUMNS

Parallel columns are columns in which the text is printed exactly as it is entered into each column. When one column is full, the text does not roll over into the next column. Figure 21-12 shows an example of parallel columns.

Figure 21-12

```
NAME                  AGE       SKILLS DESCRIPTION

Abrams, K.            35        Programming in various database
                                packages.  Expert in network
                                hardware and software.  Works
                                well with others.

Donaldson, M.         45        Speaks 32 languages.  Speaks and
                                reads 17 languages.  Expert in
                                German, Russian, Czech, Polish,
                                French, Italian, Mandarin,
                                Spanish, and Japanese.  Thesis in
                                British history.  Has an
                                unobtrusive demeanor.
```

There are two types of parallel columns:

Parallel - A column can extend beyond the page.

Parallel with Block Protect - An attempt is made to hold sets of items together in one block or area. This type of column would be used in the example in the box shown above.

As with newspaper-style columns, you must define the characteristics for parallel columns before you use them.

To show the use of parallel columns, assume that you want to prepare a schedule for your supervisor. To begin the process, center and bold the word "ITINERARY" and press ↵Enter twice.

To define parallel columns:

Choose	Layout	***Press***	*Alt*	**Press**	Alt+Shift+F9
Choose	Columns	***Select***	*Layout*	**Select**	Define
Choose	Define	***Select***	*Columns*		
		Select	*Define*		

To change the Number of Columns option to three columns:

Double-click	the Number of Columns text box	***Press***	*Alt+C to select the Number of Columns text box*	**Press**	Alt+C to select the Number of Columns text box
Type	3	***Type***	*3*	**Type**	3

To create parallel columns:

Click	the Parallel option button in the Type box	***Press***	*Alt+P to select the Parallel option button in the Type box*	**Press**	Alt+P to select the Parallel option button in the Type box

Your screen should look like Figure 21-13.

Figure 21-13

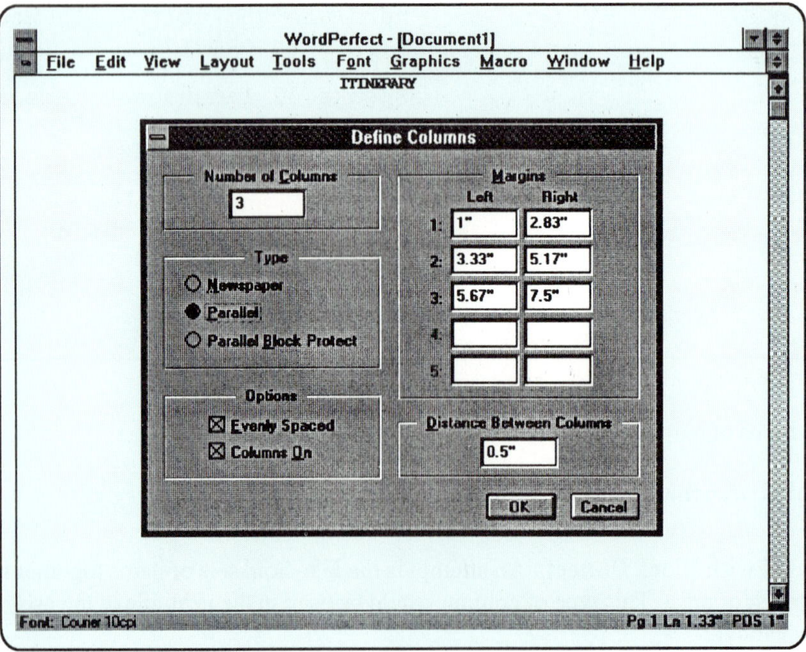

The left and right margin settings for each column are based on the number of columns that you defined and the current margins for the document. You can change the margins for each column through this screen. Select the Margins option and enter the new settings.

You should not set the column margins out of the bounds of the document margins. To avoid confusion, you should set the first column's left margin to that of the document's left margin. And you should also set the last column's right margin to that of the document's right margin.

Notice that you now have three equally spaced columns.

The Distance Between Columns option is calculated for you at approximately one-half inch. But you can change the value by selecting the Distance Between Columns text box.

To accept the column settings and turn the columns on:

Click	the OK command button	***Press***	*↵Enter*	**Press**	↵Enter

Once you have defined the characteristics of the parallel columns, you can start using the parallel columns.

As you enter text into the columns, choose Page Break from the Page option under the Layout menu or press Ctrl+↵Enter to move from one column to the next.

To center a heading over column one:

Choose	Layout	***Press***	*Alt*	**Press**	Shift+F7
Choose	Line	***Select***	*Layout*	**Type**	DATE
Choose	Center	***Select***	*Line*		
Type	DATE	***Select***	*Center*		
		Type	*DATE*		

To move to the next column:

Choose	Layout	***Press***	*Alt*	**Press**	Ctrl+↵Enter
Choose	Page	***Select***	*Layout*		
Choose	Page Break	***Select***	*Page*		
		Select	*Page Break*		

To center a heading over column two:

Choose	Layout	***Press***	*Alt*	**Press**	Shift+F7
Choose	Line	***Select***	*Layout*	**Type**	CITY
Choose	Center	***Select***	*Line*		
Type	CITY	***Select***	*Center*		
		Type	*CITY*		

To move to the next column:

Choose	Layout	***Press***	*Alt*	**Press**	Ctrl+↵Enter
Choose	Page	***Select***	*Layout*		
Choose	Page Break	***Select***	*Page*		
		Select	*Page Break*		

To center a heading over column three:

Choose	Layout	***Press***	*Alt*	**Press**	Shift+F7
Choose	Line	***Select***	*Layout*	**Type**	ACCOMMODA-TIONS
Choose	Center	***Select***	*Line*		
Type	ACCOMMODA-TIONS	***Select***	*Center*		
		Type	*ACCOMMODA-TIONS*		

To move to the next column:

Choose	Layout	***Press***	*Alt*	**Press**	Ctrl+↵Enter
Choose	Page	***Select***	*Layout*		
Choose	Page Break	***Select***	*Page*		
		Select	*Page Break*		

Your screen should look like Figure 21-14.

Figure 21-14

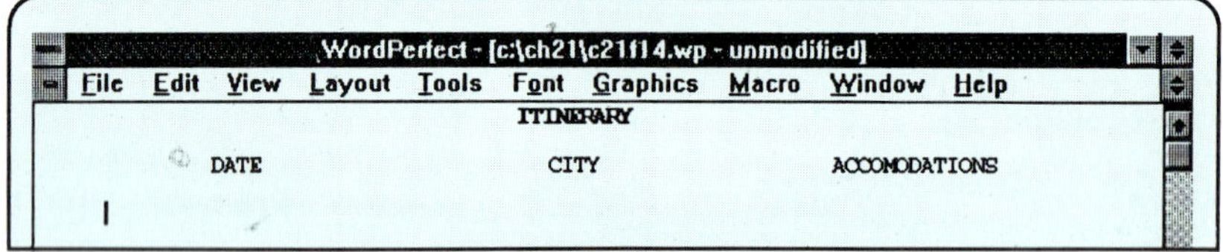

Inserting a page break from the last column moves the insertion point to the first column of a new column set. Each block of columns is separated by an extra Hard Return code.

> **In This Book**
> To insert a page break, you have been instructed to choose Page Break from the Page option under the Layout menu or to press Ctrl+↵Enter. For the remainder of this book, the steps for inserting a page break are abbreviated as "Insert a page break."

To place the first entry in the schedule:

Type	April 20, 1992	***Type***	*April 20, 1992*	**Type**	April 20, 1992
Insert	a page break	***Insert***	*a page break*	**Insert**	a page break
Type	Dallas, Texas	***Type***	*Dallas, Texas*	**Type**	Dallas, Texas
Insert	a page break	***Insert***	*a page break*	**Insert**	a page break
Type	Holiday Inn	***Type***	*Holiday Inn*	**Type**	Holiday Inn
Insert	a page break	***Insert***	*a page break*	**Insert**	a page break

The top section of your screen should look like Figure 21-15.

Figure 21-15

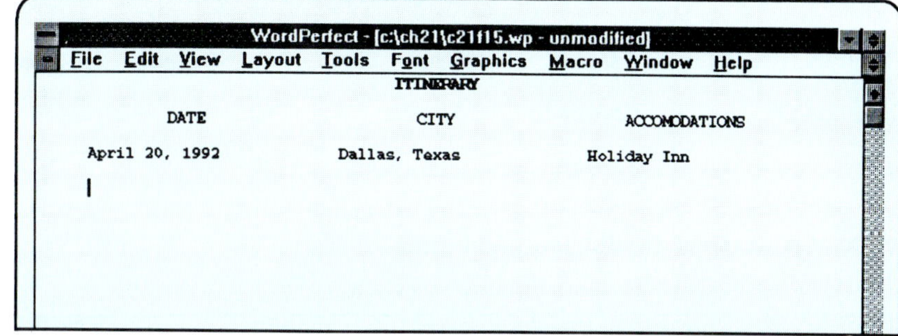

To add the second entry in the schedule:

Type	April 25, 1992	***Type***	*April 25, 1992*	**Type**	April 25, 1992
Insert	a page break	***Insert***	*a page break*	**Insert**	a page break
Type	San Francisco, California	***Type***	*San Francisco, California*	**Type**	San Francisco, California
Insert	a page break	***Insert***	*a page break*	**Insert**	a page break
Type	Ramada Inn	***Type***	*Ramada Inn*	**Type**	Ramada Inn
Insert	a page break	***Insert***	*a page break*	**Insert**	a page break

To insert the third entry in the schedule:

Type	April 28, 1992	***Type***	*April 28, 1992*	**Type**	April 28, 1992
Insert	a page break	***Insert***	*a page break*	**Insert**	a page break
Type	Los Angeles, California	***Type***	*Los Angeles, California*	**Type**	Los Angeles, California
Insert	a page break	***Insert***	*a page break*	**Insert**	a page break
Type	Holiday Inn	***Type***	*Holiday Inn*	**Type**	Holiday Inn
Insert	a page break	***Insert***	*a page break*	**Insert**	a page break

Once you have typed text in the columns, you can move the insertion point by moving the mouse to the appropriate column and clicking or by pressing Alt+→ to move right one column or Alt+← to move left one column.

You must move the insertion point below the columns before you turn off the Columns feature. This step places a Column Off code [Col Off] in the document.

To turn off the Column feature:

Click	the mouse pointer at the bottom of the document	***Move***	*the insertion point to the bottom of the document*	**Move**	the insertion point to the bottom of the document

Choose	Layout	***Press***	*Alt*	**Press**	Alt+Shift+F9
Choose	Columns	***Select***	*Layout*	**Select**	Columns Off
Choose	Columns Off	***Select***	*Columns*		
		Select	*Columns Off*		

The bottom section of your screen should look like Figure 21-16.

Figure 21-16

Notice that the "Col" indicator no longer appears on the status bar.

Save the document as "paralcol" and close the document.

EXERCISE 1

INSTRUCTIONS: Define the following terms:

1. Newspaper-style columns ______________________________

   ____

2. Column type ______________________________

   ____

3. Margins ______________________________

   ____

4. Number of columns ______________________________

   ____

5. Distance between columns ______________________________

   ____

6. Columns feature ____

____

7. Parallel columns ____

____

8. Parallel with block protect ____

____

EXERCISE 2

INSTRUCTIONS: Circle T if the statement is true and F if the statement is false.

T F 1. Newspaper-style columns allow text to continue from column to column on a page.

T F 2. When using columns, you need to define the column type, column width, number of columns, distance between columns, and the left and right margins in each column.

T F 3. You can have a maximum of ten columns in a document.

T F 4. Inserting a page break breaks a column of text before the end of the page and moves the text to the next column.

T F 5. Word wrap does not occur within a column. You must press ↵Enter after every line of text.

T F 6. In parallel columns, text does not roll over into the next column when one column is full.

T F 7. When you turn the Columns feature on, a "Col" indicator is displayed before the page indicator on the status bar.

T F 8. Inserting two page breaks turns the Columns feature off.

EXERCISE 3

INSTRUCTIONS:

1. Create the following newspaper-style document. Both columns are of equal width.
2. Save the document in a file using the name "ch21ex03."
3. Print the document.
4. Close the document.

OUR TRAINING COMMITMENT

Napier & Judd, Inc. understands that analysis and communication of information are vital to your business. We are committed to helping you develop the computer skills you need to enhance productivity and business success. We have trained more than 20,000 executives, managers, professionals, and clerical employees. We provide the highest quality instructors, materials and facilities.

ABOUT OUR COURSES

Our emphasis is on quality. Participant ratings for our courses are excellent. We consistently receive very high ratings for presentation skills, knowledge of subject matter, course materials and our facilities.

Each instructor has extensive training and business experience. All courses are "hands-on." You will be assigned your own IBM compatible 80286 microcomputer with an EGA monitor.

EXERCISE 4

INSTRUCTIONS:

1. Create the following two-column document. Break the columns so that they are approximately the same length.
2. Bold and center the title "1990 LEGISLATIVE UPDATE" at the top of the page.
3. Preview, print, and save the document in a file using the name "ch21ex04."
4. Close the document.

The following bill has been passed by the State Legislature and approved by the Governor.

SENATE BILL 1004

1. This bill extends the insurance for survivors that are disabled children over the age of 18. Under this bill, the monthly survivor benefits will continue to be paid for a disabled child who is not able to engage in any active physical or mental endeavor.

2. Removes the age 70 participation limit. Currently a person employed and age 70 would not be eligible to take benefits reserved for retirement. This change will now allow persons regardless of age to take part in the retirement system payout.

3. Adds and compounds a 4 percent automatic annual increase for all retirees.

HIGHEST AWARD FOR FINANCIAL REPORTING--OUR NEWSLETTER.

The Governor's Office has just been informed that this Newsletter has been awarded the prestigious Golden Pen Award.

This award is given to those newsletters that are found to be extremely factual and full of spirit and involvement.

The Golden Pen Award is recognized by the professional as the highest award given to non-professional newsletters.

The award was presented to James L. Smirk, Deputy Director of Finance.

There are over 20,000 newsletters in the United States that are published on a regular basis. We were one of 20 selected. Congratulations to all who have helped with the information gathering.

WORKSHOPS

The State University is sponsoring two workshops dealing with Financial Planning for Retirement.

The first will be held on May 20, at the Capital Coliseum. The title is "Planning for the Future." This session will be from 1 to 3 in the afternoon.

The second will be held June 20, an all-day affair, 8 a.m. to 4 p.m. It is entitled "Seven Common Problems to Avoid."

Reserve your space now. Call (1-800-555-9999).

Current reinvestment rate of your Funds is 8.2 percent.

EXERCISE 5

INSTRUCTIONS:

1. Create the following three-column document using the Ruler. Break the columns so that they are approximately the same length.
2. Place the titles "HAWTHORNE HERALD" and "(Inside the Office)" on the first and second lines of the page. Bold and center the titles.
3. Preview, print, and save the document in a file using the name "ch21ex05."
4. Close the document.

Announcing:

There are three new employees that have joined our ranks.

Tom Brown is the new assistant to **George Bear.** Tom will coordinate the work flow between the production area and the Dock. Glad to have you with us, Tom.

Phyllis Freemont is the new Office Receptionist. She is the new voice that you now hear over the P.A. system, the telephone and the intercom. Phyllis is married and has three children. This is her second position with our company. She was here five years ago as a student intern. Happy to have you back with us, Phyllis.

Finally, but not least, **Carrie Troester.** Carrie comes to us with a new MBA in Finance. She will be in charge of the Accounting Office. Carrie was with the Temeer Corporation for five years while she went to school part time to obtain her new degree. She has vast experience in the area of Accounting. We wish her well.

CONFERENCE TRAVEL

Bill Walton is making a presentation to the local Rotary at the September 15 meeting in Hoffman Hills. Bill will be talking about the Changing Office and its impact on the workers, production and savings.

Another traveler is **Gordon Rich.** Gordon is going to Boston for the Annual Office Equipment and Furniture Show. Gordon will be presenting his paper on "**Ergonomics.**" As you may know, Gordon is considered the leading authority on this field. This is Gordon's fourth trip to speak this year.

NEW PAYROLL SYSTEM

Carrie Troester has announced that we will be receiving our pay every two weeks. This will start the beginning of October. This is a benefit that was asked for during our last wage negotiation.

FOR SALE:

86 T-Bird, low mileage. Call Sally in Graphics.

4-Bedroom home in Flint Creek. Call Jim Arrowsmith in Communications.

Appliances: Refrig., Elec. Range, Washer, Dryer, Ice Maker. Call Howard Timms in Personnel.

If you have any news that you would like printed, give it to Sharon in Personnel.

EXERCISE 6

INSTRUCTIONS:

1. Open the document "ch21ex05."
2. Place the second title "(Inside the Office)" a double space below the first title.
3. Change "Announcing:" to all capital letters.
4. In the first column, delete the sentence that begins with "Phyllis is married...."
5. Delete the last sentence about Carrie Troester in the second column.
6. Delete the last sentence about Gordon Rich -- "This is . . . ."
7. Add the following paragraph before CONFERENCE TRAVEL.
8. Readjust any spacing to create a more attractive document. Add or delete line spacing as needed.
9. Preview and print the document.
10. Save the document in a file using the name "ch21ex06."
11. Close the document.

```
OUR PRESIDENT'S DAY

In honor of Thomas J. Wakins, our president, Wednesday, October 18
will be a day off with pay.
```

EXERCISE 7

INSTRUCTIONS:

1. Create the following document using parallel columns.
2. Use three columns.
3. Centered column headings are: Day, Date, and Destination With Comments.
4. The main title is "MEDIEVAL CASTLES." It is centered and bold.
5. The secondary title is "(France, Portugal, and Spain in October)." It is a double space below the main title.
6. Preview and print the document.
7. Save the document in a file using the name "ch21ex07."
8. Close the document.

MEDIEVAL CASTLES
(France, Portugal, and Spain)

Day	Date	Destination / Comments
Sunday	Oct. 8, 1992	Bordeaux, France. Arrive from your city by noon - Bordeaux time.
Monday	Oct. 9	Bordeaux / Dordogne. Visit Ice Age caves and local castles.
Tuesday	Oct. 10	The Castle of Beynac. The castle sits atop a 500-foot high bluff.
Wednesday	Oct. 11	Santander, Spain. Visit 13th Century Torre del Merino.
Thursday	Oct. 12	Granada, Spain. Visit the Alhambra Hill, including the citadel.
Friday	Oct. 13	Figueria da Foz, Portugal. Visit the university founded in 1290. Visit Conimbriga site of Roman castle ruins.
Saturday	Oct. 14	Barcelona, Spain. Visit the Gothic Quarters.
Sunday	Oct. 15	Return home from Barcelona.

EXERCISE 8

INSTRUCTIONS:

1. Create the following document. Use two parallel columns.
2. Set the margins for Column 1 to be a 1" left and 3" right margin. Set the margins for Column 2 to be a 3.5" left and 7.5" right margin.
3. Center the main title.
4. Preview the document.
5. Save the document in a file using the name "ch21ex08."
6. Print the document.
7. Close the document.

OFFICE INFORMATION AUTOMATION SOCIETY

OIAS PURPOSE	To offer a symposium for members to exchange ideas among business and academic members. This knowledge will facilitate research that will help the office workplace.
	To publicize Office Information Automation as a body of knowledge in analysis, design, and administrative decision support.
	To encourage members to apply research to the problems inherent to Office Information Automation for immediate needs of both the small and large business enterprise.
OIAS ACTIVITIES	**Newsletter** -- published monthly. Update activities, conferences, research projects.
	Journal -- Contains major excerpts from the research projects taken on by the members.
	Research Conference -- A two-day conference where ideas and projects are discussed in theory and reality.
STRUCTURE	1. Faculty members, students in the OIAS field.
	2. Administrators in business and government in the Office Information Automation area.
	3. Administrators, Research Directors, and Vendors in the field of Office Information.
	There is an Executive Board that oversees the organization.
MEMBERSHIP	To apply for membership, mail your check for $150 to: Dr. Wendell Harris, OIAS Treasurer. The full address will be found in the letterhead at the top of this page.

CHAPTER TWENTY-TWO

TABLES

OBJECTIVES

In this chapter, you will learn to:

- Create a table
- Edit a table
- Create a table using the Ruler

CHAPTER OVERVIEW

At times you may want to include a table in a document. This table can have numbers, text, or formulas. The Tables feature allows you to create tables and organize the information in rows and columns. This feature provides speed and flexibility. It is easy to move through the table, and formatting the text is simple.

In this chapter, the procedures for creating and editing a table are described and shown.

CREATING A TABLE

A table is a grid that is organized into columns and rows. A column is a set of information that runs down the page. A row runs across the page. A cell occurs where each column and row meet. Columns have alphabetic names and rows have numeric names. A cell's name is a combination of the column and row name. For example, cell "C5" is in the third column (C is the third letter in the alphabet) and in the fifth row. Figure 22-1 shows an example of a table.

Figure 22-1

PROJECT	BUDGETED HOURS	EST. COMPLETION	ASSIGNED TO
Jones report on therapy unit	21	9/21/90	Karen Hanson
Marketing research on diet centers	470	11/15/90	Jack Swanson Marla Masters
Summary report on all nursing units	5	9/16/90	Karen Hanson
Weekly Census Report on Patient Days	5	9/17/90	Mark Myers
Physician Summary Report	3	9/17/90	Mark Myers

Suppose you want to make a table for the office, telephone, and supplies expenses of a company. The organization has five district offices for which the data for these types of expenses are available. The table has four columns and seven rows. The columns are District name, Office expenses, Telephone expenses, and Supplies expenses. The first row contains the company name and title of the table. The second row contains headings information for the columns. The remaining rows contain the district name, the amount of office expenses, the amount of telephone expenses, and the amount of supplies expenses for a specific district.

Change the default directory to "a:\wpdocs" or to "c:\wpdocs."

To create a table:

Choose	Layout	***Press***	*Alt*	**Press**	Ctrl + F9
Choose	Tables	***Select***	*Layout*	**Select**	Create
Choose	Create	***Select***	*Tables*		
		Select	*Create*		

Your screen should look like Figure 22-2.

Figure 22-2

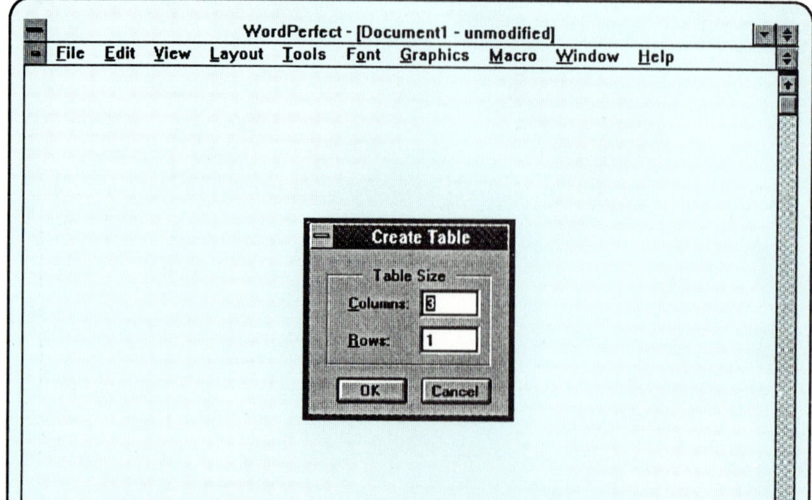

WordPerfect assumes that you want three columns.

To indicate the number of columns is four:

Type	4	***Type***	*4*	**Type**	4

Your screen should look like Figure 22-3.

Figure 22-3

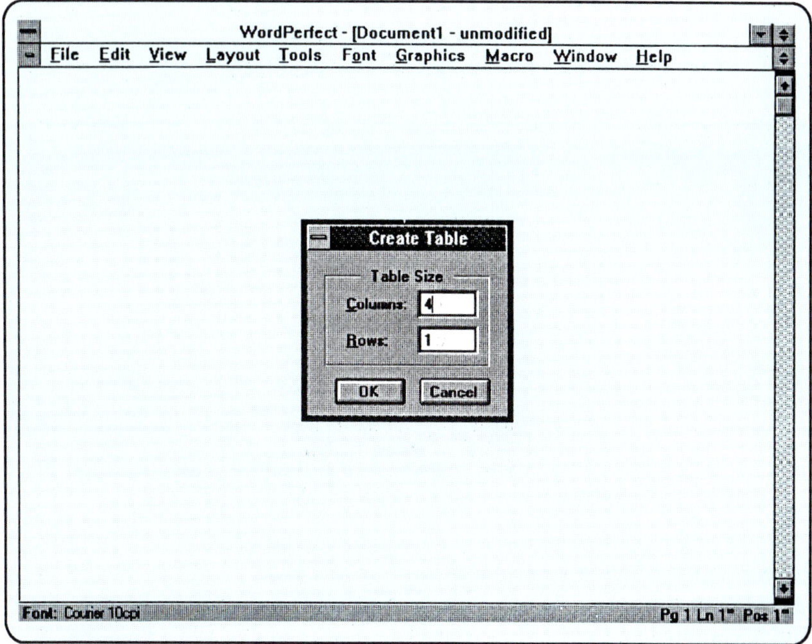

WordPerfect assumes that you want one row.

To enter the number of rows:

Double-click	the Rows text box	***Press***	*Alt+R to select the Rows text box*	**Press**	Alt+R to select the Rows text box
Type	7	***Type***	*7*	**Type**	7
Click	the OK command button	***Press***	*↵Enter*	**Press**	↵Enter

The top part of your screen should look like Figure 22-4.

Figure 22-4

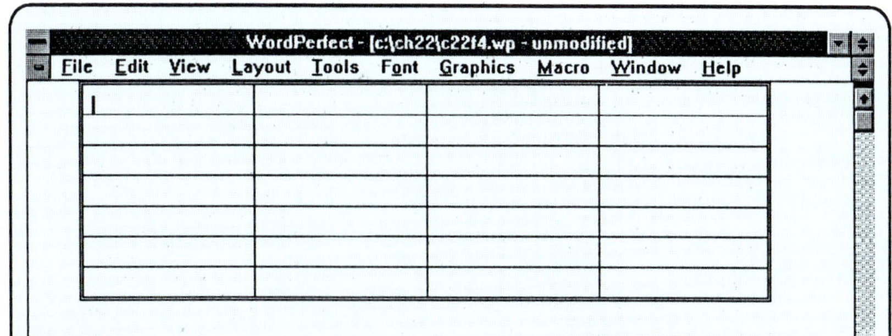

A table is shown on your screen with lines dividing the rows and columns into cells. When you are printing the table, the lines may or may not print depending on the graphics capability of your printer.

To move the insertion point to the cell at the beginning of the second row:

Click
at the beginning of the second row
Press
↓
Press
↓

The top part of your screen should look like Figure 22-5.

Figure 22-5

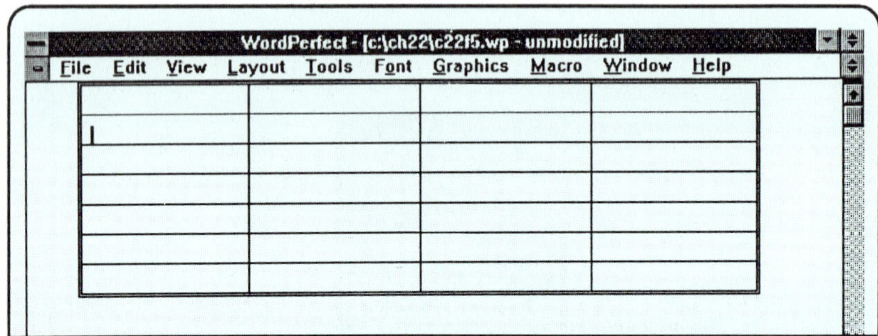

The insertion point appears in the current cell. The current cell name is displayed on the status bar after "Cell." Currently you are in cell A2.

You can use the mouse or the pointer-movement keys to move through a table. To move through a table using the mouse, point at the cell that you want to move to and click the mouse button. To move through a table using the keyboard, you press the appropriate pointer-movement keys. The following is a list of table locations and the pointer-movement keys that allow you to move to that location.

Location	Pointer-movement Keys
One cell down	↓ if the cell does not contain more than one line of text Alt+↓
One cell left	Shift+Tab Alt+←
One cell right	Tab Alt+→
One cell up	↑ if the cell does not contain more than one line of text Alt+↑
First cell in a row	Home, Home
Last cell in a row	End, End
Specific cell	Choose Edit, Go To, Specific Cell

You can enter text in the table as you normally would in any other document. You can also change the structure and format of the table.

As you format the table, you will need to select cells so that you can change them. When you are working on tables, the mouse pointer can become a selection arrow. This selection arrow allows you to easily select parts of the table.

If you move the mouse pointer to the top of a cell, the mouse pointer becomes a vertical selection arrow similar to the one in Figure 22-6.

Figure 22-6

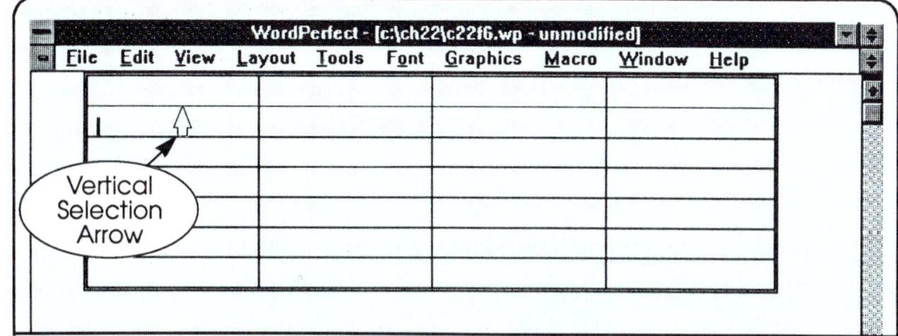

The vertical selection arrow allows you to highlight a column.

If you move the mouse pointer to the left of a cell, the mouse pointer becomes a horizontal selection arrow similar to the one in Figure 22-7.

Figure 22-7

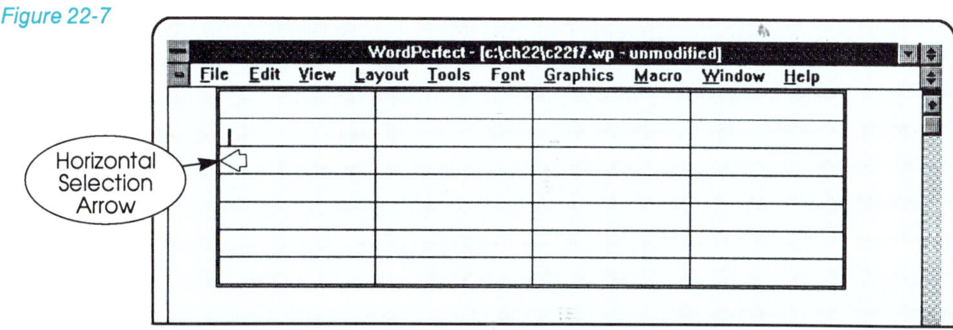

The horizontal selection arrow allows you to highlight a row.

You can also select cells in a table using the keyboard. To select cells in a table using the keyboard, press Shift+F8 and then the appropriate pointer-movement keys.

The following is a list of table selection techniques.

Selection	Mouse	Keyboard
Cell	Click while the mouse pointer is a selection arrow	Press Shift+F8
Several cells	Select the first cell and drag across the other cells	Select first cell and hold down the Shift key and a pointer-movement key to select the other cells
Column	Double-click while the mouse pointer is a vertical selection arrow	Select a cell in the column and press Ctrl+↓ or Ctrl+↑

Selection	Mouse	Keyboard
Row	Double-click while the mouse pointer is a horizontal selection arrow	Select a cell in the row and press Ctrl+→ or Ctrl+←
Table	Triple-click while the mouse pointer is a selection arrow	Select a cell in the table, press Ctrl+↓ or Ctrl+↑ and Ctrl+→ or Ctrl+←

As long as the insertion point is in the table, the "Cell" indicator appears on the status bar.

Turn on the Reveal Codes feature.

The lower part of your screen should look like Figure 22-8.

Figure 22-8

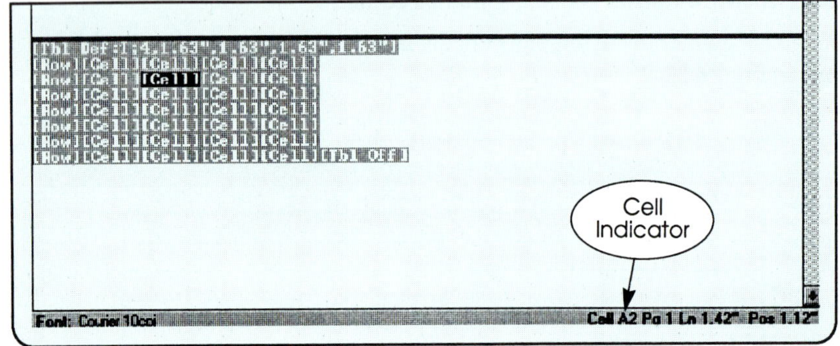

The Table Definition code and the Table Off code tell where the table begins and ends. The Row and Cell codes tell where the rows and cells begin and end.

As long as the Table Definition code exists, you cannot delete the Cell, Row, or Table Off codes. If you delete the Table Definition code, then you can delete the entire table, the contents of the table, or the table structure.

Turn off the Reveal Codes feature.

At this time, you can enter data into the table. Row 1 is set aside for the company name and title of the table, which you will enter in the next section of this chapter. Column headings are placed in row 2.

To enter the column headings in row 2:

Click	on cell A2	***Move***	*the insertion point to cell A2*	**Move**	the insertion point to cell A2
Type	District	***Type***	*District*	**Type**	District
Click	on cell B2	***Press***	*Tab*	**Press**	Tab
Type	Office	***Type***	*Office*	**Type**	Office
Click	on cell C2	***Press***	*Tab*	**Press**	Tab
Type	Telephone	***Type***	*Telephone*	**Type**	Telephone
Click	on cell D2	***Press***	*Tab*	**Press**	Tab
Type	Supplies	***Type***	*Supplies*	**Type**	Supplies

The top part of your screen should look like Figure 22-9.

Figure 22-9

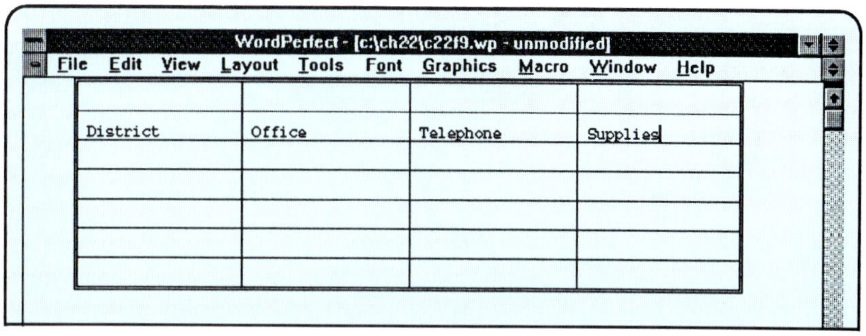

District	Office	Telephone	Supplies

Complete the table in Figure 22-10. To move the insertion point forward a cell, click on that cell or press Tab. To move the insertion point to a previous cell, click on that cell or press Shift+Tab. If you accidentally press ←Enter, press ←Backspace to return the row back to its original height. Pressing ←Enter inserts a hard return and moves the insertion point to the next line in the cell.

Figure 22-10

District	Office	Telephone	Supplies
Central	$38,000.50	$2,310.00	$11,810.98
Eastern	31,645.61	4,412.31	7,881.22
Midwest	53,760.75	3,708.78	8,544.65
Mountain	48,145.25	6,974.96	5,221.88
Western	40,746.41	8,418.77	10,550.29

■ EDITING A TABLE

After you create a table, you may want to change or edit it. You can use the Table menu to enhance the appearance of the table. If you are using the mouse, you can select the "tables.wwb" Button Bar to format and edit the table. This Button Bar contains a button for each Table menu option.

Check for the "Cell" prompt on the status bar to make sure the insertion point is in the table. If the insertion point is not in the table, move the insertion point to any cell in the table.

Choose	Layout	***Press***	*Alt*	**Press**	Ctrl+F9
Choose	Tables	***Select***	*Layout*		
		Select	*Tables*		

Your screen should look like Figure 22-11.

Figure 22-11

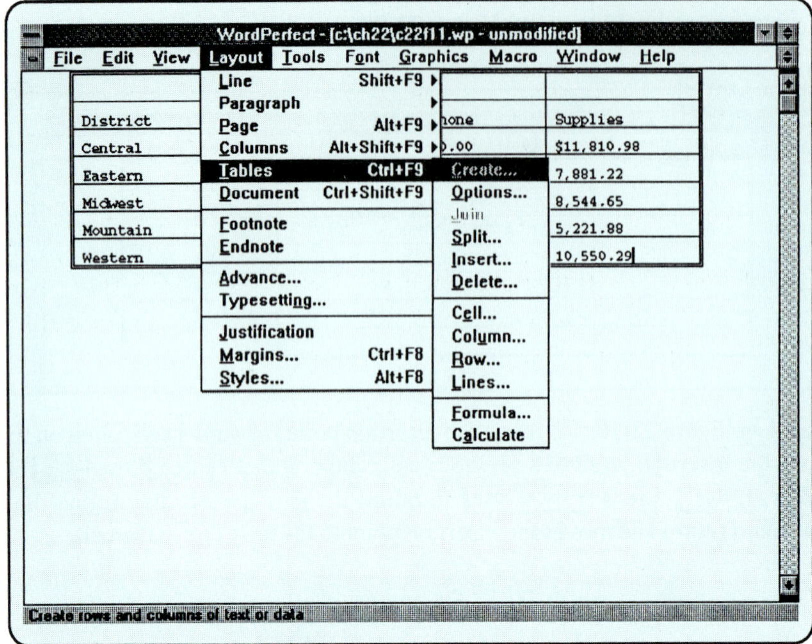

The Table menu options are described below:

Options - This option allows you to change the size, cell margins, gray shading, and negative number display of a table. You can also change the table position and designate one or more rows to appear at the top of every page for large tables. You can also turn off all cell protection using this option.

Join - Join several columns or rows together using the Select feature.

Split - Split a column or row.

Insert - Insert a column or row.

Delete - Delete a column or row.

Cell - This option allows you to change the appearance, size, justification, and alignment of text in a cell. You can also shade and protect a cell using this option.

Column - This option allows you to change appearance, size, or justification of text in a column. You can also adjust the column width or determine the number of decimal places for a column.

Row - This option allows you to set the number of lines per row and the height of a row.

Lines - The lines around a table can be changed in degrees of thickness. Use the Select feature to change the lines of more than one cell.

Formula - Tables can contain mathematical formulas. This option allows you to create formulas and place them in one or more cells.

Calculate - Calculates the formulas in a table.

To exit the Layout Tables option:

Click	on the Layout menu on the menu bar	***Press***	*Esc three times*	**Press**	Esc three times

Suppose you want to enter the company name and title of the table in the first row. You need only one cell in the first row for the entire table heading. You can use the Join option to join the four cells into one cell that stretches from the left margin to the right margin of the table. You must first select the cells that you want to join, and then choose the Join option.

To join the first row of cells:

Move	the mouse pointer to the first row of cells so that it appears as a horizontal selection arrow	***Move***	*the insertion point to the first row of cells*	**Move**	the insertion point to the first row of cells
Double-click	on the first row of cells	***Press***	*Shift+F8*	**Press**	Shift+F8
Choose	Layout	***Press***	*Ctrl+→*	**Press**	Ctrl+→
Choose	Tables	***Press***	*Alt*	**Press**	Ctrl+F9
Choose	Join	***Select***	*Layout*	**Select**	Join
		Select	*Tables*		
		Select	*Join*		

The Join option works only when the Select feature is on.

To enter the heading:

Type	JOHNSON PARTNERS	***Type***	*JOHNSON PARTNERS*	**Type**	JOHNSON PARTNERS
Press	↵Enter	***Press***	*↵Enter*	**Press**	↵Enter
Type	DISTRICT EXPENSE REPORT	***Type***	*DISTRICT EXPENSE REPORT*	**Type**	DISTRICT EXPENSE REPORT
Press	↵Enter	***Press***	*↵Enter*	**Press**	↵Enter
Type	First Quarter	***Type***	*First Quarter*	**Type**	First Quarter

You can format text in a table by choosing the Cell option from the Table menu. Through this option, the table heading can be bold and centered.

Choose	Layout	***Press***	*Alt*	**Press**	Ctrl+F9
Choose	Tables	***Select***	*Layout*	**Select**	Cell

Choose	Cell	***Select***	*Tables*		
		Select	*Cell*		

Your screen should look like Figure 22-12.

Figure 22-12

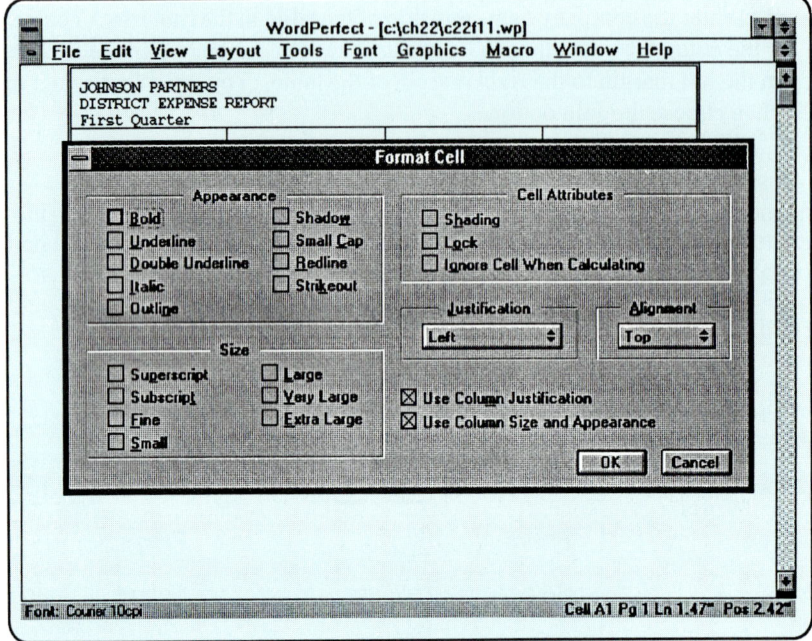

The Format Cell dialog box gives you broad formatting capabilities for the data in your table. These options are described below:

Appearance - This option allows you to change the appearance of the text in the cell.

Size - You can change the size of the text in the cell using this option.

Cell Attributes - You can shade a cell, protect or lock a cell, and restrict a cell from calculating.

Justification - You can change the justification of the cell to left, full, center, right, or decimal align.

Alignment - You can align the text at the top, bottom, or center of the cell.

To center the text in the cell:

Click	the Justification pop-up list button	***Press***	*Alt+J to select the Justification pop-up list button*	**Press**	Alt+J to select the Justification pop-up list button

Hold down	the mouse button to view the pop-up list	***Press***	*Alt+↑ to view the pop-up list*	**Press**	Alt+↑ to view the pop-up list
Choose	Center	***Type***	*C to select the Center option*	**Type**	C to select the Center option

To bold the text in the cell:

Click	the Bold check box until an X appears	***Press***	*Alt+B until an X appears in the Bold check box*	**Press**	Alt+B until an X appears in the Bold check box

To accept the cell formats:

Click	the OK command button	Press	↵Enter	Press	↵Enter

Your screen should look like Figure 22-13.

Figure 22-13

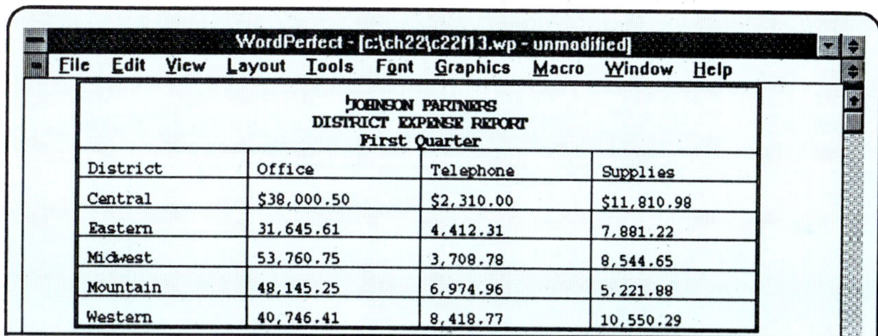

The text is now centered and bold.

To format a row, you must use the Select feature. To bold and center the column titles:

Move	the mouse pointer to the second row so that it appears as a horizontal selection arrow	***Move***	*the insertion point to the second row*	**Move**	the insertion point to the second row
Double-click	on the second row	***Press***	*Shift+F8*	**Press**	Shift+F8
Choose	Layout	***Press***	*Ctrl+→ or Ctrl+←*	**Press**	Ctrl+→ or Ctrl+←
Choose	Tables	***Press***	*Alt*	**Press**	Ctrl+F9
Choose	Cell	***Select***	*Layout*	**Select**	Cell
		Select	*Tables*		
		Select	*Cell*		

To select the bold and center options:

Click	the Bold check box until an X appears	***Press***	*Alt+B until an X appears in the Bold check box*	**Press**	Alt+B until an X appears in the Bold check box
Click	the Justification pop-up list button	***Press***	*Alt+J to select the Justification pop-up list button*	**Press**	Alt+J to select the Justification pop-up list button
Hold down	the mouse button to view the pop-up list	***Press***	*Alt+↑ to view the pop-up list*	**Press**	Alt+↑ to view the pop-up list
Choose	Center	***Type***	*C to select the Center option*	**Type**	C to select the Center option

To accept the cell formats:

Click	the OK command button	***Press***	*↵Enter*	**Press**	↵Enter

After you move to cell D3, the top part of your screen should look like Figure 22-14.

Figure 22-14

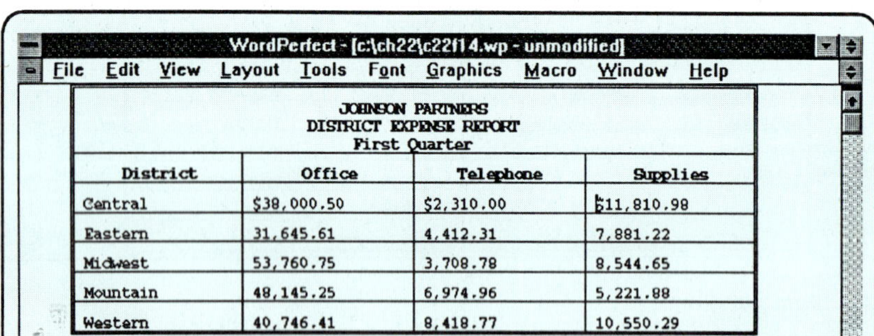

JOHNSON PARTNERS
DISTRICT EXPENSE REPORT
First Quarter

District	Office	Telephone	Supplies
Central	$38,000.50	$2,310.00	$11,810.98
Eastern	31,645.61	4,412.31	7,881.22
Midwest	53,760.75	3,708.78	8,544.65
Mountain	48,145.25	6,974.96	5,221.88
Western	40,746.41	8,418.77	10,550.29

The column titles are now centered and bold.

You can also format the numbers in the cells. To format the data so it is decimal-aligned in cell B3:

Click	on cell B3	***Move***	*the insertion point to cell B3*	**Move**	the insertion point to cell B3
Choose	Layout	***Press***	*Alt*	**Press**	Ctrl+F9
Choose	Tables	***Select***	*Layout*	**Select**	Cell
Choose	Cell	***Select***	*Tables*	**Press**	Alt+J to select the Justification pop-up list button
Click	the Justification pop-up list button	***Select***	*Cell*	**Press**	Alt+↑ to view the pop-up list
Hold down	the mouse button to view the pop-up list	***Press***	*Alt+J to select the Justification pop-up list button*	**Type**	D to select the Decimal Align option

Choose the Decimal Align option

Click the OK command button

Press *Alt+↑ to view the pop-up list*

Type *D to select the Decimal Align option*

Press *↵Enter*

Press ↵Enter

The top part of your screen should look like Figure 22-15.

Figure 22-15

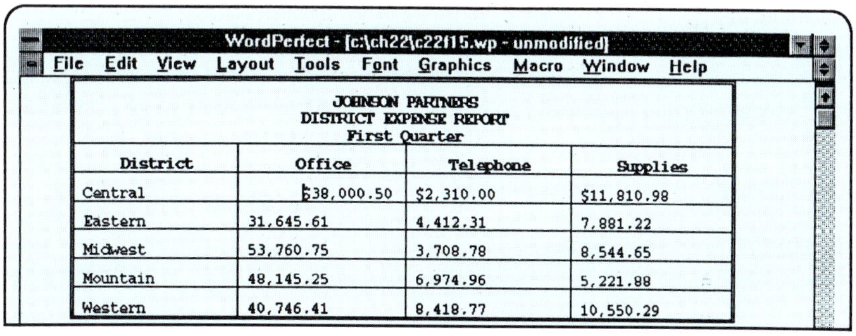

WordPerfect - [c:\ch22\c22f15.wp - unmodified]

File Edit View Layout Tools Font Graphics Macro Window Help

JOHNSON PARTNERS DISTRICT EXPENSE REPORT First Quarter			
District	Office	Telephone	Supplies
Central	$38,000.50	$2,310.00	$11,810.98
Eastern	31,645.61	4,412.31	7,881.22
Midwest	53,760.75	3,708.78	8,544.65
Mountain	48,145.25	6,974.96	5,221.88
Western	40,746.41	8,418.77	10,550.29

Notice that the number in cell B3 is right justified and aligned on the decimal point.

You can also format an entire column at a time. To decimal-align the data in column B:

Click on column B

Choose Layout

Choose Tables

Choose Column

Click the Justification pop-up list button

Hold down the mouse button to view the pop-up list

Choose Decimal Align

Click the OK command button

Move *the insertion point to column B*

Press *Alt*

Select *Layout*

Select *Tables*

Select *Column*

Press *Alt+J to select the Justification pop-up list button*

Press *Alt+↑ to view the pop-up list*

Type *D to select the Decimal Align option*

Press *↵Enter*

Move the insertion point to column B

Press Ctrl+F9

Select Column

Press Alt+J to select the Justification pop-up list button

Press Alt+↑ to view the pop-up list

Type D to select the Decimal Align option

Press ↵Enter

The top part of your screen should look like Figure 22-16.

Figure 22-16

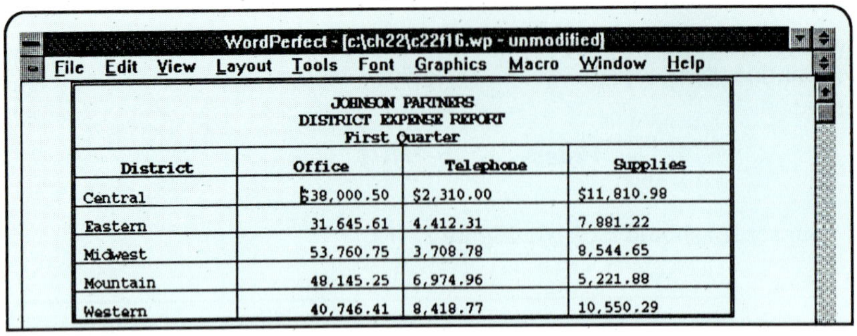

WordPerfect - [c:\ch22\c22f16.wp - unmodified]

File Edit View Layout Tools Font Graphics Macro Window Help

JOHNSON PARTNERS DISTRICT EXPENSE REPORT First Quarter			
District	**Office**	**Telephone**	**Supplies**
Central	$38,000.50	$2,310.00	$11,810.98
Eastern	31,645.61	4,412.31	7,881.22
Midwest	53,760.75	3,708.78	8,544.65
Mountain	48,145.25	6,974.96	5,221.88
Western	40,746.41	8,418.77	10,550.29

Notice that the "Office" column title stayed bold and centered. This cell was formatted with the Cell feature under the Tables options. Column formats do not affect cells that were formatted using the Cell feature.

To format column C to also be decimal aligned:

Click	on column C	***Move***	*the insertion point to column C*	**Move**	the insertion point to column C
Choose	Layout	***Press***	*Alt*	**Press**	Ctrl+F9
Choose	Tables	***Select***	*Layout*	**Select**	Column
Choose	Column	***Select***	*Tables*	**Press**	Alt+J to select the Justification pop-up list button
Click	the Justification pop-up list button	***Select***	*Column*	**Press**	Alt+↑ to view the pop-up list
Hold down	the mouse button to view the pop-up list	***Press***	*Alt+J to select the Justification pop-up list button*	**Type**	D to select the Decimal Align option
Choose	Decimal Align	***Press***	*Alt+↑ to view the pop-up list*	**Press**	↵Enter
Click	the OK command button	***Type***	*D to select the Decimal Align option*		
		Press	*↵Enter*		

To format column D to be decimal aligned:

Click	on column D	***Move***	*the insertion point to column D*	**Move**	the insertion point to column D
Choose	Layout	***Press***	*Alt*	**Press**	Ctrl+F9
Choose	Tables	***Select***	*Layout*	**Select**	Column
Choose	Column	***Select***	*Tables*	**Press**	Alt+J to select the Justification pop-up list button

Click	the Justification pop-up list button	***Select***	*Column*	**Press**	Alt+↑ to view the pop-up list
Hold down	the mouse button to view the pop-up list	***Press***	*Alt+J to select the Justification pop-up list button*	**Type**	D to select the Decimal Align option
Choose	Decimal Align	***Press***	*Alt+↑ to view the pop-up list*	**Press**	↵Enter
Click	the OK command button	***Type***	*D to select the Decimal Align option*		
		Press	*↵Enter*		

The top part of your screen should look like Figure 22-17.

Figure 22-17

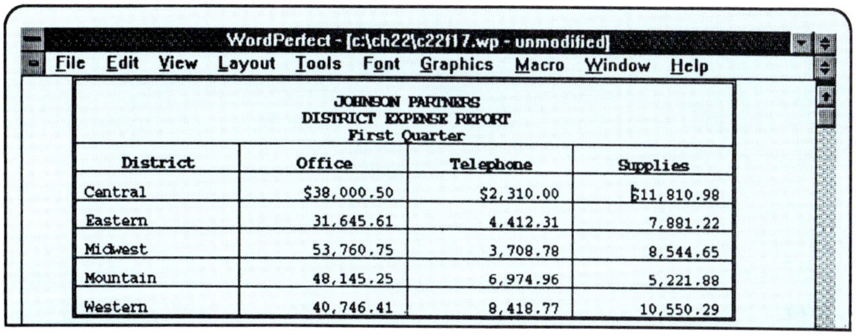

WordPerfect - [c:\ch22\c22f17.wp - unmodified]

File Edit View Layout Tools Font Graphics Macro Window Help

JOHNSON PARTNERS
DISTRICT EXPENSE REPORT
First Quarter

District	Office	Telephone	Supplies
Central	$38,000.50	$2,310.00	$11,810.98
Eastern	31,645.61	4,412.31	7,881.22
Midwest	53,760.75	3,708.78	8,544.65
Mountain	48,145.25	6,974.96	5,221.88
Western	40,746.41	8,418.77	10,550.29

In This Book

To select the cells in a table using the mouse, you move the mouse pointer in the table so that it appears as a selection arrow and click. To select cells with the keyboard, you move to the proper cell, press Shift+F8 to turn on the Select feature, and press a pointer-movement key. For the remaining portion of this book, you are asked simply to select the cells in the table. You can use either of the methods for selecting the cells.

You can also change the style of the lines surrounding the cells. To change the lines above and below the column titles so they are thicker:

Select	cells A2 through D2	***Select***	*cells A2 through D2*	**Select**	cells A2 through D2
Choose	Layout	***Press***	*Alt*	**Press**	Ctrl+F9
Choose	Tables	***Select***	*Layout*	**Select**	Lines
Choose	Lines	***Select***	*Tables*	**Press**	Alt+T to select the Top pop-up list button
Click	on the Top pop-up list button	***Select***	*Lines*	**Press**	Alt+↑ to view the pop-up list

Hold down	the mouse button to view the pop-up list
Choose	Thick
Click	the Bottom pop-up list button
Hold down	the mouse button to view the pop-up list
Choose	Thick
Click	the OK command button

Press	*Alt+T to select the Top pop-up list*
Press	*Alt+↑ to view the pop-up list*
Type	*T to select the Thick option*
Press	*Alt+B to select the Bottom pop-up list button*
Press	*Alt+↑ to view the pop-up list*
Type	*T to select the Thick option*
Press	*↵Enter*

Type	T to select the Thick option
Press	Alt+B to select the Bottom pop-up list button
Press	Alt+↑ to view the pop-up list
Type	T to select the Thick option
Press	↵Enter

Deselect the cells in the table by clicking in the document area or moving the insertion point. The top part of your screen should look like Figure 22-18.

Figure 22-18

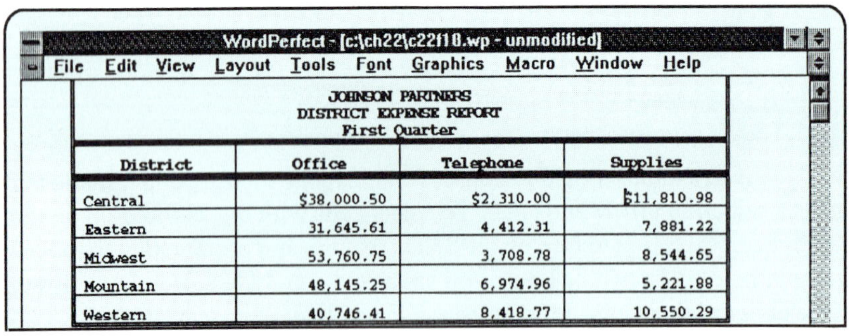

WordPerfect - [c:\ch22\c22f18.wp - unmodified]

File Edit View Layout Tools Font Graphics Macro Window Help

JOHNSON PARTNERS
DISTRICT EXPENSE REPORT
First Quarter

District	Office	Telephone	Supplies
Central	$38,000.50	$2,310.00	$11,810.98
Eastern	31,645.61	4,412.31	7,881.22
Midwest	53,760.75	3,708.78	8,544.65
Mountain	48,145.25	6,974.96	5,221.88
Western	40,746.41	8,418.77	10,550.29

You can add more information to a table by inserting rows or columns. You can use the Tables Insert feature to insert rows or columns. You can delete rows and columns using the Tables Delete feature.

You can also add a row to a table by pressing Alt+Insert. A new row is created at the insertion point. To insert a row below the row where the insertion point is located, press Alt+Shift+Insert. You can delete the current row by pressing Alt+Delete.

Suppose you want to insert a row to include the Southern district. To insert a row between Mountain and Western:

Click	on cell A7
Choose	Layout

Move	*the insertion point to cell A7*
Press	*Alt*

Move	the insertion point to cell A7
Press	Alt+Insert

Choose	Tables
Choose	Insert
Click	the Rows option button
Click	the OK command button

Select	*Layout*
Select	*Tables*
Select	*Insert*
Press	*Alt+R to select the Rows option button*
Press	*↵Enter*

If you want to insert more than one row or column, you should use the Insert option under the Tables option from the Layout menu. The top part of your screen should look like Figure 22-19.

Figure 22-19

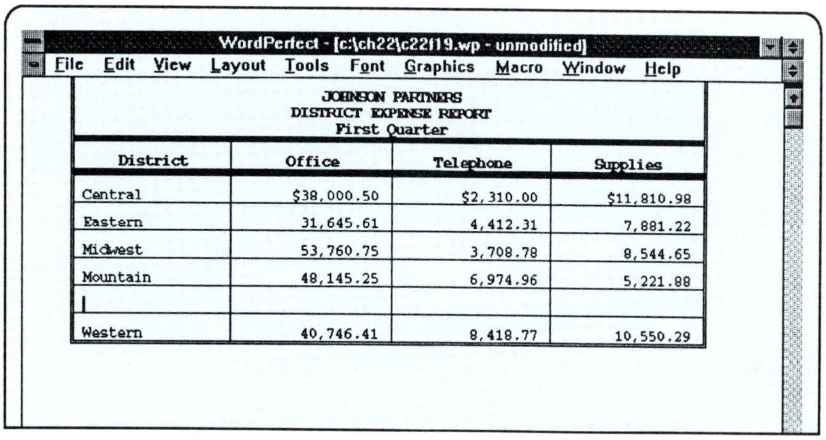

WordPerfect - [c:\ch22\c22f19.wp - unmodified]

File Edit View Layout Tools Font Graphics Macro Window Help

JOHNSON PARTNERS DISTRICT EXPENSE REPORT First Quarter			
District	**Office**	**Telephone**	**Supplies**
Central	$38,000.50	$2,310.00	$11,810.98
Eastern	31,645.61	4,412.31	7,881.22
Midwest	53,760.75	3,708.78	8,544.65
Mountain	48,145.25	6,974.96	5,221.88
Western	40,746.41	8,418.77	10,550.29

An empty row with four columns is inserted between the rows for the Mountain and Western districts. To enter data for the Southern district:

Type	Southern
Click	on cell B7
Type	34,706.21
Click	on cell C7
Type	11,142.46
Click	on cell D7
Type	15,211.75

Type	*Southern*
Press	*Tab*
Type	*34,706.21*
Press	*Tab*
Type	*11,142.46*
Press	*Tab*
Type	*15,211.75*

Type	Southern
Press	Tab
Type	34,706.21
Press	Tab
Type	11,142.46
Press	Tab
Type	15,211.75

The top part of your screen should look like Figure 22-20.

Figure 22-20

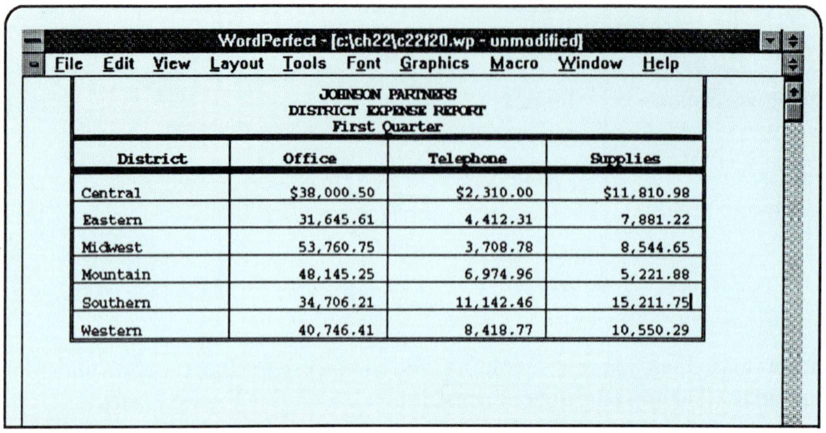

WordPerfect - [c:\ch22\c22f20.wp - unmodified]

File Edit View Layout Tools Font Graphics Macro Window Help

JOHNSON PARTNERS
DISTRICT EXPENSE REPORT
First Quarter

District	Office	Telephone	Supplies
Central	$38,000.50	$2,310.00	$11,810.98
Eastern	31,645.61	4,412.31	7,881.22
Midwest	53,760.75	3,708.78	8,544.65
Mountain	48,145.25	6,974.96	5,221.88
Southern	34,706.21	11,142.46	15,211.75
Western	40,746.41	8,418.77	10,550.29

Notice that the information is formatted using the formats previously defined.

You can also perform calculations on the numbers in a table. Suppose you want to sum the numbers in the office, telephone, and supplies columns to obtain a total for these expense categories.

The Tables Size feature allows you to increase the size of a table. To access the Tables Size feature, choose Options from the Tables option under the Layout menu. You should use the Size option to add a row to the bottom of the table or a column to the outside of the table. You can also use the Alt+Shift+Insert keys to add a row to the bottom of the table. To add a row to the bottom of the table:

Choose	Layout	***Press***	*Alt*	**Move**	the insertion point to cell A8
Choose	Tables	***Select***	*Layout*	**Press**	Alt+Shift+Insert
Choose	Options	***Select***	*Tables*		
Double-click	the Rows text box in the Table Size box	***Select***	*Options*		
Type	9	***Press***	*Alt+R to select the Rows text box in the Table Size box*		
Click	the OK command button	***Type***	*9*		
		Press	*↵Enter*		

A new row is added to the bottom of the table. This row will be used for the totals. You need to create a formula to calculate these totals. One of the easiest formulas you can create is one that sums a column. This is done by choosing Formula from the Tables option under the Layout menu.

Click	on cell B9	***Move***	*the insertion point to cell B9*	**Move**	the insertion point to cell B9
Choose	Layout	***Press***	*Alt*	**Press**	Ctrl+F9
Choose	Tables	***Select***	*Layout*	**Select**	Formula

Choose	Formula	***Select***	*Tables*		
		Select	*Formula*		

The Tables Formula dialog box appears. Your screen should look like Figure 22-21.

Figure 22-21

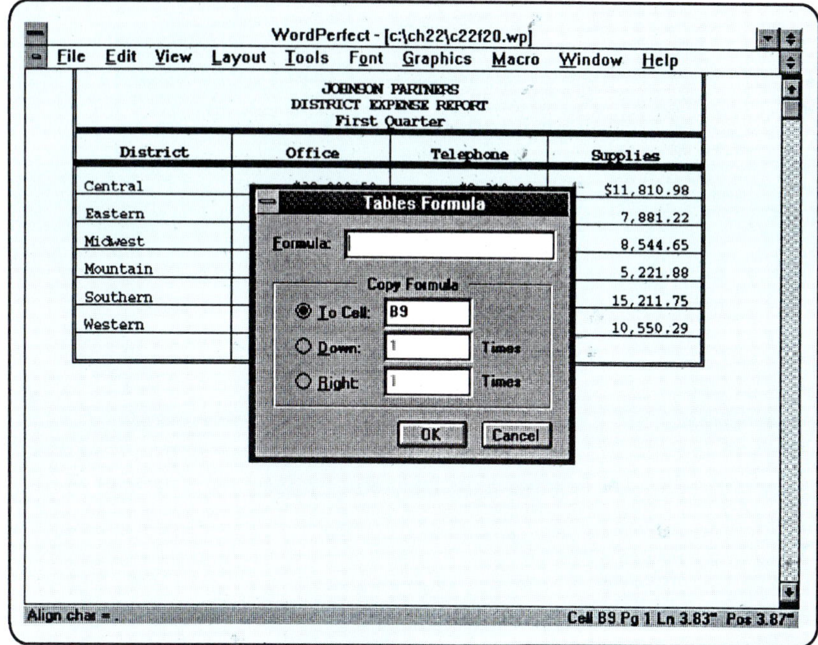

There are three types of "automatic" formulas called functions. By placing a +, =, or * in the cell, you can get a subtotal(+), total(=), or grand total(*) for the column. The grand total function sums totals. The total function sums subtotals. The subtotal function sums the numbers.

To insert the subtotal function in cell B9:

Type	+	***Type***	+	**Type**	+
Click	the OK command button	***Press***	*↵Enter*	**Press**	↵Enter

Your screen should look like Figure 22-22.

Figure 22-22

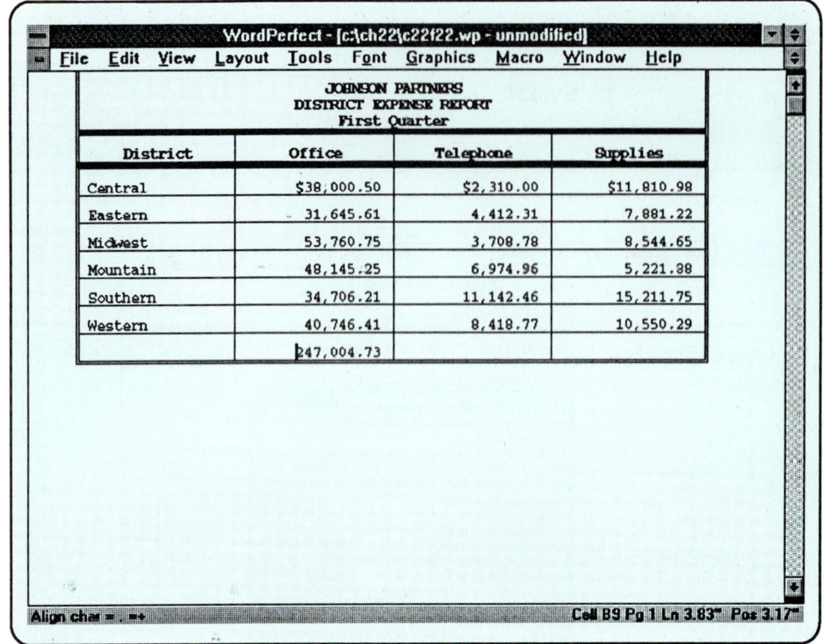

JOHNSON PARTNERS
DISTRICT EXPENSE REPORT
First Quarter

District	Office	Telephone	Supplies
Central	$38,000.50	$2,310.00	$11,810.98
Eastern	31,645.61	4,412.31	7,881.22
Midwest	53,760.75	3,708.78	8,544.65
Mountain	48,145.25	6,974.96	5,221.88
Southern	34,706.21	11,142.46	15,211.75
Western	40,746.41	8,418.77	10,550.29
	247,004.73		

The total appears in the cell. The number calculated when a formula is defined for a cell is called the "result."

To insert the subtotal function in cell C9:

Click	on cell C9	***Move***	*the insertion point to cell C9*	**Move**	the insertion point to cell C9
Choose	Layout	***Press***	*Alt*	**Press**	Ctrl+F9
Choose	Tables	***Select***	*Layout*	**Select**	Formula
Choose	Formula	***Select***	*Tables*	**Type**	+
Type	+	***Select***	*Formula*	**Press**	↵Enter
Click	the OK command button	***Type***	*+*		
		Press	*↵Enter*		

To insert the subtotal function in cell D9:

Click	on cell D9	***Move***	*the insertion point to cell D9*	**Move**	the insertion point to cell D9
Choose	Layout	***Press***	*Alt*	**Press**	Ctrl+F9
Choose	Tables	***Select***	*Layout*	**Select**	Formula
Choose	Formula	***Select***	*Tables*	**Type**	+
Type	+	***Select***	*Formula*	**Press**	↵Enter
Click	the OK command button	***Type***	*+*		
		Press	*↵Enter*		

To add a title to the row:

Click	on cell A9	***Move***	*the insertion point to cell A9*	**Move**	the insertion point to cell A9
Type	Total	***Type***	*Total*	**Type**	Total

The top part of your screen should look like Figure 22-23.

Figure 22-23

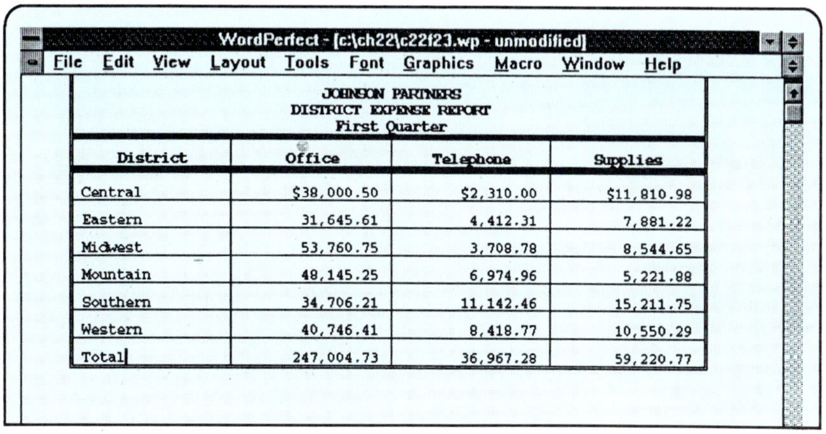

WordPerfect - [c:\ch22\c22f23.wp - unmodified]

File Edit View Layout Tools Font Graphics Macro Window Help

JOHNSON PARTNERS
DISTRICT EXPENSE REPORT
First Quarter

District	Office	Telephone	Supplies
Central	$38,000.50	$2,310.00	$11,810.98
Eastern	31,645.61	4,412.31	7,881.22
Midwest	53,760.75	3,708.78	8,544.65
Mountain	48,145.25	6,974.96	5,221.88
Southern	34,706.21	11,142.46	15,211.75
Western	40,746.41	8,418.77	10,550.29
Total	247,004.73	36,967.28	59,220.77

The totals for the expenses categories now appear on the screen.

Suppose you want to add a column so you can determine total expenses for each district. You also need to compute a grand total for all expenses. Besides using the formula functions, you can create your own formulas for a cell.

You can use the Tables Size feature to add a column to the right of the table. You can also divide the Supplies column in half by using the Split option.

To split the Supplies column into two columns:

Click	on cell D2	***Move***	*the insertion point to cell D2*	**Move**	the insertion point to cell D2
Select	the Supplies column	***Select***	*the Supplies column*	**Select**	the Supplies column
Choose	Layout	***Press***	*Alt*	**Press**	Ctrl+F9
Choose	Tables	***Select***	*Layout*	**Select**	Split
Choose	Split	***Select***	*Tables*	**Press**	Alt+C to select the Column option button
Click	the Column option button	***Select***	*Split*	**Press**	Tab to select the Column text box
Double-click	the Column text box	***Press***	*Alt+C to select the Column option button*	**Type**	2

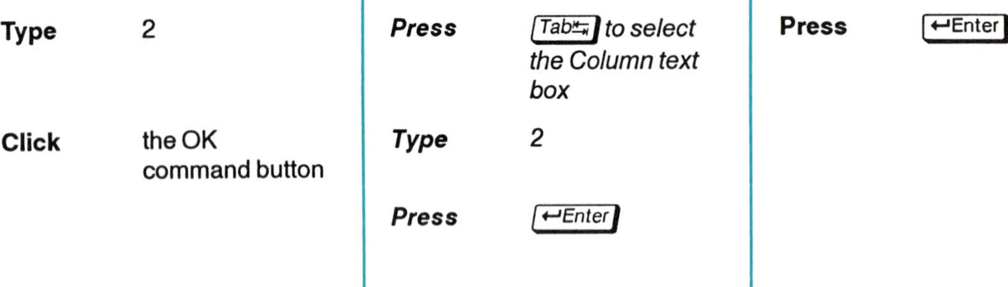

Type	2	***Press***	*Tab to select the Column text box*	**Press**	↵Enter
Click	the OK command button	***Type***	*2*		
		Press	*↵Enter*		

The top part of your screen should look like Figure 22-24.

Figure 22-24

WordPerfect - [c:\ch22\c22f24.wp - unmodified]

File Edit View Layout Tools Font Graphics Macro Window Help

JOHNSON PARTNERS
DISTRICT EXPENSE REPORT
First Quarter

District	Office	Telephone	Suppli es	
Central	$38,000.50	$2,310.0	$1,810.98	
Eastern	31,645.61	4,412.31	,881.22	
Midwest	53,760.75	3,708.78	,544.65	
Mountain	48,145.25	6,974.96	,221.88	
Southern	34,706.21	11,142.46	1,211.75	
Western	40,746.41	8,418.77	1,550.29	
Total	247,004.73	36,967.28	6,220.77	0.00

A fifth column is added to the right side of the table. The width of the Supplies column is smaller to make room for the new column. The width of the existing columns adjust to keep the table between the left and right margins of the document. You can change the width of a column by choosing Column from the Tables option under the Layout menu.

To change the width of column 1:

Click	on cell A3	***Move***	*the insertion point to cell A3*	**Move**	the insertion point to cell A3
Choose	Layout	***Press***	*Alt*	**Press**	Ctrl+F9
Choose	Tables	***Select***	*Layout*	**Select**	Column
Choose	Column	***Select***	*Tables*	**Press**	Alt+O to select the Column Width text box
Double-click	the Column Width Text box	***Select***	*Column*	**Type**	1.4
Type	1.4	***Press***	*Alt+O to select the Column Width text box*	**Press**	↵Enter

Click	the OK command button	***Type***	*1.4*		
		Press	*↵Enter*		

To change the width of column B through column E:

Select	cells B3 through E3	***Select***	*cells B3 through E3*	**Select**	cells B3 through E3
Choose	Layout	***Press***	*Alt*	**Press**	Ctrl+F9
Choose	Tables	***Select***	*Layout*	**Select**	Column
Choose	Column	***Select***	*Tables*	**Press**	Alt+O to select the Column Width text box
Double-click	the Column Width text box	***Select***	*Column*	**Type**	1.25
Type	1.25	***Press***	*Alt+O to select the Column Width text box*	**Press**	↵Enter
Click	the OK command button	***Type***	*1.25*		
		Press	*↵Enter*		

Deselect the cells in the table by clicking in the document area or moving the insertion point. The top part of your screen should look like Figure 22-25.

Figure 22-25

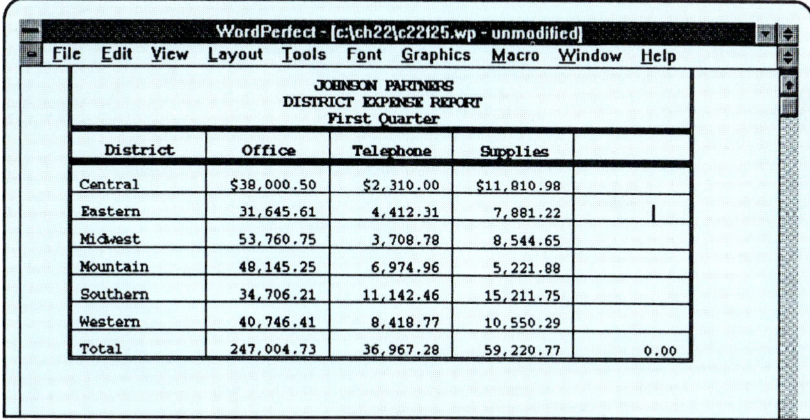

District	Office	Telephone	Supplies	
Central	$38,000.50	$2,310.00	$11,810.98	
Eastern	31,645.61	4,412.31	7,881.22	
Midwest	53,760.75	3,708.78	8,544.65	
Mountain	48,145.25	6,974.96	5,221.88	
Southern	34,706.21	11,142.46	15,211.75	
Western	40,746.41	8,418.77	10,550.29	
Total	247,004.73	36,967.28	59,220.77	0.00

If you are using a mouse, you can also change the column widths using the Ruler. When you view the Ruler and the insertion point is in a table, the margin marker displays the column widths of the table. To change the column widths, drag the appropriate marker to the new Ruler position.

You can create formulas to do calculations that the functions cannot. The four operators that you can use to create a formula are:

+ Add
- Subtract
* Multiply
/ Divide

The cell location is used in place of numbers in the formula, for example, B3+C3. The amount in each location cell referenced in the formula is used in the calculation.

To create a formula to compute the total expenses for each district, you need to add Office, Telephone, and Supplies expenses.

To create the formula for the Central District:

Click	on cell E3
Choose	Layout
Choose	Tables
Choose	Formula
Type	B3+C3+D3
Click	the OK command button

Move	*the insertion point to cell E3*
Press	*Alt*
Select	*Layout*
Select	*Tables*
Select	*Formula*
Type	*B3+C3+D3*
Press	*↵Enter*

Move	the insertion point to cell E3
Press	Ctrl+F9
Select	Formula
Type	B3+C3+D3
Press	↵Enter

When you enter the cell locations in a formula, you can use uppercase or lowercase letters. Your screen should look like Figure 22-26.

Figure 22-26

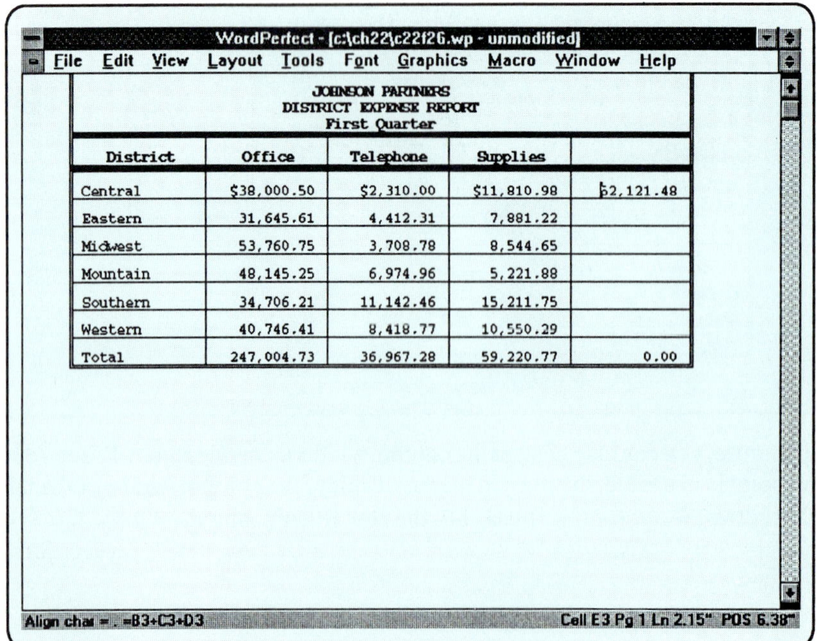

JOHNSON PARTNERS
DISTRICT EXPENSE REPORT
First Quarter

District	Office	Telephone	Supplies	
Central	$38,000.50	$2,310.00	$11,810.98	$52,121.48
Eastern	31,645.61	4,412.31	7,881.22	
Midwest	53,760.75	3,708.78	8,544.65	
Mountain	48,145.25	6,974.96	5,221.88	
Southern	34,706.21	11,142.46	15,211.75	
Western	40,746.41	8,418.77	10,550.29	
Total	247,004.73	36,967.28	59,220.77	0.00

Notice the status bar displays the formula.

When the calculation is completed, the result of the formula is displayed in the cell. You can use the same formula for several rows or columns.

To copy the formula in cell E3 to the other cells below it in the column:

Choose	Layout	***Press***	*Alt*	**Press**	Ctrl+F9
Choose	Tables	***Select***	*Layout*	**Select**	Formula
Choose	Formula	***Select***	*Tables*		
		Select	*Formula*		

The Tables Formula dialog box appears. The formula in the current cell appears in the Formula text box. To copy the formula down the column:

Click	the Down option button	***Press***	*Alt+D to select the Down option button*	**Press**	Alt+D to select the Down option button
Double-click	the Down text box	***Press***	*Tab to select the Down text box*	**Press**	Tab to select the Down text box
Type	6	***Type***	*6*	**Type**	6
Click	the OK command button	***Press***	*Enter*	**Press**	Enter

The top part of your screen should look like Figure 22-27.

Figure 22-27

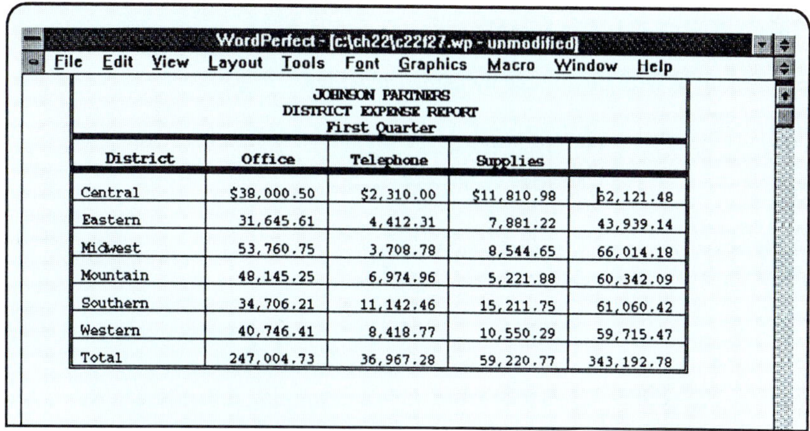

District	Office	Telephone	Supplies	
Central	$38,000.50	$2,310.00	$11,810.98	52,121.48
Eastern	31,645.61	4,412.31	7,881.22	43,939.14
Midwest	53,760.75	3,708.78	8,544.65	66,014.18
Mountain	48,145.25	6,974.96	5,221.88	60,342.09
Southern	34,706.21	11,142.46	15,211.75	61,060.42
Western	40,746.41	8,418.77	10,550.29	59,715.47
Total	247,004.73	36,967.28	59,220.77	343,192.78

The results of the copied formulas are displayed in column E.

Click	on cell E4	***Move***	*the insertion point to cell E4*	**Move**	the insertion point to cell E4

Notice that the cell location (on the left side of the status bar) in the copied formula is B4+C4+D4. When you copy formulas to other cells, WordPerfect uses "relative cell references" to change formulas in a table.

For example, if you have a formula in cell C4 that refers to cell B4 (one cell to the left) and copy that formula to cell D4, the formula will reference cell C4 (one cell to the left).

Check the cell locations in the copied formulas as you move down the column. The cell locations in each formula are changed so that the copied formulas will work for each row.

To add a title to the column:

Click	on cell E2	***Move***	*the insertion point to cell E2*	**Move**	the insertion point to cell E2
Type	Total	***Type***	*Total*	**Type**	Total

The top part of your screen should look like Figure 22-28.

Figure 22-28

WordPerfect - [c:\ch22\c22f28.wp - unmodified]

File Edit View Layout Tools Font Graphics Macro Window Help

JOHNSON PARTNERS
DISTRICT EXPENSE REPORT
First Quarter

District	Office	Telephone	Supplies	Total
Central	$38,000.50	$2,310.00	$11,810.98	52,121.48
Eastern	31,645.61	4,412.31	7,881.22	43,939.14
Midwest	53,760.75	3,708.78	8,544.65	66,014.18
Mountain	48,145.25	6,974.96	5,221.88	60,342.09
Southern	34,706.21	11,142.46	15,211.75	61,060.42
Western	40,746.41	8,418.77	10,550.29	59,715.47
Total	247,004.73	36,967.28	59,220.77	343,192.78

Save the document using the name "table.doc." Close the document.

■ CREATING A TABLE USING THE RULER

You can easily create a table with the mouse by using the Ruler.

To view the Ruler:

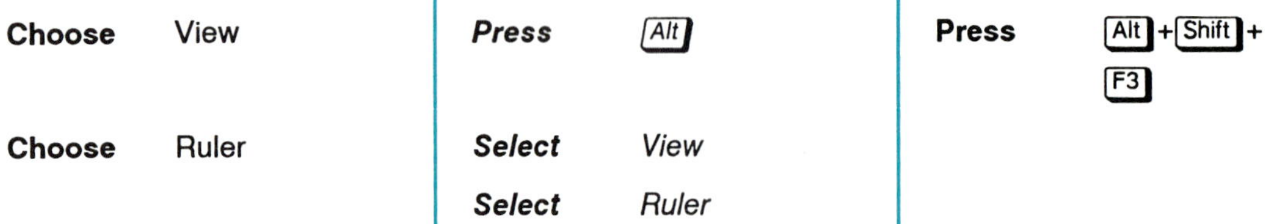

Choose	View	***Press***	*Alt*	**Press**	Alt + Shift + F3
Choose	Ruler	***Select***	*View*		
		Select	*Ruler*		

The Table button on the Ruler allows you to create a table by dragging the mouse across the table grid. The number of cells you highlight in the table grid determines the size of the table.

To create a table that is two columns and three rows:

Click the Table button on the Ruler

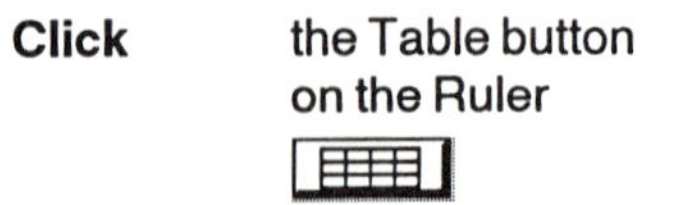

Hold down	the mouse button to view the Table grid
Drag	the mouse across two columns
Drag	the mouse down five rows

The top part of your screen should look like Figure 22-29.

Figure 22-29

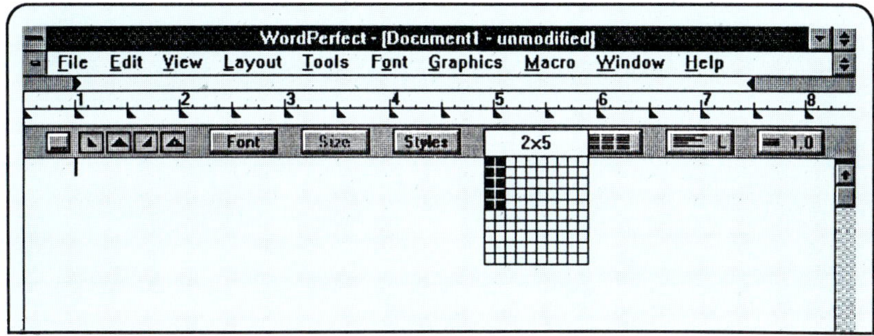

Notice the top of the table grid indicates two columns by five rows. The default table grid is ten columns by ten rows. To create a table larger than the default grid, select the Table button on the Ruler and drag the mouse to the right to increase the number of columns or down to increase the number of rows displayed on the grid.

To accept the 2x5 table size:

Release	the mouse button

The top part of your screen should look like Figure 22-30.

Figure 22-30

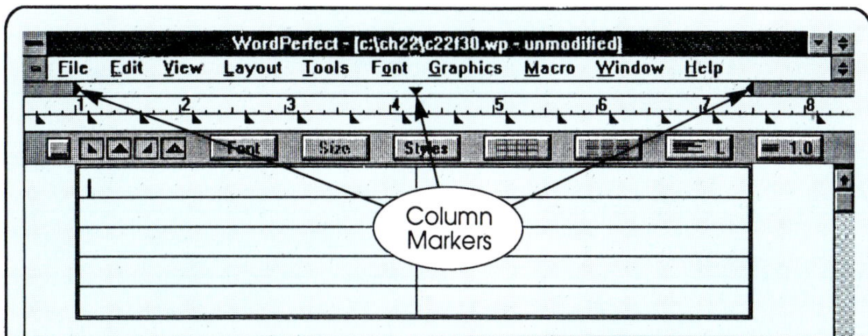

The table appears in your document. This table can be edited using the same techniques discussed in the previous section of this chapter.

Close the document without saving changes.

EXERCISE 1

INSTRUCTIONS: Define the following terms:

1. Tables feature ______________________________
2. Rows ______________________________
3. Columns ______________________________
4. Cell ______________________________
5. Insert feature ______________________________
6. Formula feature ______________________________
7. Result ______________________________
8. Functions ______________________________
9. Relative cell references ______________________________
10. Column feature ______________________________
11. Cell feature ______________________________

EXERCISE 2

INSTRUCTIONS: Circle T if the statement is true and F if the statement is false.

T F 1. Columns have numeric names, and rows have alphabetic names.

T F 2. A table is a grid that is organized into columns and rows.

T F 3. The Join option only works when the Select feature is on.

T F 4. Columns run horizontally.

T F 5. A cell occurs where each column and row meet.

T F 6. You can move from cell to cell by pressing the Tab key.

T F 7. As long as the Table Definition code exists, you cannot delete the Cell, Row, or Table Off codes.

T F 8. The Tables Size feature in the Options dialog box allows you to add only rows to a table.

T F 9. The lock option in the Insert feature enables you to prevent changes to a cell or column.

T F 10. There are four operators that you can use when creating a formula: +, -, *, and =.

EXERCISE 3

INSTRUCTIONS:

1. Create the following table. The data is for sales of three products by region.
2. The company information and column titles should be centered and bold. The row titles should be left justified and bold. The sales data should be right justified.
3. Insert a row between the North and East regions. The row title is "Central." Use the following values, from left to right, for the cells in the Central row: 17,000, 6,000, and 3,000.
4. Add a column at the end of the table and title it "Total Regional Sales."
5. The values in the "Total Region Sales" column are calculated by summing the sales value for each product in a region.
6. Add a row at the end of the table and title it "Total Product Sales."
7. Calculate the values for the cells in the "Total Product Sales" row by summing the sales for the products in each region.
8. Make the lines above and below the column titles thicker.
9. Print the document.
10. Save the document in a file using the name "ch22ex03."
11. Close the document.

JACKSON APPLIANCE INC. REGIONAL SALES REPORT Second Quarter			
Region	Washing Machines	Toasters	Mowers
North	$65,000	$10,000	$8,000
East	50,000	20,000	12,000
South	25,000	5,000	2,000
West	31,000	16,000	4,000

EXERCISE 4

INSTRUCTIONS:

1. Create the following document using the Tables feature.
2. Center the column headings.
3. Place a double line border around the outer edge of the table. All lines inside the table are single.
4. Center the table from top to bottom on the page using the Center Page feature under the Page option from the Layout menu.
5. Preview the document.
6. Print the document.
7. Save the document in a file using the name "ch22ex04."
8. Close the document.

TEN MOST POPULOUS CITIES IN THE WORLD

1985*

City	Country	Population
Tokyo	Japan	25,434,000
Mexico City	Mexico	16,901,000
Sao Paolo	Brazil	14,911,000
New York City	United States	14,598,000
Seoul	South Korea	13,665,000
Osaka-Kobe	Japan	13,562,000
Buenos Aires	Argentina	10,750,000
Calcutta	India	10,462,000
Bombay	India	10,137,000
Rio de Janeiro	Brazil	10,116,000

*Most recent figures for all cities.

EXERCISE 5

INSTRUCTIONS:

1. Create the following table.
2. Starting with "Steven J. Ross," shade every other row in the table.
3. Decimal align the third column.
4. Center the document from top to bottom on the page using the Center Page feature under the Page option on the Layout menu.
5. Center the column and table headings.
6. Preview the document.
7. Print the document.
8. Save the document in a file using the name "ch22ex05."
9. Close the document.

THE TEN HIGHEST PAID CHIEF EXECUTIVES IN 1989		
Name	Company	Total Pay
Craig O. McCaw	McCaw Cellular	$53,994,000
Steven J. Ross	Time Warner	34,200,000
Donald A. Pels	Lin Broadcasting	22,791,000
Jim P. Manzi	Lotus Development	16,363,000
Paul Fireman	Reebok International	14,606,000
Ronald K. Richey	Torchmark	12,666,000
Martin S. Davis	Paramount	11,635,000
Roberto C. Goizueta	Coca-Cola	10,715,000
Michael D. Eisner	Walt Disney	9,589,000
August A. Busch, III	Anheuser-Busch	8,816,000

EXERCISE 6

INSTRUCTIONS:

1. Open the document "ch22ex05."
2. Change the title to "THE 20 HIGHEST-PAID CHIEF EXECUTIVES."
3. Add a blank line after the title.
4. Put a double line border under the column titles.
5. Add the following ten lines at the bottom of the table.
6. Starting with "James R. Moffett," shade every other line.
7. Add the note "Data: Standard & Poor's Compustat Services Inc." a double space below the table.
8. Preview the document.
9. Print the document.
10. Save the document in a file using the name "ch22ex06."
11. Close the document.

William G. McGowan	MCI	8,666,000
James R. Moffett	Freeport McMoRan	7,300,000
Donald E. Peterson	Ford Motor	7,147,000
P. Roy Vagelos	Merck	6,764,000
W. Michael Blumenthal	Unisys	6,511,000
S. Parker Gilbert	Morgan Stanley	5,510,000
Harry A. Merlo	Louisiana-Pacific	5,314,000
Rueben A. Mark	Colgate-Palmolive	5,004,000
Robert J. Pfeiffer	Alexander & Baldwin	4,943,000
William P. Stiritz	Ralston Purina	4,854,000

Data: Standard & Poor's Compustat Services, Inc.

EXERCISE 7

INSTRUCTIONS:

1. Create the following letter and table.
2. The title of the table is centered and bold.
3. The column headings are centered. There is a thick line under the title.
4. Use the Math feature to calculate column 4. The formula is (B3-C3)/C3 100.
5. Spell check the document.
6. Preview the document.
7. Print the document.
8. Save the document in a file using the name "ch22ex07."
9. Close the document.

March 30, 1992

Mr. George Evans
Director of Sales
Eastwood Merchandise Company
1098 West Huron Street
Cleveland, OH 44101

Dear Mr. Evans:

Here is the list of top salespeople for the year. I hope that you will notice the improvement of some of the salespeople over last year's figures.

EASTWOOD MERCHANDISE COMPANY SALES LEADERS FOR 19--			
Name	This Year	Last Year	% of Change
James Bradford	$250,000	$200,000	25.00
Lenore Berger	387,000	302,000	28.15
Horace Grant	250,557	175,000	43.18
Dina Reynolds	450,000	275,000	63.64
Lincoln Tyler	315,500	150,750	109.29

These five people will be honored at the Annual Meeting for all salespeople. They will be awarded plaques and, of course, they will be substantially rewarded by their commissions.

Sincerely,

Neil Smith
Regional Sales Director

xx

EXERCISE 8

INSTRUCTIONS:

1. Create the following table.
2. Bold the state names in the first column.

3. Change the state nicknames in the second column to small print.
4. Shade the column headings line using the Tables Cell feature.
5. When done, remove all lines from the table.
6. Preview the document.
7. Print the document.
8. Save the document in a file using the name "ch22ex08."
9. Close the document.

TRIVIA INFORMATION ABOUT
SELECTED STATES

Name	Nickname	Flower
Alabama	Heart of Dixie	Camellia
Alaska	The Last Frontier	Forget-me-not
Hawaii	The Aloha State	Yellow Hibiscus
Indiana	The Hoosier State	Peony
Kentucky	The Bluegrass State	Goldenrod
New Jersey	Garden State	Purple Violet
Pennsylvania	Keystone State	Mountain Laurel
Texas	The Lone Star State	Bluebonnet

EXERCISE 9

INSTRUCTIONS:

1. Open the document "ch22ex08."
2. Change the initial font to Helvetica 10 point.
3. Add a column to the end of the table. The column heading should be "Abbr." Enter the two-letter state abbreviation for each state. The abbreviations are listed below:

   AL, AK, HI, IN, KY, NJ, PA, TX

4. The last column should be in italics.
5. Put the lines back into the table. Put a double line around the outer edges of the table.
6. Preview the document.
7. Print the document.
8. Save the document in a file using the name "ch22ex09."
9. Close the document.

EXERCISE 10

INSTRUCTIONS:

1. Create the following table.
2. Enlarge the first column to fit the names.
3. The title of the table is bold and centered.
4. The column headings are centered, shaded, and aligned at the bottom of the cell.
5. Double lines are placed around the outside of the table, the title, the Names column, and the Totals column.
6. Center the data in columns 3 and 4. Decimal align columns 2, 5, and 6.
7. Compute the totals by using this formula, B3 + E3.
8. Preview the document.
9. Print the document.
10. Save the document in a file using the name "ch22ex10.01."
11. Add the following names to the end of the table:

Farrel, S.	595	8	4	250
Vasquez, J.	595	5	7	175

12. Add a Totals row that sums each column, including the Totals column.
13. Shade the Totals row and column using the Tables Cell feature.
14. Preview the document.
15. Print the document.
16. Save the document in a file using the name "ch22ex10.02."
17. Close the document.

CONFERENCE REGISTRATION					
Names	Fees	Mtg's Pvt.	Mtg's Group	Meals	Totals
Barnes, G.	$595	4	8	$250	
Cartier, J.	595	5	7	175	
Franklin, R.	595	6	6	225	
Hoard, R.T.	595	2	10	100	
Lytle, R.S.	595	3	9	240	
Mansfield, T.	595	0	12	360	

CHAPTER TWENTY-THREE

DESKTOP PUBLISHING: CREATING GRAPHICS

OBJECTIVES

In this chapter, you will learn to:

- Import graphics
- Create a caption for graphics
- Position or anchor graphics within a document
- Change the vertical and horizontal positions of graphics
- Size graphics

CHAPTER OVERVIEW

WordPerfect includes many of the capabilities that are found in "desktop publishing" software packages. For example, you can place graphics in your document. A graphic is a picture or image. You can include borders, captions, and enhancements to the graphics in your document. The next six chapters illustrate the "desktop publishing" capabilities of WordPerfect.

In this chapter, the procedures for importing graphics are described and illustrated. Methods for creating captions, anchoring the graphics, changing the vertical and horizontal positions of graphics, and sizing graphics are also discussed.

CREATING GRAPHIC BOXES

The Graphics feature allows you to combine pictures or images into your document. You must first create a box to hold your picture. This is done by using the Graphics feature. Within a graphic box you can retrieve pictures or enter text. WordPerfect will word wrap any text that you include in the box. You can also place text outside the box and specify whether text should wrap around the box. You can change the location, appearance, and size of the graphic box at any time.

There are five box types available in WordPerfect:

> **Figure** - Place graphic images and pictures in this type of box.
>
> **Table** - This box holds WordPerfect tables and other tables containing numbers.

Text - This box holds text. It is used when you want to draw special attention to certain text on the page.

User - This is a "miscellaneous" box. If you cannot place an image in any other type of box, then use this one.

Equation - Place equations in this box. Chapter 28 explains equations in further detail.

You can also leave a box empty. Each box is numbered by WordPerfect according to its type and place in the document. Each box type has a menu of options that you can use to modify the contents and appearance of the box.

The method used for creating and editing Figure, Table, and User boxes is very similar. In Chapters 23 through 26 of this book, the procedures for creating and editing a Figure box are described and illustrated. These procedures can be applied to other graphic types.

CREATING FIGURE BOXES

After creating a figure box, you then place a graphic image into the box. You can create this image in another graphics software package. Then you retrieve the graphic into your box. In WordPerfect, retrieving a graphic is as simple as entering the name of the file. WordPerfect recognizes many different types of graphic files. See "Graphics, Formats and Programs" in the WordPerfect Reference Manual for more information about compatible graphic file types.

Many software packages, including WordPerfect, have generic graphic images already made for you. WordPerfect graphics have the extension ".wpg" and are stored in the "c:\wpwin\graphics" directory when you install the WordPerfect program. We will use one of these images in this chapter.

Change the default directory to "a:\wpdocs" or to "c:\wpdocs." Then open the document "newscol."

Suppose you want to place a picture of some daisies in the newspaper-style document that you created earlier. WordPerfect contains some standard graphic images from which you can select. One of the images is a picture of daisies.

To create a Figure box and retrieve the daisies graphic:

Click at the left margin of the second paragraph in Column 1

Choose Graphics

Choose Figure

Choose Retrieve

Move *the insertion point to the left margin of the second paragraph in Column 1*

Press *Alt*

Select *Graphics*

Select *Figure*

Select *Retrieve*

Move the insertion point to the left margin of the second paragraph in Column 1

Press F11

Your screen should look like Figure 23-1.

Figure 23-1

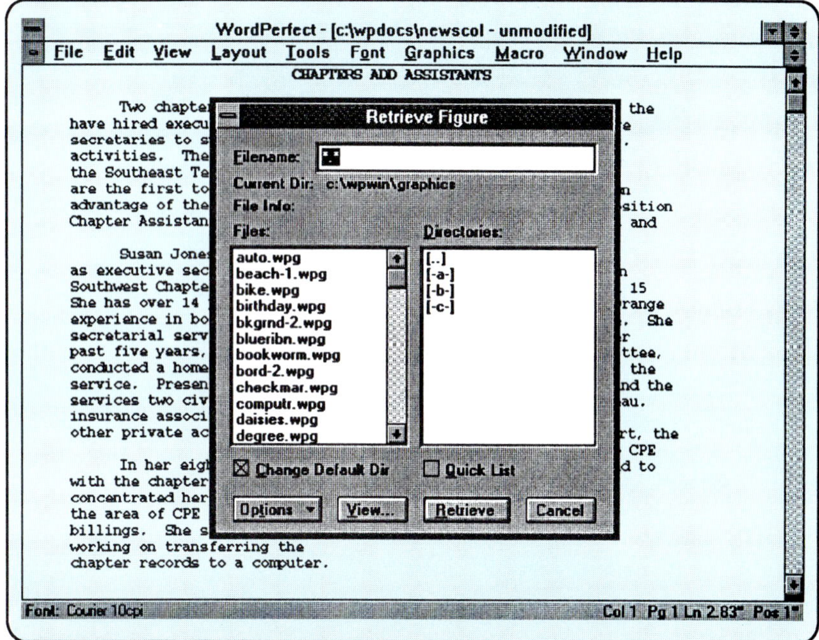

The Figure Retrieve dialog box appears. The default graphic directory appears as the Current Directory. The default graphic directory can be changed using the Location of Files command from the Preferences option under the File menu.

To retrieve a graphic image that already exists in WordPerfect, you must enter the filename of the graphic:

Click	on the "daisies.wpg" file	***Press***	*Alt+I to select the Files list box*	**Type**	**daisies.wpg**
		Press	*↓ to highlight the file "daisies.wpg"*		

WordPerfect has 36 graphic images that come with the software package. They end with a ".wpg" extension and can be used in graphic boxes. Notice that a list of the graphic files appears in the Files list box in the Retrieve Figure dialog box.

To view the picture before you retrieve it:

Click	the View command button	***Press***	*Alt+V to select the View command button*

Your screen should look similar to Figure 23-2.

Figure 23-2

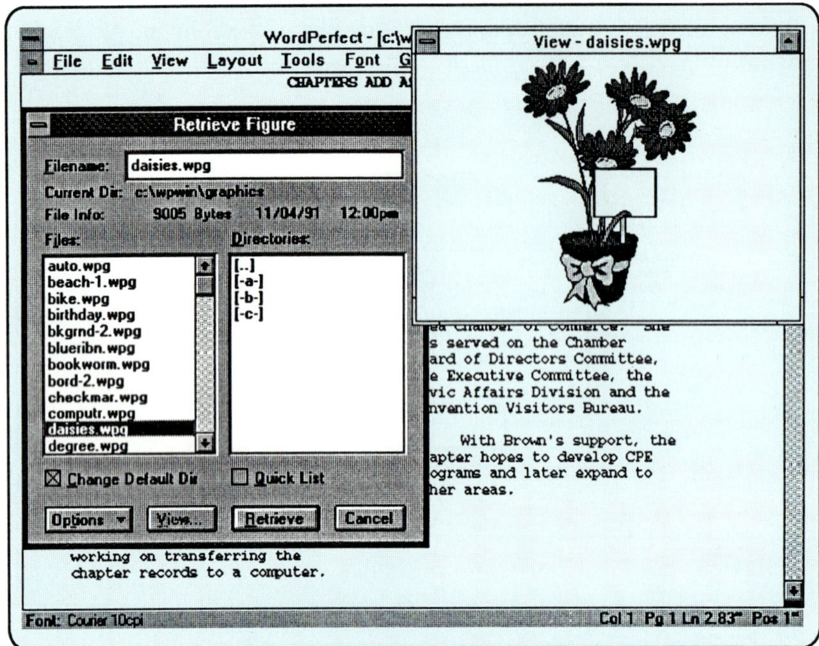

Notice that you can only view the graphic if you highlight the file name in the Files list box. You can not view the graphic if you type the file name in the Filename text box.

To retrieve the daisies graphic:

Click	the Retrieve command button	***Press***	*↵Enter to select the Retrieve command button*	**Press**	↵Enter to select the Retrieve command button

Your screen should look like Figure 23-3.

Figure 23-3

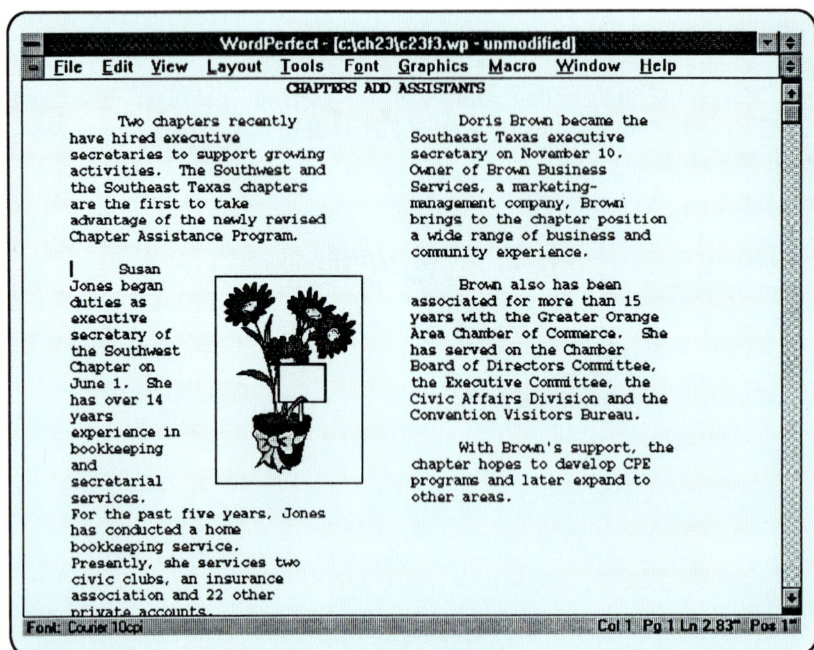

Notice that by default, the figure is placed to the right margin of the column. Notice that the text wraps around the figure box.

When you create a graphic, WordPerfect numbers the graphic box. To view the Figure number and code, turn on your reveal codes feature. The bottom part of your screen should look like Figure 23-4.

Figure 23-4

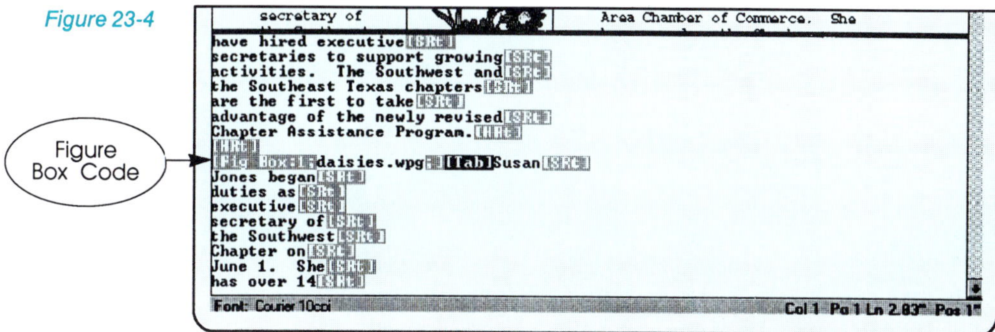

Notice the [Fig Box:1;daisies.wpg;] code. Remove the document codes from your screen using the Reveal Codes feature.

■ GRAPHIC POSITION

You can change the position and size of a graphic box by using the Position option for that particular graphic type. To change the position of a Figure box, choose Position from the Figure option under the Graphic menu.

The Position feature allows you to change the box type, the anchor type, the box size, and box position. You can also change how the box interacts with text.

To change the position of Figure 1:

Click	on the Figure 1 box with the alternate mouse button	***Press***	*Alt*
Choose	Box Position	***Select***	*Graphics*
		Select	*Figure*
		Select	*Position*
		Type	*1*
		Press	*↵Enter*

The Box Position and Size dialog box appears. Your screen should look like Figure 23-5.

Figure 23-5

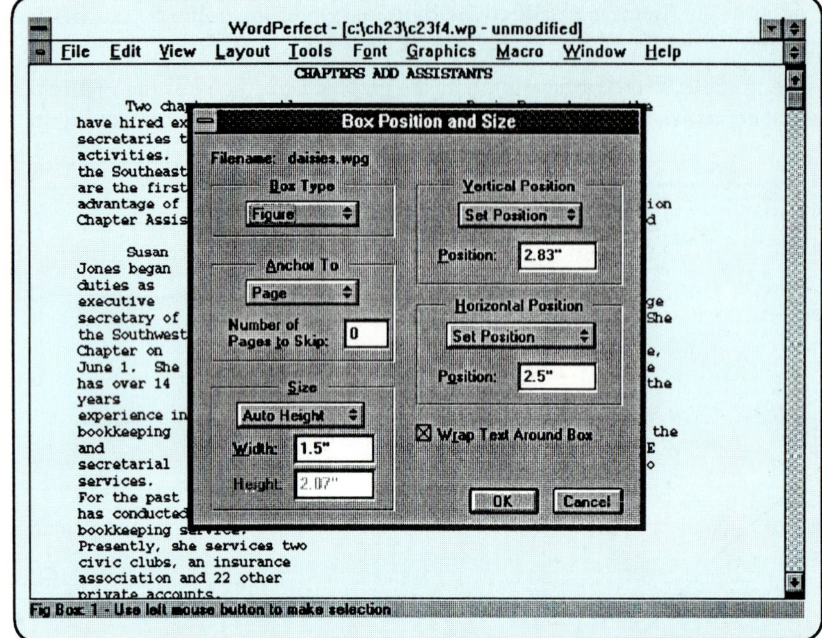

Anchor Type

The Anchor Type option defines how the graphic box "moves" on the page. It can be treated as a *character* in a line, fixed on the *page*, or associated with a *paragraph*.

Currently, the figure box has a page anchor type. This figure is fixed at a particular position on the page.

To change the anchor type so that the figure will move with the paragraph:

Click	the Anchor To pop-up list button	***Press***	*Alt+A to select the Anchor To pop-up list button*
Hold down	the mouse button to view the pop-up list	***Press***	*Alt+↑ to view the pop-up list*
Choose	Paragraph	***Type***	*P to select the Paragraph option*

Your screen should look like Figure 23-6.

Figure 23-6

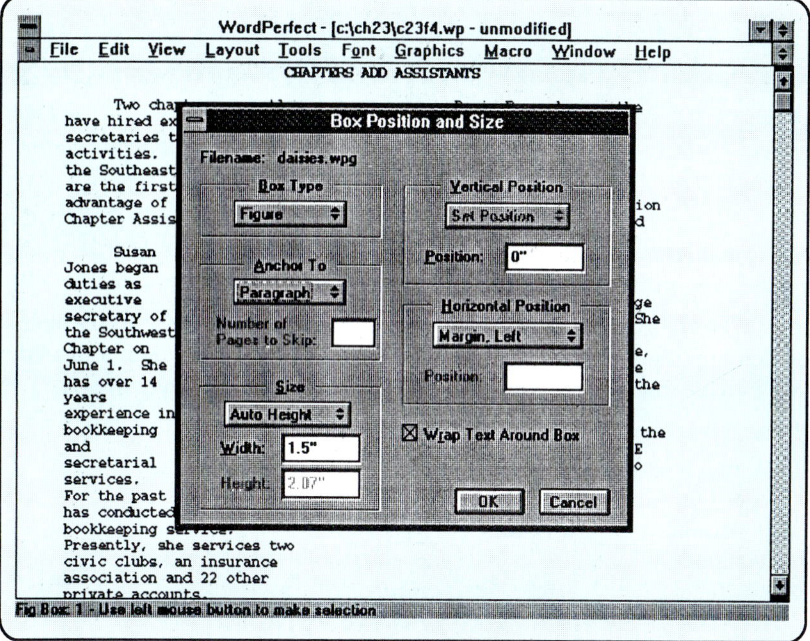

The Number of Pages to Skip option allows you to force a page-anchored graphic to appear on a different page. For example, suppose you have a page-anchored figure on page one of your document and you decide that you would like the graphic to appear on page four instead. Rather than move the graphic to page four, you can specify to skip three pages.

Vertical Position

You can move a graphic box by dragging the box with the mouse or changing the box's vertical position in the Box Position and Size dialog box.

The Vertical Position option in the Position dialog box depends on the selected anchor type. With this option, you can specify where the box is located on the page.

If the anchor type is "Paragraph," enter the amount of vertical space you want between the top of the paragraph and the graphic box. For example, if you want the graphic box to appear 1″ below the top of the paragraph, you would type a 1 in the Position text box.

If the anchor type is "Page," you can choose between top, bottom, center, full page (the graphic takes the entire page), or set the position by entering the amount of vertical space you want from the top of the page. For example, if you want the graphic to appear 1″ from the top of the page, you would choose the Set Position option from the Vertical Position pop-up list button and type 1 in the Position text box.

If the anchor type is "Character," choose between top of the line, bottom of the line, center of the line, or baseline where the figure in the box is in line with the text. For example, if you want the graphic box to align with the bottom of the text, you would choose Bottom from the Vertical Position pop-up list button.

Since you selected the Paragraph anchor type, you need to enter the amount of space you want from the top of the paragraph. The default setting is 0″ aligning the top of the graphic box even with the first line of the paragraph. You do not need to change this option.

If you want to move the graphic box below the first line of the paragraph, click the Position text box or press Alt+P and type the appropriate number of inches.

Horizontal Position

You can move a graphic box by dragging it with the mouse or you can change the Horizontal Position in the Box Position and Size dialog box.

The Horizontal Position option in the Box Position and Size dialog box depends on the selected anchor type. With this option, you can specify where the box is located across the page.

If the anchor type is "Paragraph," you can choose to have the box lined up with the left or right edge of the paragraph, centered in the paragraph, or filling the paragraph margins. For example, if you want the figure centered in the paragraph, you would choose the Margin, Center option.

If the anchor type is "Page," you can have the box lined up in relation to the margins or columns. You can also set the position any number of inches from the left margin. For example, if you want the figure centered between two columns of text, you would choose the Column, Center option.

If the anchor type is "Character," then you do not need to enter a position.

To select the Horizontal Position option:

Click	the Horizontal Position pop-up list button	***Press***	*Alt+H to select the Horizontal Position pop-up list button*
Hold down	the mouse button to view the pop-up list	***Press***	*Alt+↑ to view the pop-up list*

Since you selected the Paragraph option, you can position the box at the left of the paragraph, the right of the paragraph, the center of the paragraph, or full between the margins of the paragraph.

To place the graphic box on the left side of the paragraph:

Choose	Left	***Type***	*L to select the Left option*

Your screen should look like Figure 23-7.

Figure 23-7

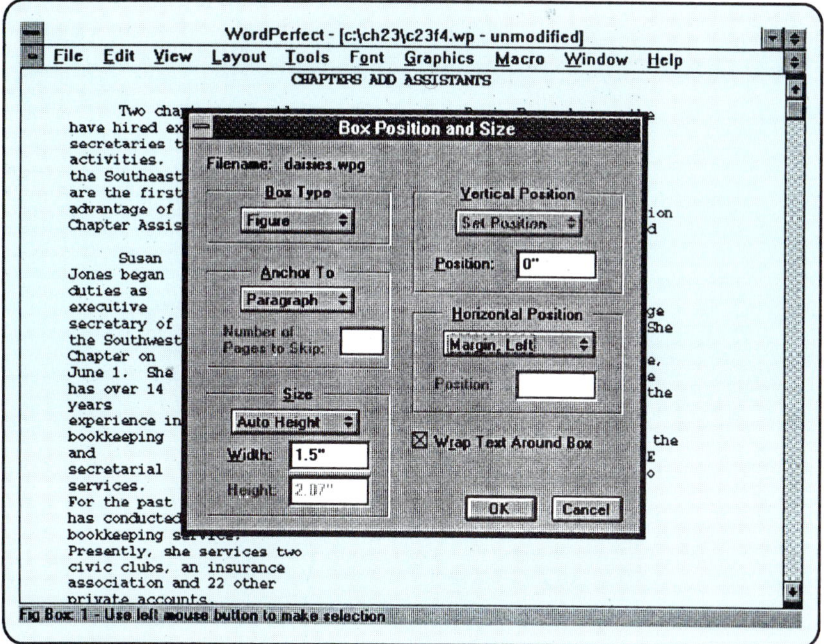

Size

The Size option in the definition menu lets you change the height and width of the box.

To select the Size option:

Click	the Size pop-up list button	***Press***	*Alt+S to select the Size pop-up list button*
Hold down	the mouse button to view the pop-up list	***Press***	*Alt+↑ to view the pop-up list*

Your screen should look like Figure 23-8.

Figure 23-8

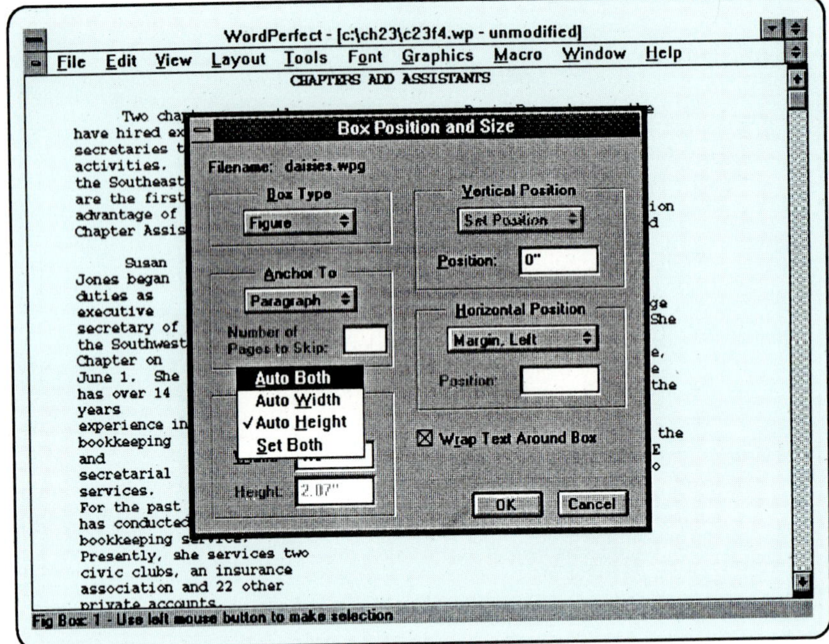

WordPerfect calculates the height and width of the image when you choose the Auto Both option.

The Auto Width option instructs WordPerfect to calculate the width and allows you to change the height. This option also keeps the original shape of the graphic image inside the box.

The Auto Height option instructs WordPerfect to calculate the height and allows you to change the width. This option keeps the original shape of the graphic image inside the box.

The Set Both option allows you to change both the height and width. The original shape of the graphic image in the box is not maintained.

To change the width but not the height:

Choose	Auto Height	***Type***	*H to select the Auto Height option*

To change the width to 2":

Double-click	the Width text box	***Press***	*Alt+W to select the Width text box*
Type	2	***Type***	*2*

Your screen should look like Figure 23-9.

Figure 23-9

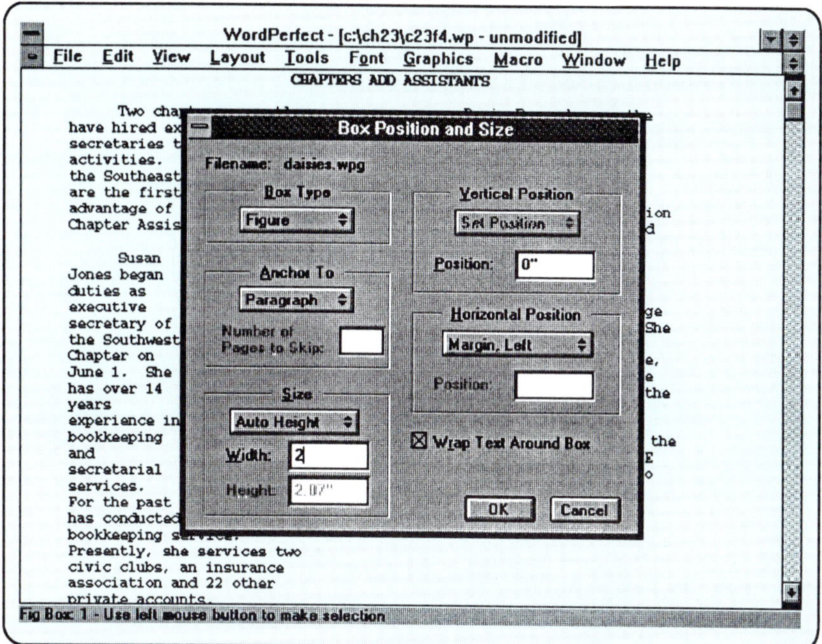

To return to the document:

Click	the OK command button	***Press***	*↵Enter*

Your figure box is displayed on the screen and should look like Figure 23-10.

Figure 23-10

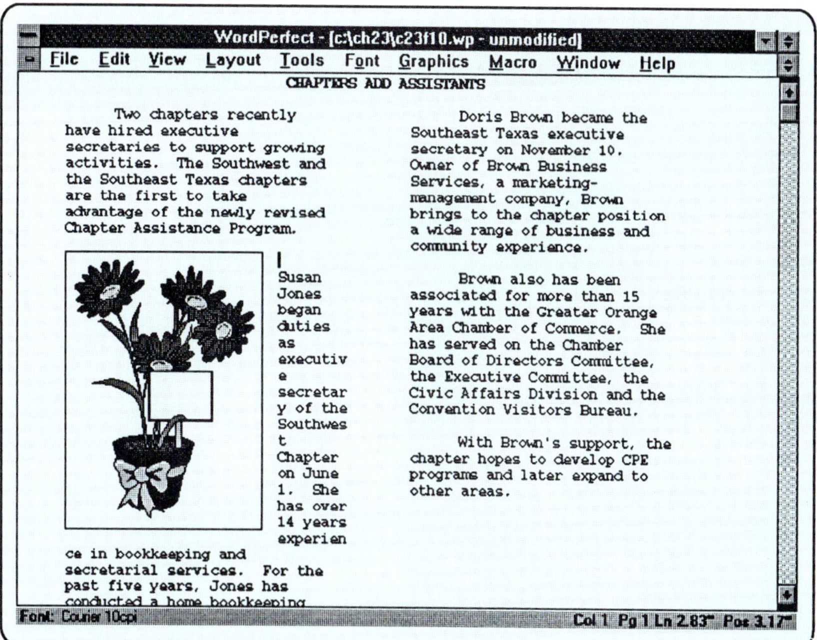

■ CAPTION

The Caption option allows you to attach a heading below or above a graphic box.

To create a caption for the daisies graphic:

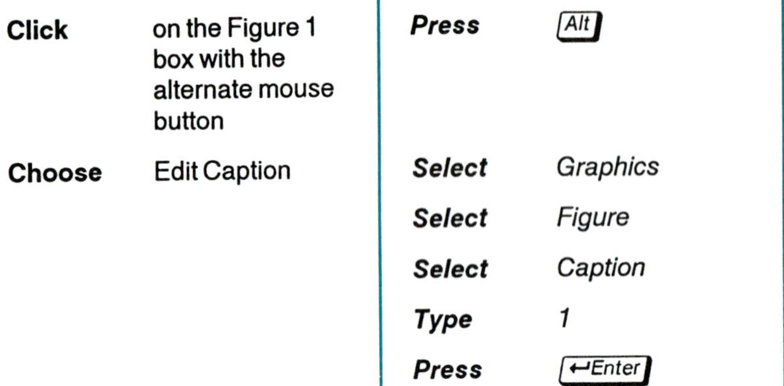

Click	on the Figure 1 box with the alternate mouse button	***Press***	*Alt*
Choose	Edit Caption	***Select***	*Graphics*
		Select	*Figure*
		Select	*Caption*
		Type	*1*
		Press	*↵Enter*

Your screen should look like Figure 23-11.

Figure 23-11

Notice that the text "Figure 1" appears on the screen. WordPerfect assumes that you want to use the caption "Figure 1." Suppose you want to use a different caption.

To delete the text "Figure 1":

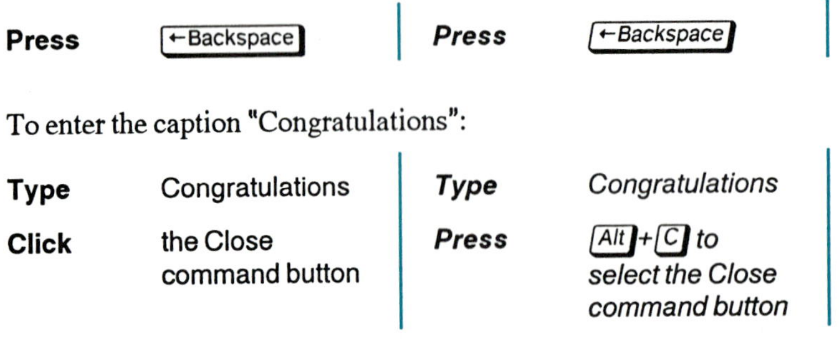

Press	←Backspace	***Press***	*←Backspace*

To enter the caption "Congratulations":

Type	Congratulations	***Type***	*Congratulations*
Click	the Close command button	***Press***	*Alt+C to select the Close command button*

Your screen should look like Figure 23-12.

Figure 23-12

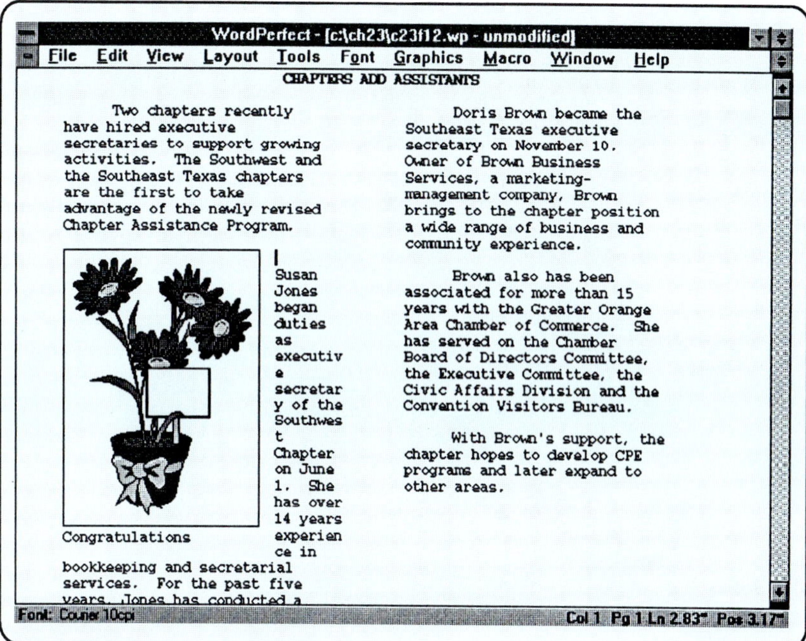

Notice that the caption appears below the graphic box.

■ CHANGING THE BOX POSITION

Currently, the size of Figure 1 causes the second paragraph to wrap incorrectly. This error can be corrected by making the box smaller. You can change the size of a graphic box using the Box Position dialog box or using the mouse. Both methods for sizing a graphic box are discussed in this section.

Using the Box Position and Size Dialog Box

You can size a box using precise measurements by using the Box Position dialog box.

To change the Size option for Figure Box 1:

Click	on the Figure 1 box with the alternate mouse button	***Press***	*Alt*
Choose	Box Position	***Select***	*Graphics*
		Select	*Figure*
		Select	*Position*
		Type	*1*
		Press	*↵Enter*

To change the width to 1.5″:

Double-click	the Width text box	***Press***	*Alt+W to select the Width text box*
Type	1.5	***Type***	*1.5*

Your screen should look like Figure 23-13.

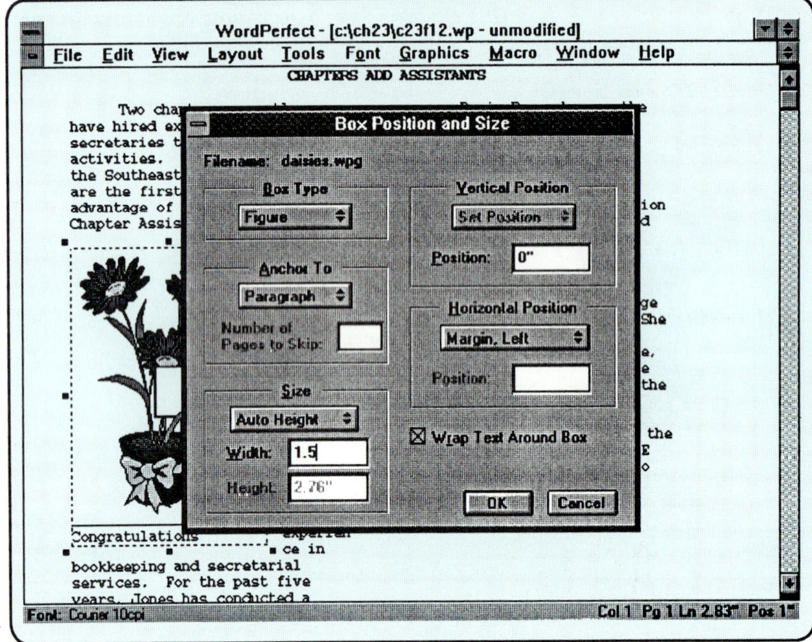

Figure 23-13

To return to the document:

Click	the OK command button	***Press***	*↵Enter*

The figure box automatically resizes to fit the options you defined for it as illustrated in Figure 23-14.

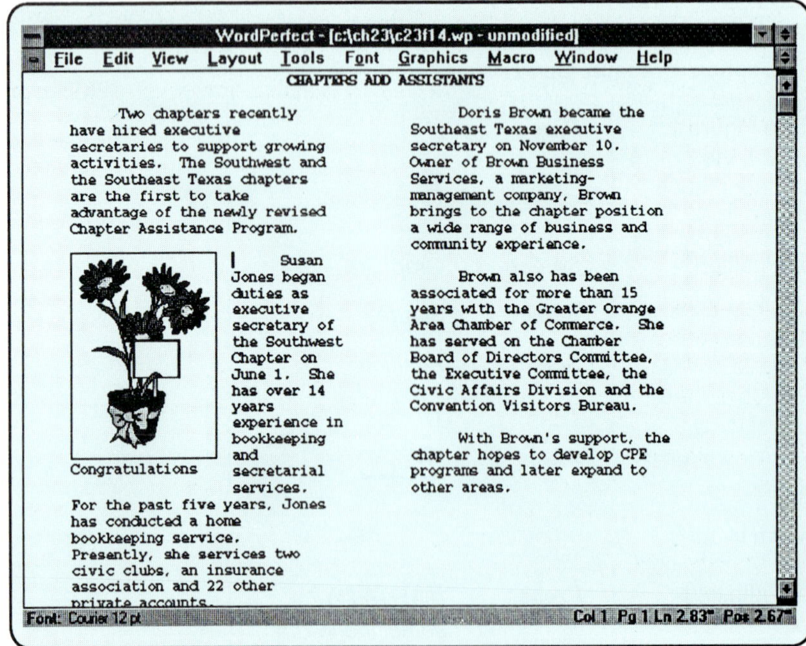

Figure 23-14

Save the document as "graphics."

Using the Mouse to Change the Box Position

You can size and move a graphic box using the mouse. To size a graphic box using the mouse, drag a sizing handle while the mouse pointer appears as a double-pointing arrow.

To change the size of Figure 1:

Click	on the Figure 1 box	

Your screen should look like Figure 23-15.

Figure 23-15

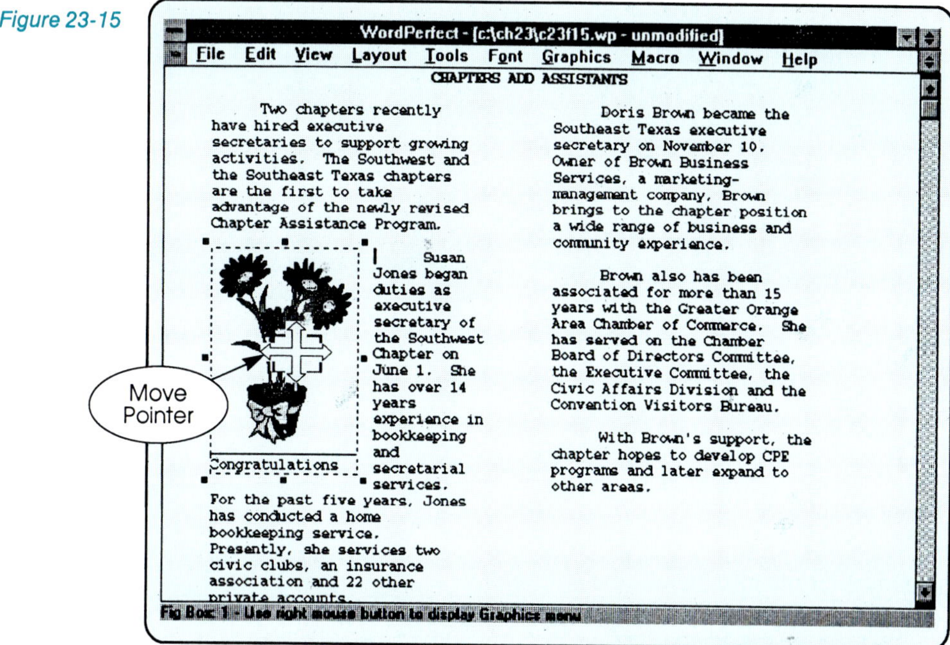

Notice a dashed line appears around the graphic and sizing handles appear on each size of the graphic and in each corner of the graphic.

To make Figure 1 wider:

Move	the mouse pointer to the middle sizing handle on the right side of the graphic until the mouse pointer appears as a double-pointing arrow	

Your screen should look like Figure 23-16.

Figure 23-16

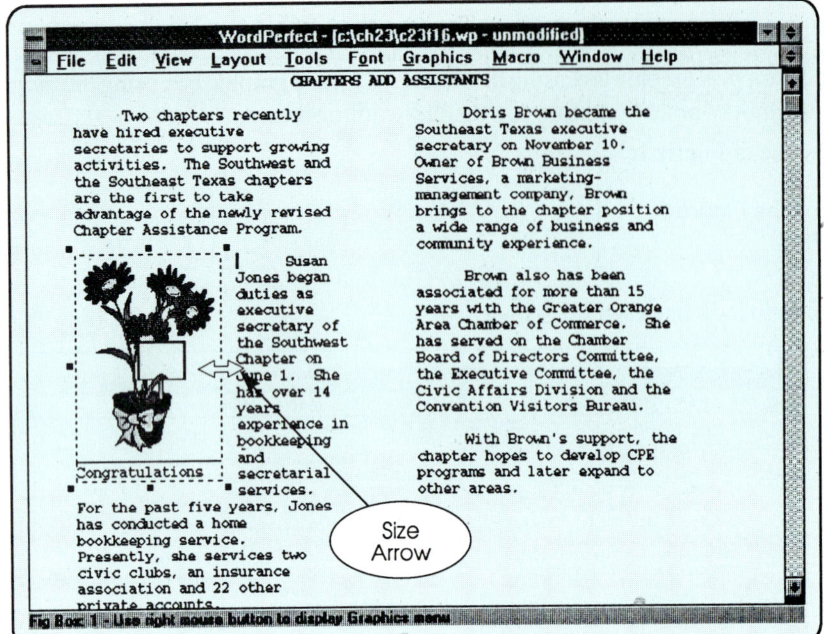

To size the graphic box:

Drag	the mouse pointer to the right
Release	the mouse button

Your screen should look similar to Figure 23-17.

Figure 23-17

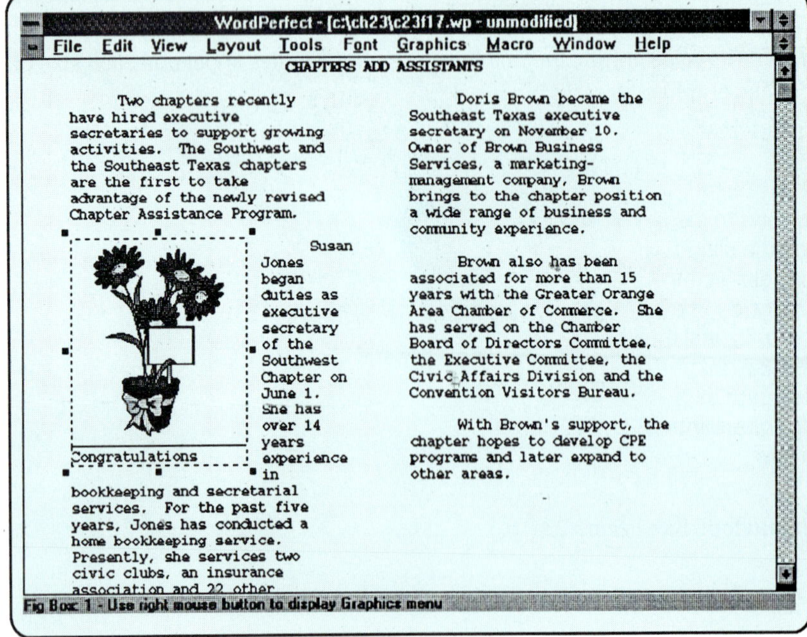

To deselect the figure, click in the document area.

You can also move a figure using the mouse. To move the graphic box, click on the figure and drag the graphic while the mouse pointer appears as a move pointer (four arrows).

To move Figure 1 to the right margin of Column 1:

Click	on the Figure 1 box
Move	the mouse pointer to the center of the figure so the mouse pointer appears as a move pointer
Drag	Figure 1 to the right margin of Column 1
Release	the mouse button

Your screen should look similar to Figure 23-18.

Figure 23-18

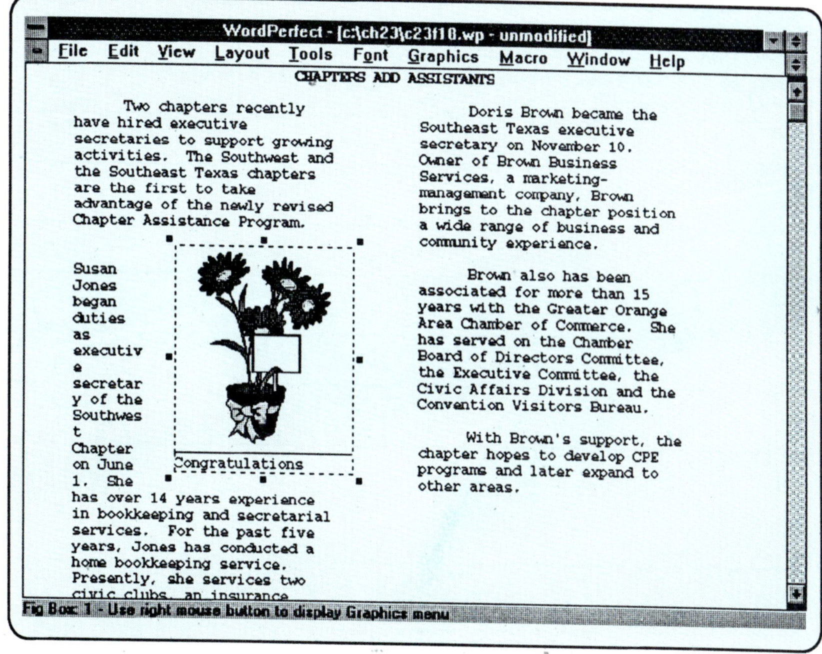

To deselect the figure, click in the document area.

Close the document without saving changes.

EXERCISE 1

INSTRUCTIONS: Define the following terms:

1. Graphics feature ____________________

   ____
2. Figure box ____________________

   ____
3. Table box ____________________

   ____
4. Text box ____________________

   ____
5. User box ____________________

   ____
6. Equation box ____________________

   ____
7. Caption ____________________

   ____
8. Anchor types ____________________

   ____
9. Size ____________________

   ____

EXERCISE 2

INSTRUCTIONS: Circle T if the statement is true and F if the statement is false.

T F 1. The Graphics feature allows you to combine pictures or text into your document.

T F 2. There are four box types available when using the Graphics feature: Figure, Table, Text, and User.

T F 3. Figure boxes can be used for graphic images and pictures.

T F 4. Table boxes can be used to display mathematical and scientific equations.

T F 5. Text boxes can be used for WordPerfect tables, maps, and statistical data.

T F 6. If the anchor type is "Paragraph," then you must enter the amount of vertical space from the top of the paragraph for the Vertical Position option.

T F 7. The Caption option allows you to attach headings to a graphic box.

T F 8. Anchor types determine how the graphic box moves within the document.

T F 9. There are two anchor types: Paragraph and Page.

EXERCISE 3

INSTRUCTIONS:

1. Create the following document.
2. Place a picture of a personal computer between the two paragraphs in the document. The name of the WordPerfect graphic is "computr.wpg."
3. Save the document in a file using the name "ch23ex03."
4. Print the document.
5. Close the document.

```
Personal computers are very popular in offices today.  A picture of
a personal computer follows.
```

```
A person can use a personal computer to prepare documents and print
them.
```

EXERCISE 4

INSTRUCTIONS:

1. Create the following document. Use the graphic "vacation.wpg."
2. Use the caption "Summer Vacation." Place it below the picture.
3. Set the height of the graphic to 3 inches.
4. Set the anchor type to paragraph.
5. Set the horizontal position to left.
6. Center the page from top to bottom.
7. Print the document.
8. Save the document in a file using the name "ch23ex04."
9. Close the document.

This graphic illustrates what the family car might look like on a summer vacation. Everything is packed up tight and the family is becoming weary of travel.

This graphic is one of 36 graphic files that come with WordPerfect for Windows. You can access these graphic files by using the Figure feature under the Graphic menu.

Figure 1 Summer Vacation

EXERCISE 5

INSTRUCTIONS:

1. Create the following document.
2. When asked in the copy, use the graphic "duckling.wpg."
3. Use the caption "Surprise!" Place it below the graphic.
4. The anchor type should be paragraph.
5. The vertical position is set to 0.
6. The horizontal position is set to centered.
7. Change the width to 2".
8. Preview the document.

9. Print the document.
10. Save the document in a file using the name "ch23ex05."
11. Close the document.

DUCKLING

We will start the paragraph with several lines of text in order to illustrate how a graphic will appear in connected text. All of the changes suggested in the instructions should now be followed. (Do not type this line or the one immediately below.)

This will show how the picture of the duckling will appear on the page. Note the position of this paragraph after you print it.

Notice how the line position in the lower right corner of the screen has jumped down to accommodate the graphic. Also notice that to the right of the picture, there is no printing.

EXERCISE 6

INSTRUCTIONS:

1. Place the graphic "wall-clk.wpg" on the page.
2. Change the width of the picture to 6".
3. Place the entire picture in the middle of the page.
4. Preview the document.
5. Print the document.
6. Save the document in a file using the name "ch23ex06."
7. Close the document.

EXERCISE 7

INSTRUCTIONS:

1. Place the graphic "bkgrnd-2.wpg" on the page. Set the height to 4″ and center it on the page.
2. Preview the document.
3. Print the document.
4. Save the document in a file using the name "ch23ex08."
5. Close the document.

CHAPTER TWENTY-FOUR

DESKTOP PUBLISHING: GRAPHIC OPTIONS

OBJECTIVES

In this chapter, you will learn to:

- Change the border style of graphics
- Change the border spacing of graphics
- Change the caption options for graphics
- Change the shading of graphics

CHAPTER OVERVIEW

Once you have created a graphic, there are options available in WordPerfect to enhance or modify the graphic's appearance. For example, you can specify a new type of border, change the caption location, and add gray shading to the graphic. In this chapter, the procedures for using these graphic options are described and illustrated.

BORDER STYLES

The Options menu can be selected from any of the graphic types under the Graphics menu. You can change the default settings for any of the five graphic box types. When you change an option, a code is inserted into your document at the insertion point location. All the boxes of that graphic type following the code are changed to reflect the new options.

Change the default directory to "a:\wpdocs" or to "c:\wpdocs." Then open the document "graphics."

To select the Figure Options menu:

Click	before the Figure Box code	***Move***	*the insertion point before the Figure Box code*
Choose	Graphics	***Press***	*Alt*
Choose	Figure	***Select***	*Graphics*
Choose	Options	***Select***	*Figure*
		Select	*Options*

The Figure Option dialog box appears. Your screen should look like Figure 24-1.

Figure 24-1

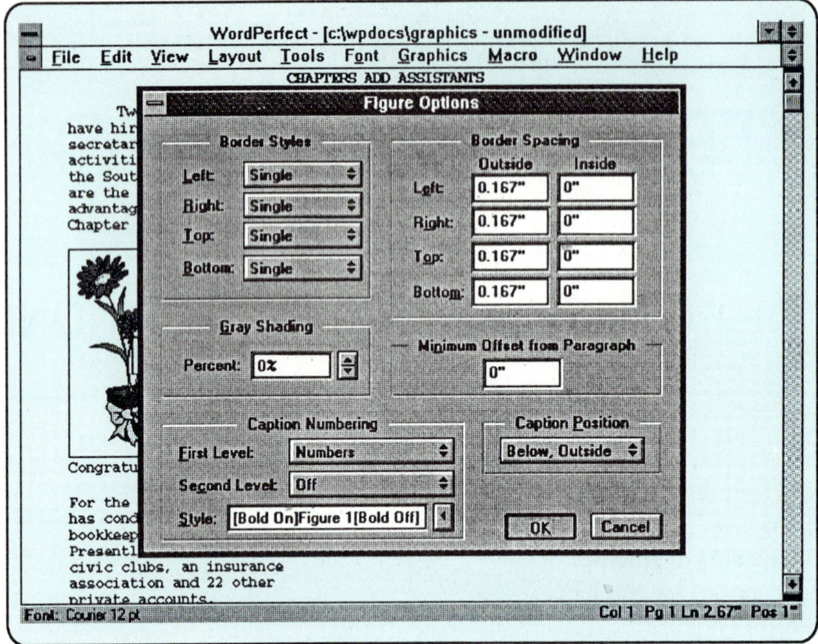

The Border Style option lets you change the appearance of the borders around a box. You can change the border style for each side of the box.

To change the Left Border Styles option:

Click	the Left pop-up list button in the Border Styles box	***Press***	*Alt+L to select the Left pop-up list button in the Border Styles box*
Hold down	the mouse button to view the pop-up list	***Press***	*Alt+↑ to view the pop-up list*

Your screen should look like Figure 24-2.

Figure 24-2

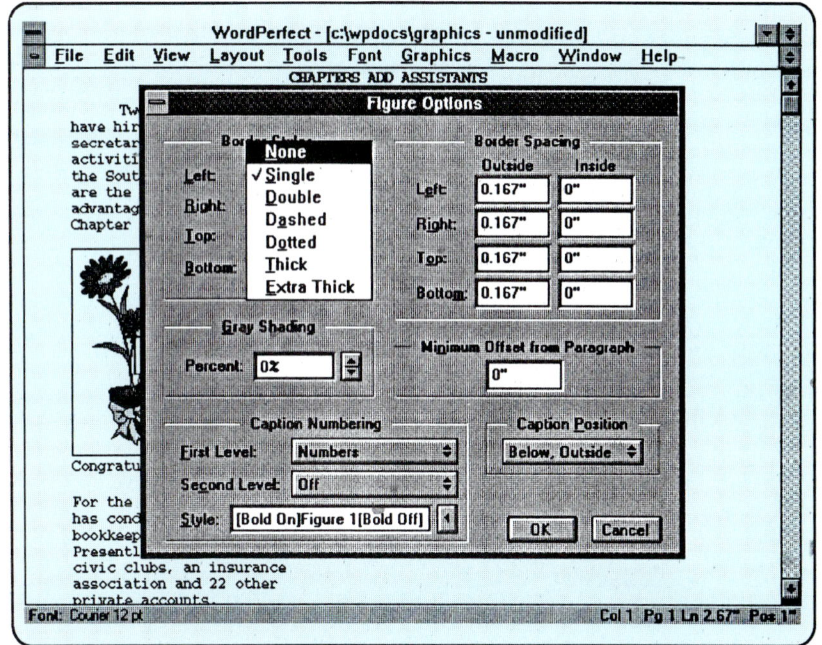

You can choose to have no border, a single line, a double line, a dashed line, a dotted line, or to make the border thick or extra thick.

Suppose you want to delete the border on the daisies graphic. To change the border style to none:

Choose	None	***Type***	*N to select the None option*
Click	the Right pop-up list button in the Border Styles box	***Press***	*Alt+R to select the Right pop-up list button in the Border Styles box*
Hold down	the mouse button to view the pop-up list	***Press***	*Alt+↑ to view the pop-up list*
Choose	None	***Type***	*N to select the None option*
Click	the Top pop-up list button in the Border Styles box	***Press***	*Alt+T to select the Top pop-up list button in the Border Styles box*
Hold down	the mouse button to view the pop-up list	***Press***	*Alt+↑ to view the pop-up list*
Choose	None	***Type***	*N to select the None option*

Click	the Bottom pop-up list button in the Border Styles box	***Press***	*Alt+B to select the Bottom pop-up list button in the Border Styles box*
Hold down	the mouse button to view the pop-up list	***Press***	*Alt+↑ to view the pop-up list*
Choose	None	***Type***	*N to select the None option*

Your screen should look like Figure 24-3.

Figure 24-3

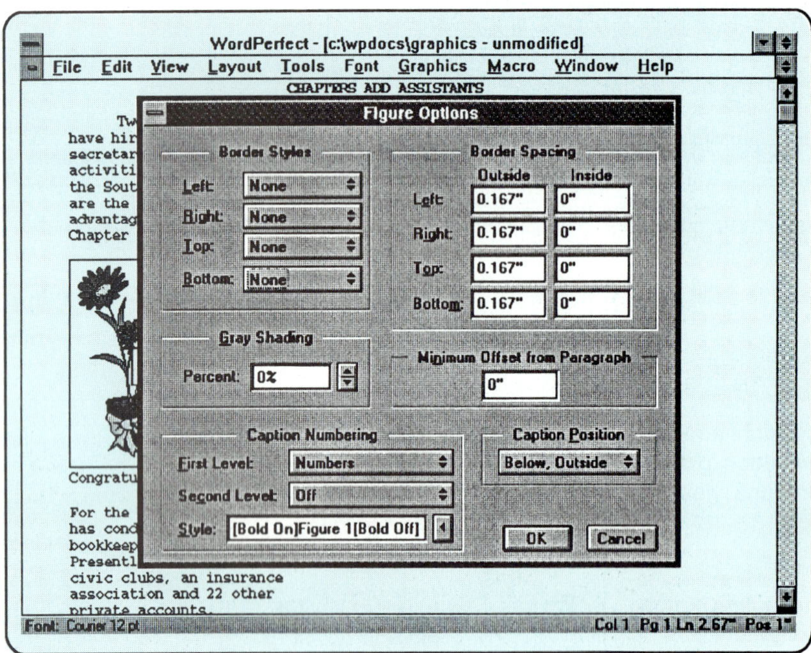

■ BORDER SPACING

The Border Spacing option is divided into two options. The Outside Border Spacing option concerns the space between the text in the document and the outer box borders. The Inside Border Spacing option concerns the space between the border of the box and the text or image inside. Notice that you can change the space on the left, right, top, and bottom of the box.

To change the Left Outside Border Spacing option:

Double-click	the Left text box in the Outside Border Spacing column	***Press***	*Alt+E to select the Left text box in the Outside Border Spacing column*

Suppose you want to change the outside border space from 0.167″ to 0.1″ on all sides of the box. To change the outside border space:

Type	.1	***Type***	*.1*
Double-click	the Right text box in the Outside Border Spacing column	***Press***	*Alt+I to select the Right text box in the Outside Border Spacing column*
Type	.1	***Type***	*.1*
Double-click	the Top text box in the Outside Border Spacing column	***Press***	*Alt+O to select the Top text box in the Outside Border Spacing column*
Type	.1	***Type***	*.1*
Double-click	the Bottom text box in the Outside Border Spacing column	***Press***	*Alt+M to select the Bottom text box in the Outside Border Spacing column*
Type	.1	***Type***	*.1*

Your screen should look like Figure 24-4.

Figure 24-4

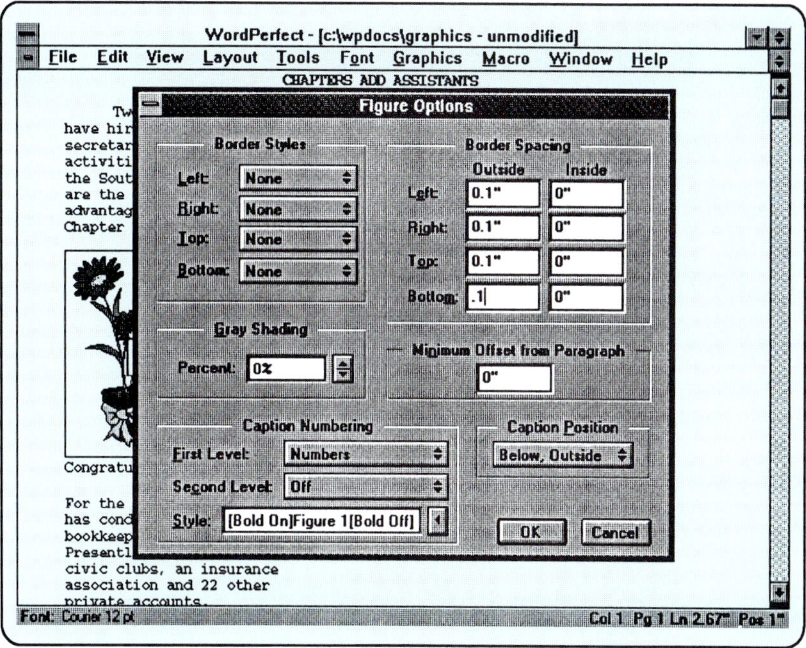

You want to leave the inside border spacing as 0″. If you wanted to change the inside border spacing, you would double-click on the appropriate text box or press the Tab key to move to the Inside Border Spacing column text boxes.

■ CAPTION

The Caption options are also divided into two options. The Caption Numbering option concerns the appearance of the numbers within a caption. The Caption Position option concerns where the caption will be placed in or around the box. The Caption Position options will vary according to the type of box you have defined.

Suppose you want to place the caption above the daisies graphic image and inside the border. To select the Caption Position option:

Click	the Caption Position pop-up list button	***Press***	*Alt+P to select the Caption Position pop-up list button*
Hold down	the mouse button to view the pop-up list	***Press***	*Alt+↑ to view the pop-up list*

Your screen should look like Figure 24-5.

Figure 24-5

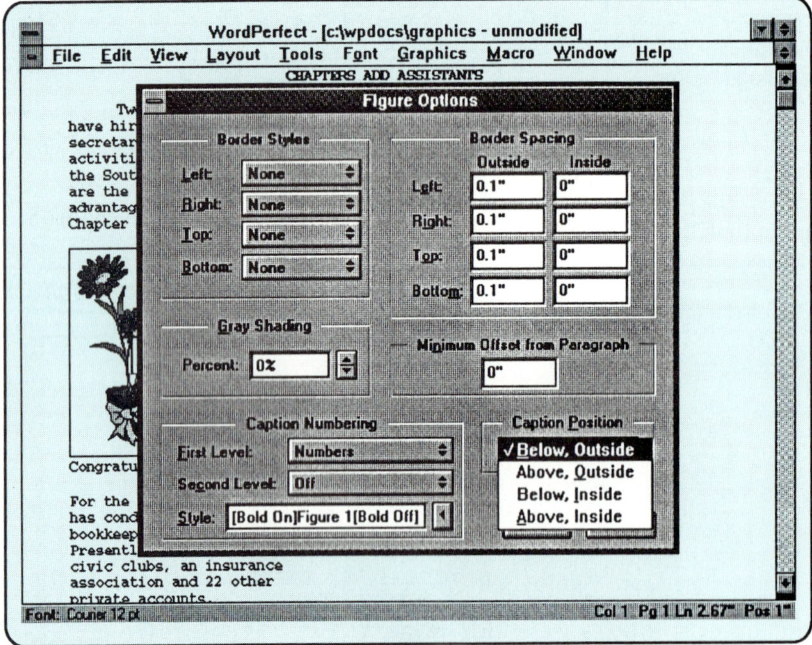

To change the caption position to above the box and inside the border:

Choose	Above, Inside	***Type***	*A to select the Above, Inside option*

Your screen should look like Figure 24-6.

Figure 24-6

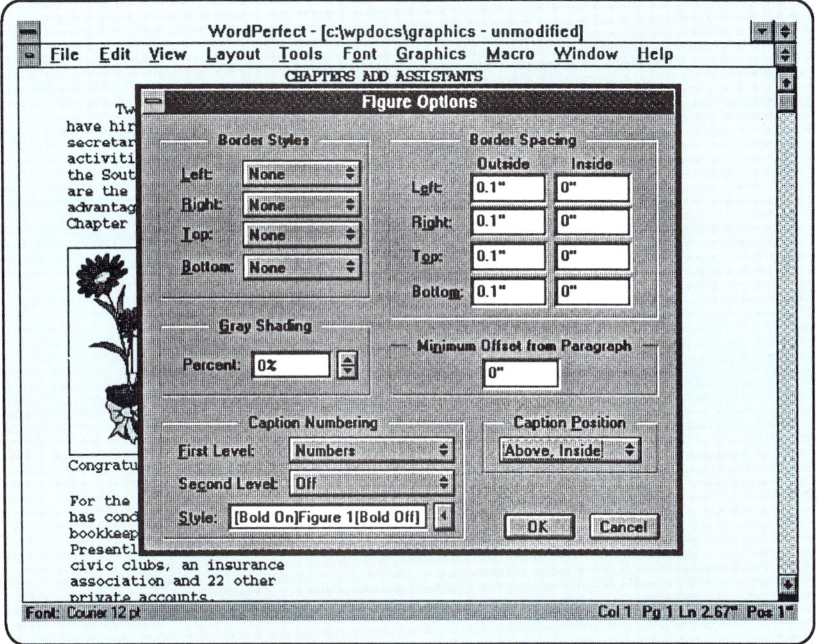

■ GRAY SHADING

The Gray Shading Percent option allows you to determine a shading for the graphic box. You enter a percentage value for the shading. A value of 100% means black and 0% means white.

Suppose you want to shade the daisies graphic. To change the gray shading percent to 15:

Double-click	the Gray Shading Percent text box	***Press***	*Alt+G to select the Gray Shading Percent text box*
Type	15	***Type***	*15*

Your screen should look like Figure 24-7.

Figure 24-7

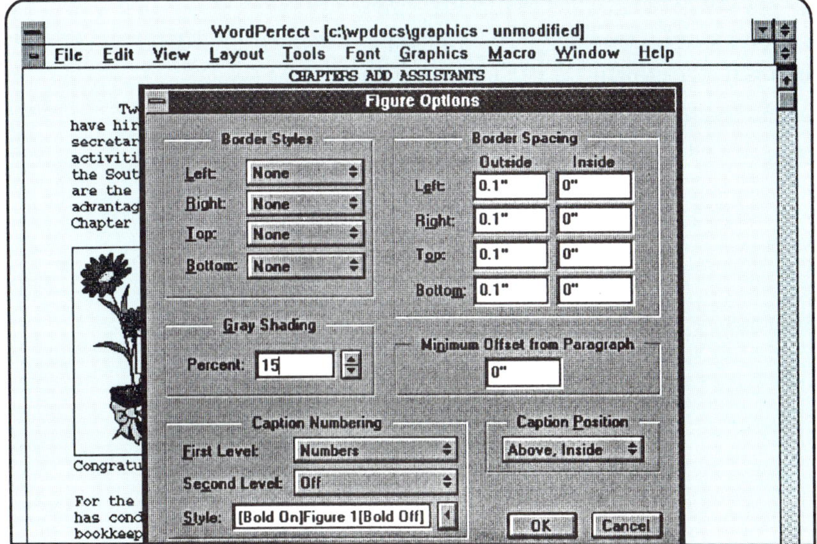

To return to your document:

Click	the OK command button	***Press***	*↵Enter*

Your screen should look like Figure 24-8.

Figure 24-8

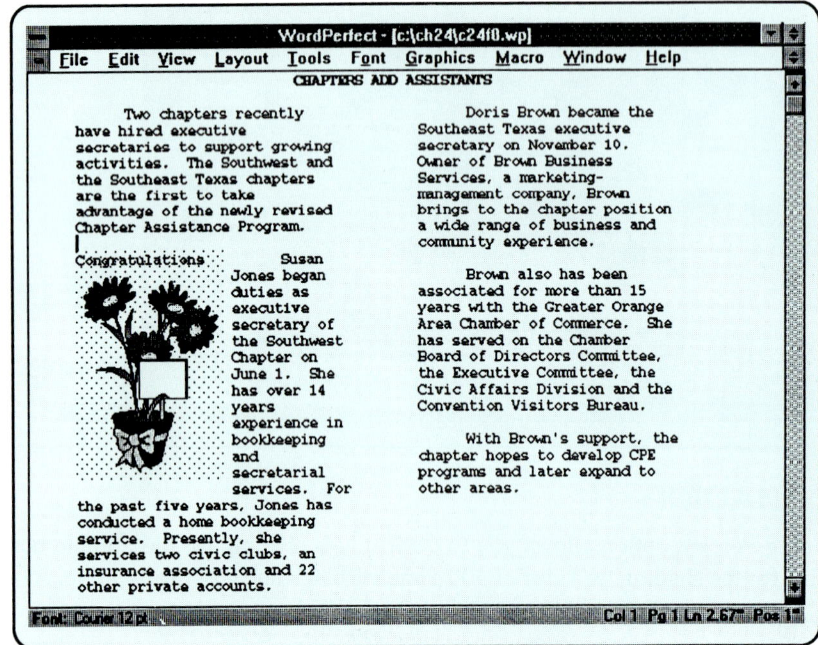

Notice that there is no border around the graphic, the text is closer to the graphic, the caption is at the top of the box and inside the box, and the gray shading is within the box.

After seeing the graphic, suppose you want to change the border style to a double line, place the caption below the daisies graphic and outside the border, and have no gray shading.

Each time that you change the graphic options for a box type, an Option code is placed in the document. Place your insertion point after the last Option code if you want to make more changes to the graphic options.

Turn on the Reveal Codes feature to see the Option codes.

A [Fig Opt] code is placed before the figure. You must move your insertion point after this code so that your new changes will take effect.

Turn off the Reveal Codes feature.

To make the changes:

Click	after the [Fig Opt] code	***Move***	*the insertion point after the [Fig Opt] code*
Choose	Graphics	***Press***	*Alt*
Choose	Figure	***Select***	*Graphics*
Choose	Options	***Select***	*Figure*

Click	the Left pop-up list button in the Border Styles box	***Select***	*Options*
Hold down	the mouse button to view the pop-up list	***Press***	*Alt+L to select the Left pop-up list button in the Border Styles box*
Choose	Double	***Press***	*Alt+↑ to view the pop-up list*
Click	the Right pop-up list button in the Border Styles box	***Type***	*D to select the Double option*
Hold down	the mouse button to view the pop-up list	***Press***	*Alt+R to select the Right pop-up list button in the Border Styles box*
Choose	Double	***Press***	*Alt+↑ to view the pop-up list*
Click	the Top pop-up list button in the Border Styles box	***Type***	*D to select the Double option*
Hold down	the mouse button to view the pop-up list	***Press***	*Alt+T to select the Top pop-up list button in the Border Styles box*
Choose	Double	***Press***	*Alt+↑ to view the pop-up list*
Click	the Bottom pop-up list button in the Border Styles box	***Type***	*D to select the Double option*
Hold down	the mouse button to view the pop-up list	***Press***	*Alt+B to select the Bottom pop-up list button in the Border Styles box*
Choose	Double	***Press***	*Alt+↑ to view the pop-up list*

Click	the Caption Position pop-up list button	***Type***	*D to select the Double option*
Hold down	the mouse button to view the pop-up list	***Press***	*Alt+P to select the Caption Position pop-up list button*
Choose	Below, Outside	***Press***	*Alt+↑ to view the pop-up list*
Double-click	the Gray Shading Percent text box	***Type***	*B to select the Below, Outside option*
Type	0	***Press***	*Alt+G to select the Gray Shading Percent text box*
Click	the OK command button	***Type***	*0*
		Press	*↵Enter*

Your screen should look like Figure 24-9.

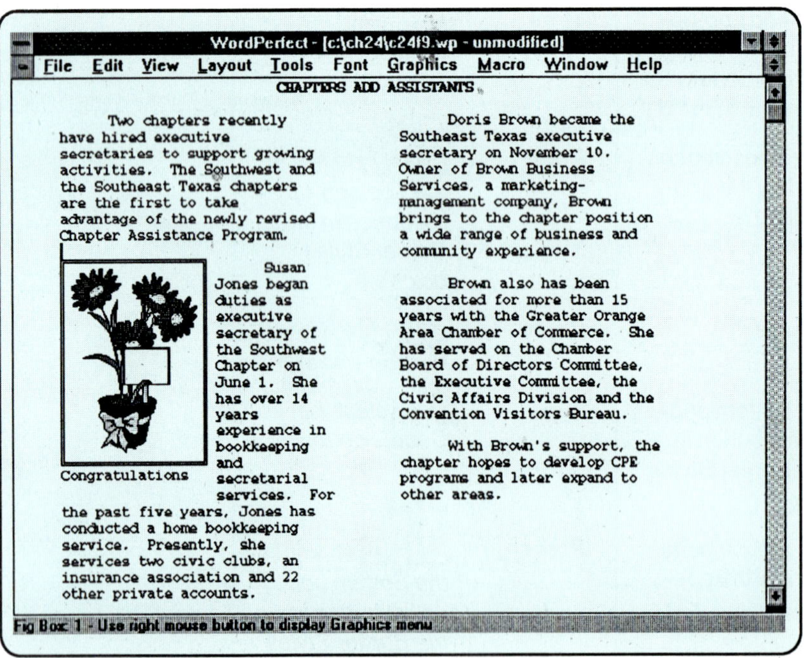

Figure 24-9

Save the document as "graphicb." Close the document.

EXERCISE 1

INSTRUCTIONS: Define the following terms:

1. Graphic Options feature ______________________________
   ____
2. Border styles ______________________________
   ____
3. Outside border spacing ______________________________
   ____
4. Inside border spacing ______________________________
   ____
5. Caption numbering style ______________________________
   ____
6. Caption position option ______________________________
   ____
7. Gray shading percent ______________________________
   ____

EXERCISE 2

INSTRUCTIONS: Circle T if the statement is true and F if the statement is false.

T F 1. The Figure Option dialog box allows you to change the default settings for any of the five graphic box types.

T F 2. The Border Styles option defines the amount of space between the border and text.

T F 3. The Outside Border Spacing option concerns the space between the border of the box and the text or image in the box.

T F 4. The Inside Border Spacing option concerns the space between double border lines.

T F 5. The Caption Numbering Style option concerns the appearance of the numbers within a caption.

T F 6. The Caption Position option concerns where the caption will be placed in or around the box.

T	F	7.	Entering 100 for the gray shading percent means the shading will be white.
T	F	8.	In order to see the option changes you define, you must view or print the document.

EXERCISE 3

INSTRUCTIONS:

1. Create the following document.
2. Place a picture of a blue ribbon where indicated. The name of the WordPerfect graphic for a blue ribbon is "blueribn.wpg."
3. Print the document.
4. Place a double line border around the blue ribbon.
5. Change the outside border space to .2" on all sides of the box.
6. Put the caption "Fun Run Prize" below the picture.
7. Change the gray shading percent to 10.
8. Print the document.
9. Save the document in a file using the name "ch24ex03."
10. Close the document.

```
Next Saturday the annual company picnic will be held.  To encourage
improved physical fitness among all employees, the first annual
special five mile fun run will be held at 9:00 a.m.

The winner of the race will receive the ribbon pictured below.
```

```
The ribbon will be imprinted with the winner's name.  A special
display will be constructed in the company cafeteria in which the
ribbon will reside until the next race is held.
```

EXERCISE 4

INSTRUCTIONS:

1. Create the following document. Use the "bookworm.wpg" and the "wall-clk.wpg" graphics.
2. Eliminate the borders around the bookworm graphic. Make the picture 3″ x 3″.
3. Make the clock graphic 1.5″ x 1.5″. Place the caption above and inside the double line borders.
4. Preview and print the document.
5. Save the document in a file using the name "ch24ex04."
6. Close the document.

THE SCIENCE CLUB
WILL
MEET NEXT TUESDAY

DON'T FORGET THE CORRECT TIME OF THE MEETING!

THE MEMBERS OF THE SCIENCE CLUB WILL HOLD THEIR NEXT MONTHLY MEETING AT 7:30 P.M. IN THE MELLON LIBRARY.

ALL MEMBERS ARE REQUESTED TO TRY TO BRING A FRIEND TO THE MEETING.

REFRESHMENTS WILL BE SERVED. WORM SLIDES FROM THE JUNGLES OF SOUTH AMERICA WILL BE SHOWN. ROBERT J. THIEDA, CURATOR OF THE NATURAL HISTORY MUSEUM WILL SPEAK.

EXERCISE 5

INSTRUCTIONS:

1. Create the following document. Use the "bkgrnd-2.wpg" graphic image.
2. Eliminate the borders of the graphic.
3. Make the graphic 5″ x 5″ and center it on the page. Change the gray shading percent to 10.
4. Add the caption "ARIZONA - THE HOME OF THE MAJESTIC GRAND CANYON." Make the caption bold and centered. Place the caption below the graphic and inside the border.
5. Preview and print the document.
6. Save the document as "ch24ex05."
7. Close the document.

ARIZONA - THE HOME OF THE MAJESTIC GRAND CANYON

EXERCISE 6

INSTRUCTIONS:

1. Create the following document. Use the "law.wpg" graphic.
2. The height of the graphic is 3.5″.
3. The borders are extra thick.
4. The percent of gray shading is 15.
5. Create the caption "LAW AND ORDER." Bold and center the caption. Place the caption above and outside the box.
6. Preview and print the document.
7. Save the document in a file using the name "ch24ex06."
8. Close the document.

LAW AND ORDER

EXERCISE 7

INSTRUCTIONS:

1. Create the following document. Use the graphic "beach-1.wpg."
2. The size of the graphic is 4″ x 4″.
3. The borders are dotted.
4. Place the caption inside and at the bottom of the box. Bold and center the caption.

5. Change the gray shading percent to 10.
6. Preview and print the document.
7. Save the document in a file using the name "ch24ex07."
8. Close the document.

SUMMER FUN!!

EXERCISE 8

INSTRUCTIONS:

1. Open the document "ch24ex07."
2. Change the size of the graphic to 5″ x 5″.
3. Change the caption to "Too much sun can lead to summer misery." Remove the bold and center features.
4. Change the borders: left is extra thick, top and right are dashed, and bottom is thick.
5. Place the caption outside the bottom of the graphic.
6. Change the gray shading percent to 5.
7. Preview and print the document.
8. Save the document in a file using the name "ch24ex08."
9. Close the document.

CHAPTER TWENTY-FIVE

DESKTOP PUBLISHING: EDITING GRAPHICS

OBJECTIVES

In this chapter, you will learn to:

- Rotate a graphic
- Scale a graphic
- Move a graphic
- Make a graphic black and white
- Outline a graphic

■ CHAPTER OVERVIEW

Whenever you include a graphic in a document, you may want to edit the graphic. The Figure Editor in WordPerfect allows you to rotate, scale, and move a graphic within the box that contains it. You can also outline a graphic or make it black and white.

In this chapter, editing graphics is described and illustrated. Some of the topics discussed are rotating a graphic, moving a graphic, scaling a graphic, and changing a graphic to black and white or an outline.

> **In This Chapter**
>
> The figures of each screen are displayed using the mouse instructions. Your screen will appear differently if you use the keyboard or function key instructions.

■ ROTATING

Change the default directory to "a:\wpdocs" or to "c:\wpdocs." Then open the document "graphicb."

Suppose you want to rotate the position of the daisies image that you used in Chapter 24. The Rotate option allows you to rotate the image in a circle.

To rotate the graphic in Figure 1:

Double-click	the daisies figure	***Press***	*Alt*	**Press**	Shift + F11
		Select	*Graphics*	**Type**	1
		Select	*Figure*	**Press**	↵Enter
		Select	*Edit*		
		Type	*1*		
		Press	*↵Enter*		

Your screen should look like Figure 25-1.

Figure 25-1

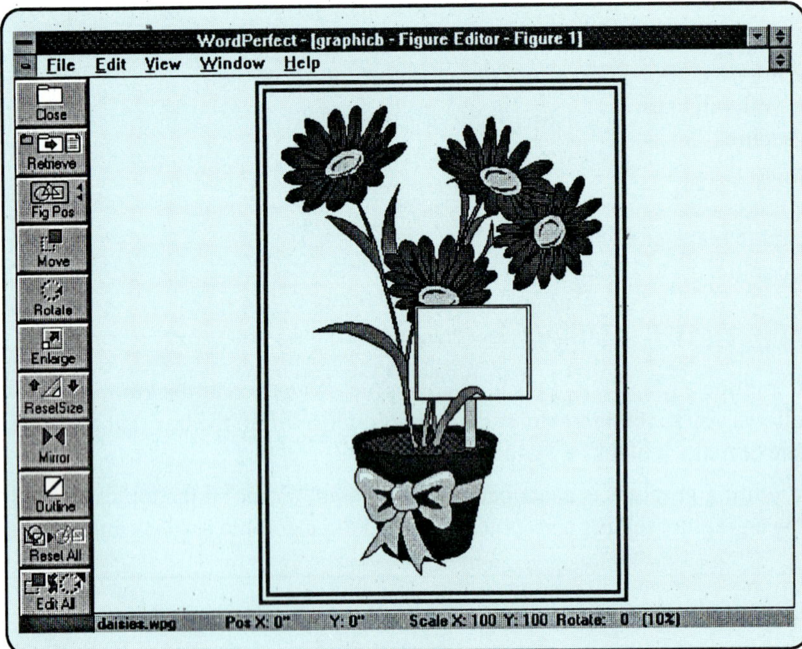

The Figure Editor has a menu and Button Bar that allows you to edit graphics. The status bar at the bottom of the Figure Editor indicates the position of your graphic in the figure box, the scale of your graphic, the number of degrees your graphic has been rotated, and the percentage of change currently selected.

The percentage of change feature allows you to specify by what percentage you want to affect the graphic when you use certain figure editing features. For example, if the percentage of change is 10% and you choose to rotate the graphic using the keyboard, the graphic would be rotated by 10% in the Figure box. To change the percentage of change, press the Insert key.

Note that the current percentage of change is 10%.

To rotate an image you can choose Rotate from the Edit menu, click the Rotate button on the Button Bar, or use the Ctrl + ← and Ctrl + → keys. When you rotate an image using the keyboard, the figure is rotated by the percentage of change.

To rotate the image 10% to the left:

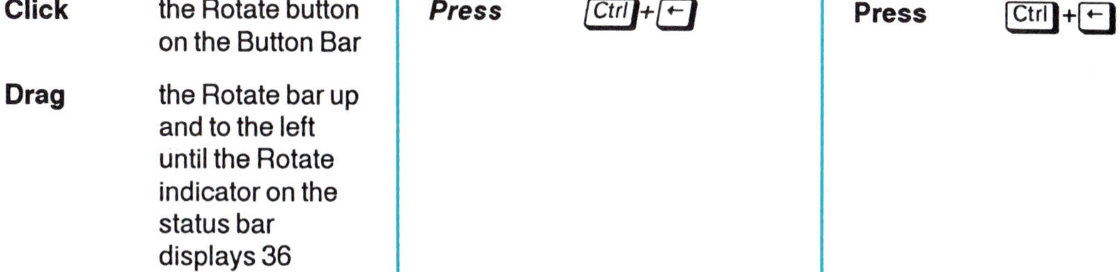

Click	the Rotate button on the Button Bar	***Press***	Ctrl+←	**Press**	Ctrl+←
Drag	the Rotate bar up and to the left until the Rotate indicator on the status bar displays 36				

Your screen should look like Figure 25-2.

Figure 25-2

To rotate the image 10% to the right:

Drag	the Rotate bar down and to the right until the Rotate indicator on the status bar displays 0	***Press***	Ctrl+→	**Press**	Ctrl+→

Your screen should look like Figure 25-3.

Figure 25-3

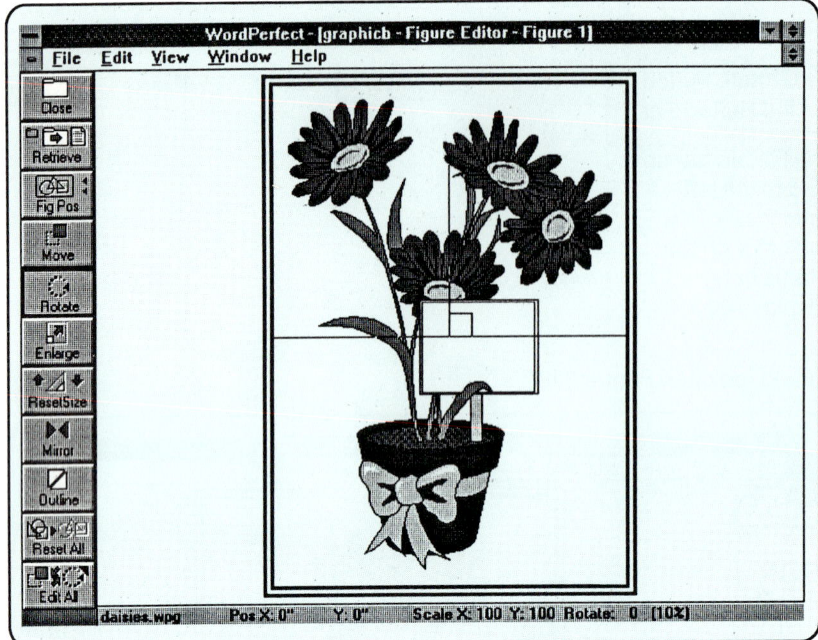

To remove the Rotate bar from the screen:

Click	the Rotate button on the Button Bar		

■ SCALE OPTION

Suppose you want to reduce the size of the daisies image. You can enlarge or reduce an image in a horizontal or vertical direction by choosing the Scale option under the Edit menu or by pressing Ctrl+↑ and Ctrl+↓.

If you want to enlarge a picture by the percentage of change, choose Enlarge % from the Scale option under the Edit menu or press Ctrl+↑. To reduce a picture by the percentage of change, choose Reduce % from the Scale option under the Edit menu or press Ctrl+↓.

Assume you want the image to be scaled to 75% of the original size, both horizontally and vertically. First, you must increase the percentage of change so that you can scale the graphic easily.

To increase the percentage of change to 25%:

Press	Insert three times	***Press***	*Insert three times*	**Press**	Insert three times

Your screen should look like Figure 25-4.

Figure 25-4

Notice the percentage of change displays 25%.

To reduce the daisies image by 25%:

Choose	Edit	***Press***	*Alt*	**Press**	Ctrl+↓
Choose	Scale	***Select***	*Edit*		
Choose	Reduce %	***Select***	*Scale*		
		Select	*Reduce %*		

Your screen should look like Figure 25-5.

Figure 25-5

Notice that the X and Y scale indicators have changed to 75.

You can also enlarge the image by using the Enlarge % choice from the Scale option under the Edit menu or by pressing Ctrl+↑.

To enlarge the image by 25%:

Choose	Edit	***Press***	*Alt*	**Press**	Ctrl+↑
Choose	Scale	***Select***	*Edit*		
Choose	Enlarge %	***Select***	*Scale*		
		Select	*Enlarge %*		

Your screen should look like Figure 25-6.

Figure 25-6

You can also enlarge part of the graphic using the Enlarge Area choice from the Scale option under the Edit menu or using the Enlarge button on the Button Bar. For more details on how to enlarge an area of the graphic see the "Figure Editor, Edit Menu" section of the WordPerfect Reference Manual.

■ MOVING

Assume that you want to move the daisies image to another location in the box. You can move an image vertically or horizontally within the box by choosing the Move option under the Edit menu or by pressing the →, ←, ↑, or ↓ keys.

To move the figure up and to the right:

Click	the Move button on the Button Bar	***Press***	→	**Press**	→
Drag	the graphic up and to the right	***Press***	↑	**Press**	↑

If you use the keyboard to move the graphic, the graphic moves up and to the right by 25%, the current percentage of change.

Your screen should look similar to Figure 25-7.

Figure 25-7

Notice the X and Y position of the graphic have changed.

■ BLACK AND WHITE OPTIONS

Most WordPerfect graphics appear in color on the screen. However, many printers can not print color documents. Most printers adapt the color graphics and print them in varying shades of gray. WordPerfect has two features that help you print graphics when you do not have a color printer and prefer not to print using a gray scale.

The Black and White feature changes any graphic colors in the picture to black. If the graphic has a number of colors in it, the Black and White option may not have the desired effect.

The Outline feature changes all colors to white and outlines the picture in black. The Outline feature does not affect black and white pictures.

Both the Black and White and Outline features are located in the Edit menu. The Outline feature also has a button on the Button Bar.

To change the picture of the daisies to black and white:

Choose	Edit	***Press***	*Alt*
Choose	Black and White	***Select***	*Edit*
		Select	*Black and White*

Your screen should look similar to Figure 25-8.

Figure 25-8

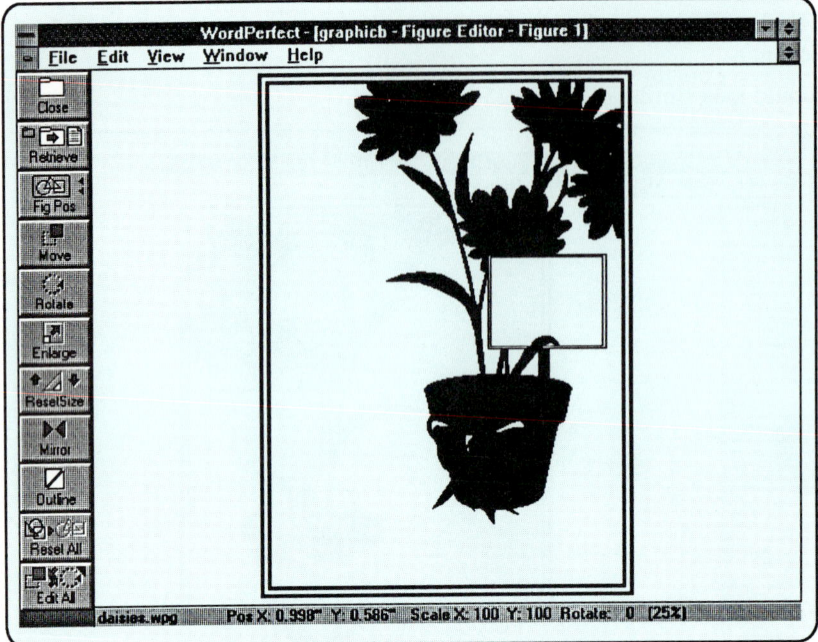

Because there are many colors in the daisies graphic, the Black and White feature makes the graphic too dark. To create a line drawing of the graphic using the Outline feature:

Click	the Outline button on the Button Bar	***Press***	Alt
		Select	*Edit*
		Select	*Outline*

Your screen should look similar to Figure 25-9.

Figure 25-9

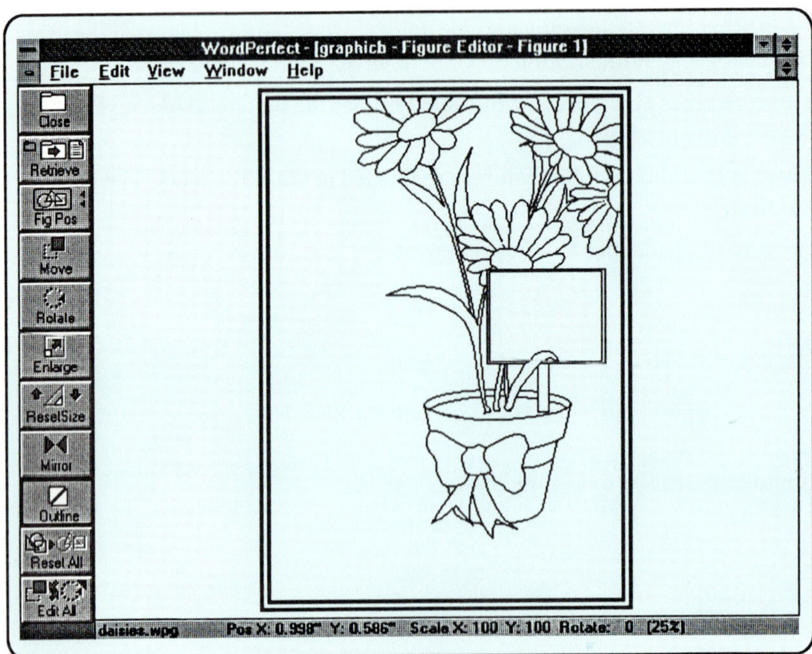

To return to your document:

Click	the Close button on the Button Bar	***Press***	Alt	**Press**	Ctrl+F4
		Select	*File*		
		Select	*Close*		

Save the document as "graphice." Close the document.

For more detailed information on the other Figure Editor features see the "Figure Editor" section of the WordPerfect Reference manual.

EXERCISE 1

INSTRUCTIONS: Define the following terms:

1. Figure Editor ______________________________

2. Rotate option ______________________________

3. Scale option ______________________________

4. Move option ______________________________

5. Black and white option ______________________________

6. Outline option ______________________________

EXERCISE 2

INSTRUCTIONS: Circle T if the statement is true and F if the statement is false.

T	F	1. The Figure Editor allows you to draw pictures and charts in WordPerfect.
T	F	2. The Rotate option allows you to rotate the image in the graphic box.
T	F	3. In the Figure Editor, pressing the → key rotates the image to the right.

T F 4. The Scale option allows you to enlarge or reduce the graphic box on the page.

T F 5. The percentage of change feature allows you to specify by what percentage you want to affect the graphic when you use the keyboard to make the graphic black and white.

T F 6. You can scale a graphic horizontally but not vertically.

T F 7. You can scale an image by pressing the pointer-movement keys.

T F 8. The Move option allows you to move the figure within the box.

T F 9. Pressing the Ctrl+↑ keys moves the image up.

T F 10. You can only move an image up or down in the box.

EXERCISE 3

INSTRUCTIONS:

1. Create the following document.
2. Place a picture of a check mark in the document where indicated. The name of the WordPerfect graphic for a check mark is "checkmar.wpg."
3. Save the document in a file using the name "ch25ex03."
4. Print the document.
5. Rotate the graphic 25% to the right.
6. Print the document.
7. Rotate the graphic to its original position.
8. Rotate the graphic 10% to the left.
9. Print the document.
10. Rotate the graphic to its original position.
11. Scale the graphic to 50% of its original size.
12. Print the document.
13. Scale the graphic back to its original size.
14. Move the graphic to the left 1/2" and down 1".
15. Print the document.
16. Move the graphic back to its original position.
17. Print the document.
18. Close the document without saving changes.

```
Check marks are often used in a document to draw attention to
specific text.  WordPerfect has prepared a picture of a check mark
that you can use.  The check mark graphic appears below.
```

```
You can rotate the check mark and change the size of the check
mark.  Also, you can move the check mark to a different location in
the graphic box.
```

EXERCISE 4

INSTRUCTIONS:

1. Create the following document. Use the "fatpencl.wpg" graphic.
2. The size of the graphic is 4″ x 4″. Rotate the figure 270°. Reduce the size of the graphic by 30%.
3. Outline the graphic.
4. Preview and print the document.
5. Save the document in a file using the name "ch25ex04."
6. Close the document.

This is an illustration on rotating a graphic 270°, and reducing the size of the graphic by 30%.

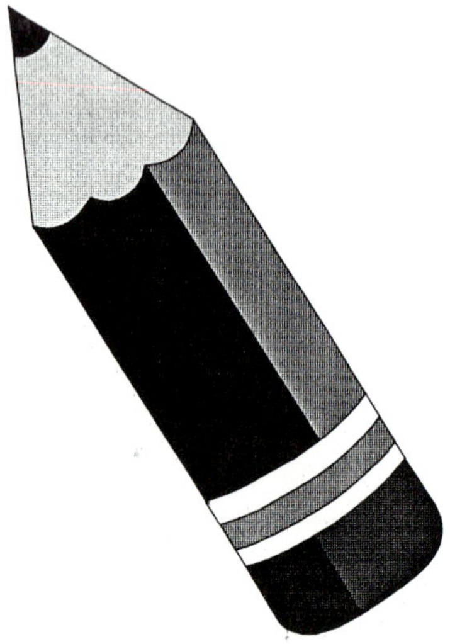

EXERCISE 5

INSTRUCTIONS:

1. Create the following document. Use the "duckling.wpg" graphic.
2. The size of the graphic is 4″ x 4″. Rotate the graphic 45° and decrease the size by 20%.
3. Preview and print the document.
4. Save the document in a file using the name "ch25ex05."
5. Close the document.

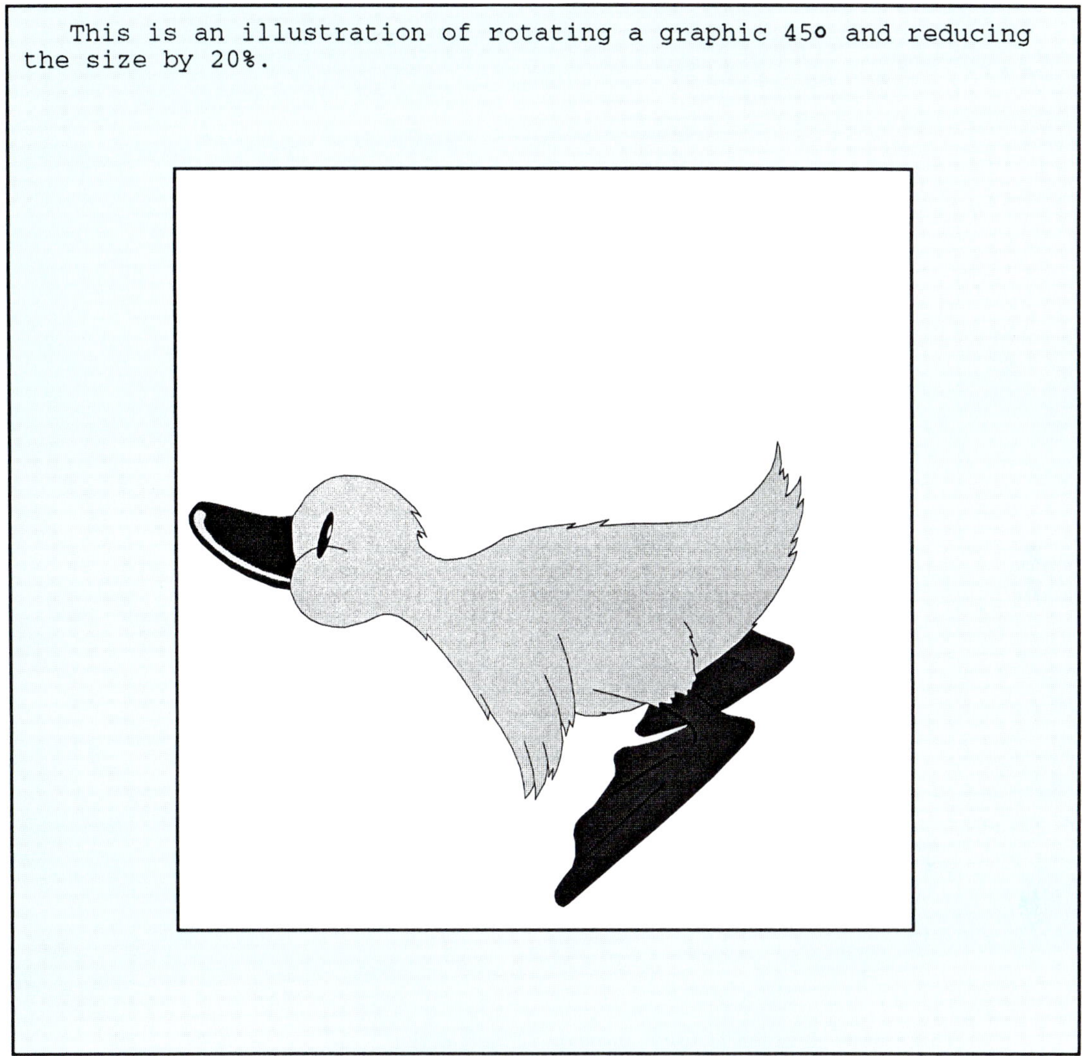

This is an illustration of rotating a graphic 45° and reducing the size by 20%.

EXERCISE 6

INSTRUCTIONS:

1. Create the following document. Use the "bookworm.wpg" graphic.
2. Center the graphic on the page. The size of the graphic is 4.5″ x 4.5″. Place the caption inside and at the bottom of the graphic.
3. Scale the graphic to 60%.
4. Move the figure up 1/2″ (Y position of .5″) and to the left 1/2″ (X position of -.5″) in the figure box.
5. Preview and print the document.
6. Save the document in a file using the name "ch25ex06."
7. Close the document.

The following illustration shows the graphic scaled at 60%. It also shows the graphic moved up 1/2" and moved to the left 1/2".

This figure is scaled to 60%, moved 1/2″ left and 1/2″ up.

EXERCISE 7

INSTRUCTIONS:

1. Create the following document. Use the "law.wpg" graphic.
2. Do not change the size. Place the caption at the top and inside the graphic box.
3. The left border is extra thick, the right border is double, the top border is single, and the bottom border is thick.
4. Place the graphic in the lower left corner of the box.
5. Preview and print the document.
6. Save the document in a file using the name "ch25ex07."
7. Close the document.

This illustration shows a graphic moved to the bottom left corner of the box. The Figure Option feature was also used to change the border of the box and the caption location.

The graphic is moved to the lower left corner of the figure box.

EXERCISE 8

INSTRUCTIONS:

1. Create the following document. Use the "bkgrnd-2.wpg" graphic.
2. The size of the graphic is 5″ x 5″. Remove the borders.
3. Enlarge the graphic by 25%. Outline the graphic.
4. Use 15% gray shading for the figure. Place the caption inside and above the graphic. Bold and center the caption.
5. Preview and print the document.
6. Save the document in a file using the name "ch25ex08."
7. Close the document.

Great Vacations!

CHAPTER TWENTY-SIX

DESKTOP PUBLISHING: GRAPHIC LINES

OBJECTIVES

In this chapter, you will learn to:

- Create graphic lines
- Edit graphic lines

CHAPTER OVERVIEW

In some situations, you may want to add horizontal or vertical lines to a document. WordPerfect has a Graphics Line feature that allows you to create and edit lines. The lines can be shaded or black.

In this chapter, the procedures for creating and editing graphic lines are described and illustrated.

CREATING LINES

Change the default directory to "a:\wpdocs" or to "c:\wpdocs." Then open the document "graphice."

Suppose you want to place a horizontal line below the "CHAPTERS ADD ASSISTANTS" text. To create the horizontal line:

Click below the main heading (Pos 1", Ln 1.17")
Choose Graphics
Choose Line
Choose Horizontal

Move *the insertion point to Pos 1", Ln 1.17"*
Press *Alt*
Select *Graphics*
Select *Line*
Select *Horizontal*

Move the insertion point to Pos 1", Ln 1.17"
Press Ctrl+F11

The Create Horizontal Line dialog box appears. Your screen should look like Figure 26-1.

Figure 26-1

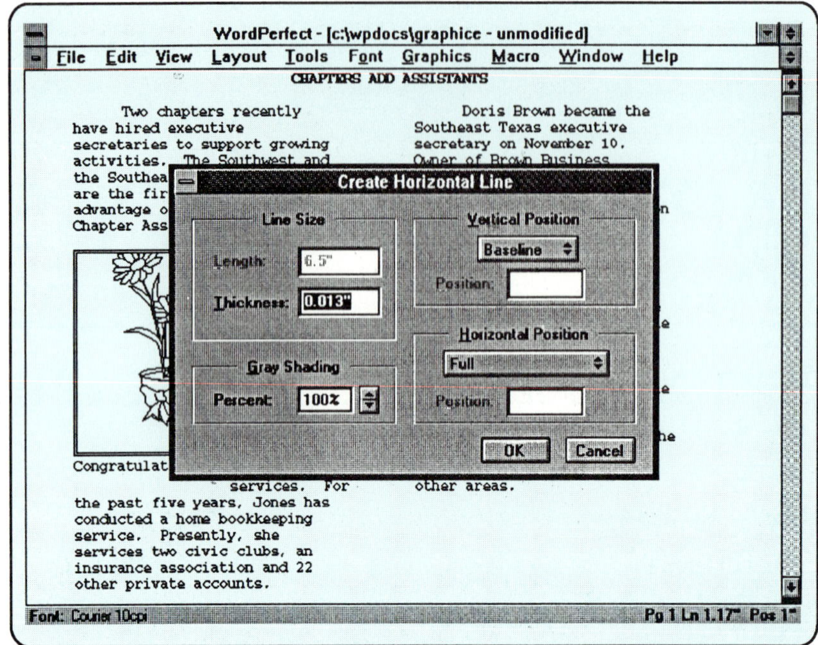

The Horizontal Position option allows you to position the line across the page. You can start the line at the left or right margin, center the line, or extend the line from margin to margin (full option). You can also set the line to begin a certain number of inches from the left side of the page.

The Vertical Position option allows you to position the graphic line on the current line (Baseline) or to set a specific position on the page where the line should be printed (Specify).

The Line Size option allows you to define the length and thickness of the line. The line length is calculated from the insertion point position to the margin set in the Horizontal Position option. If the horizontal position is defined as Full, the line length is set automatically based on the margin positions.

The Gray Shading Percent option allows you to specify how much the line should be shaded. A value of 100% is black and 0% is white.

To accept the default settings:

Click	the OK command button	***Press***	*↵Enter*	**Press**	↵Enter

The top part of your screen should look like Figure 26-2.

Figure 26-2

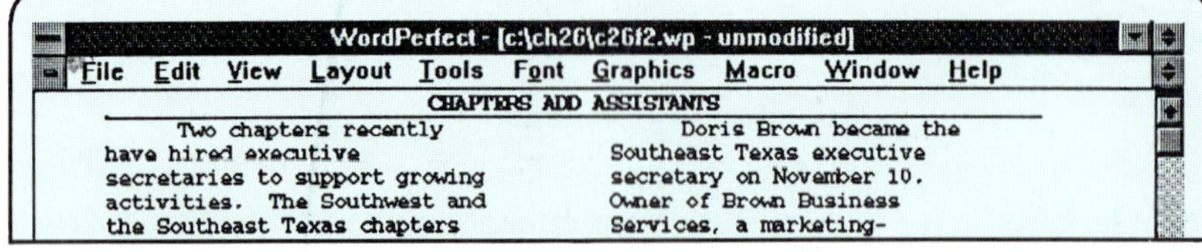

Notice that the line extends from the left to the right margins.

Suppose you want a vertical line between the columns in your document. To create the vertical line:

Click	at the left margin of the first paragraph in Column 1	***Move***	*the insertion point to the left margin of the first paragraph in Column 1*	**Move**	the insertion point to the left margin of the first paragraph in Column 1
Choose	Graphics	***Press***	*Alt*	**Press**	Ctrl+Shift+F11
Choose	Line	***Select***	*Graphics*		
Choose	Vertical	***Select***	*Line*		
		Select	*Vertical*		

The Create Vertical Line dialog box appears. Your screen should look like Figure 26-3.

Figure 26-3

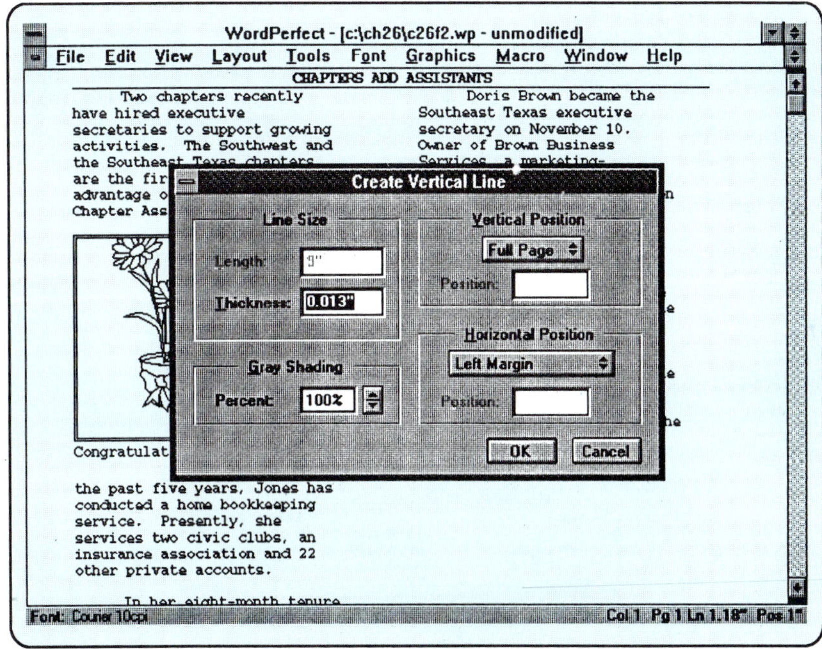

The Horizontal Position option allows you to position the line slightly to the left of the left margin, slightly to the right of the right margin, between columns, or set at a specific position.

To select the Horizontal Position option:

Click	the Horizontal Position pop-up list button	***Press***	*Alt+H to select the Horizontal Position pop-up list button*	**Press**	Alt+H to select the Horizontal Position pop-up list button
Hold down	the mouse button to view the pop-up list	***Press***	*Alt+↑ to view the pop-up list*	**Press**	Alt+↑ to view the pop-up list

Your screen should look like Figure 26-4.

Figure 26-4

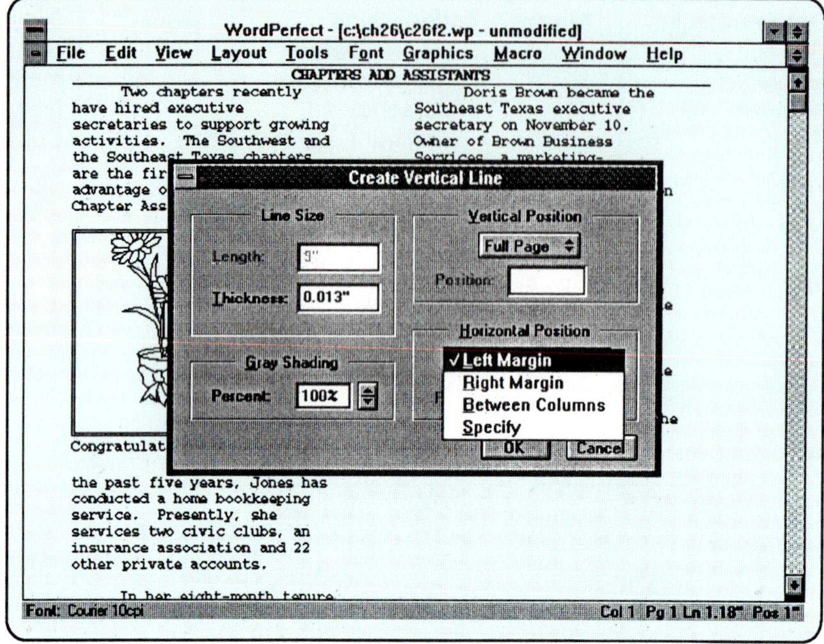

To position the line between columns:

Choose	Between Columns	***Type***	*B to select the Between Columns option*	**Type**	B to select the Between Columns option

Your screen should look like Figure 26-5.

Figure 26-5

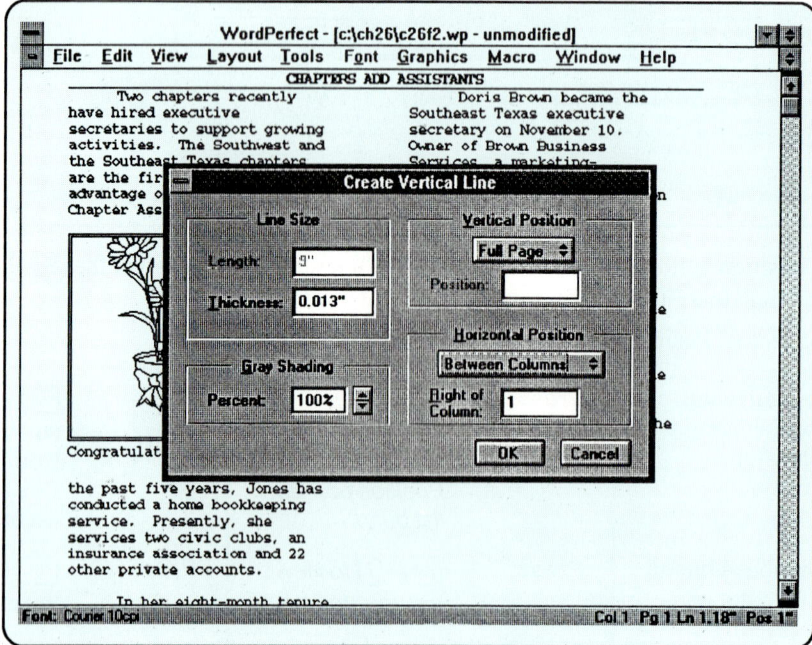

The default setting places the line to the right of column 1.

The Vertical Position option allows you to position the line at the top or bottom margin, centered between margins, extended the full length of the margins, or set to a specific position from the top of the page.

To select the Vertical Position option:

Click	the Vertical Position pop-up list button	***Press***	*Alt+V to select the Vertical Position pop-up list button*	**Press**	Alt+V to select the Vertical Position pop-up list button
Hold down	the mouse button to view the pop-up list	***Press***	*Alt+↑ to view the pop-up list*	**Press**	Alt+↑ to view the pop-up list

Your screen should look like Figure 26-6.

Figure 26-6

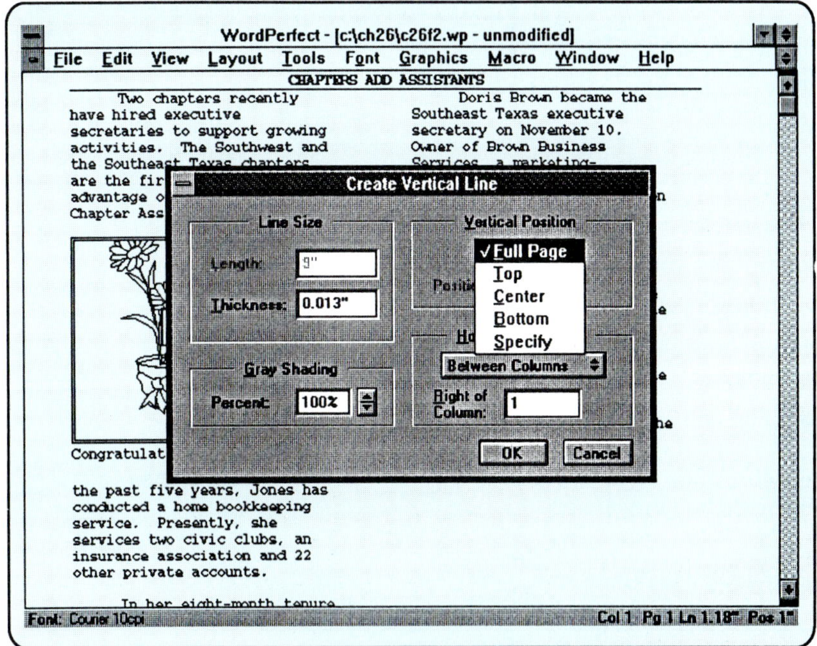

To specify that you want the line to begin where the insertion point is located:

Choose	Specify	***Type***	*S to select the Specify option*	**Type**	S to select the Specify option

Your screen should look like Figure 26-7.

Figure 26-7

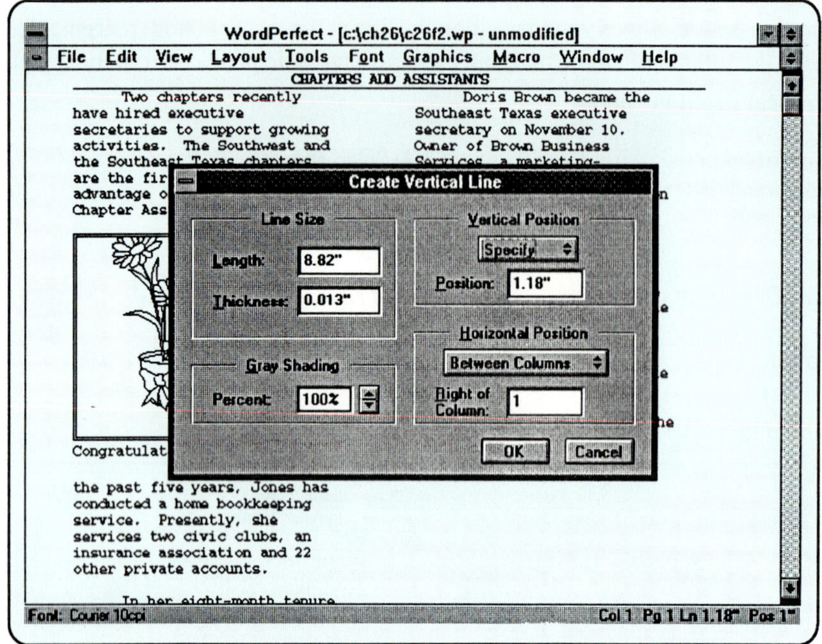

Notice that the line length has also changed.

The Length option allows you to define how long you want the line to be.

The Thickness option allows you to specify the thickness of the line.

The Gray Shading option allows you to specify how much the line should be shaded. A value of 100% is black and 0% is white.

To return to the document:

Click	the OK command button	***Press***	↵Enter	**Press**	↵Enter

Your screen should look like Figure 26-8.

Figure 26-8

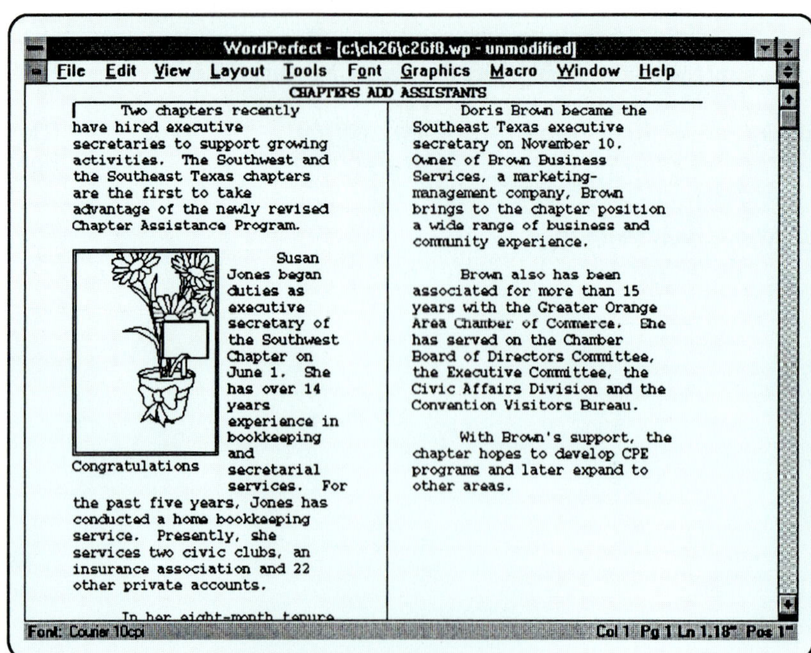

EDITING LINES

After you insert a line, you may need to modify it. Suppose you want to change the thickness of the horizontal line.

When you edit a line, select the line by clicking on it or position the insertion point immediately after the line code. WordPerfect searches backward for the first occurrence of a line.

To edit the horizontal line first:

Click	on the horizontal line	***Move***	*the insertion point after the horizontal line code*
Choose	Graphics	***Press***	*Alt*
Choose	Line	***Select***	*Graphics*
Choose	Edit Horizontal	***Select***	*Line*
		Select	*Edit Horizontal*

You can also enter the Line Edit feature by double-clicking on a graphic line.

The Edit Horizontal Line dialog box appears. Your screen should look like Figure 26-9.

Figure 26-9

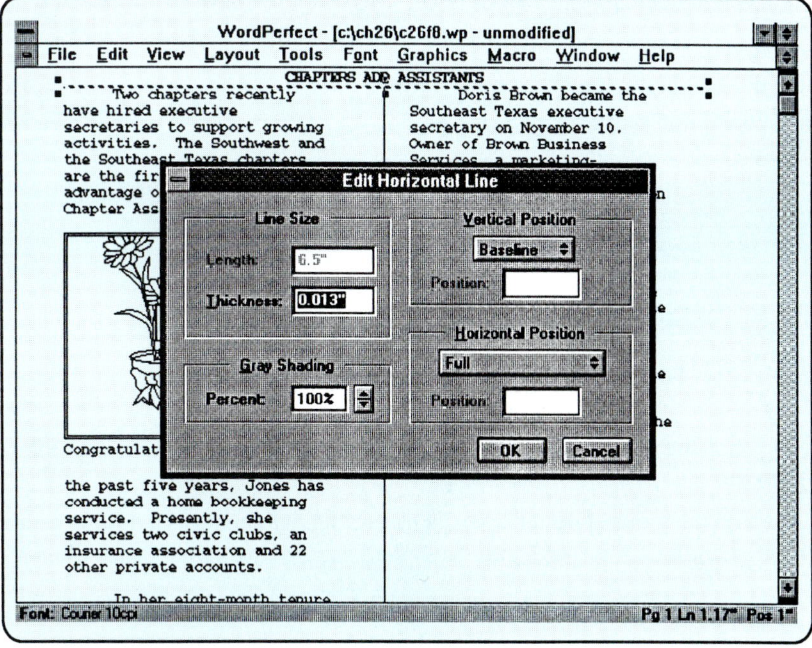

To change the thickness of the line:

Double-click	the Thickness text box	***Press***	*Alt+T to select the Thickness text box*
Type	.05	***Type***	*.05*

Your screen should look like Figure 26-10.

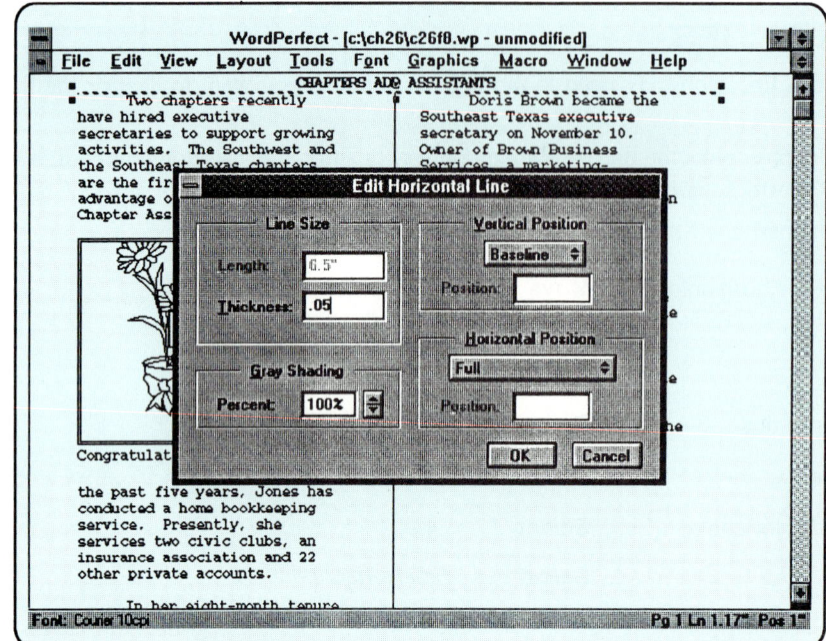

Figure 26-10

To return to the document:

Click	the OK command button	***Press***	*↵Enter*

Notice that the horizontal line is thicker. The top part of your screen should look like Figure 26-11.

Figure 26-11

You can also size and move a graphic line using the mouse. To edit a line using the mouse, select the line by clicking on it.

To move the line, position the mouse pointer over the line so that it appears as a move pointer (four pointing arrows) and drag the line.

To size the line, position the mouse pointer over the line so that it appears as a double-pointing arrow and drag one of the sizing handles. A sizing handle is a small square box that appears when a graphic line is selected.

Save the document as "graphich." Close the document.

EXERCISE 1

INSTRUCTIONS: Define the following terms:

1. Graphics Line feature ______________________________

____

2. Horizontal position option ______________________________

____

3. Vertical position option ______________________________

____

4. Line length option ______________________________

____

5. Line thickness option ______________________________

____

6. Gray shading option ______________________________

____

EXERCISE 2

INSTRUCTIONS: Circle T if the statement is true and F if the statement is false.

T F 1. The Graphics Line feature allows you to create and edit horizontal and vertical lines.

T F 2. Lines cannot be shaded.

T F 3. If the Horizontal Position option is set to "Full," the length of the line is automatically set to extend from the left to the right margin.

T F 4. When creating lines, you can set the horizontal position, vertical position, line length, line thickness, and shading of the line.

T F 5. When creating vertical lines, the Vertical Position option allows you to position the line at either the top or bottom margins.

T F 6. When creating horizontal lines, the Horizontal Position option allows you to position the line on the baseline or at a set position.

EXERCISE 3

INSTRUCTIONS:

1. Create the following document. Use the graphics "computr.wpg" and "daisies.wpg."
2. The horizontal lines at the top of the document should be full. The thickness is 0.25". Shading is 10%.
3. Size of both graphics is unchanged. Change the borders to reflect the illustration.
4. Print the document.
5. Save the document in a file using the name "ch26ex03."
6. Close the document.

THE WORD PROCESSOR

Computer mail saves paper!

We want everyone to help us reduce the amount of mail that is coming into the office.

Please try to use the computer mail system. This system was designed to reduce the paper flow in the office. Since we have instituted this system, we have reduced internal paper by 50%. We can do better!

Our next goal is to try to reduce the mail. Not all incoming mail is for product orders. We are receiving too much "junk mail." If you have any customers that send us more information than we need, please ask them to send you only the essential information.

We would like to take this opportunity to welcome the new employees. In the Word Processing department, **Ginny Moritz** has been with us for three weeks. Ginny has seven years of experience in the field of word processing.

In the Executive Division, **Tom Sheerer** has just been employed to help with the traffic. Tom has been a Traffic Manager for the past 10 years with the Dibow company.

The new face you see in the Payroll department belongs to **Jorge Escobar**. Jorge has just graduated from MidState University with a B.S. in Accounting.

We wish all these new employees "good luck" with their new positions.

WELCOME NEW EMPLOYEES!!!

EXERCISE 4

INSTRUCTIONS:

1. Create the following document. Use the "computr.wpg" graphic.
2. The width of the horizontal lines is 0.1″.
3. The size of each graphic is 1″ x 1″.
4. Print the document.
5. Save the document in a file using the name "ch26ex04."
6. Close the document.

THE NATIONAL COMPUTER SOCIETY

EXERCISE 5

INSTRUCTIONS:

1. Create the following document. Use the "map-worl.wpg" graphic.
2. The horizontal lines for the heading are full and 0.05″ wide.
3. The height of the graphics is 0.5″.
4. Create a two-column document with a vertical line between the columns. The vertical line should extend to the bottom of the page.
5. Print the document.
6. Save the document in a file using the name "ch26ex05."
7. Close the document.

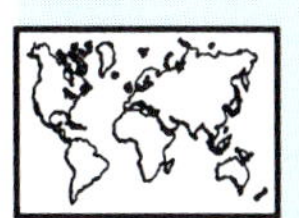

THE DAILY UNIVERSE

EXERCISE 6

INSTRUCTIONS:

1. Create the following document. Use the following graphics: "daisies.wpg," "owl-wise.wpg," "computr.wpg," and "map-worl.wpg."
2. Use horizontal lines that are .25" thick and use 50% shading for the heading. Place vertical lines between the columns. The vertical lines should extend to the bottom of the page.
3. Print the document.
4. Save the document in a file using the name "ch26ex06."
5. Close the document.

THE COMPANY NEWSLETTER

We take this time to express congratulations to the staff members with newborn babies. Betty Sue was born on July 4 to Tom and Mary Brown. Tim Ryan was born on May 7 to Gene and Rose Gunther.

Do you have an idea that can be used by the company????

We are willing to pay for any sound ideas that will save us money. Cash awards will be based on the amount of money saved in one year.

Management is really serious about this idea. They will pay 1 percent of any saved amount.

The rumors that have been going around the office about new computers are really true.

Everyone in the company will be given a new computer for their desktops by the end of the year. We will be connected to each other by something called a LAN.

The new LAN will allow us to talk to one another on the computer as easily as on the phone. In fact, if you have a computer at home and a modem, you will be able to get your messages over the phone-modem at home. This will allow us to leave detailed messages to each other and receive answers back without coming into the office.

There is also another feature on this system that will allow us to check each other's calendars to set up meetings that will not conflict with each other.

As you may have heard, the company will be merging with a company from West Germany. We will become a multinational organization in just a short time. This will have definite advantages for those who own stock in the company. It is expected that the stock will split at least 3 to 1 in our favor.

It will mean many positions will be available for transfer. There will be a procedure for you to follow if you would like an overseas assignment.

EXERCISE 7

INSTRUCTIONS:

1. Create the following document. Use the graphic "manufact.wpg."
2. The size of the graphic is 4" x 3".
3. The horizontal lines above and below the heading are 5" long.
4. The vertical line extends to the bottom of the page.
5. Print the document.
6. Save the document in a file using the name "ch26ex07."
7. Close the document.

THE WEEKLY CLARION

CONTRACT NEGOTIATIONS

Once again, we are troubled with the type of contract negotiated by our bargaining team with management.

Have you read the section on Overtime Pay? If we follow this contract, we will be receiving less for working overtime now than any previous time.

Management has given us some good benefits, but in this case, they have stripped us of a very lucrative increase in our weekly paychecks.

Ask your local negotiator how this new clause of **not paying for overtime until after 40 hours are worked** came to be.

There are some really good items in this new contract. I would like to personally thank everyone for basically a fine contract. If the overtime section can be reworked, we could have the best contract ever.

MOVING

If you plan to move out of the area in the next year, you should contact Jim O'Donnell for help. Jim moves all the executives and is very good. He offers great rates as well!

CHAPTER TWENTY-SEVEN

DESKTOP PUBLISHING: ADVANCED GRAPHIC FEATURES

OBJECTIVES

In this chapter you will learn to:

- Change the typesetting of a document
- Place a graphic box on another graphic box
- Access special WordPerfect characters
- Create a text box

■ CHAPTER OVERVIEW

In this chapter, the Typesetting feature is discussed and demonstrated. The procedures for creating a text box and for placing a graphic on a graphic are illustrated. The WordPerfect Characters feature is described and the process for inserting special characters in a document is given.

■ TYPESETTING FEATURES

When creating newsletters, manuscripts, and large reports, the appearance of the text on each page is very important. WordPerfect provides several typesetting features that allow you to change the amount of space between letters, between words, between lines of text, and between paragraphs.

Suppose you create a monthly corporate newsletter. When you create the newsletter using the default settings in WordPerfect, there is not enough space between the headings and the following paragraphs, the words are too far apart, and the letters in each word are too close together. You can change each of these options using the Typesetting feature. To use the Typesetting features, choose Typesetting from the Layout menu.

Before beginning this section, change the default document directory to "c:\wpdocs" or "a:\wpdocs." Create the document in Figure 27-1. To format the document properly, set the initial font to TmsRmn 12pt (Z1A), use two equally spaced newspaper-style columns, and set the justification to full. The newsletter heading is TmsRmn 14pt Bold (Z1A) and is centered. Bold each section heading. Force column two to begin with the "Issue Awareness Committee" section. Indent each item in the list in the "Issue Awareness Committee" section using a tab set at 4.75".

Figure 27-1

THE COMPANY NEWSLETTER

New Employees
Welcome! We have several new employees this month. Please extend a welcome to Julia Brown, Finance; Oliver Hunt, Human Services; and James Sharp, PC Support.

Happy Birthday!
A warm Happy Birthday wish to all of our employees with June birthdays. This month's birthday bunch includes Doris Boyd, Mark Cohn, Ross James, Samantha Cooley, and Belinda Meyers. The monthly birthday celebration will be held in Conference Room 2 on the 15th.

Annual Meeting
The annual meeting of the stockholders is June 28-July 2. All meetings and conferences will be held at the Boliver Hotel. There are still rooms available if you would like accommodations at the hotel rather than having to commute. You can obtain a room for a special discount of $50 per night. Please contact Janice Johnson if you would like more information.

Issue Awareness Committee
The IAC has distributed packets containing important employee information to each employee. Each packet should contain:

New insurance forms for medical, life, and disability plans
Information on the company 401K plan
Stock and money market fund options
Company-provided day care information
Car pool matching forms

Please turn in your completed copy of each of these forms to your direct supervisor by June 30. If you need a form, please contact Mike Rogers, the IAC chair.

Brown Bag Seminar
A lunch seminar will be presented on June 12. The topic this month is "Advanced Graphic Features in WordPerfect for Windows." The workshop will begin promptly at 11:45.

Save the document as "newslet."

Line Height Adjustment

Notice that the section headings are directly above the first paragraph in the section. A single hard return between the section heading and the paragraph is not quite enough, but two hard returns would be a little too much space between the heading and the paragraph. To change the amount of space between paragraphs:

Click	at the beginning of Column 1	***Move***	*the insertion point to the beginning of Column 1*

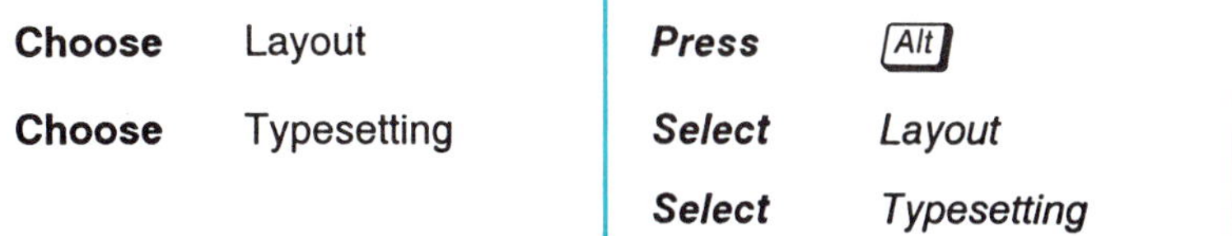

Choose	Layout	***Press***	*Alt*
Choose	Typesetting	***Select***	*Layout*
		Select	*Typesetting*

Your screen should look like Figure 27-2.

Figure 27-2

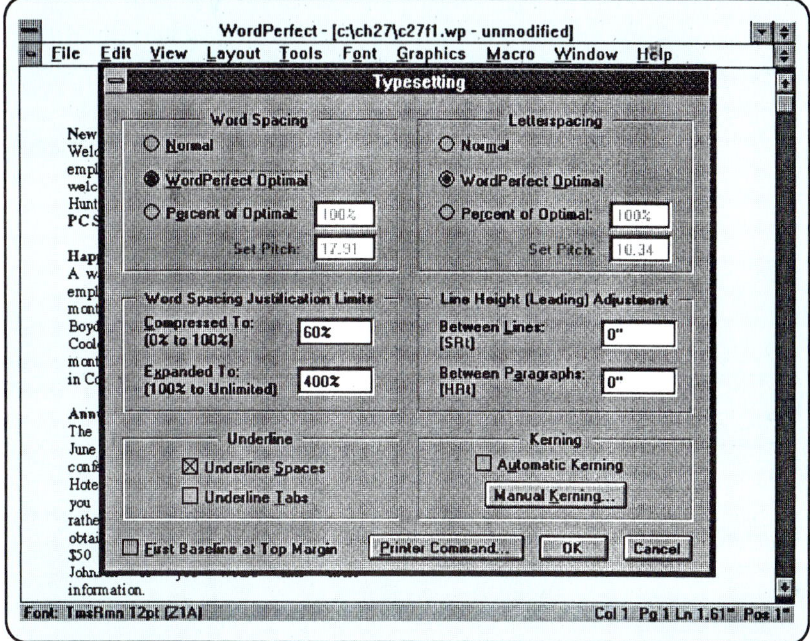

The Typesetting dialog box appears. Several typesetting features are available. Each feature is described in the following list:

Word Spacing - adjusts the spacing between words in your document.

Letterspacing - changes the amount of spacing between the letters in your document.

Word Spacing Justification Limits - compresses or expands the justified text in your document. If your justified text is too close together, then you should increase the percentage under the Compressed to option. If the justified text is too far apart, then you decrease the number in the Expanded to option.

Line Height (Leading) Adjustment - increases or decreases the amount of white space between lines of text. You can specify to change the amount of white space or leading for lines ending with soft return codes [SRt] or lines ending with hard return codes [HRt].

Underline - allows you to specify whether you want spaces and tabs underlined in your document when the Underline feature is used.

Kerning - Manual kerning allows you to change the spacing between individual letter pairs in your document. Unlike letter spacing, manual kerning affects letters on a selected basis. Letter spacing affects large portions of the document, not individual letter pairs.

First Baseline at Top Margin - specifies the first baseline on each page as the position of the top margin. Normally, the first baseline on each text is at the bottom of the first line of text. When your fonts differ from page to page, then your baseline also changes from page to page. By setting the first baseline at the top margin, you can have each page's first baseline start in the same place.

Printer Command - sends special commands to your printer which WordPerfect may not normally support.

To change the line height adjustment between paragraphs:

Double-click	the Between Paragraphs text box in the Line Height (Leading) Adjustment box	***Press***	*Alt+A to select the Between Paragraphs text box in the Line Height (Leading) Adjustment box*
Type	.05	***Type***	*.05*
Click	the OK command button	***Press***	*↵Enter*

Your screen should look like Figure 27-3.

Figure 27-3

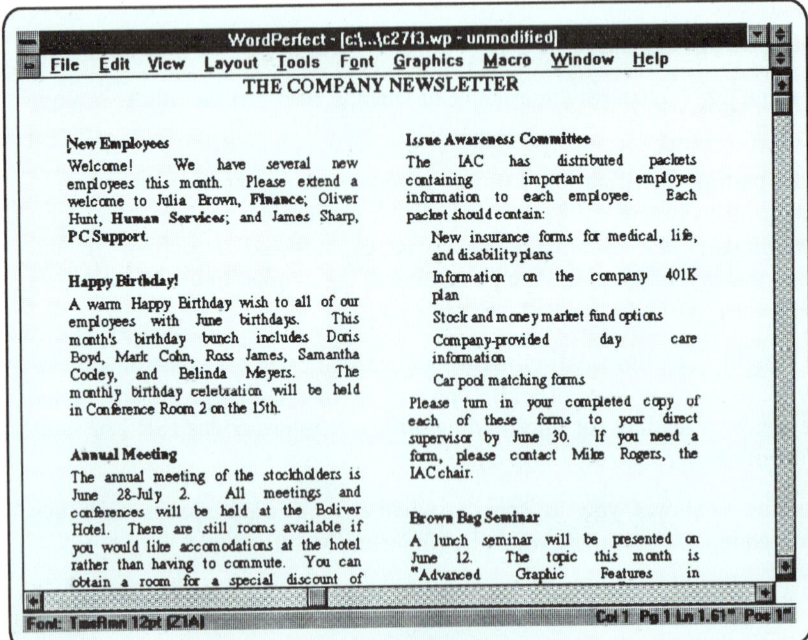

Notice the extra space between each paragraph.

Word Spacing and Letterspacing

The Word Spacing and Letterspacing options in the Typesetting feature allow you to change the amount of space between the words or letters in your document.

You can change the amount of space between words using the Word Spacing option. The Word Spacing option changes the amount of space between words regardless of the justification. The Word Spacing Justification Limits option changes the spacing between words only when full justification is being used.

You can change the amount of space between letters using the Letterspacing option. The Letterspacing option changes the amount of space between letters in a group of text. The Kerning option changes the spacing between letters for specific letter pairs.

Suppose you want to decrease the amount of space between words in the newsletter and increase the amount of space between letters in the newsletter. To change the amount of letter and word spacing in the body of the newsletter:

Click	at the left margin of Column 1	***Move***	*the insertion point to the left margin of Column 1*
Choose	Layout	***Press***	*Alt*
Choose	Typesetting	***Select***	*Layout*
		Select	*Typesetting*

Four settings can be used to change the Word Spacing option. The Normal option instructs WordPerfect to change the word spacing to what the printer manufacturer considers appropriate. The WordPerfect Optimal option instructs WordPerfect to set the word spacing to what WordPerfect considers optimal. The Percent of WordPerfect Optimal allows you to increase or decrease the amount of word spacing based on a percentage of what WordPerfect considers optimal. The Pitch option allows you to change the word spacing based on a certain numbers of characters per inch.

To change the amount of space between words to 95% of optimal:

Click	the Percent of Optimal option button in the Word Spacing box	***Press***	*Alt+E to select the Percent of Optimal option button in the Word Spacing box*
Double-click	the Percent of Optimal text box in the Word Spacing box	***Press***	*Tab to select the Percent of Optimal text box in the Word Spacing box*
Type	95	***Type***	*95*

Your screen should look like Figure 27-4.

Figure 27-4

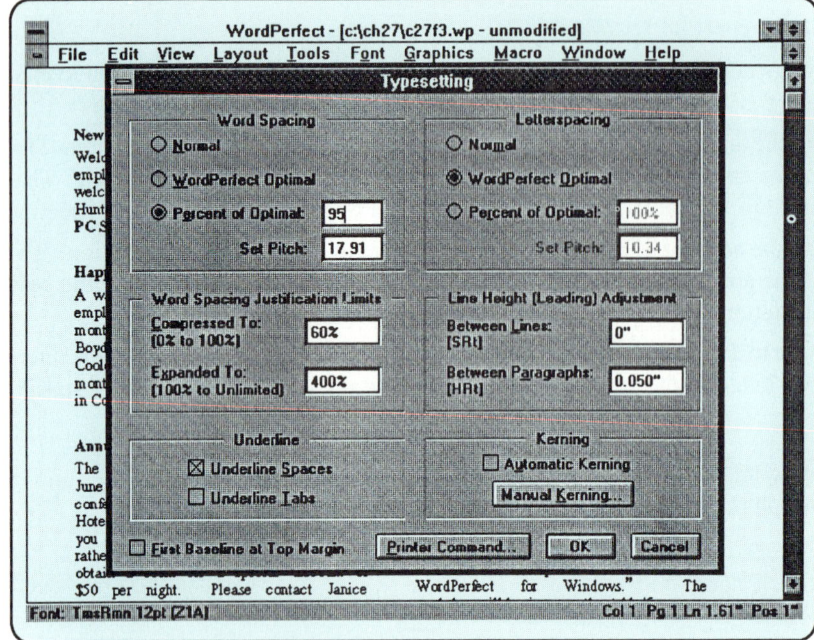

Four settings can be used to change the Letterspacing option. The Normal option instructs WordPerfect to change the letter spacing to what the printer manufacturer considers appropriate for that font. The WordPerfect Optimal option instructs WordPerfect to set the letterspacing to what WordPerfect considers optimal. The Percent of WordPerfect Optimal allows you to increase or decrease the amount of letterspacing based on a percentage of what WordPerfect considers optimal. The Pitch option allows you to change the letterspacing based on a certain numbers of characters per inch.

To increase the Letterspacing option to 110% of optimal:

Click	the Percent of Optimal option button in the Letterspacing box	***Press***	*Alt+R to select the Percent of Optimal option button in the Letterspacing box*
Double-click	the Percent of Optimal text box in the Letter-spacing box	***Press***	*Tab to select the Percent of Optimal text box in the Letter-spacing box*
Type	110	***Type***	*110*

Your screen should look like Figure 27-5.

Figure 27-5

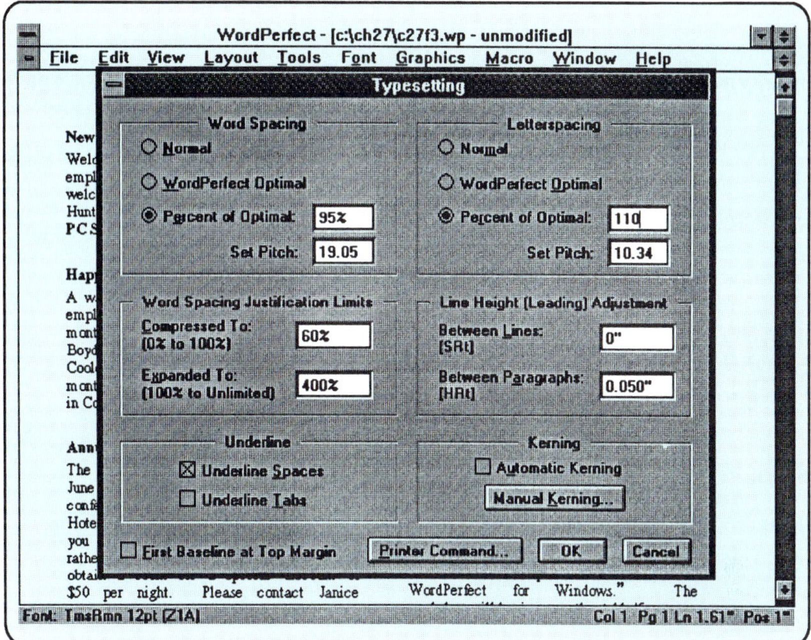

To accept the word spacing and letterspacing changes:

Click	the OK command button	***Press***	*↵Enter*

Your screen should look like Figure 27-6.

Figure 27-6

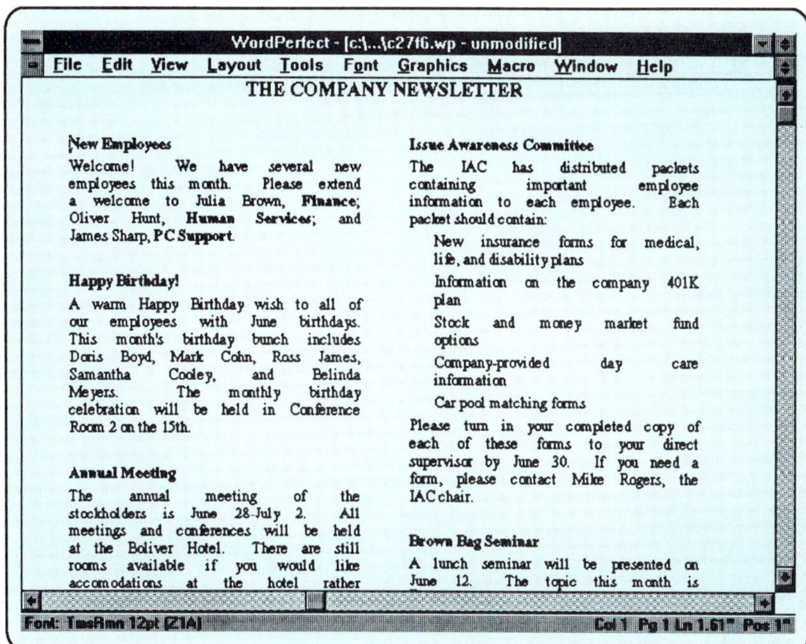

Kerning

The Kerning option allows you to manually increase or decrease the amount of space between two characters. Notice the title of the newsletter. The two "T"s in the word "newsletter" are very close together since you are using a TmsRmn font. To add space between these two characters only, you use the Manual Kerning option in the Typesetting dialog box.

To add space between the two "T"s in the title:

Click	between the two "T"s in the word "NEWSLETTER" in the title of the document	***Move***	*the insert point between the two "T"s in the word "NEWSLETTER" in the title of the document*
Choose	Layout	***Press***	*Alt*
Choose	Typesetting	***Select***	*Layout*
		Select	*Typesetting*

To select the Manual Kerning feature:

Click	the Manual Kerning command button	***Press***	*Alt+K to select the Manual Kerning command button*

Your screen should look like Figure 27-7.

Figure 27-7

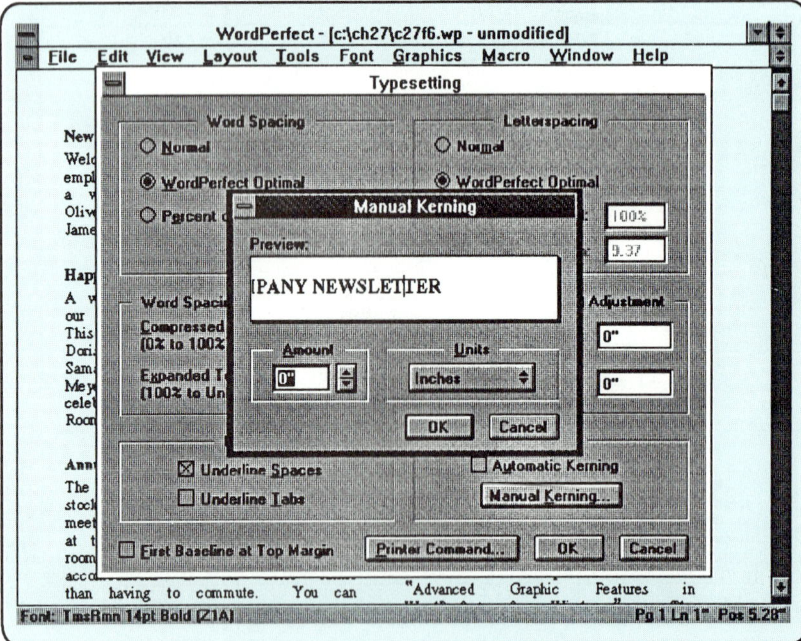

The Manual Kerning dialog box appears. Notice the preview of the characters appears at the top of the dialog box. To increase the space between the characters:

Click	the up triangle button next to the Amount text box	***Press***	*[↑] to increase the number in the Amount text box*

Your screen should look like Figure 27-8.

Figure 27-8

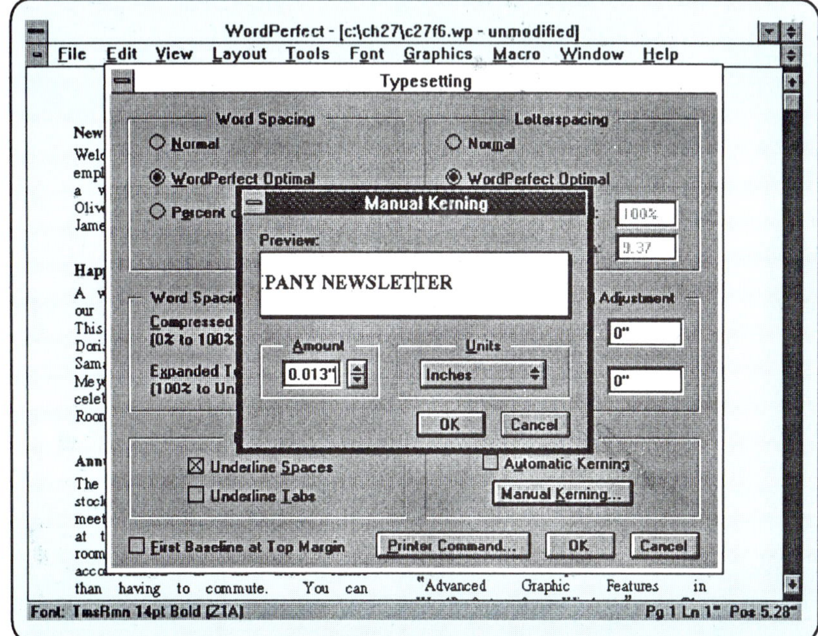

The preview in the Manual Kerning dialog box displays the characters with the increase of .013″ between them.

To accept the change in kerning and return to your document:

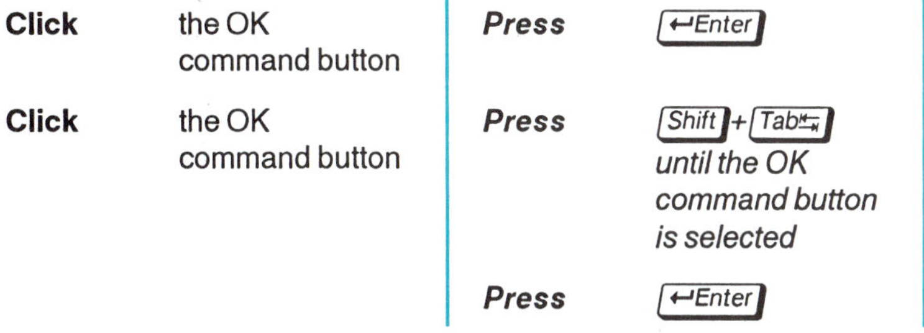

Click	the OK command button	***Press***	*[↵Enter]*
Click	the OK command button	***Press***	*[Shift]+[Tab] until the OK command button is selected*
		Press	*[↵Enter]*

The top part of your screen should look like Figure 27-9.

Figure 27-9

Save the document as "newslet1."

■ PLACING A GRAPHIC ON A GRAPHIC

WordPerfect provides several graphic files in the "c:\wpwin\graphics" directory. You can use these graphics individually or combine graphics to create new figures. The Wrap Text Around Box option in the Position and Size dialog box provides the capability to place a graphic on top of another graphic.

Suppose you want to include the "birthday.wpg" graphic under the "Happy Birthday" section of the newsletter. This graphic by itself looks adequate but, by combining it with the "bord-2.wpg" graphic, you can create a very decorative graphic.

To overlay the two graphics, first retrieve the border graphic, "bord-2.wpg." To retrieve the graphic:

Click	on the blank line below the "Happy Birthday" section	***Move***	*the insertion point to the blank line below the "Happy Birthday" section*	**Move**	the insertion point to the blank line below the "Happy Birthday" section
Choose	Graphics	***Press***	*Alt*	**Press**	F11
Choose	Figure	***Select***	*Graphics*	**Type**	**bord-2.wpg**
Choose	Retrieve	***Select***	*Figure*	**Press**	↵Enter to select the Retrieve command button
Click	on the file "bord-2.wpg" in the Files list box	***Select***	*Retrieve*		
Click	the Retrieve command button	***Type***	***bord-2.wpg***		
		Press	*↵Enter to select the Retrieve command button*		

Your screen should look like Figure 27-10.

Figure 27-10

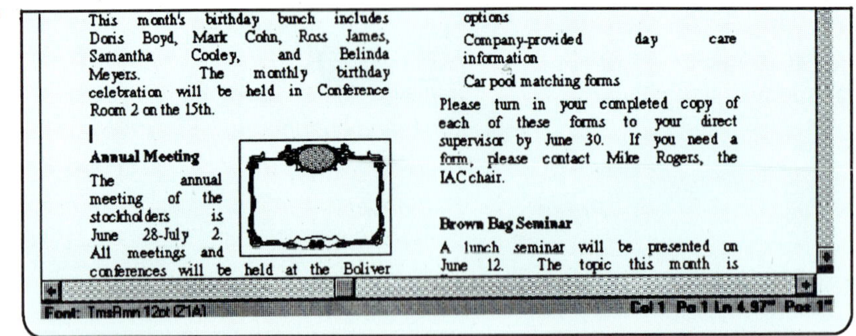

The figure is created using the figure box defaults. You want to change the anchor type to paragraph so that it will move with the text. You also want to change the box size to automatic and turn off the Wrap Text Around Box feature so that you can place the birthday graphic on top of the border. To change the position and size of the Figure box:

Click	on the border figure with the alternate mouse button	***Press***	Alt
Choose	Box Position	***Select***	*Graphics*
Click	the Anchor To pop-up list button	***Select***	*Figure*
Hold down	the mouse button to view the pop-up list	***Select***	*Position*
Choose	Paragraph	***Type***	*1*
Click	the Size pop-up list button	***Press***	↵Enter
Hold down	the mouse button to view the pop-up list	***Press***	Alt+A *to select the Anchor To pop-up list button*
Choose	Auto Both	***Press***	Alt+↑ *to view the pop-up list*
Click	the Wrap Text Around Box check box until the X disappears	***Type***	*P to select Paragraph*
Click	the OK command button	***Press***	Alt+S *to select the Size pop-up list button*
		Press	Alt+↑ *to view the pop-up list*
		Type	*A to select Auto Both*
		Press	Alt+R *until the X disappears from the Wrap Text Around Box check box*
		Press	↵Enter

Your screen should look like Figure 27-11.

Figure 27-11

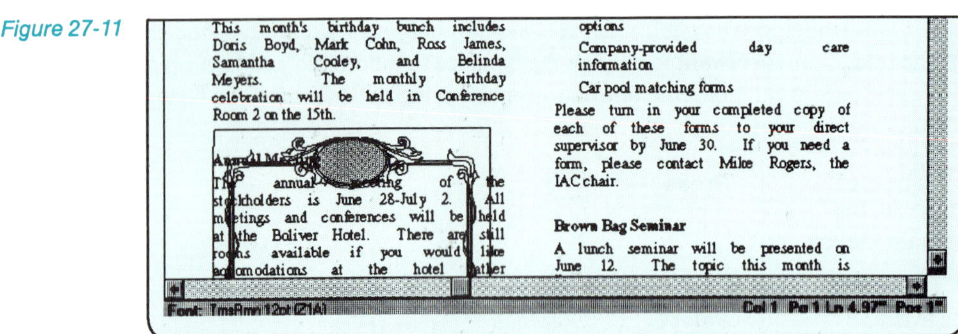

When you turn off the Wrap Text Around Box option, the text of the next section moves into the border graphic. To move the text down:

Press	↵Enter seven times	***Press***	*↵Enter seven times*

The text will move down further after the second graphic is placed in the document. To move to the location where the birthday graphic should be placed, turn on the reveal codes feature.

Click	after the [Fig Box:1] code	***Move***	*the insertion point after the [Fig Box:1] code*

The bottom part of your screen should look like Figure 27-12.

Figure 27-12

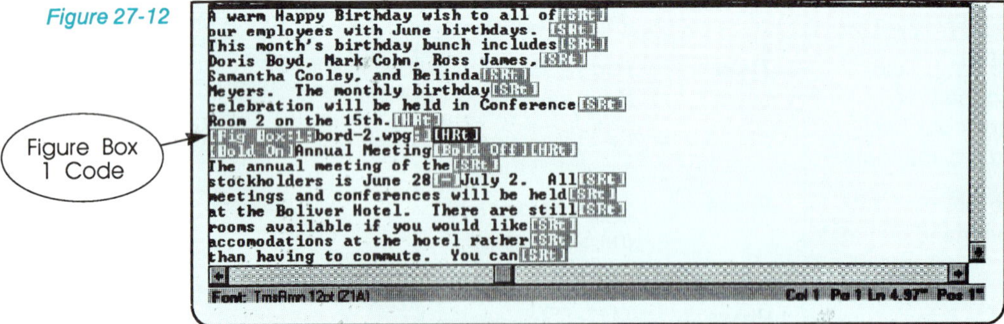

Remove the Reveal Codes from your screen. You do not want a border around the birthday graphic. To change the figure options so that the graphic does not have a border:

Choose	Graphics	***Press***	*Alt*
Choose	Figure	***Select***	*Graphics*
Choose	Options	***Select***	*Figure*
Click	the Left pop-up list button in the Border Styles box	***Select***	*Options*
Hold down	the mouse button to view the pop-up list	***Press***	*Alt+L to select the Left pop-up list button*

Choose	None	***Press***	*Alt+↑ to view the pop-up list*		
Click	the Right pop-up list button in the Border Styles box	***Type***	*N to select the None option*		
Hold down	the mouse button to view the pop-up list	***Press***	*Alt+R to select the Right pop-up list button*		
Choose	None	***Press***	*Alt+↑ to view the pop-up list*		
Click	the Top pop-up list button in the Border Styles box	***Type***	*N to select the None option*		
Hold down	the mouse button to view the pop-up list	***Press***	*Alt+T to select the Top pop-up list button*		
Choose	None	***Press***	*Alt+↑ to view the pop-up list*		
Click	the Bottom pop-up list button in the Border Styles box	***Type***	*N to select the None option*		
Hold down	the mouse button to view the pop-up list	***Press***	*Alt+B to select the Bottom pop-up list button*		
Choose	None	***Press***	*Alt+↑ to view the pop-up list*		
Click	the OK command button	***Type***	*N to select the None option*		
		Press	*↵Enter*		

To retrieve the birthday graphic:

Choose	Graphics	***Press***	*Alt*	**Press**	F11
Choose	Figure	***Select***	*Graphics*	**Type**	**birthday.wpg**
Choose	Retrieve	***Select***	*Figure*	**Press**	↵Enter to select the Retrieve command button
Click	on the file "birthday.wpg" in the Files list box	***Select***	*Retrieve*		

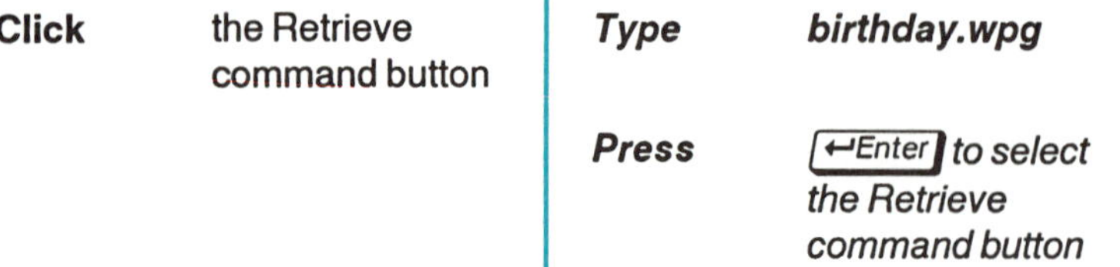

Click	the Retrieve command button	***Type***	***birthday.wpg***
		Press	*[↵Enter] to select the Retrieve command button*

Your screen should look like Figure 27-13.

Figure 27-13

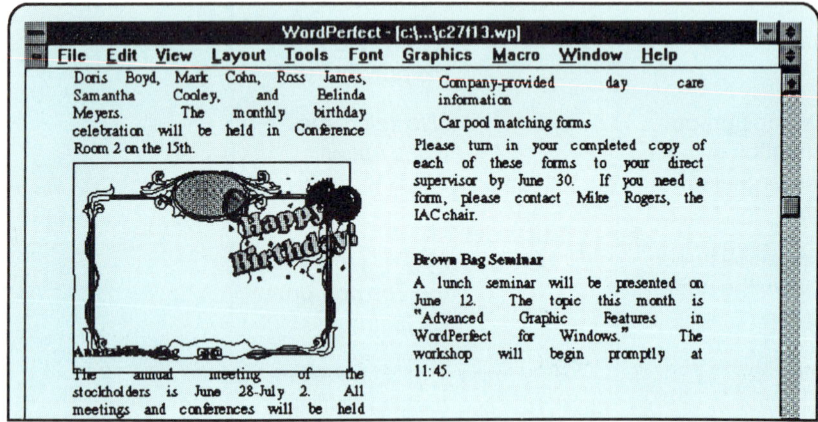

To change the box position:

Click	on the right side of the Figure 2 box until the box is selected	***Press***	*[Alt]*
Click	on the box with the alternate mouse button	***Select***	*Graphics*
Choose	Box Position	***Select***	*Figure*
Click	the Anchor To pop-up list button	***Select***	*Position*
Hold down	the mouse button to view the pop-up list	***Type***	*2*
Choose	Paragraph	***Press***	*[↵Enter]*
Click	the Horizontal Position pop-up list button	***Press***	*[Alt]+[A] to select the Anchor To pop-up list button*
Hold down	the mouse button to view the pop-up list	***Press***	*[Alt]+[↑] to view the pop-up list*

Choose	Margin, Center	***Type***	*P to select the Paragraph option*
Click	the OK command button	***Press***	*Alt+H to select the Horizontal Position pop-up list button*
		Press	*Alt+↑ to view the pop-up list*
		Type	*C to select the Margin, Center option*
		Press	*↵Enter*

Your screen should look like Figure 27-14.

Figure 27-14

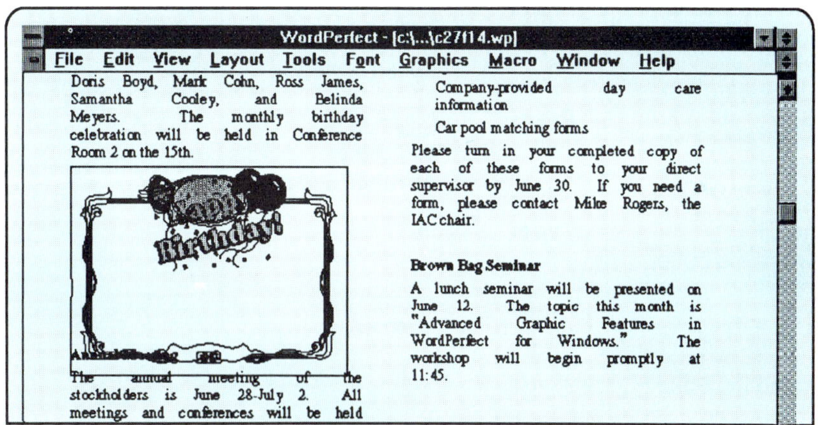

The birthday graphic is still too far up in the border box. To advance the graphic down a certain number of inches, you can use the Advance option under the Layout menu. The Advance feature allows you to move text up, down, left, or right a specific number of inches.

Turn on the Reveal Codes feature. To move before the Figure 2 code:

Click	on the [Fig Box:2] code	***Move***	*the insertion point on the [Fig Box:2] code*

The bottom part of your screen should look like Figure 27-15.

Figure 27-15

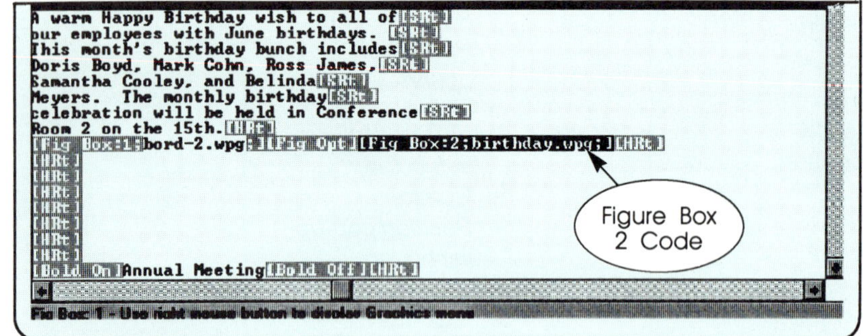

Remove the Reveal Codes from your screen.

To advance the graphic down .6″:

Choose	Layout	***Press***	*Alt*
Choose	Advance	***Select***	*Layout*
Click	the Down option button	***Select***	*Advance*
Double-click	the Advance text box	***Press***	*Alt+D to select the Down option button*
Type	.6	***Press***	*Alt+A to select the Advance text box*
Click	the OK command button	***Type***	*.6*
		Press	*↵Enter*

Your screen should look like Figure 27-16.

Figure 27-16

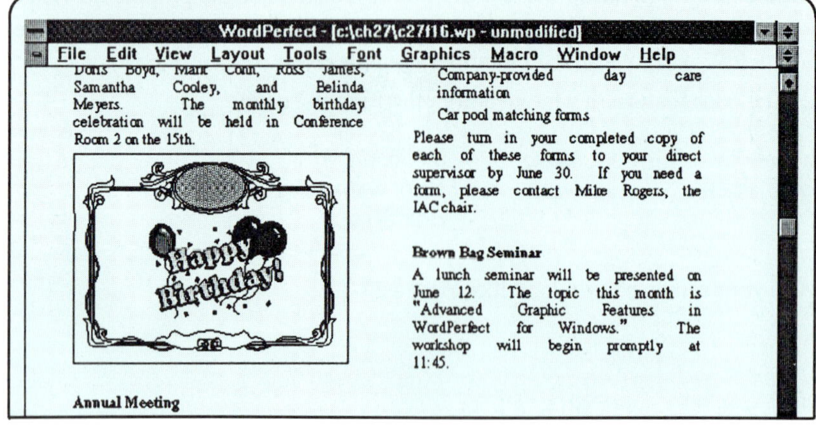

Save the document.

WORDPERFECT CHARACTERS

WordPerfect provides special characters that you can use when you are creating your documents. These characters are called WordPerfect Characters.

The WordPerfect Characters feature provides you with 13 sets of special characters. These character sets include ASCII, Multinational 1, Multinational 2, Box Drawing, Typographic Symbols, Iconic Symbols, Math/Scientific, Math/Scientific Ext., Greek, Hebrew, Cyrillic, Japanese, and User-Defined. Some of the characters include bullets, copyright symbols, special characters for foreign languages, and mathematic symbols like the square root symbol.

To use a WordPerfect Character, choose WP Characters from the Font menu or press Ctrl+W and select the proper character set.

Suppose you want to add bullets to the list under the "Issue Awareness Committee" section. To add a solid round bullet:

Click	at the left margin of the "New Insurance" paragraph in the list
Choose	Font
Choose	WP Characters

Move	*the insertion point to the left margin of the "New Insurance" paragraph in the list*
Press	*Alt*
Select	*Font*
Select	*WP Characters*

Move	the insertion point to the left margin of the "New Insurance" paragraph in the list
Press	Ctrl+W

The WordPerfect Characters dialog box appears. Your screen should look like Figure 27-17.

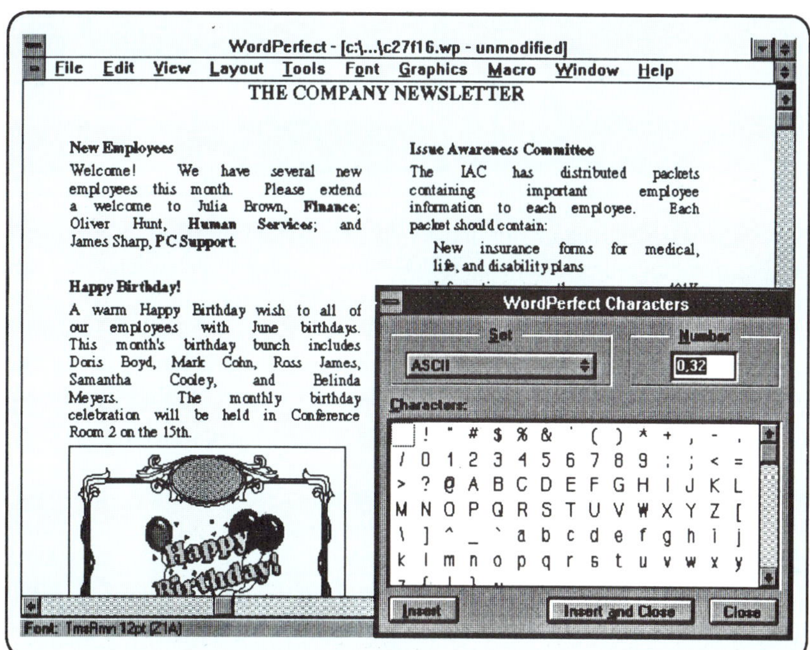

Figure 27-17

The bullet is in the Typographic Symbols set. To change the set:

Click	the Set pop-up list button	***Press***	*Alt+S to select the Set pop-up list button*	**Press**	Alt+S to select the Set pop-up list button
Hold down	the mouse button to view the pop-up list	***Press***	*Alt+↑ to view the pop-up list*	**Press**	Alt+↑ to view the pop-up list
Choose	Typographic Symbols	***Type***	*T to select the Typographic Symbols option*	**Type**	T to select the Typographic Symbols option

Your screen should look like Figure 27-18.

Figure 27-18

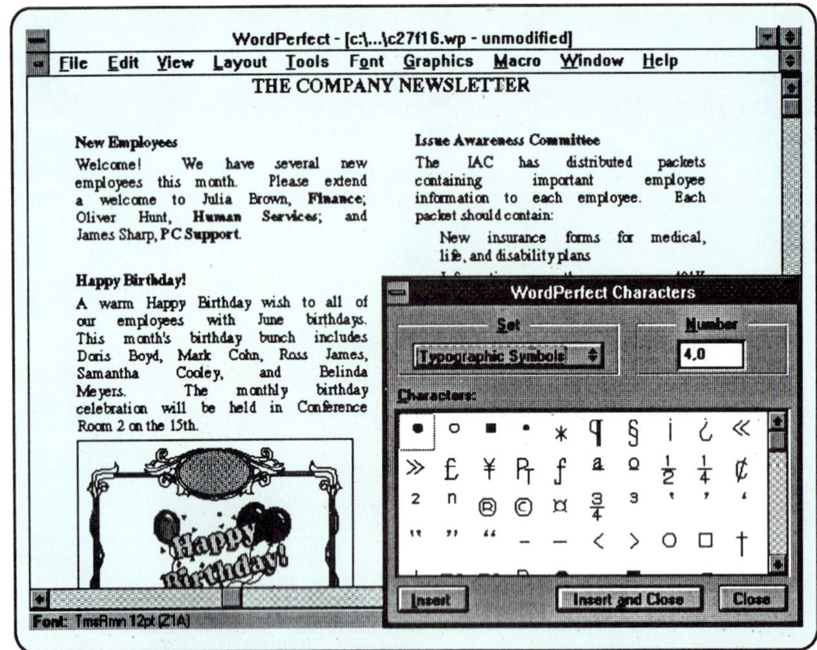

The medium filled bullet is the first character in the Typographic Symbols set. Notice the numbers in the Number text box. The medium bullet is number 4,0. The first number in a character number represents the set. The Typographic Symbols set is the fourth character set. The second number represents the character number. Each set of characters begins with the number zero. Since the bullet is the first character, its number is zero. As you become more familiar with the special characters, you can type the number representing the character rather than switching to the character set and highlighting the number.

To insert the bullet in the document at the insertion point and close the dialog box:

Click	the Insert and Close command button	***Press***	*Alt+A to select the Insert and Close command button*	**Press**	Alt+A to select the Insert and Close command button

Your screen should look like Figure 27-19.

Figure 27-19

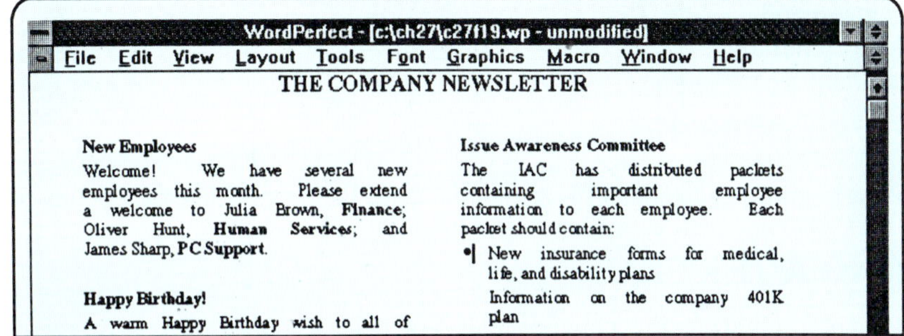

To insert a bullet at the second paragraph:

Click	at the left margin of the "Information" paragraph in the list	***Move***	*the insertion point to the left margin of the "Information" paragraph in the list*	**Move**	the insertion point to the left margin of the "Information" paragraph in the list
Choose	Font	***Press***	*Alt*	**Press**	Ctrl+W
Choose	WP Characters	***Select***	*Font*		
		Select	*WP Characters*		

Your screen should look like Figure 27-20.

Figure 27-20

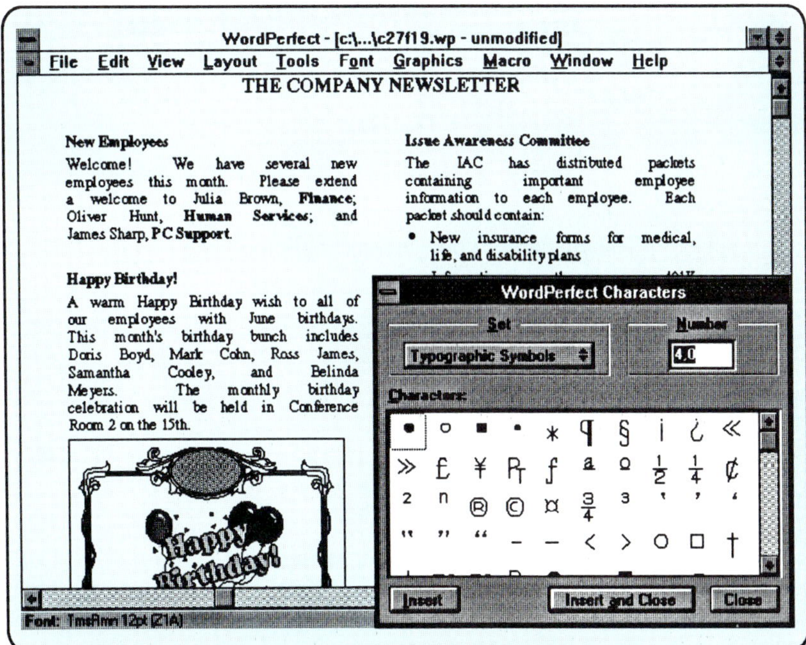

Notice the Typographic Symbols set is still selected. Once you select a set during a session of WordPerfect, the set will appear the next time you enter the WordPerfect Characters feature.

To select the bullet and close the dialog box:

Click	the Insert and Close command button	***Press***	*Alt+A to select the Insert and Close command button*	**Press**	Alt+A to select the Insert and Close command button

Insert a bullet at the beginning of each of the remaining three list items. Save the document.

■ CREATING A TEXT BOX

A text box is a type of graphic box that contains text. You can use a text box to draw attention to text in a document. You enter the text in a text box in the same way that you enter text in a document. You can format and enhance the text as you would in a document.

You can change the options and position of a text box using the Text Box option under the Graphics menu. The procedures for changing graphic options and position are discussed in Chapters 23 and 24.

Suppose you want to add a reminder to the end of the newsletter. To draw attention to the reminder, you will place it in a text box.

To create the text box:

Click	at the end of the "Brown Bag Seminar" section	***Move***	*the insertion point to the end of the "Brown Bag Seminar" section*	**Move**	the insertion point to the end of the "Brown Bag Seminar" section
Press	↵Enter twice	***Press***	*↵Enter twice*	**Press**	↵Enter twice
Choose	Graphics	***Press***	*Alt*	**Press**	Alt+F11
Choose	Text Box	***Select***	*Graphics*		
Choose	Create	***Select***	*Text Box*		
		Select	*Create*		

The Text Box Editor appears. The top part of your screen should look like Figure 27-21.

Figure 27-21

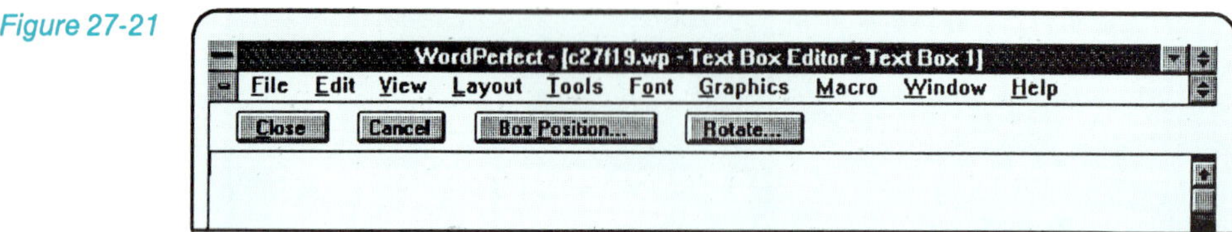

To enter the text:

Type	Don't forget the company picnic on June 3rd!!	***Type***	*Don't forget the company picnic on June 3rd!!*	**Type**	Don't forget the company picnic on June 3rd!!

The upper part of your screen should look like Figure 27-22.

Figure 27-22

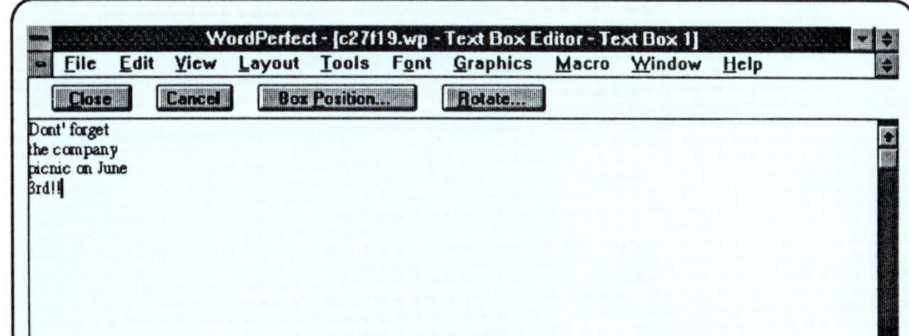

To close the Text Box Editor:

Click	the Close command button	***Press***	*Alt+C to select the Close command button*	**Press**	Alt+C to select the Close command button

The bottom part of your screen should look like Figure 27-23.

Figure 27-23

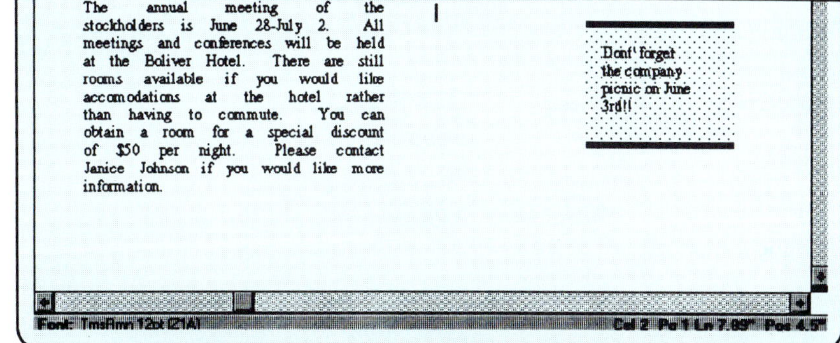

Notice the text box has a thick border on the top and bottom and no border on the left and right. The text box also has gray shading.

The text box is not positioned correctly. Suppose you want to change the position of the text box so that it is centered in the column and to change the width to 2.25". You also want the text box anchored as a paragraph.

To change the text box position:

Click	Text Box 1 with the alternate mouse button	***Press***	*Alt*
Choose	Box Position	***Select***	*Graphics*
Click	the Anchor To pop-up list button	***Select***	*Text Box*
Hold down	the mouse button to view the pop-up list	***Select***	*Position*
Choose	Paragraph	***Type***	*1*
Click	the Size pop-up list button	***Press***	*↵Enter*

Hold down	the mouse button to view the pop-up list
Choose	Auto Height
Double-click	the Width text box
Type	2.25
Click	the Horizontal Position pop-up list button
Hold down	the mouse button to view the pop-up list
Choose	Margin, Center
Click	the OK command button

Press	*Alt+A to select the Anchor To pop-up list button*
Press	*Alt+↑ to view the pop-up list*
Type	*P to select the Paragraph option*
Press	*Alt+S to select the Size pop-up list button*
Press	*Alt+↑ to view the pop-up list*
Type	*H to select the Auto Height option*
Press	*Alt+W to select the Width text box*
Type	*2.25*
Press	*Alt+H to select the Horizontal Position pop-up list button*
Press	*Alt+↑ to view the pop-up list*
Type	*C to select the Margin, Center option*
Press	*↵Enter*

The bottom part of your screen should look like Figure 27-24.

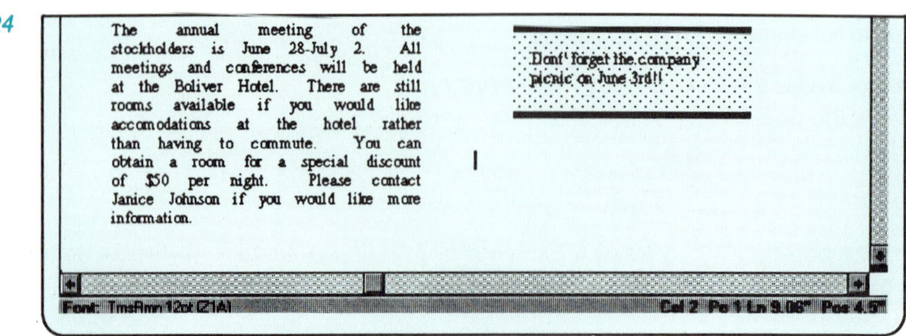

Figure 27-24

Save the document. Close the document.

EXERCISE 1

INSTRUCTIONS: Define the following terms:

1. Typesetting feature ______________________________

2. Word spacing ______________________________

3. Letterspacing ______________________________

4. Line height adjustment ______________________________

5. Manual kerning ______________________________

6. Wrap text around box feature ______________________________

7. WordPerfect characters ______________________________

8. Text box feature ______________________________

EXERCISE 2

INSTRUCTIONS: Circle T if the statement is true and F if the statement is false.

T F 1. You can change the amount of space between words using the Typesetting feature.

T F 2. Manual kerning changes the amount of space between a group of characters.

T F 3. The Letterspacing feature changes the amount of space between a specific pair of characters.

T F 4. The way you change the text box options is different than the way you change the options for other graphic boxes.

T F 5. You can format and enhance text in a text box as you would text in a document.

T F 6. If you turn off the wrap text around box feature, then you can place a graphic on another graphic or place text on a figure.

T F 7. The line height adjustment feature can change the amount of space between paragraphs or between lines.

T F 8. WordPerfect provides six character sets in the WordPerfect Characters feature.

EXERCISE 3

INSTRUCTIONS:

1. Create the following document. Set the initial font to TmsRmn 12pt (Z1A) and the justification to full.
2. Change the line height adjustment between paragraphs to .03". Change the line height adjustment between lines to .01".
3. Change the word spacing feature to 95% of optimal.
4. Save the document as "ch27ex03."
5. Print the document.
6. Close the document.

NEW EXPENSE GUIDELINES

So that the XYZ Company does not have to cut more significant areas of our budget, we have revised our expense guidelines. Please begin implementing these new guidelines immediately.

- All employees must use the company mileage schedule for travel expenses. Departments that were previously using special schedules must convert to the corporate schedule effective today.
- All client expenses must be approved in advance by your department supervisor. Client expenses include client lunches, entertainment, and transportation expenses. If you think you will be incurring expenses during a client meeting, have the expenses approved. If the expenses are unnecessary, then you can discard the approval form.
- Office supplies will be cut back to a minimum. For example, we will no longer order four types of legal pads. Each department will use the same legal pads. Special orders must be requested through your department supervisor. If a department exceeds its office supply budget, employees will be asked to compensate the difference.
- We will no longer order preformatted diskettes or special mouse pads as part of our computer supplies.
- An immediate freeze has been placed on all purchases of office equipment. Department needs will be examined on an individual basis.

Thank you for your cooperation in implementing these guidelines. By cutting our travel and office expenses we may be able to avoid cuts in more important areas.

EXERCISE 4

INSTRUCTIONS:

1. Open the document "ch26ex07." If you have not created the document yet, do so at this time.
2. Change the line height adjustment between paragraphs to .05″. Change the line height adjustment between lines to .01″
3. Change the word spacing to 98% of optimal and the letterspacing to 103% of optimal.
4. Save the document as "ch27ex04."
5. Print the document.
6. Close the document.

EXERCISE 5

INSTRUCTIONS:

1. Create the following company logo. Use the font Helv 14pt Bold (Z1A) for the first letter of each word. Use the font Helv 12pt (Z1A) for the other characters.
2. Use the manual kerning feature to overlap the first two letters of each word. Decrease the space between each letter approximately .05″.
3. Use the graphic "map-worl.wpg" in the figure. Remove the figure borders and anchor the figure as a character. Size the graphic to .5″ width and .5″ height.
4. Save the document as "ch27ex05."
5. Print the document.
6. Close the document.

Worldwide **C**omputing 

EXERCISE 6

INSTRUCTIONS:

1. Create the following document using the WordPerfect Characters feature.
2. Save the document as "ch27ex06."
3. Print the document.
4. Close the document.

WORDPERFECT CHARACTERS

The WordPerfect Characters feature offers many symbols that you can use in documents. Some of the more commonly used character sets include the multinational, iconic, and typographic symbols sets. The following list describes some uses for these character sets.

Multinational 1	accented letters as in résumé or fiancée
Typographic Symbols	round bullets such as • or squares such as ■
	copyright symbols © or trademark symbols ™ or ®
Iconic Symbols	special symbols like ☺ or ♥ or ☎
Math/Scientific	special math symbols like $\sum$ or $\geq$ or $\pm$
Greek	Greek letters that can create organization names like ΦΒΚ

All of these symbols and many more are available by choosing WP Characters from the Font menu.

EXERCISE 7

INSTRUCTIONS:

1. Create the following document by placing the "jet-2.wpg" figure on the "bkgrnd-2.wpg."
2. The background picture should have a page anchor type, be centered between the margins, and be 5″ wide and 5″ tall. Turn off the wrap text around box feature. Add the caption "West Airlines brings you to the canyons!"
3. The jet figure has a page anchor type, placed horizontally on the left margin, and uses the default size.
4. Remove all borders from the figure options and place the caption above and outside the figure box.
5. Save the document as "ch27ex07."
6. Print the document.
7. Close the document.

West Airlines brings you to the canyons!

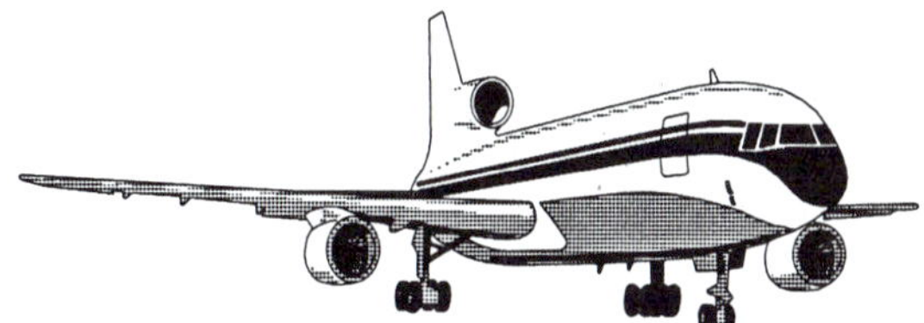

EXERCISE 8

INSTRUCTIONS:

1. Create the following document by placing a text box on the "bord-2.wpg" figure.
2. Set the border graphic to have a page anchor type. Change the size of the figure to 5″ wide and 5″ tall. Center the figure between the margins. Turn off the wrap text around box feature.
3. Change the figure options to include no borders.
4. Create the text using the largest TmnsRmn font available. Make the text bold and italic. The text box has a page anchor type and is 3″ wide by 1.3″ tall. Center the text box between the margins and within the border graphic.
5. Change the text box options to include no borders and 10% gray shading.
6. Save the document as "ch27ex08."
7. Print the document.
8. Close the document.

Congratulations
on your record
sales performance!

CHAPTER TWENTY-EIGHT

EQUATION EDITOR

OBJECTIVES

In this chapter, you will learn to:

- Define an equation
- Use the Equation Palette
- Save an equation
- Retrieve an equation
- Print an equation
- Edit an equation

CHAPTER OVERVIEW

Some documents require complex equations. For example, you may need to include an equation for the average salary for a group of employees. This equation would look like Figure 28-1.

Figure 28-1

$$\mu = \frac{\sum_{i=1}^{n} SAL}{N}$$

The Equation Editor feature allows you to create and edit mathematical and scientific equations. Once you create an equation, you can save the equation to be used in other documents as well. These topics are discussed and illustrated in this chapter.

CREATING AN EQUATION

The Equation Editor feature allows you to include mathematical and scientific equations in a document. This feature does not calculate the equation for you. Instead, it helps you create the complex characters that make up an equation so that you do not have to draw them manually.

Each equation is placed in a graphics box in your document. You create the equation that is placed in that box.

Change the default directory to "a:\wpdocs" or to "c:\wpdocs."

Suppose you need to create an equation that adds the variable A to the quantity of 6 minus the variable Y divided by another variable Z. Your completed equation will look like Figure 28-2.

Figure 28-2

$$A+\frac{6-Y}{Z}$$

To create a graphics box for the equation:

Choose	Graphics	***Press***	Alt
Choose	Equation	***Select***	*Graphics*
Choose	Create	***Select***	*Equation*
		Select	*Create*

Your screen should look like Figure 28-3.

Figure 28-3

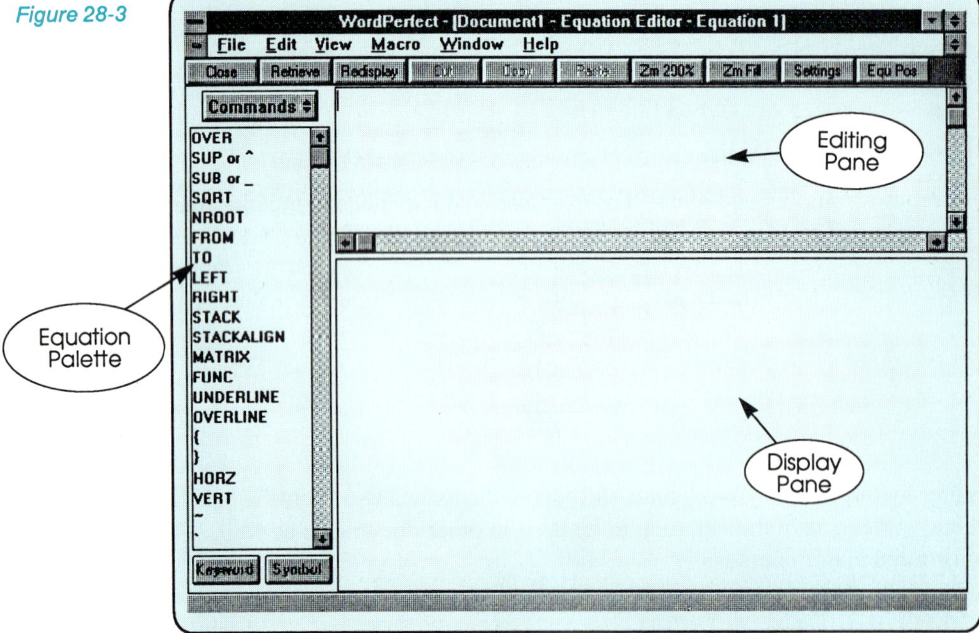

The Equation Editor is divided into three panes. The Editing pane at the top of the screen is where you create and edit an equation. The Display pane at the bottom of the screen shows how the equation will look when printed. The Equation Palette on the left side of the screen provides lists of commands and symbols that you use to build an equation.

The following list describes the commands available on the Equation Editor Button Bar.

Close the Equation Editor. This button is equivalent to choosing Close from the File menu or pressing Ctrl+F4.

Retrieve an equation stored on disk into the Equation Editor. This button is equivalent to choosing Retrieve from the File menu.

Redisplay draws the commands and symbols entered in the editing pane in the display pane. This button is equivalent to choosing Redisplay from the View menu or pressing Ctrl+F3.

Cut the selected text from the editing pane to the Windows Clipboard. This button is equivalent to choosing Cut from the Edit menu or pressing Shift+Delete.

Copy the selected text from the editing pane to the Windows Clipboard. This button is equivalent to choosing Copy from the Edit menu or pressing Ctrl+Insert.

Paste the text in the Windows Clipboard to the editing pane. This button is equivalent to choosing Paste from the Edit menu or pressing Shift+Insert.

Zm 200% displays the formula at 200% in the display pane. This button is equivalent to choosing 200% from the View menu. Zm 200% does not change the actual size of the equation in the document.

Zm Fill displays the equation so that it fills the display pane. This command does not actually change the size of the equation in the document. This button is equivalent to choosing Zoom Fill from the View menu.

Settings allows you to change the Font, Horizontal Alignment, Vertical Alignment, and print settings of the equation. This button is equivalent to choosing Settings from the File menu.

Equ Pos allows you to change the equation box position and size in the document. This button is equivalent to choosing Box Position from the File menu.

In most cases, you can type an equation just as you would say it. You need to create an equation that adds the variable A to the quantity 6 minus the variable Y divided by another variable Z.

To create the equation:

Type	A+6-Y over Z	***Type***	*A+6-Y over Z*	**Type**	A+6-Y over Z

The upper part of your screen should look like Figure 28-4.

Figure 28-4

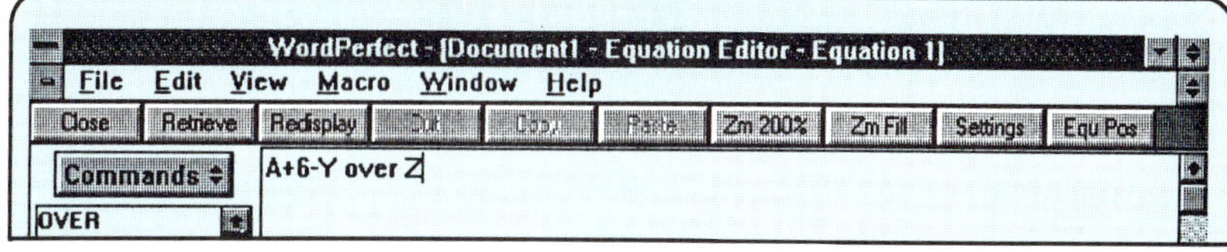

The text you typed is displayed in the editing pane. To see the equation in the display pane:

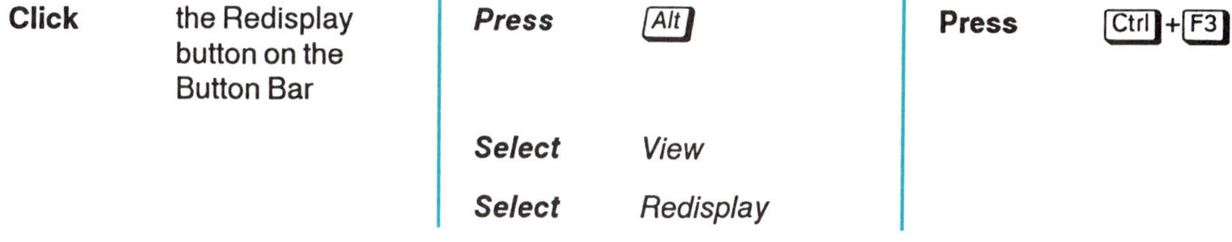

Click	the Redisplay button on the Button Bar	***Press***	*Alt*	**Press**	Ctrl+F3
		Select	*View*		
		Select	*Redisplay*		

The bottom part of your screen should look like Figure 28-5.

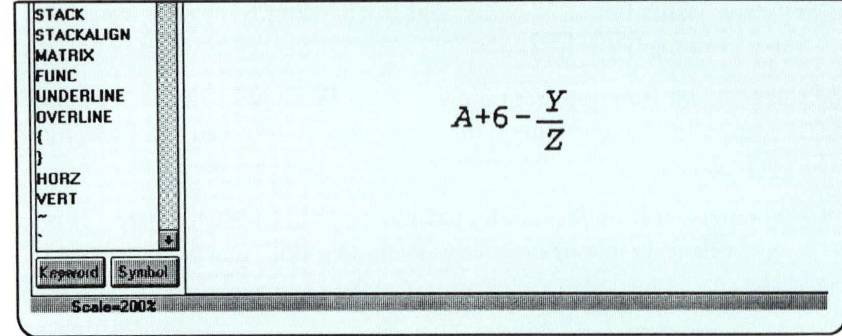

Figure 28-5

The equation appears in the display pane, but this is not the correct formula. Only the "Y" is over the "Z." You want the entire "6 - Y" over the "Z."

The "OVER" command makes a fraction. It places the character to the left of the command over the character to the right. To have WordPerfect recognize (6 - Y) as a single character to the left of the "OVER" command, you must place braces { } around the characters.

To edit the equation:

Click	before the "6" in the equation in the editing pane	***Move***	*the insertion point before the "6" in the equation in the editing pane*	**Move**	the insertion point before the "6" in the equation in the editing pane
Type	{	***Type***	*{*	**Type**	{
Click	after the letter "Y" in the editing pane	***Move***	*the insertion point after the letter "Y" in the editing pane*	**Move**	the insertion point after the letter "Y" in the editing pane
Type	}	***Type***	*}*	**Type**	}

The top part of your screen should look like Figure 28-6.

Figure 28-6

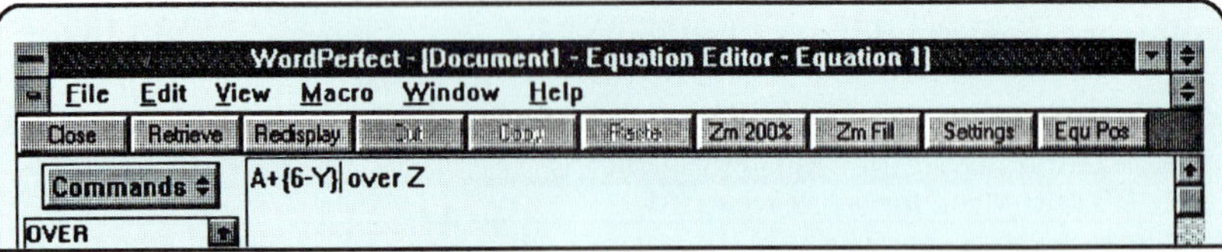

To display the edited equation:

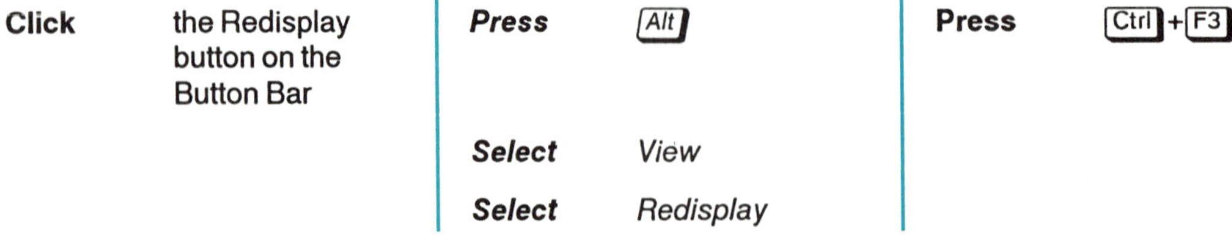

Click	the Redisplay button on the Button Bar	***Press***	*Alt*	**Press**	Ctrl+F3
		Select	*View*		
		Select	*Redisplay*		

The lower part of your screen should look like Figure 28-7.

Figure 28-7

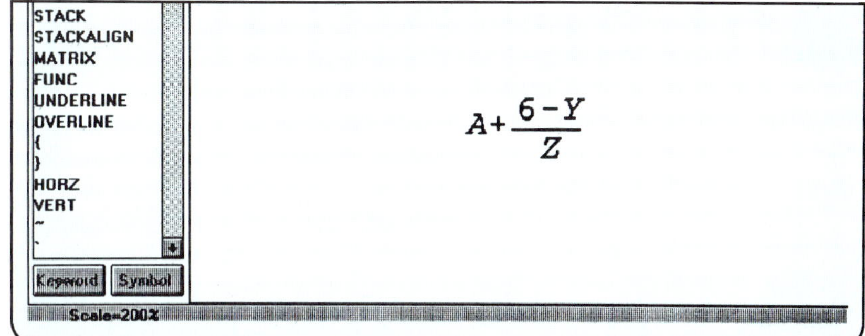

To return to the normal editing screen:

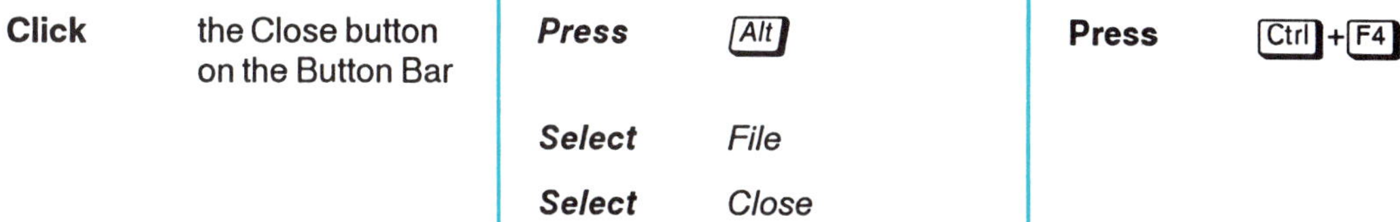

Click	the Close button on the Button Bar	***Press***	*Alt*	**Press**	Ctrl + F4
		Select	*File*		
		Select	*Close*		

The top part of your screen should look like Figure 28-8.

Figure 28-8

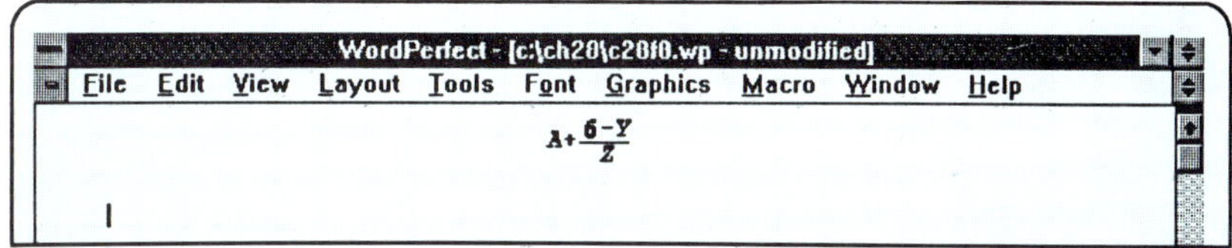

The equation appears in your document. The equation is much smaller in the document than in the Equation Editor. By default, equation boxes are centered horizontally in the document. You can change the box position and the box options of an equation box in the same way that you change the box position and options of other graphic boxes.

Save the document as "equate1." Close the document.

■ USING THE EQUATION PALETTE

At times, you may need to create an equation that requires the use of scientific and mathematical symbols. WordPerfect provides an Equation Palette that contains such symbols.

Suppose you want to create the equation for computing the average age for all of the people in a class. This equation looks like Figure 28-9.

Figure 28-9

$$\mu = \frac{\Sigma x_i}{N}$$

> **In This Chapter**
> Equations are given to you for the purpose of examples and exercises. While the format is provided, an explanation of each character will not accompany the formula. For more detailed information about the different equation symbols, see "Appendix B, Equation Palette" in the WordPerfect Reference Manual.

To create the equation:

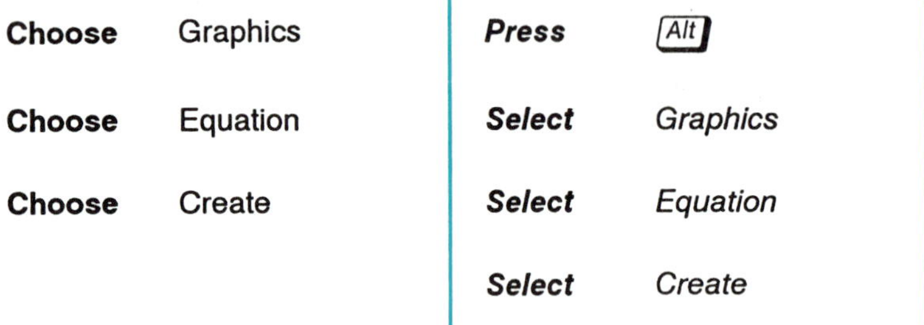

Choose	Graphics	***Press***	Alt	
Choose	Equation	***Select***	*Graphics*	
Choose	Create	***Select***	*Equation*	
		Select	*Create*	

The Equation Editor appears on the screen.

To move the insertion point to the Equation Palette:

Click	on the Palette list	***Press***	F6	**Press**	F6

Your screen should look like Figure 28-10.

Figure 28-10

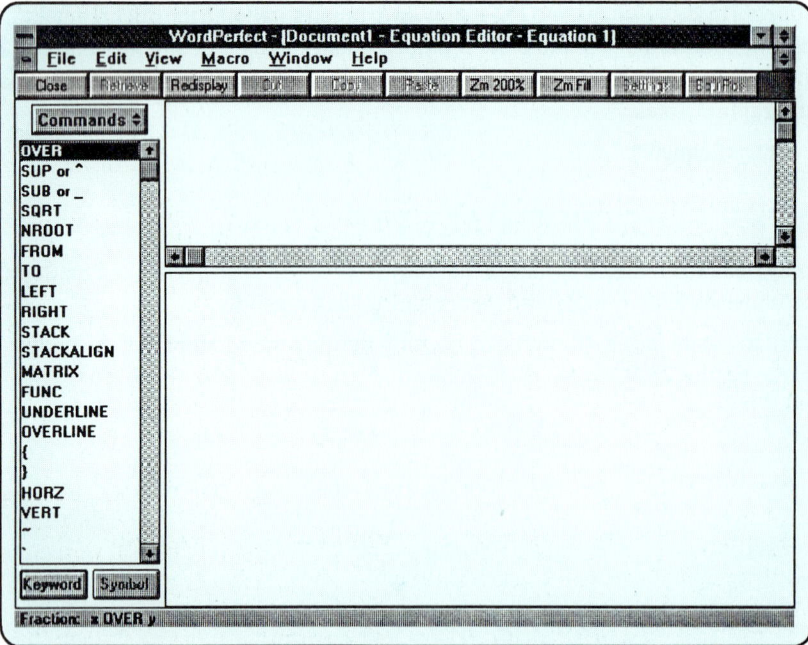

The name of the current palette appears on the palette pop-up list button. The current selection in the palette is highlighted. You can view other commands by using the scroll bars or by pressing the ↑ or ↓ keys.

A definition of each command or symbol appears on the left corner of the status bar. For example, if the current palette selection is "OVER," the message "Fraction: x OVER y" appears in the left corner of the status bar.

There are eight equation palettes. You can view the different equation palettes by selecting a new palette from the palette pop-up list or by pressing PageUp or PageDown.

To rotate through all the palettes:

Click	the Palette pop-up list button	***Press***	*PageDown twelve times*	**Press**	PageDown twelve times
Hold down	the mouse button to view the pop-up list				
Select	a different palette until you have seen each palette				

Before creating the equation, make sure the Commands palette is selected in the equation palette.

To create the Average equation:

Click	the Palette pop-up list button	***Press***	*PageDown five times to select the Greek palette*	**Press**	PageDown five times to select the Greek palette
Hold down	the mouse button to view the pop-up list				
Select	the Greek palette				

Your screen should look like Figure 28-11.

Figure 28-11

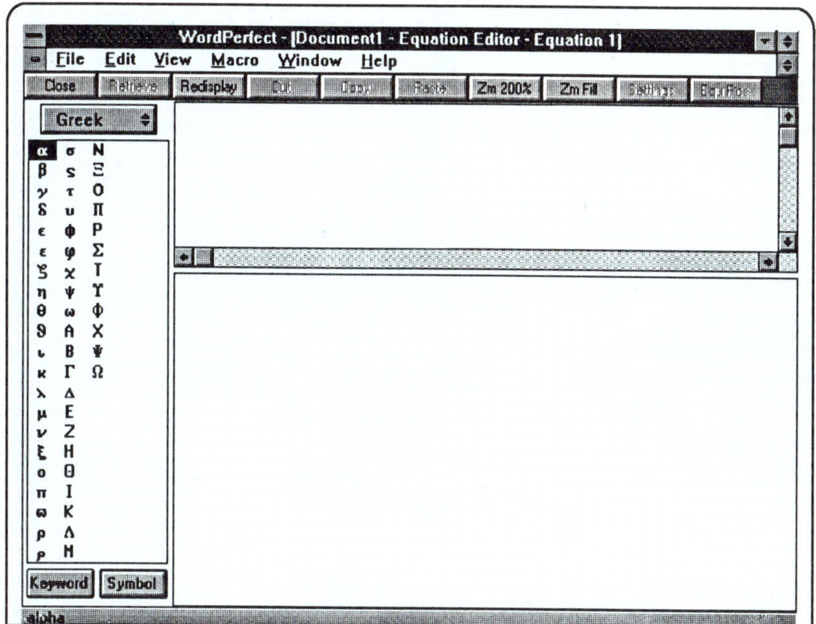

The Greek symbols are displayed on your screen. The names of the symbols are shown on the status bar. To select the "mu" symbol:

Click	on the μ (mu) symbol	***Press***	*[↓] thirteen times*	**Press**	[↓] thirteen times
Click	the Keyword command button	***Press***	*[↵Enter] to select the Keyword command button*	**Press**	[↵Enter] to select the Keyword command button

The upper part of your screen should look like Figure 28-12.

Figure 28-12

The Keyword command button places the name of the symbol in the editing pane. The Symbol command button places the actual symbol in the editing pane.

To continue the formula:

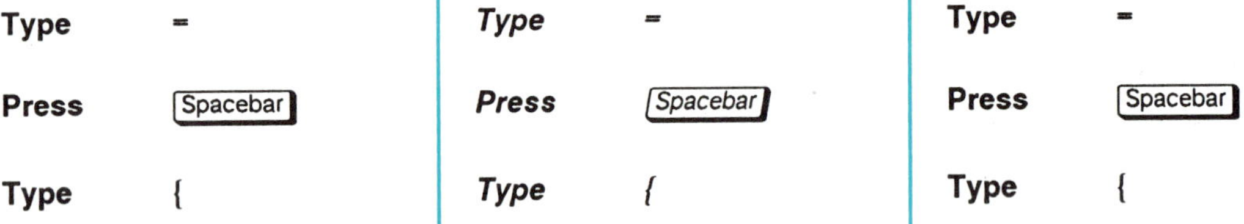

Type	=	***Type***	*=*	**Type**	=
Press	[Spacebar]	***Press***	*[Spacebar]*	**Press**	[Spacebar]
Type	{	***Type***	*{*	**Type**	{

To select the "SMALLSUM" symbol from the Large palette:

Click	the Palette pop-up list button	***Press***	*[F6]*	**Press**	[F6]
Hold down	the mouse button to view the pop-up list	***Press***	*[PageUp] twice to view the Large palette*	**Press**	[PageUp] twice to view the Large palette
Select	the Large palette	***Press***	*[↓] to select the SMALLSUM symbol*	**Press**	[↓] to select the SMALLSUM symbol
Click	on the SMALLSUM symbol (the second symbol in the first column)	***Press***	*[↵Enter] to select the Keyword command button*	**Press**	[↵Enter] to select the Keyword command button
Click	the Keyword command button				

The top part of your screen should look like Figure 28-13.

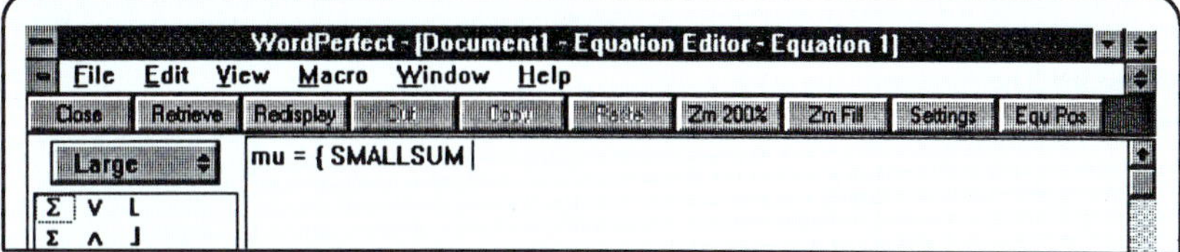

Figure 28-13

The X in the equation includes a subscript "i" which can be created using the "SUB" command.

Type	X	***Type***	*X*	**Type**	X

To select the SUB command:

Click	the Palette pop-up list button	***Press***	*F6*	**Press**	F6
Hold down	the mouse button to view the pop-up list	***Press***	*PageUp to select the Commands palette*	**Press**	PageUp to select the Commands palette
Select	the Commands palette	***Press***	*↓ twice to select the SUB or _ command*	**Press**	↓ twice to select the SUB or _ command
Click	on the SUB or _ command	***Press***	*↵Enter to select the Keyword command button*	**Press**	↵Enter to select the Keyword command button
Click	the Keyword command button	***Type***	*i*	**Type**	i
Type	i	***Type***	*}*	**Type**	}
Type	}	***Press***	*Spacebar*	**Press**	Spacebar
Press	Spacebar	***Type***	*over N*	**Type**	over N
Type	over N				

The top part of your screen should look like Figure 28-14.

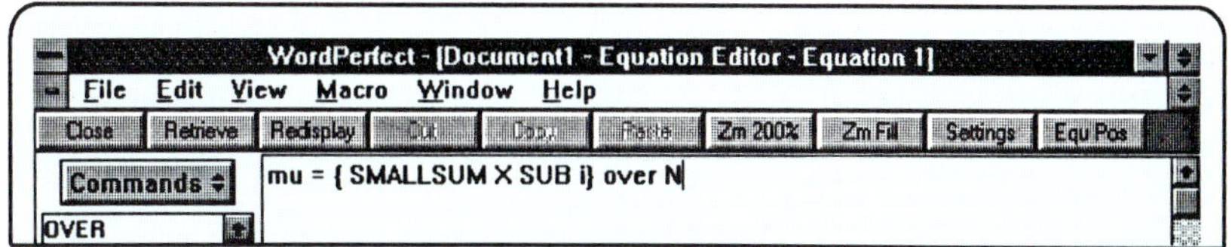

Figure 28-14

To display the equation:

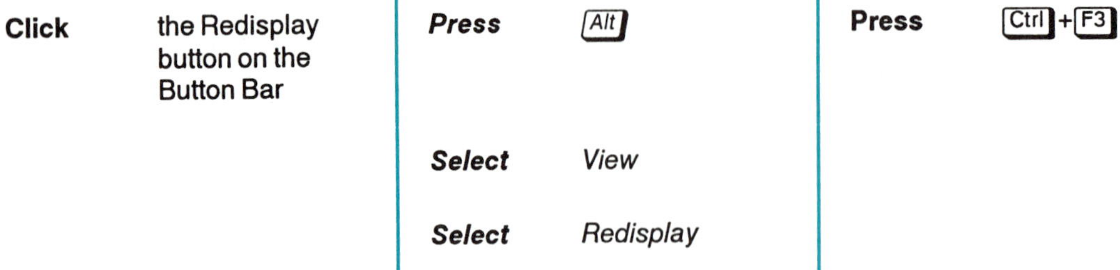

Click	the Redisplay button on the Button Bar	***Press***	*Alt*	**Press**	Ctrl + F3
		Select	*View*		
		Select	*Redisplay*		

The bottom portion of your screen should look like Figure 28-15.

Figure 28-15

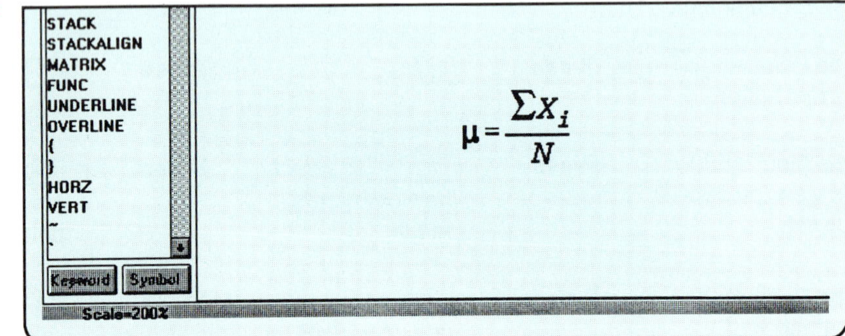

■ SAVING AN EQUATION

After you create an equation, you may want to save the equation so that you can use it in other documents. Saving an equation is not the same as saving the entire document. In order to save the document, you must be in the normal editing screen.

To save an equation that you have created to a separate file:

Choose	File	***Press***	*Alt*	**Press**	F3
Choose	Save As	***Select***	*File*		
		Select	*Save As*		

Your screen should look like Figure 28-16.

Figure 28-16

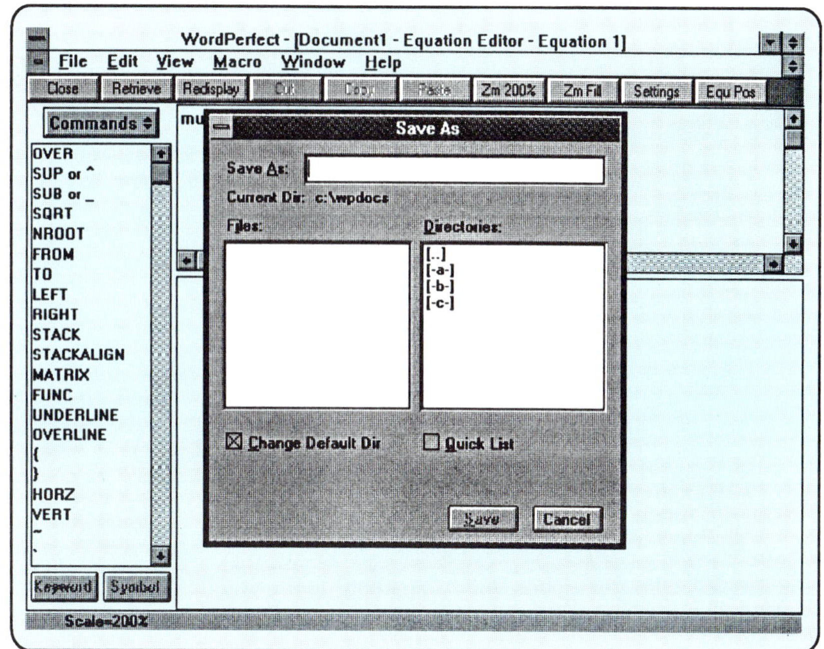

WordPerfect does not automatically add an extension to the equation file name when you save the file. However, when retrieving an equation file, WordPerfect looks for files with the extension ".eqn." To locate equation files easily, you should add the ".eqn" extension to equation file names.

Type	**avg.eqn**	***Type***	***avg.eqn***	**Type**	**avg.eqn**
Click	the Save command button	***Press***	*↵Enter to select the Save command button*	**Press**	↵Enter to select the Save command button

The equation is saved in the documents directory "c:\wpdocs" or "a:\wpdocs."

To return to the normal editing screen:

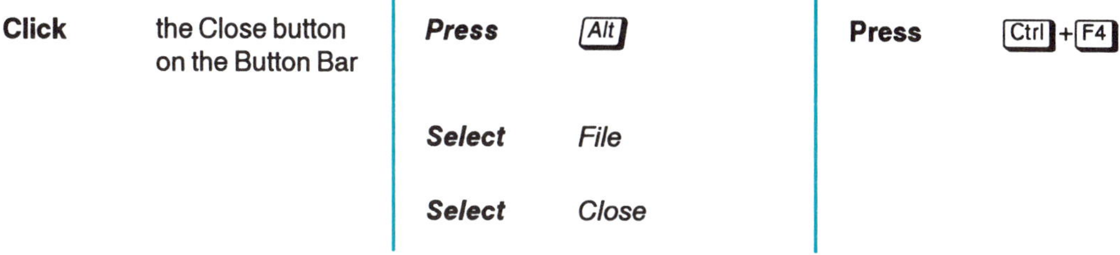

Click	the Close button on the Button Bar	***Press***	*Alt*	**Press**	Ctrl+F4
		Select	*File*		
		Select	*Close*		

Close the document without saving changes.

■ USING AN EQUATION IN A DOCUMENT

This section shows how an equation fits into a document containing text. Create the document shown in Figure 28-17. In the last paragraph, make sure the **i** in $\mathbf{X_i}$ is a subscript.

Figure 28-17

```
Suppose you need to know the average age of the students in a
WordPerfect class.  The average age can be computed by summing
the ages of all the people in the class and dividing by the
number of students.

The formula for computing the average for a group of items is:



where u is the symbol for the arithmetic mean, Xi represents the
value for each of the items for which you are computing the mean,
and N is the number of items.
```

Suppose you want to insert the equation saved in "avg.eqn" in the middle of your document. To move to the location where you want to insert the equation and then enter the Equation Editor:

Click	at the second line after the line beginning "The formula"	***Move***	*the insertion point to the second line after the line beginning "The formula"*
Choose	Graphics	***Press***	Alt
Choose	Equation	***Select***	*Graphics*
Choose	Create	***Select***	*Equation*
		Select	*Create*

To retrieve the equation saved in the file "avg.eqn":

Click	the Retrieve button on the Button Bar	***Press***	Alt
Click	on the file "avg.eqn"	***Select***	*File*
Click	the Retrieve command button	***Select***	*Retrieve*
		Type	***avg.eqn***

		Press	*[↵Enter] to select the Retrieve command button*		

To return to the normal editing screen:

Click	the Close button on the Button Bar	***Press***	*[Alt]*		
		Select	*File*		
		Select	*Close*		

The top part of your screen should look like Figure 28-18.

Figure 28-18

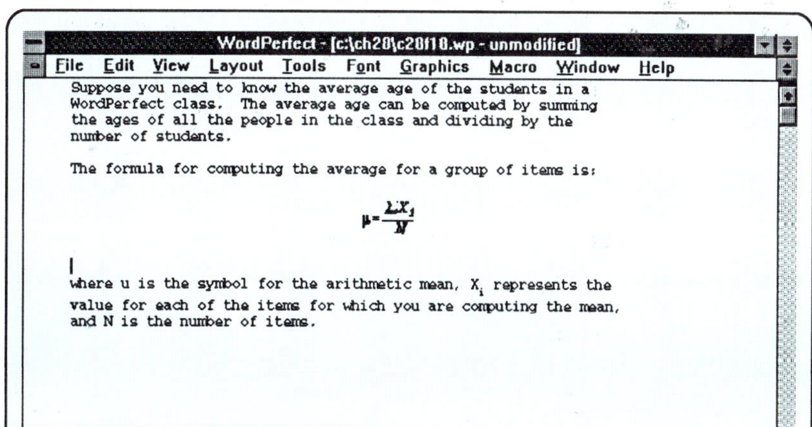

You can replace the "u" in the first line of the last paragraph with the Greek "mu" symbol. You could create an equation consisting of only one character, the mu symbol. However, WordPerfect also has special character sets that contain many mathematical and scientific symbols. Using the WordPerfect Characters feature is much simpler for one symbol.

To delete the "u" out of the document and enter the WP Characters feature:

Click	before the "u" in the first line of text after the equation	***Move***	*the insertion point before the "u" in the first line of text after the equation*	**Move**	the insertion point before the "u" in the first line of text after the equation
Press	[Delete]	***Press***	*[Delete]*	**Press**	[Delete]
Choose	Font	***Press***	*[Alt]*	**Press**	[Ctrl]+[W]
Choose	WP Characters	***Select***	*Font*		
		Select	*WP Characters*		

To access the Greek character set:

Click	the Set pop-up list button	***Press***	*Alt+S to select the Set pop-up list button*	**Press**	Alt+S to select the Set pop-up list button
Hold down	the mouse button to view the pop-up list	***Press***	*Alt+↑ to view the pop-up list*	**Press**	Alt+↑ to view the pop-up list
Choose	Greek	***Type***	*G to select Greek*	**Type**	G to select Greek

To select the "mu" symbol:

Click	on the μ symbol in the Characters list box	***Press***	*Alt+C to select the Characters list box*	**Press**	Alt+C to select the Characters list box
		Press	*↓*	**Press**	↓
		Press	*→ ten times*	**Press**	→ ten times

Your screen should look like Figure 28-19.

Figure 28-19

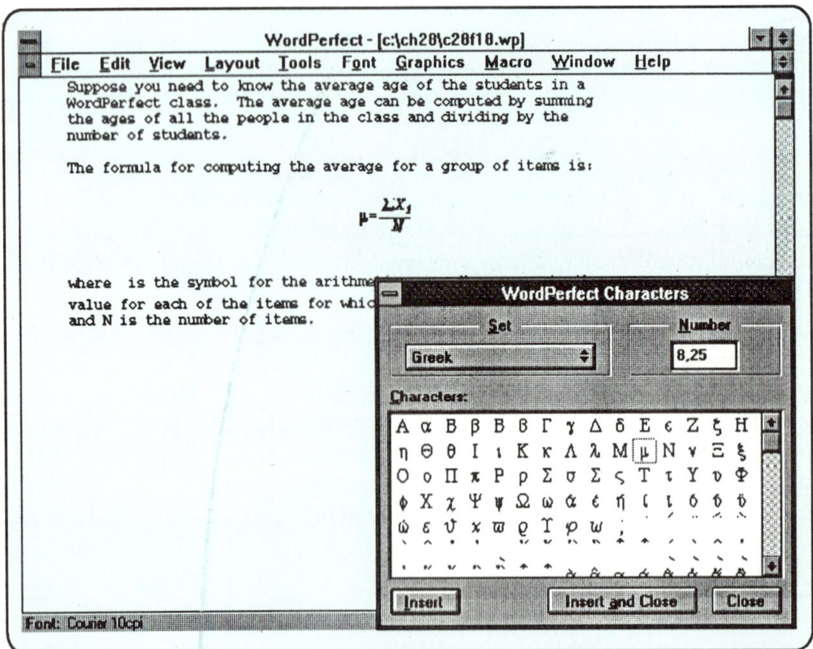

Notice the text "8,25" in the Number text box. The μ symbol is number 25 in the eighth character set.

To insert the symbol and close the dialog box:

Click	the Insert and Close command button	***Press***	*Alt+A to select the Insert and Close command button*	**Press**	Alt+A to select the Insert and Close command button

The top part of your screen should look like Figure 28-20.

Figure 28-20

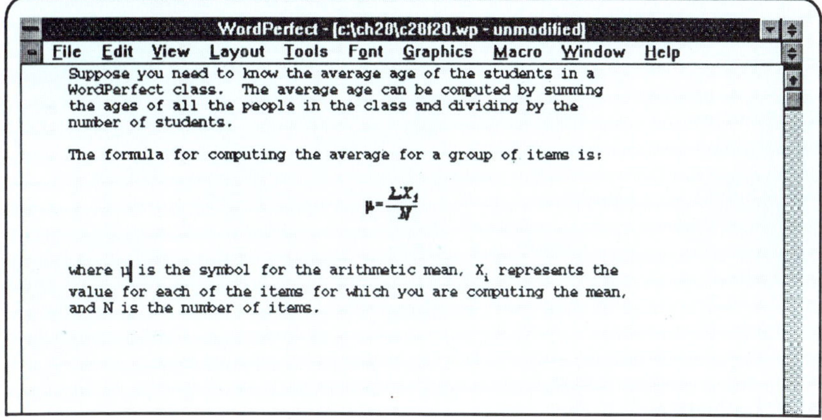

Notice that the µ symbol appears in the document. Save the document as "equate2."

PRINTING AN EQUATION

When you send an equation to your printer, WordPerfect uses the printer settings to reproduce the equation you see on the screen.

If your printer can print graphics, you should have no problem printing equations. If your printer cannot print graphics, characters that cannot be printed will be replaced with a space.

Print the document.

EDITING AN EQUATION

Each equation in a document is numbered by WordPerfect. When editing an equation, you are asked to enter the equation number.

To edit equation 1:

Double-click	the Equation 1 box	***Press***	*Alt*
		Select	*Graphics*
		Select	*Equation*
		Select	*Edit*
		Type	*1*
		Press	*↵Enter*

To change "over" to a "/" in the equation:

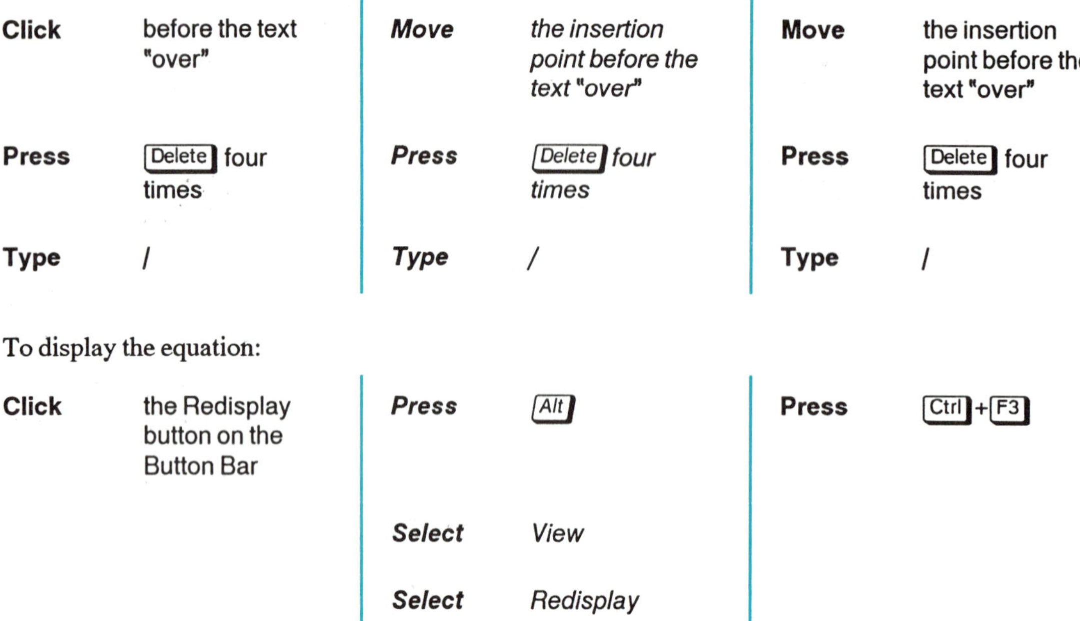

Click	before the text "over"	***Move***	*the insertion point before the text "over"*	**Move**	the insertion point before the text "over"
Press	[Delete] four times	***Press***	*[Delete] four times*	**Press**	[Delete] four times
Type	/	***Type***	*/*	**Type**	/

To display the equation:

Click	the Redisplay button on the Button Bar	***Press***	*[Alt]*	**Press**	[Ctrl]+[F3]
		Select	*View*		
		Select	*Redisplay*		

Your screen should look like Figure 28-21.

Figure 28-21

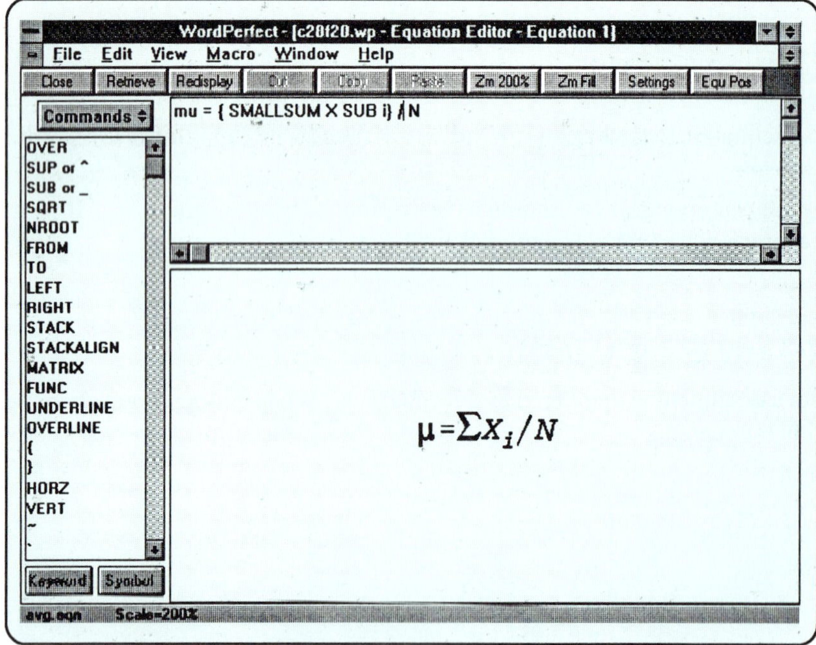

You can not use the spacebar to add a space between characters in the display of your equation. To create a space between characters in your equation, you insert a tilde (~).

To add a space before and after the equal sign in this equation:

Click	before the = sign	***Move***	*the insertion point before the = sign*	**Move**	the insertion point before the = sign
Type	~	***Type***	*~*	**Type**	~
Click	after the = sign	***Move***	*the insertion point after the = sign*	**Move**	the insertion point after the = sign
Type	~	***Type***	*~*	**Type**	~

To view the changes in the equation:

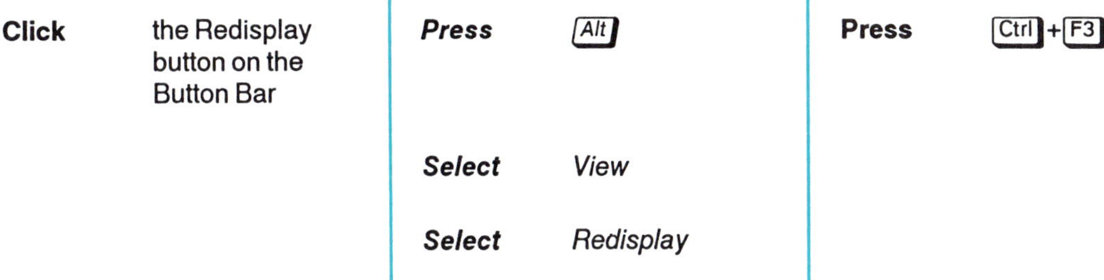

Click	the Redisplay button on the Button Bar	***Press***	*Alt*	**Press**	Ctrl + F3
		Select	*View*		
		Select	*Redisplay*		

Your screen should look like Figure 28-22.

Figure 28-22

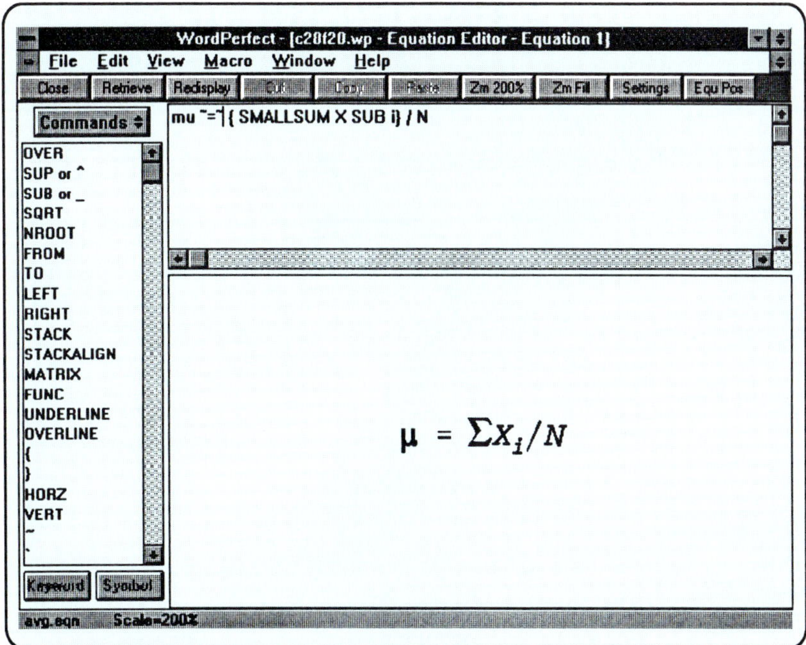

$\mu = \Sigma X_i / N$

To return to the normal editing screen:

Click	the Close button on the Button Bar	***Press***	*Alt*	**Press**	Ctrl + F4

Select	*File*
Select	*Close*

Save the document as "equate3." Close the document.

EXERCISE 1

INSTRUCTIONS: Define the following terms:

1. Equation feature ______________________________

2. Equation editor ______________________________

3. Editing pane ______________________________

4. Display pane ______________________________

5. Equation palette ______________________________

6. Over command ______________________________

7. Redisplay ______________________________

EXERCISE 2

INSTRUCTIONS: Circle T if the statement is true and F if the statement is false.

T F 1. The Equation feature allows you to include mathematical or scientific equations in a document.

T F 2. The Equation Editor enables you to create equations.

T F 3. The Equation Editor can create and calculate equations for you.

T F 4. The Equation Editor is divided into four parts: the editing pane, the display pane, the equation palette, and the calculation window.

T F 5. The equation palette shows how the equation will look when printed.

T F 6. The display pane provides lists of commands and symbols that you use for building an equation.

T F 7. The "OVER" command creates a fraction.

T F 8. To recognize (5 x T x W) as a single character to the left of the Over command, place brackets [ ] around the characters.

T F 9. Saving an equation saves the document, too.

EXERCISE 3

INSTRUCTIONS:

1. Create the following formula that computes the interest owed on a loan for a specific time period.

$$I=P\ x\ \frac{R}{12}$$

2. Save the formula in a file using the name "interest.eqn."
3. Print the formula.
4. Close the document.
5. Create the following document and insert the formula as indicated.
6. Save the document in a file using the name "ch28ex03."
7. Print the document.
8. Close the document.

Sometimes it is necessary to compute the amount of interest due for a loan during a specific month. The following formula can be used to calculate the interest due for a particular month.

$$I=P\ x\ \frac{R}{12}$$

The letter I is the variable for Interest. P is the variable for the Principal or loan amount owed. R is the annual interest rate, for example, 10%. The annual interest rate is divided by 12, because you need to calculate the monthly interest amount rather than the annual interest amount.

EXERCISE 4

INSTRUCTIONS:

1. Create the following document.
2. Use the "SMALLSUM" symbol from the Large palette for the voltage formula.
3. Print the document.
4. Save the document in a file using the name "ch28ex04."
5. Close the document.

```
Loop Equations:

Kirchoff's Voltage Law
```

$$\Sigma Erises = \Sigma Vdrops$$

```
Area of a Circle
```

$$A = \pi r^2$$

EXERCISE 5

INSTRUCTIONS:

1. Create the following financial formulas.
2. Save the present value formula as "pv.eqn." Save the future value formula as "fv.eqn."
3. Print the document.
4. Save the document in a file using the name "ch28ex05."

```
The Present Value of an Annuity formula allows you to determine the
present value of an investment based on a number of equal payments
(p), discounted at a specific interest rate (i), over a certain
period of time (n).
```

$$p\ x\ \frac{1-(1+i)^{-n}}{i}$$

```
The Future Value of an Annuity formula allows you to determine the
future value of an investment based on a number of equal payments
(p), earning a periodic interest rate (i), over a certain period of
time (n).
```

$$p\ x\ \frac{(1+i)^{n}-1}{i}$$

EXERCISE 6

INSTRUCTIONS:

1. Create the following statistical equations. Use the "SQRT" command to create the square root symbol. Use the "sigma" command in the Greek palette for the character σ.
2. Save the first equation as "stddev.eqn." Save the second formula as "variance.eqn."
3. Print the document.
4. Save the document in a file using the name "ch28ex06."
5. Close the document.

CALCULATING THE STANDARD DEVIATION

$$\sigma = \sqrt{\frac{\Sigma(x-\mu)^2}{n}}$$

CALCULATING THE VARIANCE

$$\sigma^2 = \frac{\Sigma\ (x-\mu)^2}{n}$$

where μ is the average of the numbers

EXERCISE 7

INSTRUCTIONS:

1. Create the following math equations. Use the "SQRT" command in the Command palette to create the square root symbol. Use the vertical line in the Large palette to create the vertical line in the second equation. Use the "sigma" and "mu" characters from the Greek palette for the characters σ and μ respectively.
2. Print the document.
3. Save the document in a file using the name "ch28ex07."
4. Close the document.

Standard Density Function

$$\frac{1}{\sqrt{2\pi}}e^{-\frac{1}{2}U^2}$$

Tchebycheff's Inequality Formula

$$P\ (\ |x-\mu|\ \geq k\sigma)\ \leq \frac{1}{k^2}$$

EXERCISE 8

INSTRUCTIONS:

1. Create the following math equations. Use the "INTEGRAL" symbol from the Large palette for the $\int$ symbol. To place the characters above and below the integral, use the "FROM" and "TO" commands in the Command palette. The syntax for the "FROM" and "TO" commands is "FROM a TO b."
2. Print the document.
3. Save the document in a file using the name "ch28ex08."
4. Close the document.

Integral Formula

$$\int_a^b f(x)d(x)$$

Logarithmic Rule

$$\int \frac{1}{x}\ dx\ =\ 1nx+c\ (x>0)$$

CHAPTER TWENTY-NINE

DOCUMENT STYLE SHEETS

OBJECTIVES

In this chapter, you will learn to:

- Create a style
- Edit a style
- Save a style
- Retrieve a style
- Apply a style using the Ruler
- Delete a style

■ CHAPTER OVERVIEW

There may be times when you want to use the same format within a document. At other times, you may require the use of the same format for several different documents. To repeat a format, you can use the Styles feature. In this chapter, the procedures for creating, editing, saving, retrieving, and deleting a style sheet or format are described and illustrated.

■ CREATING AND USING A STYLE

A style allows you to repeat formats easily. A style can have text and any number of format codes associated with it. A style is placed into the document as a code. You can use several styles within one document.

Change the default directory to "a:\wpdocs" or to "c:\wpdocs." Create the document in Figure 29-1.

Figure 29-1

```
Beginning:  Word Processing Basics.  Create, modify, save, and
print documents.  Topics include pull-down menus, file retrieval,
scrolling, deleting, search and replace, text enhancements,
reveal codes, line spacing, tabs, margin settings, pagination,
headers and footers, and page format options.  The block, switch
and move functions are also covered.  No prior knowledge of word
processing is required.

Dates:       April 18    May 16      June 18

Intermediate:  Form Letters, Merge, and Macros.  This course
covers macros, math calculations, text columns, the table
feature, the document merge feature, sorting, creating, and
editing a graphic image, forms fill-in, creating mailing labels
using the merge feature, and file conversion.  A preview of style
sheets and generating an index is also presented.

Dates:       April 19    May 17      June 19

Advanced:  Graphics, Style Sheets, and Indexing.  This course is
currently in the planning stage.  ABC Can Company plans to offer
this class in July.
```

Save the document using the name "schedule."

Suppose you want to create styles that will do the following:

1. Bold the words "Beginning," "Intermediate," and "Advanced."
2. Italicize and underline the names of the courses, like "Word Processing Basics."
3. Italicize the lines containing the dates.

To access the Styles feature:

Choose	Layout	***Press***	Alt	**Press**	Alt+F8
Choose	Styles	***Select***	*Layout*		
		Select	*Styles*		

The Styles dialog box appears. Your screen should look like Figure 29-2.

Figure 29-2

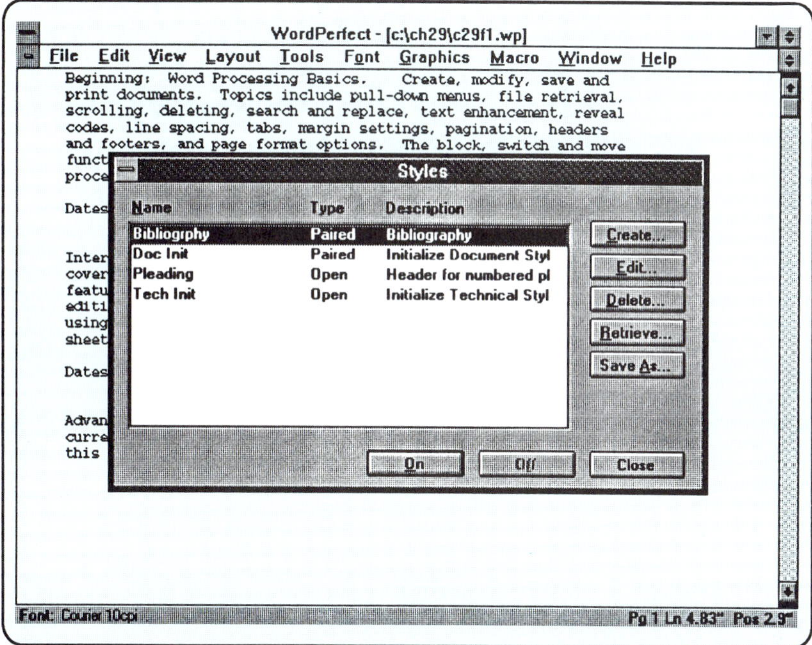

Notice that four styles automatically appear in the Styles dialog box. These styles are the default styles that WordPerfect has available. The default styles are saved in a file called "library.sty" in the "c:\wpwin" directory. The default styles will automatically appear when you choose Styles from the Layout menu or press Alt+F8. You can change the default style sheet and the default styles directory if you choose Location of Files from the Preferences option under the File menu or press Ctrl+Shift+F1 and select Location of Files.

To create a style:

Click	the Create command button	***Press***	*Alt+C to select the Create command button*	**Press**	Alt+C to select the Create command button

Your screen should look like Figure 29-3.

Figure 29-3

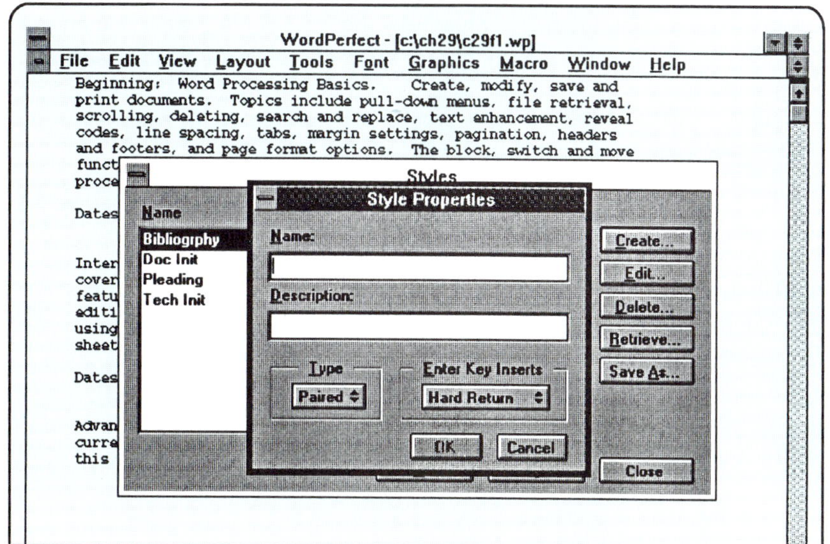

The Style Properties dialog box appears. Options are available for entering a style name, type, description, and how the ↵Enter key operates in the style.

You can give a style a name by selecting the Name option. Approximately 33 characters will fit in the Name text box. The name can contain spaces.

To name the style:

Double-click	on the Name text box	***Press***	*Alt+N to select the Name text box*	**Press**	Alt+N to select the Name text box
Type	Course Level	***Type***	*Course Level*	**Type**	Course Level

The Description option is used to enter text that describes the style that you are creating. A description of the style is helpful, since a name cannot tell all the features that a particular style can perform. Approximately 33 characters will fit in the Description text box.

To enter a description:

Double-click	the Description text box	***Press***	*Alt+D to select the Description text box*	**Press**	Alt+D to select the Description text box
Type	Bold Course Levels	***Type***	*Bold Course Levels*	**Type**	Bold Course Levels

There are two types of styles:

Paired - This style type uses On and Off codes to turn on the features defined with the style, and then turns off the style at a later point in the text.

Open - An Open style type turns on the features associated with the style once. These features are used to the end of the document.

The default setting for the style type is Paired. Since you are creating a style to bold the course level headings, you do not need to change the style type.

The Enter Key Inserts option allows you to change how the ↵Enter key works when you are using that particular style. The ↵Enter key can perform three actions when used with a paired style.

Hard Return - A hard return code is placed in your document when you press the ↵Enter key while using the style.

Style Off - A Style Off code is placed in your document when you press the ↵Enter key while using this style.

Style Off/On - A Style Off code is placed in your document when you press the ↵Enter key once. When you press the ↵Enter key a second time, a Style On code is placed in the document.

The default setting for the Enter Key Inserts option is Hard Return. A hard return code will be inserted in your document when you press the ↵Enter key while using the style. You do not need to change the Enter Key Inserts option.

To accept the style settings and insert the formatting codes for a Paired style type:

Click	the OK command button	***Press***	*↵Enter*	**Press**	↵Enter

Your screen should look like Figure 29-4.

Figure 29-4

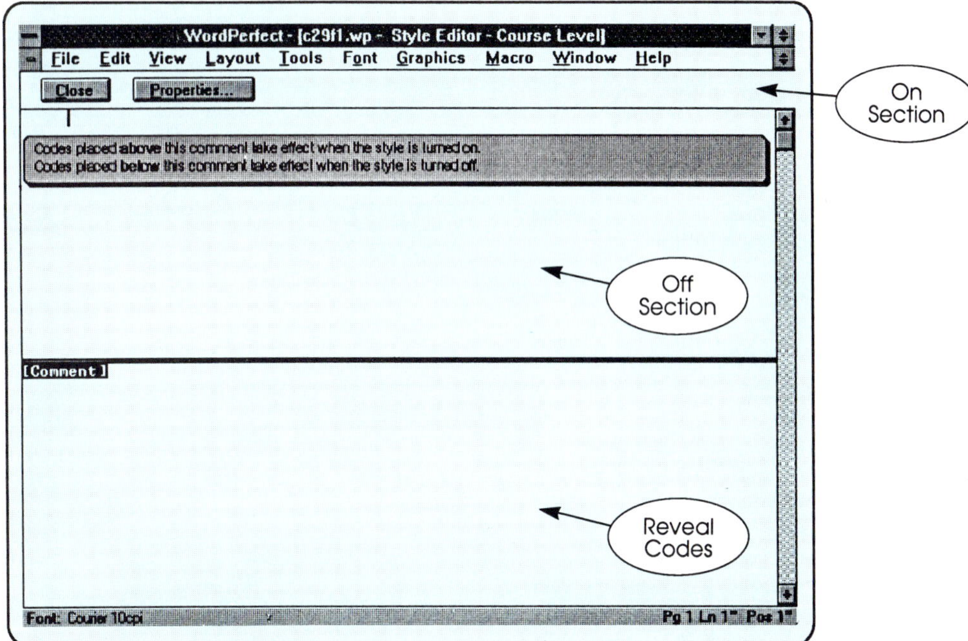

The Style Editor allows you to associate feature codes and text with a style. The codes and text are placed in a style in the same way that they are placed in a document.

Recall that style types affect how these codes operate in the document. The codes in the Open style type are on until the end of the document.

The codes in a Paired style type are on in a document until the Style Off code is reached.

Your screen displays the Style Editor for a Paired style type. The screen has two sections. The top part of the screen is the On section. The On section contains codes that are executed when the style is turned on, i.e., a Style On code is placed in the document. The On section is located before the [Comment] code in the bottom part of the screen.

The bottom part of the screen is the Off section. This section contains codes that are executed when the style is turned off. The Off section is located after the [Comment] code in the bottom part of the screen.

When a style is turned off, any document setting that was changed when the style was turned on is returned to its original value.

To place a Bold On code [Bold On] to the left of the [Comment] code in the On section:

Choose	Font	***Press***	*Alt*	**Press**	Ctrl+B
Choose	Bold	***Select***	*Font*		
		Select	*Bold*		

The bottom section of your screen should look like Figure 29-5.

Figure 29-5

To close the Style Editor:

Click	the Close command button	***Press***	*Alt+C to select the Close command button*	**Press**	Ctrl+F4

Your screen should look like Figure 29-6.

Figure 29-6

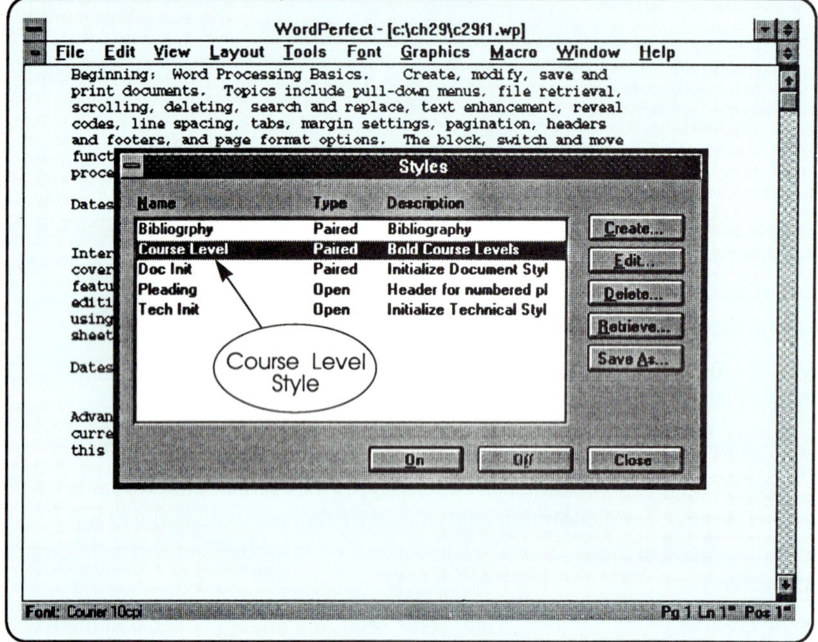

The Course Level style is now shown in the Styles dialog box.

You must now create two more styles for the course title and the date lines. To create the Course Title style:

Click	the Create command button	***Press***	*Alt+C to select the Create command button*	**Press**	Alt+C to select the Create command button
Double-click	the Name text box	***Press***	*Alt+N to select the Name text box*	**Press**	Alt+N to select the Name text box
Type	Course Title	***Type***	*Course Title*	**Type**	Course Title

Double-click	the Description text box	***Press***	*Alt+D to select the Description text box*	**Press**	Alt+D to select the Description text box
Type	Italicize and Underline Course Titles	***Type***	*Italicize and Underline Course Titles*	**Type**	Italicize and Underline Course Titles
Click	the OK command button	***Press***	*↵Enter*	**Press**	↵Enter
Choose	Font	***Press***	*Alt*	**Press**	Ctrl+I
Choose	Italic	***Select***	*Font*	**Press**	Ctrl+U
Choose	Font	***Select***	*Italic*		
Choose	Underline	***Press***	*Alt*		
		Select	*Font*		
		Select	*Underline*		

The bottom part of your screen should look like Figure 29-7.

Figure 29-7

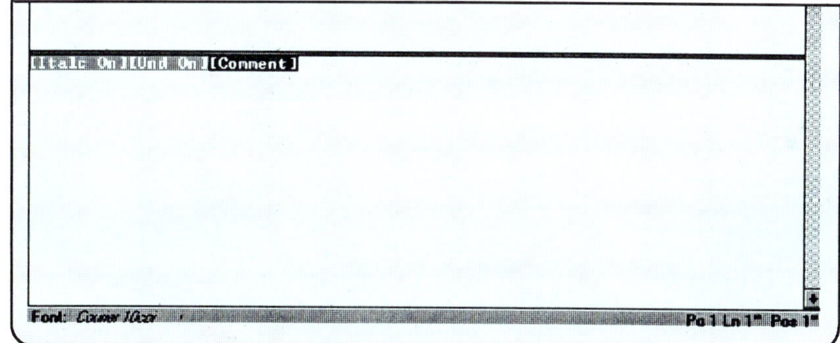

To return to the list of styles:

Click	the Close command button	***Press***	*Alt+C to select the Close command*	**Press**	Ctrl+F4

The Course Title style now appears in the list.

To create a style for the date lines:

Click	the Create command button	***Press***	*Alt+C to select the Create command button*	**Press**	Alt+C to select the Create command button
Double-click	the Name text box	***Press***	*Alt+N to select the Name text box*	**Press**	Alt+N to select the Name text box
Type	Dates	***Type***	*Dates*	**Type**	Dates

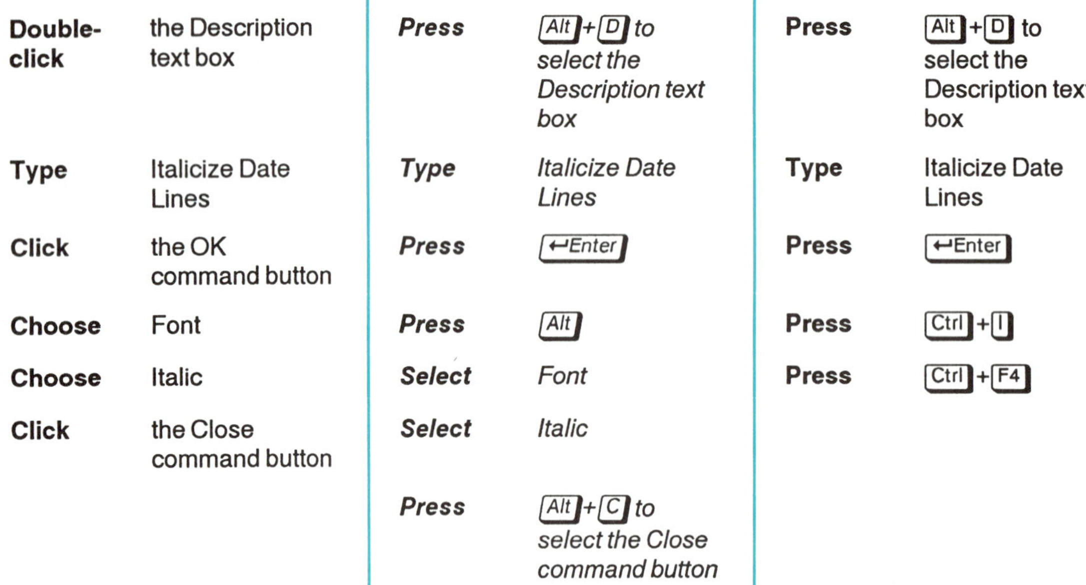

Double-click	the Description text box	***Press***	*Alt+D to select the Description text box*	**Press**	Alt+D to select the Description text box
Type	Italicize Date Lines	***Type***	*Italicize Date Lines*	**Type**	Italicize Date Lines
Click	the OK command button	***Press***	*↵Enter*	**Press**	↵Enter
Choose	Font	***Press***	*Alt*	**Press**	Ctrl+I
Choose	Italic	***Select***	*Font*	**Press**	Ctrl+F4
Click	the Close command button	***Select***	*Italic*		
		Press	*Alt+C to select the Close command button*		

Your screen should look like Figure 29-8.

Figure 29-8

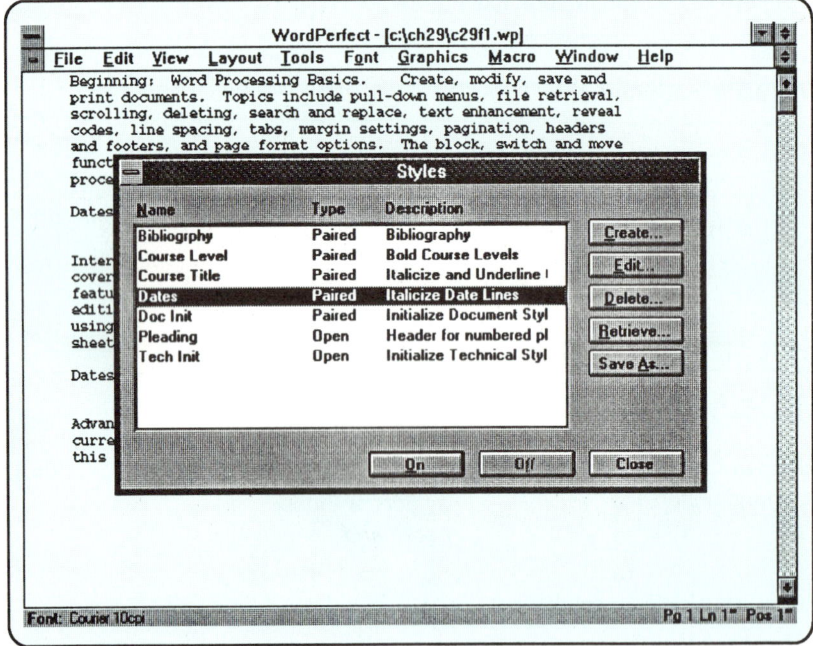

The Dates style now appears in the list.

To return to your document:

Click	the Close command button	***Press***	*Esc*	**Press**	Esc

To use the Course Level style:

Select	the text "Beginning:"	***Select***	*the text "Beginning:"*	**Select**	the text "Beginning:"
Choose	Layout	***Press***	*Alt*	**Press**	Alt+F8
Choose	Styles	***Select***	*Layout*		
		Select	*Styles*		

To turn on the Course Level style:

Click	on Course Level in the Name list box	***Press***	*Alt+N to select the Name list box*	**Press**	Alt+N to select the Name list box
Click	the On command button	***Press***	*the pointer-movement keys to select Course Level*	**Press**	the pointer-movement keys to select Course Level
		Press	*↵Enter to select the On command button*	**Press**	↵Enter to select the On command button

Repeat the steps to select and turn on the Course Level style for the "Intermediate:" and "Advanced:" text.

Your screen should look like Figure 29-9.

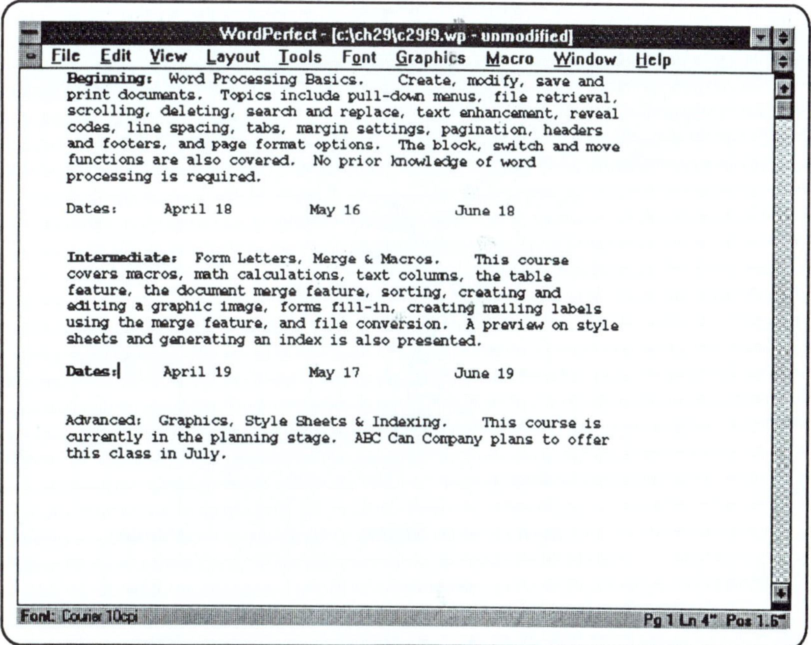

Figure 29-9

The course levels are now bold.

Display the Reveal Codes to see the Style On and Off codes. When you move the insertion point on top of the Style On code, the code expands to show the codes that you placed in the On section (to the left of the [Comment] code). When you move your insertion point on top of the Style Off code, the code expands to show the contents of the Off section. Turn off the Reveal Codes feature.

To use the Course Title style:

Select	the text "Word Processing Basics."	***Select***	*the text "Word Processing Basics."*	**Select**	the text "Word Processing Basics."
Choose	Layout	***Press***	*Alt*	**Press**	Alt+F8
Choose	Styles	***Select***	*Layout*	**Press**	Alt+N to select the Name list box
Click	on Course Title in the Name list box	***Select***	*Styles*	**Press**	the pointer-movement keys to select Course Title
Click	the On command button	***Press***	*Alt+N to select the Name list box*	**Press**	↵Enter to select the On command button
		Press	*the pointer-movement keys to select Course Title*		
		Press	*↵Enter to select the On command button*		

Repeat the steps to select and turn on the Course Title style for the "Form Letters, Merge & Macros." and "Graphics, Style Sheets & Indexing." text.

To use the Dates style:

Select	the date line for the Beginning class	***Select***	*the date line for the Beginning class*	**Select**	the date line for the Beginning class
Choose	Layout	***Press***	*Alt*	**Press**	Alt+F8
Choose	Styles	***Select***	*Layout*	**Press**	Alt+N to select the Name list box
Click	on Dates in the Name list box	***Select***	*Styles*	**Press**	the pointer-movement keys to select Dates
Click	the On command button	***Press***	*Alt+N to select the Name list box*	**Press**	↵Enter to select the On command button

Press	*the pointer-movement keys to select Dates*
Press	*↵Enter to select the On command button*

Repeat the steps to select and turn on the Dates style for the line containing the dates for the Intermediate class.

Your screen should look like Figure 29-10.

Figure 29-10

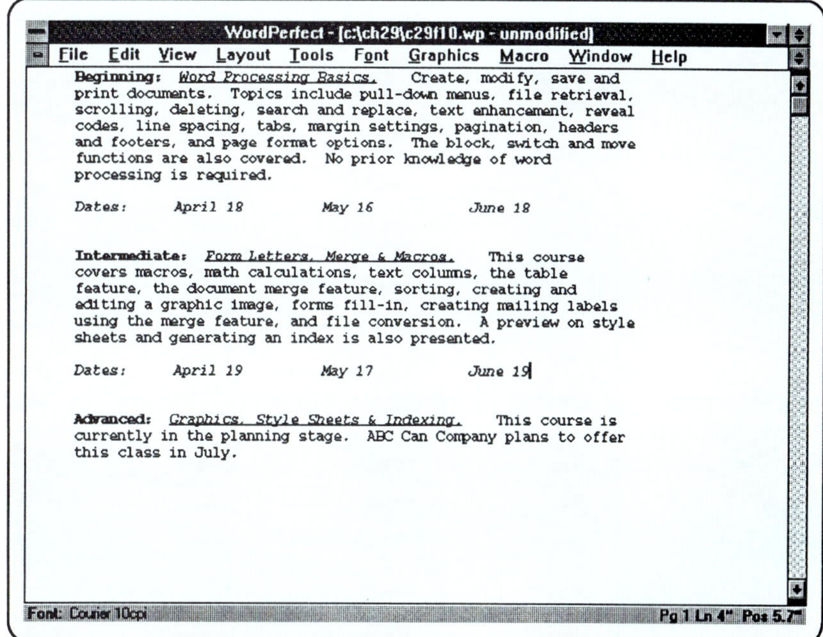

Suppose you want to place the title "WordPerfect 5.1" at the top of the schedule. Assume that you want the text to be centered and in the Helvetica 14pt bold font style.

To create a style for the format of the heading:

Choose	Layout	***Press***	*Alt*	**Press**	Alt+F8
Choose	Styles	***Select***	*Layout*	**Press**	Alt+C to select the Create command button
Click	the Create command button	***Select***	*Styles*	**Press**	Alt+N to select the Name text box
Double-click	the Name text box	***Press***	*Alt+C to select the Create command button*	**Type**	Schedule Title

Type	Schedule Title	***Press***	*Alt+N to select the Name text box*	**Press**	Alt+D to select the Description text box
Double-click	the Description text box	***Type***	*Schedule Title*	**Type**	Helv 14pt Bold and Centered
Type	Helv 14pt Bold and Centered	***Press***	*Alt+D to select the Description text box*	**Press**	↵Enter
Click	the OK command button	***Type***	*Helv 14pt Bold and Centered*		
		Press	*↵Enter*		

To change the font to Helvetica 14pt Bold:

Choose	Font	***Press***	*Alt*	**Press**	F9
Choose	Font	***Select***	*Font*	**Press**	the pointer-movement keys to select Helv 14pt Bold (Z1A)
Click	the scroll arrows to view Helv 14pt Bold (Z1A)	***Select***	*Font*	**Press**	↵Enter
Click	on Helv 14pt Bold (Z1A)	***Press***	*the pointer-movement keys to highlight Helv 14pt Bold (Z1A)*		
Click	the OK command button	***Press***	*↵Enter*		

To insert a [Center] code:

Choose	Layout	***Press***	*Alt*	**Press**	Shift+F7
Choose	Line	***Select***	*Layout*		
Choose	Center	***Select***	*Line*		
		Select	*Center*		

The bottom part of your screen should look like Figure 29-11.

Figure 29-11

To return to the list of styles:

Click	the Close command button	***Press***	*Alt+C to select the Close command button*	**Press**	Ctrl+F4

The Schedule Title now appears in the Styles dialog box.

To return to your document:

Click	the Close command button	***Press***	*Esc*	**Press**	Esc

You have already formatted existing text with a paired style by selecting the text and then selecting the Course Level, Course Title, and Dates styles. You can also select a paired style first and then type the text.

To position the insertion point where the heading is to be typed:

Click	at the beginning of the document	***Move***	*the insertion point to the beginning of the document*	**Move**	the insertion point to the beginning of the document
Press	↵Enter three times	***Press***	*↵Enter three times*	**Press**	↵Enter three times
Click	at the beginning of the document	***Move***	*the insertion point to the beginning of the document*	**Move**	the insertion point to the beginning of the document

To select a style before entering the text:

Choose	Layout	***Press***	*Alt*	**Press**	Alt+F8
Choose	Styles	***Select***	*Layout*		
		Select	*Styles*		

To turn on the Schedule Title style:

Click	on Schedule Title in the Name list box	***Press***	*Alt+N to select the Name list box*	**Press**	Alt+N to select the Name list box
Click	the On command button	***Press***	*the pointer-movement keys to select Schedule Title*	**Press**	the pointer-movement keys to select Schedule Title
		Press	*↵Enter to select the On command button*	**Press**	↵Enter to select the On command button

To enter the heading:

Type	WordPerfect 5.1	***Type***	*WordPerfect 5.1*	**Type**	WordPerfect 5.1

The top part of your screen should look like Figure 29-12.

Figure 29-12

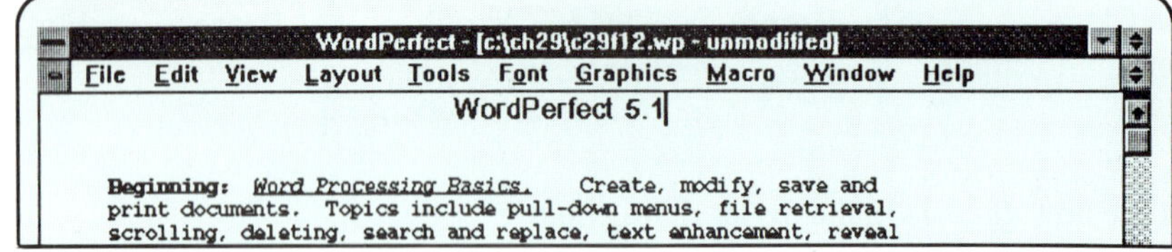

Format codes that affect an entire document are normally placed in a group at the beginning of a document. By including these codes in a style, you can easily select the style to format the entire document. Because the format codes will affect the entire document, the style should be placed in an Open style type.

Suppose you want to format the schedule with 2″ left and right margins, 1.5″ top margin, 1″ bottom margin, full justification, page numbering, and an initial font set to Helvetica 12 point. When adding format codes to your style, select the Layout menu options as you would in a normal document or press the appropriate function keys.

To create the Schedule Format style:

Choose	Layout	***Press***	*Alt*	**Press**	Alt+F8
Choose	Styles	***Select***	*Layout*	**Press**	Alt+C to select the Create command button
Click	the Create command button	***Select***	*Styles*	**Press**	Alt+N to select the Name text box
Double-click	the Name text box	***Press***	*Alt+C to select the Create command button*	**Type**	Schedule Format
Type	Schedule Format	***Press***	*Alt+N to select the Name text box*	**Press**	Alt+D to select the Description text box
Double-click	the Description text box	***Type***	*Schedule Format*	**Type**	Margins, justification, font, and page number
Type	Margins, justification, font, and page number	***Press***	*Alt+D to select the Description text box*	**Press**	Alt+T to select the Type pop-up list button
Click	the Type pop-up list button	***Type***	*Margins, justification, font, and page number*	**Press**	Alt+↑ to view the pop-up list
Hold down	the mouse button to view the pop-up list	***Press***	*Alt+T to select the Type pop-up list button*	**Type**	O to select Open

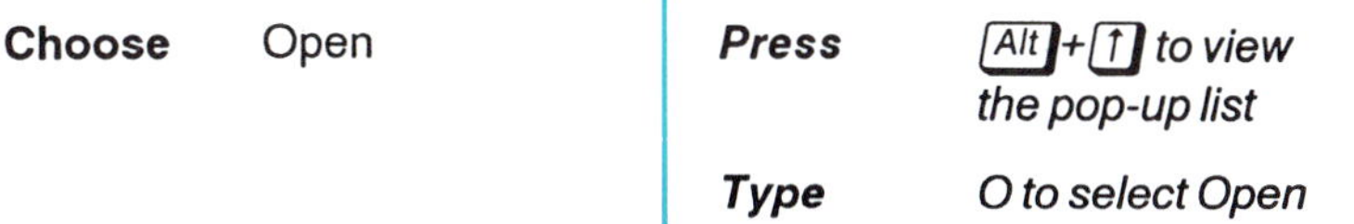

Choose	Open	***Press***	*Alt+↑ to view the pop-up list*
		Type	*O to select Open*

Your screen should look like Figure 29-13.

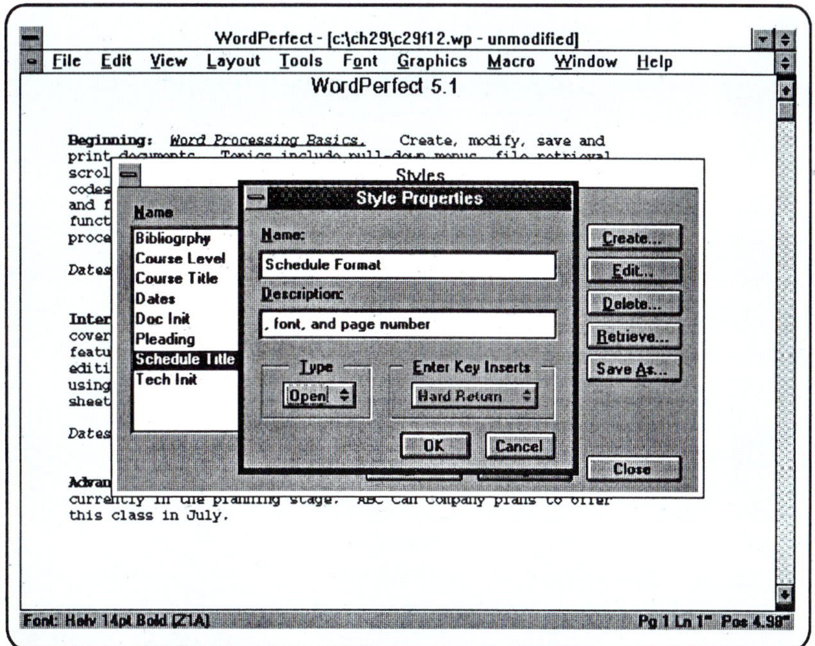

Figure 29-13

To insert the format codes for the style:

Click	the OK command button	***Press***	*↵Enter*	**Press**	↵Enter

To create the formats for the document:

Set	the left and right margins at 2" and the top margin at 1.5"	***Set***	*the left and right margins at 2" and the top margin at 1.5"*	**Set**	the left and right margins at 2" and the top margin at 1.5"
Select	full justification	***Select***	*full justification*	**Select**	full justification
Select	page numbering at the bottom center of every page	***Select***	*page numbering at the bottom center of every page*	**Select**	page numbering at the bottom center of every page
Select	Helv 12pt (Z1A) as the font	***Select***	*Helv 12pt (Z1A) as the font*	**Select**	Helv 12pt (Z1A) as the font

The bottom part of your screen should look like Figure 29-14.

Figure 29-14

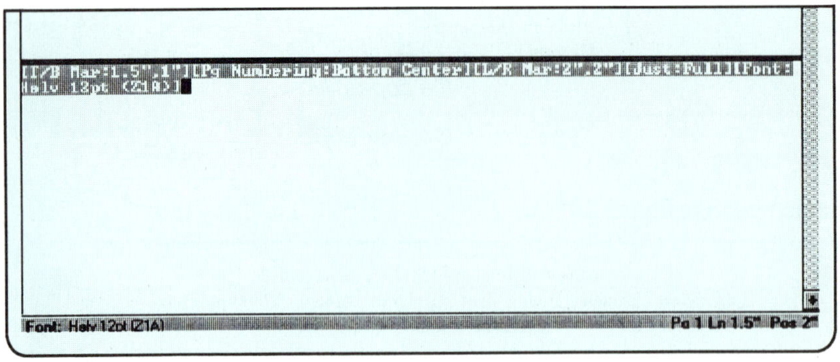

To return to your document:

Click	the Close command button	***Press***	*Alt+C to select the Close command button*	**Press**	Ctrl+F4
Click	the Close command button	***Press***	*Esc*	**Press**	Esc

To format the entire document:

Click	at the beginning of the document	***Move***	*the insertion point to the beginning of the document*	**Move**	the insertion point to the beginning of the document
Choose	Layout	***Press***	*Alt*	**Press**	Alt+F8
Choose	Styles	***Select***	*Layout*		
		Select	*Styles*		

To turn on the Schedule Format style:

Click	on Schedule Format in the Name list box	***Press***	*Alt+N to select the Name list box*	**Press**	Alt+N to select the Name list box
Click	the On command button	***Press***	*the pointer-movement keys to select Schedule Format*	**Press**	the pointer-movement keys to select Schedule Format
		Press	*↵Enter to select the On command button*	**Press**	↵Enter to select the On command button

Your screen should look like Figure 29-15.

Figure 29-15

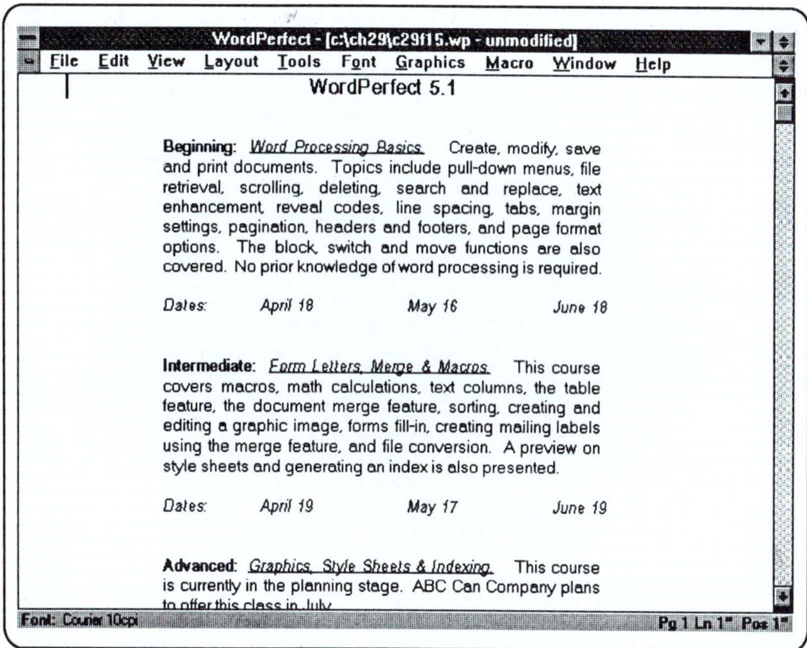

Notice that the text is in Helvetica 12 point, the document margins have changed, and a page number appears at the center of the bottom line.

Preview the document. Select full page. Notice that a page number appears at the bottom of the page. Return to your document.

EDITING A STYLE

When you want to edit a style, select the Style feature and change the information as necessary. The text in your document will reflect the changes wherever the edited style is used.

Suppose you want to change the Course Title style so that the titles are no longer in italics. Instead the titles are to be underlined and bold.

To edit the Course Title style:

Choose	Layout	***Press***	*Alt*	**Press**	Alt+F8
Choose	Styles	***Select***	*Layout*	**Press**	Alt+N to select the Name list box
Click	on Course Title in the Name list box	***Select***	*Styles*	**Press**	the pointer-movement keys to select Course Title
Click	the Edit command button	***Press***	*Alt+N to select the Name list box*	**Press**	Alt+E to select the Edit command button
Click	the Properties command button	***Press***	*the pointer-movement keys to select Course Title*	**Press**	Alt+P to select the Properties command button

Double-click	the Description text box
Type	Bold and Underline Course Titles
Click	the OK command button

Press	*Alt+E to select the Edit command button*
Press	*Alt+P to select the Properties command button*
Press	*Alt+D to select the Description text box*
Type	*Bold and Underline Course Titles*
Press	*↵Enter*

Press	Alt+D to select the Description text box
Type	Bold and Underline Course Titles
Press	↵Enter

To delete the [Italc] code and replace it with the [Bold] code:

Click	on the [Italc On] code
Press	Delete
Choose	Font
Choose	Bold

Move	*the insertion point on the [Italc On] code*
Press	*Delete*
Press	*Alt*
Select	*Font*
Select	*Bold*

Move	the insertion point on the [Italc On] code
Press	Delete
Press	Ctrl+B

The lower part of your screen should look like Figure 29-16.

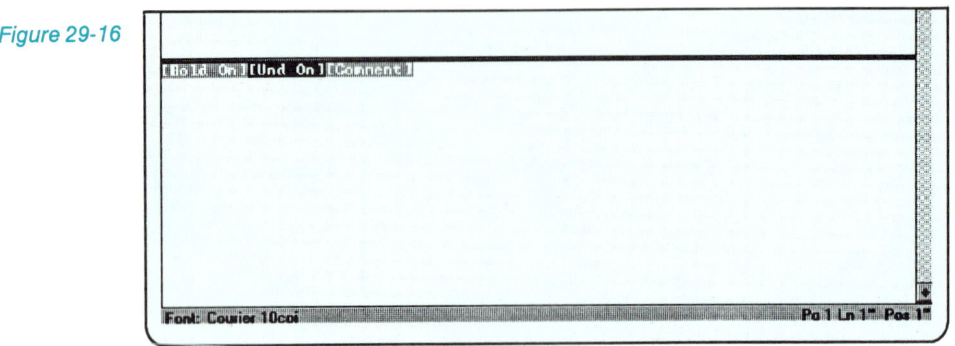

Figure 29-16

To return to your document:

Click	the Close command button
Click	the Close command button

Press	*Alt+C to select the Close command button*
Press	*Esc*

Press	Ctrl+F4
Press	Esc

Your screen should look like Figure 29-17.

Figure 29-17

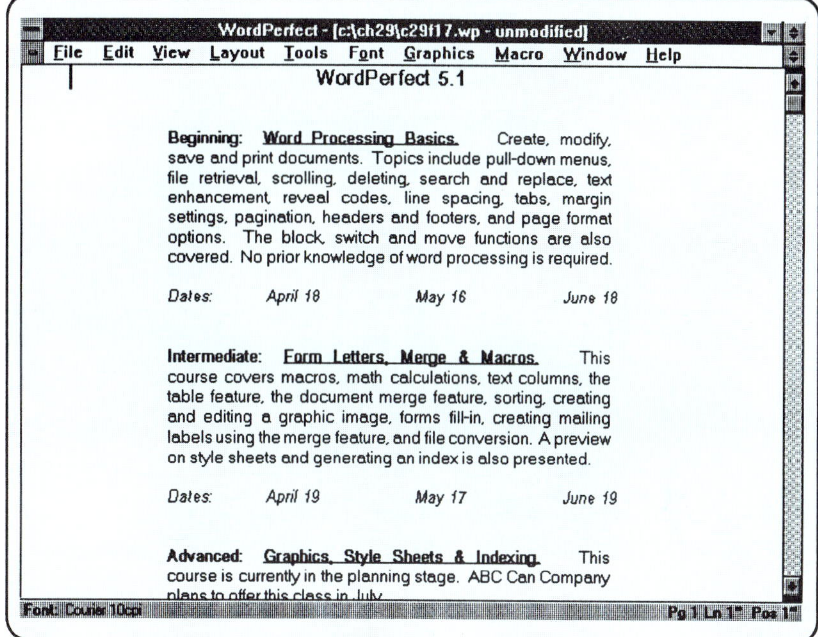

Notice that the course titles are bold and underlined.

■ SAVING STYLES

Once you create a list of styles, you may want to use the same styles to format other documents. By saving the list as a file, you can retrieve the list into any WordPerfect document.

Suppose you want to save the styles that you created for use with other documents.

To save a list of styles:

Choose Layout

Choose Styles

Click the Save As command button

Press *Alt*

Select *Layout*

Select *Styles*

Press *Alt+A to select the Save As command button*

Press Alt+F8

Press Alt+A to select the Save As command button

Your screen should look like Figure 29-18.

Figure 29-18

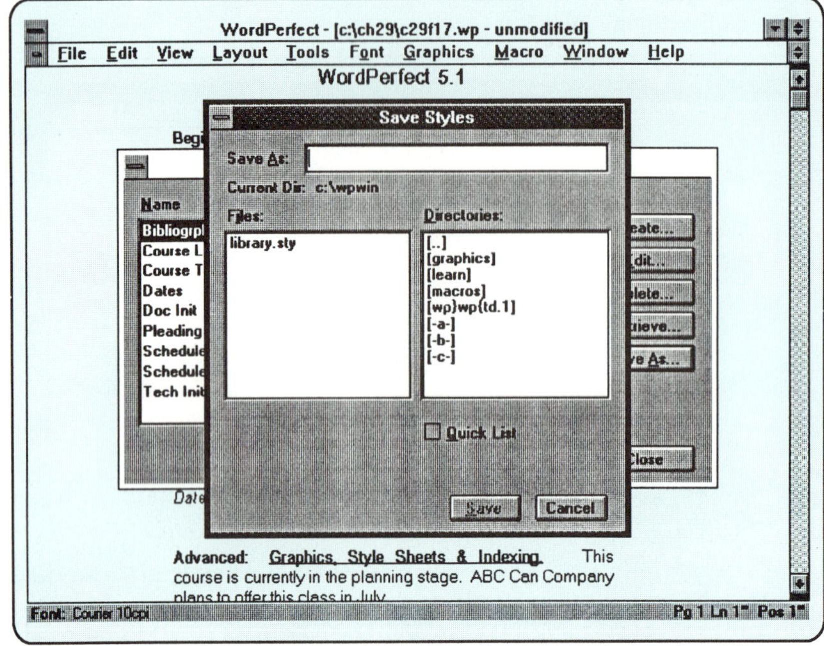

Type	**sched.sty**	***Type***	***sched.sty***	**Type**	**sched.sty**
Click	the Save command button	***Press***	*[↵Enter] to select the Save command button*	**Press**	[↵Enter] to select the Save command button

The ".sty" filename extension is not necessary, but it can help you quickly identify files that contain styles.

The styles are now saved in the "sched.sty" file. They can be retrieved into any other WordPerfect document. The styles are saved in the "c:\wpwin" directory by default. To change the location where styles are stored, use the Location of Files option under the Preferences option in the File menu.

To return to your document:

Click	the Close command button	***Press***	*[Esc]*	**Press**	[Esc]

Save the document as "stysched" and close the document.

■ RETRIEVING A STYLE

You can retrieve a list of styles that was saved at an earlier time. If any style names in your current list match those in the file that you are retrieving, you can replace the matches. Otherwise, the new styles are added to your current list.

To retrieve a list of styles:

Choose	Layout	***Press***	*[Alt]*	**Press**	[Alt]+[F8]
Choose	Styles	***Select***	*Layout*	**Press**	[Alt]+[R] to select the Retrieve command button

Click	the Retrieve command button	***Select***	*Styles*	**Type**	**sched.sty**
Click	on the file "sched.sty" in the Files list box	***Press***	*Alt+R to select the Retrieve command button*	**Press**	↵Enter to select the Retrieve command button
Click	the Retrieve command button	***Type***	*sched.sty*		
		Press	*↵Enter to select the Retrieve command button*		

Your screen should look like Figure 29-19.

Figure 29-19

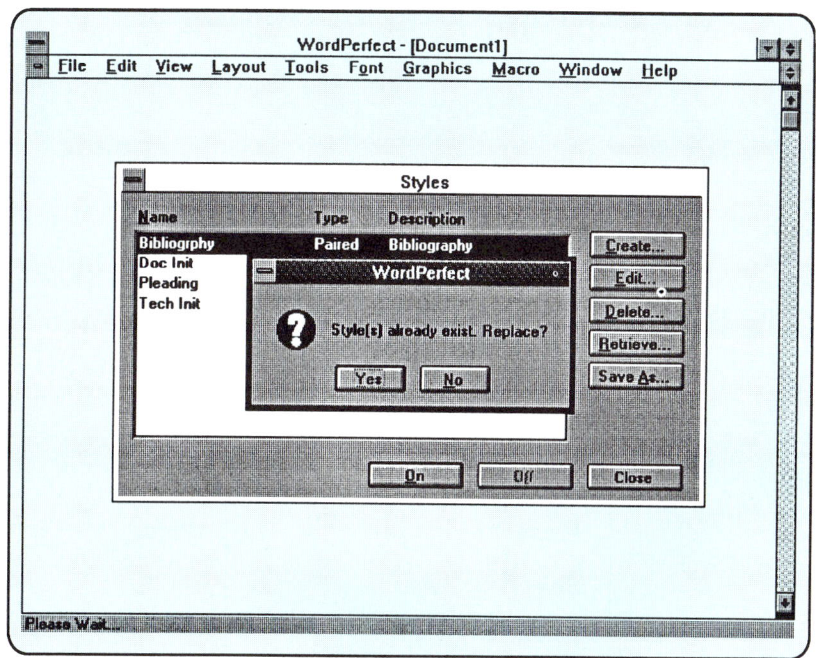

To replace existing styles:

Click	the Yes command button	***Press***	*Alt+Y to select the Yes command button*	**Press**	Alt+Y to select the Yes command button

Your screen should look like Figure 29-20.

Figure 29-20

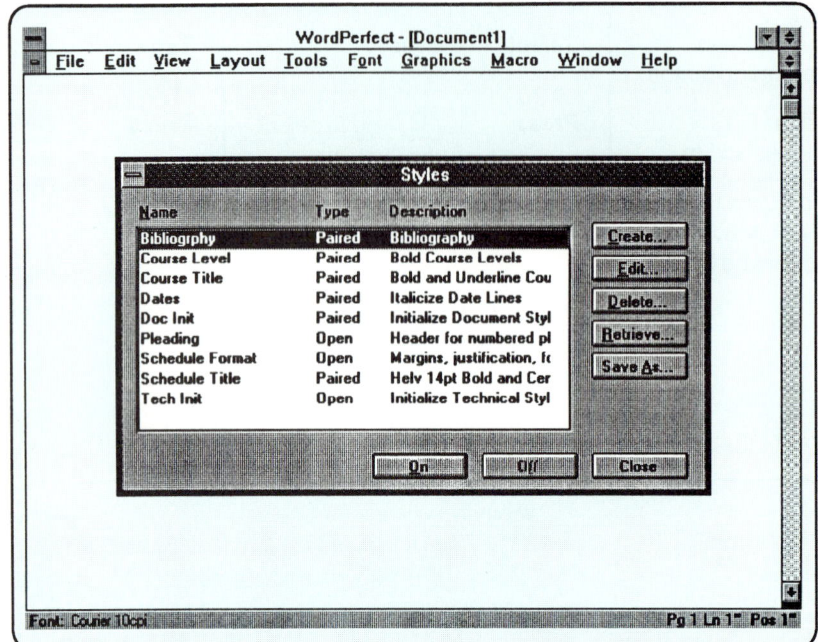

Now you can apply theses styles to your document without having to recreate the styles. Close the Styles dialog box.

■ APPLYING STYLES WITH THE RULER

You can use the Ruler to apply styles in your document. The Styles button on the Ruler allows you to quickly access a list of the styles in your document. Double-clicking on the Styles button produces the Styles dialog box.

To view the Ruler:

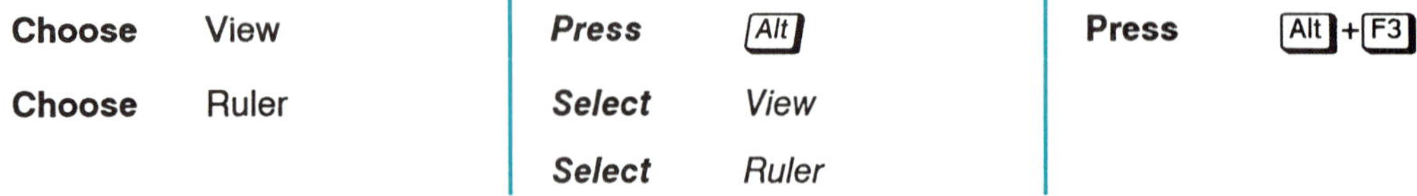

Choose	View	***Press***	Alt	**Press**	Alt+F3
Choose	Ruler	***Select***	*View*		
		Select	*Ruler*		

The top portion of your screen should look like Figure 29-21.

Figure 29-21

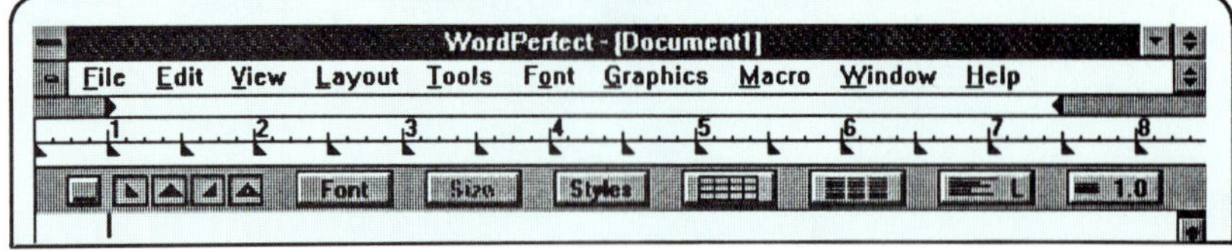

Notice the Styles button on the Ruler. You can use this button to quickly access the styles in your document.

When using paired styles, WordPerfect turns the style on the first time you choose the style from the pop-up list. The second time you select the style from the pop-up list WordPerfect turns the style off.

When you choose an open style from the pop-up list, the style is turned on at the insertion point.

To apply the Schedule Format open style:

Click	the Styles button on the Ruler [Styles]
Select	Schedule Format

Notice the change in the margins of your document. The Ln indicator on the status bar is set at 1.5″ and the Pos indicator is 2″. Since the Schedule Format style is an open style, you do not have to turn it off.

To turn on the Schedule Title style:

Click	the Styles button on the Ruler
Select	Schedule Title

The Font indicator on the status displays the new font.

To enter the text and turn the style off:

Type	WordPerfect for Windows
Click	the Styles button on the Ruler
Select	Schedule Title

The top part of your screen should look like Figure 29-22.

Figure 29-22

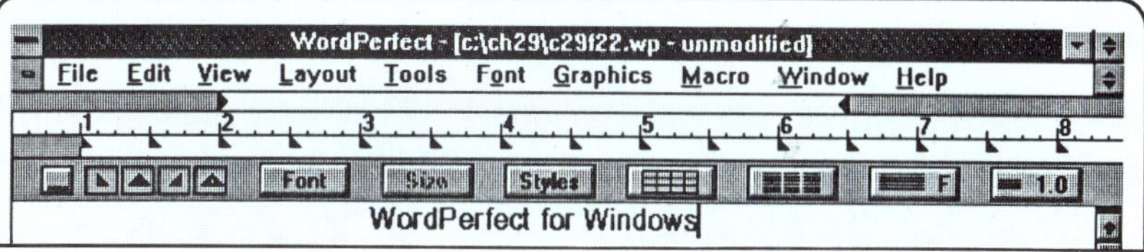

Notice the Font indicator has returned to Helv 12pt (Z1A), the document font in the Schedule Format style.

To continue the document:

Press	[↵Enter] twice
Type	Beginning:

To apply a style when the text appears in the document:

Select	the text "Beginning:"
Click	the Styles button on the Ruler
Choose	Course Level

The top part of your screen should look like Figure 29-23.

Figure 29-23

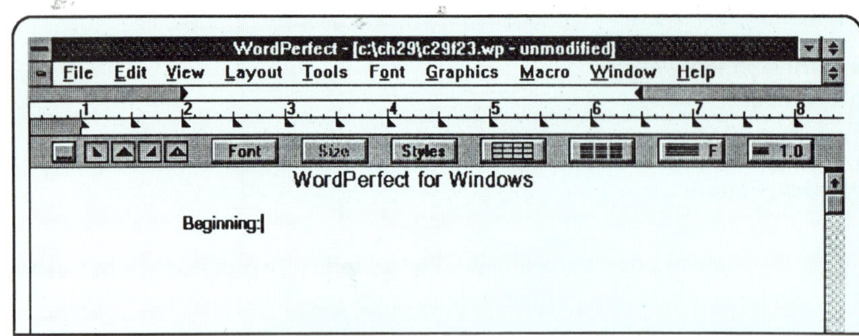

When you select the text before choosing the style, you do not have to turn the style off.

Move the insertion point to the end of the document. Complete the document in Figure 29-24. Apply the styles for Course Level, Course Title, and Dates to each course offering.

Figure 29-24

WordPerfect for Windows

Beginning: **Word Processing Basics.** Create, modify, save, and print documents. Topics include using menus and function keys, opening files, scrolling, deleting, searching and replacing text, enhancing text, using reveal codes, line spacing, tabs, margin settings, pagination, headers and footers, and page format option. The WordPerfect Button Bar and Ruler are also discussed. The select feature and the move and copy features are covered. No prior knowledge of word processing is required.

Dates: April 20 May 18 June 20

Intermediate: **Form Letters, Merge & Macros.** This course covers macros, text columns, the table feature, document merge feature, sorting, creating and editing graphics, and using multiple windows. A preview of advanced topics is also presented.

Dates: April 21 May 19 June 21

Advanced: **Style Sheets & Indexing.** This course is currently being developed. ABC Can Company plans to offer this class in July.

Save the document as "styruler." Close the document.

DELETING A STYLE

There are three options available to you when deleting a style. These options are described below:

Leave Format Codes - The style is deleted from the list, and all style codes referring to this style are removed from the document. However, all format and feature codes contained in the style are placed into the document at the location of each style code.

Delete Format Codes - The style is deleted from the list, and all references to the style are removed from the document. No codes are placed back into the document.

Delete Definition Only - The style is deleted from the list, but the references to the style remain in the document. If you scroll through the document from top to bottom, WordPerfect will recreate every style that is used in the document. Therefore, only those styles that the document uses are put back into the list.

Open the "stysched" document.

To delete the Dates style including the codes:

Choose	Layout	***Press***	*Alt*	**Press**	Alt+F8
Choose	Styles	***Select***	*Layout*	**Press**	Alt+N to select the Name list box
Click	on Dates in the Name list box	***Select***	*Styles*	**Press**	the pointer-movement keys to select Dates
Click	the Delete command button	***Press***	*Alt+N to select the Name list box*	**Press**	Alt+D to select the Delete command button
Click	the Delete Format Codes option button	***Press***	*the pointer-movement keys to select Dates*	**Press**	Alt+D to select the Delete Format Codes option button
Click	the OK command button	***Press***	*Alt+D to select the Delete command button*	**Press**	↵Enter
		Press	*Alt+D to select the Delete Format Codes option button*		
		Press	*↵Enter*		

Your screen should look like Figure 29-25.

Figure 29-25

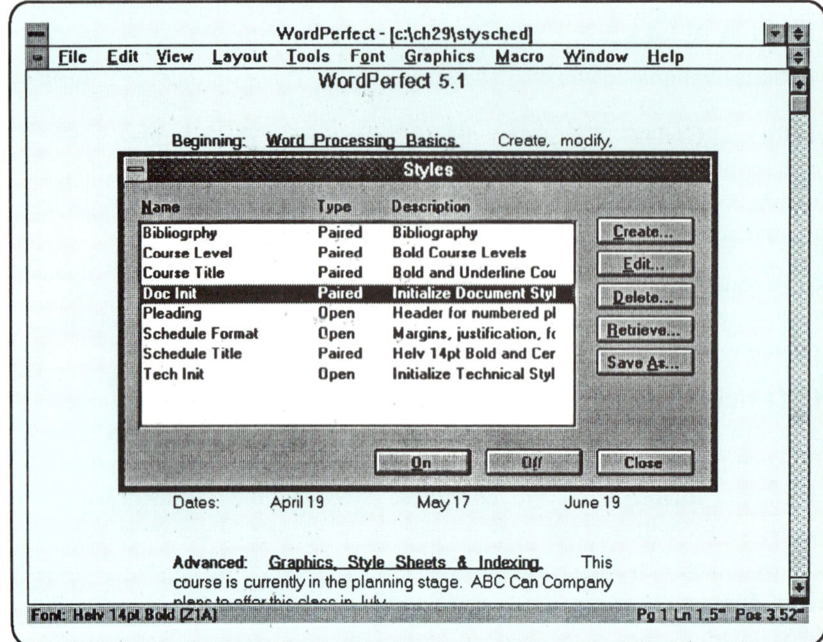

Notice the Dates style has been deleted from the Styles dialog box. To return to your document:

Click	the Close command button	***Press***	Esc	**Press**	Esc

Your screen should look like Figure 29-26.

Figure 29-26

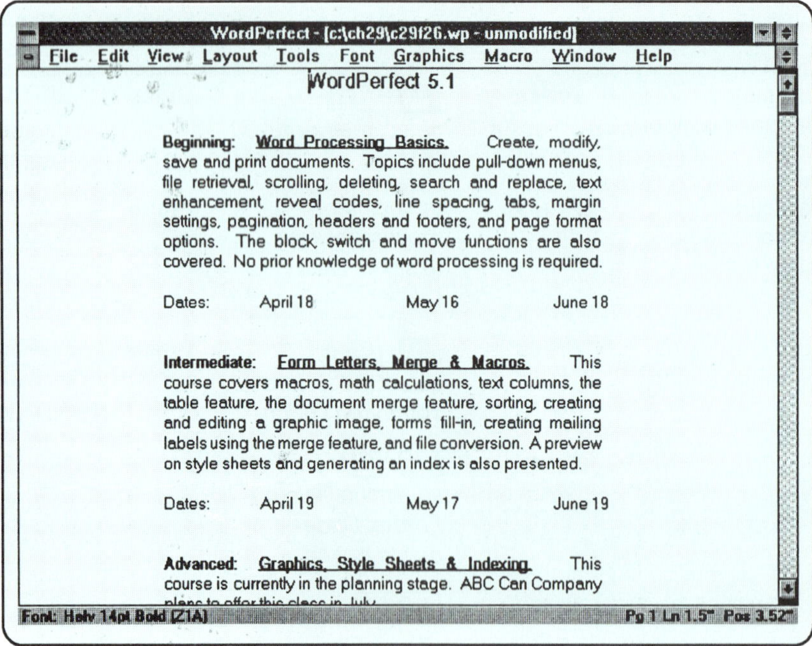

The dates are no longer italicized and the style code is deleted from your document. Close the document without saving changes.

EXERCISE 1

INSTRUCTIONS: Define the following terms:

1. Styles feature ______________________________

   ____

2. Style editor ______________________________

   ____

3. Style name ______________________________

   ____

4. Style type ______________________________

   ____

5. Style description ______________________________

   ____

6. Style codes ______________________________

   ____

7. Paired type ______________________________

   ____

8. Open type ______________________________

   ____

EXERCISE 2

INSTRUCTIONS: Circle T if the statement is true and F if the statement is false.

T F 1. The Styles feature helps you control repeating formats in a document.

T F 2. The Style Editor allows you to associate format codes and text with a style.

T F 3. There are two types of styles that you can create: Paired and Open.

T F 4. The Paired style type turns on the features associated with the style once. The features are used to the end of the document.

T F 5. The Open style type uses On and Off codes to turn on the features defined with the style, and then turns off the style at a later point in the text.

T F 6. You cannot use the Ruler to apply styles.

T F 7. There are three options when deleting a style: Leave Format Codes, Delete Format Codes, and Delete Definition Only.

T F 8. The Leave Format Codes option places all format codes contained in the style at the location of each style code.

T F 9. The Delete Definition Only option deletes the style codes from the document.

T F 10. A style can have text and any number of format codes associated with it.

EXERCISE 3

INSTRUCTIONS:

1. Create the following document.
2. Print the document.
3. Create a style to center and bold the title "CONSULTING SPECIALTIES."
4. Create a style to bold and underline the headings.
5. Use the styles on the document.
6. Print the document.
7. Save the final document in a file using the name "ch29ex03."
8. Save the styles in a file using the name "ch29ex03.sty."

```
CONSULTING SPECIALTIES

Information Systems Consulting

      Information Systems Assessment
      Information Systems Planning

Software and Hardware Selection

      Requirements Analysis
      System Evaluation
      Implementation Assistance

Systems Development

      Database Applications
      Multi-User Applications
      Distributed Processing

Local Area Network Consulting

      Selection
      Installation
      Training
```

EXERCISE 4

INSTRUCTIONS:

1. Create the following styles for a very short letter (body of letter contains less than 75 words).
2. Set the left and right margins to 1.75″.
3. Set justification to left.
4. Turn on hyphenation.
5. If possible, set the initial font to Times Roman 14 point.
6. Save the style in a file using the name "short.sty."
7. Close the document.

EXERCISE 5

INSTRUCTIONS:

1. Create the following styles for a left-bound manuscript.
2. Change the left margin to 1.5″. The right margin remains the same. The body of the document is double spaced. Page numbers are placed at the top right of the page and start on the second page. Suppress the page number on the first page only. Turn on hyphenation. Set justification to left.
3. The title starts at the 2″ line on the page and is centered.
4. Side headings are underlined.
5. Save the styles in a file using the name "leftman.sty."
6. Close the document.

EXERCISE 6

INSTRUCTIONS:

1. Retrieve your styles for a short letter, "short.sty," that you created in Exercise 4.
2. Create the following document using the short letter style.
3. Save the letter in a file using the name "ch29ex06."
4. Print the letter.
5. Close the document.

```
current date


Johnston and Hovell Company
855 N. Lafayette Street
Sioux Falls, SD  57101

Ladies and Gentlemen:

This will acknowledge that we have received your Purchase Order
#23AB421 for 100 gross of "OOO" Springs.

We are currently back ordered on this part and do not expect to
make shipment for six more weeks.  Please advise.

Sincerely,

ROLF SPRING COMPANY




Robert R. Rolf
Vice President



xx
```

EXERCISE 7

INSTRUCTIONS:

1. Retrieve the styles for a left-bound manuscript "leftman.sty" that you created in Exercise 5.
2. Create the document written below and on the next page using the left bound style.
3. Save the document in a file using the name "ch29ex07."
4. Print the document.
5. Close the document.

Preparing For A Speech

The person who does not get excited before giving a speech is a rare individual. Almost everyone is on the verge of panic. This is especially true for first-time speakers, or those students in speech class. Everyone is fearful of the unknown. How does my voice sound? Am I prepared enough? Are my notes easy to read? How sincere am I? Do I believe in what I am saying?

These and other questions will always race through your mind—you may also feel it in your stomach. The result may be near hysteria at the podium. Here are some time-worn suggestions to help ease the panic and make your talk interesting.

Overcoming Fear

Always select a subject with which you are very familiar. If this is not possible, make sure you have adequate time to prepare. Set up a schedule for gathering data. Try to incorporate the information into real-life situations. you can do this by relating it to examples or your own personal experiences.

Make contact with your audience. you need not look people directly in the eyes, but a good trick is to look at their foreheads.

If you are not using a voice amplifier, make certain everyone can hear you. Practice talking in an empty room with a tape recorder in the back. Check it out to see how you sound.

Be yourself. Whenever possible talk from your background. Be honest, be enthusiastic. Try to make your speech enjoyable for yourself and it will be enjoyable for your listeners.

Make your Talk Interesting

A good speech should inform the listeners. Use facts and references to set the framework. Be careful though, not to use too many. Be selective. Use round numbers. Leave out insignificant details and incidents.

Try to confine your speech to only three or four main points. Remember your audience. They do not know your subject as well as you do. Make your last point clear by using anything that will add clarity — charts, graphs, pictures. Always make sure that those in the back of the room can clearly see your visuals.

If possible, try to use humor. This is a powerful tool, if you are up to it. Search your library for books on stories or jokes that relate to the point you are trying to make.

Conclude your talk by summing up the points clearly and concisely. Remember, a good speaker always finishes his speech before the audience finishes listening.

EXERCISE 8

INSTRUCTIONS:

1. Retrieve the short letter styles "short.sty" that you created in Exercise 4.
2. Edit the style to change the left and right margins of the letter to 1.5″.
3. Turn off hyphenation.
4. Enter the document shown below. Save it in a file using the name "ch29ex08."
5. Print the document.
6. Close the document.

```
current date


Taylor and Holmes Electronics
1201 West Moss Avenue
Red Bank White Oak, TN 37415

Dear Sir or Madam:

We find that your account is 60 days overdue.  Is there a problem
with our merchandise?  If not, why have you not responded to our
last three notices?

If we do not hear from you within ten days, we will be forced to
report this matter to the Red Bank White Oak Credit Bureau.

Respectfully yours,


James Arthur Dillon
Accounts Manager

xx
```

EXERCISE 9

INSTRUCTIONS:

1. Open the document "ch29ex07."
2. Edit the style so that the side headings are bold instead of underlined.
3. Change both margins to 1″.
4. Move the page numbers to the bottom center of the page.
5. Print preview the document.
6. Print the document.
7. Save the document in a file using the name "ch29ex09."

8. Save the style changes in the file "leftman.sty."
9. Close the document.

EXERCISE 10

INSTRUCTIONS:

1. Create the following styles for an invoice. A sample invoice is shown below.

```
                    Norma Dijkstra, PC
                    One Riverway Plaza
               1800 Davis Boulevard, Suite 1550
                 New Orleans, LA 82110-0998


                         INVOICE


Company: Name                           current date
         Address

Contact: Name                           Invoice:   #nnnn
                                        Total:     $99,999.99

Paragraph describing invoice activity and the period of
invoice - in italics.

   Class Date   Location                          Amount
    mm/dd/yy    Course location                $nn,nnn.nn
```

2. Create an open style for the invoice heading and addressee section. This style should do the following:
   a. Set the left and right margins to 1.5″. Set the bottom margin to 0.5″.
   b. Set justification to left.
   c. Set the base font to Helvetica 12 point.
   d. Bold and center the following text which is the invoice heading:

      Norma Dijkstra, PC
      One Riverway Plaza
      1800 Davis Boulevard, Suite 1550
      New Orleans, LA 82110-0998

      INVOICE

   e. Set tabs for the invoice addressee section. This is the section that contains the company name, address, date, and invoice number. Use your own discretion for tab spacing.

3. Create a paired style for a paragraph describing the invoice activity and period. This paragraph is in italics.
4. Create another open style for the itemized class section of the invoice located at the bottom. This style should do the following:
   a. Set tabs for the column headings. Use your own discretion for tab spacing. The column headings should be bold and underlined.
   b. Set tabs for the column data. The amount column should have a decimal tab. Use your own discretion for tab placement.
5. Save the style in a file using the name "invoice.sty."
6. Create the following two invoices. Keep the two invoices in one document. Place a page break between each one. Use the "invoice.sty" style to create the invoices. Print the invoices. Save the document in a file using the name "ch29ex10."

```
Company: ABC Training Services
         1100 Sam Houston Parkway
         Suite 1500
         Aberdeen, TX 79220

Contact: Mr. John J. McPherson              Invoice:  #901000
                                            Total:    $9,721.87

For training services rendered during the period of April 1, 1990
to June 30, 1990.  Payment due thirty days after receipt.  The
following classes were taught during the period:

4/3/90     Moynihan Oil Company, Houston          1,200.00

4/11/90    Best Metal Products, Los Angeles       3,521.87

5/5/90     Allied Health Services, New Orleans    2,500.00

6/3/90     Allied Health Services, New Orleans    2,500.00
```

```
Company: Hemlock PC Seminars
         One Peachtree Plaza
         Suite 3400
         Atlanta, GA 79220

Contact: Ms. Janice K. Hemlock              Invoice:  #901205
                                            Total:    $22,533.44

For training services rendered during the period of May, 1990.
Payment due fifteen days after receipt.  The following classes were
taught during the period:

5/3/90     Caladium Airlines, New York City       6,000.00

5/10/90    Caladium Airlines, Los Angeles         6,500.55

5/12/90    Percy Shelley Insurance, Miami         3,600.00

5/16/90    Caladium Airlines, Houston             1,110.44

5/23/90    Monstrosity Shoes, New York City       5,322.45
```

CHAPTER THIRTY

OUTLINES

OBJECTIVES

In this chapter, you will learn to:

- Create an outline
- Edit an outline

CHAPTER OVERVIEW

An outline is a way of organizing the ideas and information that you want to present in a long document or report. The Outline feature allows you to create several types of outlines. The procedures for creating and editing an outline are described and shown in this chapter.

CREATING AN OUTLINE

An outline is made up of paragraph numbers. In WordPerfect you can have up to eight levels of numbers within a document. An example of an outline is shown in Figure 30-1.

The levels in this outline are displayed through numbers and letters. You may use keyboard characters, WordPerfect characters, or styles within a level.

Figure 30-1

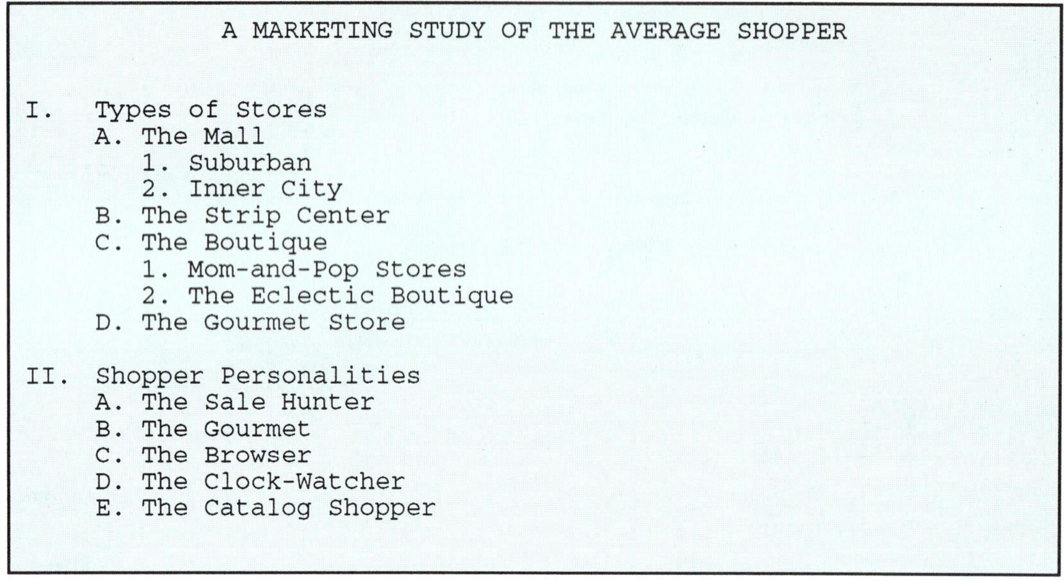

A MARKETING STUDY OF THE AVERAGE SHOPPER

I. Types of Stores
  A. The Mall
    1. Suburban
    2. Inner City
  B. The Strip Center
  C. The Boutique
    1. Mom-and-Pop Stores
    2. The Eclectic Boutique
  D. The Gourmet Store

II. Shopper Personalities
  A. The Sale Hunter
  B. The Gourmet
  C. The Browser
  D. The Clock-Watcher
  E. The Catalog Shopper

Change the default directory to "a:\wpdocs"or to "c:\wpdocs."

To start using the Outline feature:

Choose	Tools	***Press***	Alt
Choose	Outline	***Select***	*Tools*
Choose	Outline On	***Select***	*Outline*
		Select	*Outline On*

Your screen should look like Figure 30-2.

Figure 30-2

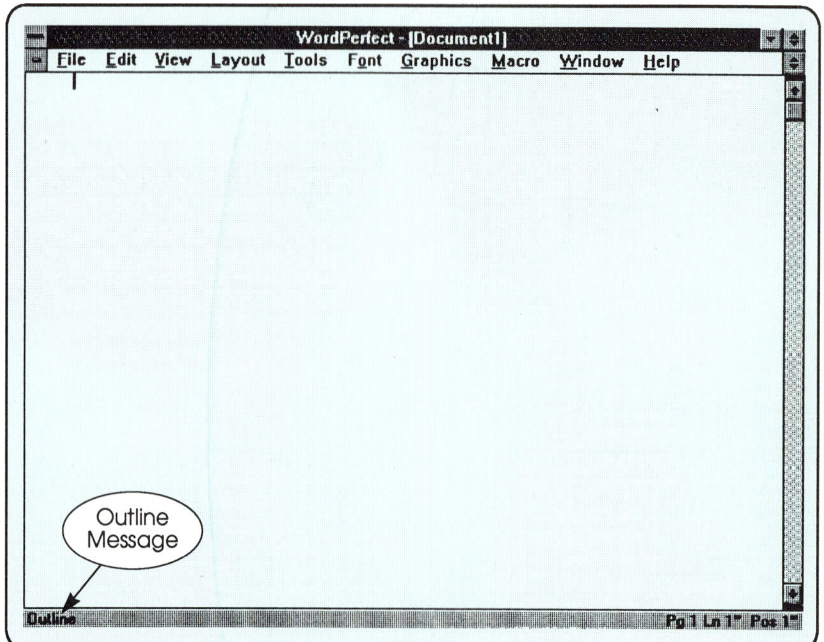

Notice that "Outline" is displayed on the status bar to let you know that the Outline feature is on.

Now that the Outline feature is active, WordPerfect is ready to help you create an outline by inserting the numbers and letting you type the headings. Press [↵Enter] to insert a first-level paragraph number. Press [Tab] as many times as needed to change the current level to the next level paragraph. Press [Shift]+[Tab] to reverse the direction.

To insert a first level paragraph number:

The top part of your screen should look like Figure 30-3.

Figure 30-3

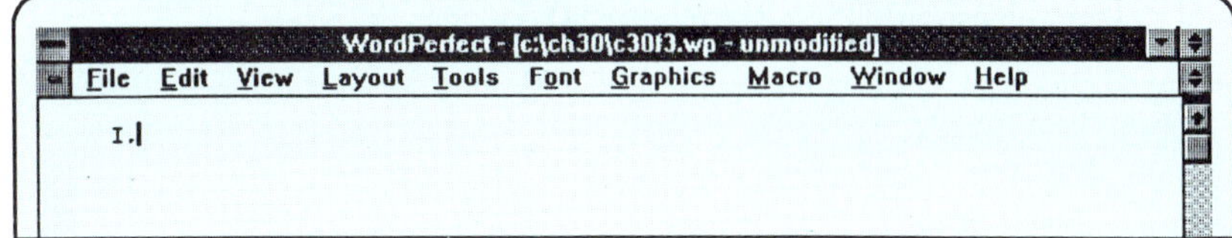

An Automatic Paragraph Number code [Par Num:Auto] has been added to the outline and is displayed as a Roman numeral "I." on your screen.

The Indent feature is used to set the text off from the numeral. Also, if the text on a level should word wrap, the indent aligns the text properly on the next line. This situation is most likely to occur on the higher level numbers.

To enter the text for the first outline level:

Choose	Layout	***Press***	*Alt*	**Press**	F7
Choose	Paragraph	***Select***	*Layout*	**Type**	INTRODUC-TION
Choose	Indent	***Select***	*Paragraph*		
Type	INTRODUC-TION	***Select***	*Indent*		
		Type	*INTRODUC-TION*		

The top part of your screen should look like Figure 30-4.

Figure 30-4

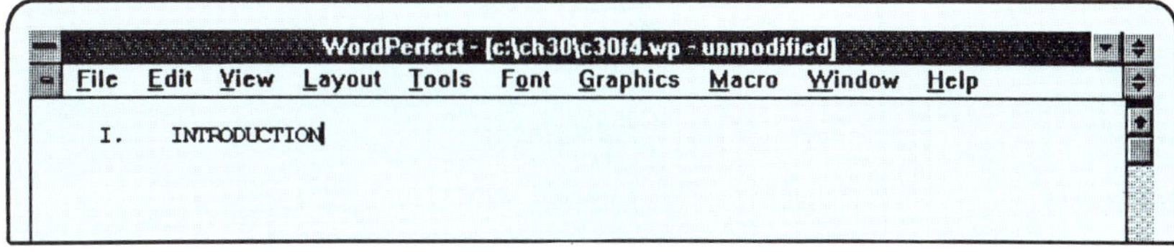

To enter another first-level paragraph number and insert a blank line:

Press	↵Enter twice	***Press***	*↵Enter twice*	**Press**	↵Enter twice
Choose	Layout	***Press***	*Alt*	**Press**	F7
Choose	Paragraph	***Select***	*Layout*	**Type**	HARDWARE
Choose	Indent	***Select***	*Paragraph*		
Type	HARDWARE	***Select***	*Indent*		
		Type	*HARDWARE*		

The top section of your screen should look like Figure 30-5.

Figure 30-5

To insert a second-level paragraph number:

Press	↵Enter	***Press***	*↵Enter*	**Press**	↵Enter
Press	Tab	***Press***	*Tab*	**Press**	Tab

The top part of your screen should look like Figure 30-6.

Figure 30-6

Pressing the Tab key moves the number to the next tab stop and updates the number to the next level. If you want to move the number back a level, press Shift+Tab.

To enter the text for the second outline level:

Choose	Layout	***Press***	*Alt*	**Press**	F7
Choose	Paragraph	***Select***	*Layout*	**Type**	Keyboard
Choose	Indent	***Select***	*Paragraph*		
Type	Keyboard	***Select***	*Indent*		
		Type	*Keyboard*		

The upper part of your screen should look like Figure 30-7.

Figure 30-7

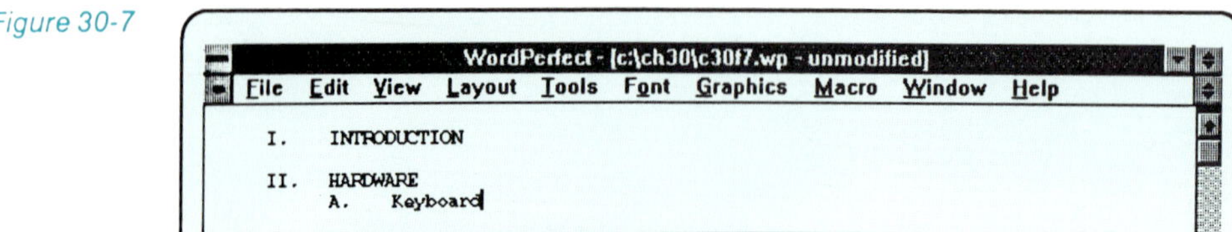

Press [↵Enter] to add a paragraph at the same level. Use the [Tab] key and the [Shift]+[Tab] keys to change the level numbers.

> **For the Remaining Portion of This Chapter**
>
> In the steps for creating an outline, you will be asked to use the Indent feature, but no steps will be provided. To indent using the menus, choose Indent from the Paragraph option under the Layout menu. To indent using the function keys, press the [F7] key.

To insert another second-level paragraph number:

Press	[↵Enter]	***Press***	*[↵Enter]*	**Press**	[↵Enter]
Choose	Indent	***Select***	*Indent*	**Select**	Indent
Type	Monitor	***Type***	*Monitor*	**Type**	Monitor

To insert a third-level paragraph number:

Press	[↵Enter]	***Press***	*[↵Enter]*	**Press**	[↵Enter]
Press	[Tab]	***Press***	*[Tab]*	**Press**	[Tab]
Choose	Indent	***Select***	*Indent*	**Select**	Indent
Type	Monochrome	***Type***	*Monochrome*	**Type**	Monochrome

To insert a fourth-level paragraph number:

Press	[↵Enter]	***Press***	*[↵Enter]*	**Press**	[↵Enter]
Press	[Tab]	***Press***	*[Tab]*	**Press**	[Tab]
Choose	Indent	***Choose***	*Indent*	**Choose**	Indent
Type	No Graphics Capability	***Type***	*No Graphics Capability*	**Type**	No Graphics Capability
Press	[↵Enter]	***Press***	*[↵Enter]*	**Press**	[↵Enter]
Choose	Indent	***Choose***	*Indent*	**Choose**	Indent
Type	MGA	***Type***	*MGA*	**Type**	MGA
Press	[↵Enter]	***Press***	*[↵Enter]*	**Press**	[↵Enter]
Choose	Indent	***Choose***	*Indent*	**Choose**	Indent
Type	MVGA	***Type***	*MVGA*	**Type**	MVGA
Press	[↵Enter]	***Press***	*[↵Enter]*	**Press**	[↵Enter]

To return to the third-level:

Press	[Shift]+[Tab]	***Press***	*[Shift]+[Tab]*	**Press**	[Shift]+[Tab]

Use Tab, Shift+Tab, and the Indent feature to complete the remaining items in the outline shown in Figure 30-8. Remember that Tab advances one paragraph level (moves to the right) and that Shift+Tab reduces one paragraph level (moves to the left).

Figure 30-8

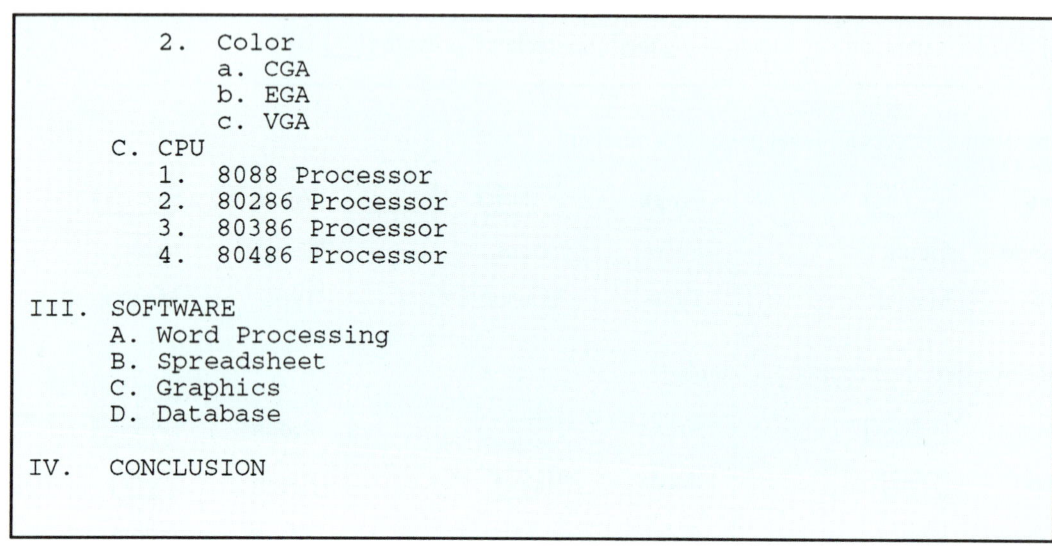

```
            2.  Color
                a. CGA
                b. EGA
                c. VGA
        C. CPU
            1.  8088 Processor
            2.  80286 Processor
            3.  80386 Processor
            4.  80486 Processor

III.    SOFTWARE
        A. Word Processing
        B. Spreadsheet
        C. Graphics
        D. Database

IV.     CONCLUSION
```

To turn off the Outline feature:

Choose	Tools	***Press***	*Alt*
Choose	Outline	***Select***	*Tools*
Choose	Outline Off	***Select***	*Outline*
		Select	*Outline Off*

Suppose you want to add the title "COMPUTER BOOK" to the outline.

Click	at the beginning of the document. Be sure the insertion point is before the [Outline On] code	***Move***	*the insertion point to the beginning of the document. Be sure the insertion point is before the [Outline On] code*	**Move**	the insertion point to the beginning of the document. Be sure the insertion point is before the [Outline On] code
Press	↵Enter twice	***Press***	*↵Enter twice*	**Press**	↵Enter twice
Click	at the beginning of the document	***Move***	*to the beginning of the document*	**Move**	to the beginning of the document
Choose	Layout	***Press***	*Alt*	**Press**	Shift+F7
Choose	Line	***Select***	*Layout*	**Type**	COMPUTER BOOK

Choose	Center	***Select***	*Line*		
Type	COMPUTER BOOK	***Select***	*Center*		
		Type	*COMPUTER BOOK*		

Save the document in file "bookout."

Your screen should look like Figure 30-9.

Figure 30-9

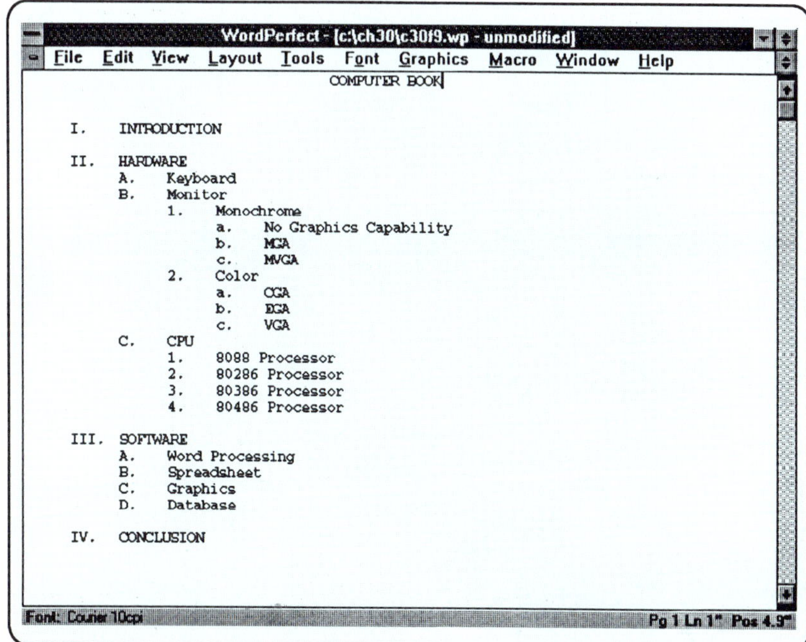

■ EDITING AN OUTLINE

WordPerfect defines a "family" in an outline as the paragraph number on the current line plus the paragraph numbers under that line. Any text included on these levels is also considered a part of the family.

There are Move, Copy, and Delete Family options available in WordPerfect. These options make it very easy for you to move, copy, or delete complete outline families. With these "group" options, you can edit your outline. Whenever you edit an outline, the paragraph numbers are automatically updated to reflect any changes you make.

Suppose you want to add more items in the Software family.

Click	at the end of the line "D. Database"	***Move***	*the insertion point to the end of the line "D. Database"*	**Move**	the insertion point to the end of the line "D. Database"
Press	↵Enter	***Press***	*↵Enter*	**Press**	↵Enter
Choose	Indent	***Select***	*Indent*	**Select**	Indent
Type	Desktop Publishing	***Type***	*Desktop Publishing*	**Type**	Desktop Publishing

Suppose you want to add an item under "VGA" in the Color Monitor family.

Click	at the end of the line "c. VGA"	***Click***	*at the end of the line "c. VGA"*	**Click**	at the end of the line "c. VGA"
Press	↵Enter	***Press***	↵Enter	**Press**	↵Enter
Press	Tab	***Press***	Tab	**Press**	Tab
Choose	Indent	***Choose***	*Indent*	**Choose**	Indent
Type	Regular	***Type***	*Regular*	**Type**	Regular
Press	↵Enter	***Press***	↵Enter	**Press**	↵Enter
Choose	Indent	***Choose***	*Indent*	**Choose**	Indent
Type	Super-VGA	***Type***	*Super-VGA*	**Type**	Super-VGA

Your screen should look like Figure 30-10.

Figure 30-10

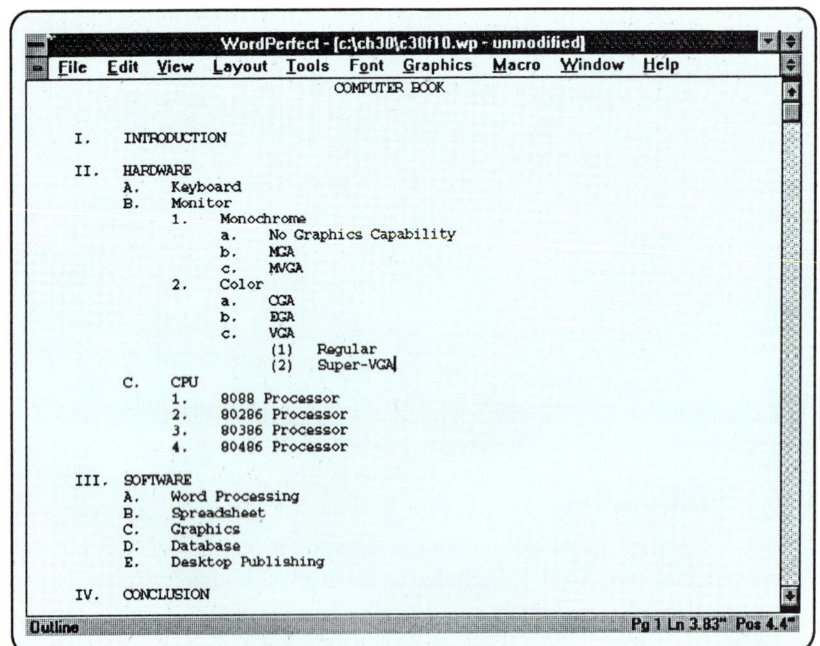

Suppose you want to copy the family associated with "SOFTWARE."

To copy the family:

Click	before the heading "III. SOFTWARE"	***Move***	*the insertion point before the heading "III. SOFTWARE"*
Choose	Tools	***Press***	Alt
Choose	Outline	***Select***	*Tools*
Choose	Copy Family	***Select***	*Outline*
		Select	*Copy Family*

Your screen should look similar to Figure 30-11.

Figure 30-11

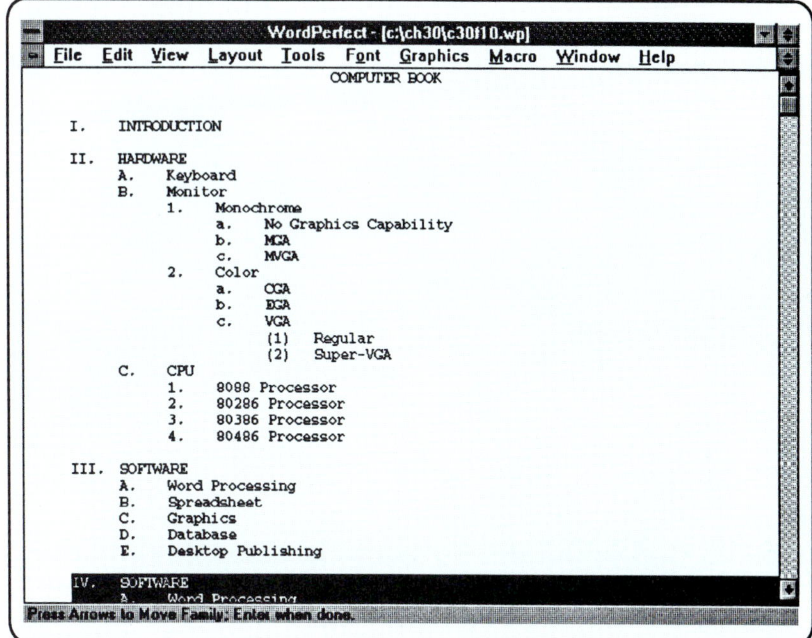

A copy of the family is highlighted and displayed below the original family.

To move a copy of the Software family above the Hardware family:

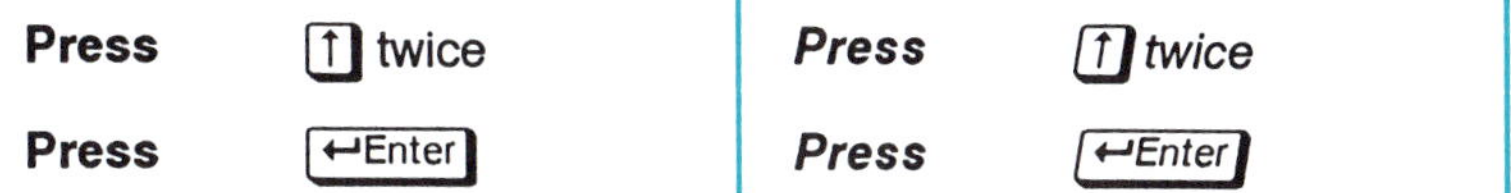

You cannot use the mouse to move a copy of the outline family. If you move the mouse into the document area, the no symbol (⃠) appears. You must use the pointer-movement keys.

Your screen should look like Figure 30-12.

Figure 30-12

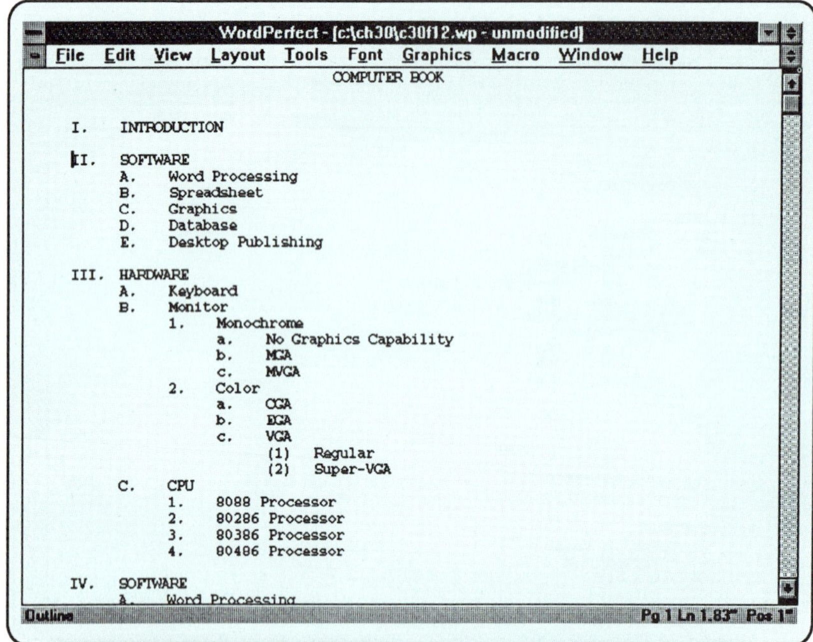

Notice the paragraph numbers are automatically updated to reflect the change.

The original Software family is still in the outline. To delete the original Software family:

Click	before the heading "IV. SOFTWARE"	***Move***	*the insertion point before the heading "IV. SOFTWARE"*
Choose	Tools	***Press***	*Alt*
Choose	Outline	***Select***	*Tools*
Choose	Delete Family	***Select***	*Outline*
Click	the Yes command button	***Select***	*Delete Family*
		Press	*Alt+Y to select the Yes command button*

Your screen should look like Figure 30-13.

Figure 30-13

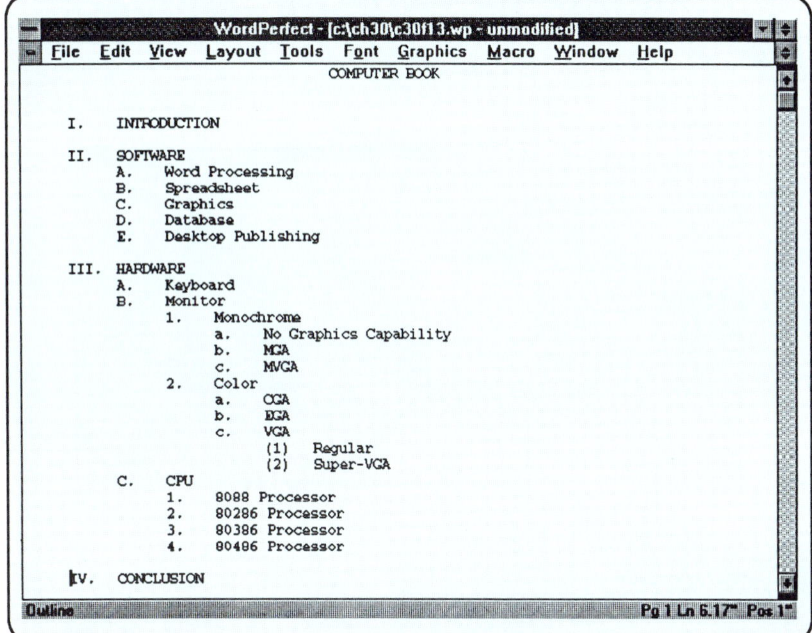

After you edit an outline, family paragraph numbers automatically update.

You may not want to use the automatic paragraph numbering scheme provided by WordPerfect. The Outline Define option lets you change the numbers and other outline features according to your specification.

To display the Define Paragraph Numbering dialog box:

Click	at the beginning of the document	***Move***	*the insertion point to the beginning of the document*	**Move**	the insertion point to the beginning of the document
Choose	Tools	***Press***	*Alt*	**Press**	Alt+Shift+F5
Choose	Outline	***Select***	*Tools*		
Choose	Define	***Select***	*Outline*		
		Select	*Define*		

The Define Paragraph Numbering dialog box appears. Your screen should look like Figure 30-14.

Figure 30-14

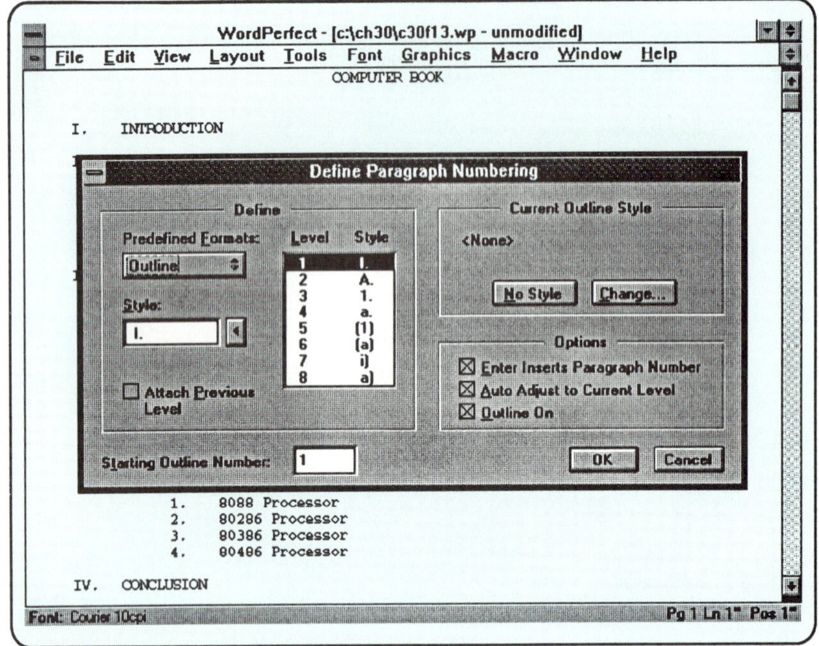

The current outline definition is displayed in the Define box. You can see each of the eight outline levels and that level's corresponding style. You can use the Predefined Formats button to change the outline format. The current outline format is outline. The other predefined formats include paragraph, legal, and bullets. You can also create your own outline format called user.

To change the current definition to Legal:

Click	the Predefined Formats pop-up list button	***Press***	*Alt+F to select the Predefined Formats pop-up list button*	**Press**	Alt+F to select the Predefined Formats pop-up list button
Hold down	the mouse button to view the pop-up list	***Press***	*Alt+↑ to view the pop-up list*	**Press**	Alt+↑ to view the pop-up list
Select	Legal	***Type***	*L to select Legal*	**Type**	L to select Legal

Your screen should look like Figure 30-15.

Figure 30-15

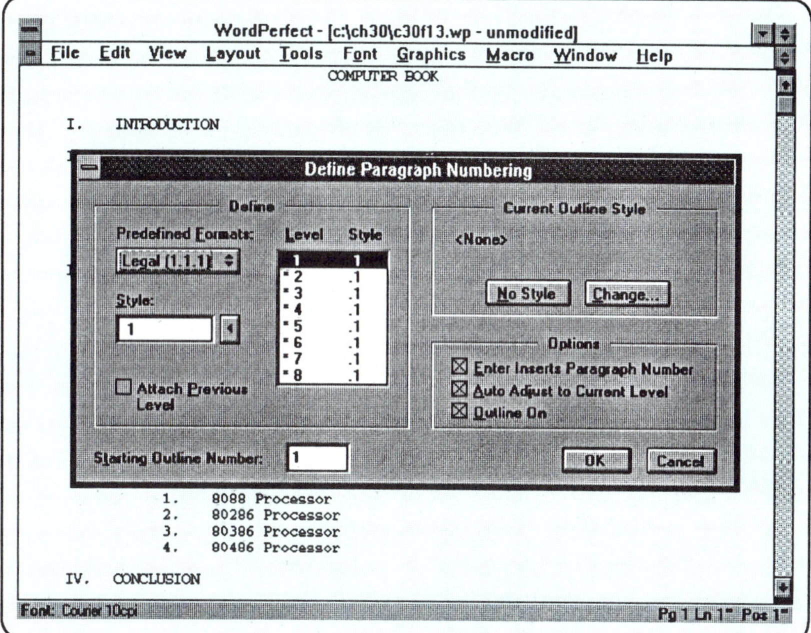

Notice that the current definition changed to reflect the legal definition.

To return to your document:

Click	the OK command button	***Press***	*↵Enter*	**Press**	↵Enter

Your screen should look like Figure 30-16.

Figure 30-16

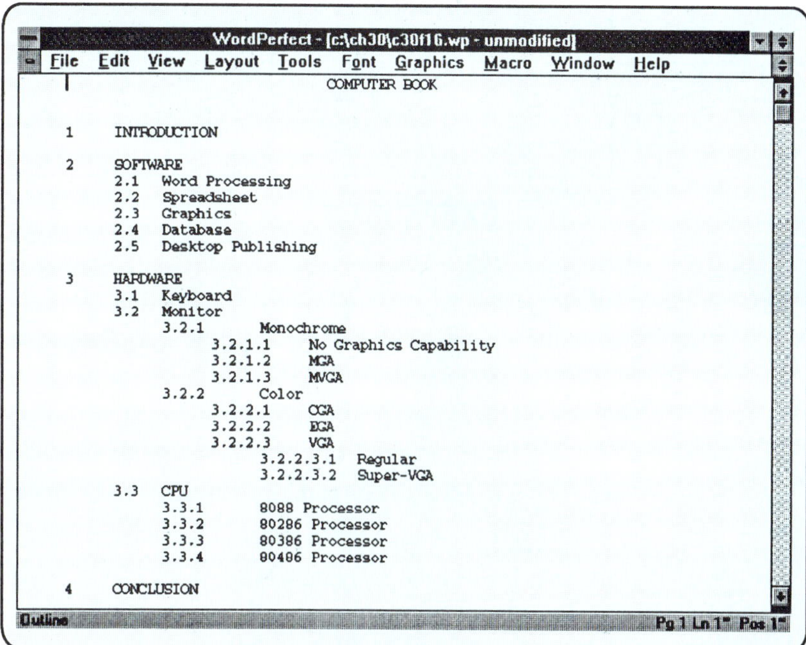

The other outline formats are described in the "Outline, Define" section of the WordPerfect Reference Manual.

Save the document as "bookout2" and close the document.

EXERCISE 1

INSTRUCTIONS: Define the following terms:

1. Outline ______________________________

2. Family ______________________________

3. Move family ______________________________

4. Copy family ______________________________

5. Delete family ______________________________

6. Define paragraph number definition dialog box ______________________________

EXERCISE 2

INSTRUCTIONS: Circle T if the statement is true and F if the statement is false.

T F 1. An outline is a way of organizing the ideas and information that you want to present in a long document or report.

T F 2. Outlines are made up of paragraph numbers.

T F 3. You can have up to nine levels of paragraph numbers within a document.

T F 4. Press Tab to advance one paragraph level.

T F 5. Press Enter to advance one number in the same paragraph level.

T F 6. If you want to move the paragraph number back a level, press Shift+Tab.

T F 7. An outline "family" is the paragraph number on the current line plus the paragraph numbers under that line or level.

T F 8. There are Move, Copy, Delete, and Add Family options available in WordPerfect.

T F 9. In the Define Paragraph Numbering dialog box, you can choose between the Paragraph, Outline, Legal, Letter, and Bullets numbering styles or you can make your own style.

EXERCISE 3

INSTRUCTIONS: 1. Create the following outline.

```
              A MARKETING STUDY OF CONSUMER SHOPPING

I.     Introduction

II.    Types of Stores
       A.     The Mall
              1.     Suburban
              2.     Inner City
       B.     The Strip Center
       C.     The Boutique
              1.     Mom-and-Pop Stores
              2.     The Eclectic Boutique
       D.     The Gourmet Store

III.   Shopper Personalities
       A.     The Sale Hunter
       B.     The Gourmet
       C.     The Browser
       D.     The Catalog Shopper

IV.    Conclusion
```

2. Save the document in a file using the name "ch30ex03.ot1."
3. Print the document.
4. Add the following information after Section III.

```
IV.    Shopping Seasons
       A.     Valentine's Day
       B.     Easter
       C.     Mother's Day
       D.     Father's Day
       E.     Fall
       F.     Christmas
```

5. Print the document.
6. Change the paragraph number definition to Paragraph.
7. Print the document.
8. Change the paragraph number definition to Bullets.
9. Print the document.
10. Move the "Shopper Personalities" family immediately after the "Introduction" family.
11. Print the document.
12. Save the document in a file using the name "ch30ex03.ot2."
13. Close the document.

EXERCISE 4

INSTRUCTIONS:

1. Create the following outline using the Outline feature.
2. Preview the document.
3. Print the document.
4. Save the document in a file using the name "ch30ex04."
5. Close the document.

```
               SELECTED TOPICS OUTLINE FOR WORD PROCESSING


I.      TYPING LETTERS
        A.      Personal Letters
        B.      Business Letters
                1.      Modified block style
                2.      Block style

II.     TYPING BUSINESS CORRESPONDENCE
        A.      Memorandums
        B.      Letters on Executive-size Paper
        C.      Reports
        D.      Tables

III.    STATISTICAL COMMUNICATIONS
        A.      Business Forms
        B.      Statistical Reports
        C.      Administrative Forms
```

EXERCISE 5

INSTRUCTIONS:

1. Create the following outline using the Outline feature.
2. Preview the document.
3. Print the document.
4. Save the document in a file using the name "ch30ex05."
5. Close the document.

```
                    OUTLINE STRUCTURE

I.    PRIMARY HEADINGS IN ALL CAPITAL LETTERS
      A.    Identify Major Divisions of an Outline
            1.    Primary headings by Roman Numerals
            2.    Secondary headings by capital letters
                  a.   Subdivisions by
                  b.   Arabic numerals or
                  c.   Small letters or
                  d.   Parentheses surrounding Arabic numerals or
                  e.   Parentheses surrounding small letters or
                  f.   Right parentheses next to Arabic numerals or
                  g.   Right parentheses next to small letters
      B.    Spacing the Outline
            1.    Double-space before the main headings
            2.    Single-space between subdivisions

II.   THE SENTENCE STRUCTURE
      A.    Identify Divisions as Topics
      B.    Punctuating and Spacing the Outline
            1.    Punctuate complete sentences as in normal writing
            2.    Use regular sentence spacing
```

EXERCISE 6

INSTRUCTIONS:

1. Create the following outline using the Outline feature.
2. Preview the document.
3. Print the document.
4. Save the document in a file using the name "ch30ex06."
5. Close the document.

LEFT-BOUND MANUSCRIPTS

I. MARGINS AND SPACING
  A. Margins
    1. Left margin 1½"
    2. Top, bottom, and right margins 1"
    3. Top, first page: 12 pitch 2"; 10 pitch 1½"
    4. Additional page: 1"
  B. Spacing
    1. General style: double spacing, 5-space paragraph indentions
    2. Business style: single spacing with blocked paragraphs
    3. Always leave 2 lines of a paragraph at the top and bottom of each page
    4. Quoted material: Single-space quotes of four or more lines; indent from left margins all lines of quote

II. PAGE NUMBERING
  A. First Page: Optional, but if used, Centered at bottom of the Page
  B. Other Pages: Typed even at the right top margin

EXERCISE 7

INSTRUCTIONS:

1. Open the document "ch30ex06."
2. Under Division I, move the "Spacing" family before the "Margins" family.
3. Change the text under Division I to "SPACING AND MARGINS."
4. Change the numbering style to Bullets.
5. Preview the document.
6. Print the document.
7. Save the document in a file using the name "ch30ex07."
8. Close the document.

EXERCISE 8

INSTRUCTIONS:

1. Create the following outline using the Outline feature.
2. Preview the document.
3. Print the document.
4. Save the document in a file using the name "ch30ex08."
5. Close the document

```
                              AUSTRALIA

I.     PEOPLE
       A.     Age distribution
              1.     Age 0-14 approx. 22%
              2.     Age 15-59 approx. 62%
              3.     Age 59+ approx. 15%
       B.     Ethnic groups
              1.     Europeans 93%
              2.     Asians 5%
              3.     Aborigines 1.5%
       C.     Languages
              1.     English
              2.     Aboriginal
       D.     Religions
              1.     Anglican 26%
              2.     Protestant 25%
              3.     Roman Catholic 25%

II.    GEOGRAPHY
       A.     Area
              1.     2,966,200 sq. mi.
              2.     Almost as large as continental U.S.
       B.     Location:  SE of Asia
       C.     Neighbors
              1.     North
                     a.     Indonesia
                     b.     Papua New Guinea
              2.     East
                     a.     Solomons
                     b.     Fiji
                     c.     New Zealand

III.   GOVERNMENT TYPE
       A.     Democratic Federal State System
              1.     Head of State:  Queen Elizabeth
              2.     Head of Government:  Prim Min. Robert Lee Hawke
              3.     Local Division
                     a.     6 states
                     b.     2 territories
```

EXERCISE 9

INSTRUCTIONS:

1. Open the document "ch30ex08."
2. Copy the entire document to a new document. Make the following changes to Document2.
3. Delete family C under Division II.
4. Add the following family under Division III, subdivision 3a:
   (1) New South Wales
   (2) Victoria
   (3) Queensland
   (4) South Australia
   (5) Western Australia
   (6) Tasmania
5. Add the following family under Division III, subdivision 3b:
   (1) Australian Capital Territory
   (2) Northern Territory
6. Preview the document.
7. Print the document.
8. Save the document in a file using the name "ch30ex09." Close the document.
9. Close the "ch30ex08" document without saving any changes.

EXERCISE 10

INSTRUCTIONS:

1. Open the document "ch30ex09."
2. Move the Geography family before the People family.
3. Delete the Religions family.
4. Change the numbering style to "Paragraph."
5. Preview the document.
6. Print the document.
7. Save the document in a file using the name "ch30ex10."
8. Close the document.

CHAPTER THIRTY-ONE

FOOTNOTES AND ENDNOTES

OBJECTIVES

In this chapter, you will learn to:

- Create footnotes
- Create endnotes

■ CHAPTER OVERVIEW

Footnotes and endnotes are a method of documenting sources of quotations, facts, and ideas in a report. A footnote appears at the bottom of the page that contains its reference. Endnotes appear at the end of the document.

In this chapter, the procedures for creating and editing footnotes and endnotes are described and shown.

■ FOOTNOTES

The Footnote feature is used by choosing the Footnote option from the Layout menu. As you create, edit, add, or delete a footnote, WordPerfect manages the numbering of the footnote and the format of the page so the footnote will fit.

Change the default directory to "a:\wpdocs" or to "c:\wpdocs." Create the document shown in Figure 31-1.

Figure 31-1

```
                         CHAPTERS ADD ASSISTANTS

Southwest Chapter

   Susan Jones began duties as executive secretary of the Southwest
Chapter on June 1.  She has over 14 years experience in bookkeeping
and secretarial services.  For the past five years, Jones has
conducted a home bookkeeping service.
   In her eight-month tenure with the chapter, Jones has
concentrated her efforts in the area of CPE and dues billings.  She
says she is working on transferring the chapter records to a
computer.

Southeast Chapter

   Doris Brown became the Southeast Texas executive secretary on
November 10.  Owner of Brown Business Services, a marketing-
management company, Brown brings to the chapter position a wide
range of business and community experience.
   Brown also has been associated for more than 15 years with the
Greater Orange Area Chamber of Commerce.  She has served on the
Chamber Board of Directors Committee, the Executive Committee, the
Civic Affairs Division, and the Convention Visitors Bureau.
```

Format the document in the following manner:

Set	the left and right margins to 2"	***Set***	*the left and right margins to 2"*	**Set**	the left and right margins to 2"
Set	the line spacing to double	***Set***	*the line spacing to double*	**Set**	the line spacing to double

Save the document as "endfoot1.doc."

To create a footnote:

Click	after the word "Jones" on the first line of the first paragraph	***Move***	*the insertion point after the word "Jones" on the first line of the first paragraph*
Choose	Layout	***Press***	*Alt*
Choose	Footnote	***Select***	*Layout*
Choose	Create	***Select***	*Footnote*
		Select	*Create*

The top part of your screen should look like Figure 31-2.

Figure 31-2

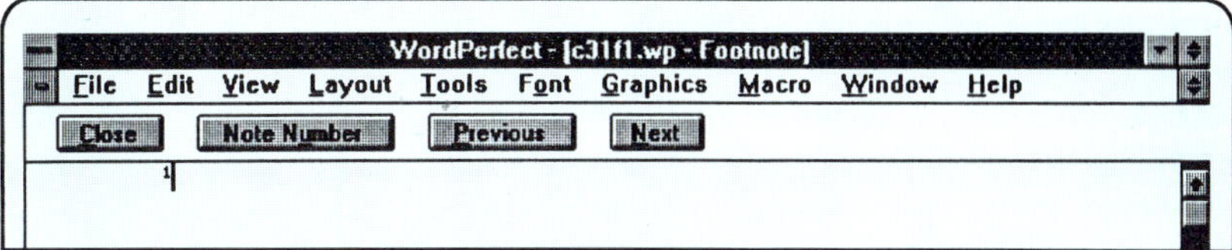

You are placed in the Footnote screen. The word "Footnote" appears on the title bar.

A footnote number is already provided for you. All you need to do is type the text of the footnote.

Type	Southwest Chapter, Main Office, (806) 498-5833	***Type***	*Southwest Chapter, Main Office, (806) 498-5833*
Click	the Close command button	***Press***	*Alt+C to select the Close command button*

The top part of your screen should look like Figure 31-3.

Figure 31-3

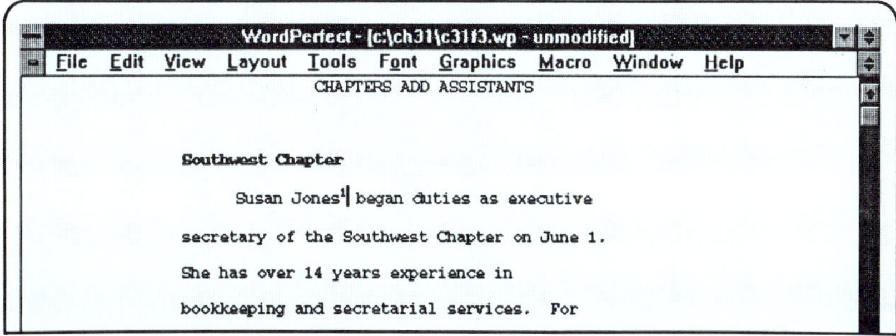

The Footnote code is represented by a number 1 on the screen.

Turn on the Reveal Codes feature.

The bottom part of your screen should look like Figure 31-4.

Figure 31-4

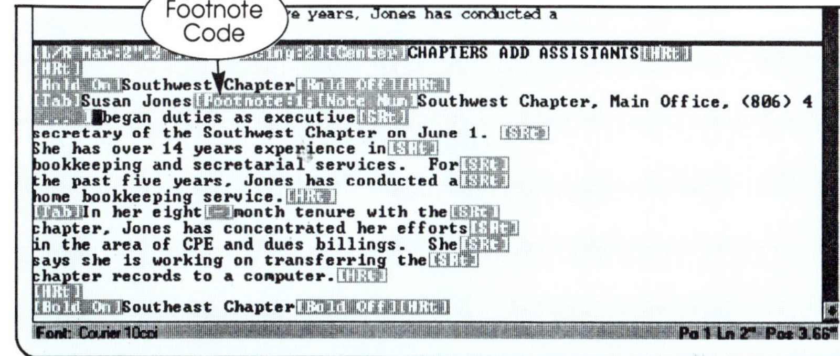

A Footnote code is placed in the document. The first part of the footnote text is shown. This makes finding a particular footnote easier for you.

Turn off the Reveal Codes feature.

To create another footnote:

Click	after the word "Brown" on the first line of the third paragraph	***Move***	*the insertion point after the word "Brown" on the first line of the third paragraph*
Choose	Layout	***Press***	*[Alt]*
Choose	Footnote	***Select***	*Layout*
Choose	Create	***Select***	*Footnote*
Type	Southeast Chapter, Main Office, (409) 898-1569	***Select***	*Create*
Click	the Close command button	***Type***	*Southeast Chapter, Main Office, (409) 898-1569*
		Press	*[Alt]+[C] to select the Close command button*

The lower part of your screen should look like Figure 31-5.

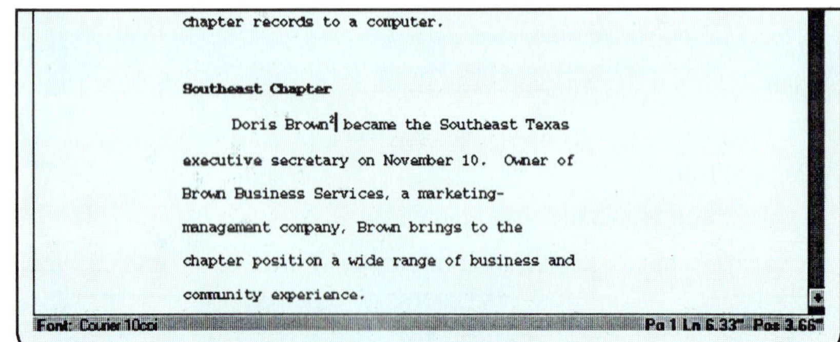

Figure 31-5

The Footnote code is represented by a number 2 on the screen.

Preview the document. Your screen should look like Figure 31-6.

Figure 31-6

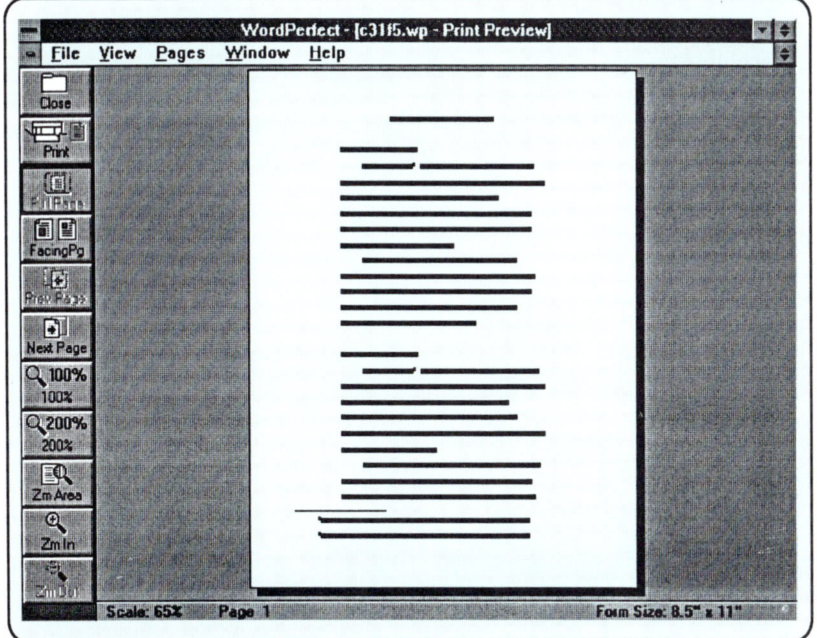

Notice that the footnotes appear at the bottom of the page. Text that did not fit on the first page has been moved to the second page to make room for the footnotes.

Return to your document.

You may need to edit the contents of an existing footnote. Suppose you need to modify the second footnote.

To edit the second footnote:

Choose	Layout	***Press***	Alt
Choose	Footnote	***Select***	*Layout*
Choose	Edit	***Select***	*Footnote*
		Select	*Edit*

The Edit Footnote dialog box appears. Your screen should look like Figure 31-7.

Figure 31-7

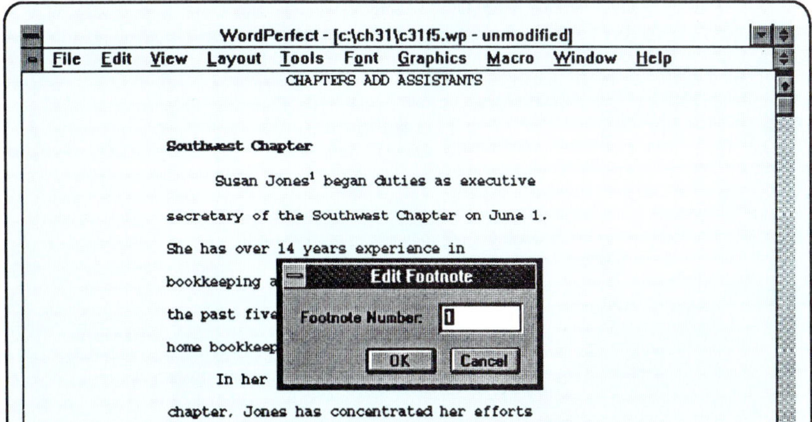

Your insertion point does not have to be located on the second footnote in order to modify it. You open each footnote by its number.

To edit footnote 2:

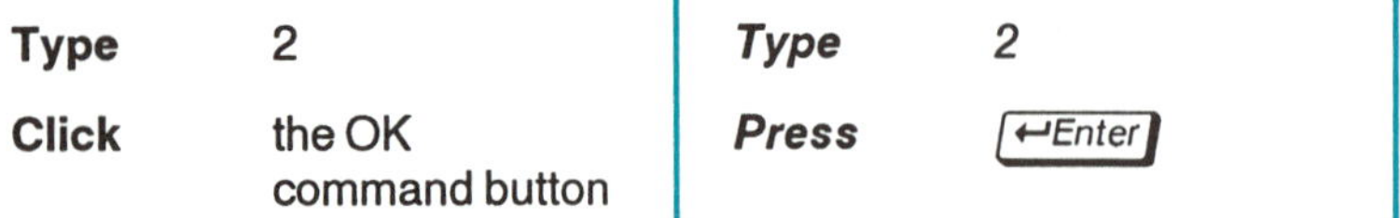

Type	2	***Type***	*2*
Click	the OK command button	***Press***	*↵Enter*

The top part of your screen should look like Figure 31-8.

Figure 31-8

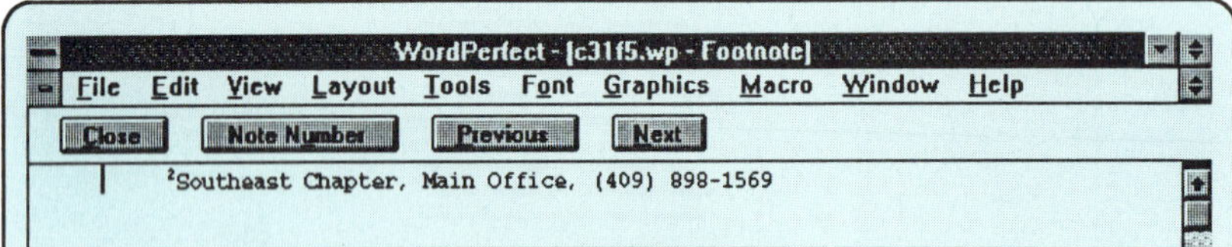

To change the last digit in the phone number from "9" to "8":

Click	before the last 9	***Move***	*the insertion point before the last 9*
Press	Delete	***Press***	*Delete*
Type	8	***Type***	*8*
Click	the Close command button	***Press***	*Alt+C to select the Close command button*

You can change the way WordPerfect numbers the footnotes and formats them on the page. This is done by selecting Options under the Footnote option from the Layout menu. A Footnote Option code [Ftn Opt] is placed in your document. The option changes are in effect from the location of the code until the end of the document. Place the code at the beginning of the document if you want all footnotes to reflect your option changes. You can also place your Footnote Option code in a document style.

Suppose you want to have the line separating the text on a page from the footnote to extend from margin to margin (rather than a half-line as shown in Figure 31-6).

To change the footnote options:

Click	at the beginning of the document	***Move***	*the insertion point to the beginning of the document*
Choose	Layout	***Press***	*Alt*
Choose	Footnote	***Select***	*Layout*
Choose	Options	***Select***	*Footnote*
		Select	*Options*

The Footnote Options dialog box appears. Your screen should look like Figure 31-9.

Figure 31-9

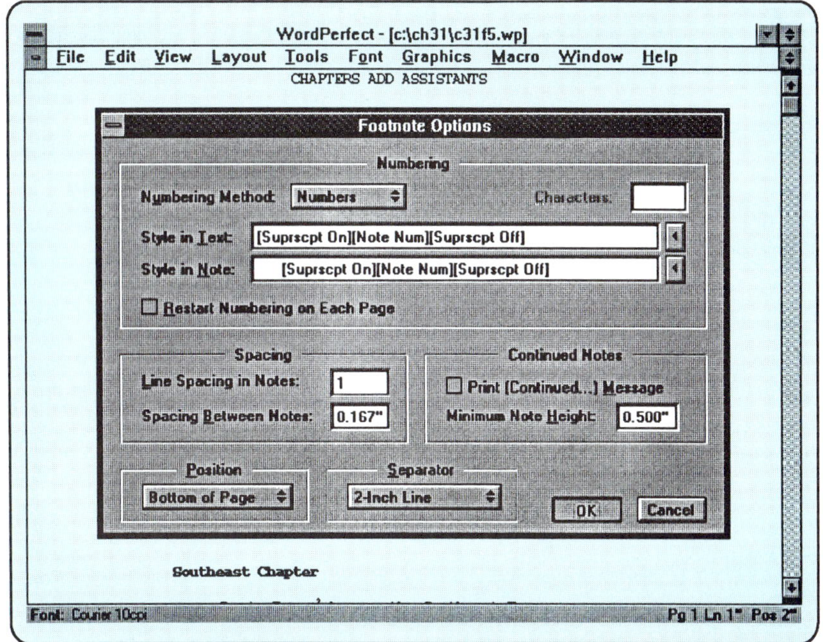

For detailed information regarding each of these options, see "Footnotes, Options" in the WordPerfect Reference Manual.

To change the option separator:

Click	the Separator pop-up list button	***Press***	*Alt+S to select the Separator pop-up list button*
Hold down	the mouse button to view the pop-up list button	***Press***	*Alt+↑ to view the pop-up list*

To have a line print from margin to margin:

Choose	Margin to Margin	**Type**	M to select Margin to Margin

The lower part of your screen should look like Figure 31-10.

Figure 31-10

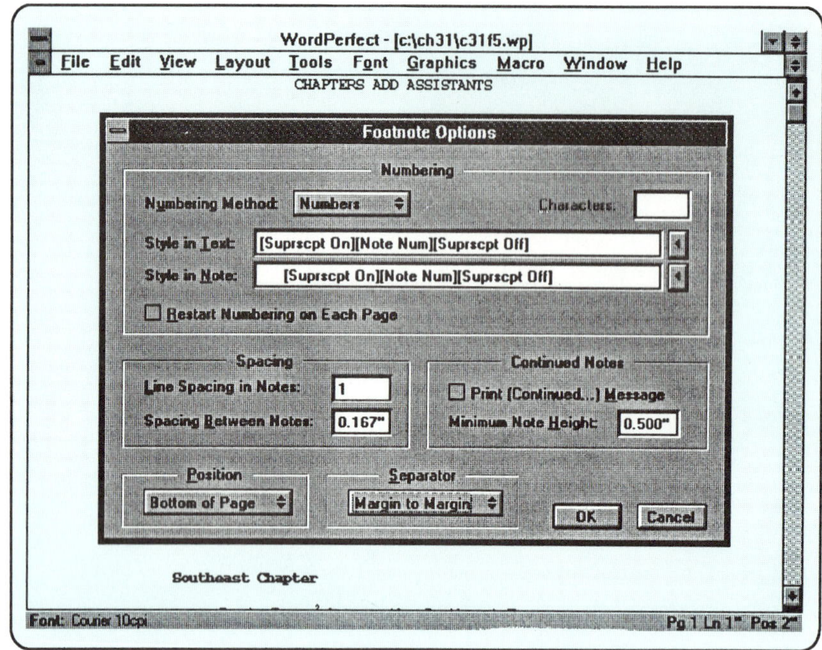

To return to your document:

Click	the OK command button	***Press***	*↵Enter*

Preview the document. Notice that a line appears from margin to margin. Your screen should look like Figure 31-11.

Figure 31-11

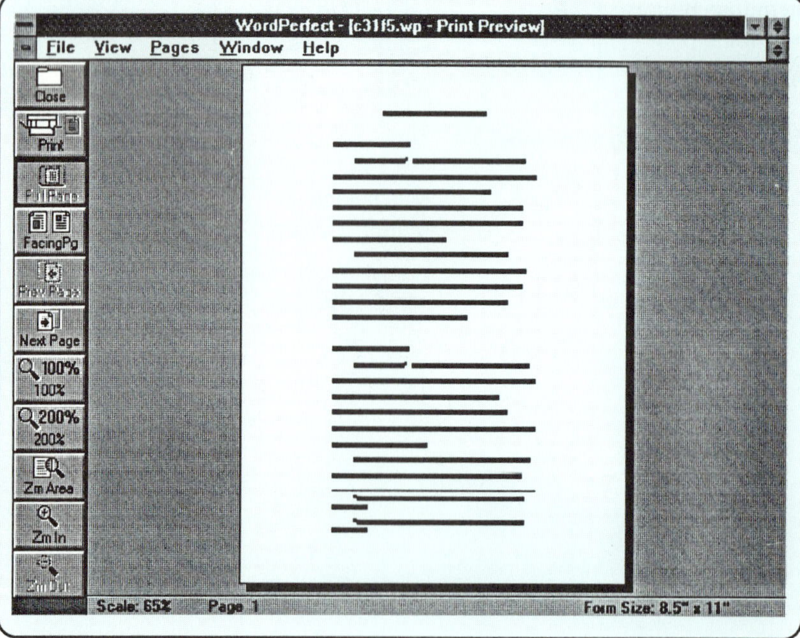

Return to your document. Save the document as "endfoot2.doc" and close the document.

■ ENDNOTES

The Endnote feature is used by choosing the Endnote option from the Layout menu. As you create, edit, add, or delete an endnote, WordPerfect manages the numbering of the endnote and places it at the end of the document.

Open the "endfoot1.doc" document.

To create an endnote:

Click	after the word "Jones" on the first line of the first paragraph	***Move***	*the insertion point after the word "Jones" on the first line of the first paragraph*
Choose	Layout	***Press***	*Alt*
Choose	Endnote	***Select***	*Layout*
Choose	Create	***Select***	*Endnote*
		Select	*Create*

The top part of your screen should look like Figure 31-12.

Figure 31-12

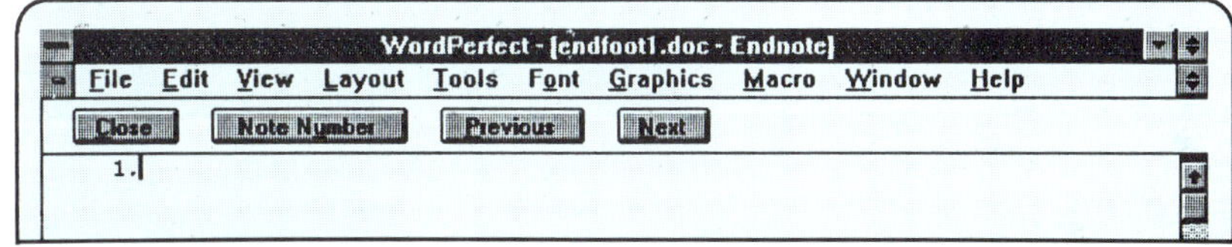

You are placed in the Endnote screen. The word "Endnote" appears on the title bar.

An endnote number is already provided for you. All you need to do is type the text of the endnote.

Press	the Spacebar twice	***Press***	*the Spacebar twice*
Type	Southwest Chapter, Main Office, (806) 498-5833	***Type***	*Southwest Chapter, Main Office, (806) 498-5833*
Click	the Close command button	***Press***	*Alt+C to select the Close command button*

The top part of your screen should look like Figure 31-13.

Figure 31-13

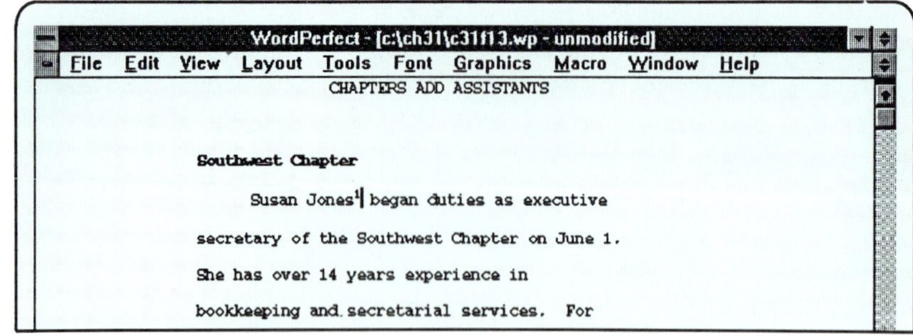

The Endnote code is represented by a number 1 on the screen.

Turn on the Reveal Codes feature.

The bottom part of your screen should look like Figure 31-14.

Figure 31-14

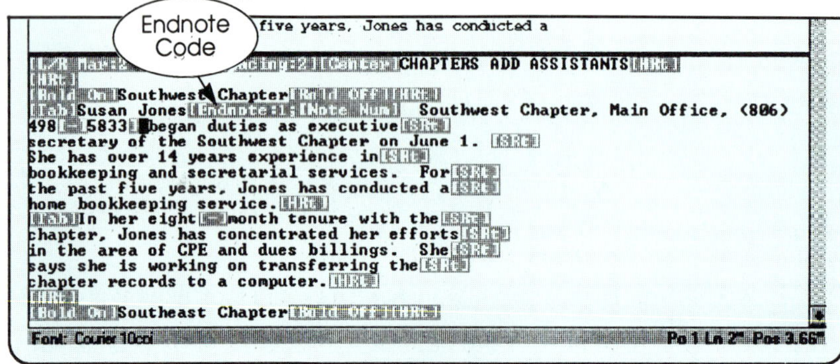

An Endnote code is placed in the document. The first part of the endnote text is shown. This makes finding a particular endnote easier for you.

Turn off the Reveal Codes feature.

To create another endnote:

Click	after the word "Brown" on the first line of the third paragraph	***Move***	*the insertion point after the word "Brown" on the first line of the third paragraph*
Choose	Layout	***Press***	*Alt*
Choose	Endnote	***Select***	*Layout*
Choose	Create	***Select***	*Endnote*
Press	the Spacebar twice	***Select***	*Create*
Type	Southeast Chapter, Main Office, (409) 898-1569	***Press***	*the Spacebar twice*

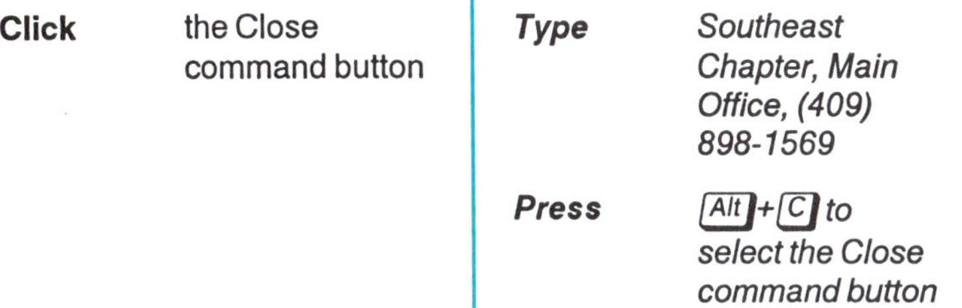

Click	the Close command button	***Type***	*Southeast Chapter, Main Office, (409) 898-1569*
		Press	*Alt+C to select the Close command button*

The lower part of your screen should look like Figure 31-15.

Figure 31-15

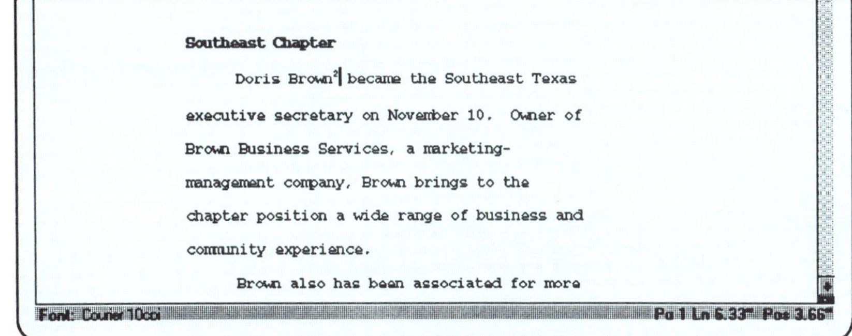

The Endnote code is represented by a number 2 on the screen.

Preview page 2 of the document. The top part of your screen should look like Figure 31-16.

Figure 31-16

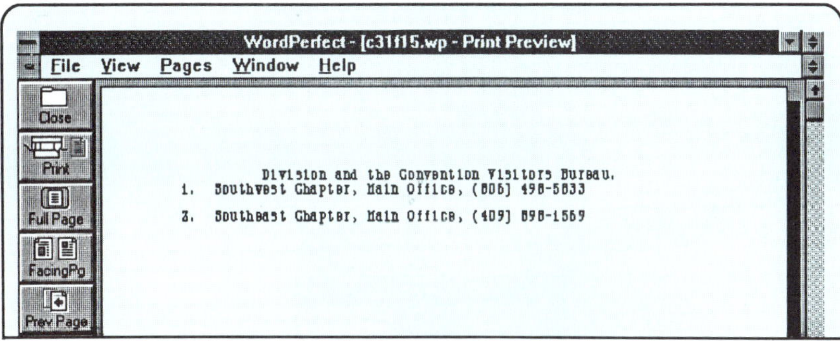

Notice that the endnotes appear at the end of the document. You can place a Hard Page code at the end of your document to force the endnotes to begin on a separate page.

Return to your document.

To place the endnotes on a separate page:

Click	at the end of the document	***Move***	*the insertion point to the end of the document*
Insert	a page break	***Insert***	*a page break*

Preview page 3 of the document. Your screen should look like Figure 31-17.

Figure 31-17

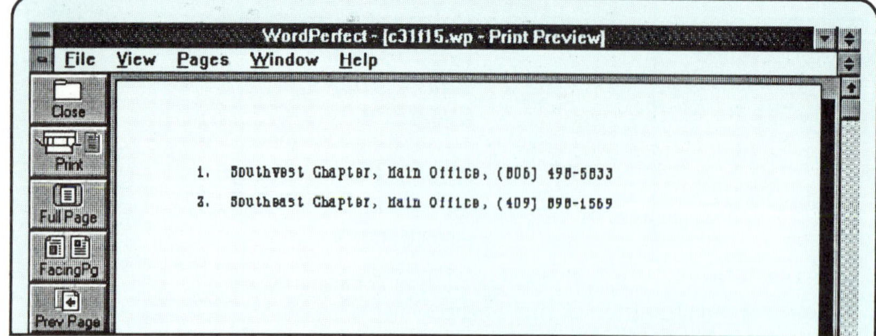

Notice that the endnotes appear on a separate page. Return to your document.

You may need to edit the contents of an existing endnote. Suppose you need to modify the second endnote. To edit the second endnote:

Choose	Layout	***Press***	*Alt*
Choose	Endnote	***Select***	*Layout*
Choose	Edit	***Select***	*Endnote*
		Select	*Edit*

The Edit Endnote dialog box appears. Your screen should look similar to Figure 31-18.

Figure 31-18

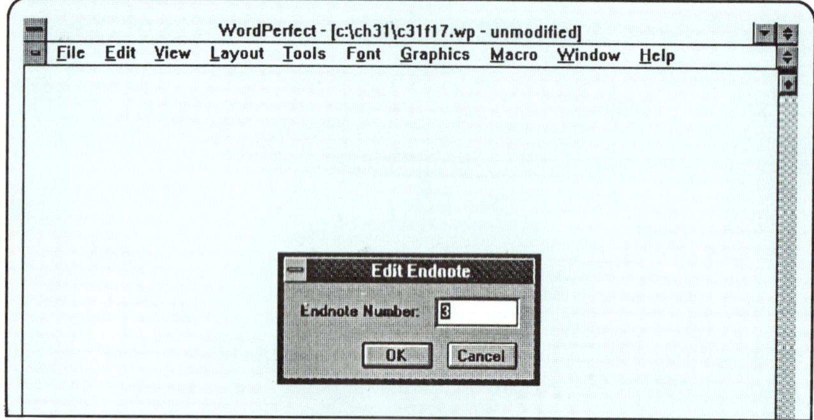

Your insertion point does not have to be located on the second endnote in order to modify it. You open each endnote by its number.

To edit endnote 2:

Type	2	***Type***	*2*
Click	the OK command button	***Press***	*↵Enter*

The top part of your screen should look like Figure 31-19.

Figure 31-19

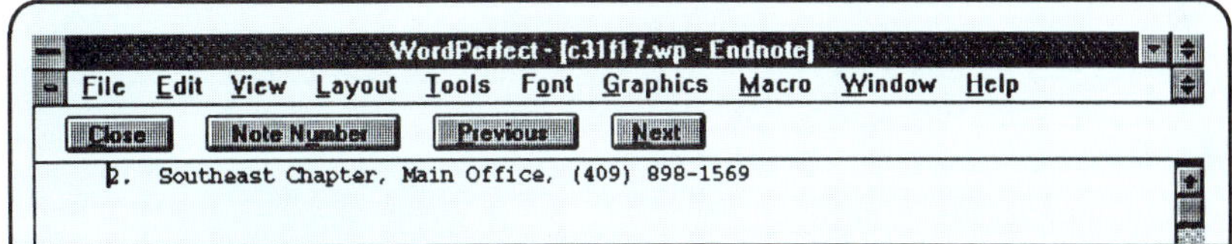

To change the last digit in the phone number from "9" to "8":

Click	before the last 9	***Move***	*the insertion point before the last 9*
Press	Delete	***Press***	*Delete*
Type	8	***Type***	*8*
Click	the Close command button	***Press***	*Alt+C to select the Close command button*

You can change the way WordPerfect numbers the endnotes and formats them on the page. This is done by choosing Options under the Endnote option from the Layout menu. An Endnote Option code [End Opt] is placed in your document. The option changes are in effect from the location of the code until the end of the document. Place the code at the beginning of the document if you want all endnotes to reflect your option changes. You could also place your Endnote Option code in a document style.

Suppose you want to change the numbers (1, 2, etc.) for the endnotes to letters (a, b, etc.).

To change the endnote options:

Click	at the beginning of the document	***Move***	*the insertion point to the beginning of the document*
Choose	Layout	***Press***	*Alt*
Choose	Endnote	***Select***	*Layout*
Choose	Options	***Select***	*Endnote*
		Select	*Options*

The Endnote Options dialog box appears. Your screen should look like Figure 31-20.

Figure 31-20

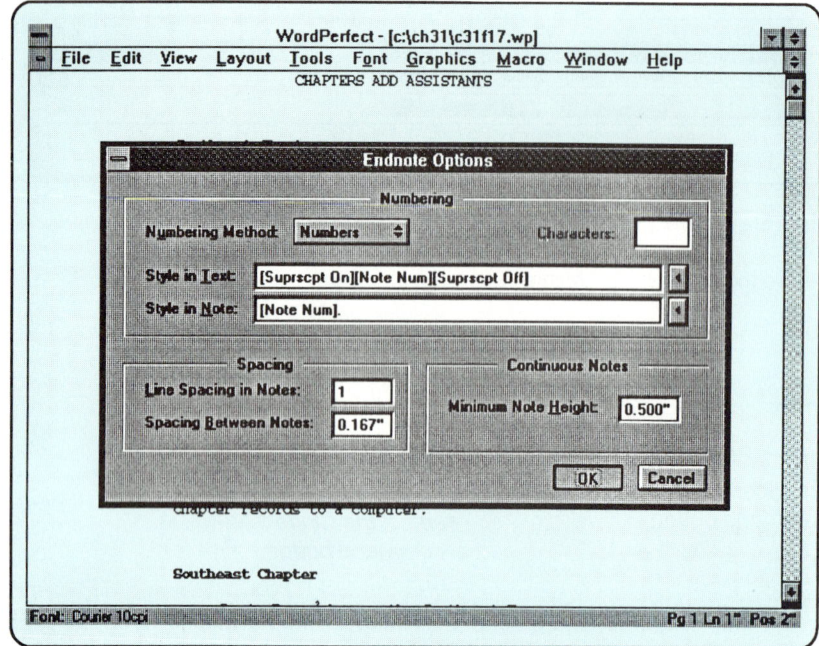

For detailed information regarding each of these options, see "Endnotes, Options" in the WordPerfect Reference Manual.

To change the Numbering Method option:

Click	the Numbering Method pop-up list button	***Press***	*Alt+U to select the Numbering Method pop-up list button*
Hold down	the mouse button to view the pop-up list button	***Press***	*Alt+↑ to view the pop-up list*

To select letters:

Choose	Letters	***Type***	*L to select Letters*

Your screen should look like Figure 31-21.

Figure 31-21

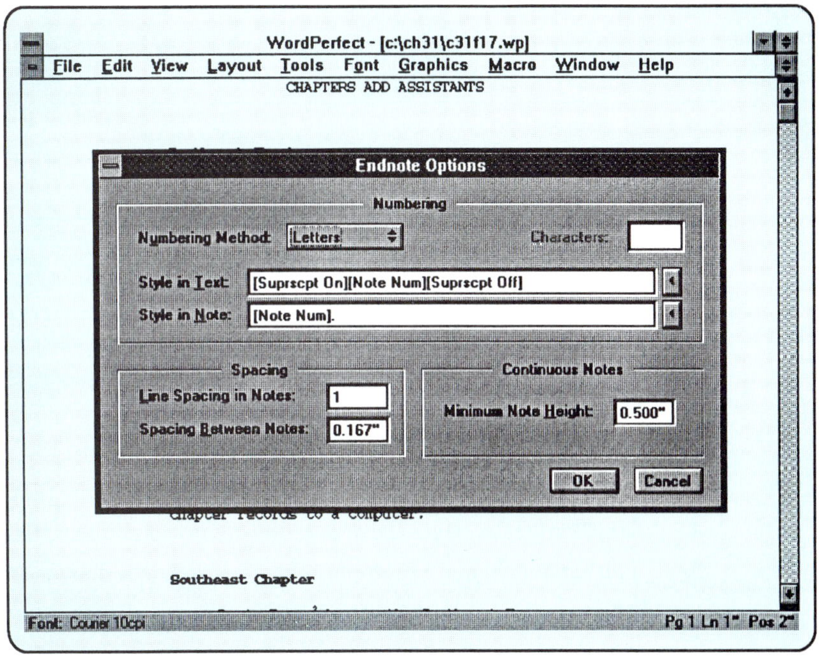

To return to your document:

Click	the OK command button	***Press***	↵Enter

Preview page 3 of the document. Notice that a letter appears next to each endnote. The top part of your screen should look like Figure 31-22.

Figure 31-22

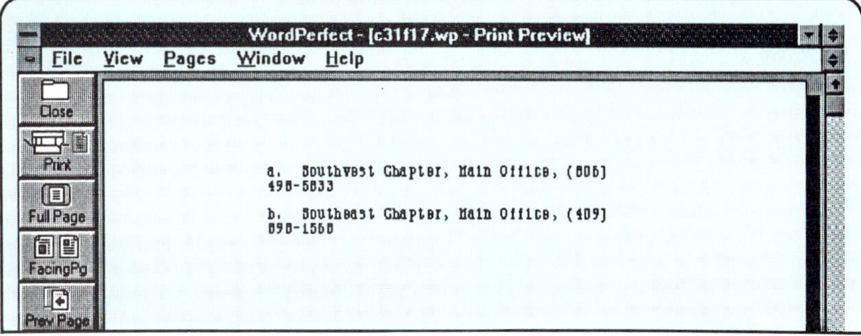

Return to your document. Save the document as "endnote3.doc" and close the document.

EXERCISE 1

INSTRUCTIONS: Define the following terms:

1. Footnotes ____

____

2. Endnotes ____

____

EXERCISE 2

INSTRUCTIONS: Circle T if the statement is true and F if the statement is false.

T F 1. Footnotes and endnotes are a method of documenting sources of quotations, facts, and ideas in a report.

T F 2. Footnotes are usually listed at the end of the document.

T F 3. Endnotes are usually listed at the end of the page where they are used.

T F 4. WordPerfect manages the numbering of the footnotes and endnotes for you.

T F 5. You cannot change a footnote. You must delete it first, and then add a new one.

T F 6. If you look closely, you can see the actual endnote at the bottom of each page on the normal editing screen.

T F 7. You can change the way WordPerfect numbers the footnotes and formats them on the page.

T F 8. Your insertion point must be at the top of the document in order to edit an endnote.

T F 9. WordPerfect formats the pages for you so that the footnotes will fit.

EXERCISE 3

INSTRUCTIONS:

1. Create the following document.
2. Print the document with the following footnote information.

   Wall Street Journal, Vol. 85, No. 77, April 19, 1990, p.1.
3. Save the document in a file using the name "ch31ex03"
4. Remove the footnote.
5. Place an endnote on a separate page from the text using the information in step 2.
6. Print the document.
7. Close the document.

```
The following quote appeared in the Wall Street Journal concerning
Eastern Airlines:

   Eastern Airlines was turned over to a trustee by a bankruptcy
   judge, who took control of the financially battered carrier
   away from Texas Air and Chairman Frank Lorenzo.  Named as
   trustee was Martin R. Shugrue, who was ousted last year as
   president of Continental Airlines, Texas Airline's other
   airline unit.  Unsecured creditors sought a trustee because
   they blamed management for Eastern's ever growing losses.[1]
```

EXERCISE 4

INSTRUCTIONS:

1. Create the following document using footnotes. The footnotes are listed in the second box. The footnotes should appear at the bottom of the page separated by a 2″ line from the body of the text.
2. Spell check the document.
3. Preview the document.
4. Print the document.
5. Save the document in a file using the name "ch31ex04".
6. Close the document.

```
Springer defined "Ergonomics as the study of humans at work,"[1]
Yet, we have a different definition from Popham, "..ergonomics
integrates both the physiological and psychological factors
involved in creating an effective work area."[2]
```

```
1. T.J. Springer, "Ergonomics:  The Real Issue," Office
Administration and Automation, May, 1984, p. 69.

2. Estelle L. Popham, Rita Sloan Tilton, J. Howard Jackson, and J.
Marshall Hanna, Secretarial Procedures and Administration
(Cincinnati: South-Western Publishing Co., 1983), p.31.
```

EXERCISE 5

INSTRUCTIONS:

1. Create the following document using footnotes. The footnotes are listed in the second box. The footnotes should appear at the bottom of the page separated by a 2″ line from the body of the text.
2. Spell check the document.

3. Preview the document.
4. Print the document.
5. Save the document in a file using the name "ch31ex05."
6. Close the document.

```
    In his Pulitzer Prize-winning book, Dumas Malone makes the

following statement about Thomas Jefferson,

    Jefferson would not have placed on and select list the bill on
    this subject (slavery), for it was merely a digest of existing
    laws.  By the time that the revisor submitted their formal
    report they did not need to recommend that the importation of
    slaves be prohibited. The Assembly had already seen to that,
    and, according to Jefferson's later account, the action was
    taken on his motion.[1]

    Accordingly, Jefferson, proposed discontinuance of the slave

trade before the American Revolution.  Before he could make his

statement to the House, it was introduced in 1778.[2]
```

```
1. Dumas Malone, Jefferson The Virginian, (Boston, Little, Brown
and Company, 1948), p. 264.

2. Ford, I, 51-52: Hening IX, 471-72.  As given in the Delegates
Journal, the legislative history is as follows: On October 14,
1778, it was ordered that leave be given to bring in a bill to
prevent the future importation of slaves, and that the committee of
trade prepare and bring in the same.  On October 15, Richard Kello,
of Southhampton presented a bill.  This passed the house of
Delegates on October 22, under a slightly different title.  On
October 27, as amended by the Senate, it was agreed to.  Jefferson
did not appear in the house until November 30.
```

EXERCISE 6

INSTRUCTIONS:

1. Open the document "ch31ex05."
2. Add the following sentence to the end of footnote 2. (Do not include the double quotes.)

   "I have found no evidence of his intimacy with any member of the committee of trade."
3. Spell check the document.

4. Preview the document.
5. Print the document.
6. Save the document in a file using the name "ch31ex06."
7. Close the document.

EXERCISE 7

INSTRUCTIONS:

1. Create the following document using endnotes. Double-space the document. The endnotes are listed in the second box. Place the endnotes at the bottom of the last page. The title "ENDNOTES" should be centered and placed above the endnotes.
2. Spell check the document.
3. Preview the document.
4. Print the document.
5. Save the document in a file using the name "ch31ex07."
6. Close the document.

The Modern Language Association[1] has recommended using endnotes. These endnotes should appear at the end of a paper, and they should be listed in order of citation. They should appear under a heading "Endnotes." In either footnotes or endnotes, the number used to identify each should be a superior (raised) figure at the point of reference in the text.

At one time, only footnotes were acceptable as documentation of a reference. This presented problems with providing enough room at the bottom of the page to accommodate the material in the footnotes.

Endnotes and textual citation are similar. In each, the author, publication date, and page number(s) (if needed) of the material cited are given. The list is usually presented in alphabetic order on a separate page at the end of the report. Seybold and Young[2] strongly endorse this procedure because it is easy to use with a typewriter or personal computer.

1. MLA Handbook for Writers of Research Papers. New York: Modern Language Association, 1984, pp. 28-31.

2. Seybold, Catherine and Bruce Young. The Chicago Manual of Style. 13th ed. Chicago: The University of Chicago Press, 1982, p. 400.

EXERCISE 8

INSTRUCTIONS:

1. Create the following document using endnotes. Place the endnotes at the end of the document. The title "ENDNOTES" should be centered and placed at the top of the page.
2. Spell check the document.
3. Preview the document.
4. Print the document.
5. Save the document in a file using the name "ch31ex08."
6. Close the document.

THE STRUCTURE OF EVERYDAY LIFE[1]

In Braudel's book, he comments that the present world population is over 4 billion people. Comparing this with the very approximate figures of the past shows that this number is five times the population of 1800, twelve times that of 1300.[2]

Cologne, at the intersection of two Rhine waterways, one up, and the other down-stream, and important overland routes, was the largest town in Germany in the Fifteenth Century. Despite this fact, it numbered only 20,000 people.[3]

In 1451 a plague killed off 21,000 people in Cologne; over the next few years 4,000 marriages were celebrated.[4]

Increases and declines therefore alternated in the short term, regularly compensating each other. Those most vulnerable— young children and the aged were always at risk.

Endnotes

1. Fernard Braudel, The Structure of Everyday Life, New York: Harper + Row, Publishers, 1979.

2. If anyone accepts the figure of 350 million for 1300 and 1,000 million for 1800. These are the figures on which the calculations are based.

3. Heinrick Bechtel, Wirtschaftsgeschichte Deutschlands vol. 16, 1952, pp. 25-26.

4. Erich Schonfelder, Die Wirtschaftliche Entwicklung, translated in 1970, says 30,000 deaths.

CHAPTER THIRTY-TWO

PREPARING TABLES OF CONTENTS, INDEXES, AND LISTS

OBJECTIVES

In this chapter, you will learn to:

- Create, define, and generate a table of contents
- Create, define, and generate an index
- Create, define, and generate a list

CHAPTER OVERVIEW

When you prepare reports or long documents, you may need to make a table of contents, an index, or a list of items such as figures, maps, or tables. In this chapter, the procedures for creating, defining, and generating a table of contents, index, and list are described and illustrated.

TABLES OF CONTENTS

A table of contents appears at the front of large reports or books. It lists the headings of each chapter and the sections that divide each chapter. There can be several levels of subsections listed in the table of contents, depending on the level of detail you want to maintain. A page number is defined for each item in the table of contents. An example of a table of contents is shown at the front of this book.

The Table of Contents feature creates a table of contents automatically from a document that you prepare. A maximum of five levels of chapters and subsections can be maintained. The first level is placed at the left margin. Levels two through five are placed at the next four tab stops. You can specify how you would like the numbers to appear for each level.

Change the default directory to "a:\wpdocs" or to "c:\wpdocs." Then create the document in Figure 32-1. Set the initial font to Helvetica 12 point. Use the Outline feature to create the document. To create the paragraphs without paragraph numbers, delete the paragraph number and choose the Indent feature. Save the document as "inform.rpt."

Figure 32-1

I. Introduction

Last year a decision was made to install new information processing equipment at the corporate office. The target date for installation and full operation is August 1.

II. History

Prior to the installation of the information processing equipment last August, the document preparation group consisted of seven individuals. There are now five people in the department today.

III. New Information Processing Equipment

A. Future Installations

The company is beginning to install additional information processing systems in all of the organization's departments.

B. Long-Range Plans

The consultant that assisted us in the design and installation of the initial information processing equipment will work with us on a continuing basis to determine our long-term needs.

Creating a table of contents involves three steps. First, you must mark the headings or text in your document that you want to appear in the table of contents. You can do this while you are creating your document, or after you are finished entering it. To mark text for the table of contents, select the text, choose Table of Contents from the Mark Text option under the Tools menu or press F12, and enter a table of contents level number (1 - 5) for the text.

The second step in creating a table of contents is to specify where you would like the table placed in the document and to define how the numbers should appear for each level in the table.

The third step is to choose the Generate feature that creates the table of contents.

Creating a Table of Contents

To mark the first heading "I. Introduction":

Select the heading "I. Introduction"

Choose Tools

Choose Mark Text

Select *the heading "I. Introduction"*

Press *Alt*

Select *Tools*

Select the heading "I. Introduction"

Press F12

Select Table of Contents

Choose	Table of Contents	***Select***	*Mark Text*		
		Select	*Table of Contents*		

The Mark Table of Contents dialog box appears. The top of your screen should look like Figure 32-2.

Figure 32-2

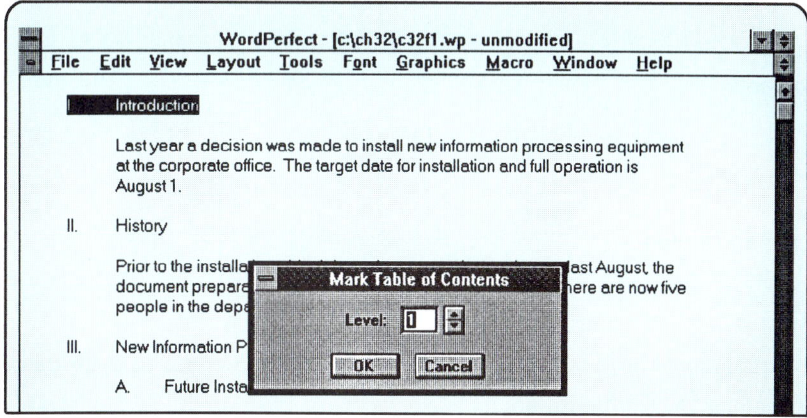

To enter the level:

Type	1	***Type***	*1*	**Type**	1
Click	the OK command button	***Press***	*↵Enter*	**Press**	↵Enter

To display the codes that mark the heading for the table of contents, turn on the Reveal Codes feature.

A [Mark:ToC,1] code is placed in the document to indicate a level-one table of contents marker. An [End Mark:ToC,1] indicates the end of the text that is placed in the table of contents.

Turn off the Reveal Codes feature.

To mark the second heading "II. History":

Select	the heading "II. History"	***Select***	*the heading "II. History"*	**Select**	the heading "II. History"
Choose	Tools	***Press***	*Alt*	**Press**	F12
Choose	Mark Text	***Select***	*Tools*	**Select**	Table of Contents
Choose	Table of Contents	***Select***	*Mark Text*	**Type**	1
Type	1	***Select***	*Table of Contents*	**Press**	↵Enter
Click	the OK command button	***Type***	*1*		
		Press	*↵Enter*		

To mark the third heading "III. New Information Processing Equipment":

Select	the heading "III. New Information Processing Equipment"	***Select***	*the heading "III. New Information Processing Equipment"*	**Select**	the heading "III. New Information Processing Equipment"
Choose	Tools	***Press***	*Alt*	**Press**	F12
Choose	Mark Text	***Select***	*Tools*	**Select**	Table of Contents
Choose	Table of Contents	***Select***	*Mark Text*	**Type**	1
Type	1	***Select***	*Table of Contents*	**Press**	↵Enter
Click	the OK command button	***Type***	*1*		
		Press	*↵Enter*		

The "A. Future Installations" heading is a subheading to the section, and needs to be marked for level 2.

To mark the subheading "A. Future Installations":

Select	the subheading "A. Future Installations"	***Select***	*the subheading "A. Future Installations"*	**Select**	the subheading "A. Future Installations"
Choose	Tools	***Press***	*Alt*	**Press**	F12
Choose	Mark Text	***Select***	*Tools*	**Select**	Table of Contents
Choose	Table of Contents	***Select***	*Mark Text*	**Type**	2
Type	2	***Select***	*Table of Contents*	**Press**	↵Enter
Click	the OK command button	***Type***	*2*		
		Press	*↵Enter*		

Turn on the Reveal Codes feature.

A [Mark:ToC,2] code marks the beginning of the level two text for the table of contents. An [End Mark:ToC,2] marks the end of the text.

Turn off the Reveal Codes feature.

Mark the subheading "B. Long-Range Plans" for entry in the second level of the table of contents.

Defining a Table of Contents

After marking the text, you must tell WordPerfect where to place the table in the document and how to format the page numbers.

To create a separate page for the table of contents at the beginning of the document:

Click	at the beginning of the document before the Outline code	***Move***	*the insertion point to the beginning of the document before the Outline code*	**Move**	the insertion point to the beginning of the document before the Outline code
Insert	a page break	***Insert***	*a page break*	**Insert**	a page break
Click	at the beginning of the document	***Move***	*the insertion point to the beginning of the document*	**Move**	the insertion point to the beginning of the document

The top part of your screen should look like Figure 32-3.

Figure 32-3

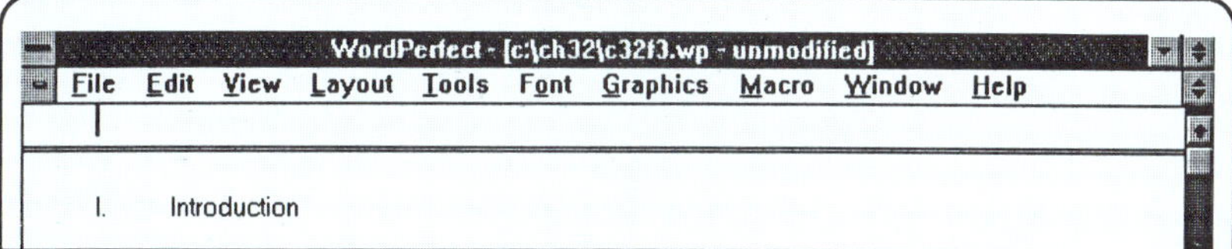

To define the table of contents:

Choose	Tools	***Press***	*Alt*	**Press**	Shift+F12
Choose	Define	***Select***	*Tools*	**Select**	Table of Contents
Choose	Table of Contents	***Select***	*Define*		
		Select	*Table of Contents*		

The Define Table of Contents dialog box appears. Your screen should look like Figure 32-4.

Figure 32-4

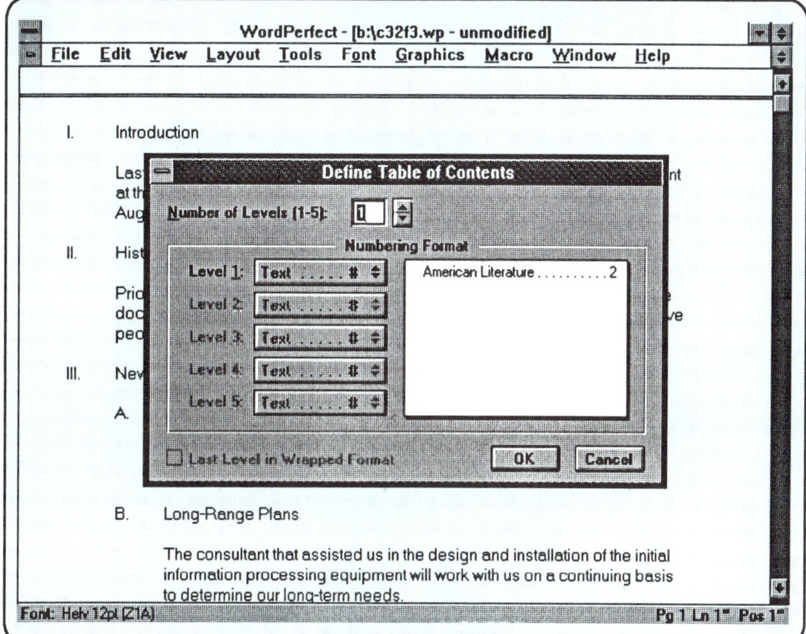

The Define Table of Contents dialog box appears. You can select the number of levels, the page numbering style, and whether the last level should be word wrapped.

There are five page numbering styles that you can choose:

1. No page numbers
2. Page numbers directly following the text in the table of contents
3. Page numbers in parentheses that directly follow the text in the table of contents
4. Page numbers against the right margin (flush right)
5. Page numbers flush right with dots (leaders) placed between the headings and the numbers

To change number of levels to 2:

Click	the up triangle button next to the Number of Levels text box	***Press***	*Alt+N to select the Number of Levels text box*	**Press**	Alt+N to select the Number of Levels text box
		Type	*2*	**Type**	2

Your screen should look like Figure 32-5.

Figure 32-5

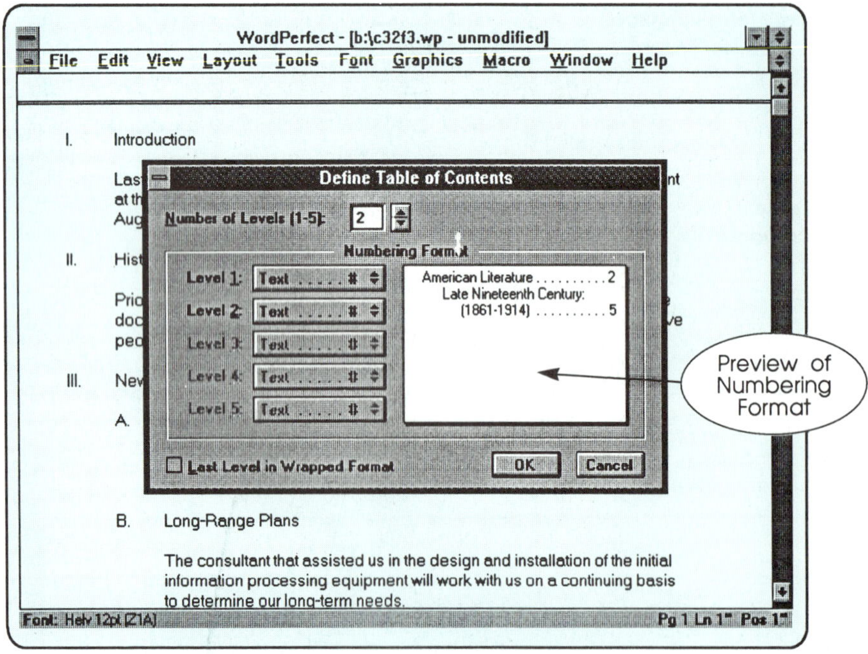

To return to the document:

Click	the OK command button	***Press***	*↵Enter*	**Press**	↵Enter

Turn on the Reveal Codes feature.

A Definition code [Def Mark:ToC,2:FlRgtDotLdr,FlRgtDotLdr] is placed in the document where the table will be located. This code indicates the Table of Contents will have two levels. Each level will be formatted with the page numbers flush right and preceded by dot leaders.

Turn off the Reveal Codes feature.

Generating a Table of Contents

Once the text is marked and the table of contents defined, all you need to do is generate a table of contents.

To generate a table of contents:

Choose	Tools	***Press***	*Alt*	**Press**	Alt+F12
Choose	Generate	***Select***	*Tools*		
		Select	*Generate*		

The top part of your screen should look like Figure 32-6.

Figure 32-6

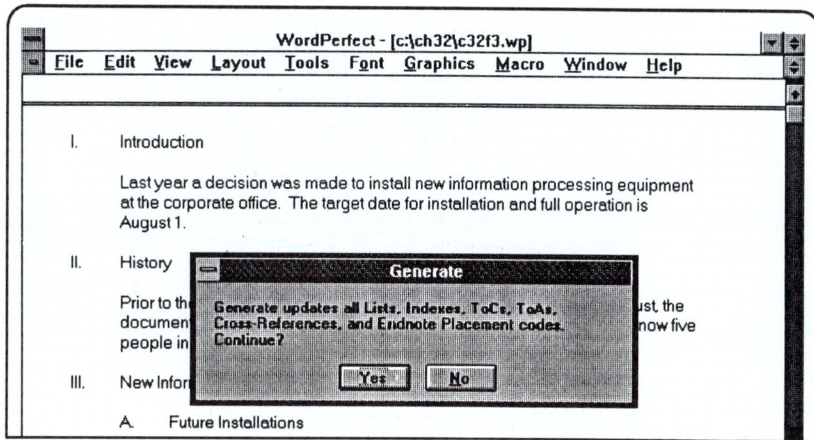

You are asked if you want to replace any existing tables, lists, and indexes. Choose Yes to replace or No to return to your document without generating the table of contents.

To generate the table of contents:

Click	the Yes command button	***Press***	*Alt+Y to select the Yes command button*	**Press**	Alt+Y to select the Yes command button

A counter shows the progress of the table generation. When complete, the table of contents is displayed on your screen as in Figure 32-7.

Figure 32-7

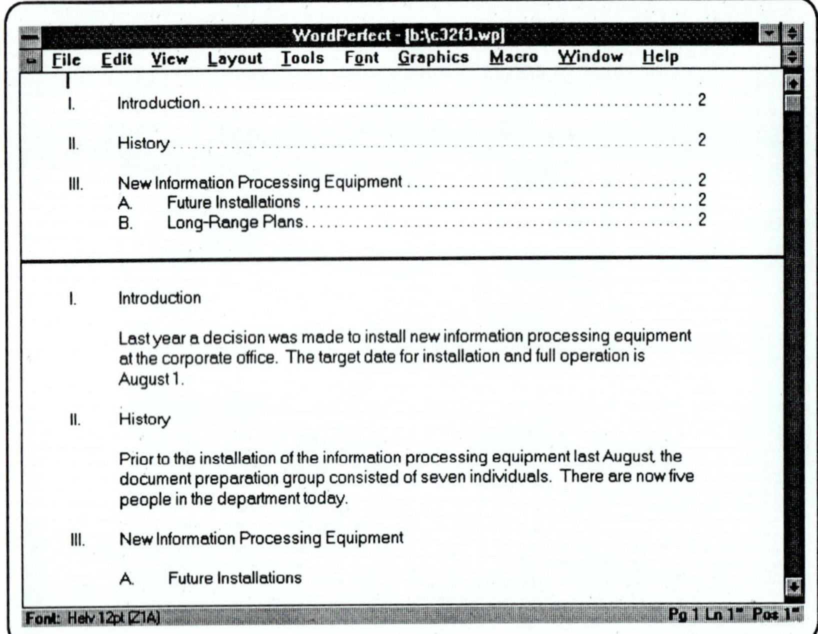

Turn on the Reveal Codes feature.

Notice that Indent, Margin Release, and Flush Right codes have been added to format the text in the table of contents. Page numbers for the table of contents are displayed at the right margin.

Turn off the Reveal Codes feature. Save the document as "toc." Close the document.

INDEXES

An index appears at the back of a long report or book. It matches key words and phrases to page numbers. An example of an index appears at the back of this book.

The procedure for creating an index is very similar to that of a table of contents. First, you mark the words or phrases that you want in the index. Then specify where you want the index located in the document and how you want the page numbers to appear. You can choose one of five numbering styles. Finally, you create the index through the Generate feature.

Open the document "inform.rpt."

Creating an Index

You can create your own index topic heading, or you can select text in the document and use it as an index heading. For example, suppose you want to include the phrase "information processing" as an index heading. The phrase appears five times in the report.

There are two types of "information processing" included in the report: "equipment" and "systems." It would probably be best to list "Information Processing" in the index as a heading, with "equipment" and "systems" as subheadings.

To mark the text "information processing" for the index:

Select	the text "information processing" in the first paragraph	***Select***	*the text "information processing" in the first paragraph*	**Select**	the text "information processing" in the first paragraph

Choose	Tools	***Press***	*Alt*	**Press**	F12
Choose	Mark Text	***Select***	*Tools*	**Select**	Index
Choose	Index	***Select***	*Mark Text*		
		Select	*Index*		

The Mark Index dialog box appears. Your screen should look like Figure 32-8.

Figure 32-8

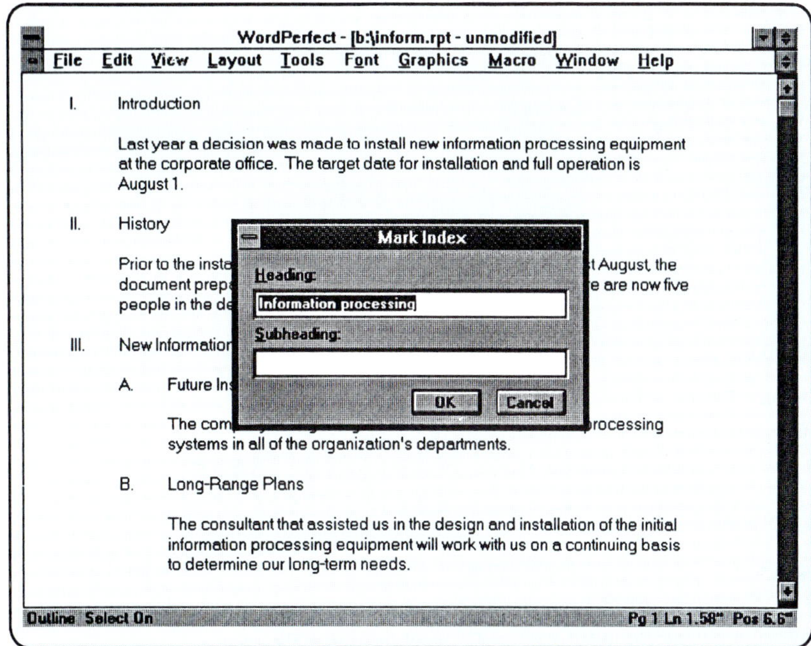

The selected word is offered as an index heading.

To enter a subheading:

Double-click	the Subheading text box	***Press***	*Alt+S to select the Subheading text box*	**Press**	Alt+S to select the Subheading text box
Type	equipment	***Type***	*equipment*	**Type**	equipment
Click	the OK command button	***Press***	*↵Enter*	**Press**	↵Enter

Turn on the Reveal Codes feature.

An Index code [Index:Information processing;equipment] is placed in the document for the heading and subheading.

Turn off the Reveal Codes feature.

To enter the heading "Information processing" and the subheading "systems":

Select	the text "information processing" in the third paragraph	***Select***	*the text "information processing" in the third paragraph*	**Select**	the text "information processing" in the third paragraph
Choose	Tools	***Press***	*Alt*	**Press**	F12
Choose	Mark Text	***Select***	*Tools*	**Select**	Index
Choose	Index	***Select***	*Mark Text*		
		Select	*Index*		

To enter the subheading:

Double-click	the Subheading text box	***Press***	*Alt+S to select the Subheading text box*	**Press**	Alt+S to select the Subheading text box
Type	systems	***Type***	*systems*	**Type**	systems
Click	the OK command button	***Press***	*↵Enter*	**Press**	↵Enter

Defining an Index

You can specify where the index is located in the document and how the page numbers should appear through the Define Index dialog box.

To create a separate page for the index at the end of the document:

Click	at the end of the document	***Move***	*the insertion point to the end of the document*	**Move**	the insertion point to the end of the document
Insert	a page break	***Insert***	*a page break*	**Insert**	a page break

The bottom part of your screen should look like Figure 32-9.

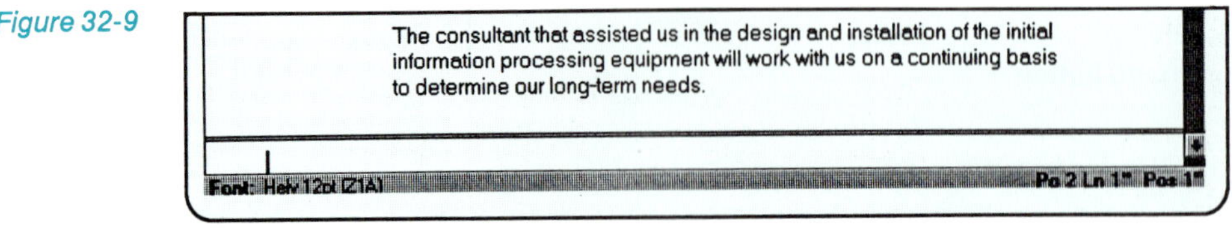

Figure 32-9

To define the index:

Choose	Tools	***Press***	*Alt*	**Press**	Shift+F12
Choose	Define	***Select***	*Tools*	**Select**	Index
Choose	Index	***Select***	*Define*		
		Select	*Index*		

The Define Index dialog box appears. The top part of your screen should look like Figure 32-10.

Figure 32-10

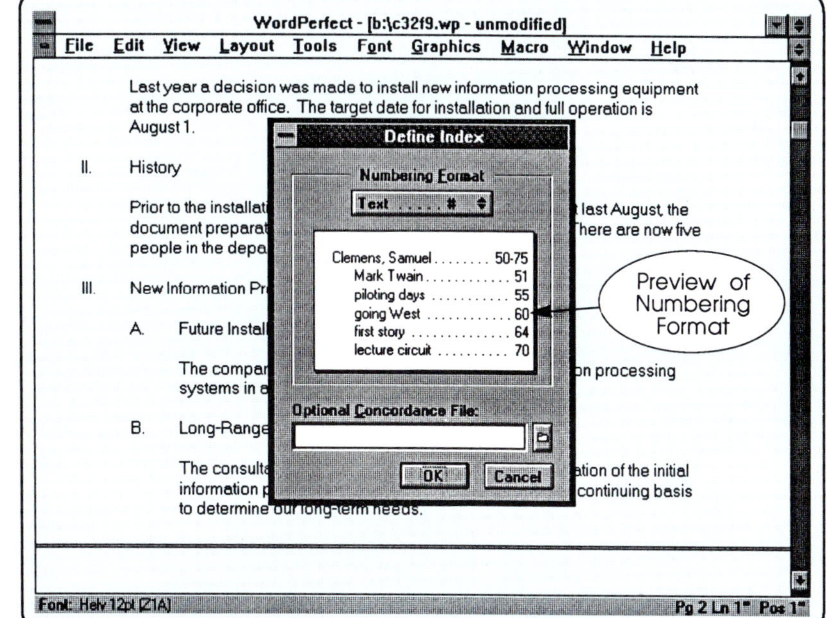

The Define Index feature allows you to determine the numbering format for the index or suggest an option concordance file. A concordance file is a special file that you can create. The file contains a list of all the index entries that you want to define for your document. You simply type in each index entry on a line. WordPerfect compares this list with the document and creates an index. For more information on how to use a concordance file, see the section "Index, Concordance and Mark Text" in the WordPerfect Reference Manual.

The page numbering formats are the same as the formats available for the Table of Contents feature. To select a numbering style:

Click	the Numbering Format pop-up list button	***Press***	*Alt+F to select the Numbering Format pop-up list button*	**Press**	Alt+F to select the Numbering Format pop-up list button
Hold down	the mouse button to view the pop-up list	***Press***	*Alt+↑ to view the pop-up list*	**Press**	Alt+↑ to view the pop-up list
Choose	Text #	***Type***	*# to select Text #*	**Type**	# to select Text #
Click	the OK command button	***Press***	*↵Enter*	**Press**	↵Enter

Turn on the Reveal Codes feature.

An Index Definition code [Def Mark:Index,TxtSpcPg] is placed in the document where the index will be located. This code indicates the Index will be formatted with the page numbers directly following the index entries.

Turn off the Reveal Codes feature.

Generating an Index

Once the text is marked and the index is defined, all you need to do is generate the index.

To generate the index:

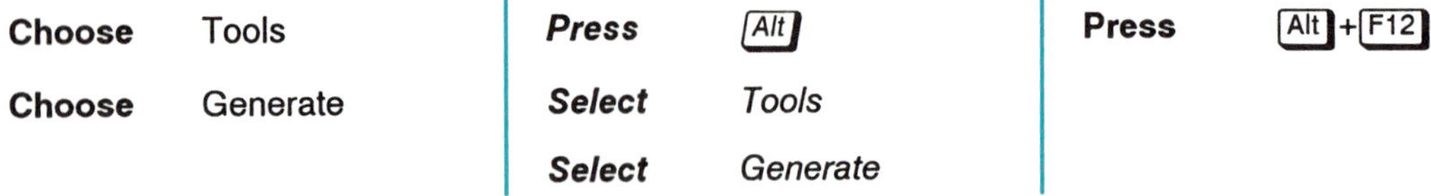

Choose	Tools	***Press***	*Alt*	**Press**	Alt+F12
Choose	Generate	***Select***	*Tools*		
		Select	*Generate*		

Your screen should look like Figure 32-11.

Figure 32-11

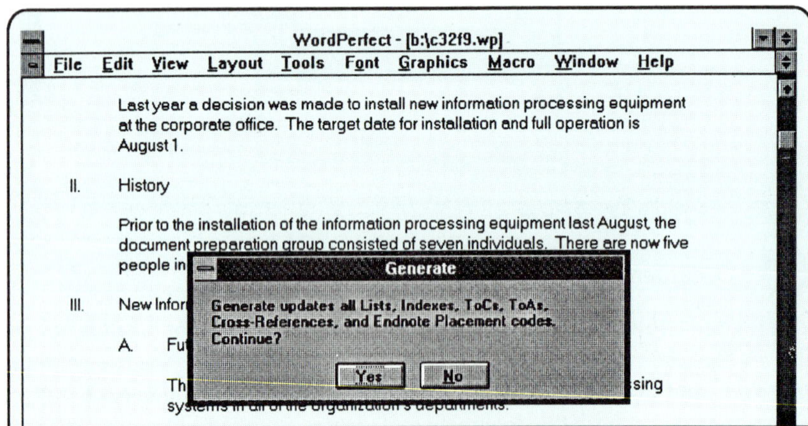

You are asked if you want to replace any existing tables, lists, and indexes. Choose Yes to replace or No to return to your document without generating the index.

To generate the index:

Click	the Yes command button	***Press***	*Alt+Y to select the Yes command button*	**Press**	Alt+Y to select the Yes command button

A counter shows the progress of the index generation. When the generating is complete, the index is displayed on your screen as in Figure 32-12.

Figure 32-12

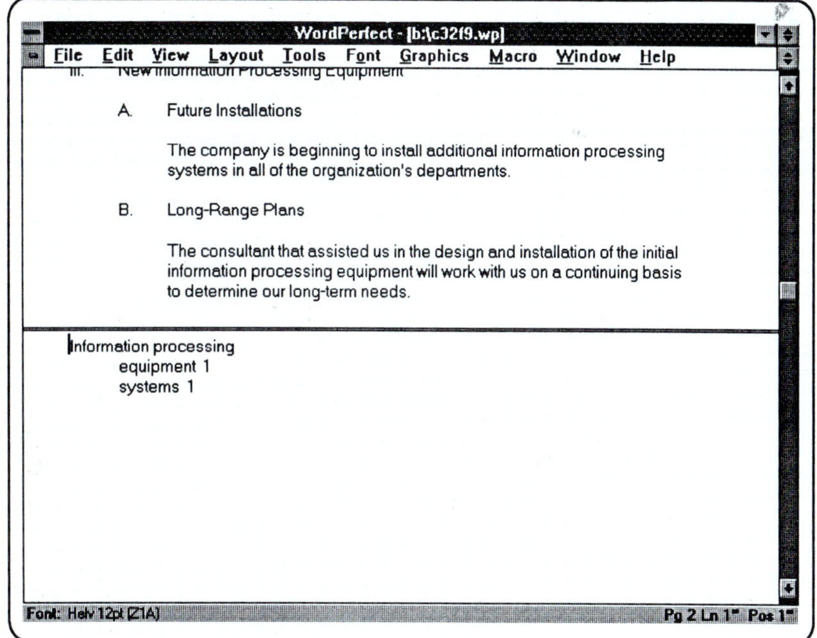

Turn on the Reveal Codes feature.

Notice that Indent and Margin Release codes have been added to format the text in the index. Each index entry is separated from the page number by a space.

Turn off the Reveal Codes feature. Save the document as "index." Close the document.

■ LISTS

You can create a list of figures, tables, maps, or illustrations that are used in a long report or book. A page number is placed with each item on the list so you can easily find it in the text. A list can appear at the front or back of the report or book. The entries appear in the order in which they are presented in the document.

You can create up to ten lists within a WordPerfect document. Recall that you can attach captions to equations. Actually, you can attach captions to any graphic box, figure, table, or equation. If you have done so, then you can use the captions as the entries in your list. You do not have to mark any text. You can define a list of captions for one of the graphic types when generating the list. Lists six through ten have been assigned to graphic objects. The following is a list of each List number and its predefined graphic type.

List 6	Figure Box Captions
List 7	Table Box Captions
List 8	Text Box Captions
List 9	User Box Captions
List 10	Equation Box Captions

The procedure for creating a list, other than the graphic lists, is very similar to that of a table of contents or index. First, you mark the text that you want in the list. Then, you specify where you want the list located in the document and how you want the page numbers to appear. You can choose one of five numbering styles. Last, you create the list through the Generate feature.

Open the document "inform.rpt."

Creating a List

Suppose you want to make a list of the first level headings in your document.

To mark the first heading "I. Introduction":

Select	the heading "I. Introduction"	***Select***	*the heading "I. Introduction"*	**Select**	the heading "I. Introduction"
Choose	Tools	***Press***	*Alt*	**Press**	F12
Choose	Mark Text	***Select***	*Tools*	**Select**	List
Choose	List	***Select***	*Mark Text*		
		Select	*List*		

The Mark List dialog box appears. Your screen should look like Figure 32-13.

Figure 32-13

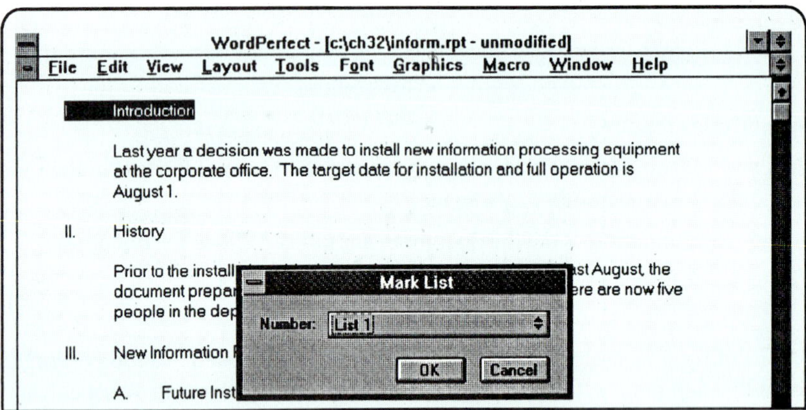

To enter the List Number:

Click	the Number pop-up list button	***Press***	*Alt+↑ to view the pop-up list*	**Press**	Alt+↑ to view the pop-up list
Hold down	the mouse button to view the pop-up list	***Type***	*1 to select List 1*	**Type**	1 to select List 1
Choose	List 1	***Press***	*↵Enter*	**Press**	↵Enter
Click	the OK command button				

To display the codes that mark the text for the list, turn on the Reveal Codes feature.

A [Mark:List,1] code is placed in the document to indicate a list 1 marker. An [End Mark:List,1] indicates the end of the text for the list.

Turn off the Reveal Codes feature.

To mark the second heading "II. History":

Select	the heading "II. History"	***Select***	*the heading "II. History"*	**Select**	the heading "II. History"

Choose	Tools
Choose	Mark Text
Choose	List
Click	the Number pop-up list button
Hold down	the mouse button to view the pop-up list
Choose	List 1

Press	*Alt*
Select	*Tools*
Select	*Mark Text*
Select	*List*
Press	*Alt+↑ to view the pop-up list*
Type	*1 to select List 1*
Press	*↵Enter*

Press	F12
Select	List
Press	Alt+↑ to view the pop-up list
Type	1 to select List 1
Press	↵Enter

To mark the heading "III. New Information Processing Equipment":

Select	the heading "III. New Information Processing Equipment"
Choose	Tools
Choose	Mark Text
Choose	List
Click	the Number pop-up list button
Hold down	the mouse button to view the pop-up list
Choose	List 1

Select	*the heading "III. New Information Processing Equipment"*
Press	*Alt*
Select	*Tools*
Select	*Mark Text*
Select	*List*
Press	*Alt+↑ to view the pop-up list*
Type	*1 to select List 1*
Press	*↵Enter*

Select	the heading "III. New Information Processing Equipment"
Press	F12
Select	List
Press	Alt+↑ to view the pop-up list
Type	1 to select List 1
Press	↵Enter

Defining a List

After marking the text, you must tell WordPerfect where to place the list in the document and how to format the list.

To create a separate page for the list at the end of the document:

Click	at the end of the document
Insert	a page break

Move	*the insertion point to the end of the document*
Insert	*a page break*

Move	the insertion point to the end of the document
Insert	a page break

The bottom part of your screen should look like Figure 32-14.

Figure 32-14

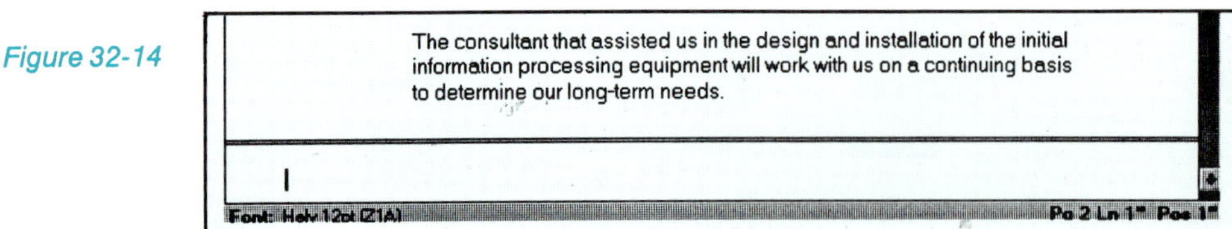

To define the list:

Choose	Tools	***Press***	*Alt*	**Press**	Shift + F12
Choose	Define	***Select***	*Tools*	**Select**	List
Choose	List	***Select***	*Define*		
		Select	*List*		

The Define List dialog box appears. Your screen should look like Figure 32-15.

Figure 32-15

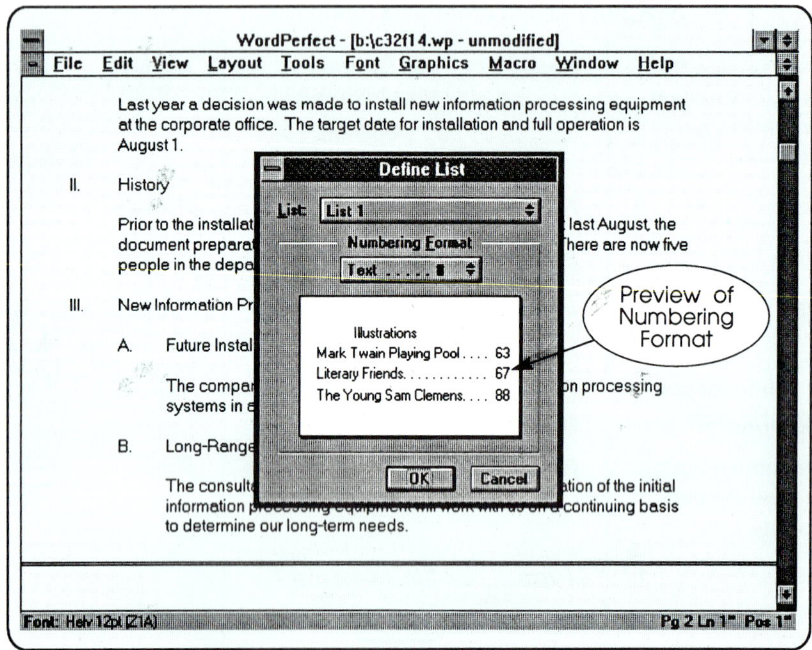

Recall that you can have up to ten lists per document. To indicate that this is the first list for the document:

Click	the List pop-up button	***Press***	*Alt + L to select the List pop-up button*	**Press**	Alt + L to select the List pop-up button
Hold down	the mouse button to view the pop-up list	***Press***	*Alt + ↑ to view the pop-up list*	**Press**	Alt + ↑ to view the pop-up list
Choose	List 1	***Type***	*1 to select List 1*	**Type**	1 to select List 1

The possible page numbering styles are the same as those for the table of contents. To select a page numbering style:

Click	the Numbering Format pop-up list button	***Press***	*Alt+F to select the Numbering Format pop-up list button*	**Press**	Alt+F to select the Numbering Format pop-up list button
Hold down	the mouse button to view the pop-up list	***Press***	*Alt+↑ to view the pop-up list*	**Press**	Alt+↑ to view the pop-up list
Select	Text (#)	***Type***	*T to select Text (#)*	**Type**	T to select Text (#)
Click	the OK command button	***Press***	*↵Enter*	**Press**	↵Enter

Turn on the Reveal Codes feature.

A List Definition code [Def Mark:List,1:TxtParenPg] is placed in the document where the list will be located. This code indicates the list is list one and that each item in the list will be formatted with the page numbers following the item in parentheses.

Turn off the Reveal Codes feature.

Generating a List

Once the text is marked and the list is defined, all you need to do is generate the list.

To generate a list:

Choose	Tools	***Press***	*Alt*	**Press**	Alt+F12
Choose	Generate	***Select***	*Tools*		
		Select	*Generate*		

You are asked if you want to replace any existing tables, lists, and indexes. Choose Yes to replace or No to return to your document without generating the list.

To generate the list:

Click	the Yes command button	***Press***	*Alt+Y to select the Yes command button*	**Press**	Alt+Y to select the Yes command button

A counter shows the progress of the list generation. When complete, the list is displayed on your screen as in Figure 32-16.

Figure 32-16

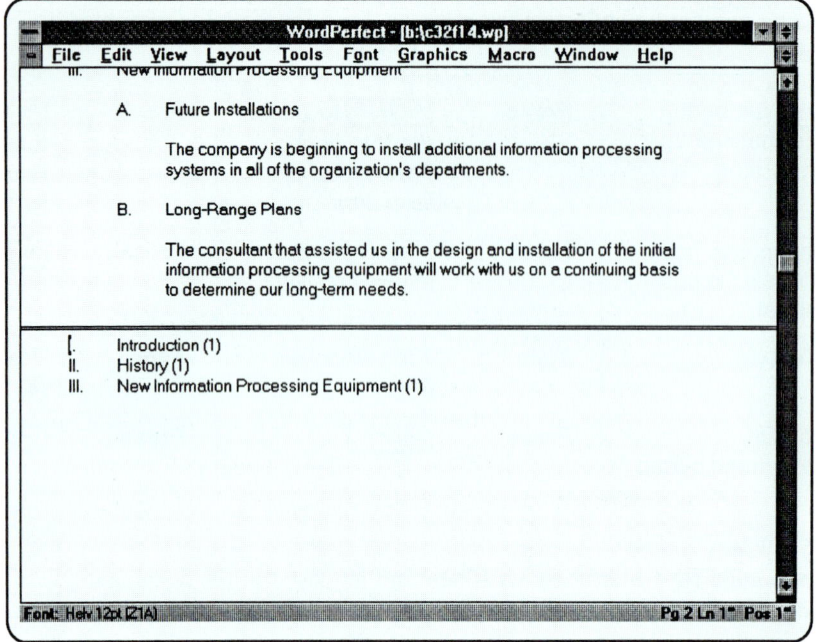

Turn on the Reveal Codes feature.

Notice that Double Indent, Indent, and Margin Release codes have been added to format the text in the list. Page numbers are enclosed in parentheses and separated by a space.

Turn off the Reveal Codes feature. Save the document as "list." Close the document.

EXERCISE 1

INSTRUCTIONS: Define the following terms:

1. Table of contents ______________________________

   ____

2. Index ______________________________

   ____

3. Lists ______________________________

   ____

4. Mark text feature ______________________________

   ____

5. Define feature ______________________________

   ____

6. Generate feature ______________________________

   ____

EXERCISE 2

INSTRUCTIONS: Circle T if the statement is true and F if the statement is false.

T F 1. WordPerfect can manage a maximum of six levels of chapters and subsections in a table of contents.

T F 2. When creating a table of contents, the next step after marking the headings and text in the document is actually generating the table of contents.

T F 3. The first step in creating a table of contents, index, or list is to specify where you would like the table, index, or list placed in the document and how the numbers should appear.

T F 4. An index matches key words and phrases to page numbers.

T F 5. An index appears at the front of a long report or book.

T F 6. The Define Index dialog box allows you to change the page numbering style.

T F 7. You can create up to twenty lists in a WordPerfect document.

T F 8. An index is made up of a heading and a subheading.

T F 9. The Define List code is placed before each item of text that should appear in the list.

T F 10. You can create a table of contents, index, or list with no page numbers.

EXERCISE 3

INSTRUCTIONS:

1. Create the following document using the Outline feature.
2. Save the document in a file using the name "ch32ex03.01"
3. Place a page break between each section.
4. Create a table of contents.
5. Place the table of contents on a separate page at the beginning of the document.
6. Create an index for the words "quality" and "committee."
7. Place the index on a separate page at the end of the document.
8. Print the document.
9. Save the document in a file using the name "ch32ex03.02."
10. Close the document.

```
I.     Introduction

       In a recent announcement, the president of the company
       indicated the importance of improving the quality of our
       services.  A task force has been organized to consider ways
       for enhancing our quality efforts.

II.    History

       Our company has consistently been among the producers of
       quality services in its industry.  However, there is always
       room for improvement.  In the last industry update report, we
       placed fourth among 20 companies in quality.  While this is a
       very high rating, we slipped from number two to number four.

III.   Quality Task Force Members

       The individuals assigned to the quality task force are the
       chief operating officer, the controller and division vice
       presidents.  There are a total of eight people on the
       committee.  The president has asked the group to report their
       results by October 31.
```

EXERCISE 4

INSTRUCTIONS:

1. Create the following document.
2. Use double spacing.
3. Create a table of contents. Side headings are first level. Underlined paragraph phrases are secondary.
4. Print the document.
5. Save the document in a file using the name "ch32ex04."
6. Close the document.

IMPRESSIONS

Visual Impressions

First Impressions. Whenever we meet someone for the first time, a first impression is made. As you are introduced, you form a judgment about that person. The way the person behaves or dresses may affect your impression. Your first impression may accept or reject the person without knowing anything else but their names.

Letter Impressions. When you write a letter, the reader views the document as his or her first impression of you and the company you represent. The placement on the page, the quality of the paper, the correctness of format, grammar, punctuation, and spelling all create impressions. The recipient of the letter makes judgments based on a piece of paper about you and your company.

Effective Images. Always try to develop an effective image with the written document. Make sure that placement, formatting, grammar, punctuation, and spelling are correct. The use of good-quality paper adds to a good impression. Demonstrate your ability to make effective good impressions for your company in everything you do.

EXERCISE 5

INSTRUCTIONS:

1. Create the following document.
2. Double space the document.
3. Create a table of contents using two levels.
4. Create an index of the following words:

paycheck	commissions
Overtime	Personnel Board
holiday	vacation
terminated	retirement

5. Print the document.
6. Save the document in a file using the name "ch32ex05."
7. Close the document.

PAYROLL PROCEDURES

Change in Compensation Procedures

Payroll schedule changes. All employees will begin receiving their paycheck every two weeks commencing July 28. This is the regular payday for that time period. After July 28, you will receive 1/26th of your pay every two weeks.

Exempt personnel. Those employees who are scheduled to receive their pay once a month will continue to do so. These employees will receive their commissions every two weeks instead of once a month. This will begin on July 28.

Part-time personnel. All part-time personnel will continue to receive their checks once a month. If there is sufficient interest in changing this procedure, it will be considered by the Personnel Board.

Payroll Compensation

Overtime hours. Overtime pay will begin each day after a worker has worked his or her regular hours. This is changed from working 37 1/2 hours before receiving overtime pay.

Rate of pay. All overtime pay will be compensated at the rate of one and one-half times that of the regular pay.

Weekend pay. All employees (regardless of company status) will be paid at the rate of twice their regular hourly pay if they work four or more hours per day on the weekend.

Holiday pay. Any employee that must work on a regular scheduled holiday, will be compensated at the rate of three times their regular hourly rate.

Vacation pay. All employees will be paid their regular pay for 37 1/2 hours (normal work week) for vacation pay. The regular vacation pay will be issued according to the schedule of vacation pay for years work.

Separation Pay

Separation pay for leaving company. Employees will receive one week's pay for every three years of service upon termination.

Terminated employees. Any employee terminated by request of the company will receive two weeks severance pay. If terminated because of inappropriate conduct, no pay will be received.

Retirement pay. All employees who retire at age 70 after serving at least 10 years with the company will be eligible for the regular retirement plan.

Questions About New Procedures

If you have questions about any of the above procedures, please check with your foreman, supervisor, or manager.

EXERCISE 6

INSTRUCTIONS:

1. Create the following document. Double space the document.
2. Create a table of contents on a separate page with the heading "Table of Contents." Use flush right numbers with leaders (dots).

3. Create an index of the following words and place the page numbers in parentheses:

literature	extensive vocabulary
audience	listener
intelligence	dictionary

4. Print the document.
5. Save the document in a file using the name "ch32ex06."
6. Close the document.

<u>Good Vocabulary</u>

How is your vocabulary? A good vocabulary is very important to business people. Those individuals with extensive vocabulary usually receive greater benefits. Words help you think. Reading good literature will help you increase your vocabulary.

<u>Vocabulary Recognition</u>

We all recognize someone who has an extensive vocabulary. The greater our recognition of the words, the greater our understanding. Occasionally, someone with a very extensive vocabulary will try to impress everyone by overusing it. You must always consider your audience when using your vocabulary. If you send the reader or listener to the dictionary with every other word, you are not communicating, you are confusing that person.

<u>Vocabulary Power</u>

There is a high correlation between intelligence and vocabulary. This will usually translate to one's position within the firm. Just having a large, useful vocabulary is not enough. Hard work is the major criteria for promotion. Having a good vocabulary and being able to use it at the proper time will only enhance your position and power.

<u>Word Power</u>

Good managers will read, speak, listen and write well. They did not automatically get this way. Most are avid readers. They either join book clubs or read learned professional journals extensively.

Everyone can acquire word power. Become a reader. Take an interest in using new words in the proper context and place. Acquire an interest in the dictionary. Learn to look up words you do not know. Learn to pronounce and use them. As you gain confidence, you will find that your appetite will become insatiable for more. Once you start, you may never want to stop.

EXERCISE 7

INSTRUCTIONS:

1. Create the following document using the Outline feature.
2. Create a list of the first level headings and place the page numbers in parentheses. Generate the list on a separate page at the beginning of the document.
3. Print the document.
4. Save the document in a file using the name "ch32ex07."
5. Close the document.

```
I.     Introduction
       A.     Changes
       B.     Trends

II.    Getting Acquainted
       A.     Creating a document
       B.     Editing a document
       C.     Printing a document

III.   Capabilities of WP Software
       A.     Editing Features
       B.     Formatting
       C.     Print Enhancements
       D.     Strikeover

IV.    Data Base

V.     Spreadsheets
```

EXERCISE 8

INSTRUCTIONS:

1. Create the following document for making a table of contents.
2. Place page breaks as they appear in the copy.
3. Use double spacing.
4. Number the pages in the upper right corner of the page.
5. After entering the text, create a table of contents page with the title "TABLE OF CONTENTS". Use side headings and paragraph introductions as items in the table of contents. The table of contents should be on a separate page.
6. In the table of contents, place the numbers against the right margin with dots between the headings and the numbers.
7. Print the document.
8. Save the document in a file using the name "ch32ex08."

AUSTRALIA

Introduction

Australia was founded over 200 years ago when prisoners were exiled to this new land. It was their punishment to create a new way of life on a continent for white people with its only inhabitants being Aborigines. **(Page Break)**

Early History

British sea captain, James Cook. He was the first to reach the east coast of Australia in 1770. He claimed the land for the Crown.

Colonies. By 1856 six separate colonies were established. New South Wales and Tasmania were founded mostly by convicts. Victoria was founded by business people of Europe. Even today, Melbourne can remember its founding through the grid pattern of its streets.**(Page Break)**

Some Basic Facts

Size. Australia is roughly the size of the United States if you exclude Hawaii and Alaska.

Continent. Australia is the only nation that is a continent. This also means that it is the smallest of all continents. **(Page Break)**

Unusual Facts

Australia is the flattest and the driest continent. Less than 10 percent of the land is usable for growing crops.

Rocks. The oldest known fragments of the earth's crust is found in Jack Hills. It is estimated to be 4.3 billion years old. **(Page Break)**

Continued on next page.

Statistical Information

Per Capita. Australians have it better than most. The per capita income is $14,458. This is one of the highest in the world.

Citizenry. The life expectancy is 76 years. This is one of the world's longest.

Literacy. The literacy rate is considered 100 percent. This is an amazing statistic considering that the Aborigines have a very difficult time being accepted by many people, and they resist efforts to be educated.

Work force. The workers of this country earn six weeks of vacation annually. **(Page Break)**

Resources

Uranium. More than 28 percent of the free world's uranium can be found in this country.

Opals. Almost all of the world's supply of opals can be found in Australia. The main spot for opals is Coober Peedy. This unique community is one in which over half of the residents live underground. The reason for underground living is the intense heat of the summer. Temperatures reach 120°.

Meat. Australia leads the world in the export of beef and veal. It is second to New Zealand in mutton and lamb.

APPENDIX A: PROOFREADER'S MARKS

DEFINED		EXAMPLES
Paragraph	¶	¶ Begin a new paragraph at this
Insert a character	^	point. Insrt a letter here.
Delete		Delete these words. Disregard
Do not change	stet or	the previous correction. To
Transpose	tr	transpose is to around turn.
Move to the left	[	Move this copy to the left.
Move to the right	]	Move this copy to the right.
No paragraph	No ¶	No ¶ Do not begin a new paragraph
Delete and close up		here. Delete the hyphen from pre-empt and close up the space.
Set in caps	Caps or ≡	a sentence begins with a capital
Set in lower case	lc	letter. This Word should not
Insert a period	⊙	be capitalized. Insert a period ⊙
Quotation marks		Quotation marks and a comma
Comma		should be placed here he said.
Insert space	#	Space between thesewords. An
Apostrophe		apostrophe is whats needed here.
Hyphen	=	Add a hyphen to AfroAmerican. Close
Close up		up the extra spa ce.
Use superior figure		Footnote this sentence. Set
Set in italic	Ital. or ___	the words, sine qua non, in italics.
Move up		This word is too low. That word is
Move down		too high.

APPENDIX B: LINKING DATA BETWEEN WINDOWS APPLICATIONS

WordPerfect for Windows includes a feature that allows you to access and transfer data to and from other Windows applications. Dynamic Data Exchange (DDE) allows you to link data between WordPerfect for Windows and other Windows applications.

Lotus 1-2-3 for Windows is a popular spreadsheet package that specializes in complex numerical calculations and number manipulation. These abilities are not available in a word processing package. You can link a Lotus 1-2-3 for Windows spreadsheet to a WordPerfect for Windows document. If you change the spreadsheet in 1-2-3 for Windows when both files are open, then the WordPerfect document will automatically update.

In order to create a link, you must first be using a Windows application that supports DDE. Refer to the reference manual of your Windows application to determine if that application supports Dynamic Data Exchange. Both WordPerfect for Windows and 1-2-3 for Windows support DDE.

The simplest way to create a DDE link is to copy information from one application to another. First, copy the source information, in this example the spreadsheet data, using the Edit, Copy command. Then, switch to the target application, in this example WordPerfect, and move to the location where you want to place the link. Choose Paste Link from the Link option under the Edit menu to create the link and place the data.

Suppose you want to link a spreadsheet to a WordPerfect document. To switch to Lotus 1-2-3 from WordPerfect:

Click	the program control menu box	***Press***	*Ctrl+Esc to produce the Windows Task List*	**Press**	Ctrl+Esc to produce the Windows Task List
Choose	Switch To	***Select***	*Program Manager*	**Select**	Program Manager
Click	on Program Manager	***Press***	*↵Enter to select the Switch To command button*	**Press**	↵Enter to select the Switch To command button
Click	the Switch To command button	***Press***	*Alt*	**Press**	Ctrl+Tab until the Lotus Applications group is selected
Double-click	the Lotus Applications program group	***Select***	*Window*	**Press**	the pointer-movement keys to select the 1-2-3 for Windows program icon
Double-click	the 1-2-3 for Windows program icon	***Select***	*Lotus Applications*	**Press**	↵Enter

		Press	*the pointer-movement keys to select the 1-2-3 for Windows program icon*		
		Press	*↵Enter*		

Create the spreadsheet in Figure B-1.

Figure B-1

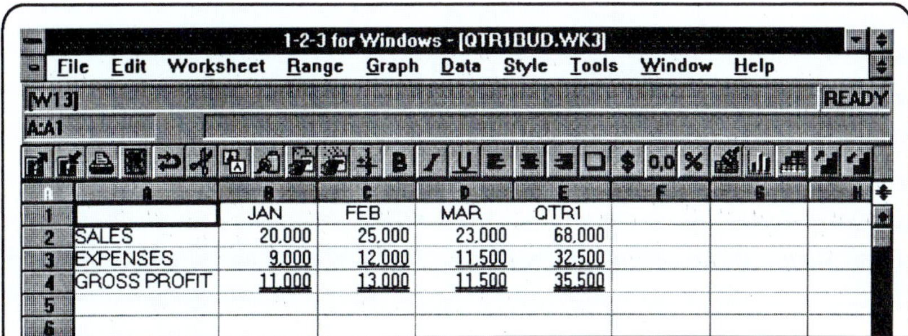

Save the spreadsheet file as "qtr1bud.wk3."

To copy the data to the Windows clipboard:

Select	cells A1 to E4	***Select***	*cells A1 to E4*	**Select**	cells A1 to E4
Choose	Edit	***Press***	*Alt*	**Press**	Ctrl + Insert
Choose	Copy	***Select***	*Edit*		
		Select	*Copy*		

To place the data in the WordPerfect document:

Click	the program control menu box	***Press***	*Ctrl + Esc*	**Press**	Ctrl + Esc
Choose	Switch To	***Select***	*WordPerfect for Windows*	**Select**	WordPerfect for Windows
Choose	WordPerfect for Windows	***Press***	*↵Enter to select the Switch To command button*	**Press**	↵Enter to select the Switch To command button
Click	the Switch To command button				

Close any open documents. Create the document in Figure B-2. Press ↵Enter four times to leave three blank lines between the text and the spreadsheet data.

Figure B-2

```
The following is an example of a file linked from Lotus 1-2-3 for
Windows.
```

Choose	Edit	***Press***	Alt
Choose	Link	***Select***	*Edit*
Choose	Paste Link	***Select***	*Link*
		Select	*Paste Link*

Your screen should look like Figure B-3.

Figure B-3

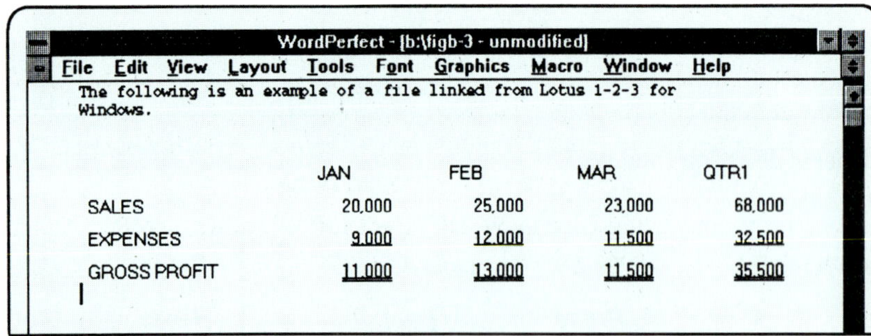

When both the WordPerfect document and the 1-2-3 spreadsheet are open, any changes in the 1-2-3 spreadsheet will be reflected in the WordPerfect document. You can update the WordPerfect document by choosing Update from the Link option under the Edit menu when both files are open. If the 1-2-3 spreadsheet is changed and the WordPerfect document is not open, then the changes are not reflected in the word processing document. If the 1-2-3 spreadsheet is not open when you open the WordPerfect document, previous changes in the spreadsheet are not reflected in the word processing document.

Pasting a link does not work with every application that supports DDE. In certain applications you may have to create a link manually using the Edit, Link, Create Link command. If you have to create a link manually, you may want to refer to the section "DDE Link" of the WordPerfect for Windows Reference Manual for more information.

APPENDIX C: CONVERTING TO/FROM WORDPERFECT FOR WINDOWS

The most current version of the WordPerfect software package is WordPerfect for Windows. You may have some documents that were created with an earlier version of WordPerfect, such as 4.2, 5.0, or 5.1. The different versions of WordPerfect use different document codes. You will want to update your documents so that WordPerfect for Windows can work with them.

WordPerfect for Windows files are saved in a WordPerfect 5.1 format. To use a WordPerfect 5.1 for DOS file in WordPerfect for Windows, open the old document in WordPerfect for Windows. All document codes from WordPerfect 5.1 for DOS are compatible with WordPerfect for Windows. You can also use your WordPerfect for Windows files in WordPerfect 5.1. Simply retrieve the WordPerfect for Windows file into the WordPerfect 5.1 for DOS program.

If you are updating a document created in WordPerfect 5.0, 4.2, or earlier, open the document in WordPerfect for Windows. When you select the file and click the Open command button, a Convert File Format dialog box appears on your screen. The name of the program in which the document was created should appear in the Convert File Format From drop down list box. If the program name is incorrect, you can select a program from the drop down list by clicking the down arrow next to the program name and scrolling through the list. When you have the correct program name selected, click the OK command button.

If you need to convert a WordPerfect for Windows document to WordPerfect 5.0 or WordPerfect 4.2, change the File Format in the File, Save As command. To change the file format, click the down arrow of the Format drop down list box in the Save As dialog box and select the proper format. When you choose the OK command button, the file will be saved in the proper format.

For more information on converting files in WordPerfect for Windows, see the "Open" or "Save As" sections of the WordPerfect Reference Manual.

APPENDIX D: ADDITIONAL WORDPERFECT FOR WINDOWS FEATURES

An interim release of WordPerfect for Windows was released on April 30, 1992. This release contains additional WordPerfect features and enhancements to existing features. Two of the features added in this interim release were the Drag and Drop feature and the View Zoom feature. Both of these features are discussed in this appendix.

Drag and Drop

The Drag and Drop feature allows you to move and copy text without using the Windows Clipboard application. To move text using the Drag and Drop feature, select the text, drag the text to the desired location, and release the mouse button.

At this point, change the default directory to "c:\wpdocs" or "a:\wpdocs" and open the document "johnson.ltr."

To move the first paragraph of your document and place it below the third paragraph using the Drag and Drop feature:

Select	the first paragraph
Move	the mouse pointer over the selected text
Drag	the mouse pointer before the "S" in "Sincerely"
Release	the mouse button

The bottom portion of your screen should look similar to Figure D-1.

Figure D-1

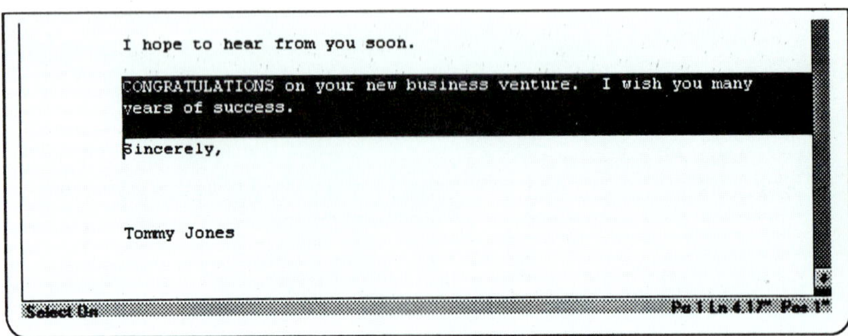

You can also copy text using the Drag and Drop feature. To copy text using the Drag and Drop feature, hold down the Ctrl key while dragging the text. Do not release the Ctrl key until you release the mouse button.

To copy the inside address using the Drag and Drop feature and to place it at the end of the document:

Click	at the end of the document
Press	↵Enter twice to skip one line before copying the text to the end of the document
Highlight	the inside address
Hold down	the Ctrl key
Drag	the inside address to the bottom of the document
Release	the mouse button
Release	the Ctrl key

Deselect the inside address by clicking in the document area. The lower part of your screen should look like Figure D-2.

Figure D-2

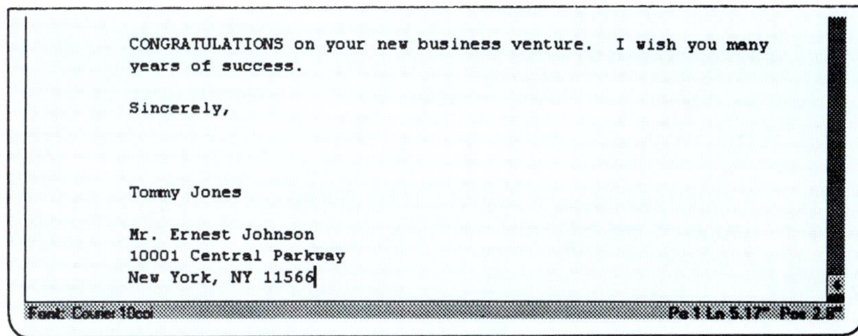

Zoom

The Zoom feature allows you to view your document at a different perspective. For example, you can look at your text close up using the 200% option or you can view your page from a distance by choosing the 50% option.

To change the view of your document, choose Zoom from the View menu and select the desired percentage option. You can also choose a zoom percentage using the Zoom button on the Ruler. The Zoom button is located between the Styles button and the Table button.

To view the document "johnson.ltr" at 50%:

Choose	View	***Press***	*Alt*
Choose	Zoom	***Select***	*View*
Choose	50%	***Select***	*Zoom*
		Select	*50%*

Your screen should look similar to Figure D-3.

Figure D-3

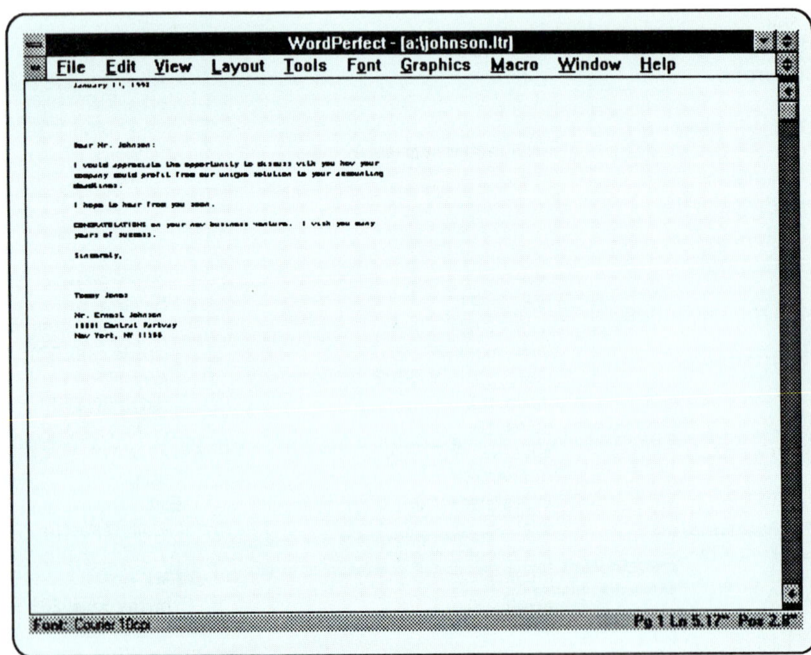

Notice that you can view an entire page at one time. When you are viewing the document using zoom, you can edit and format the document as you would when you view the document at 100%. Notice the insertion point still appears on the screen.

To return to 100% view:

Choose	View	***Press***	*Alt*
Choose	Zoom	***Select***	*View*
Choose	100%	***Select***	*Zoom*
		Select	*100%*

Your document should return to the normal view. Close the document without saving changes.

For more detailed information about the features in the Interim release of WordPerfect for Windows, refer to the Software Change Notice for the April 30, 1992 release.

INDEX